A Manager's Guide to Quant

ABOUT THE AUTHOR

Michael Cuming took a degree in Natural Science at Trinity College, Dublin and an MA in Quantitative Social Sciences at the University of Kent at Canterbury. He has taught practising managers for 18 years on short courses, the Diploma in Management Studies and at Masters level. In his role as a Consultant and an Industrial Tutor, he has had a wide experience of industrial, commercial and local government operations around the United Kingdom. He is married with 2 children and is a Senior Lecturer at Ealing College of Higher Education.

A Manager's Guide to Quantitative Methods

Michael Cuming

ELM Publications

© Michael Cuming, 1984.

Published by Elm Publications, Seaton House,
Kings Ripton, Cambs PE17 2NJ and printed
by Biddles Ltd, Martyr Road, Guildford, Surrey.

No part of this book may be reproduced or transmitted in any
form or by any means without prior, written permission from
the publisher.
October, 1984.

 British Library Cataloguing in Publication Data

Cuming, Michael
 A manager's guide to quantitative methods.
 1. Management——Mathematical models
 I. Title
 658.4   HD30.25

ISBN 0-946139-0-16

BSD CS7

CONTENTS

Preface		vii
Introduction : for the Reader		xi
Acknowledgements/Permissions		xiii
1.	Frequency distributions	1
2.	Getting the right answer from your calculator	40
3.	Summarising distributions	74
4.	The language of uncertainty	118
5.	Simplifying data	154
6.	Compound interest and discounting	182
7.	Correlation and regression — a statistical minefield	223
8.	Tracking things in time	259
9.	Finding out by sampling	295
10.	Drawing conclusions	329
11.	Managing with the computer	355
12.	Problems with data	395

APPENDIX CHAPTERS — 414

A 3.	Summarising distributions	415
A 4.	The language of uncertainty	417
A 6.	Compound interest and discounting	420
	Technical Note : Complications over compounding	427
A 7.	Correlation and regression	430
A 8.	Tracking things in time	434
A 9.	Finding out by sampling	441
A10.	Drawing conclusions	447

APPENDICES

1.	Critical values of the normal distribution	453
2.	How the critical values for the 't' distribution vary with the degrees of freedom	454
3.	How the critical values for the chi-square distribution (x^2) vary with degrees of freedom	455
4.	Critical values of the sign test	456
5a.	Compound amount factors or inflation factors	457

5b.	Discount factors	459
5c.	Capital recovery factors	460
6.	Normal distribution tables	462
7.	Table of random digits	463
	Answers	465

References 473
Index 477

PREFACE

This book is intended as an introductory guide to quantitative methods for working managers, such as those attending general management courses like the Diploma in Management Studies (DMS) and the Certificate in Management Studies (CMS). It aims to provide practising managers with an insight into the principles and concepts underlying widely used quantitative techniques as well as giving an introduction to a set of elementary manual and computer-based techniques that they can implement themselves in the work place. It should also be suitable for undergraduate students who intend to follow a career in business and who are not studying quantitative methods as a specialist subject.

The term 'manager' is used in its most general sense to indicate people within a wide range of organisations responsible for analysing, planning, monitoring and controlling business operations. They will range from senior executive down to supervisory levels and will vary greatly in the degree of quantitative expertise which they possess. Those with a scientific and engineering background can often cope with the mathematics of existing texts. The great majority, however, seem to have a negative experience of quantitative techniques which makes them unable or unwilling to acquire the necessary mathematical language to cope with the standard texts available.

Research carried out by Gallagher and Metcalfe (1981) has shown that few quantitative techniques are in common use by practising managers, and those that are are usually the simplest ones. They point out that managers express an interest in those techniques that they can understand and also in those suitable for computing. Armed with realistic objectives, this book sets out to explain basic fundamental techniques and concepts in a language which is comprehensible to most managers. It avoids the use of mathematical language, except in the appendix chapters (those with prefix A) and introduces new ideas within the context of a practical problem rather than in the abstract.

The language employed is familiar, and deliberately avoids the abstract, formal style of so many standard texts, whilst deliberately setting out to engage the interest of the reader. Far from being condescending in intent, this approach is chosen in recognition of the fact that working managers have not got the time or the motivation to acquire a formal scientific training at a point in their careers when they are mainly occupied with developing their managerial expertise, and are often studying a number of totally new subjects on a general management course. The style of this book aims to bring the basic concepts and skills to the manager where he can accept them on his own terms, rather than forcing him onto unfamiliar ground where he lacks confidence.

I have been encouraged to adopt this approach by following the current trends in computing. Whereas the student of statistics in the past spent much time on the computational aspects of techniques, modern software makes it possible for the manager to obtain from a cheap personal computer the necessary statistical results by merely pointing at the screen of the VDU! For example, 20 years ago the correlation coefficient could only be obtained by many minutes hard work on a noisy electro-mechanical calculator operated with the assistance of ear-muffs. On a modern spreadsheet system, the same quantity, and many others besides, can be obtained instantaneously and effortlessly and with the exercise of little or no skill. The computational aspects of statistics are no longer a problem, so it is essential now that the manager be provided with a guide to the correct interpretation and use of what can now be so easily obtained without expert help. Furthermore, an emphasis on problems and difficulties now becomes essential and this also features within this book.

In Chapter 1, emphasis is placed on the variety of distributions to be found in the world of business. The role of the normal distribution and other theoretical distributions is played down and the reader, instead, is encouraged to seek out and discover the nature of actual distributions within his own field of study. In spite of the widespread occurrence of irregular and skewed distributions, many texts give the impression that the normal distribution crops up widely in the business world, whereas its principal importance lies in its role in sampling theory and in quality control. I have been faced by students who have *apologised,* when showing me a distribution from their work area, because it does not conform to any of the theoretical distributions that they have studied!

Chapter 2 spends considerable time on the use of calculators and the approximate arithmetic which is essential for their correct use. The users are encouraged to develop routines or 'programs' for their calculators that will carry out procedures efficiently and *accurately*.

Chapter 3 explains what averages and measures of dispersion represent, using graphical techniques rather than computational formulae. The methods of computation are also clearly shown.

In Chapter 4, the practical use in business of simple probabilities is described with special emphasis on the manager's role in applied probability theory. A realistic assessment of the concept of expected monetary value is coupled with a practical exercise designed to show the subjective nature of utility functions.

Chapter 5 deals with the mundane matter of simplifying data with percentages and graphs. Although lacking in academic status, these are simple quantitiative techniques that managers need most of all in their day-to-day working lives.

The content of Chapter 6 is more complex than most other chapters. Financial mathematics is of vital importance in business because of the dual effects of interest and inflation. A special feature of this chapter is the way in which the wide applicability of the concept of interest is stressed.

The widespread availability of packages which fit correlation coefficients and lines of regression at the touch of a finger, justifies the negative title of Chapter 7. The potential for misuse is so great that the subject is truly a 'minefield'. I have before me a computer package which brazenly promises to 'forecast' sales from past sales and advertising expenditure figures. Managers need more than ever to develop a natural suspicion of the easy answers offered by these modern 'witch-doctors'. Within this chapter, the concept of significance is explained with the aid of a sampling experiment.

In Chapter 8, more emphasis is placed on the use of index numbers than on their construction. For the manager, the subtle differences between different forms of index are less important than knowing how to neutralise the confounding effects of inflation by deflating series. The difficulties of Time Series analysis are emphasised for those working in an uncertain world subject to sudden changes in traditional patterns and trends. Again, the widespread availability of 'oversold' package programs makes a cautious approach advisable. The naive idea of equating forecasting with projecting straight lines, which is still being offered by some texts, is replaced by an encouragement for managers to use such projections merely as a base line from which inevitable shifts can be detected.

The fundamental principles of sampling theory and the central limit theorem are explained by means of sampling experiments in Chapter 9. Unlike most texts, equal emphasis is given to bias and sampling error. This is in recognition of the fact that bias is potentially a more important source of error than sampling error and one to the elimination of which the manager can make a vital contribution. Whereas sampling error follows laws well understood and documented by the statistician, identifying the potential for bias requires specialist knowledge and experience of the work area, which the manager can provide.

The concept of significance testing is discussed in Chapter 10. It is prefaced by a discussion of experimentation as it can be applied in industry and business. A simple example of a significance test is chosen so that the totality of the procedure can be covered, with emphasis on the 'power' concept, so neglected in some texts. A brief description is given of some of the principal tests in use.

Chapter 11 encourages managers to re-assess their relationship with the computer, thinking positively and creatively about the new systems becoming available. The chapter stresses the changes in the computer world which will reduce the gap that has grown up between user and machine system. Spreadsheets are described and sufficient **BASIC** is provided to enable someone with access to a personal computer to use it as an advanced calculator. The last Chapter, 12, deals with the problem of data itself. So many sophisticated techniques fail in business because of the problem of finding data that makes sense. Although other texts have emphasised problems with published statistics, this book concentrates mainly on how business data can become corrupted or misleading.

In the A chapters, technical notes to amplify the main text are provided together with mathematical statements of formulae and simple **BASIC** routines.

INTRODUCTION : FOR THE READER

This book aims to provide working managers with an introduction to quantitative methods which will not only explain basic concepts and invite imaginative thinking about data, but which will also help the reader to improve his general level of numeracy. The reader is invited to attempt all the exercises provided, answers being shown at the end of the book.

The references given throughout the book have been selected for relevance and readability for the non-specialist rather than because they represent the definitive texts on the subject. General texts for further reading abound in the libraries but Ehrenburg (1982), Sprent (1979), Huff (1973), Tanur (1972) and Martin (1982) are particularly recommended.

The reader who boasts few quantitative skills might tackle Chapter 2 first having first obtained a *simple* calculator possessing

$\boxed{\text{M+}}$ $\boxed{\text{MR}}$ $\boxed{\sqrt{}}$ $\boxed{1/x}$ and $\boxed{+/-}$

keys. Unless you are an engineer or a scientist, avoid the scientific calculators that offer a whole range of facilities which you will never need.

In the A chapters, which correspond to the main chapters of the same number, summaries of the main formulae using conventional mathematical notation can be found. There are also a number of computer routines (hardly worth the name 'program'). These are provided in a form of BBC.B **BASIC** compatible with most forms of **BASIC** operating on currently available machines. You are encouraged to use these programs as an aid to learning **BASIC** and as a starting point for developing your own programs.

ACKNOWLEDGEMENTS/PERMISSIONS

A book such as this inevitably draws on the ideas and experiences of many students of management and colleagues whom I have encountered over the years. In particular I would like to thank my colleagues at Ealing College of Higher Education who, as a group, have helped to form my ideas and teaching methods. A few of the examples in this book have formed part of the communal teaching material of that group over the years.

Lecturing on courses such as the Diploma in Management Studies has the great advantage that the teacher learns from the taught. Amongst those students whose ideas and experiences have particularly influenced this book are David Beck, Iqbal Cader, D James, Mike Kipp, Graham Morrison, and George Noble.

I would like to thank all those who have read and commented on the manuscript:- Pete Dawson, Ray Holloway, Phil Jones, Dick Martin, John Mingers, and also Anthony and Genevieve Cuming. The Normal Distribution table shown in Appendix 6 was calculated by John Mingers.

Permission to reproduce material was given by the following organisations and individuals, whom I thank:-

Permissions
No. Reference

1 — Pergamon Press allowed the use of the material in Figure 1.7 (p. 20), which is taken from Sissouras & Moores (1976).

2 — The (American) Institute of Management Sciences gave permission for Figure 5.3 (p. 172) to be reproduced from Canen & Galvao (1980).

3 — British Airways allowed the figures used in Table 5.7 (p.175) to be taken from their 1980/1981 Annual Report.

4 — Det norske Veritas permitted the use of the figures quoted in Table 3.1 (p. 80) from Veritas(1980).

5 — Graham Morrison and Geoff Fish gave permission for the survey results shown in Figure 7.9 (p.241) to be reproduced.

6 — The Controller of H M S O gave permission for the following material to be reproduced:-

Table 3.9.5   (p.109)   Table 5.17   (p.174)
Table 4.3   (p.123)   Figure 8.1   (p.268)
Example 4.7.5 (p.140–1)   Figure 8.2   (p.268)
Tables 5.1 & 5.2 (p.155–156)   Table 8.5   (p.265)
Table 7.2   (p.228)   Table 8.6   (p.265)
Exercise 1   (p.157)   Table 8.7   (p.269)
Exercise 2   (p.163)

CHAPTER 1 : FREQUENCY DISTRIBUTIONS

This chapter consists of two main parts. Sections 1.1 to 1.9 introduce you to a variety of frequency distributions based on actual problem situations. In the remaining sections, 1.10 to 1.15, practical details are given to help you to use the technique for yourself.

1.1 Introduction

Management has to carry out the vital functions of planning and control without precise forecasts and in the face of imperfect knowledge of the environment. Often there is a vast amount of raw data to hand which may lead the manager to take refuge in the over-simplifications of averages rather than be swamped. This chapter discusses a simple, yet powerful, technique for handling large quantities of data which is easy to understand and implement. It gives access to the inner structure of the data which is so often lost in the crude process of averaging.

We'll start by looking at examples drawn from a wide range of situations. They can't all be discussed fully until some simple techniques have been mastered, and so I will refer back to them at later points in the book. The purpose of all these examples is to highlight the practical importance of frequency distributions.

You must always bear in mind that each of the following examples only discusses one small aspect of a complex business situation, so in each case I will describe the broader context. As to technical details, remember I promised no algebra and no Greek alphabet! In return I ask you to be prepared, if it proves necessary, to develop a greater sense of numeracy. It is a fundamental principle of this book that the basic concepts of quantitative analysis can be established without the use of specialised algebra and mathematical language. The reader who is prepared to brush up his numerate skills will be rewarded by a greater understanding of business problems and of the capabilities of the specialists queuing up to assist him.

1.2 Too Much Gold?

In this first example we are in a medium-sized company on the fringes of a large city manufacturing high-quality electrical connectors. Although made of brass, these are gold-plated to ensure good contact performance and to avoid corrosion.

QUANTITATIVE METHODS

The plating is carried out in a small laboratory, not very different in appearance from a school laboratory. There is little noise about, apart from some typical lab sounds: the buzzing of electrical equipment, the trickling of taps and the gentle churning sound of the plating equipment on a bench.

One small but vital part of the manufacturing process involves plating the brass connectors with gold. The gold is supplied in the form of a white powder, a salt of gold (remember, gold dissolves in *aqua regia*!). Powder or not, it is still a very expensive raw material. In order to apply the required gold coating, the connectors are 'tumbled' in gold solution, within a mechanism that works something like a tumble drier. As the connectors tumble in the solution, the gold is electroplated onto their surface. A thickness of two microns (2 millionths of a metre) is required in order to meet the product specification. Less than that and the anti-corrosive nature of the product will not be achieved. Too thick a coating, and gold will be wasted and, what's more, customers may have difficulty in soldering onto the connectors.

Fig 1.1a : Frequency Distribution of Gold Thicknesses on Connectors (Batch Size : Large)

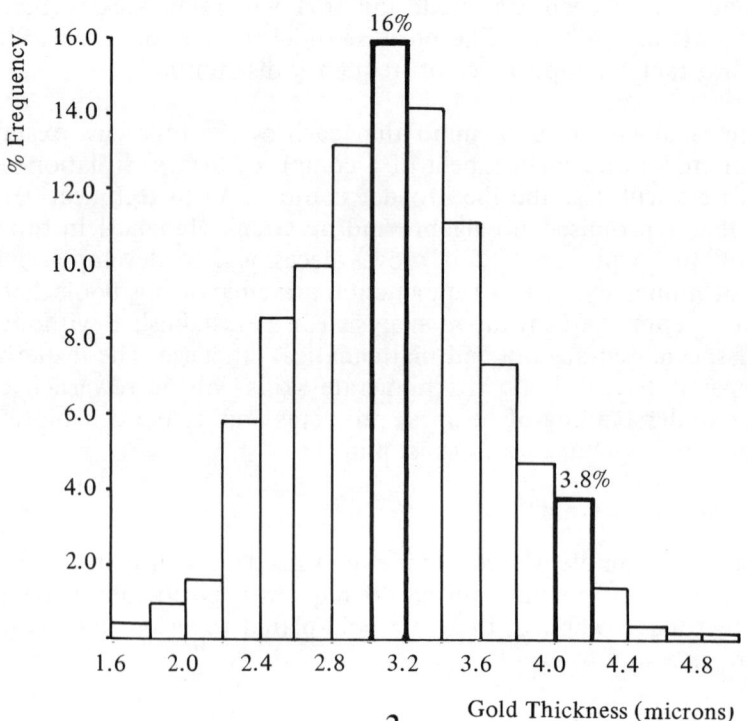

FREQUENCY DISTRIBUTIONS

One of the many problems facing management arises from the fact that the thickness of gold deposited onto connectors within the same batch varies. Using this fundamental technique of statistical analysis we can see at a glance the scale of the problem. Fig. 1.1a shows the distribution pattern of gold thicknesses produced by this technique. The height of each column indicates the percentage of the batch which received a coating of gold within the range of microns indicated at the base of the column. Thus 16% of the batch had a coating of three microns up to, but not including, 3.2 microns, and 3.8% of the batch had a coating of between 4.0 microns up to, but not including, 4.2 microns.

The distribution provides the manager with a picture of the 'shape' of the measurement data. Now let's see how this distribution can be put to immediate use to improve the economic performance of this company. Let us remind ourselves once again: we are not interested in elegant diagrams for their own sake, but only to the extent to which they can help the manager.

To start with, the production manager, with overall responsibility for producing the finished product and for whom this is only one irritating problem amongst many, can immediately see that most of the connectors are obtaining a sufficient coating of gold. However 1.4% receive marginally too little (Fig. 1.1b).

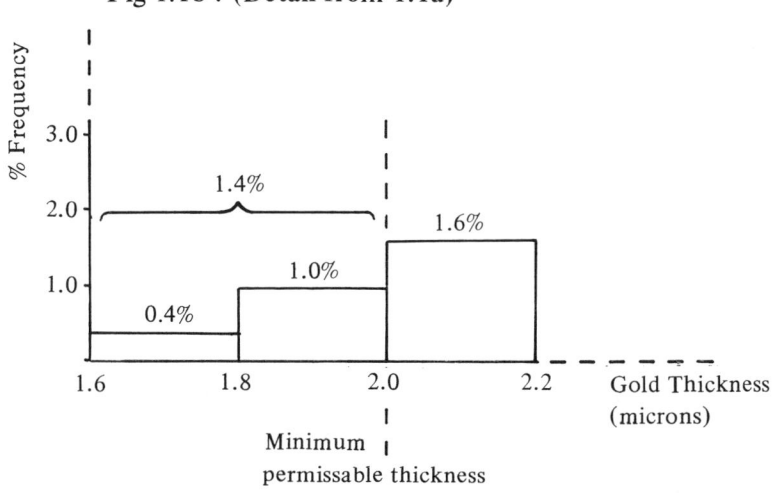

QUANTITATIVE METHODS

Fig 1.1c Comparison of the Distributions of Gold Thickness for different batch sizes

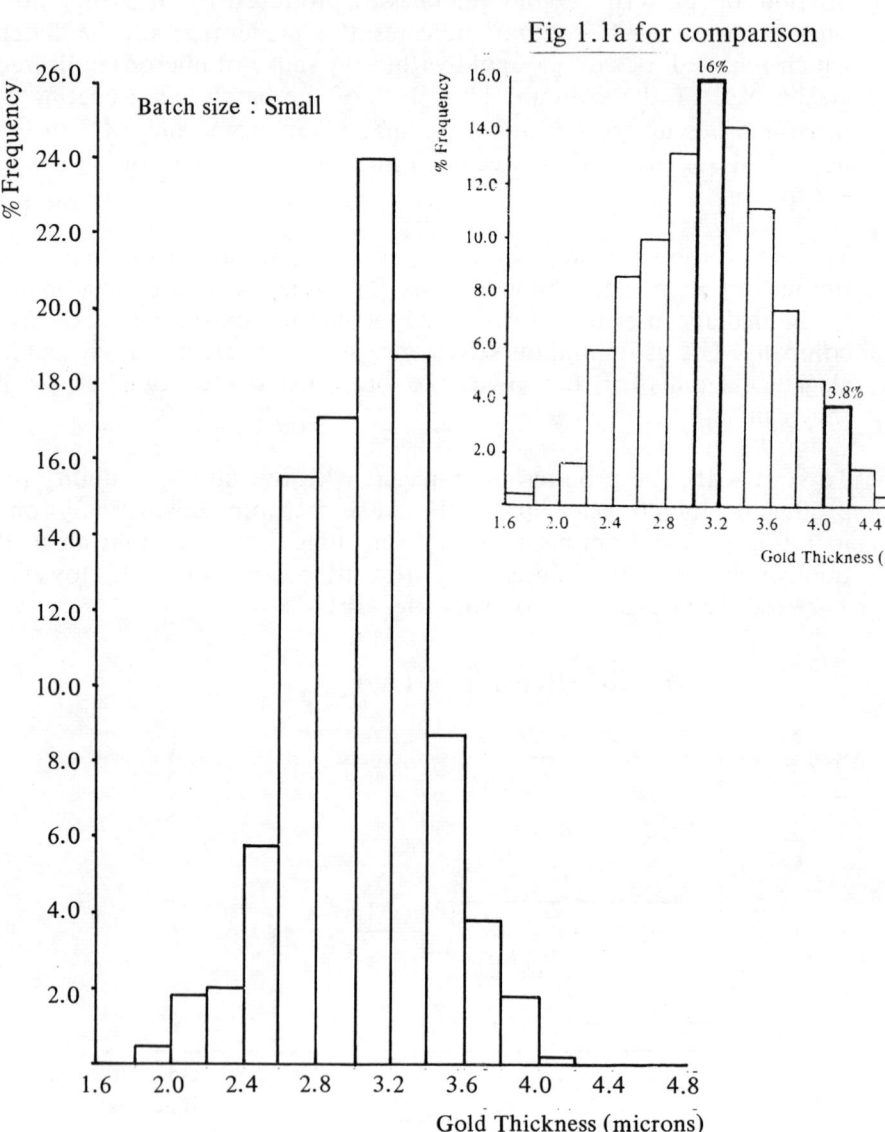

FREQUENCY DISTRIBUTIONS

It is also immediately obvious that most connectors are receiving more gold than is strictly necessary. The distribution makes it clear why. The process has a limited accuracy and the gold coatings cover a range of about 3 microns. This range or spread in the coatings achieved is related, in some way, to the technique used. The connectors tumbling together receive slightly different exposures to the metal being deposited. In order to ensure a minimum coating of 2 microns, the controller of the process has to aim much higher than that level in order to keep the left hand 'tail' from falling below 2 microns.

The distribution makes it clear that if the spread could be reduced, gold could be saved. With less spread, the distribution could be shifted downward to the left without the 'tail' dipping too far below 2 microns. By trial and error or by design the 'aiming point' has clearly been set between 3.0 and 3.2 microns, the peak of the distribution. Clearly management will be very concerned because gold constitutes a high proportion of the final cost of the product. It is also a raw material which can often rise dramatically in price.

Fig 1.1c shows the situation which arises when a smaller batch size is used. The batch size indicates the number of connectors which are tumbled together in the gold solution.

Compared with the larger batch size, the spread has been reduced. Very few connectors now receive more than 4 microns and the proportion below 2 microns has been reduced to about ½%. However the saving in gold will be offset by higher production costs. Smaller batch sizes mean a smaller throughput. The fixed costs of setting up a batch will be spread over a smaller number of connectors. But at least the production manager can now see for himself that through some planned experimentation, an appropriate compromise could be reached. Fig 1.1c shows that the spread of values are of economic significance. Gold costs money and should not be wasted. They also suggest that there is hope for cost reduction if ways of controlling the spread of gold coatings in the process can be found.

This simple technique, the frequency distribution has not provided answers, but it has shown that there can be shape and order hidden within the uncertainties and variability of a business situation and it has provided a means of measuring and communicating the performance of the process to management.

QUANTITATIVE METHODS

1.3 Too Much Steel?

And now for a complete contrast. Imagine that you are in the steel plant of a large integrated works producing steel ingots from molten iron. The molten iron is tapped from the blast furnace and is poured in 'measured' amounts into the converter. A hollow lance is inserted and oxygen passed through the liquid iron to burn out the carbon. In marked contrast to the gold plating operation this is a violent, noisy process and the steel plant is a dirty, rough and dangerous place. Whilst the process is under way, a mould train is waiting. The moulds have, typically, capacities lying between ten and twenty tons and rest on a railway bogey. When ready, the steel is poured into the moulds, producing ingots once the steel has solidified. If the amount of steel produced were to be exactly equal to the capacity of the moulds on the train, there would be no problem. If too much steel is produced, then the excess becomes scrap. Clearly excess molten steel cannot be carried forward to the next pouring, as it could in similar circumstances in many industries. It is hot, it is dangerous and it is already beginning to solidify.

If too little steel is produced than the last mould to be filled will be incomplete. As long as it is not too short, it can be rolled into sheet and then downgraded. Below a certain point, however, the resulting ingot can only be treated as scrap.

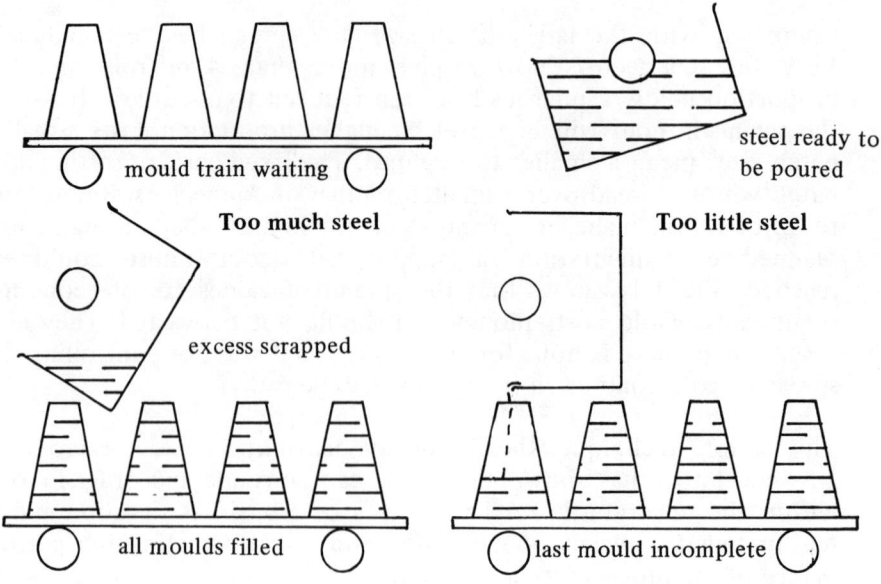

FREQUENCY DISTRIBUTIONS

The economics of the situation are complex. One crucial factor (there are of course many others) in determining an appropriate production policy is the accuracy with which the final quantity of steel produced can be predicted. For various reasons this is not as simple as it may seem. You might think that all you have to do is to add up the capacity of the moulds on the mould train and then put together the ingredients which will yield just that amount of steel. But remember, in the infernal environment of a steel plant, precise measurements are impossible and minor spillages are bound to occur.

Fig 1.2 shows the distribution of the *difference* between the tonnage actually produced and available for pouring into moulds and that which was scheduled.

Fig 1.2 : Difference between Converter & Scheduled Steel Tonnage.

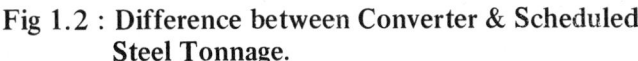

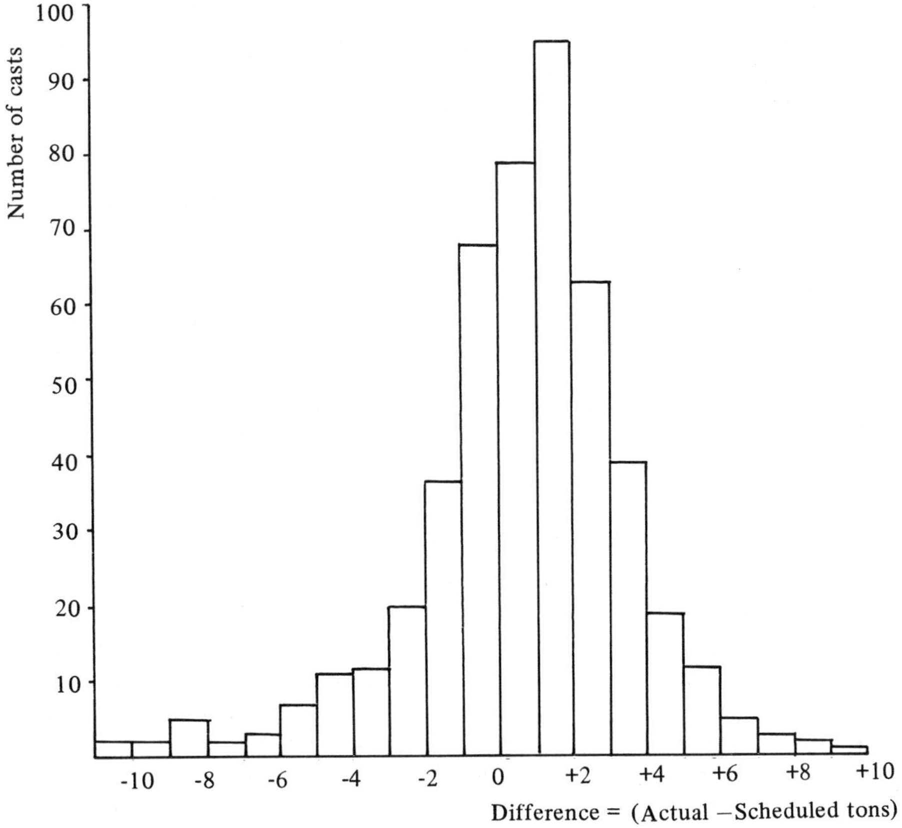

Difference = (Actual − Scheduled tons)

Even if we disregard the freak values at the lower end of the distribution, which may be due to special circumstances, there is still a wide variation inherent in the process. Sometimes the actual tonnage produced has fallen short of that scheduled and sometimes it has exceeded it. Overall there seems to be a spread of about 20 tons. We can say that the aiming point seems to be about 1 ton over schedule. By trial and error or by design, the policy has been to aim to produce slightly more than the scheduled quantity. The distribution provides us with a 'picture' of the accuracy of the steel conversion process. It reminds us that whatever tonnage is scheduled, a different tonnage, more or less, will almost certainly be produced. It provides the planner with a picture of the uncertainties facing him, but more than just a picture, it helps him to quantify the error that is likely to be encountered.

As was the case with the gold plating process, management can use the distribution to see the effect of changing the aiming point. They can consider different strategies towards building up the mix of moulds on the mould train for different production schedules. They can then see what the economic outcome of adopting different aiming points will be. For each strategy, they will be able to forecast the proportion of last-moulds which will be short and therefore down-graded or scrapped and the proportion of occasions on which excess steel will be produced.

So far in the discussion we have assumed that management will accept the spread or error displayed in Fig 1.2 as fixed. The distribution also poses the question: is it not possible to reduce the error? If this could be done then the potential cost savings could be estimated. A study of physical processes involved would be necessary to answer that question. The possibility of more accurate weighing of ingredients and the avoidance of spillages could be investigated.

1.4 The Manager and the Statistician

We have looked at two examples so far. In both, the scale of operations has been widely different. The statistician will recognise in both examples similar statistical characteristics. In both cases they have been quasi-symmetrical distributions around a central aiming point in Figs 1.1a & c the aiming point was the thickness of gold to be plated and the spread around that aiming point derived from the process of electroplating. In Fig 1.2, the aiming point was a quantity of steel to be produced from liquid iron and the spread around that aiming point came from the error inherent in the processes involved

FREQUENCY DISTRIBUTIONS

and the difficulty of weighing or measuring accurately in a steel plant.

The scientist is instictively attracted to finding common patterns in widely different settings. That is why he may be able to see a similar opportunity to assist management in a situation which has not yet been recognised. Managers generally have no such interest in the universal applicability of science. For the production manager responsible for producing electrical connectors, the problem of excessive gold consumption and adequate plating thicknesses is only one of many problems which beset him. The steel plant manager also has a whole set of problems specific to his plant: cranes mal-functioning, budgets exceeded, and, of course, the inevitable industrial relations problems. He does not want to know about gold plating. He has enough problems producing steel.

The moral goes something like this. Managers should realise that statisticians can recognise familiar patterns in the chaotic and highly specific world of the businessman. This facility can help the manager to do his job more efficiently. The statistician's ability to recognise these structures and patterns is due to his interests *outside* the specific business situation of the manager. In other words it is the statistician's relative detachment from the specific situation at hand that is his strength.

Statisticians must recognise, for their part, that what management wants is enlightenment on specific issues. They do not particularly want to take part in the advance and spread of human knowledge and they do not want to know that gold-plating thicknesses or steel production variances provide nice examples of statistical theory in practice.

The two examples above, and those that follow, are ample evidence that there is plenty of common ground for the statistician and the business manager to meet for their mutual benefit. All that is needed is the ability to

COMMUNICATE

It is to assist in the process of communication that this book has been written.

Blocks to communication are often set-up by management's fear of what is perceived to be the higher level of *academic* attainment of the specialist adviser. This fear often expresses itself in a retreat behind a barrier made up of the manager's experience. An extreme version goes a bit like this:

QUANTITATIVE METHODS

> 'Look my lad, I've spent 20 years plating gold (casting steel). When you've got as much experience you can come and give me advice!'

There are many more subtle, but equally negative versions which amount to the same thing. What line management could more usefully say might go like this:

> 'Look my lad, I've spent 20 years plating gold (casting steel). I've still got more problems than I can cope with. Seeing as you have only limited experience of my field, maybe you can shed some new light on some of my problems. Keep talking to me as you carry on your study (if you can find me, that is). Smith here will give you all the gen you need to know. Give me your findings in a language that I and my colleagues can understand.'

The statistician for his part sets up barriers to communication in two ways. Firstly he is trained to use a language, mathematics, which is alien to his client. The fact that he may use mathematics to develop his proposals does not mean that he should then use mathematics in communicating the results. That is why maths language has been banned from this part of the book. Secondly he may hide behind the barriers made up of his academic training. The world of theoretical statistics is highly structured. The subject, as laid out in the text books, follows a clear logical sequence. The business environment is fast-moving and complex. Data collection is often rudimentary and mathematics, except for engineering environments, is usually 'not spoken.'

For the statistician to contribute usefully to management's task, it is essential for these barriers to be removed. Both parties need to cooperate closely in a critical appraisal of the data employed and the objectives of the study. This problem of data and data collection is taken up in Chapter 12.

Both the distributions we have looked at so far have been quasi-symmetrical. A symmetrical distribution is one in which the left hand side is an exact mirror image of the right hand side. I use the term 'quasi-symmetrical' to refer to Figs 1.1 and 1.2 because they only approximate to the description 'symmetrical'. To see what a non-symmetrical distribution looks like, look at Figs 1.3a and 1.3b. They represent the distribution of the ages of the caretakers in schools in a London borough.

FREQUENCY DISTRIBUTIONS

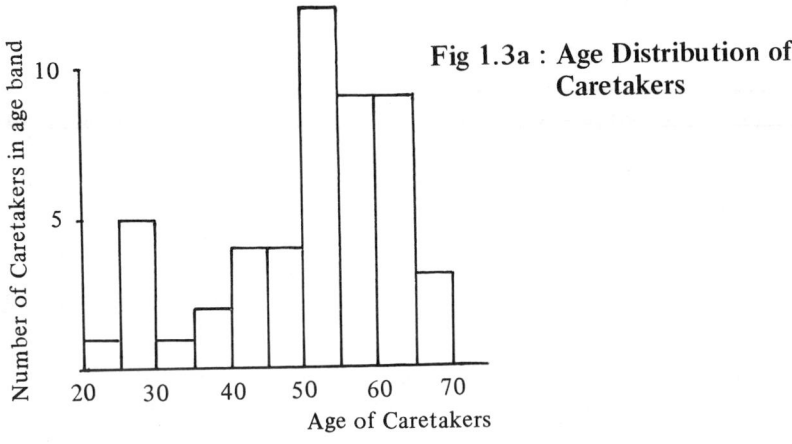

Fig 1.3a : Age Distribution of Caretakers

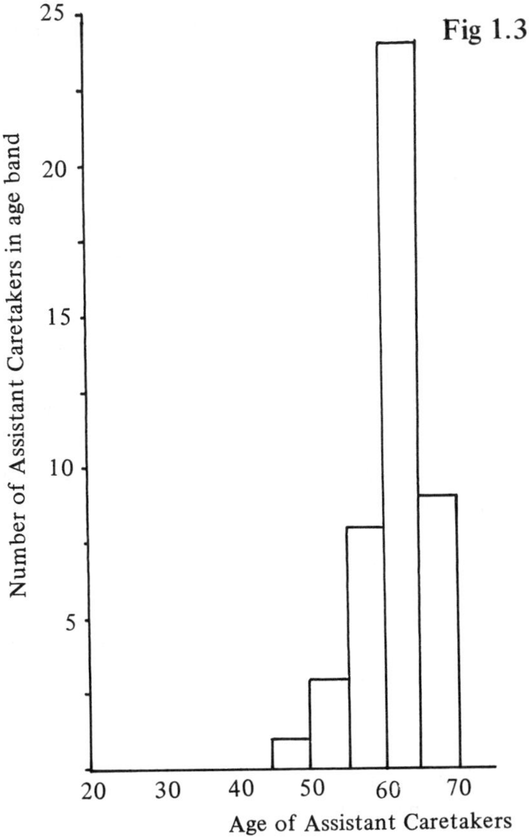

Fig 1.3b : Age Distribution of Assistant Caretakers

QUANTITATIVE METHODS

1.5 How Old are the Caretakers?

The distribution of the ages of employees is a subject of great interest to personnel managers. The age structure of an organisation can develop an undesirable form, especially when there is little staff turnover. An ageing workforce can lead to a loss of corporate vigour. Age bulges, where a high proportion of employees are collected within a narrow age band, can be an indicator of future retirement complications especially if a lowering of the retirement age is introduced.

The difference between the two distributions shown in Figs 1.3a and b is very striking.

Although most assistant caretakers are quite old, amongst the caretakers there seems to be a group of very young persons. It is important not to expect distribution analysis like this to provide answers. On the contrary it poses a number of questions. That's good. Techniques that help us to ask probing questions are useful techniques. They also have the advantage of encouraging communication between management and analyst. Here are some of the questions that come to mind:

1. Are assistant caretakers very badly paid?
2. Have young caretakers always formed part of the work force or is this a reflection of some new policy?
3. What are the rules governing the retirement of caretakers?
4. What changes are envisaged in employment policy, if any?

Hopefully you can think of a few more. Note how the distributions give some form and structure to one aspect of employment in the public service. The answers to questions 2 and 3 have a major bearing on the way the distribution will evolve into the future. For example, if the employment of young caretakers is part of a relatively new employment policy, then the younger group in the distribution will grow with the passage of time and spread to the right, while the older group will dwindle as the existing caretakers retire.

On the other hand, maybe some younger caretakers have always been taken on as well as relatively old recruits, in which case the distribution may remain very much the same as it is now.

Both 1.3a and 1.3b have a shape that we will describe as 'negatively skewed'. This is a term that describes their characteristic 'tail to the left' shape.

FREQUENCY DISTRIBUTIONS

Fig 1.3c, by contrast shows the age distribution and length of service distribution of a large manufacturing company.

Fig 1.3c : Ages of a sample of 242 employees in Company X

Fig 1.3d : Length of service of a sample of 242 employees in Company X

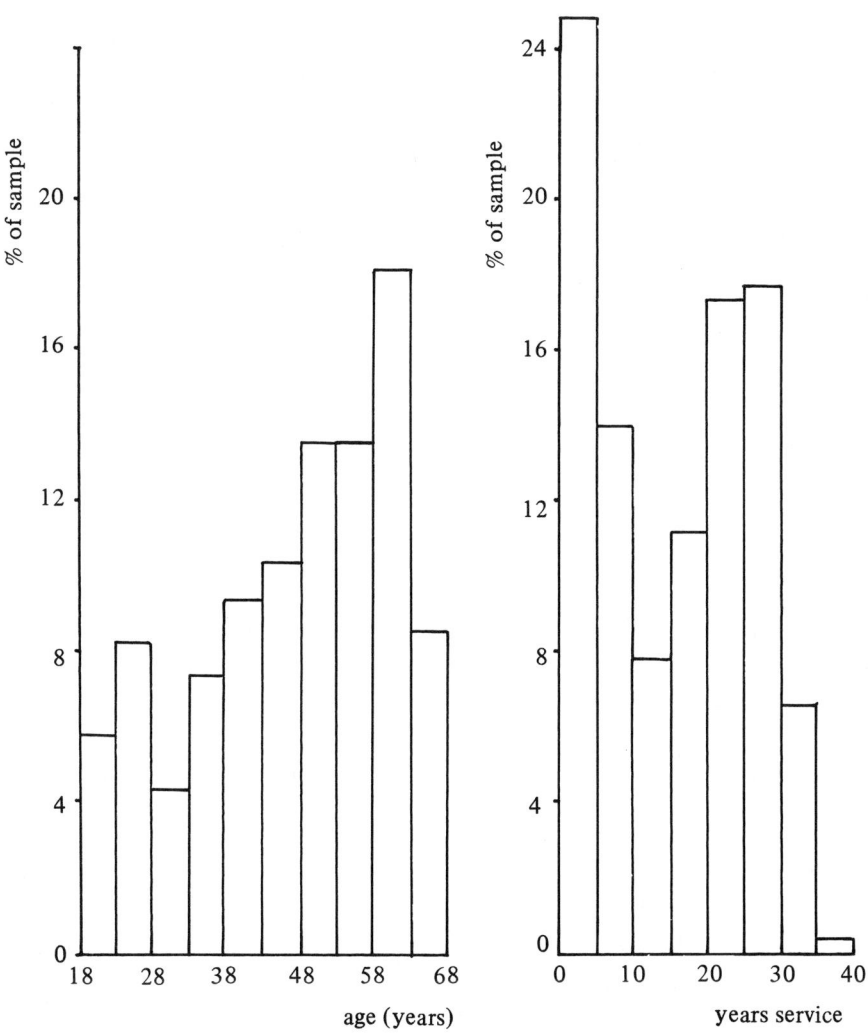

QUANTITATIVE METHODS

Note how well Fig 1.3c shows up the relatively high age of the workforce. (The age bands were chosen to start at 18 because the distribution ranged from 18.9 years to 67 years). The distribution is negatively skewed and a majority of workers are aged over 40. At a glance you can see that if retirement at 60 were brought in, about 25% of the workforce would go within two years.

Turning to the length of service distribution (Fig 1.3d), it follows that just under half of the workforce has put in no less than 20 years service or more. Obviously many of the workforce taken on in the post-war years are still there. Think how ill-fitted they would be to face redundancy. Both distributions help to provide a picture of an ageing traditional manufacturing company.

1.6 How long did the Job Take?

Fig 1.4 shows an example of a distribution which is 'positively

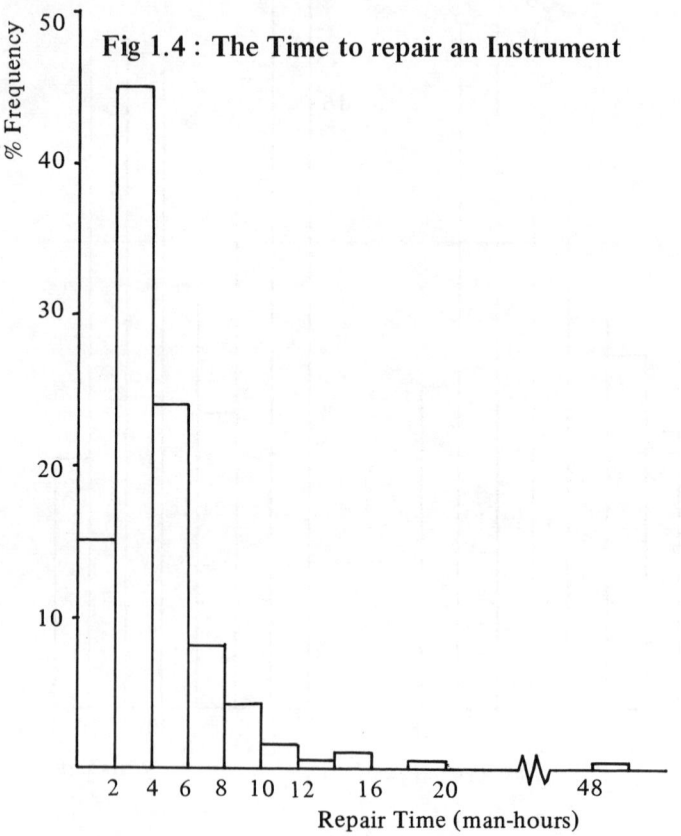

Fig 1.4 : The Time to repair an Instrument

FREQUENCY DISTRIBUTIONS

skewed'. This is a useful term to describe an asymmetrical distribution which has a tail stretching out to the right. The distribution shows the time, in man-hours, that it took to repair an instrument in an engineering workshop. Notice that although most instruments take less than 6 hours, some take more than double that time. Would you expect job-time distributions to be symmetrical or to be positively skewed? Under what circumstances would job-times be expected to be negatively skewed? I would expect job-times for any complex operation to be positively skewed because of the possibility that some jobs, a small minority perhaps, will involve snags and cause special difficulties thus leading to the tail to the right. That certainly seems to be the case with this instrument.

Of course I don't believe that 48 hour figure! It's so far out of line with the others that I suspect that what happened was that some error has got into the data. After all, 48 man-hours spent on one instrument seems hardly cost effective. I would like very much to find out precisely how the man-hours were recorded.

Note how seeing the whole distribution helps to put the extreme values into context. The 48 hours figure was so high that I had to break the horizontal axis in order to indicate that it has been foreshortened.

To decide whether this rogue figure is genuine or not I will need to talk with someone who works close to the workshop environment.

1.7 How Much Stock should they hold?

Fig 1.5 shows us 4 positively skewed distributions. Each represents the number of units of a consumable item of stock withdrawn from stores in a large engineering centre attached to an airline.

To understand the stock control problems found in the engineering works of an airline you must appreciate that when an airliner is pulled to bits, you end up with an awful lot of different parts. An airliner can easily be made up of more than 100,000 different sorts of components.

Stock control is usually a specialist function within an organisation. It is, however, an area of general interest because stock-holding situations in one form or another are found in most organisations, public and private, and because most aspects of business systems are affected by the failure or success of the stock control system employed.

QUANTITATIVE METHODS

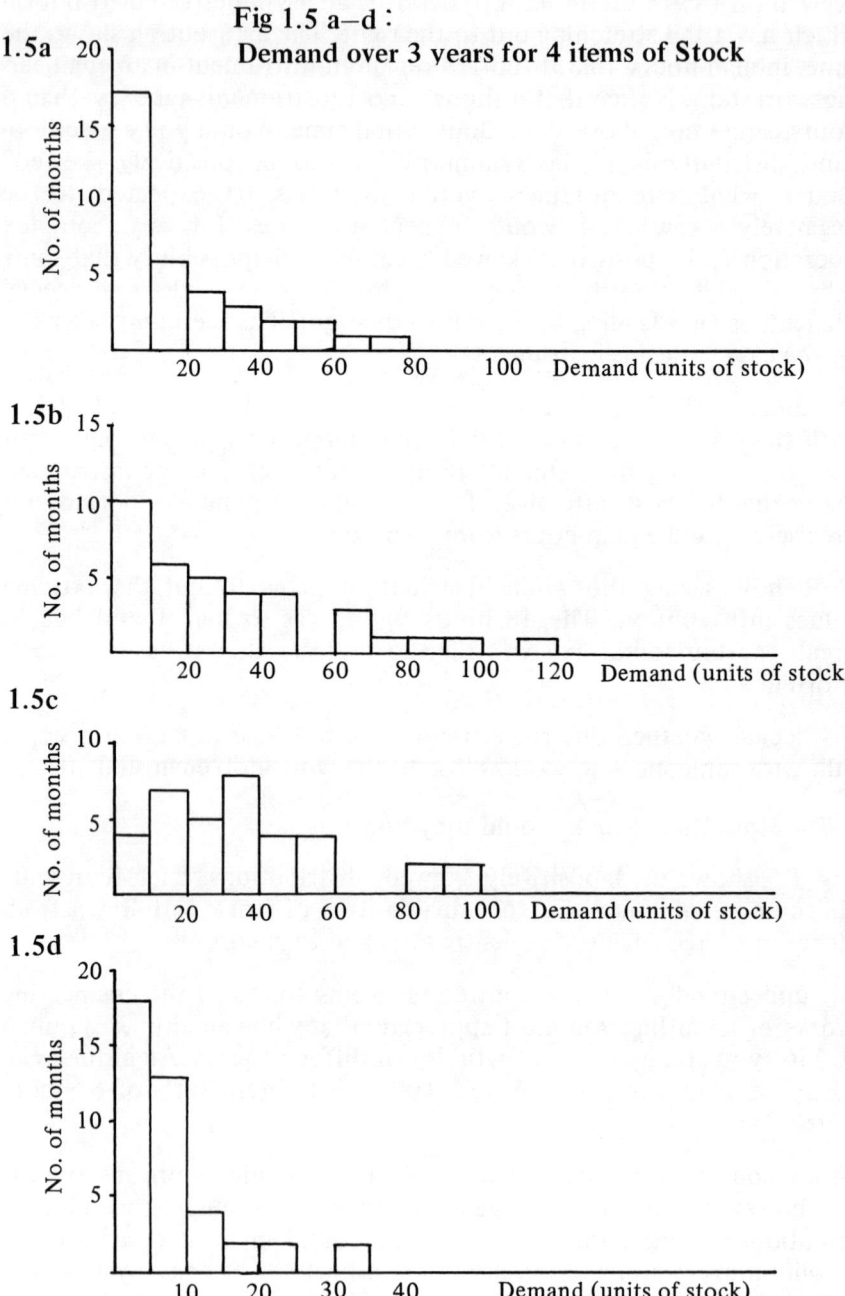

Fig 1.5 a–d : Demand over 3 years for 4 items of Stock

FREQUENCY DISTRIBUTIONS

Fig 1.5a tells us that in many months there has been little demand for the item while in others there has been a demand for more than 50. At first sight it would seem that such skewed distributions would suggest the need for relatively high stock holdings. If, as is the case in Fig 1.5b, stores may be required in some months to issue around 100 units, then surely the stock level will have to be maintained at a high level to meet that eventuality. Now bear in mind that item (b) cost around £2 (in 1984 prices) *each* and there are many thousands of similar items. Before deciding how serious the problem is, the data will have to be subjected to greater scrutiny. This will be done in Chapter 12.

Suffice it to note at this state that the distributions in Fig 1.5 give us a good picture of one aspect of the headache which the stock controller has to cope with given a limited budget, serving line managers who expect service on demand.

1.8 Breaking down a Distribution

Some distributions are very rich in features and defy straight-forward classification. Fig 1.6a is a highly irregular distribution. It represents the life until removal, in flying hours, for an aircraft component (a flying hour is clocked up each time an aircraft flies for one hour). This is a rotable component. That means that once removed from an aircraft, it is repaired, tested, and made available for another aircraft.

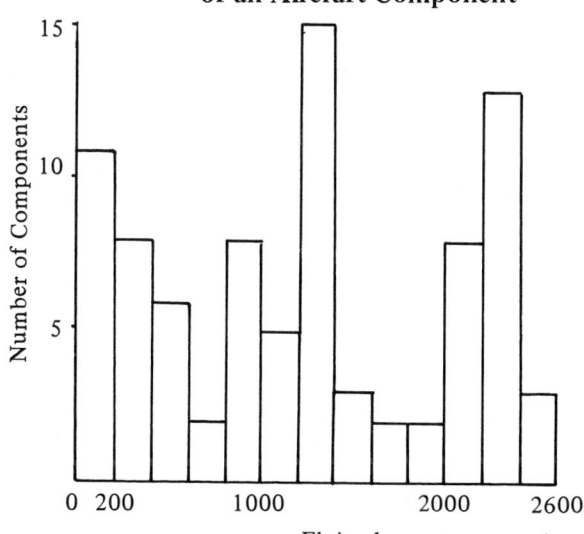

Fig 1.6a : Life (flying hours) to Removal of an Aircraft Component

Flying hours to removal

QUANTITATIVE METHODS

There are a number of strange features about this distribution. It seems to have three main peaks. A surprising number of components fail very early on and everything comes to an abrupt halt after 2600 hours. What you know of your own car might suggest to you that a component that can function satisfactorily for 2000 hours should have a reasonable chance of keeping going for some considerable time after that. Wouldn't you expect the distribution of lives to have a long right hand tail?

Some further information will explain at least some of these features. At the time this data was collected, the component had an allowed life of 2400 flying hours. Once 2400 hours had been clocked up, the component was removed and sent to the workshops. (Note, the distribution shows clearly that in a few instances an extension had been granted for up to 200 hours beyond 2400 hours).

Because of this information, we now realise that the life up to removal is not the same as the life up to failure. Obvious perhaps, but the sort of error an inexperienced statistician might make.

As it happens, in this instance we can obtain a more detailed breakdown of the data, Figs 1.6b, c, d. Fig 1.6b shows the hours to removal of those components which were removed and which were then confirmed as having failed. Fig 1.6c shows those which were removed as 'failures' but which were not confirmed as such by the workshops. The fact that they functioned correctly in the workshops doesn't mean that they were necessarily working on the aircraft, but in some cases certainly the removal was certainly due to faulty diagnosis. It seems that sometimes a component can fail to function on an aircraft because of some mismatch or other and yet still pass a workshop test. The statistician will only learn of such peculiarities, well known to the engineers, if he communicates with those who have accumulated experience in this specialised field. Fig 1.6d shows those components that were routine removals.

As is usually the case, this breakdown of the data poses as many questions as it answers. There's nothing wrong with that. This is a healthy sign. While analysing a problem, techniques that throw up questions are doing a good job of work. For example, Fig 1.6d shows routine removal of components that had reached the limit of 2400 hours. But why, you might well wonder, should one remove a component which has only flown 1200 hours or even 600 hours? I describe these questions as healthy because to get the answers, the statistician must communicate with those engineers who spend their

FREQUENCY DISTRIBUTIONS

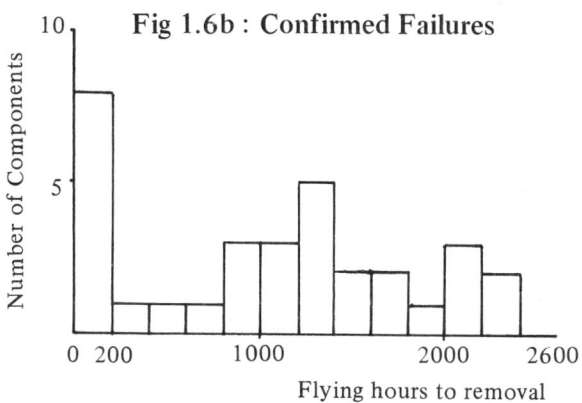

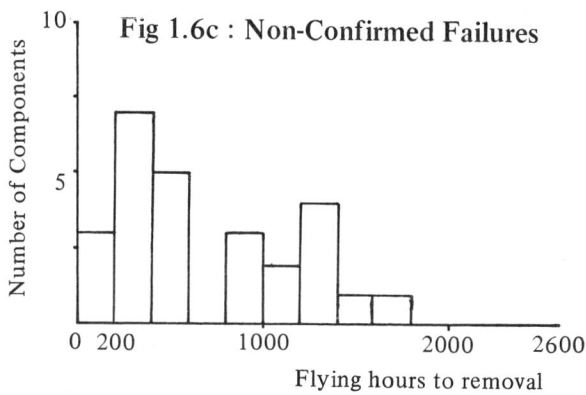

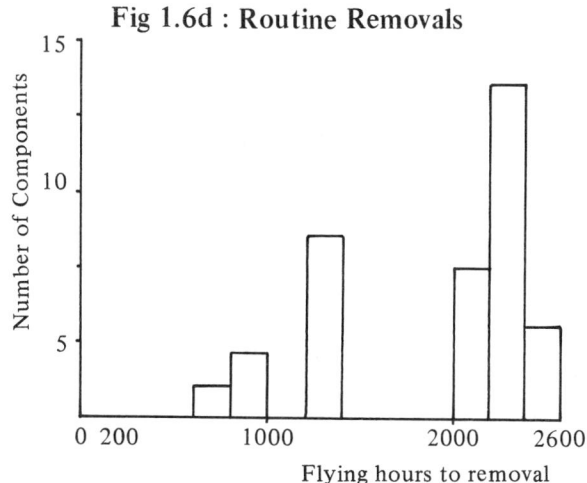

QUANTITATIVE METHODS

life working in this environment. The distributions of Figure 1.6 can now form common ground for a two-way discussion between the statistician and line-management staff. In fact part of the answer lies in the timing of aircraft maintenance. If an aircraft is undergoing a major maintenance programme, it can make sense to remove a component prematurely if it has a fixed allowed life. By sacrificing 1000 hours or so, you save the trouble of having to remove it from the aircraft at a later date.

All the distributions we have looked at so far are known as 'continuous distributions'. In these, the horizontal scale is subdivided into bands and the frequency or percentage frequency count on the vertical axis indicates the number or percentage of values which fall within the given bands. In situations where the values can only take on a limited number of discrete values, we draw up a 'discrete frequency distribution'. To illustrate this type of distribution, here is an interesting example drawn from the public sector.

1.9   Coronary Care

Fig 1.7a shows a percentage frequency distribution for the number of admissions per day to a coronary care unit in Salford. A coronary

Fig 1.7 : Admissions per day to a Coronary Care Unit

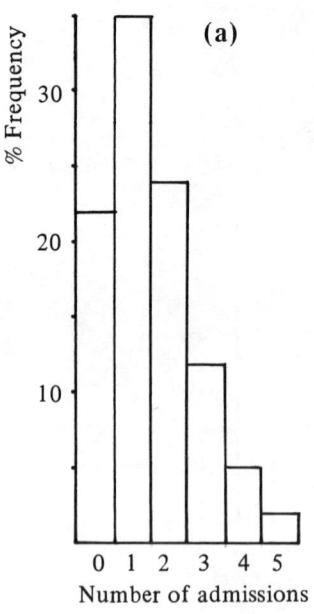
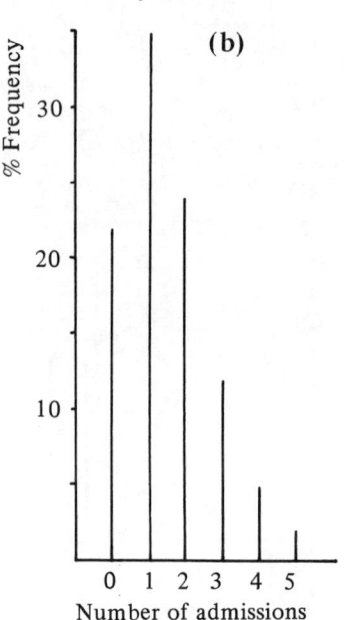

(Permission No. 1)

FREQUENCY DISTRIBUTIONS

care unit is a special treatment unit attached to a hospital. Obviously only whole numbers of patients can be admitted so the horizontal axis is marked off in whole numbers.

The first two columns therefore read:

Col. 1 : On 22% of days, 0 admissions were made to the unit

Col. 2 : On 35% of days, 1 admission was made.

Fig 1.7b shows a method of presenting the distribution which emphasises the discrete nature of the data but Fig 1.7a is a more common version and will be used here.

The distribution highlights the problem that the variability of one part of the system gives to management. It would be convenient if emergency coronary cases presented themselves to the unit in a neat orderly fashion. Management could then plan to receive them. Of course in the real world things don't happen like that. In fact, as we have seen, anything from 0 to 5 cases can arrive in any one day *and cannot be turned away.* Here is a queuing system with a difference; no queue is permitted! Instead patients in the unit are 'ejected', that is the treatment of some patients is reduced from the ideal time required. This study set out to examine, using simulation techniques, the effect on the ejection level of varying levels of demand that might be expected when allowing for different sizes of the care units.

Another vital feature of this study was the distribution of the length of stay in the unit. It would help, wouldn't it, if a standard length of stay could be assumed. A glance at Fig 1.7c and d (page 22) shows that this is far from being the case. In fact the length of stay is variable and is quite different from those who have suffered a 'myocardial infarction' (a coronary blockage) and those who have not.

1.10 We've seen how useful frequency distributions can be. Now let us find out how to set them up. This is a technique that you can usefully employ yourself so it's worth facing up to a few of the practical problems involved. I promised no complicated maths in this section. Well, drawing up frequency distributions doesn't involve much maths, but it does need some care and technical skill and so a few practical hints will come in handy.

QUANTITATIVE METHODS

Fig 1.7c : Myocardial Infarction   Fig 1.7d : Non-Myocardial Infarction

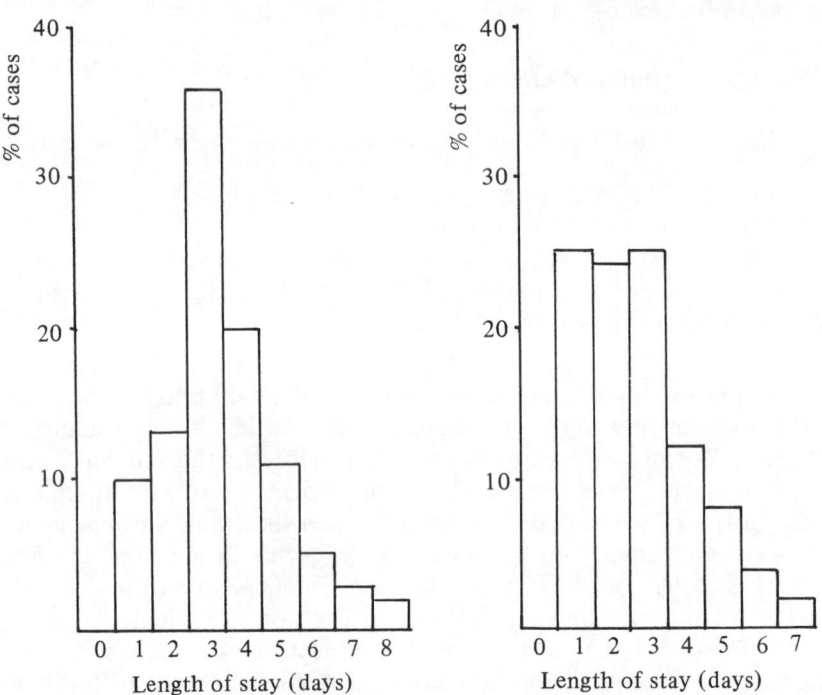

Here is the original data showing us the ages of school caretakers.

Ages of School Caretakers (years)

50	26	60	30	41	53	58	54	53	28
56	68	42	67	53	46	59	66	36	57
41	54	62	24	62	54	29	61	56	49
58	29	53	53	47	64	59	55	60	45
56	51	61	44	52	38	62	26	64	52

First I establish the minimum and maximum values, in this case 24 and 68 years respectively. It's always worth considering whether these extreme values make sense. Schoolboy or octagenarian caretakers would be ridiculous. It's never worth making a fool of yourself just because the typist has hit the wrong keys!

In this case, 24 seems reasonable enough and I can just believe 68 although I raise a query in my mind as to whether there might be a legal limit to the upper age of caretakers. I make a mental note to check my facts at the first opportunity.

FREQUENCY DISTRIBUTIONS

Five years seems a reasonable class interval for data spanning about 40 years so I set out the intervals as follows:

Age Interval

20 — 24
25 — 29
30 — 34
35 — 39
40 — 44
45 — 49
50 — 54
55 — 59
60 — 64
65 — 69

Running down the first column, the ages slot into the class intervals thus:

Age Interval

20 — 24
25 — 29
30 — 34
35 — 39
40 — 44   41
45 — 49
50 — 54   50
55 — 59   56,56,58
60 — 64
65 — 69

Now the whole point of choosing class intervals is to treat all numbers falling within the given intervals as being the same, so I replace the numbers with a tally count thus:

Age Interval	Tally Count
20 — 24	
25 — 29	
30 — 34	
35 — 39	
40 — 44	/
45 — 49	
50 — 54	/
55 — 59	///
60 — 64	
65 — 69	

23

QUANTITATIVE METHODS

Adding the next two columns I get

Age Interval	Tally Count
20 – 24	
25 – 29	//
30 – 34	
35 – 39	
40 – 44	//
45 – 49	
50 – 54	////
55 – 59	///
60 – 64	///
65 – 69	/

Note how the shape of the distribution is starting to build up in front of you.

Adding another two columns, making the first five in all, the picture continues to build up. Note how I batch my tally marks in bundles of 5. It's much easier to read.

50 – 54 /̶/̶/̶/̶/ //   than   50 – 54 ///////

Age Interval	Tally Count
20 – 24	/
25 – 29	//
30 – 34	/
35 – 39	
40 – 44	////
45 – 49	/
50 – 54	/̶/̶/̶/̶/ //
55 – 59	///
60 – 64	////
65 – 69	//

The complete distribution ends up looking like this:

Age of Caretakers (Years)

Age Range	Tally Count	Frequency
20 – 24	/	1
25 – 29	/̶/̶/̶/̶/	5
30 – 34	/	1
35 – 39	//	2
40 – 44	////	4
45 – 49	////	4
50 – 54	/̶/̶/̶/̶/ /̶/̶/̶/̶/ //	12
55 – 59	/̶/̶/̶/̶/ ////	9
60 – 64	/̶/̶/̶/̶/ ////	9
65 – 69	///	3
		50

FREQUENCY DISTRIBUTIONS

The distribution can be represented graphically in the form of a *histogram* (Fig 1.3a on page 11). Note that the tally marks on their own provide quite a good histogram. What's more, as you have just seen, you can watch the picture build up as you are processing the raw data. This is particularly useful if you are working through grubby work-sheets where the figures are difficult to extract.

Many of the technical problems which arise in the use of quantitative techniques make expert advice advisable. However building up frequency distributions is a fundamental, useful and rewarding technique and well worth practising yourself even if you can afford to pay someone to do most of your analysis. The technique described looks simple enough. When you try and put it into practice, problems can arise. Here are a few of them together with hints as to how to overcome them.

1.11 Problem 1 : How to represent the frequencies and class intervals graphically, yet unambiguously

The first three class intervals read

Age	Frequency
20 – 24	1
25 – 29	5
30 – 34	1

Graphically I have represented these as

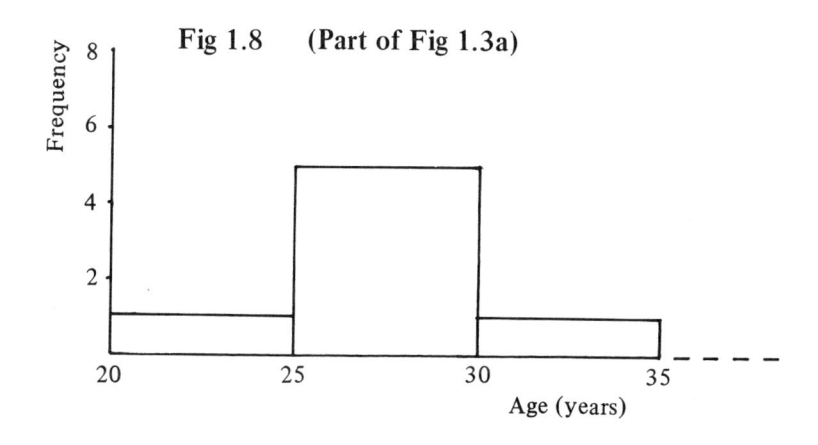

Fig 1.8   (Part of Fig 1.3a)

QUANTITATIVE METHODS

Someone might read this histogram as

Age	Frequency
20 – 25	1
25 – 30	5
30 – 35	1

and wonder where a caretaker aged 25 exactly should be placed.

Now assuming a caretaker doesn't count as 25 until his 25th birthday, we should, to avoid any ambiguity, draw the graph with a break thus:

Fig 1.9

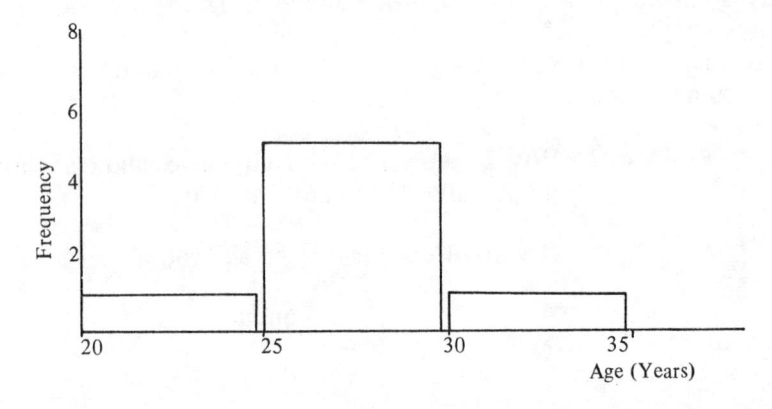

Alternatively, if their ages are rounded off to the nearest whole number of years, we would represent the diagram thus:

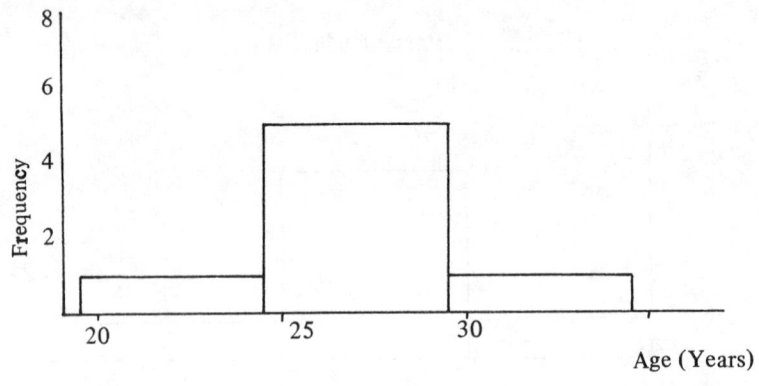

The old interval 20 – 24 becomes 19.5 – 24.5. A caretaker aged 19.6 years old will then count as 20 and one aged 24.3 will count as 24.

FREQUENCY DISTRIBUTIONS

I think you'll agree that in both cases the effect is confusing for the general user. In some specialised cases this degree of precision may be required. In the interests of clarity, we will adopt the convention that Fig 1.3a is read as indicating that 1 caretaker has an age falling within the interval 20 up to, but not including 25, 5 caretakers have ages in the range 25 up to, but not including 30 etc.

This is often represented in a frequency distribution as

$$20 \; - \; <25$$
$$25 \; - \; <30 \text{ etc.}$$

or somewhat more ambiguously as

20	–	25	or better as	20	–	
25	–	30 etc.		25	–	etc.

Exercise

1. The weekly demand over 50 weeks for two items of stock A & B are shown below.

Item A : Number of units per week

2	1	3	5	1	6	2	8	4	2
0	4	2	3	2	3	1	7	5	3
2	1	5	2	5	4	2	3	3	8
3	3	1	7	0	4	2	5	1	2
1	4	3	2	6	9	2	2	4	0

Item B : Number of units per week

2	3	2	4	3	3	3	4	2	3
3	1	4	3	5	2	4	3	6	3
4	2	5	3	4	3	3	3	4	2
3	3	4	3	3	2	5	1	4	3
2	4	3	5	2	4	3	3	4	3

i) Draw up separate discrete frequency distributions for each item and plot the histograms one at the top and the other at the bottom of the graph paper. Do not use class intervals. Build up the tallies for each possible discrete value.

ii) How would the appearance of these distributions influence your decision about re-stocking the items given that it takes a week for an order to be delivered.

QUANTITATIVE METHODS

2. Draw up a frequency distribution and histogram based on the following workshop repair times and comment on the results. Use a class interval of 10 minutes.

Repair Times (minutes)

16	42	21	11	23	16	13	34	22	17
30	6	15	29	25	24	19	39	13	28
20	41	68	41	4	42	10	46	9	19
27	14	17	42	17	18	32	21	44	
86	36	72	62	15	28	12	23	26	

3. Suppose that the weight of material A used to make up part of a sack of fertilizer has been measured as follows.

Weight of Material A (kilos) used to make 1 sack of fertilizer. (46 observations)

41.3	52.6	58.9	49.3	53.6
66.8	46.3	51.3	54.4	65.1
45.3	62.3	42.4	46.8	48.8
48.7	51.7	48.3	56.2	53.2
54.1	64.7	63.8	47.2	64.6
46.1	57.5	49.4	65.2	59.3
63.8	42.6	62.9	42.9	47.4
52.8	62.0	45.9	48.0	54.2
48.9	56.2	45.1	52.0	48.2
45.0				

i) Draw up frequency distribution and histogram of the usage recorded for material A using suitable class intervals.

ii) What questions would be worth posing to management given that the standard usage laid down is 40 kilos. Bear in mind that the data was collected on 3 different days and that two different operators were involved.

1.12 Problem 2 : Class intervals of unequal width

Suppose, for some reason, we had combined the first two class intervals so that instead of

Age	Frequency
20 − 24	1
25 − 29	5
30 − 34	1
35 − 39	2 etc.

FREQUENCY DISTRIBUTIONS

we had produced

Age	Frequency
20 – 29	6
30 – 34	1
35 – 39	2 etc.

We would then obtain a histogram looking like Fig 1.11 the original histogram (Fig 1.3a) is shown with it for the purposes of comparison.

Fig 1.11 : Incorrect Handling of Unequal Intervals

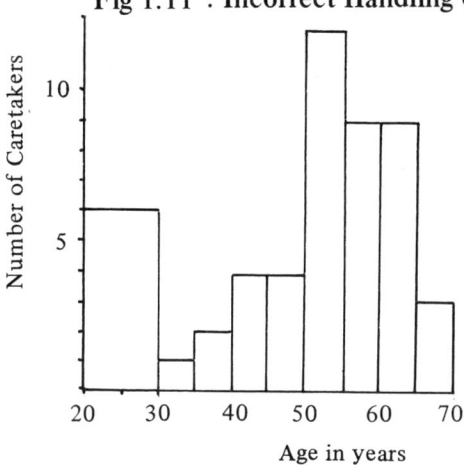

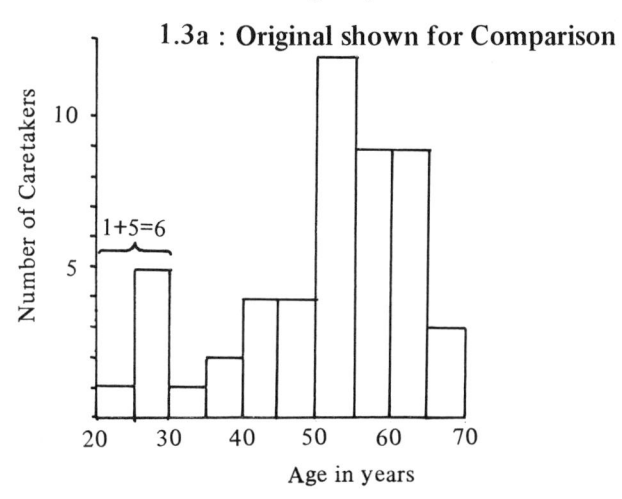

1.3a : Original shown for Comparison

Although strictly correct, the picture is misleading. Someone might try to argue that:

29

QUANTITATIVE METHODS

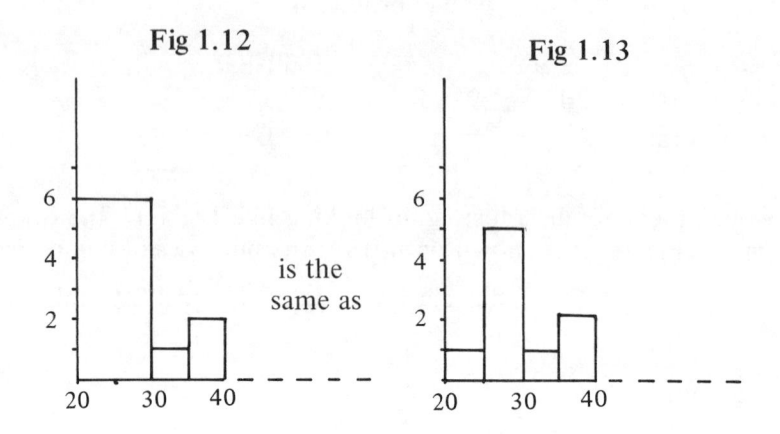

Fig 1.12 is the same as **Fig 1.13**

'Look, he might say. Fig 1.12 says that 6 caretakers have ages lying between 20 and 29. What's wrong with that?' The eye, however, assesses the relative frequencies by comparing the relative areas in the histogram. Now a histogram is a *visual* representation of a frequency distribution. Therefore anything which is visually confusing should be avoided. In such a situation we should halve the frequencies on the histogram for those class intervals which have been doubled (Fig 1.14).

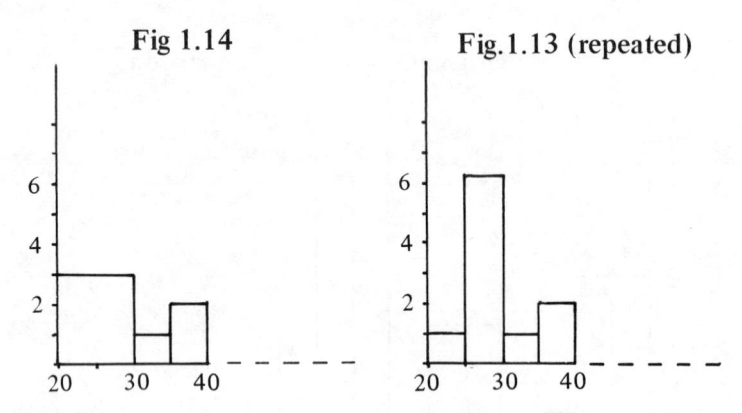

Fig 1.14   **Fig.1.13 (repeated)**

Of course some perverse reader may now interpret this as '3 caretakers with ages in the range 20 – 29'. As so often happens in statistical representation, we have to choose between two evils.

As a general guide

i) Avoid class intervals of differing widths where possible.

FREQUENCY DISTRIBUTIONS

ii) Where this can't be avoided or where it is thought desirable, divide the larger class interval into a standard width and allocate the frequencies in proportion.

1.12.1 Example

Values	Frequency	
0 – 9	4	width = 10
10 – 19	5	width = 10
20 – 59	6	width = 40

Here we must sub-divide the third interval into 4 equal intervals and assign ¼ of the frequency of 6 to each thus:

Value	Frequency
0 – 9	4
10 – 19	5
20 – 9	1.5
30 – 39	1.5
40 – 49	1.5
50 – 59	1.5

Don't worry about the fractional values. We're not calculating frequencies here, we're simply working out how high to draw the frequency columns on the histogram. In drawing the histogram, we will not show the artificial sub-division of the larger interval.

Fig 1.15

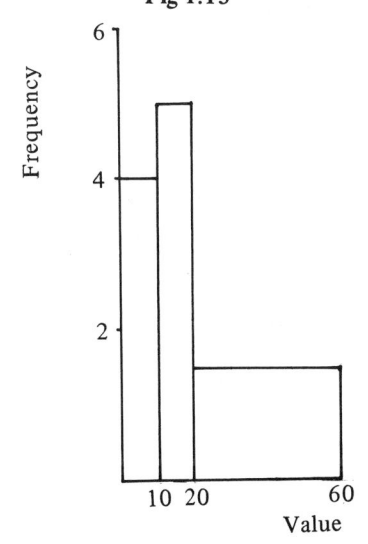

QUANTITATIVE METHODS

Without that adjustment, we would have the following histogram which is surely totally misleading!

Fig 1.16 : Incorrect Version of Fig 1.15

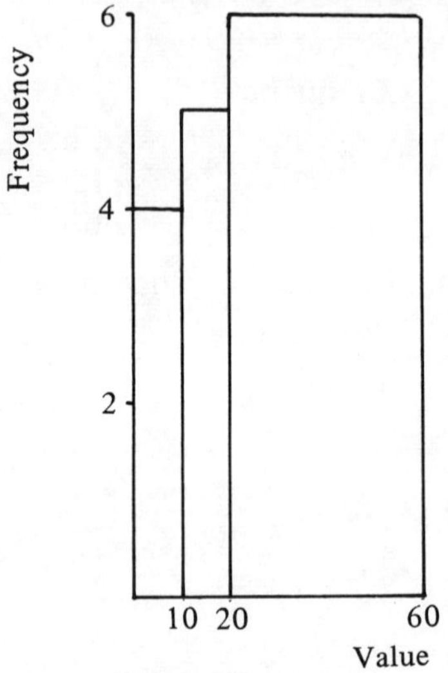

Exercise

1. Draw up a histogram of the following distribution of the sales volume (£) per customer per annum.

Sales per Customer (£)	Number of Customers
10,000 — < 20,000	10
20,000 — < 30,000	50
30,000 — < 40,000	40
40,000 — < 60,000	30
60,000 — < 80,000	20
80,000 — <100,000	10

2. Draw up a histogram of the following frequency distribution representing the earnings of employees in an organisation.

Earnings of Employees	Number of Employees
6,000 — < 7,000	340
7,000 — < 8,000	120
8,000 — < 9,000	80
9,000 — < 10,000	60
10,000 — < 12,000	40
12,000 — < 14,000	20
14,000 — < 20,000	10

FREQUENCY DISTRIBUTIONS

Hint: reduce all intervals to a common interval of £1,000 and adjust the frequencies accordingly.

1;13 Problem 3 : How big should the class intervals be?

The answer is simple. Not too big and not too small! A useful guide is to err on the side of making them too small, especially at the data collection stage. You can always double up class intervals later on, but you can't divide them up. A few examples will explain what I mean.

1.13.1 Example

Values	Frequency
0 — 4	1
5 — 9	0
10 — 14	2
15 — 19	1
20 — 24	4
25 — 29	8

Suppose that I now wish that I had chosen class intervals of width 10, I can simply double up the intervals without going back to the original figures.

Values	Frequency		
0 — 9	1 + 0	=	1
10 — 19	2 + 1	=	3
20 — 29	4 + 8	=	12

1.13.2 Example

Value	Frequency
0 — 19	4
20 — 39	8
40 — 59	1

Suppose I now wish I had chosen intervals of width 10. To do this I will have to refer back to the original data. I know that there are 8 data values in the range 20 — 39, but there is no way that I can deduce how many fall in the range 20 — 29 and how many in the 30 — 39. Remember too that referring back to the original data may involve deciphering semi-legible scribbles on work-sheets and the amount of work could be considerable. So *think ahead* and in the first instance keep your intervals small.

QUANTITATIVE METHODS

1.13.3 Even when you have all the data readily available and sorted into small class intervals, you may still wonder how to judge what is the best size of interval to employ. Let's refer back to the caretaker data (Fig 1.3a). Suppose we have it sorted neatly as follows:

Class Interval	Ages of Caretakers	
20 – 24	24	1
25 – 29	26,26,28,29,29	5
30 – 34	30	1
35 – 39	36,38	2
40 – 44	41,41,42,44	4
45 – 49	45,46,47,49	4
50 – 54	50,51,52,52,53,53,53,53,53,54,54,54	12
55 – 59	55,56,56,56,57,58,58,59,59	9
60 – 64	60,60,61,61,62,62,62,64,64	9
65 – 69	66,67,68	3
		50

Fig 1.17 shows histograms representing the data but using different widths of class intervals, 1,2,5,10 and 20. It seems clear that intervals of 5 or 10 *in this case* give good results. Widths of 1 and 2 display much irrelevant detail and a width of 20 obscures most of what is interesting.

Fig 1.17 : Version of Fig 1.3a using Different Class Intervals

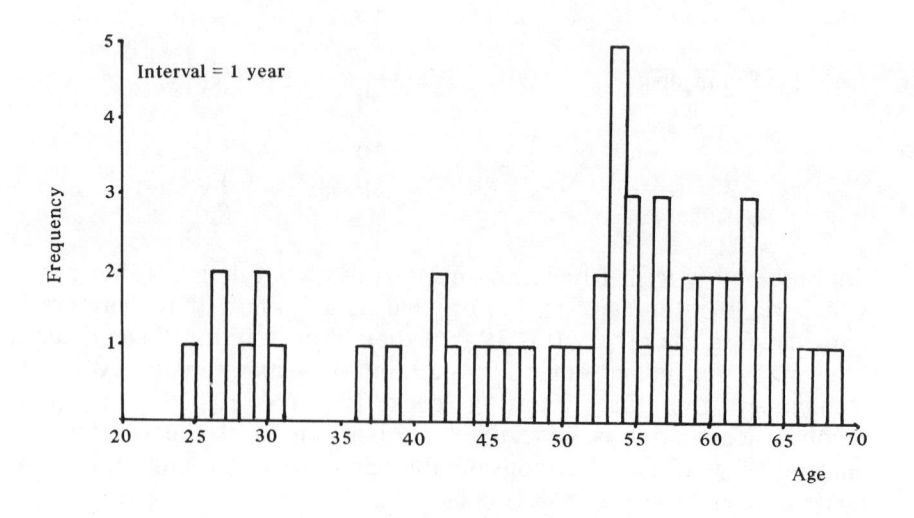

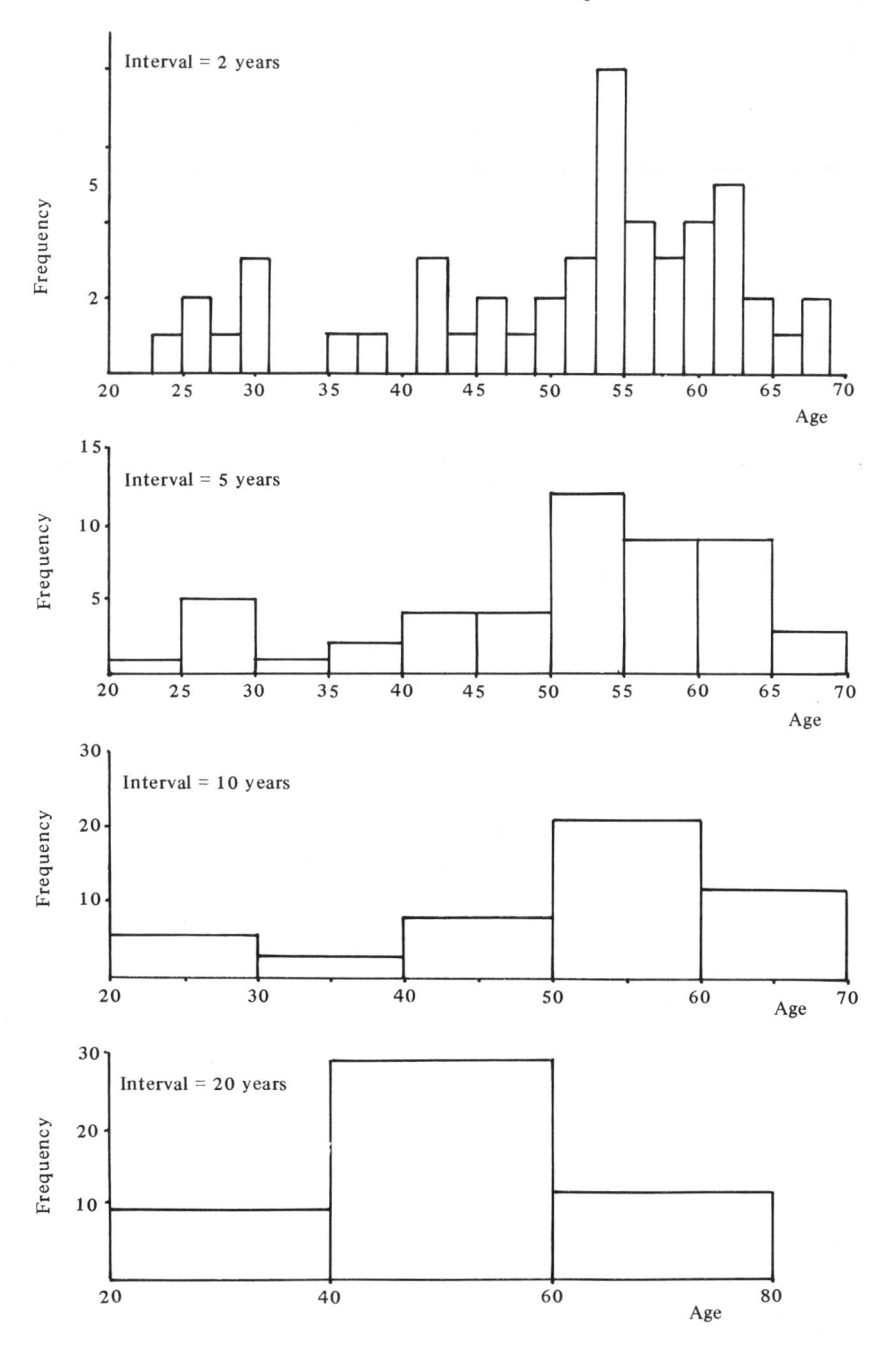

FREQUENCY DISTRIBUTIONS

QUANTITATIVE METHODS

In the end it is experience that will help you to develop a sense of judgment. While developing that judgment, choose small class intervals and see how the distribution looks. Then double the width of the intervals and see whether the result is more appropriate.

Exercise

Repeat Exercises 2 and 3 on page 28 with class intervals of varying sizes and comment on the effects.

For question 2 try intervals of 5 minutes, 20 minutes and 50 minutes.

For question 3 try intervals of 2, 5, 10 and 20 kilos.

1.14 Problem 4 : I know what width I want, but where should the first interval start.

1.14.1 This is a more subtle problem. Assuming intervals of 5 years, should the first one be 20 – 24 or, given that the lowest figure is 24, should the first interval be 24 – 28?

The lowest figure is 24 and the highest figure is 68. Logically a first interval of 24 – 28 (implying a last interval fo 64 – 68) covers the data best. However the intervals that result look a bit perverse. It's probably better to stick to class intervals that look less contrived. To show how much difference the choice can make to the end result, Fig 1.18 shows the same caretaker data plotted using class intervals of width 5 but employing different starting points. Note how the superficial detail changes but the overall shape remains the same.

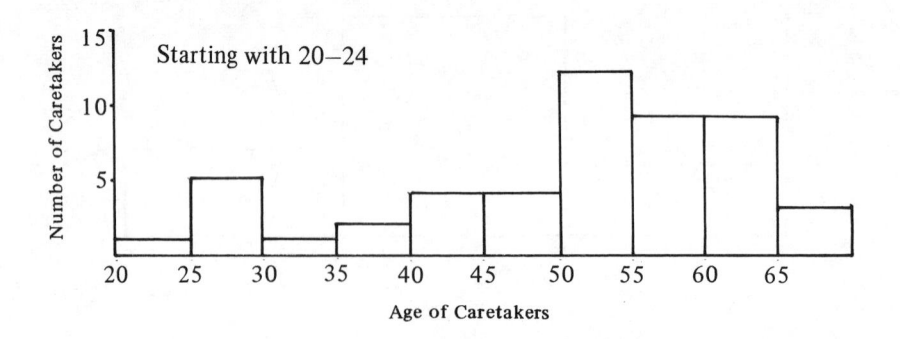

Fig 1.18 : Fig 1.3a with varying starting points for class intervals

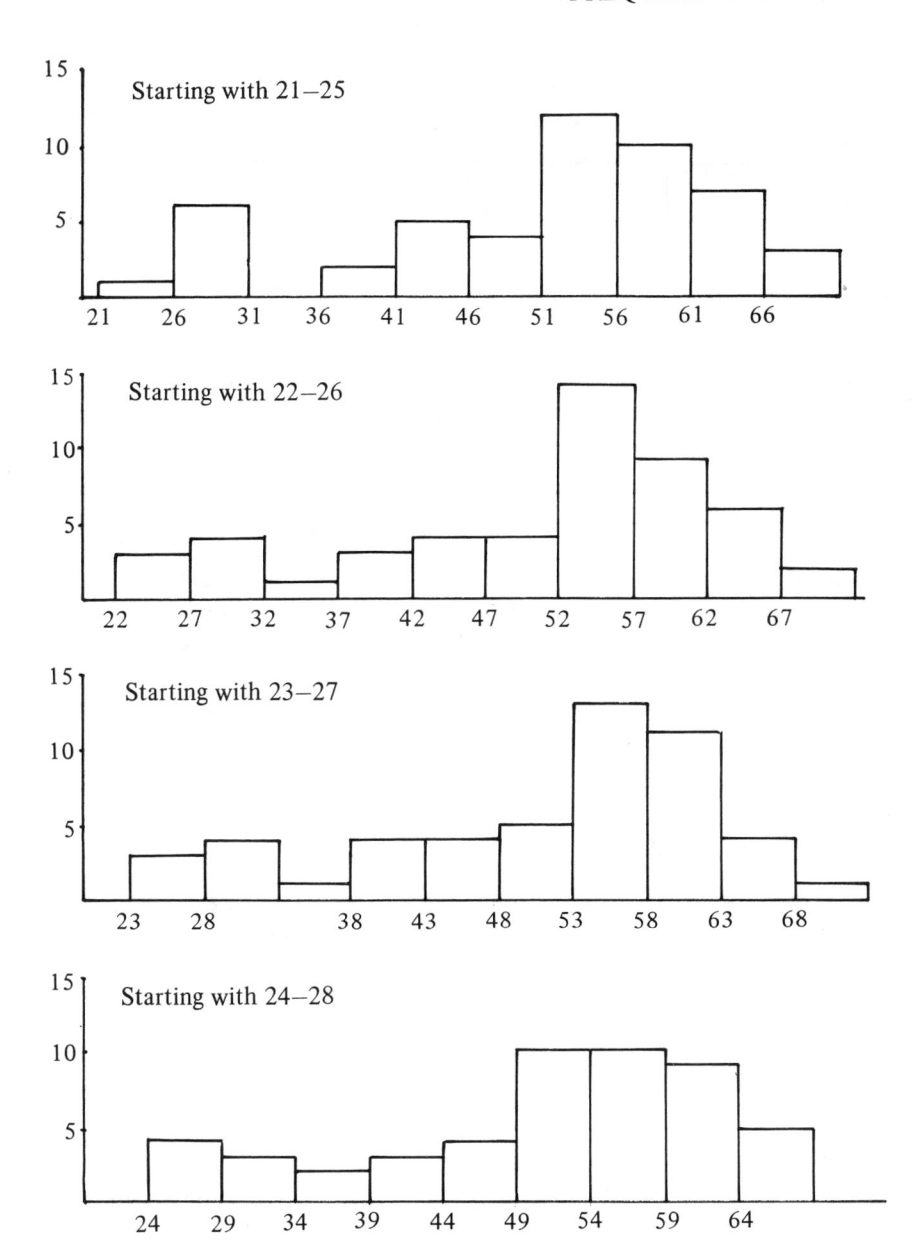

FREQUENCY DISTRIBUTIONS

QUANTITATIVE METHODS

1.14.2 Fig 1.18 also helps to make an important point. The superficial detail in the distribution changes merely because of an arbitary change in the class intervals. So remember, when you are examining a histogram, you should concentrate on the overall shape of the distribution and not try to read too much into superficial points of detail. In particular beware of making too much of differences between the frequencies attached to adjoining class intervals.

For example, look at the last two distributions in Fig 1.18; the one starting with the interval 23 – 27 and the other with the interval 24 – 28. There seems to be a dramatic difference between the right-hand portions of the histograms even though they are derived from the same figures. This arises from a peculiarity of this data. There are exactly 5 caretakers aged 53. In the last two histograms, the intervals shift from 53 – 57 to 54 – 58 with the result that those 5 people move into the lower class interval. Of course there is no significance to the existence of 5 of the caretakers being aged exactly 53, it is just a peculiarity of this data. Most data will have some odd features which are of no general significance, so concentrate on the overall shape and be cautious about going overboard on the detail.

1.15 Problem 5: What do I do with an Open-ended Class Interval?

This is an irritating problem. Suppose you were looking at the size of the work forces in a number of companies and wished to draw a histogram of the following distribution where one class interval has no specified upper or lower limit.

Size of Workforce	Number of Companies
0 – 50	4
50 – 100	20
100 – 200	10
200 – 400	10
400 – 1,000	6
1,000 + (or 'over 1,000')	8

All we know is that there are 8 companies under consideration with work forces in excess of 1,000 employees. To draw up a histogram assuming that the last class interval is, say, 1,000 – 2,000 employees is sheer speculation in the absence of any evidence to support it.

So unless some information is available about the likely limits to the

FREQUENCY DISTRIBUTIONS

open interval, the best plan is to make the position quite clear as is shown in Fig 1.19.

Fig 1.19 : Distribution of Number of Employees in 58 companies.

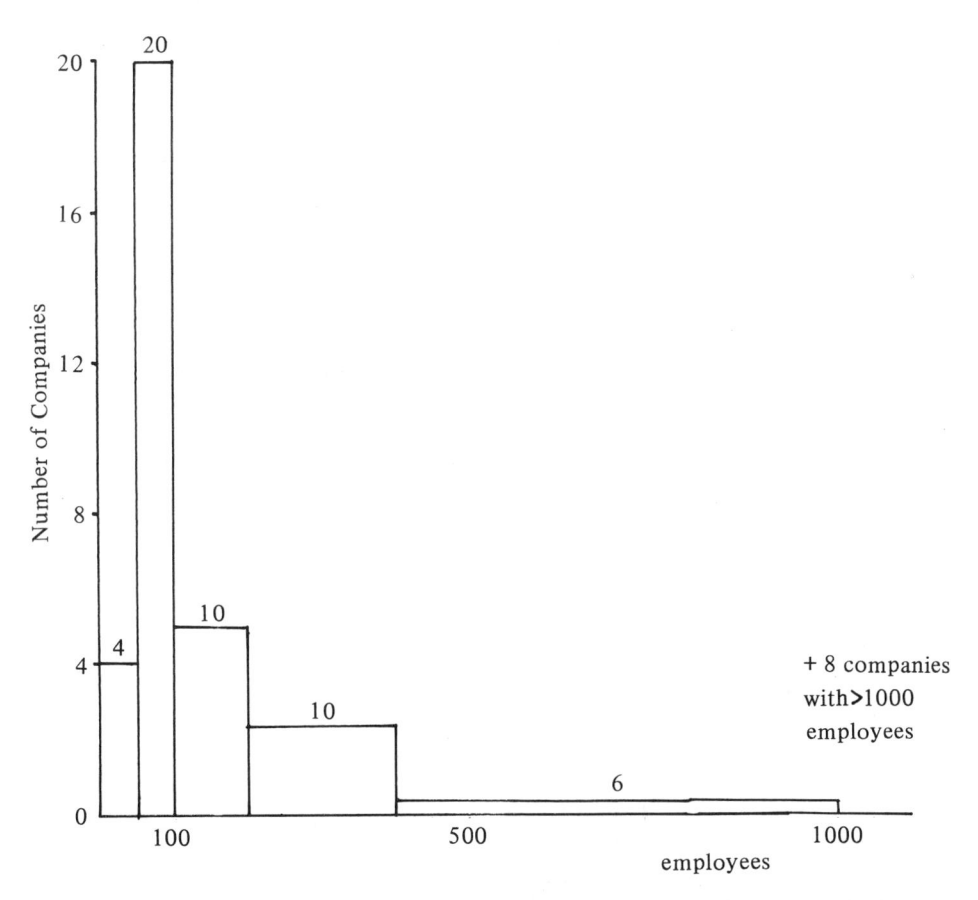

+ 8 companies with >1000 employees

Note that in this case, because of the added complication of the irregular class intervals, I have written the actual number of companies at the top of the histogram blocks. The truth is that there is inevitably an element of confusion when such irregularities arise.

CHAPTER 2 : GETTING THE RIGHT ANSWER FROM YOUR CALCULATOR

2.1 Introduction

Before moving on you are advised to brush up on basic numeracy and the use of the common calculator. Even if you believe that you can do without such a revision, I suggest that you at least skim the contents. In my experience many people do not know how to use a calculator effectively and most people have problems with some aspect of the basic skills of numeracy.

2.1.1 The First Rule of Using Calculators

Calculators do strange things when they start running out of power. Without blinking an eyelid, they will announce that 2 + 2 = 6.3 and so on. So buy a liquid-crystal calculator and avoid the all-singing and dancing varieties that consume a lot of power. Otherwise make sure that there is a way that you can tell when there is insufficient supply of power available or use a mains power pack.

Figure 2.1 : a Basic Calculator

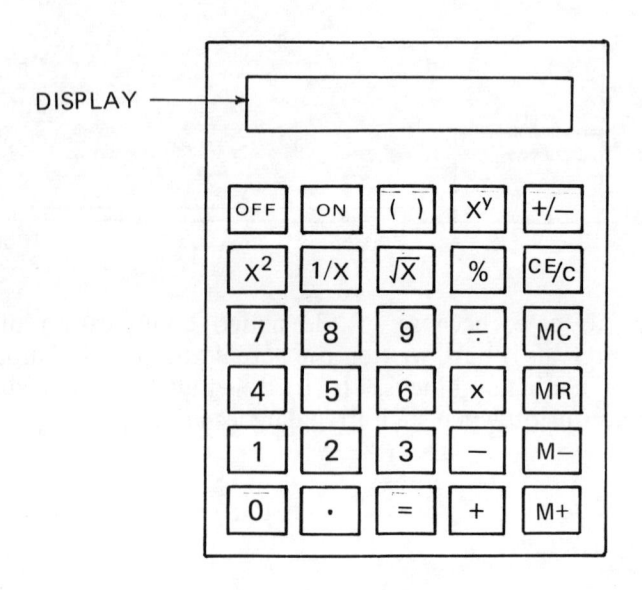

(Additional useful keys, not present on this machine, e^x, ln x, log x,).

2.1.2 The Calculator

I've no doubt that there are many good calculators around, but mine has proved to have all the features I need. It was cheap and it has proved reliable for several years and it will serve as a useful basis for illustrating the use of calculators in general. Your calculator may not have all the features present on mine. If there are major differences, then you'll have to work out your own operating rules with the help of the instructions.

2.1.3 The Basic Principle of Calculator Use

Calculators are very accurate, *but your fingers are not*!

However careful you may be, it is easy to hit the wrong keys, or leave out a decimal point. On some calculators, if you hold your finger down on a key, say '2', the key can register twice or more. Thus '2' would become '22' or even '222'. When buying, try and get this effect while in the shop and reject the machine if it has that tendency. Sometimes you may think that you have hit a key but in fact it hasn't registered. Thus 504 might be registered as 54 or 50. On my calculator, there is an optional sound switch. If it is engaged, a bleep indicates that a key has registered. It's a good system but it can drive people mad. Often there is nothing wrong with the machine, it is simply that the operator botches the operation. Working fast, you hit the wrong keys in sequence and produce rubbish. In other words the chances are that the results of your calculators will sometimes be incorrect and you had better face up to the inevitability of that happening.

For all these reasons,

> IT IS ESSENTIAL TO HAVE AN ESTIMATE OF THE FINAL ANSWER IN YOUR HEAD, OR ON PAPER, BEFORE PERFORMING THE REQUIRED CALCULATION.

This means learning how to do approximate arithmetic quickly. This principle will be illustrated as the discussion of calculator operations proceeds. Remember

> CALCULATORS DO NOT REMOVE THE NEED TO DEVELOP THE BASIC SKILLS OF NUMERACY.

Most calculators allow you to delete the incorrect entry you have just

QUANTITATIVE METHODS

made while preserving any running total. On my machine the $\boxed{\text{CE/C}}$ key has that effect. You need to experiment with your machine and see whether this applies in your case.

2.2 Addition

Most people know how to add on a calculator. I will use that fact to introduce a way of describing calculator operations in an unambiguous fashion.

The basic procedure is as follows:

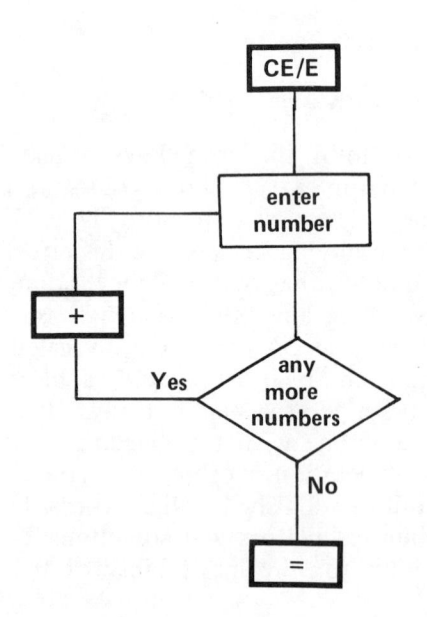

Start by clearing the machine then enter the first number on the keyboard. Continue by pressing the 'plus' key and entering further numbers, repeating the procedure until you have entered all the numbers. Once all the numbers have been entered, press the equals sign and read off the answer on the screen.

I hope you find the logical flow diagram above easy to follow. It avoids turgid instructions like those on the right hand side of the page. From now on the flow diagram will be used to describe the procedures. Even if you don't like it, you might as well get used to it. The manager in the computer age will often be required to check out system procedures which will be expressed in a logical flow diagram of this kind.

Do remember that your calculator may not work quite like the one I am using. You'll need to experiment for yourself. The procedures I describe will at least give you an idea of how a calculator can be used.

42

GETTING THE RIGHT ANSWER FROM YOUR CALCULATOR

2.2.1 Example

$$\begin{array}{r} 403 \\ 29 \\ 163 \\ 521 \\ 430 \\ \underline{500} \end{array}$$

Before adding these, do an approximate addition. Remember this is not just designed to exercise the brain. It is your only protection against gross errors in entering figures, calculator malfunctions and so on.

I would do it like this: count up the hundreds column only. We would then have

$$\begin{array}{r} 4\;*\;* \\ *\;* \\ 1\;*\;* \\ 5\;*\;* \\ 4\;*\;* \\ \underline{5\;*\;*} \\ 1\,9\;*\;* \end{array}$$

so the answer must be at least 1900. Now I give a quick glance at the 10's column. There I see a '6' and a few small digits. This suggests one more in the hundreds column, so I raise my estimate to about 2000, certainly no more than 2100. The machine gives me the precise result, 2046. As it is well within my estimate, I accept it.

If the result was particularly crucial I would repeat the addition just to be sure. Producing a rough estimate will not pick up all errors, but it will detect major ones. For example in the above calculation:

Nature of Error	Final Answer	Action Given Rough Estimate
Leave out 500	1546	Rejected
162 instead of 163	2045	Accepted
430, with the '3' not registered i.e. 40 entered	1656	Rejected
403 registerd with an additional '3' at the end i.e. 4033 entered.	5676	Rejected

43

QUANTITATIVE METHODS

2.2.2 Example

```
  17349
  29864
  53413
  97625
 115382
```

With all these digits around, slips on entry are particularly easy to make. I add the first two columns in my head like this

```
    1 * * * *
    2 * * * *
    5 * * * *
    9 * * * *
  1 1 * * * *
  2 8 *,* * *
```

Looking at the third column and doing some very rough and ready arithmetic, my eye picks up

```
  * 7 * * *
  * 9 * * *
  * 3 * * *
  * 7 * * *
  * 5 * * *
  3 *,* * *
```

so I add 3*,*** to the 28*,*** giving me an estimate of at least 31*,***.

My calculator yields 313,633.

2.2.3 Example

```
  2 . 0 6 3
  5 . 9 3 6
  7 . 6 1 2
  0 . 0 5 2
  9 . 6 2 3
```

The first stage of my rough estimate goes as follows:

```
   2 . * * *
   5 . * * *
   7 . * * *
   0 . * * *
   9 . * * *
  2 3 . * * *
```

Now I move on to the first place of decimals

44

GETTING THE RIGHT ANSWER FROM YOUR CALCULATOR

```
    * . 0 * *
    * . 9 * *
    * . 6 * *
    * . 0 * *
    * . 6 * *
    ───────────
    2 . * * *
```

I haven't added the column accurately. All I have done is mentally to register that there is a 'carry' of 2 to be added to the 23 that I already have. In my head I am carrying out the following sum

```
    2 3 . * * *
        2 . * * *
    ───────────
    2 5 . * * *
```

so my estimate is between 25 and 26.

my calculator gives me the precision that I need, 25.286.

2.2.4

Some readers may get very annoyed by having to carry out this sort of preliminary approximate calculation. 'Why bother with a calculator,' they say. 'if I am going to have to do a major arithmetical job first? I might as well do the whole thing by hand!'

Three responses. Firstly, with practice, it doesn't take very long. Secondly, even if you did do it wholly by hand, the calculator would provide a quick check and thirdly, you don't really have any choice. Calculator errors are inevitable.

The ability to do approximate arithmetic is one of the most valuable skills that the numerate analyst or manager can develop. Unfortunately it is a skill ignored in our schools where the emphasis is placed on precision and method. Who ever heard of a school giving children sums and asking them to guess the answers? However that is the very skill which I am suggesting that you develop. It is even more important now that calculators are freely available. The well judged guess ensures that your answer makes sense. The calculator gives you the precision required.

What I am suggesting is that you work with a calculator in the same way that people used to use a slide rule. In those days everybody accepted that it was essential to have a rough answer in your head. It

QUANTITATIVE METHODS

still is today!

In fact this is nothing new for most managers. It is a version of a skill which they already possess. They can't check all the information which passes through their offices: budgets, sales figures, expenses, etc. What they can do in the time available is to see if they 'look about right'. They can spot anything out of the ordinary because they already have, in advance, a rough idea of the values they're going to see. It is that very skill which I am asking you to employ when using the calculator.

2.2.5 Addition using M+

This accumulator key has the effect of adding the quantity displayed to whatever is already in the memory. Unless you have cleared the memory first by using the MC key, you run the risk of corrupting the values transferred.

Using this key, addition can be carried out by accumulating the figures in memory. This is particularly useful if you tend to make mistakes entering numbers. If you botch an entry you can clear the display leaving the total accumulated so far safely held in memory.

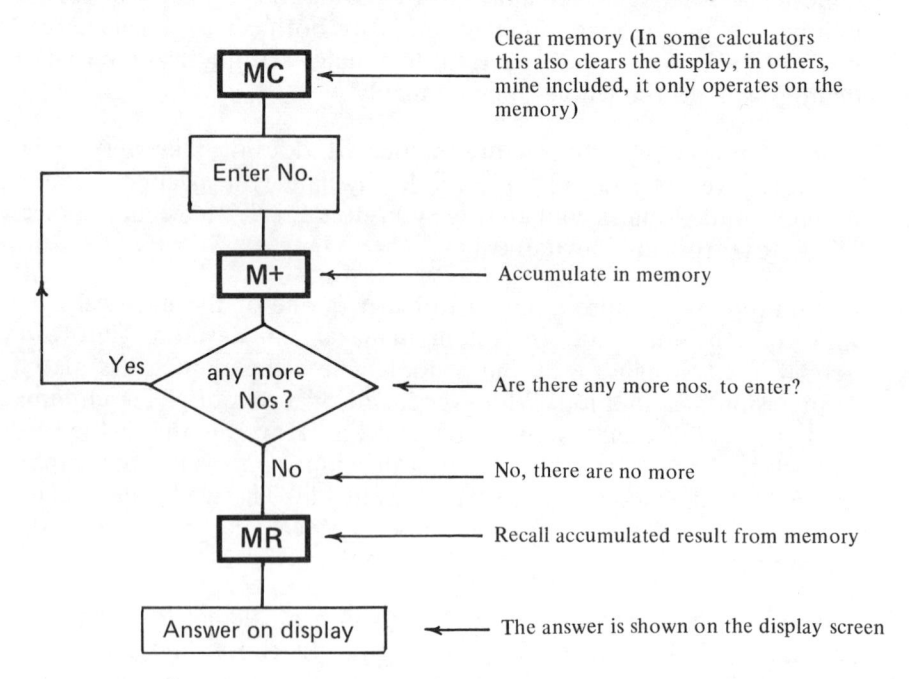

```
        MC      ←——  Clear memory (In some calculators
                     this also clears the display, in others,
                     mine included, it only operates on the
                     memory)

      Enter No.

        M+      ←——  Accumulate in memory

   Yes
      any more   ←——  Are there any more nos. to enter?
       Nos?

        No      ←——  No, there are no more

        MR      ←——  Recall accumulated result from memory

   Answer on display  ←——  The answer is shown on the display screen
```

GETTING THE RIGHT ANSWER FROM YOUR CALCULATOR

This method is particularly useful when you have to carry out an operation on each of the numbers you are adding.

Suppose I want to calculate the following

```
   23              116              36
   47      +        23       +      49
  163              417             620
```

I want each separate sum *and* the total overall. I use the following procedure:

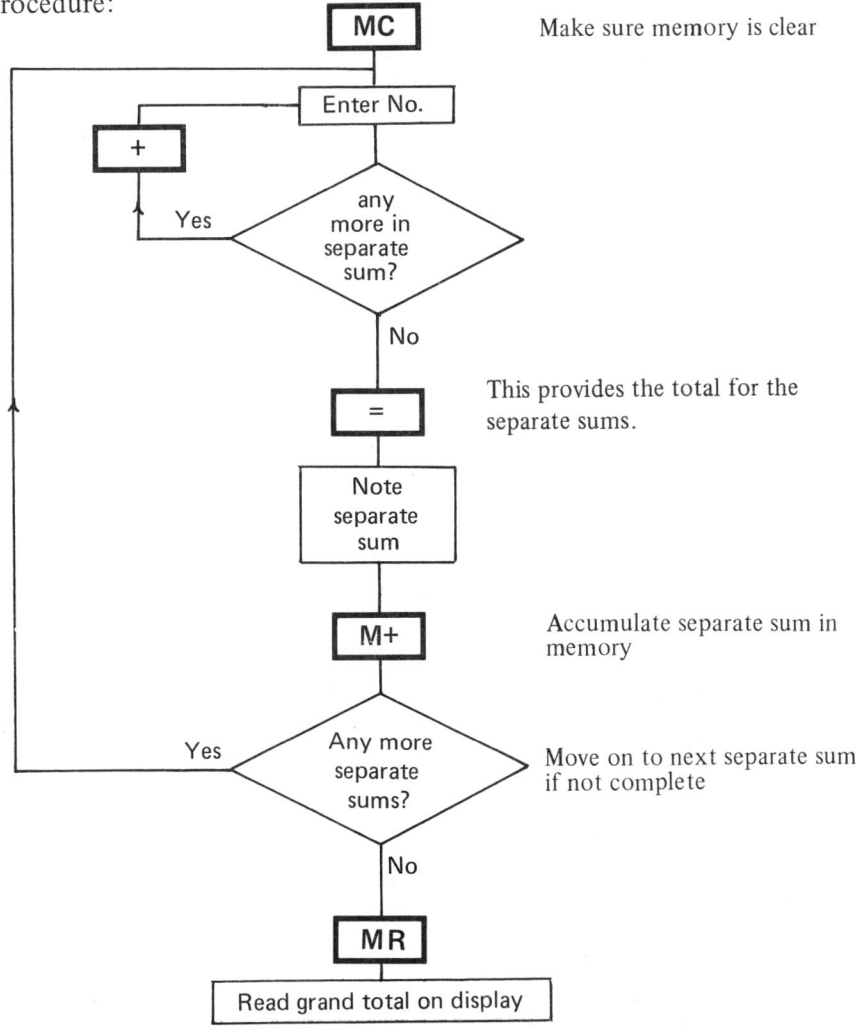

- **MC** — Make sure memory is clear
- Enter No.
- **+**
- any more in separate sum? → Yes: loop back to Enter No.
- No ↓
- **=** — This provides the total for the separate sums.
- Note separate sum
- **M+** — Accumulate separate sum in memory
- Any more separate sums? → Yes: loop back. Move on to next separate sum if not complete
- No ↓
- **MR**
- Read grand total on display

47

QUANTITATIVE METHODS

Rough calculation: the separate sums are *roughly*

230   550   700

therefore the grand total is *roughly* 1500.

The actual results for the separate sums using the calculator are

233   556   705

and the grand total is 1494, all of which tallies with my estimates.

2.3 Rounding

Rounding figures plays a vital role in doing approximate arithmetic and doing quantitative work in general. Examples of rounding are given below

		to the nearest whole no.	
	3.6	to the nearest whole no.	4
	3.4	"	3
*	3.5	"	4
*	2.5	"	2
	2.51	"	3
	196	to the nearest 100	200
	714	"	700
	12496	"	12500
	0.16395	to two decimal places	0.16
	0.16935	"	0.17
*	0.165	"	0.16
*	0.175	"	0.18
**	0.20007	"	0.20

* Where there is ambiguity about the direction in which to round, I adopt the rule of rounding to the nearest even digit. Other people use other rules. My method is designed to spread the errors around, sometimes rounding down, sometimes rounding up. Whatever you do, be consistent.

* * I have written the rounded result as 0.20 rather than 0.2 to show that it is accurate to 2 decimal places. If I had just written 0.2 it might have given the impression that it was only accurate to 1 place of decimals.

GETTING THE RIGHT ANSWER FROM YOUR CALCULATOR

Exercise

1. The number of micro-computers sold in 6 different branches of a chain store during the months of January, February, March was:

	January	February	March
Branch No 1	61	48	59
2	3	9	5
3	19	26	31
4	18	42	9
5	12	17	36
6	86	77	68

i) Roughly estimate the total sales across all branches for each of the three months separately (sum the columns).

ii) Roughly estimate the total sales for each branch for the quarter Jan–March (sum the rows).

iii) Use the calculator to obtain accurate answers to i and ii.

2. The number of visitors to a museum in each of 12 months is given below.

21,379
28,573
14,631
18,582
8,883
7,612
9,553
14,671
53,779
49,411
38,882
31,499

i) Guess the total number of visitors during the year.

ii) Work out the approximate sum on the calculator, rounding off each figure to the nearest thousand as you go along.

iii) Calculate the exact sum to the nearest visitor and compare it to the answer to (ii).

49

QUANTITATIVE METHODS

3. Below are 5 measurements of the thickness in inches of a metal foil produced on a machine.

$$0.001134$$
$$0.000926$$
$$0.001735$$
$$0.000882$$
$$0.000776$$

These sheets are packed together and we need to know the thickness of the resulting combined sheet.

i) Guess the combined thickness by roughly adding the individual thicknesses. To do this, round the figures to four places of decimals first.

ii) Sum the total on the calculator.

iii) Repeat (ii) but this time work in thousands of an inch so that, for example, 0.0008" becomes 0.8 thou".

The method of (iii) is more reliable when dealing with awkward decimals.

2.4 Subtraction

2.4.1 Example   437
                    196

Rough calculation: 440 − 200 = 240 roughly.

NB: Here I am rounding the figures to the nearest 10 in order to obtain an approximate result.

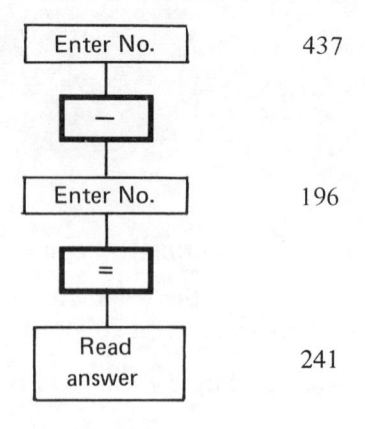

Enter No.	437
−	
Enter No.	196
=	
Read answer	241

GETTING THE RIGHT ANSWER FROM YOUR CALCULATOR

2.4.2 Example

Suppose we have to subtract a sum from another number

1463.21 − 140.2
             39.6   +
             44.1
            122.5

we could do this as follows

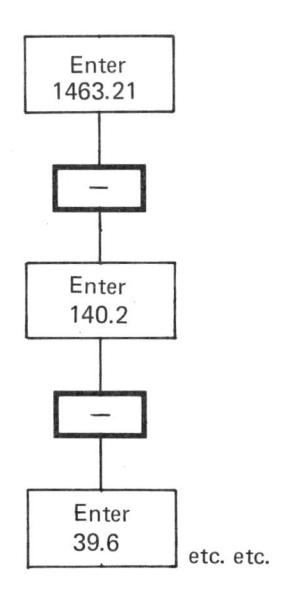

```
┌───────────┐
│  Enter    │
│ 1463.21   │
└─────┬─────┘
      │
┌─────┴─────┐
│     −     │
└─────┬─────┘
      │
┌─────┴─────┐
│  Enter    │
│  140.2    │
└─────┬─────┘
      │
┌─────┴─────┐
│     −     │
└─────┬─────┘
      │
┌─────┴─────┐
│  Enter    │
│  39.6     │
└───────────┘  etc. etc.
```

Often, however, we could do with the separate sum as well.

Rough calculation: separate sum = 200 (from 1st column)
                               + 100 (from 2nd column)
                               = 300+
                               about 350, I'd say for the separate sum.

So overall, roughly 1500 − 350 = 1150 for the final answer

QUANTITATIVE METHODS

Method 1 : Using the +/− key

The +/− key simply changes the sign of the number held in the register. So we can follow the following procedure using the same figures.

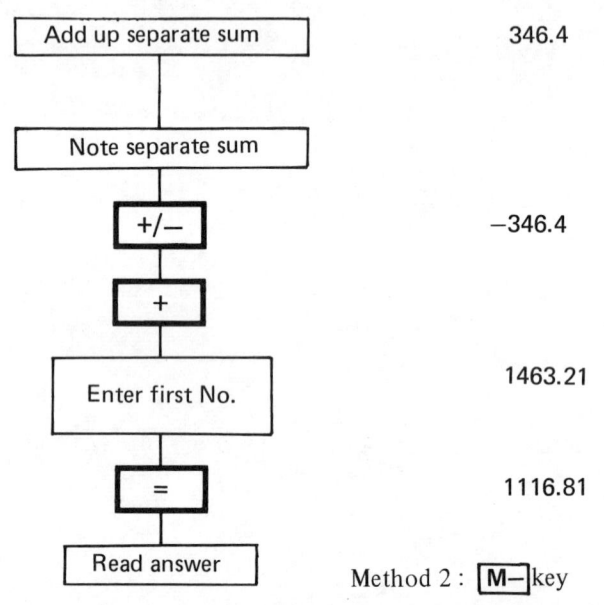

Add up separate sum	346.4
Note separate sum	
+/−	−346.4
+	
Enter first No.	1463.21
=	1116.81
Read answer	

Method 2 : M− key

The M− key acts like the M+ key but subtracts the value on display from the memory. It is equivalent to +/− M+

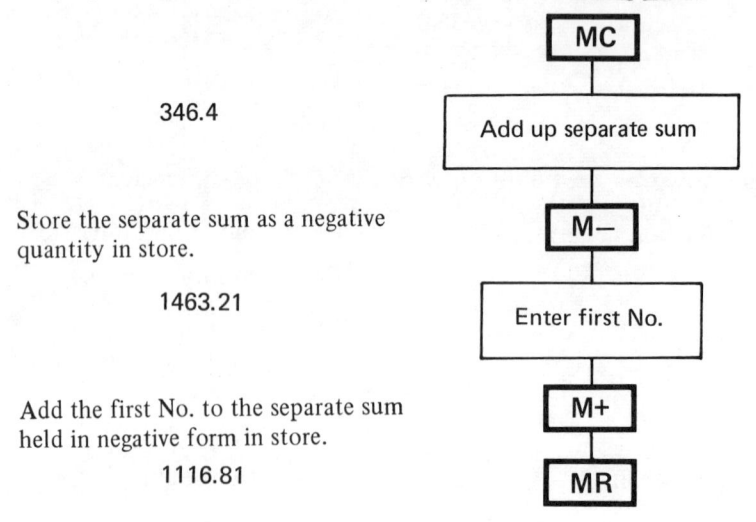

346.4

Store the separate sum as a negative quantity in store.

1463.21

Add the first No. to the separate sum held in negative form in store.

1116.81

| MC |
| Add up separate sum |
| M− |
| Enter first No. |
| M+ |
| MR |

52

GETTING THE RIGHT ANSWER FROM YOUR CALCULATOR

Exercise

1. Calculate the following:

   $366.52 - (1.635 + 2.319 + 4.173)$

2. A businessman has £8,416 in the bank. He has made the following purchases:

Materials	£1,942
Wages	£ 633
Electricity	£ 719
Rates	£2,413

i) Write down a rough estimate of the balance remaining in his account after he has paid all these bills.

ii) Calculate the sum of the bills and the balance left in his account.

3. A machine has produced 20,000 tubes of paste, most of which have been packed and stored away. Those not stored have been accounted for by the production manager as follows:

Damaged and scrapped	276
Sent for inspection	107
Retained for standards	40
Awaiting packing	1635

i) Estimate, by subtraction, the number that have been stored.

ii) Calculate the number that have been stored.

iii) How reliable is your answer to (ii) likely to be in practice given the method of calculation.

2.5 Multiplication

2.5.1 Example

23.6×48.1

Rough calculation: 20×50 = 2×5 00
= 10 00
= 1000 roughly

Enter no.   23.6

$\boxed{\times}$

Enter no.   48.1

$\boxed{=}$ 1135.16

QUANTITATIVE METHODS

2.5.2 Example   317.53 x 796.38

Rough calculation: 300 x 800 = 3x8 0,000
                              = 24 0,000
                              =   240,000

Accurate answer: 252,874.54

Here the rough calculation is very useful in ensuring that you don't mis-copy the number shown on the display. (Some calculators, not mine, put in the comma, which is very nice).

2.5.3 Example   1.364 x 11.312

Rough calculation: 1 x 11 = 11

Accurate answer: 15.429568.

The rough calculation is a bit disappointing here. It has done little more than ensure a result of the right order of magnitude.

A more refined rough calculation: 1.4 x 11 → 1.4 x 10 = 14 x 1

giving an estimate of about 14. The result is more accurate because in this case I took into account two significant figures in the first number (Here → means 'roughly equal to').

2.5.4 Example

I find people have great difficulties in multiplying decimals. Even with a calculator, it is very easy to 'drop' zeros

$$0.16 \times 0.93$$

Rough calculation: $0.2 \times 0.9 = \frac{2}{10} \times \frac{9}{10}$

$$\frac{2 \times 9}{10 \times 10} = \frac{18}{100} = 0.18, \text{ roughly}$$

Accurate answer: 0.1488.

GETTING THE RIGHT ANSWER FROM YOUR CALCULATOR

2.5.5 Example   0.016 x 0.0003

Rough calculation:

first note $0.016 = \dfrac{0.16}{10} = \dfrac{1.6}{100} = \dfrac{16}{1000}$

therefore $0.016 \times 0.0003 = \dfrac{16}{1000} \times \dfrac{3}{10,000}$

which is roughly $\dfrac{15 \times 3}{1000 \times 10,000} = \dfrac{45}{10,000,000}$

i.e. the rough answer is   0.0000045
Accurate answer   0.0000048

Exercise

1. Calculate the following

   a) 2.7   x 0.34
   b) 11.6 x 5.31
   c) 0.2   x 0.07
   d) 0.83 x 0.65

2. The sales price and number of units of a selection of products sold in a high street shop on a particular day is given below:

Item	Number of Units Sold	Sales Price (£)	Revenue
Records	69	4.50	
Computers	7	350.00	
Magazines	26	0.80	
Diaries	64	3.65	
Newspapers	270	0.23	
Biros	45	0.40	
Puzzles	16	3.20	

i) Roughly estimate and write down the revenue arising from the sale of each individual item. Remember all that's needed is a rough guess. For instance 270 newspapers at £0.23 each is roughly 300 at £0.2 each or 30 at £2 each which is about £60.

QUANTITATIVE METHODS

ii) Now calculate accurately the individual revenue figures.
iii) Estimate the total revenue using the rough answers to (i).
(iv) Accurately calculate the total revenue and check it against your guess in (iii).

3. The following represents the frequency distribution for the salaries of the employees in a large company:

Mean Salary	Number of Employees
6,725	136
8,946	232
11,462	86
14,632	15

i) Estimate the total salary bill. (You will probably need to jot down some of your approximate workings as you go along).
ii) Calculate the accurate value and check it against (i).

2.6 Multiplication using a constant

Most calculators have the facility of multiplying by a constant. Mine works like this:

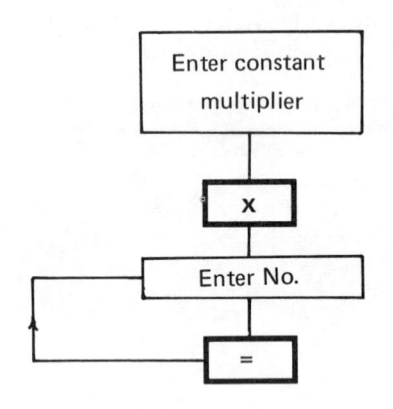

Note the ☒ is only used once. After each result, merely enter the new no. and press ☐=☐

Of course your calculator may not quite work like that but it's worth seeing how it does the equivalent operation.

GETTING THE RIGHT ANSWER FROM YOUR CALCULATOR

2.6.1 Example

Suppose I want to convert the following franc sums into sterling at an exchange rate of 1 NF = £0.09

$$\begin{array}{c} NF \\ 110 \\ 250 \\ 330 \end{array}$$

Rough calculation: about 700 NF in £

$$= 700 \times 0.09 = 7 \times 0.09 \times 100$$
$$= £ 7 \times 9 = £63 \text{ roughly.}$$

* **Method 1**

```
         MC
          │
  Enter constant
    multiplier
          │
          ×
          │
  Enter francs ←─────┐
          │         │
          = **      │
          │         │
         M+         │
          │         │
    Yes ╱ any ╲─────┘
       ╲ more ╱
          │ No
         MR
          │
  Answer on display
```

Method 2

```
         MC
          │
  Enter constant
    multiplier
          │
         M+
          │
  Enter francs ←─────┐
          │         │
          ×         │
          │         │
         MR         │
          │         │
          = ────────┘
```

* N.B. This facility is not avilable on some calculators. If so, use Method 2.

** Here, if the answer isn't sensible, go back and re-enter the constant multiplier leaving the accumulated £ total in memory

Accurate answer: £62.10

57

QUANTITATIVE METHODS

The smart reader will ask 'why not just add up the franc total first and then multiply by 0.09? This is quite correct, but the other method gives the sterling equivalent of each sum in francs as you go along.

You can also use $\boxed{M+}$ to carry out the above transaction. This is especially useful if your calculator doesn't have the facility used in Method 1, but then you don't now have the memory available for accumulating the results (see Method 2).

Exercise

1. Multiply the following by 0.83
    a) 163.5
    b) 6.3
    c) 0.00217

2. Repeat (1) multiplying by 73.9

3. Convert the following sterling prices into their equivalent dollar prices assuming an exchange rate of £1 = S1.43. (Remember to write down your rough answer first).

	Sterling Price	Dollar Price
Car	£3543.00	
Newspaper	£ 0.23	
Cigarettes	£ 0.86	
Wine	£ 2.43	
Book	£ 6.96	

4. Repeat exercise 3 but converting the prices into French francs (FF) using an exchange rate of 13.37 FF = £1.

2.7 Division

2.7.1 Example   36 ÷ 25

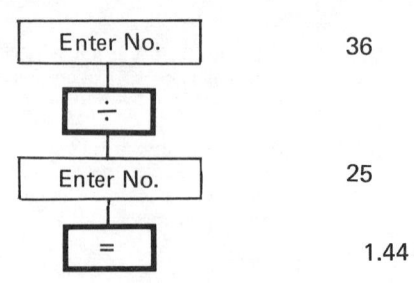

Enter No.	36
÷	
Enter No.	25
=	1.44

GETTING THE RIGHT ANSWER FROM YOUR CALCULATOR

Rough calculation: $\dfrac{36}{25} \to \dfrac{35}{25} = \dfrac{35 \times 4}{25 \times 4} = \dfrac{140}{100}$

$= 1.4$ roughly.

A cruder rough calculation which provides the right order of magnitude is

$$\dfrac{36}{25} \to \dfrac{40}{20} = 2$$

Accurate answer: 1.44

2.7.2 Example $\dfrac{3146.38}{29.41}$

Rough calculation: $\dfrac{3000}{30} = \dfrac{300}{3} = 100$ roughly.

Accurate result: 106.98333

2.7.3 Example $\dfrac{9.4632}{719.83}$

Rough calculation: $\dfrac{10}{700} = \dfrac{1}{70}$

which I see as lying between two more familiar fractions

$\dfrac{1}{100}$ is less than $\dfrac{1}{70}$ which is less than $\dfrac{1}{50} = \dfrac{2}{100}$

$0.01 \qquad\qquad \dfrac{1}{70} \qquad\qquad 0.02$

so my rough answer is between 0.01 and 0.02.

Accurate result: 0.0131464.

2.7.4 Example $\dfrac{0.016}{0.003}$

Rough calculation: $\dfrac{0.02}{0.003} = \dfrac{0.02 \times 1000}{0.003 \times 1000}$

$= \dfrac{20}{3} \to \dfrac{21}{3} = 7$

Accurate result: $5.33333333 = 5.3$

Alternative rough calculation: $\dfrac{0.016}{0.003} \to \dfrac{0.015}{0.003} = \dfrac{15}{3} = 5.$

QUANTITATIVE METHODS

Exercise

1. Calculate the following:

   a) $\dfrac{36.4}{0.02}$

   b) $\dfrac{9.91}{82.7}$

   c) $\dfrac{0.073}{0.0043}$

   d) $\dfrac{0.012}{0.0007}$

   e) $\dfrac{416.2}{0.011}$

   f) $\dfrac{0.003}{0.11}$

2. The following table shows the forecast number of man-hours available in three TV service centres next month together with the mean number of hours required to repair a set (it varies from centre to centre). Produce an estimate of the number of sets which can be processed (Repair Capacity) in each centre rounded to the nearest set.

Service Centre	Estimated Man-hours Available	Mean time to repair and test (hours)	Repair Capacity (sets)
A	3,050	0.6	
B	1,700	0.7	
C	863	0.75	

3. The table below shows the quantity of material (in kilos) which goes into making 5 different products. Calculate the maximum number of units of each product that could be made out of 2473 kilos of material, assuming that there is no waste. In each calculation assume that only one product is being made.

	Kilos of material needed per unit of product	Maximum possible number of units which can be made
Product 1	0.7	
2	0.03	
3	0.56	
4	365.2	
5	436.19	

4. Repeat exercise 3 assuming 20% material wastage in each case.

GETTING THE RIGHT ANSWER FROM YOUR CALCULATOR

2.8 Division using a constant divisor

This is particularly useful when working out percentages.

2.8.1 Method 1

One method is to use a special facility found in some calculators

Method 2

Another method is to hold the constant divisor in memory and proceed as follows

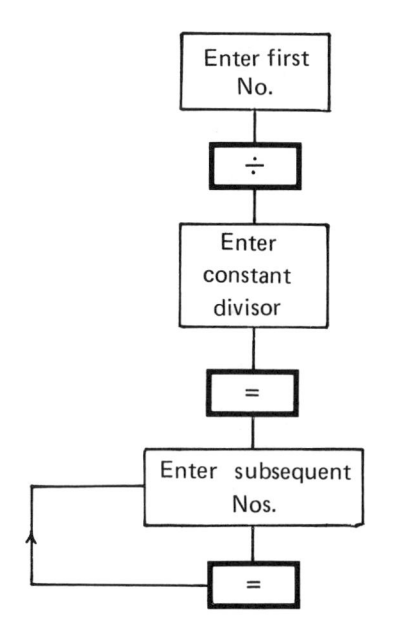

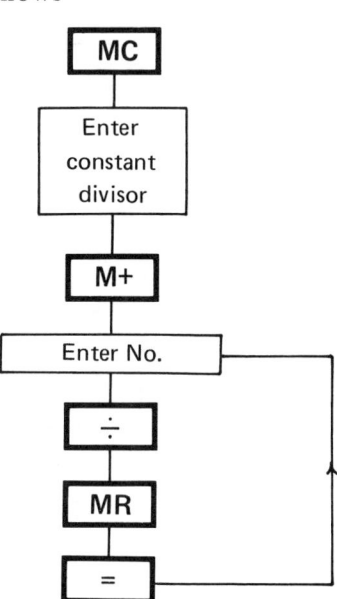

```
Enter first No.
    ↓
   ÷
    ↓
Enter constant divisor
    ↓
    =
    ↓
Enter subsequent Nos.  ←┐
    ↓                   │
    =  ──────────────────┘
```

```
   MC
    ↓
Enter constant divisor
    ↓
   M+
    ↓
Enter No.  ←────────────┐
    ↓                   │
   ÷                    │
    ↓                   │
   MR                   │
    ↓                   │
    =  ──────────────────┘
```

2.8.2 In some calculators, instead of finishing with $\boxed{=}$, one can use $\boxed{\%}$, to give the answer as a percentage. An example will illustrate this facility.

Example 1	Area No.	Sales for area £ '000
	1	11
	2	22
	3	34
	4	16

QUANTITATIVE METHODS

Problem: to express the sales per area as a % of the total. (Here we need no rough calculation. It will suffice to check that the percentages add up to 100).

Alternative Method

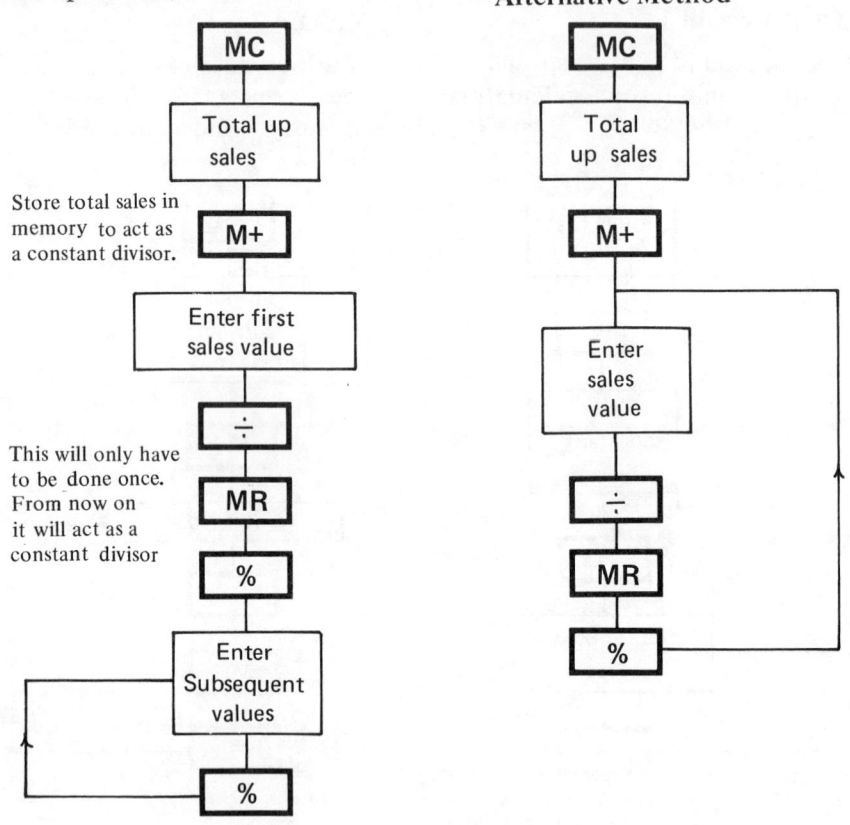

```
                    MC                              MC
                     |                               |
              ┌─────────────┐               ┌─────────────┐
              │  Total up   │               │   Total     │
              │   sales     │               │  up sales   │
              └─────────────┘               └─────────────┘
                     |                               |
Store total sales in                                 
memory to act as     M+                              M+
a constant divisor.  |                               |
              ┌─────────────┐               ┌─────────────┐
              │ Enter first │               │   Enter     │
              │ sales value │               │   sales     │
              └─────────────┘               │   value     │
                     |                      └─────────────┘
                     ÷                               |
This will only have  |                               ÷
to be done once.    MR                               |
From now on          |                              MR
it will act as a     %                               |
constant divisor     |                               %
              ┌─────────────┐
              │   Enter     │
              │ Subsequent  │
              │   values    │
              └─────────────┘
                     |
                     %
```

The results obtained are

%

13.25
26.51
40.96
19.28

Now all we need to do is to check that these add up to 100.

62

GETTING THE RIGHT ANSWER FROM YOUR CALCULATOR

Exercise

1. Convert the following frequency distributions into percentage frequency distributions. (Divide each frequency in turn by the total frequency and then check that your percentages add up to 100).

   a) **Length of Service Distribution for 272 Employees**

Length of Service (Years)	Number of Employees	Percentage of Total Employees
0	86	
1	25	
2	39	
3	67	
4	23	
5+	32	

   b) **Analysis of 146 tyres replaced in a Service centre.**

Nature of Fault in Tyre	Number of Tyres	Percentage of Total Tyres
Bald	84	
Puncture	43	
Damaged walls	17	
Unknown	2	

2. Convert the following sums in marks (DM) into sterling given 4.3 DM = £1. (Remember to obtain a rough estimate for the answers first!).

Sum in DM	Sum in £
3,416.33	
46.19	
1,349.7	
989.49	

3. Work study has shown that the mean time to weld a joint in a particular job is 7.4 minutes. Calculate the number of weldings that can be carried out in the following time periods given that 1 minute must be allowed between each welding:

   a) 1 hour
   b) a 40 hour week
   c) a 40 hour week allowing 10 minutes rest after each hour.

63

QUANTITATIVE METHODS

2.9 The $\boxed{1/x}$ key

The $\boxed{1/x}$ key simply has the effect of inverting the number held in the display. It's very useful when all the action is in the denominator.

Example $\qquad \dfrac{26}{31 + 40 + 90}$

Rough calculation: $\qquad \dfrac{25}{150} = \dfrac{5}{30} = \dfrac{1}{6} \rightarrow \dfrac{1}{5} = 0.2$

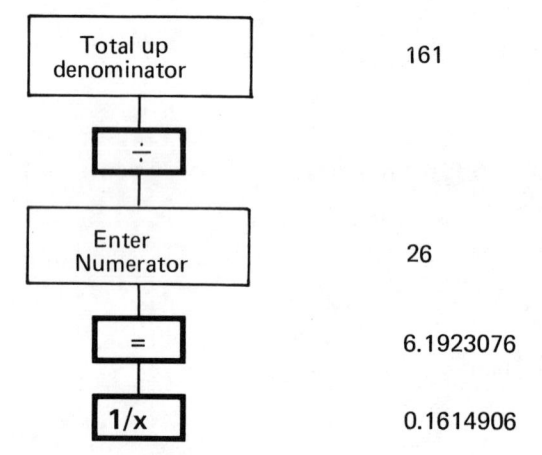

Step	Display
Total up denominator	161
÷	
Enter Numerator	26
=	6.1923076
1/x	0.1614906

It's often more convenient, as in this case, to calculate the bottom of the fraction first, divide it by the top and then invert the result. If you don't have such a facility, then you can total the denominator, put it into memory, enter the numerator and then divide by the number held in memory.

Exercise

1. Calculate the sum of 3.6, 4.9, 2.3 and 8.7 and also the result of subtracting the sum from 100.

2. Use the $\boxed{1/x}$ key to calculate the market share (by volume) of a company selling 50,000 units per annum whose competitors sell 60,000, 20,000, and 90,000 units per annum. (Add the sum, divide by 50,000 and then hit the $\boxed{1/x}$ key.)

3. Evaluate the following (a form of calculation which will occur a lot in Chapter 6).

GETTING THE RIGHT ANSWER FROM YOUR CALCULATOR

a) $$\frac{1}{(1.31)}$$

b) $$\frac{1}{(1 + \frac{6}{7})}$$

c) $$\frac{1}{2.3 + 3.9 + 4.7 + 1.9}$$

2.10 Powering up

This will be very important when we come to look at compound interest and discounting in Chapter 6.

2.10.1 Example

$(2.3)^2$ which means 2.3×2.3

Rough calculation: $2^2 = 4$

$3^2 = 9$

therefore my estimate lies between 4 and 9.

Method using $\boxed{x^2}$ This key is absent from many calculators.

Enter no.   2.3

$\boxed{x^2}$ 5.29

Method using $\boxed{x}$ $\boxed{=}$

Enter no.   2.3   This facility is found on most calculators.

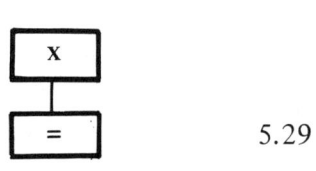

$\boxed{x}$
$\boxed{=}$ 5.29

2.10.2 Example

$(2.3)^3$ which means $2.3 \times 2.3 \times 2.3$

Rough calculation: $2^3 = 8$

$3^3 = 27$

therefore I expect an answer between 8 and 27, but nearer to 8 than 27.

QUANTITATIVE METHODS

Method 1

There is no key which will do this directly but a bit of ingenuity does the trick.

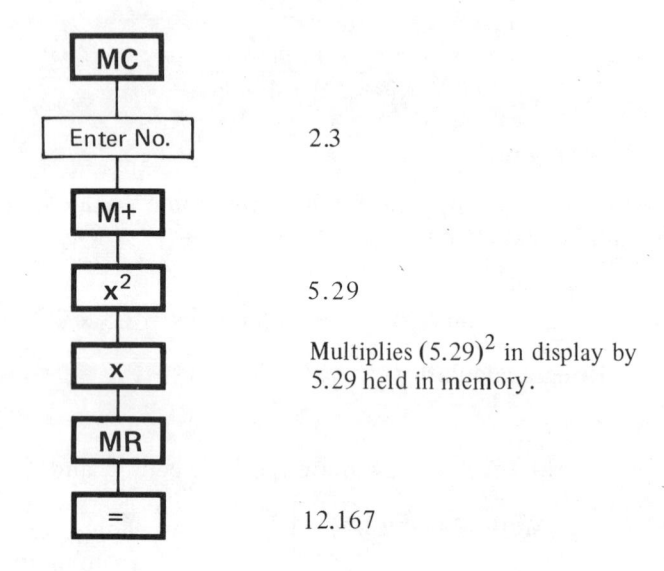

| MC |
| Enter No. | 2.3 |
| M+ |
| x^2 | 5.29 |
| × | Multiplies $(5.29)^2$ in display by 5.29 held in memory. |
| MR |
| = | 12.167 |

Method 2

NB: This useful procedure is not available on all machines so check it out first.

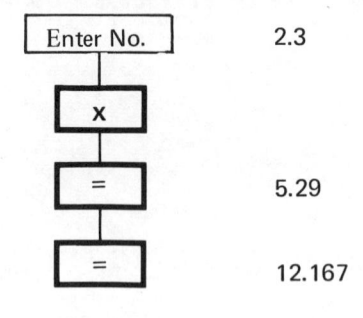

| Enter No. | 2.3 |
| × |
| = | 5.29 |
| = | 12.167 |

Note the way successive pressing of the = key produces successive powers of the original number entered.

Method 3

Some calculators have an x^n, y^x /or an a^b key. This automatically powers up a number by the given index.

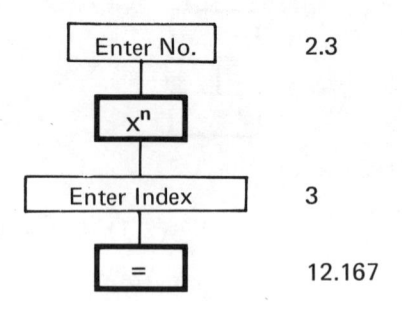

| Enter No. | 2.3 |
| x^n |
| Enter Index | 3 |
| = | 12.167 |

GETTING THE RIGHT ANSWER FROM YOUR CALCULATOR

2.10.3 Example

$$(4.7)^5$$

Rough calculation:

4^5 = 4x4x4x4x4 = 16 x 16 x 4
     = 256 x 4 ⟶ 250 x 4 = 1000

5^5 = 25 x 25 x 5 = 625 x 5
     ⟶ 600 x 5 = 3000

therefore I expect an answer between 1000 and 3000.

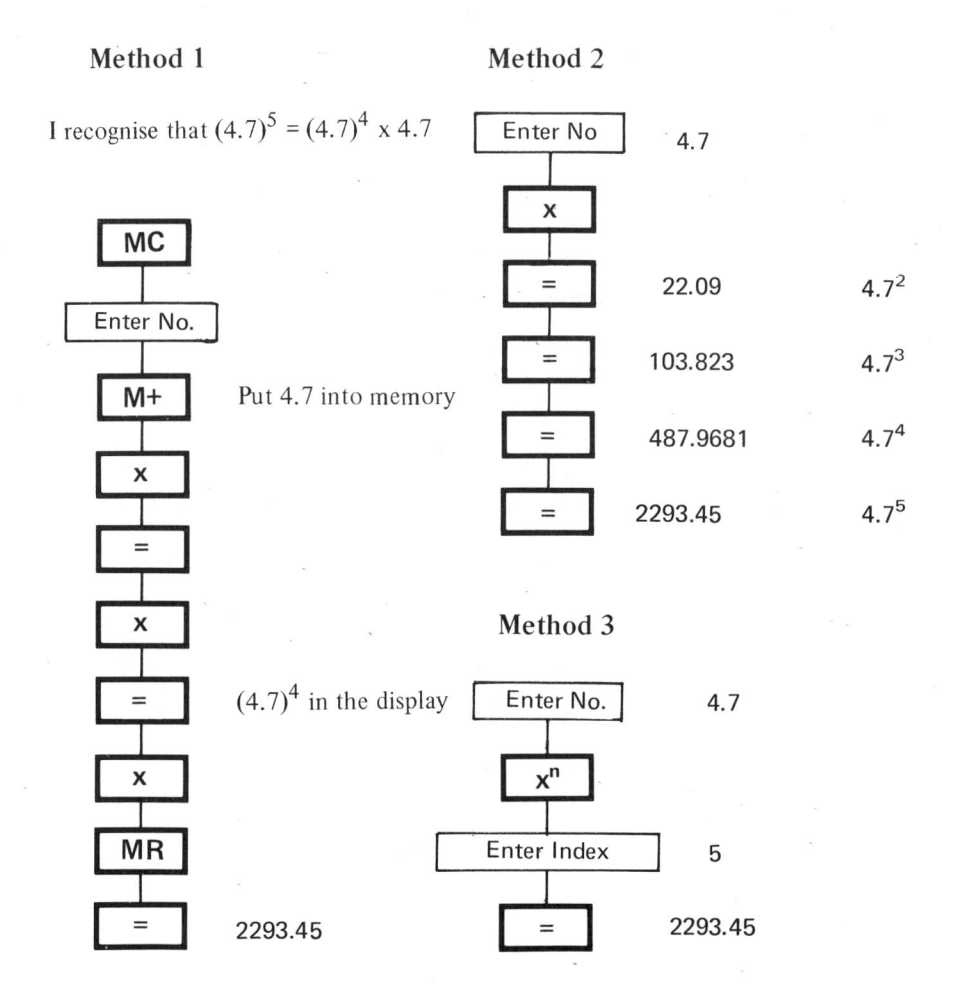

Method 1

I recognise that $(4.7)^5 = (4.7)^4 \times 4.7$

| MC |
| Enter No. |
| M+ | Put 4.7 into memory
| x |
| = |
| x |
| = | $(4.7)^4$ in the display
| x |
| MR |
| = | 2293.45

Method 2

| Enter No | 4.7 |
| x |
| = | 22.09 | 4.7^2
| = | 103.823 | 4.7^3
| = | 487.9681 | 4.7^4
| = | 2293.45 | 4.7^5

Method 3

| Enter No. | 4.7 |
| x^n |
| Enter Index | 5 |
| = | 2293.45 |

QUANTITATIVE METHODS

2.10.4 Example

When powering up decimals, the rough calculation requires a certain amount of care.

$$(0.6219)^3$$

$$\text{Rough calculation: } (0.6)^3 = \frac{6}{10} \times \frac{6}{10} \times \frac{6}{10}$$

$$= \frac{36 \times 6}{1000}$$

$$\longrightarrow \frac{40 \times 6}{1000} = \frac{240}{1000}$$

$$= 0.24, \text{ roughly.}$$

Accurate result: 0.2405

2.10.5 Example

$$(1.05)^{34}$$

In the absence of an $\boxed{x^n}$ key this presents some problems. The thing to do is to break the quantity down into powers of 2.

$$(1.05)^{34} = (1.05)^{32} \times (1.05)^2$$

Now $(1.05)^2$ will be calculated and stored in memory, then $(1.05)^{32}$ can be built up on the display and multiplied by the contents of memory

$$= 4.765 \times 1.1025$$

$$= 5.2534$$

2.10.6 Example

$$(1.12)^{22}$$

This is a nasty one: we can try to simplify it as:

$$(1.12)^{22} = (1.12)^{16} \times (1.12)^6$$
$$= (1.12)^{16} \times (1.12)^4 \times (1.12)^2$$

GETTING THE RIGHT ANSWER FROM YOUR CALCULATOR

On my calculator I can build it up by the following stratagem (or do yourself a favour and *demand* a calculator with an $\boxed{x^n}$ key!

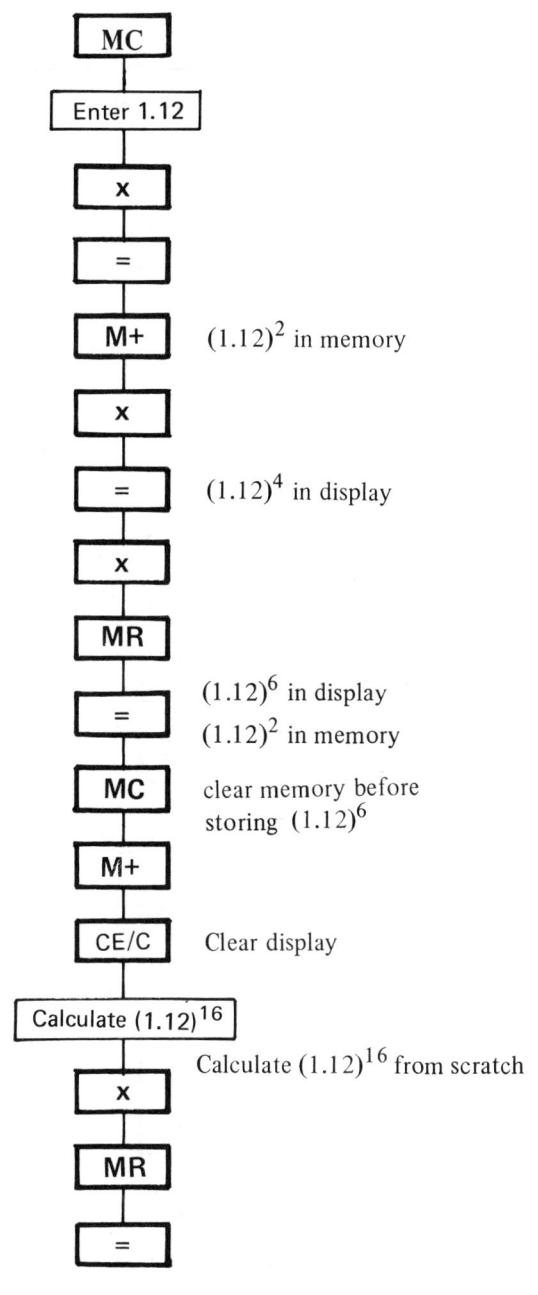

```
         MC
      Enter 1.12
          ×
          =
         M+          (1.12)² in memory
          ×
          =          (1.12)⁴ in display
          ×
         MR
          =          (1.12)⁶ in display
                     (1.12)² in memory
         MC          clear memory before
                     storing (1.12)⁶
         M+
        CE/C         Clear display
   Calculate (1.12)¹⁶
                     Calculate (1.12)¹⁶ from scratch
          ×
         MR
          =
```

69

QUANTITATIVE METHODS

Exercise

The facility described in the foregoing section will be widely used in Chapter 6. Here in the meanwhile are a few technical exercises:

1. $(1.05)^2$
2. $(1.02)^4$
3. $(1.02)^{10}$
4. $(1.07)^{25}$
5. $(1.11)^{17}$
6. $(1.13)^{37}$

2.11 The ( ) key

Note this is a feature absent on many calculators, but it is becoming more common. It enables you to operate with some figures set in brackets.

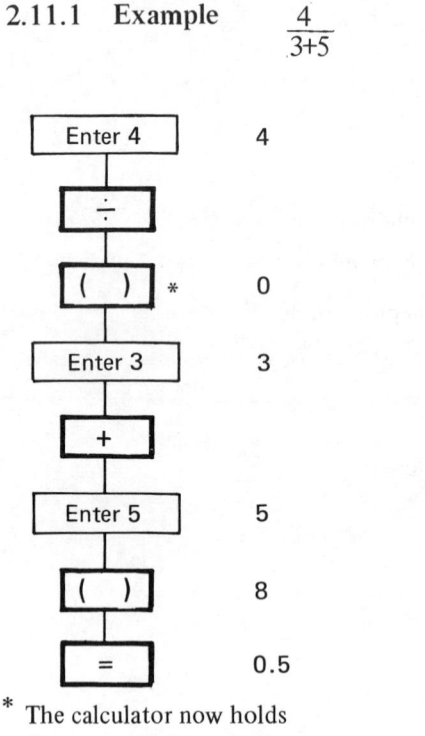

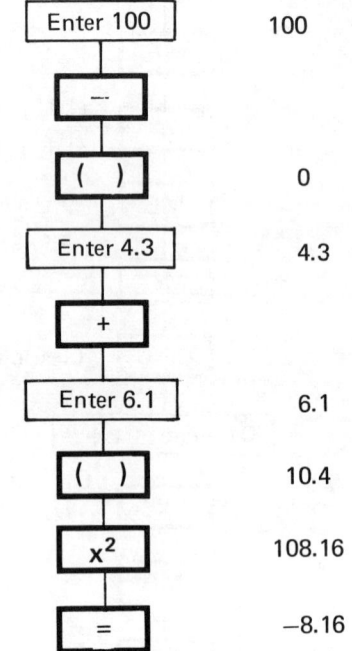

2.11.1 Example $\quad \dfrac{4}{3+5}$

Enter 4	4
÷	
( )*	0
Enter 3	3
+	
Enter 5	5
( )	8
=	0.5

* The calculator now holds the 4 — until the quantity in brackets has been evaluated.

2.11.2 Example $\quad 100 - (4.3 + 6.1)^2$

Enter 100	100
−	
( )	0
Enter 4.3	4.3
+	
Enter 6.1	6.1
( )	10.4
x^2	108.16
=	−8.16

Rough calculation: $100 - (10 +)^2$
As $10^2 = 100$, I expect a small negative result.

GETTING THE RIGHT ANSWER FROM YOUR CALCULATOR

Exercise

If you have the ☐( )☐ key you can use it on calculations like the following:

1. 4 − (1.1 x 3.6)
2. 7 − (2.9 x 4.6)
3. $\dfrac{1}{2+(3.6-1.9)}$

2.12 The Personal Computer as a Calculator

You don't have to be a programmer to get some work out of a micro. For instance in the case of the BBC.B, and most other personal computers, if you just switch it on, you can use it straight away as a calculator as shown below. What the computer gives you is underlined. Don't forget to press the return key [R] otherwise you will wait until Doomsday for a response!

    PRINT   4.2 * 3.7 [R]   Note that you don't have to put
              <u>15.54</u>   in any line numbers.

BASIC uses * as the multiplication sign so as to avoid confusion with the letter x, and uses / in place of ÷ which would require a non-standard character.

Brackets are used to cope with more complex expressions. So in order to calculate

    3 x (4 − 3.6 x 2.1)

you type in

        PRINT   3* (4−3.6*2.1)
                 <u>−10.68</u>

or to evaluate

$$\dfrac{3}{4.6 - 3.3}$$

you type

        PRINT   3/(4.6−3.3)
                 <u>2.30769231</u>

The brackets ensure that the computer calculates 4.6 − 3.3 *before* dividing into 3.

QUANTITATIVE METHODS

Even more complicated expressions can be dealt with in one operation. Suppose you wanted to calculate this horrible expression

$$\frac{1}{1 - \frac{1}{(1+0.03)^2}} \times 4000$$

you would type

    PRINT   (1/(1−(1/(1+0.03)↑2)))*4000
       69681.4455

Dissecting this to show how it works we get

PRINT (1 / (1 − (1 / (1 + 0.03)↑2))) * 4000

$$(1+0.03)^2$$

$$\frac{1}{(1+0.03)^2}$$

$$1 - \frac{1}{(1+0.03)^2}$$

$$\frac{1}{1 - \frac{1}{(1+0.03)^2}}$$

The micro is particularly useful when powering up or taking square roots.

$(1.7)^3$ PRINT   (1.7)↑3
                           4.913

$(1.26)^{17}$.   PRINT   (1.26)↑17
                           50.8509728

$\sqrt{2.9}$ PRINT   (2.9)↑0.5
                           1.70293864

GETTING THE RIGHT ANSWER FROM YOUR CALCULATOR

But of course the computer is much more powerful than these simple examples demonstrate. The machine really comes into its own when some simple programs are written. A simple guide to elementary programming can be found in Chapter 11 on page 364.

Exercise

To practice the use of the personal computer as a calculating machine, work through a selection of the exercises in this chapter and check your answers. Here are a few blockbusters to check your ability to use brackets to sort out the logic.

1. $$\frac{1}{\left(1 - \frac{1}{(1.03)^4}\right)}$$

2. $(1.07)^{41}$

3. $$\frac{2.6 - (1.9 \times 4.3)^2}{1 - 0.6 \times 0.12}$$

CHAPTER 3 : SUMMARISING DISTRIBUTIONS

This chapter starts by defining a number of averages and explaining why they can be confusing (Sections 3.1 to 3.3). Section 3.4 shows how to calculate the averages from frequency distributions while Sections 3.5 to 3.7 explain when they should and should not be used. Section 3.8 demonstrates how the loose definition of terms can be another source of confusion while the last section deals with measures of dispersion around the mean.

3.1 Much ado about nothing

The subject of averages is an unhappy one. They are widely used, but they are also widely despised and misunderstood. Often this contempt is merited; the misuse of averages is fairly common and is reinforced by the media who have the job of informing the public on a very large number of highly complex matters. This abuse of averages has often formed the basis of a variety of jokes. For instance people like to have a good laugh over the average 1.8 children borne by women. What does that 0.8 of a child look like? How tall is she or he? Which bit is missing? they ask sarcastically. Or maybe you have heard the one about the mother who complained to the headmaster because she was told that a report had shown that no less than 50% of the children in the school were under average intelligence. They're pretty rotten jokes, I agree, but they are a symptom of something that is seriously wrong with the state of relations between the statisticians and you, the users. I suggest that we all use our common sense and get to the bottom of this once and for all.

Let me put this proposition to you. When intelligent men produce an average number of children of 1.8 in a family, then it must surely be for a reason. The statisticians are well aware that you cannot rear 8/10 of a child. To see the result as a joke must be evidence of some basic misunderstanding of what the figure is supposed to be portraying. The trouble is that people do not appreciate a little known but vital truth:

THERE IS NO SUCH THING AS THE AVERAGE

What's more, just to avoid any misunderstanding on the matter, there never has been any such thing as *the* average and in fact there never will be such a thing as *the* average.

Once you've got that on board we can start to clear away the clouds

SUMMARISING DISTRIBUTIONS

of misunderstanding. Clearly if people keep on talking about something that doesn't exist, misunderstanding is inevitable. Obviously if the media bombard us daily with information about such things as *the* average rate of inflation, then this misunderstanding is inevitably going to be reinforced.

3.2 Averages and averages

Let's start by deciding why we should have averages at all. What are they for?

An average is a figure which summarises one aspect of a distribution. More precisely, it is a figure which summarises the central tendency of a distribution. (There are other measures, as we shall see later, which summarise other aspects of a distribution such as the spread of the data or its skewness.) The cause of all the trouble lies in the fact that there are many different ways of producing an average. The reduction of a distribution down to one single figure is a drastic step. It is important, therefore, to choose an appropriate average to suit each situation.

To illustrate the different ways in which an average can be calculated, consider Fig. 1.3a on page 11. Here we have the distribution of the ages of caretakers, a distribution full of information and one which stimulates a number of searching questions as we saw in Chapter 1.

3.2.1 The Mean

One way of producing an average is to calculate the mean. For many people, this is 'the' average. It is found by totalling the data items and then dividing by the number of items involved. We can express this procedure in the form of a formula:

$$\text{The mean} = \frac{\text{The total of the values of the data items.}}{\text{The number of data items.}}$$

Well, the data is available on page 22 of Chapter 1 and so, to calculate the mean age, I add up the data, column by column:

But remember, first I do a rough calculation. Most of the ages I am going to add up will be in the sixties or the fifties. Some, however are in the twenties and thirties. On balance I expect a mean in the fifties.

$$\text{Mean age of} = \frac{50 + 56 + 41 + 58 + 56 + 26 + \ldots + 45 + 52}{50}$$

$$= \frac{2524}{50} = 50.48$$

QUANTITATIVE METHODS

The mean age of caretakers = 50.5 years.

Let's postpone discussion of this figure until we have calculated a few more averages.

3.2.2 The Median

The median is that value above which and below which 50% of the data items lie. In other words, it is a value which divides the distribution into two equal parts. Looking at the breakdown on page 34 of Chapter 1, the first 25 values end with the age 53, the next 25 values start with 54. The median age therefore lies between these two values

The median age of caretakers = 53.5 years.

3.2.3 The Mode

This is simply the most frequently occurring value. Inspection of the data shows that this value is an age of 53 years.

The modal age of caretakers = 53 years.

To summarise, we have found three different averages as follows:

The mean	=	50.5	years.
The median	=	53.5	years.
The mode	=	53	years.

3.2.4 Note that, although all different, they are all of the same order of magnitude. Each gives us some idea of the location of the centre of the distribution while serving a slightly different purpose and yet are not all of them decidedly disappointing when compared with the detail shown in the original distribution? Of course this is hardly surprising given the amount of information that must be thrown away when reducing a distribution to one wretched little figure.

The mode claims to be the most typical value as it occurs the most often, and yet to say that the typical caretaker is aged 53 gives only a poor summary of the overall distribution. The median is perhaps more precise in what it is trying to say. It asserts that there are as many caretakers aged 54 or over as there are aged 53 or less. The mean is the centre of gravity or balance point for the distribution (Fig 3.1):

SUMMARISING DISTRIBUTIONS

Fig 3.1 : The Mean as 'Centre of Gravity'

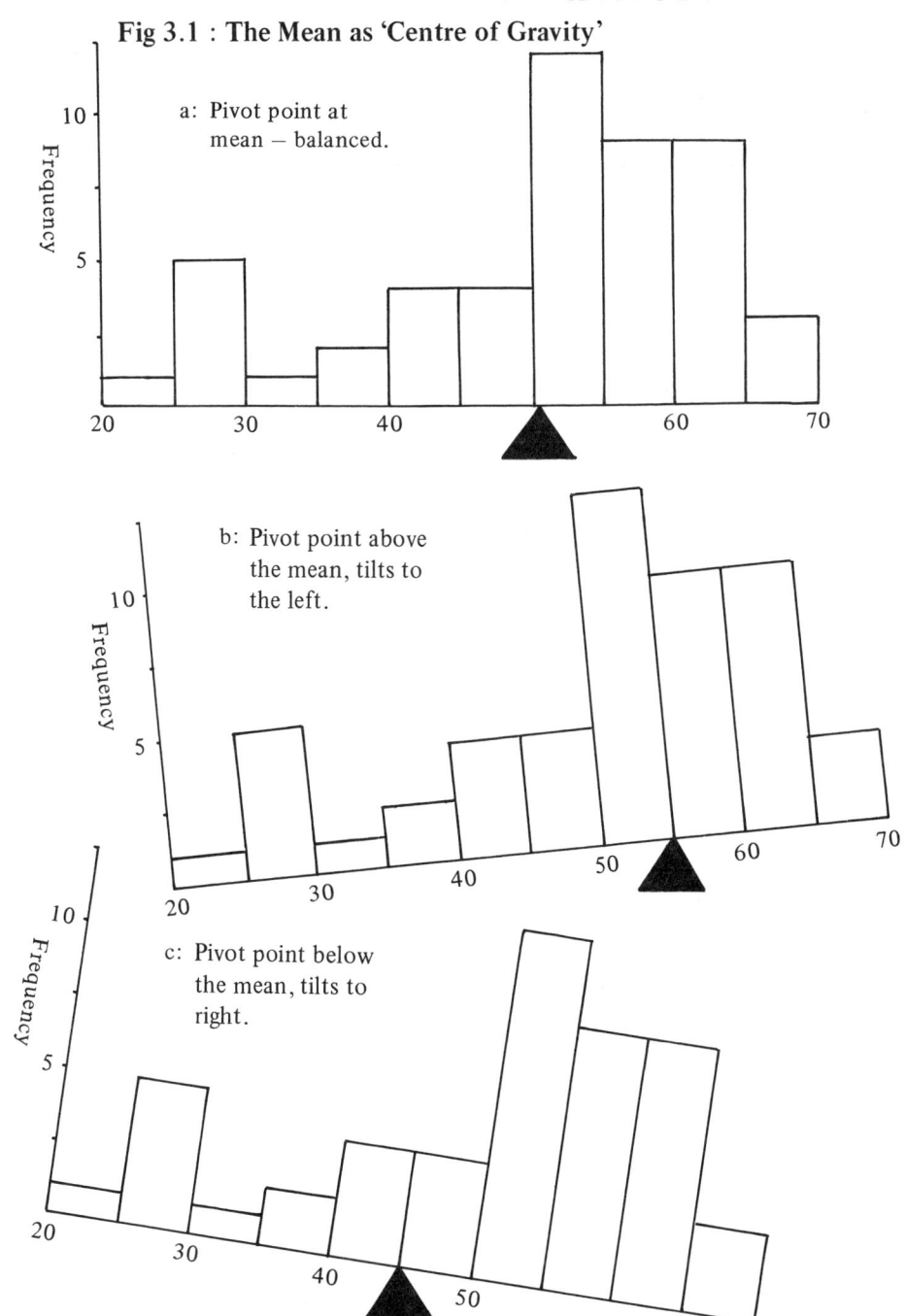

a: Pivot point at mean — balanced.

b: Pivot point above the mean, tilts to the left.

c: Pivot point below the mean, tilts to right.

and as the distribution is negatively skewed, the secondary peak at lower values 'pulls' the mean down below the other averages.

QUANTITATIVE METHODS

Fig 3.2 : The Mean as Centre of gravity

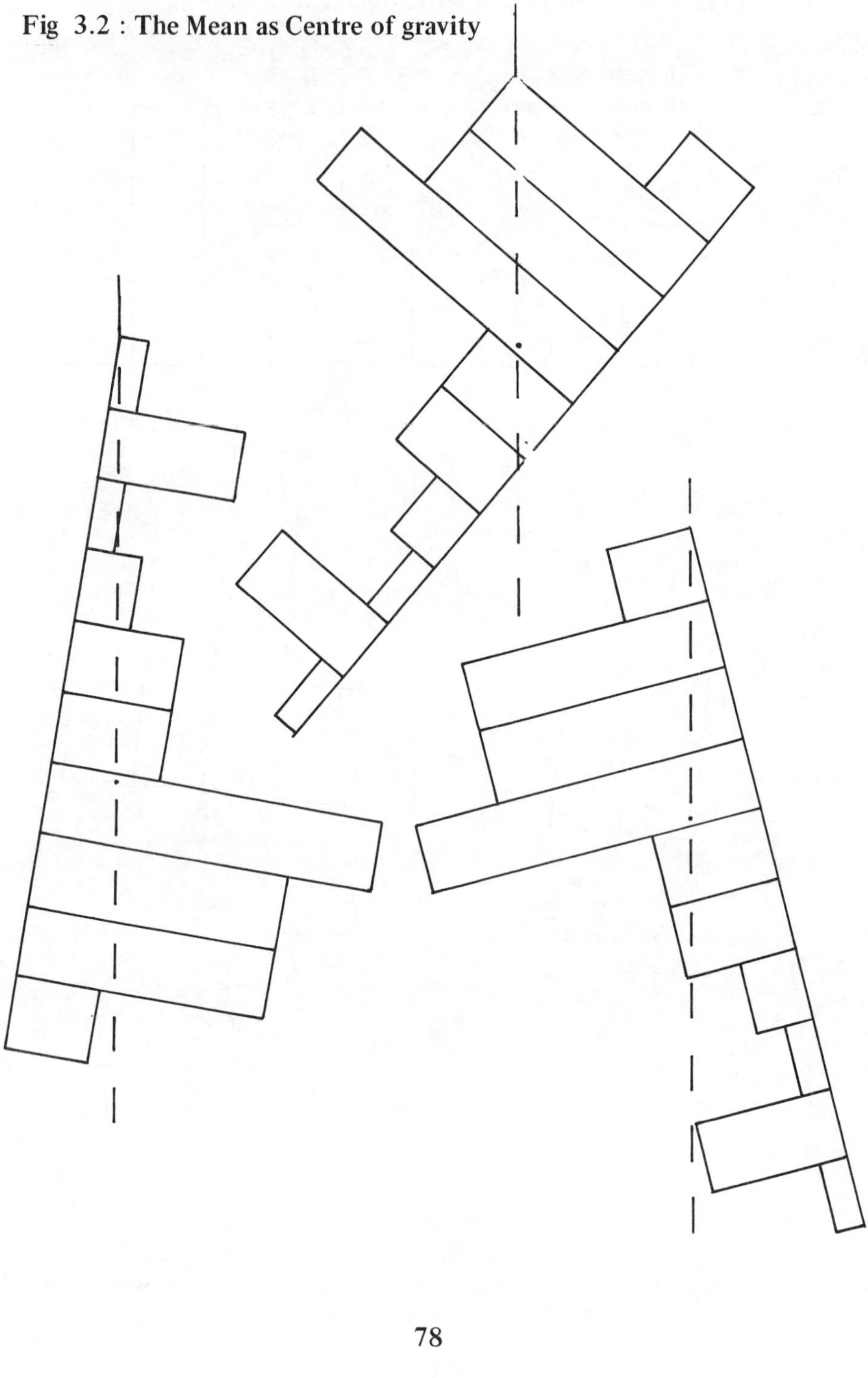

SUMMARISING DISTRIBUTIONS

Fig 3.2 (cont.)

Centre of gravity projected on scale = 50.3

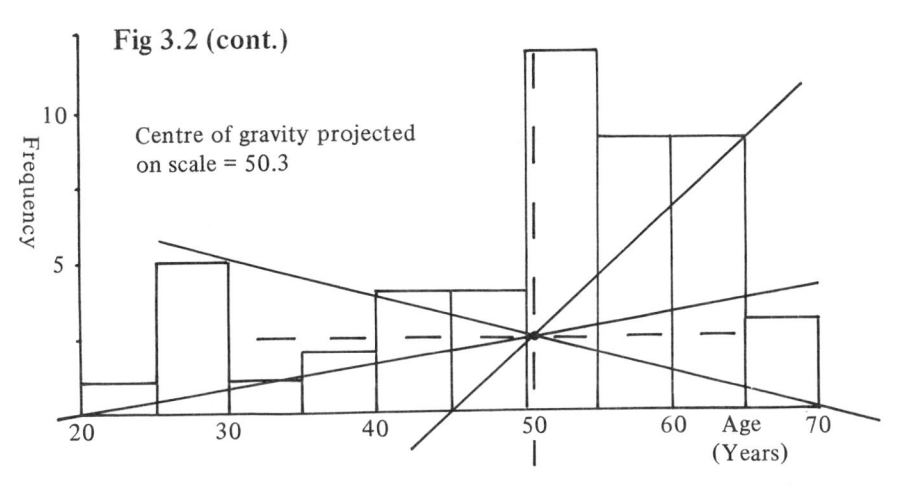

This analogy is a perfect one. You could actually calculate the mean by drawing the histogram to scale on heavy, quality board and then finding the centre of gravity by suspending the cut-out distribution from three points of suspension. The projection of the centre of gravity onto the horizontal axis would yield the mean. Not a very practical method I agree but enlightening all the same!

Exercise

1. Calculate the mean, median and modal job time given the following:

   Job time in hours   6   2   9   4   3   3   11

2. Calculate the mean, median and modal stay in hospital for these 12 patients:

   Length of Stay (days)   1   23   1   1   2   17
                             6   11   14   7   9   1

3.3 The Overworked Average

As we have seen, each average is saying something different about the distribution. All of them, however, contain less information than can be found in the distribution from which they are derived. We expect too much from our averages. We expect more from them than they can possibly deliver. What's more we confound them all and allow ourselves to perpetuate the myth that there exists a single quantity called the average. I would like to propose what I call the law of the confusion of averages.

QUANTITATIVE METHODS

'When asked for the average, people calculate the mean, think of it as the mode, endow it with the properties of the median and then wonder why everyone is confused'.

In other words, when asked for 'the' average, everyone 'knows', don't they, that you just add up all the values and divide by the number of values. Having achieved the average, people will expect it to be 'typical' and, as everyone 'knows', there are as many values above 'the' average as there are below it.

Alas, only in special circumstances can an average achieve all those functions at the same time. As an example, suppose that you are told that the average number of people killed in 13 accidental spills during the transport of toxic and inflammable gases is 19 people. That certainly sounds pretty bad. Even if we are told that that is the mean, can we help but envisage that figure as a typical death roll? Don't we go away with the impression that each time there is an accident in this category we can expect a double-figure death roll? In fact only one of these 13 accidents involved as many as 19 deaths and that was a quite exceptional catastrophe when no fewer than 180 people were killed. In this instance, the mode and the median values were both 6. Looking at the original figures I think you'll agree that 6 is a better average and yet even then it conceals the potential for disaster demonstrated by the Spanish accident when, by mere chance, a camping site was engulfed in flames coming from a crashed tanker.

TABLE 3.1 : Fatalities from some accidental spills during the Transport of Toxic and Inflammable Liquified Gases.

Year	Place	Spill from	No. of Fatalities
1968	France		5
1969	U.S.A.	Rail Tank	6
1970	G.B.		2
1970	U.S.A.		6
1972	U.S.A.		1
1973	France		6
1974	U.S.A.	Rail Tank	1
1975	U.S.A		4
1976	U.S.A.		6
1978	U.S.A	Rail Tank	8
1978	Spain		180
1978	Mexico		8
1978	U.S.A.		12

N.B. Unless otherwise stated, the spills were from a Road Tanker

(Permission No. 4)

SUMMARISING DISTRIBUTIONS

3.3.1 Once we put averages in their place and ban the use of the word 'the' when used to imply that there exists a single measure, then much of the humbug of this aspect of statistics vanishes. As an experiment, you can try replacing the word 'the' with the word 'an' every time you come across 'the' average. Her's a sample so that you can judge the effect.

    Union negotiator: 'Do you realise that *the* average wage of workers in this factory is only £80 per week?'

How do you follow that? An interminable discussion is likely to follow to determine whether the 'average' quoted is 'correct' or not. Now try replacing 'the' with 'an'.

    Union negotiator: 'Do you realise that *an* average wage for workers in this factory is only £80 per week?'

Note how much weaker this is as a statement and yet how much more constructive. It invites the immediate reply:

    Management: 'Oh really, and which average is that may I ask? How was it calculated? Which other averages did you consider before deciding to use that one?'

The effect of replacing 'the average' with 'an average' is to take away the dominating assertiveness of the statistic and replace it with a more tentative, constructive attempt at summarising the underlying information. The meaningless expression 'the average' is an aggressive term and is often used to bully rather than to persuade. The use of the definite article implies that the figure is definitive and not capable of being queried. Its replacement by the indefinite article suggests the need for agreement, opening up the possibility of alternative measures.

Of course when discussing average wages it is not just a question of which of the three averages mentioned above should be used. There is also the question of which values should be averaged in the first place. Should overtime and bonus be included and if so, then on what basis? All these other complications make the determination of one agreed average impossible except on the basis of constructive discussion.

3.3.2 Before going on to discuss which averages should be used in which circumstances, let us briefly speculate on the reasons which

QUANTITATIVE METHODS

drive people, against their common sense, to expect so much from averages. I believe that it arises partly as a natural response to the complexity of the world of business and of our lives in general. Nowadays we expect to be informed about a wide range of topics. We also know that facts are needed if we are to get away from mere generalisations. We cling therefore to the illusion that science can push aside the complexity of the world and boil it down to a few figures which we can easily grasp. Unfortunately, even though the media try to reinforce this illusion, our common sense tells us that this cannot be true.

Let me make one thing quite clear. I am not saying that averages are not useful; far from it. All I am saying is that for each average that you come across there are alternatives that could also have been chosen. No average can fully summarise the distribution from which it is derived. Soon we will look at each average in turn and discuss the circumstances under which they provide the best of a bad deal. But first we need to see how the three averages can be calculated.

3.4 Calculating Averages

We have already seen how to calculate three averages for simple data in Section 3.2. Now we turn to the calculation of the 'weighted mean' as a prelude to the treatment of frequency distributions.

3.4.1 The Weighted Mean

Weighted means are widely used. They form the basis of the system of index numbers dealt with in Chapter 8.

Example

Suppose a businessman uses two raw materials A and B which cost £10 and £20 per kilo respectively. What is the mean price per kilo of the materials? To calculate the mean by averaging £10 and £20 to give £15 would only be correct if the materials were used in equal quantities. If on the other hand 4 kilos of A are used for every kilo of B then we really need a weighted mean. This would be the mean price of a 'basket' of materials consisting of 4 kilos of A and 1 kilo of B. The relative usage of the materials are used as the 'weights' in the calculation.

$$\text{Weighted Mean} = \frac{\text{Price of A} \times \text{weight} + \text{Price of B} \times \text{weight}}{\text{Sum of the weights}}$$

SUMMARISING DISTRIBUTIONS

$$= \frac{£10 \times 4 + £20 \times 1}{4 + 1}$$

$$= \frac{£40 + £20}{4 + 1}$$

$$= £12$$

Note how the higher weighting ascribed to A has pulled the weighted mean down towards the price of A.

Look at Figs 1.3a and b on page 11 showing the distributions of the ages of caretakers. Let us suppose that instead of the original data, we only had the frequency distributions available. How would we then calculate, or rather estimate, the three averages considered so far?

3.4.2 The Mean of a Frequency Distribution

If all I had to go by was the frequency distribution on page 24, then all I would know is that I have one value in the range 20 – 24, 5 values in the range 25 – 29 and so on. How can I calculate the mean? Surely for that purpose I need the original values? In place of the original values I assume that all the values falling within a given interval have the value of the mid-point of that interval. In the case of the first interval, that mid-point is 22 years. I work this out by assuming that the ages of caretakers have been rounded off to the nearest whole number. The interval then covers all ages from 19.5 to 24.5; 19.4 would be rounded down to 19, and 24.6, up to 25. This interval, 19.5 – 24.5, is 5 years wide. Half way across is therefore 19.5 + 5/2 = 22 years. If, on the other hand, the age recorded is the age at the last birthday, so that a man aged 24 years 11 months is recorded as being aged 24, then the interval is effectively 20 – 24.99 which is 5 years wide and has a mid-point of 22.5 years, slightly higher than is the case under the other assumption. Often, the precise way in which the class intervals have been defined is not known. Fortunately the potential error involved is fairly small.

So, to calculate the mean, I assume that the ages of all those falling within a given band have the value of the mid-point. I will assume that the ages have been rounded off so that the mid-point of the first interval is 22 years. Effectively

QUANTITATIVE METHODS

Age band in Years	Frequency
20 – 24	1
25 – 29	5
30 – 34	1 etc.

is treated as

20 – 24	22
25 – 29	27,27,27,27,27
30 – 34	32 etc.

and the mean is calculated, as usual, by adding up the total of the ages and then dividing by the total number of values thus:

$$\text{mean age} = \frac{(1 \times 22) + (5 \times 27) + (1 \times 32) + \text{.. etc, etc.}}{1 + 5 + 1 + \text{.. etc, etc.}}$$

Remember we are calculating the mean as if we did not have the original data available. The work can best be laid out as follows:

Table 3.2 : Calculation of the Mean using the mid-points of class intervals.

Assumed mid-point	Frequency	Frequency x mid-point
22	1	22
27	5	135
32	1	32
37	2	74
42	4	168
47	4	188
52	12	624
57	9	513
62	9	558
67	3	201
	50	2515

$$\text{Mean age} = \frac{2515}{50} = 50.3$$

Note that this differs from the true mean of 50.48 calculated on page 75 because here we are using the mid-points of class intervals and not the original data.

SUMMARISING DISTRIBUTIONS

The exercise is not difficult on a calculator, but don't forget that it is essential to do a rough calculation first.

Rough calculation: looking at the distribution I can see that the modal age is about 52. The secondary peak lies at about 27 and this will bring the mean (centre of gravity) down to a balance point of somewhere between 48 and 52.

The procedure is more straightforward when dealing with a discrete distribution (there is no need to estimate the mid-points of class intervals). The following example will illustrate such a calculation while at the same time demonstrating how to deal with a percentage frequency distribution.

In Fig 1.7a on page 20, we don't know the actual frequencies with which a given number of admissions to the coronary unit occurred, only the relative frequencies. On 22% of days 0 admissions were made, on 35% of days 1 admission was made, and so on. We calculate the mean as if these percentages were actual frequencies. If you like, we treat the distribution as if it represented the results for 100 days observed.

First we need to do a rough calculation. As always with the mean, this amounts to guessing the 'centre of gravity' of the distribution. If you tried to balance the distribution at 1.0, it would clearly tip over; similarly with an attempted balance point of 2.0, but in the other direction.

Fig 3.3 : Estimating the Mean by seeking a Balance Point

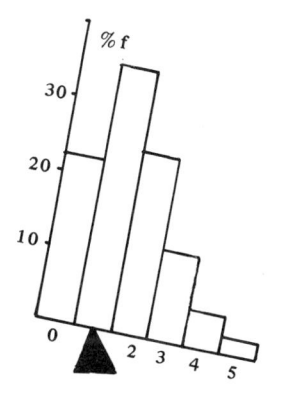

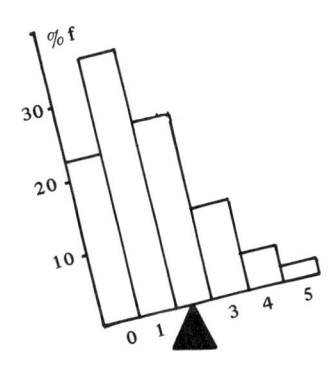

QUANTITATIVE METHODS

So I am expecting a mean lying between 1.0 and 2.0 admissions per day. I carry out this rough estimate *before* carrying out the detailed calculations. The balancing trick, of course, I do in my head; the diagram merely shows you how my mind works when carrying out the exercise. You'll be surprised just how accurately you can estimate the mean using this method. As a race we may not be naturally numerate, but we are endowed with a phenomenal sense of balance!

This guessing technique has another important use for managers who have someone else to do the dirty work. It enables them to check the mean calculated by others. When presented with a distribution, their sense of balance will provide them with an estimate of the mean in a second or two. This will enable them to check the figure quoted to see whether or not it is reasonable. Also if the distribution is asymmetrical and 'the' average is quoted, without the type being specified, a glance at the distribution will indicate whether the average quoted is the mean or not.

The work can be laid out as follows:

Table 3.3 : Calculation of the Mean of a Percentage Frequency Distribution

Number of Admissions	% Frequency	% Frequency x Admissions
0	22	0
1	35	35
2	24	48
3	12	36
4	5	20
5	2	10
	100	149

Mean number of admissions per day = $\frac{149}{100}$, which is about 1.5 per day.

3.4.3 : The Median

A rough estimate of the median of a frequency distribution can be obtained by working out the likely location of the middle item. This is made relatively easy because the data items are already ordered into class intervals, and is particularly true if there are a large number of such intervals.

Suppose we have the distribution of the time (in minutes) to serve a

SUMMARISING DISTRIBUTIONS

customer in a drive-in repair shop.

Table 3.4 : Distribution of Service Times

Class Intervals for Service Times (minutes)	Frequency (Number of Customers)	Cumulative Frequency
0 – < 20	6	6
10 – < 20	15	21
20 – < 30	8	29
30 +	2	31
	31	

The median is the service time of the 16th customer when these are taken in order i.e. there will be 15 customers who were served quicker and 15 who were served slower than the median customer. Obviously its value lies somewhere in the range 10 – 20 minutes. As there are 6 customers already in the first interval, we are looking for the 10th customer in order in the middle interval (16 – 6 = 10) and there are 15 customers in all in that interval. The median service time is therefore roughly 10/15ths of the way along the middle interval giving a value of 16 or 17 minutes.

Applying the same rough approach to Table 3.2 on page 84 it seems that the median of the caretaker distribution must lie in the interval 50 – 54 and be nearer 54 than 50.

The most accurate way of calculating the median of a frequency distribution is by drawing up a graph showing the cumulative percentage frequency. An example will illustrate the technique.

Step 1: If the distribution is not already in that form, convert the frequency distribution into the percentage form. The % frequencies are found by dividing each of the frequencies by the total of the frequencies and then multiplying by 100. Thus in the case of the caretaker distribution where the frequencies total 50, a frequency of 1 in the range 20 – 24 becomes 1/50 x 100% = 2%. On my calculator I can use the constant divisor facility here.

(Of course in this example you could do the arithmetic in your head. Usually the numbers won't be so nice so get the practice in here when you can see straight away if you go wrong!)

QUANTITATIVE METHODS

The fact that the % frequencies should add up to 100 usually provides a sufficient check on the arithmetic. However, because of rounding error, the sum may not be exactly 100. The sum should be shown as 100 all the same.

Step 2: Convert the percentage frequencies into cumulative percentage frequencies. This is done by progressively accumulating the percentage frequency column.

Table 3.5 : Caretakers : Percentage & Cumulative Percentage Frequency

Age of Caretakers	Frequency	Percentage Frequency	Cumulative Percentage Frequency
20 – 24	1	2	2
25 – 29	5	10	12
30 – 34	1	2	14
35 – 39	2	4	18
40 – 44	4	8	26
45 – 49	4	8	34
50 – 54	12	24	58
55 – 59	9	18	76
60 – 64	9	18	94
65 – 69	3	6	100
	50	100	

This additional column tells you that 2% of caretakers were aged 24 or less, 12% were aged 29 or less, 14% were aged 34 or less, etc. This can be represented graphically as follows in the form of an 'Ogive'.

Fig 3.4 : Ogive for Caretaker's Distribution

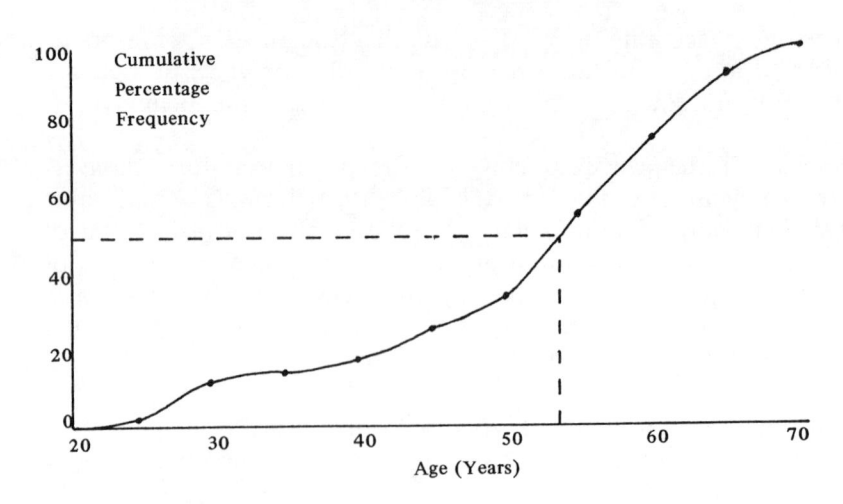

SUMMARISING DISTRIBUTIONS

A technical note: in drawing the graph above, I have plotted the cumulative percentage frequencies, 2%, 12% and 14% against the *upper* end of the class intervals: 24.5, 29.5 and 34.5 years respectively.

Fig 3.5 : Detail of Fig 3.4

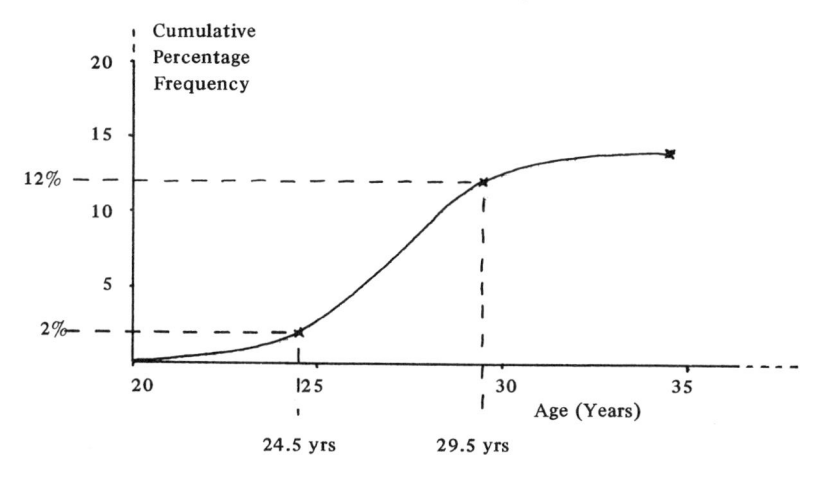

This is because, by rounding down, all caretakers aged 24.5 or less would be recorded as 24. If on the other hand, the data had been recorded on the basis of age at last birthday, the cumulative % frequency points would have to be plotted against 24.99, 19.99 and 34.99 respectively as shown below.

Fig 3.6 : On the basis of age at last birthday (detail)

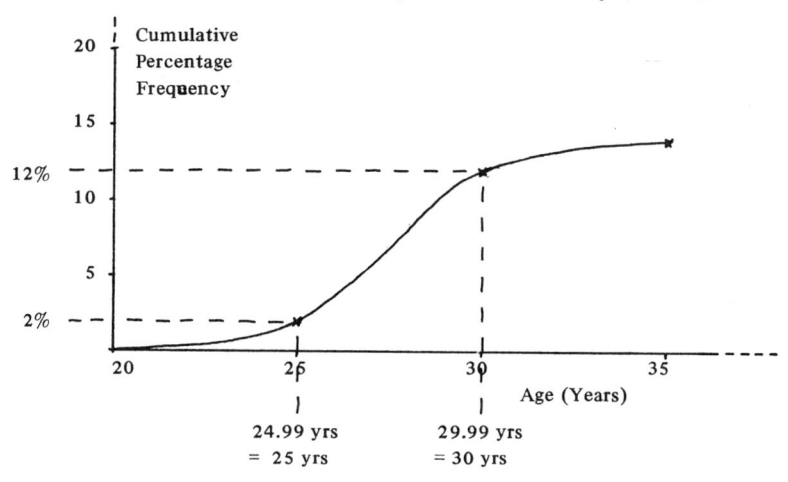

QUANTITATIVE METHODS

The potential error is not great, but given that some very precise work can be carried out with the median, it is as well not to accumulate more error than is strictly necessary.

Having produced the ogive, the median can be read off on the horizontal axis as shown in Fig. 3.4, yielding a value of 53 years. Although this method is not as accurate as that which uses the original data (the true value was 53.5), the results are usually quite good, as in this case. Remember that often you won't have the original raw data before you, only the frequency distribution.

3.4.4 The Mode

For a discrete frequency distribution, the mode is easily read off except in awkward cases where there exists more than one mode as in Fig. 1.7d on page 22. Frankly, this is a hopeless case. Strictly speaking the mode is both 1 and 3 days. In fact 1, 2 and 3 days in the unit are all roughly equi-frequent.

For a continuous distribution, the approximate for estimating the mode is as follows:

Fig 3.7 : Estimated Mode of Distribution of the Age of Caretakers

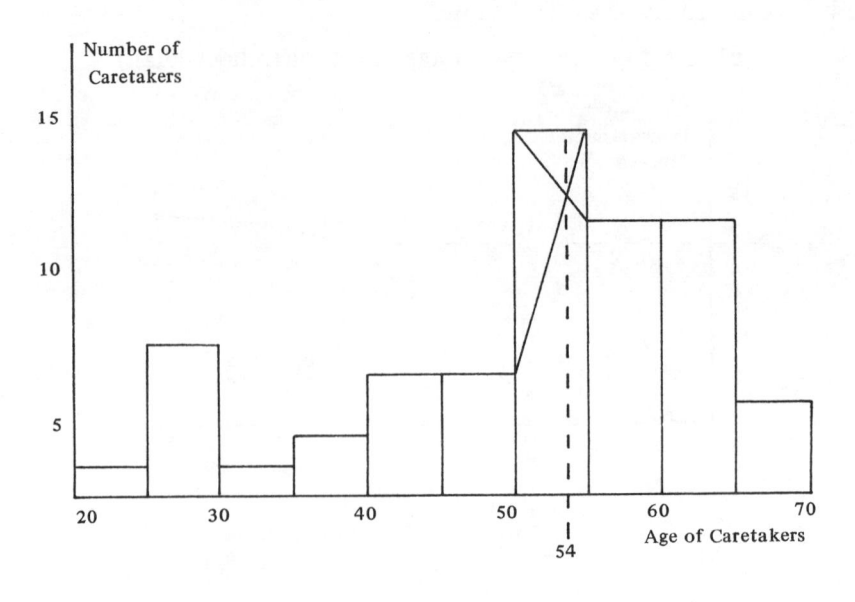

SUMMARISING DISTRIBUTIONS

giving an estimate of about 54 years for the mode. We know, because we have the raw data, that the true mode is 53. However, often we do not have access to the original data and therefore need to use an approximate method. The method above is better than selecting a point half way across the class interval because it takes into account the fact that the next class interval, 55 – 59, above the model class interval, 50 – 54, has a higher frequency count than the class interval immediately preceding, 45 – 49. Logically, the mode in this instance is more likely to lie towards the upper end of the modal class interval. This point is best illustrated by an extreme case.

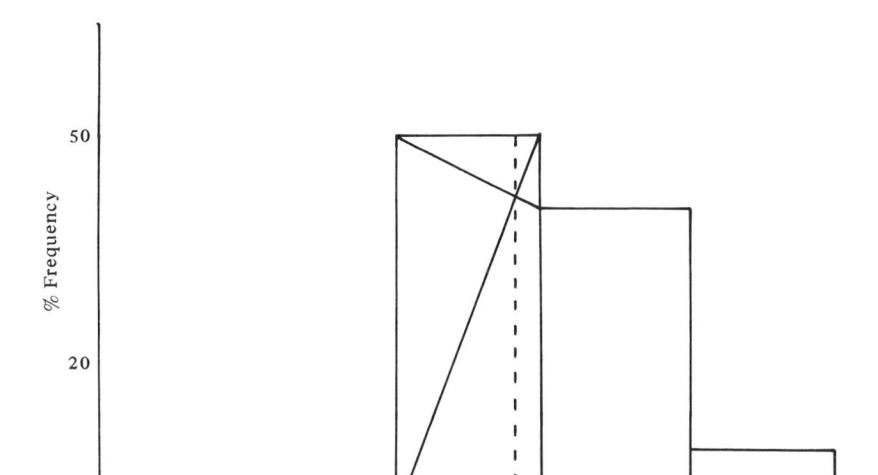

Fig 3.8 : Estimating the Mode, an extreme case

Given almost no values in the interval 10 – 20, we would expect the majority of values in the 20 – 30 interval to arise in the upper end of the interval. The method described, in fact, yields a value of 28. This method should *not* be used when the modal class interval is the first interval in the distribution. In this situation, use the mid-point of the interval.

QUANTITATIVE METHODS

Exercise

Estimate the median and the mean of the following frequency distributions. Then if you want to practice the detailed workings, calculate the precise value and compare your results with the estimates.

1. Age of New Recruits to a Company

Age Range	Number of Recruits
20 –<30	24
30 –<40	10
40 –<50	6
50 –<60	4

2. Number of faults

Faults arising	Number of of days
0	45
1	10
2	2
3	4
4	20

3. Turn to your answers to the first of the exercises in Section 1.11 on page 27. Estimate the mean, mode and median for items A and B. Then calculate the true values from the frequency distributions and comment on the results. If you have time you can check your results against the raw data.

N.B: You don't have to draw up an ogive to calculate the median as these are discrete distributions.

4. Do the same for exercise 2 on page 28, using the mid-point of the class intervals to obtain the mean and by drawing an ogive to get the median. If you have time, check out the results with the true values obtained from the raw data.

3.5 When to use which average?
The Mean

This is the best average for quantitative estimation rather than for descriptive work. As we shall see in Chapters 9 and 10, it also plays a major role as does the median, in what is known as 'Statistical Inference', that is the drawing of conclusions on the basis of statistical evidence.

3.5.1 Example

Suppose the average repair time is required for the instrument whose repair time distribution is shown in Fig 1.4 on page 14. The average repair times are as follows:

SUMMARISING DISTRIBUTIONS

                mean   = 4.34 manhours
                median = 3.6   "   "
                mode   = 3.2   "   "

Which average should be chosen? When asked for an average the initial response should always be the same:

WHAT DO YOU WANT THE AVERAGE FOR?

If an average is needed to give a rough idea of how long the job usually takes, then it would be best to choose the mode, 3.2 hours, the most frequently occurring time and therefore the one most likely to arise. Alternatively the median time could be given, 3.6 hours, of which it can be said that as many instruments take as long to repair as take less. Both of these averages give a figure which is 'typical' in some sense, so when should the mean be chosen?

Suppose that I expect that 100 instruments will pass through my workshop next month and that I need to produce a manpower utilisation forecast. I can estimate the *total* manhours to be used as follows. I know from the way that the mean is calculated that

The mean repair time   =   Total manhours employed
for instruments   ─────────────────────────────
                             Number of instruments repaired.

From which it follows that:

Total manhours employed = Mean repair × Total number of instru-
                          time   ments to be repaired

                        =   4.34 × 100 = 434 manhours.

Clearly if I had employed the median as the average in this situation I would have obtained an estimate of 3.6 × 100 = 360 manhours. This typical average, ideal for descriptive purposes, would have led to a gross underestimate of the total manhours required next month. The point is that for my manpower forecast, I need an average that takes account of the fact that some jobs, allbeit a minority, will take substantially longer than the 'typical' figure of 3.6 hours.

'Horses for courses', as the saying goes. Don't overwork the average concept. Don't expect an average to do more than one simple job at a time, they're simply not up to it.

3.5.2 Example 2

Suppose I need to estimate the quantity of a particular impure raw material in kilos that will be required to produce a given quantity of

QUANTITATIVE METHODS

pure, refined final product. Because of difficulties in the process leading to losses, the quantity of raw material needed varies. Suppose the distribution is as follows:

Fig 3.9 : % of occasions on which a specified quantity of new material was needed to produce 1000 kilos of final product.

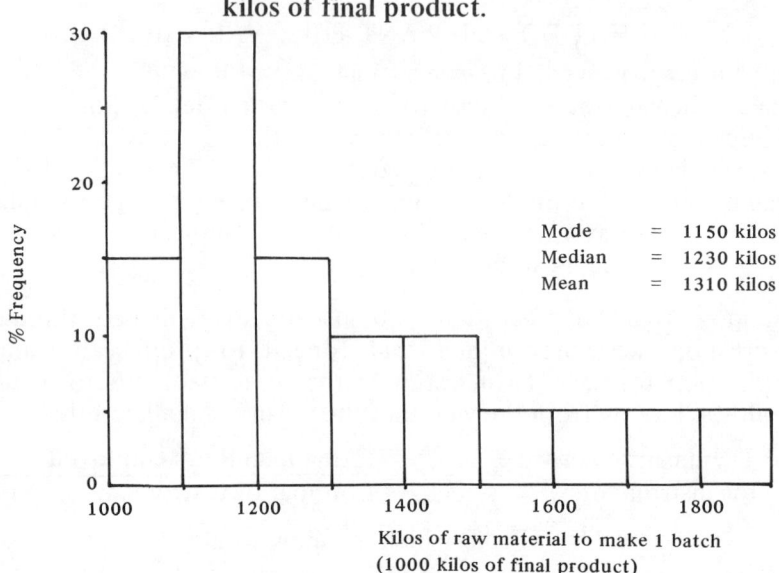

```
Mode   = 1150 kilos
Median = 1230 kilos
Mean   = 1310 kilos
```

Kilos of raw material to make 1 batch
(1000 kilos of final product)

We require to know the quantity of raw material needed to meet a production target next month of 10 batches of 1000 kilos of refined product. To estimate the raw material required, we should use the mean estimate of 1310 kilos per batch thus:

Raw material to produce   =   10 x mean raw material
10 batches of final product   utilisation per batch.

$\qquad\qquad\qquad\qquad\qquad\quad$ =   10 x 1310   = 13100 kilos.

However, as a descriptive average the mean is highly misleading. It seems to imply a very low conversion efficiency ($\frac{1000}{1310}$ x 100 = 76%) whereas in 60% of batches, the quantity used was less than 1300 lbs. If we had used the median, 1230 lbs, implying an efficiency of $\frac{1000}{1230}$ x 100 = 81%, we would have had a figure more typical in the sense that there were as many instances above as below it. Using the median for estimating usage, however, we would have obtained an estimate for next month of 12,300 lbs, representing a shortfall of 800 lbs.

Confused? You shouldn't be as long as you bear in mind that there is

SUMMARISING DISTRIBUTIONS

no such thing as the average and that the right average to use depends on what you are trying to do. This is particularly important with highly skewed distributions such as the one found above.

The essential point to learn from these examples is that when producing typical averages, we need measures that are not influenced by extreme values. In producing quantitative forecasts, we need a measure, the mean, which takes account of the extreme values. Of course it may have occurred to you that it would be worth finding out why these extreme values exist, why on some occasions we need nearly 2000 lbs of raw material to produce 1000 lbs of product. Until production procedures have been improved, we still have to budget for such extremes by using the mean to provide the raw material forecasts.

Of course where the mean is affected by extreme values *which are not likely to occur again within the planning period* then, quite frankly, the figures should be adjusted. Suppose, in the above example, you were able to establish that all raw material usage greater than 1500 lbs was due to faulty equipment which has now been replaced.

In that case the raw material estimate based on the revised mean of 1212.5 kilos would become 12,125 kilos rather 13,100 kilos.

3.5.3 Example 3

We often need the mean to provide the accurate 'centre of gravity' of a distribution. Look again at the two distributions in 1.1a and 1.1c on pages 2 and 4. They show, you will remember, the thickness of gold plated onto electrical connectors using different batch sizes. It is clear that the spread, or dispersion, of the measurements is reduced when the smaller batch size is employed. It isn't so clear as to whether the mean has also been reduced. The precise values of the means are as follows:

        Batch size :   large , mean coating 3.13 microns
        batch size :   small ,   "   "   3.05 microns

The precision of the mean indicates that not only the spread, but also the mean coating has been marginally reduced. From the mean, also, the expected quantity of gold to be used can be estimated. Later, in Chapter 10, we will consider whether such figures are significantly different, that is whether the small difference observed represents a real improvement or not.

QUANTITATIVE METHODS

Example 4

Look again at Fig 1.7a on page 20. This distribution shows the number of admissions per day to a coronary unit. The mean number of admissions per day turned out to be 1.49 per day; let's call it 1.5 admissions per day on average. Faced with one and a half coronary admissions per day, you may still be tempted to smile and say 'but of course that's only 'theory', you can't have half an admission'. If you are tempted to follow that line then you are still following the law of the confusion of averages enunciated on page 80. Some people might even be tempted to make a sick joke. 'Does the half admission have the half with the heart in it?'

Well of course it's perfectly reasonable to talk of a mean value of 1.5 admissions per day. It's only another way of saying 15 every 10 days. What's so ridiculous about that? What's more, for quantitative purposes, the mean is precisely the average that you need. Suppose the unit needs 1 packet of a certain instrument, X say, for each admission and suppose I wish to estimate the number of packets that I need for a 30 day period, I calculate using the mean:

Estimated number of = Number of x Mean number
packets of X to be used   days   of admissions
                                           per day.

= 30 x 1.5

= 45 packets per day.

If I had used the mode or the median for this estimation purpose, 1 admission per day in both cases, I would have obtained an estimate of 30 packets, thereby grossly underestimating the consumption to be expected.

Example 5

Look at Fig 1.6a on page 17. It represents the life until replacement of a component. The mean life is 1230 flying hours. No average can typify such an irregular distribution. The mode is ill-defined and the median is of little use as it is unaffected by extremes and in this example, the extremes are interesting and of great practical significance. What use could there possibly be for the mean of such a distribution?

Suppose that I estimate that next year the fleet which uses this item will clock up 60,000 flying hours. How can I estimate the number of

SUMMARISING DISTRIBUTIONS

components that will be replaced.

Estimated number of components to be replaced = $\dfrac{\text{Total flying hours}}{\text{Mean flying hours per component to replacement}}$

$$= \frac{60,000}{1,230} = 48.78$$

Given the inaccuracies in the estimates and data used, I will round this off to 50 components.

Example 6

Lets go back to 1.8 children per family. Why should it be reasonable to talk about family size in such a provocative way? Well, if you want to compare the average size of families from one year to the next then clearly the mode is useless, it remains, from year to year, at 1 per family for the moment at least. The median suffers from the same disadvantage, being too imprecise for discrete distributions of low values. The total number of children born is no indicator as the number of families varies from year to year as does the number of women capable of bearing children. The obvious way to compare the birth rates in different years is either on the basis of births per child-bearing woman, births per woman of child-bearing age or children per family. In each case the result will turn out in the form of a fraction. Of course 1.8 children per family is just another way of saying 1800 children per 1000 families. If the latter sounds reasonable, why shouldn't the former? The reason is simple: people expect all their averages to have the property of the mode. It's yet another demonstration of the Law of the Confusion of Averages.

In all these examples, we have seen how the mean is used for quantitative estimates even though it is not usually as typical or representative as other averages used for descriptive purposes.

3.6 The Median

The median is a nice friendly average. It is reasonably easy to understand what it means and it is not difficult to calculate. While providing an excellent average for descriptive purposes, a whole set of precise quantitative tests have been built up around it (see Chapter 10). It is not widely recognised in business although it has long been used in Social Statistics where skewed distributions with extreme values are common. It is worthy of more recognition from managers.

QUANTITATIVE METHODS

Why is the median so easy to understand? Suppose a man is being interviewed for a job. The wage offered is £80 per week. If he is told that the median wage for workers in that category is £78 per week, then he knows that there are fewer people earning more than him than are earning less. It is relatively easy for the worker to judge his position relative to other workers. Extreme values, those values which tend to shift the mean considerably, have no effect on the value of the median. So, for instance, consider two workforces of 10 people each. Their weekly earnings are :

Table 3.6 : The weekly Earnings of Two Workforces

	Workforce 'A'		Workforce 'B'
Median = 80	75	Median = 80	71
	76		73
Mean = 80.8	78	Mean = 87.8	76
	78		77
	79		79
	....		....
	81		81
	82		83
	85		88
	86		115
	88		135

The two wage distributions are very different. The second is more skewed than the first having extreme values at the upper end. That's why, although the median is the same in each case, the mean for the second workforce is higher than for the first. The high values in workforce B have shifted the centre of gravity upwards. For a worker to be told that the median wage in both cases is £80 p.w. is not misleading. In each workforce, he knows that there are 5 workers earning more than that figure and 5 less. Of course it doesn't give him the whole picture but then one figure cannot do that. I cannot stress enough that one figure cannot satisfactorily summarise *all* aspects of a distribution.

For some discrete distributions, however, the median is pretty useless. Consider Fig 1.7a on page 20. The median number of admissions per day is 1. On 22% of days there were 0 or less admissions and on 57% of days there were 1 or less. In this case the median does not convey

SUMMARISING DISTRIBUTIONS

precise information. Certainly, on 50% of days, 1 or more admissions arose, but then on 50% of days 1 or less arose. The median is therefore ambiguous and possibly misleading. Suppose I tell someone that the median is one admission per day, he might interpret that as meaning that on 50% of days 2 or more admissions were made, which is not true; or he might say that on 50% of days less than 1 admission, that is 0 admissions were made, which is also not the case. In this case the mode is a much better average to use for descriptive purposes. Confused? Well, as I explained earlier, you must face up to the truth. No single average is suitable for all purposes. All you can do is to decide, in each case, what you are trying to get over and then use that average which most effectively and unambiguously achieves your purpose. There is, of course, another alternative. You can rely less on averages and more on the actual distributions themselves.

It is quite easy to present a distribution to the reader in reduced form if necessary. The *shape* immediately helps the user to avoid misinterpreting quoted averages.

3.7 The Mode

The mode is a fickle average. At times it is an effective way of summarising a distribution, at other times it is ambiguous or even useless. 1 admission per day on average, the mode, is a good way of describing Fig 1.7a if one figure is all you can employ. But there are other distributions where the mode is ill-defined. In Fig 1.6a on page 17, the theoretical mode is 1280 flying hours but in cases like this where there are a number of peaks it is better to use the concept of multiple modes. We can describe Fig 1.7a as being a distribution with 3 modes.

Main mode	=	1280 flying hours
Second mode	=	2270 ” ”
Third mode	=	100 ” ”

Quoting all three modes gives a good summary of the distribution.

With the distribution of the ages of caretakers, we have a bi-modal distribution:

Main mode	=	53 years
Second mode	=	27.5 years.

In general terms the mode is good for summarising very discrete distributions. It can be employed in a flexible way to describe the principle peak or peaks of a distribution. To describe the Alps in terms

QUANTITATIVE METHODS

of Mt. Blanc alone is highly misleading. Adding the Matterhorn and the Jungfrau does a little more justice to the whole!

A special case can arise when the mode is the best quantitative average to use. If a clothing manufacturer is going to make a shoe of just one size, then it would be foolish of him to make it to suit the mean foot size of the market. The mean would be untypical if influenced by extreme values. In this case by producing his shoe to fit the modal foot size, it will then provide a perfect fit for the largest single group of potential purchasers.

Exercise

1. Suppose that the following histogram shows the distribution of the mean monthly sales achieved by each of 35 salesmen in a typical year (Sales do not show any seasonal pattern).

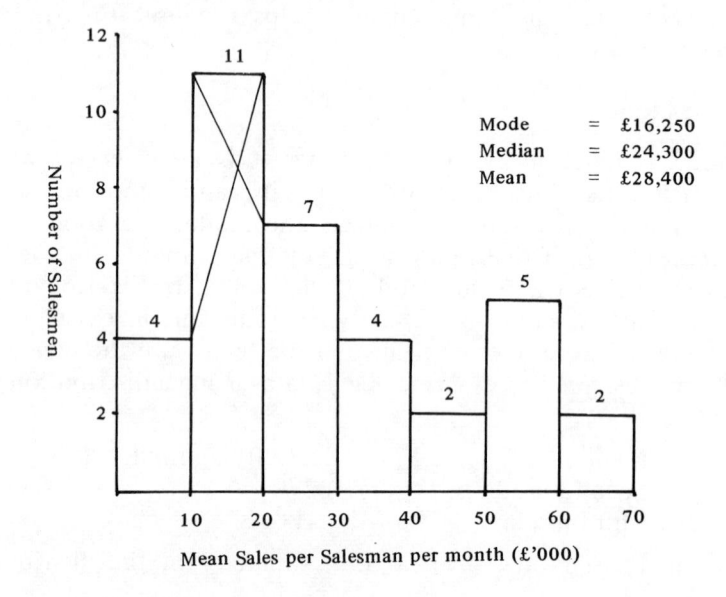

Mode = £16,250
Median = £24,300
Mean = £28,400

In each of the following cases indicate which average derived from the distribution would be most appropriate:

i) To estimate the value of the total sales in a typical month given 35 salesmen in the field.

ii) To give a salesman an idea of what is the most usual value for the monthly sales achieved.

iii) To give a salesman a yardstick against which he can measure his

SUMMARISING DISTRIBUTIONS

achievement against that of his colleagues.

NB: These questions should form the basis for discussion. Clear-cut answers can't be given.

2. To what extent does the total distribution supply the answers to (i) (ii) and (iii) in Exercise (1) without the need for averages?

3. A local authority consumes 30,000 packets of a material every year. Each order consists of 20,000 packets. What is the mean number of orders made per year and how can the answer be meaningfully interpreted?

4. Suppose the distribution of the number of breakdowns per week for a computer system in a factory is as shown below together with the values of three averages.

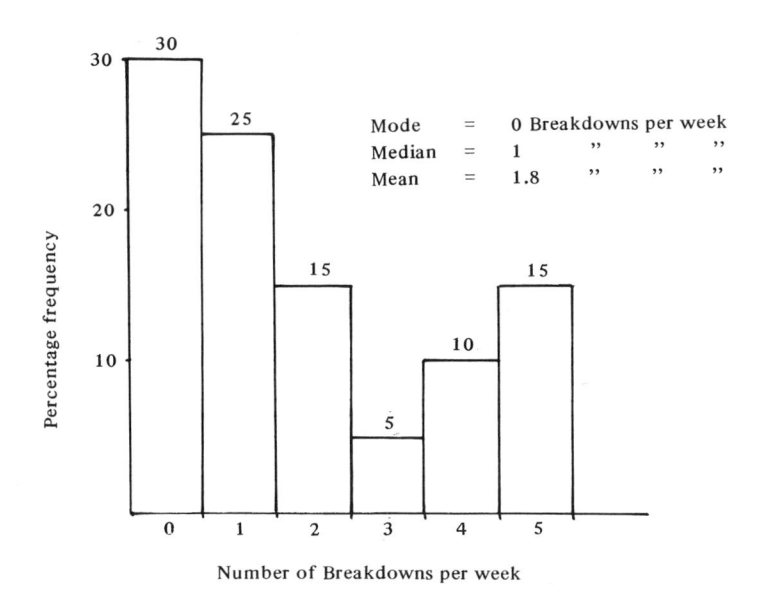

```
Mode   = 0 Breakdowns per week
Median = 1      ”      ”    ”
Mean   = 1.8    ”      ”    ”
```

Percentage frequency values: 30, 25, 15, 5, 10, 15 at breakdowns 0, 1, 2, 3, 4, 5 respectively.

Number of Breakdowns per week

i) What are the uses and limitations of each average in this context?

ii) Give a precise interpretation of the mean in this case for the benefit of someone who says 'You can't have 1.8 of a breakdown'.

101

QUANTITATIVE METHODS

3.8 Other ways in which averages can be deceptive
3.8.1 The Loose Definition of Terms

It should be stressed that the confusion about averages that exists is not limited to a confusion between means, modes and medians. Often the problem arises from the way in which the data has been defined. The whole subject of the quality of data is discussed in detail in Chapter 12, and the problems of Indices, a special form of average, are discussed in Chapter 7. Here it will suffice to show how an agreed type of average can still cause confusion.

Suppose that during wage negotiations it has been agreed that the weighted mean is an appropriate average to be used to describe wage rates. Confusion can arise from the ambiguity surrounding the definition of the term 'wage'. The facts are as follows:

Table 3.7

	Workers Category		
	A	B	C
Number of workers per category last year	10	20	5
Estimated number of workers per category next year	8	20	10
Basic wage rate for a 40 hour week last year	£2/hr	£2.5/hr	3.5/hr
Basic wage last year	£80	£100	£140
Overtime basis	time + ¼	time + ¼	time + ½
Mean weekly overtime hours worked last year	10.5	8.4	9.6
Mean weekly overtime hours worked in previous month	20.4	18.6	19.2
Forecast weekly overtime hours for next year	6.0	4.0	5.0

SUMMARISING DISTRIBUTIONS

From the above data it is quite possible to calculate all of the following averages.

1. Mean wage based on basic wage rate

$$= \frac{10 \times 80 + 20 \times 100 + 5 \times 140}{10 + 20 + 5}$$

$$= £100 \text{ per week.}$$

2. Mean earnings based on on mean weekly overtime for preceding year weighted by last year's workforce. $= £129.70$ per week.

3. Mean earnings based on mean weekly overtime worked in preceding month weighted by last year's workforce. $= £162.19$ per week

4. Mean earnings based on estimated mean overtime for next year using last year's workforce for weighting. $= £115.18$ per week.

5. As for 4. above but using projected workforce next year for weighting $= £122.96$ per week.

etc. etc. . . .

The source of all this confusion does not lie in the choice of statistical average used, nor is it 'yet another example of how statistics can be used to prove anything'. In each case a weighted mean has been used, the weights being the relative sizes of the three components of the workforce. The problem lies in the complexity of the world in which we work. Remember, in real life remuneration systems are much more complicated than this simple example. To avoid confusion a clear definition of the terms used must be agreed before meangful discussion can start.

Unfortunately terms are often not clearly defined and we would often be considered pedantic or obstructive if we were to insist on such clarification. Figures are quoted on TV and in the newspapers for 'unemployement' and 'crime' as if these terms were unambiguous. A clear definition would involve a lot of complex discussion and this

QUANTITATIVE METHODS

would not sell newspapers or keep viewers fingers away from the 'off' button of the set. In fact if you try to explain and harden up the definition of your terms, people start to get suspicious and feel that you are perhaps trying to pull the wool over their eyes. Nobody thanks you these days for showing how complicated things are. People cling to the myth that deep down things are simple.

Let's be realistic and accept that for every average quoted, resonable alternatives exist. Providing that we are comparing like with like, we can avoid major confusion. The problem is that this is often easier said than done. Given a changing workforce and a changing workload it is not easy to know how to compare earnings in one year to those in the next. Ulitmately in wage negotiations, as in politics, the choice of statistics often becomes part of the negotiation itself.

3.8.2 Is there an Alternative to Averages?

Yes there is. Even the averages most suitable for a given purpose cannot do justice to the information contained within the underlying distribution. There are two ways out of this trap. The first is to provide, in association with the chosen average, some summary statistic which measures the spread or scatter round the average used. The second is to provide the user with the distribution itself to back up and provide background in depth for the summary statistics being used. In each case there is a price to be paid: a willingness on the part of all concerned to cope with more sophisticated statistical summaries of aspects of the systems affecting them.

3.9   Measures of Dispersion or Scatter around an Average

As is the case with averages, we must fall back on the old dictum:

> 'Horses for courses'.

The measure appropriate in a given situation depends on the purpose at hand and more particularly it depends on which average is being used.

3.9.1 Minimum and Maximum Values

You might think that quoting a minimum and a maximum value in association with the mean or the median would provide a good summary of a distribution as a whole providing, as it would, an idea of the extent to which the distribution spreads out around the chosen average. Unfortunately such a method yields erratic results. Most distributions have one or two outlying figures at either end which are

SUMMARISING DISTRIBUTIONS

then given excessive prominence if published with the chosen average. Extreme values will then define the dispersion of the distribution which is not a good idea except in certain special circumstances.

3.9.2 The Range
A similar argument can be used against the use of the range which is defined to be:

The Range = (Maximum value − minimum value).

As the minimum and maximum values are often very erratic, so too will be the range. However for small samples, less than 10 say, the range is often used. It has the advantage in many Quality Control applications of being easy to calculate, and as the samples are small you would have to be very unlucky to pick up an extreme value in the small sample. In the rough and tumble of many industrial production systems the calculation of sample ranges on the shop floor gives a quick measure of the spread in the values being measured.

3.9.3 The Semi-interquartile range and the Median
This is an excellent descriptive measure of dispersion. Unfortunately it has got itself stuck with an unpleasant, although accurate, name. Once you get used to the name, you have a measure which people can easily understand. Just as the median divides a distribution into two equal halves.

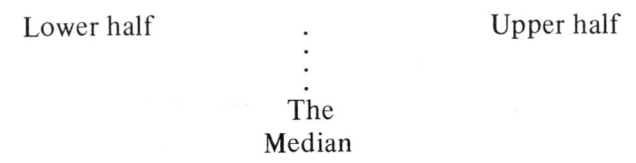

| Lower half | | Upper half |

The Median

so the distribution can be divided into four equal quarters or 'quartiles'.

	First Quartile	Second Quartile	Third Quartile	Fourth Quartile
Variable Value − 20	44	53	59	69

The interquartile range
59 − 44 = 15 yrs.

The interquartile range is the width of that part of the distribution which comprises the central 50%.

The values for the caretaker distribution are shown above. They are easily obtained from the ogive which has been drawn up for the purpose of estimating the median. Just as the median is obtained from

QUANTITATIVE METHODS

the 50% point on the ogive, the other quartiles are obtained by reading off the 25% and 75% points.

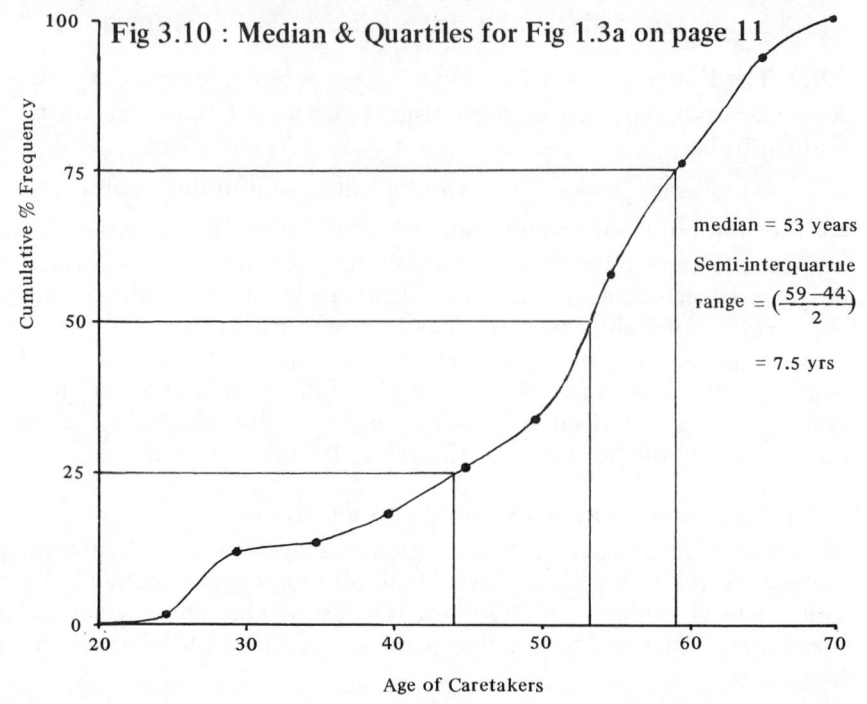

Fig 3.10 : Median & Quartiles for Fig 1.3a on page 11

median = 53 years

Semi-interquartile range $= (\frac{59-44}{2})$

= 7.5 yrs

Age of Caretakers

The value of the interquartile range is 59 −44 = 15 years. In other words the central 50% of caretakers have ages spanning 15 years.

The figure that is usually quoted is half this quantity, the semi-interquartile range.

$$\text{semi-interquartile range} = \frac{\text{interquartile range}}{2}$$

$$= \frac{15}{2} = 7.5 \text{ years.}$$

This measure is the mean width of the second and third quartiles

Width of second quartile = 53 − 44 = 9 years
Width of third quartile = 59 − 53 = 6 years
Mean of second and
third quartiles $= \frac{(9+6)}{2} = 7.5$ yrs.

This is a measure of spread or dispersion around the median which is

SUMMARISING DISTRIBUTIONS

reasonably easy to interpret. The median age is 53 years and the 25% of caretakers above and below the median cover ± 7.5 years on average.

Let us use the semi-interquartile range to obtain a precise comparison of the dispersion around the centres of the distributions of gold coatings shown in Figs 1.1a and c on pages 2 and 4. Note how closely the median coincides with the mean. This is a characteristic of symmetrical and quasi-symmetrical distributions: the mean, mode and median tend to be roughly equal.

Table 3.8 : Dispersion of Thickness of Gold Coatings shown in Figure 1.1a and 1.1c

	Batch size = Large	Batch size = Small
Mean	3.125	3.05
Median	3.12	3.06
Lower Quartile	2.76	2.80
Upper Quartile	3.46	3.28
Interquartile range	3.46–2.76 = 0.70	3.28–2.8 = 0.48 microns
Semi-interquartile range	0.35	0.24 microns

The dispersion of the second distribution as measured by the semi-interquartile range represents a reduction of $\frac{(0.35 - 0.24)}{0.35} \times 100\% = 31\%$. We can interpret this figure as meaning that, on average, the middle 50% of connectors have gold coatings ± 0.35 microns around the median with a large batch size, and ± 0.24 microns with a small batch size.

Exercise

1. Suppose the ogive below is derived from a distribution for the length (in hours) of messenger runs for a firm in the City of London. Read off, from the ogive, the median and the upper and lower quartiles and calculate the semi-interquartile range.

Explain what the figures mean.

QUANTITATIVE METHODS

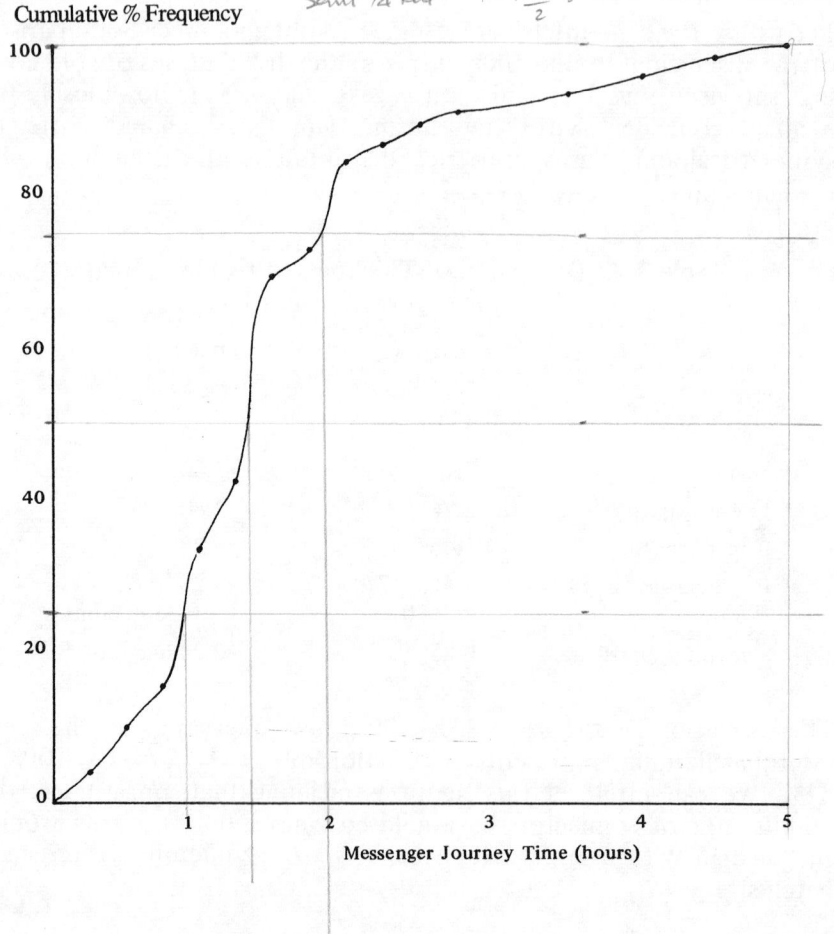

Handwritten annotations:
median = 1.5 Hrs.
Lower ¼ tile = 0-1
Upper " = 2.5
inter ¼ tile = 1-2
Semi ¼ tile = $\frac{2-1}{2}$ = 0.5

Cumulative % Frequency plotted against Messenger Journey Time (hours).

2. Return to Exercise 1 on page 92. Calculate the semi-interquartile range and the upper and lower deciles for the age of new recruits. Express in words what it means.

3. The table below shows the duration of unemployment for men and women of different ages.

SUMMARISING DISTRIBUTIONS

Table 3.9.5 : Unemployment : age and duration : Oct 13, 1983

(Permission No. 6)

	Men		Women	
Duration of Unemployment in weeks	Aged under 18	Aged 35–44	Aged under 18	Aged 35–44
1 or less	5,939	8,362	4,768	3,013
1 – < 2	6,643	9,422	5,429	3,576
2 – < 4	13,437	13,483	10,653	5,308
4 – < 6	43,348	12,013	36,163	5,104
6 – < 8	6,337	9,765	4,548	3,917
8 – < 13	12,138	21,016	8,233	7,995
13 – < 26	21,087	39,329	14,217	15,321
26 – < 39	16,115	30,200	11,391	11,929
39 – < 52	6,839	25,232	5,098	8,354
52 – < 65	8,560	21,166	6,497	5,845
65 – < 78	1,858	17,459	1,268	4,045
78 – <104	371	32,228	229	5,565
104 – <156	4	41,029		5,258
156 – <208		27,942		2,829
208 +		22,546		2,394
Total	142,676	331,192	108,494	90,453

Calculate approximate medians and semi-interquartile ranges for the four categories shown.

To calculate precise values you will need to calculate the percentage frequency distribution. I would round the given figures off to the nearest 1000 first. Then calculate the cumulative percentage frequency distribution and draw up the ogive. From this the median and quartiles can be read off.

1) Why should great care be taken when comparing the figures for the two *age* categories?

ii) What differences between men and women are highlighted by the figures?

3.9.6 Mean deviation around the mean

The mean is the most important average for quantitative work. Clearly there must be some measure of dispersion which is appropriate for use with such an important average.

An obvious way of measuring spread around the mean is to measure the mean deviation of each value from the mean. The mean is a very precise measure of the location of the centre of the distribution and one which uses all the data. It should not be surprising then, that we use a measure of dispersion which is also precise and uses each value of the distribution, including extreme values.

QUANTITATIVE METHODS

Refer back to the data representing the weekly earnings of the members of two workforces (see page 98). The mean earnings for workforce B is £87.8 per week. The lowest earner earns £71 p.w., a a sum £16.8 p.w. below the mean. The highest earner earns a sum of £135 p.w. or a sum £47.2 p.w. above the mean. The total picture of the deviations of individual earnings from the mean are shown in Table 3.9 and can be represented graphically as in Fig. 3.11.

Table 3.9 : Deviations from the Mean

Workforce B earnings £ p.w.	Mean earnings	Deviation from the mean	Absolute deviation from mean
71	87.8	−16.8	16.8
73	87.8	−14.8	14.8
76	87.8	−11.8	11.8
77	87.8	−10.8	10.8
79	87.8	− 8.8	8.8
81	87.8	− 6.8	6.8
83	87.8	− 4.8	4.8
88	87.8	+ 0.2	0.2
115	87.8	+ 27.2	27.2
135	87.8	+ 47.2	47.2
		0.0	149.2

Because the mean is the 'centre of gravity', a balance point for the distribution, the deviations around the mean cancel each other out. We can, however, calculate a pretty obvious measure of scatter around the mean by looking at the absolute deviations, also shown in Fig 3.11. These measure the magnitude of the dispersion around the mean regardless of sign. The mean of these, £14.92 in our example, is called the 'mean absolute deviation'. This measure is easy to understand, expressing as it does how far all the values are on average from the mean. There is only one snag. Despite its simplicity it is not widely used. This has nothing to do with its unfortunate abbreviation, M.A.D., it is simply that statisticians prefer to use an alternative average deviation from the mean, a root mean square deviation from the mean. Fig. 3.12 (on page 112) illustrates the principle of this measure. The squares of the deviations are produced, represented in Fig. 3.12 by the areas of the squares. The mean square deviation is represented by a square whose area is the mean of the areas representing the squared deviations. It is a very important quantity known as *'The Variance'*.

SUMMARISING DISTRIBUTIONS

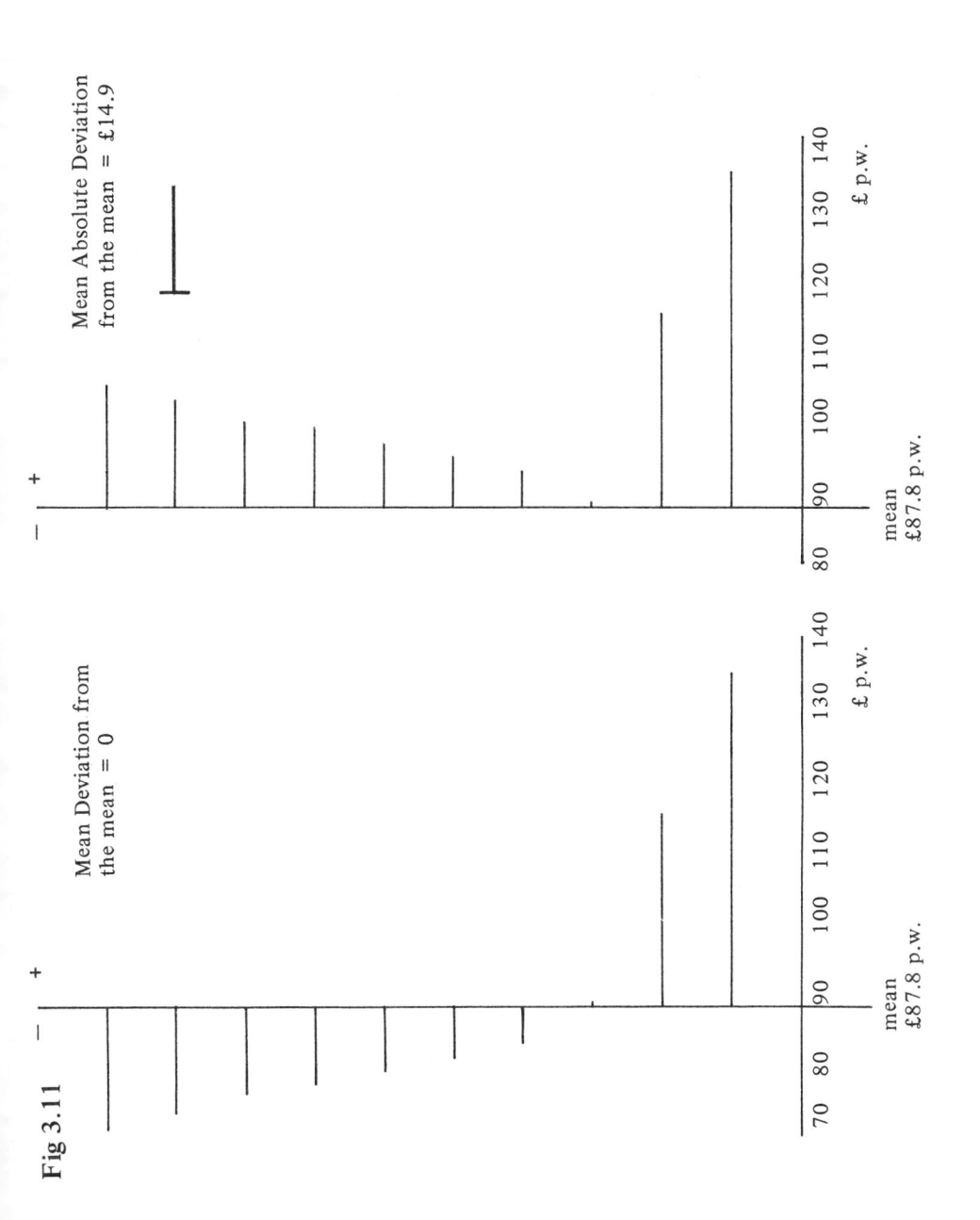

Fig 3.11

Mean Absolute Deviation from the mean = £14.9

Mean Deviation from the mean = 0

QUANTITATIVE METHODS

Fig 3.12 : Standard Deviation and Variance

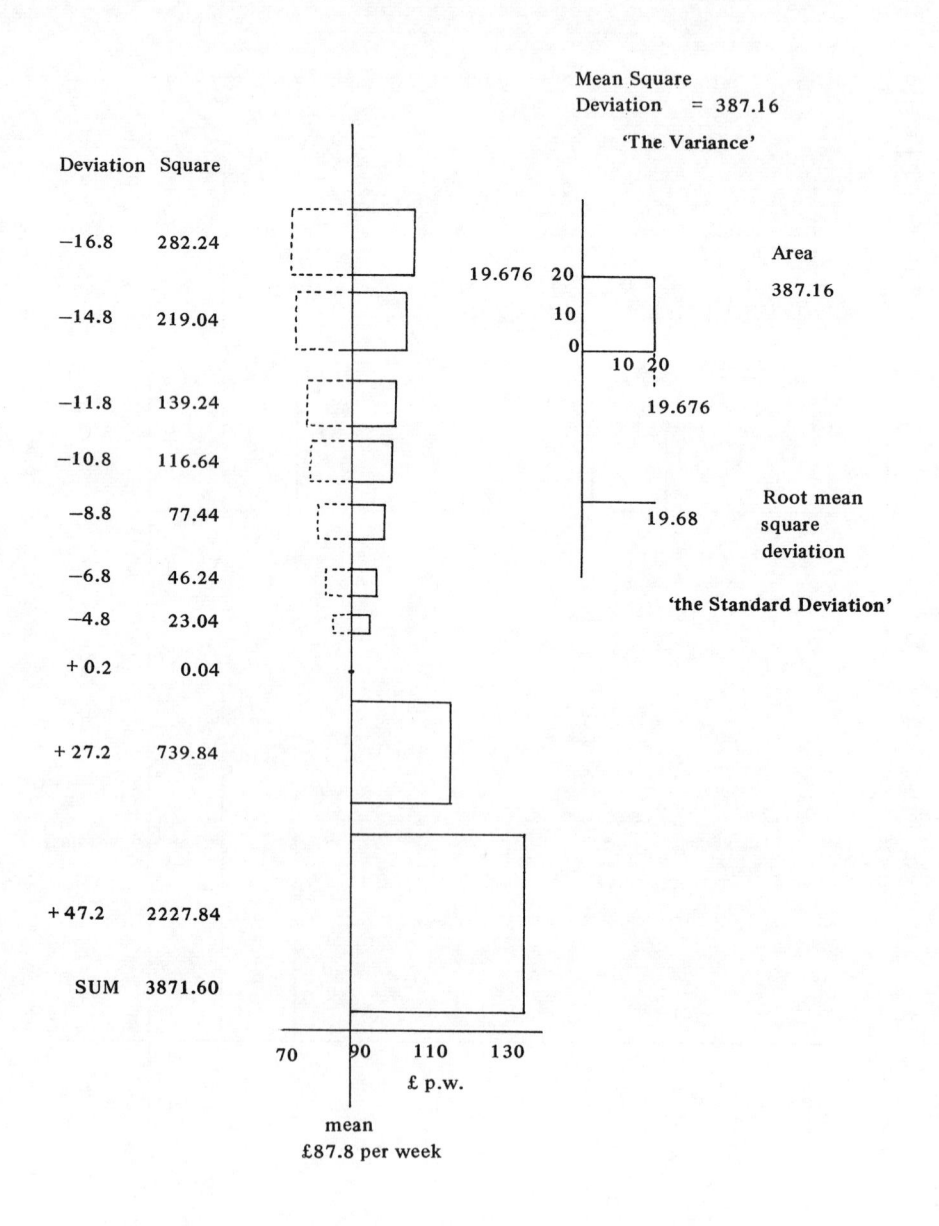

Deviation	Square
−16.8	282.24
−14.8	219.04
−11.8	139.24
−10.8	116.64
−8.8	77.44
−6.8	46.24
−4.8	23.04
+ 0.2	0.04
+ 27.2	739.84
+ 47.2	2227.84
SUM	3871.60

Mean Square Deviation = 387.16

'The Variance'

Area 387.16

19.676

Root mean square deviation
19.68

'the Standard Deviation'

70   90   110   130
£ p.w.

mean
£87.8 per week

112

SUMMARISING DISTRIBUTIONS

The side of that square, £19.68 represents the 'root mean square deviation from the mean'. It is known as the *'Standard Deviation'*.

Why on earth, you might well ask, should statisticians use such a weird and complicated measure of dispersion when they already have a perfectly good measure in the mean absolute deviation? The answer is simple. It is just more useful, and most statistical theory has been built up around it. Actually the root mean square is a respectable average which is widely used in science. For example electrical engineers use it to average alternating current flow which varies from positive to negative and which in one sense has an average value of zero. It suits them because the heating effect of an electrical current is proportional to the square of that current. Just as the mean has an exact physical analogy in the centre of gravity of a body with the same shape, so it turns out that the standard deviation has an exact analogy in the radius of gyration of a body around a line drawn vertically through the centre of gravity. In fact you could calculate the mean and standard deviation of a distribution by evaluating the centre of gravity and the radius of gyration of a body cut out in the shape of the distribution. I must confess I've never tried it myself!

If you are an engineer you will have appreciated this digression. If you are not, you will at least realise that, strange though it may seem, there is some logic behind the use of a root mean square measure of dispersion. In any case you don't have much choice. The science of statistics is largely built up on this measure of dispersion and it will be referred to from time to time in this book.

3.9.8 Important though it is in quantitative statistics, the standard deviation has certain disadvantages. It is not easy to explain to non-specialists precisely what it represents. Furthermore it is not pleasant to calculate and has the disadvantage for descriptive purposes of being unduly influenced by extreme values. The semi-interquartile range therefore has distinct advantages over the standard deviation for descriptive purposes.

The standard deviation is a measure which you will often find quoted as a descriptive measure of dispersion despite its unsuitability for that purpose in many cases. When on the receiving end it is best to think of it as a sort of inflated mean deviation from the mean. For certain special distributions, such as the normal distribution, it has a very precise interpretation as we will see when looking at samples in Chapter 9.

QUANTITATIVE METHODS

3.10 Using the distribution itself for descriptive purposes

Quoting an appropriate average together with a measure of dispersion gives a better summary of a distribution than an average on its own. However one vital element is still missing: the shape of the distribution. Fig 3.13 shows three distributions which have exactly the same mean and standard deviation.

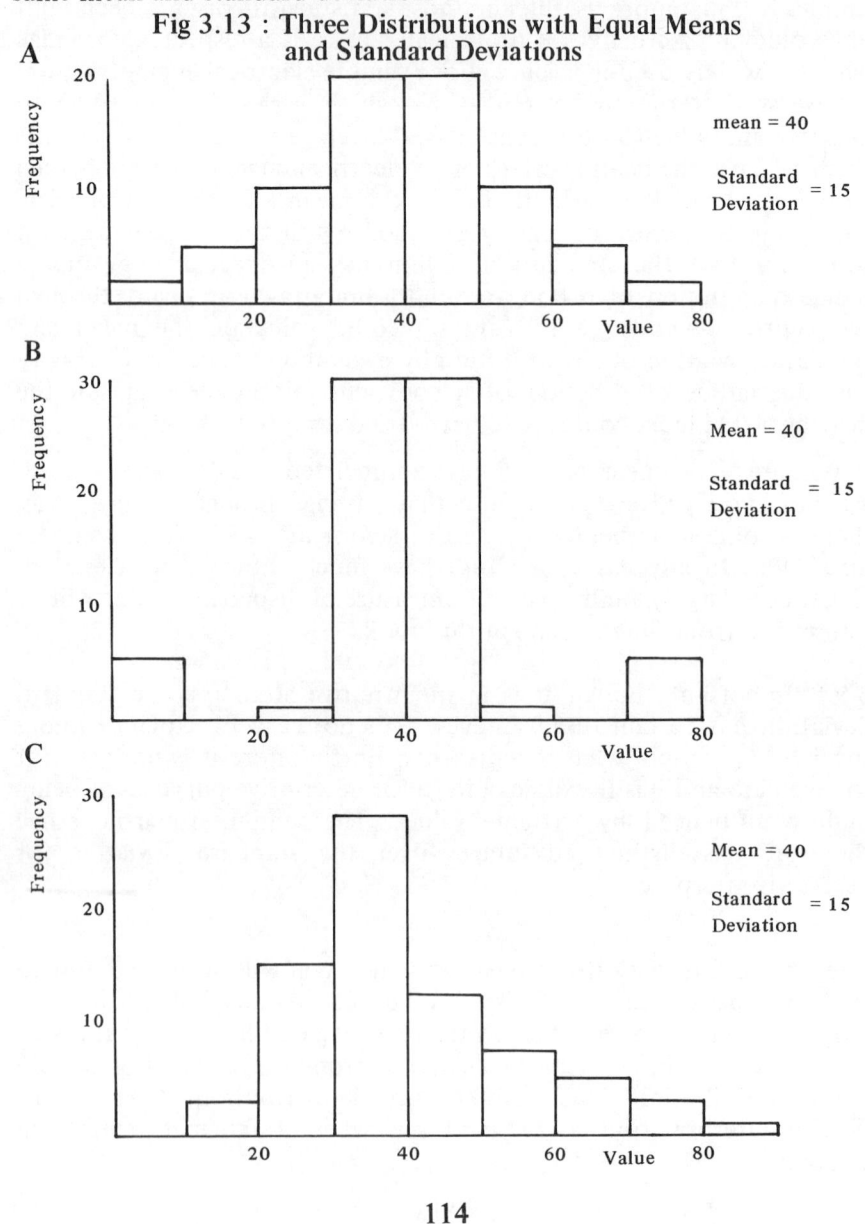

Fig 3.13 : Three Distributions with Equal Means and Standard Deviations

A

mean = 40

Standard Deviation = 15

B

Mean = 40

Standard Deviation = 15

C

Mean = 40

Standard Deviation = 15

SUMMARISING DISTRIBUTIONS

Although the distributions have been contrived to make the point, they remind us that the mean together with the standard deviation cannot be expected to represent the totality of a distribution.

Given this inadequacy, and especially when irregular distributions are likely to occur, why not present the distributions themselves? The argument is usually that they would take up too much room or be difficult to understand. To show that this disadvantage is not as great as all that, Fig 3.14 (Page 116) shows the three distributions of Fig 3.13 in miniaturised form. They provide instant information to supplement the summary statistics provided. I say 'instant' because the eye can pick up shapes very quickly.

As another example, consider Figs. 1.3a and 1.3b on page 11, showing the ages of caretakers and assistant caretakers. Now suppose that you are told that the mean age of caretakers is 50 years with standard deviation of 12 years, whereas for assistant caretakers it is 61 years with a standard deviation of 5 years. Given these combined figures you might imagine that the distribution for assistant caretakers is higher and, because of its lower standard deviation, more compact than that for the caretakers. Of course you would be quite correct, but the figures do not tell you about the interesting difference in the *shapes* of the two distributions. In particular the summary statistics conceal the existence of a secondary peak in the caretaker distribution. Using the median and semi-interquartile ranges is no more helpful in this respect:

	Median	Semi-interquartile range	
Caretakers	53	7.5	
Assistant Caretakers	61.5	2.1	Years

These figures present effectively the same picture as that suggested by the mean and standard deviation.

By providing the distributions themselves in miniature form, the user can get an immediate idea of the comparative shapes of the distributions even if the presentation is too miniaturised for detailed information to be read off.

QUANTITATIVE METHODS

Fig 3.14 : Miniaturised Frequency Distributions

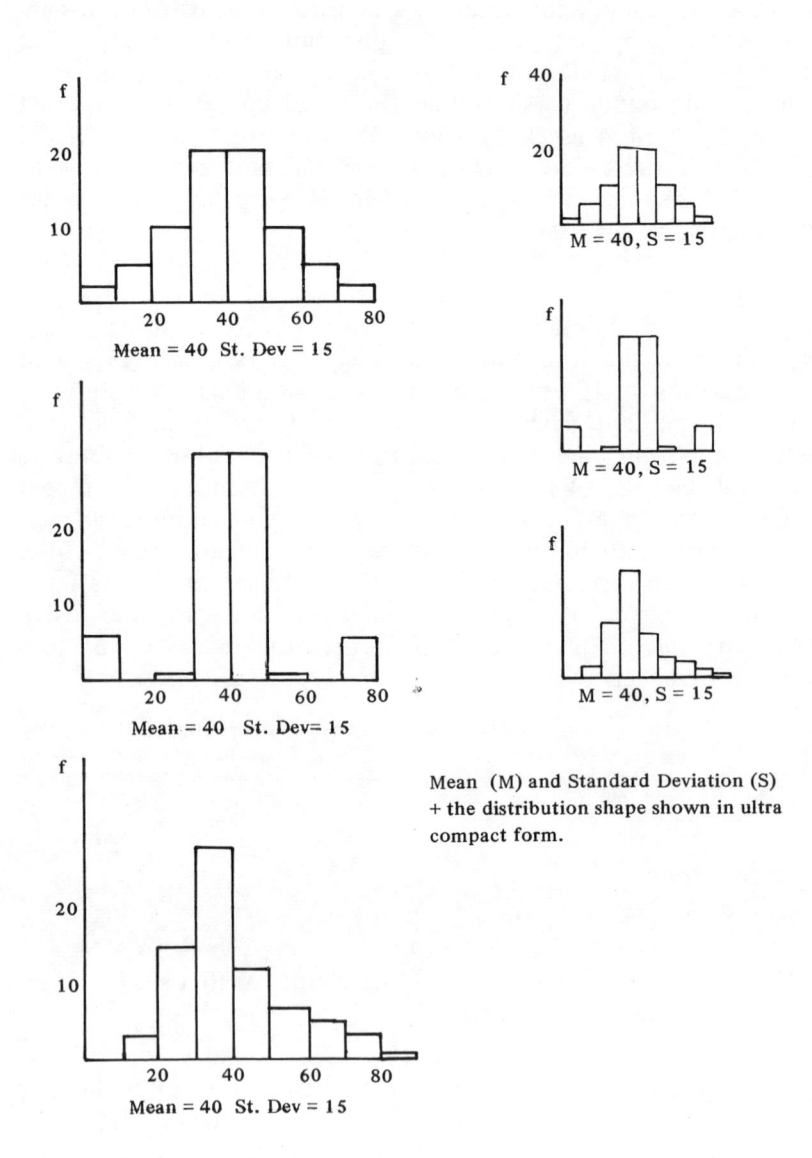

Mean (M) and Standard Deviation (S) + the distribution shape shown in ultra compact form.

116

SUMMARISING DISTRIBUTIONS

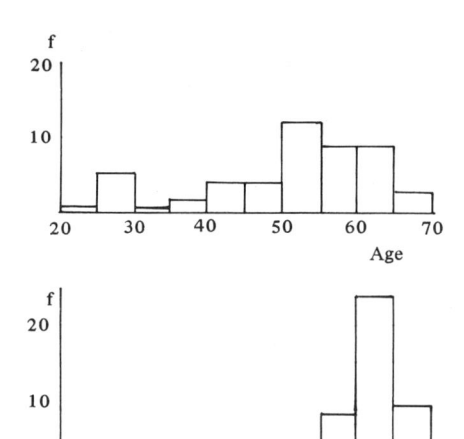

Fig 3.15 : The Caretakers' Distributions in Miniature

I've deliberately made these small (Fig 3.15) to demonstrate how little space a histogram can occupy and still convey a lot of information that summary statistics can never do. This approach also has the advantage of encouraging people to think more in terms of distributions, the heart of statistics, and less in terms of averages.

CHAPTER 4 : THE LANGUAGE OF UNCERTAINTY

Sections 4.1 to 4.4 deal with the way probabilities are used to describe the uncertainty in business situations. Section 4.5 uses simulation to discuss the concept of random and non-random sequences. Section 4.6 to 4.8 shows how the probability of complex events can be handled and the chapter ends in Section 4.9 with the valuation of risky ventures involving potential losses and gains.

4.1 Talking about probability

Managers operate in an unpredicatable world. Their forecasts let them down, their costs fluctuate and without warning, competitors, governments, and authorities take decisions which can have a marked influence on their organisation. However they are still expected to plan and control the area for which they are responsible.

Managers have to use language to express their views and expectations in an uncertain world. One of the problems of language lies in its ambiguities. Ambiguity may be the essence of poetry, but to the businessman it is a source of confusion. To make this point clearer you are invited to take part in an experiment to test the degree of precision in the language that businessmen use. Moore and Thomas (1975) quote 10 expressions culled from an article discussing some forecasts that had been made in the consumer durables field. Here they are:

> probable
> quite certain
> unlikely
> hoped
> possible
> not unreasonable that
> expected
> doubtful
> not certain
> likely

Before looking at Moore and Thomas' results, you, and any of your colleagues that you can rope in for the occasion, are invited to rank these ten words or phrases in decreasing order of certainty. Assign the rank 1 to the word or phrase which most closely suggests certainty and continue until the rank 10 has been assigned to that which seems least so. Where you can't choose between two words or phrases, then

THE LANGUAGE OF UNCERTAINTY

they should share the ranks; thus if two words come equally at the top of your list, they should share the first and second ranks and score 1.5 each. Make the ranks sum to 55 and remember that the ranks 1 – 10 are to be assigned starting with the most certain and running down to the least certain.

If you can get enough of your colleagues to join you in the experiment, record your combined results on a grid. Do it now without turning the page. Table 4.1 shows a summary of Moore and Thomas' results. They were derived from 250 executives on management programmes at the London Business School.

You can now compare your rankings with their averages. What is most striking about the results is the range of the ranks assigned to each word or phrase. For example 'quite certain' always fell within the top three ranks, but 'expected' was ranked anywhere from 1 to 6 and and 'probable' anywhere from 2 to 9. This suggests that managers do not agree about the relative ranking of terms commonly used to describe uncertainty in management reports. Thus in order to avoid ambiguity, there is a need for some commonly agreed scale for describing uncertainty if managers are to be able to communicate effectively with one another.

4.2. The Scale of Probabilities

4.2.1: The probability scale runs between two extremes, that of impossibility on the one hand and absolute certainty on the other and which are given the values 0 and 1 respectively.

```
|..............................................|
0                                                1
Impossible                                  Certain
```

Sometimes this scale is replaced by a percentage scale

```
|..............................................|
0%                                            100%
```

As nothing can be more certain than certain or more doubtful than an impossibility, negative probabilities or probabilities greater than one cannot, by definition, exist. The probability of any event occurring must therefore lie somewhere between these two extremes. Let us fill in some values on the scale making use of the device of drawing from a shuffled pack of 52 playing cards (jokers excluded). Irritating though it may seem to some people, the simple pack of cards has the

QUANTITATIVE METHODS

Table 4.1 : Ranking of Uncertainty Expressions

Expressions	Mean Rank	Range of Ranks
Quite certain	1.10	1 − 3
Expected	2.95	1 − 6
Likely	3.85	2 − 7
Probable	4.25	2 − 9
Not unreasonable that	4.65	3 − 7
Possible	6.10	3 − 9
Hoped	7.15	3 − 10
Not certain	7.80	3 − 10
Doubtful	8.6	7 − 10
Unlikely	8.75	3 − 10

advantage of having a structure which is almost universally familiar:

```
13  spades coloured  black
13  clubs      "        "
13  hearts     "       red
13  diamond    "        "
```

The pack can be well mixed by the process of shuffling and therefore although there is uncertainty about which card is going to be drawn next, the chance of drawing specified cards can be precisely calculated. It is useful to use gambling devices such as the drawing of cards from a shuffled pack or the thowing of dice, in order to discuss simple probability ideas before getting tangled up with any practical problems. Here are the promised probabilities:

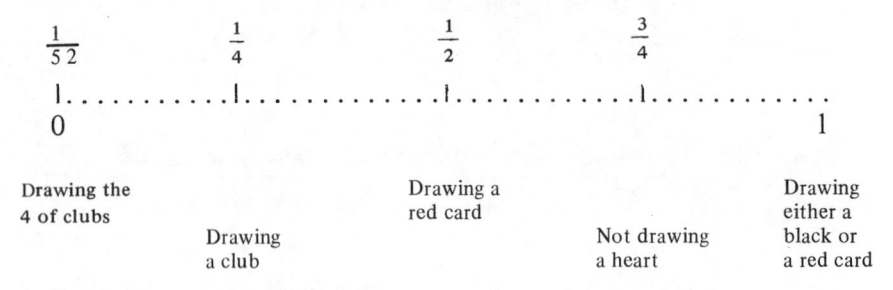

$$\frac{1}{52} \qquad \frac{1}{4} \qquad \frac{1}{2} \qquad \frac{3}{4}$$

|..............|..............|..............|..............|.........
0   1

Drawing the 4 of clubs

Drawing a club

Drawing a red card

Not drawing a heart

Drawing either a black or a red card

All the probabilities and odds quoted are derived from the known structure of a pack of cards. Lets see where the figures came from and what they mean. The probability of an event occurring can be interpreted as indicating the proportion of occasions, in the long run, that the event will occur on repeated fair trials. Given the structure of a pack of cards it follows that.

THE LANGUAGE OF UNCERTAINTY

Probability of drawing a red card = $\dfrac{\text{Number of red cards}}{\text{number of cards overall}}$

$$= \dfrac{26}{52} = \dfrac{1}{2}$$

After each card is drawn, it is replaced and the pack shuffled before the next card is drawn. Logic, not experimentation, tells us that in the long run, on repeated trials, the proportion of outcomes showing a red card will tend to be ½. To have any other long-term ratio, $\dfrac{20}{52}$ for instance, we would have to imagine a bias towards black cards. But as the cards of both colours are present in equal numbers and the drawing of the cards is fair, this cannot be the case.

An alternative way of looking at the long run is to imagine a large number of people each of whom draws a card just once from a pack of cards. The term

'in the long run the proportion drawing a red card = ½'

means that over the large number of people making just one draw, the proportion of people getting a red card will tend to be ½. One more example follows:

Probability of *not* drawing a heart = $\dfrac{\text{number of cards which are not hearts}}{\text{number of cards in pack overall}}$

$$= \dfrac{13 + 13 + 13}{52}$$

$$= \dfrac{39}{52} = \dfrac{3}{4}$$

Exercise

1. From a well shuffled pack of cards what is the probability of drawing:

   a) a diamond
   b) a card below 4 (aces counting high, i.e. not as 1)
   c) a card showing an even number

2. A roulette wheel is inscribed with 36 numbers together with the number 0 on which the house wins. Half the numbers are coloured black and the other half are red (0 is not coloured). What is the probability of the following coming up:

QUANTITATIVE METHODS

a) a red number *(rouge)*.
b) an uneven number *(impair)*
c) an uneven red number
d) any individual specified number.

4.2.2 The 'odds' scale

For people who enjoy gambling, it may be useful to show how the probability scale compares with a scale of odds.

Table 4.2 : Odds and Probabilities

Odds quoted	Equivalent probabilities
6 to 1 against	1/7
3 to 1 against	1/4
evens	1/2
3 to 1 on	3/4
6 to 1 on	6/7

In terms of odds, the probability of *not* getting a heart, 3/4, is '3 to 1 on'. A clumsy but familiar term it means, for the benefit of the non-gambling reader, that you lay on £3 to win £1 together with the return of your stake in the event of the card drawn not being a heart. On average, over 4 bets, the gambler will win 3x£1 in 3 bets but lose his stake on one other bet leaving him on balance neither winning or losing. The problem with the odds scale is that in order to obtain the necessary definition, clumsy odds must be quoted. For instance, it is not immediately obvious that '6 to 4 on' is the equivalent of 0.6 or that '11 to 9 on' is the equivalent of 0.55. The probability scale has the advantage that it provides a continuous scale of probabilities.

4.3 Probabilities Based on Past Experience
The Relative Frequency approach

4.3.1 The statement that the probability of drawing a red card from a pack is 1/2 is derived from logical deduction based on the known make-up of a pack of cards. In business situations, probabilities are often calculated on the basis of past long-term performance on the basis that such arisings are a guide to what is likely to happen in the future. A classic example of this approach is found in the way that Insurance companies calculate the probability of their clients dying and making claims on the company. Table 4.3 shows the probability that a person in the specified age group will die within a year. The probabilities are, thankfully, very small and a convenient way of expressing such low risks is to multiply them by an arbitary value, in this case 1,000.

THE LANGUAGE OF UNCERTAINTY

Table 4.3 : Death rates for Men and Women
1980 (HMSO, 1983)

Age Groups	Men Probability of dying in 1 year	Men Death rate per 1000 per year	Women Death Rate per 1000 per year
0 – 4	0.0034	3.4	2.7
5 – 9	0.0003	0.3	0.2
10 – 14	0.0003	0.3	0.2
15 – 19	0.0009	0.9	0.3
20 – 24	0.0009	0.9	0.4
25 – 34	0.0009	0.9	0.6
35 – 44	0.0020	2.0	1.4
45 – 54	0.0066	6.6	4.0
55 – 64	0.0187	18.7	10.0
65 – 74	0.0476	47.6	25.1
75 – 84	0.1103	110.3	68.1
85 +	0.2344	234.4	189.1

(Permission No. 6)

These probabilities are based on a study of death rates in the past. As time passes, of course, these death rates may well change and have to be updated. Remember that the statement:-

'Probability of drawing a red card = 1/2'

was interpreted as meaning that 'in the long run' on repeated draws from a shuffled pack, the proportion of red cards arising would tend towards a value of 1/2. In the case of mortality risk figures, if we assume that these rates will apply in the future as they have done in the past, then they represent the proportion of a large number of people in the given age groups who will die within one year. The 'long run' in this context can be read as 'over a large number of cases'.

Exercise

In each of the following exercises estimate the probability required on the basis of the past observations given. Then consider the extent to which the past is a reliable guide to the future giving your reasons.

1. In 968 throws of a dice, '3' came up 158 times. What is the probability of a '3' coming up on the next throw.

2. A life insurance salesman made 163 telephone calls during the previous week out of which 27 showed some interest. What is the probability that on his next call, some interest will be shown.

3. A work study engineer personally monitored 323 stores-counter

QUANTITATIVE METHODS

transactions and found that in 25 cases, the time exceeded 5 minutes. What is the probability that a fitter going to the stores will experience a service time which exceeds 5 minutes?

4. In 3742 flights, an automatic pilot system has never failed. What is the probability of the system failing in a given flight?

5. In 632 journeys by road carrying chemicals at all times of the year, a transport company has had 3 accidents. In no case was any loss of chemicals recorded. What is the probability of there being an accident on a journey? Might the time of the year make any difference to the calculation? How should statistics be recorded in this instance in order to enable reasonable probability estimates to be made in the future?

4.3.2 Risk Analysis

Another application of probabilities which are derived from past experience is to be found in *Risk Analysis*. With the development of large scale construction work in the North Sea and the creation of complex and potentially dangerous petrochemical complexes on land, there is a need to calculate the risks of accidents occurring and of death and injury being inflicted on society.

Before looking at a real-life example, consider a simplified example. Suppose a small ferry has been making an estuary crossing daily for 10 years. During those 10 years, it has been involved in 20 minor incidents with other vessels and 3 'serious' incidents. We might estimate the minor incident rate as follows:

Over 10 years there have been
365×10 2-way crossings

The minor incident rate is then

$$\frac{20}{365 \times 10} = 0.0054794 \text{ per 2-way crossing}$$

or to use the jargon of the trade and rounding off the figures

5.5×10^{-3} per 2-way crossing

or

5.5×10^{-3} 2-way crossing^{-1}

(Remember $5^{-1} = \frac{1}{5}$, $10^{-1} = \frac{1}{10}$ etc.)

You may not like this way of expressing probabilities but it is widely

THE LANGUAGE OF UNCERTAINTY

used in the trade to express awkward small probabilities and so it is worth becoming familiar with such terminology.

As to whether that rate, based on past occurrences, can be used as the probability of a future occurrence depends on whether the future is likely to be a reflection of the past. In this sort of work it is common for the historic rate to be adjusted to take account of new factors. This of course inevitably brings a subjective element into the calculations which is unavoidable. If new speed limits on the river had recently been brought in, this would almost certainly reduce the risk of collision. It would then seem reasonable to reduce the estimated risk calculated on the basis of historical arisings providing that the assumptions underlying the subjective adjustment are made clear.

Exercise

1. Express in decimal form
    a) 10^{-4}
    b) 1.7×10^{-3}
    c) 3.4×10^{-6}

2. Express in terms of powers of 10 (as in question 1)
    a) 0.0037
    b) 0.000073
    c) 0.000001

3. A lorry carrying a dangerous chemical makes about two trips a week from London to Birmingham. It unloads and then returns empty to London. Over the past three years the following data has been collected.

Year	Number of lorries operating	Number of Accidents when loaded Winter	Summer
1	2	2	1
2	2	1	0
3	3	3	1

Estimate the probability of a loaded lorry having an accident on a trip, for both winter and for summer. Are there likely to be better ways in practice of estimating the risk of an accident?

4.3.3 We can see this sort of procedure being adopted in an example taken from a Government report on the potential hazards of oper-

QUANTITATIVE METHODS

ations in the Canvey Island/Thurrock area (HMSO 1981). This is a highly technical and specialised field of study but the example will illustrate some of the practical problems of estimating risk probabilities in the real world. As part of this study the Health and Safety Executive carried out a review of accident data on the transport of Liquid Petroleum Gas (LPG). The delivery of this product to jetties on Canvey Island constitutes only one potential hazard amongst many in that industrial complex. A typical calculation involves the following steps:

1. LPG Carriers (>5000 cubic ft) delivered about 19000 cargoes over the period 1964–1974.

2. There were 37 'serious incidents' although none of these involved any loss of the cargo.

3. A delivery from a Port A to a single Port B involves 2 loaded movements, that is the ship is under way loaded with cargo.
    i) Leaving A
    ii) Arriving at B
At all other times the ship is empty.

4. A delivery from A to two ports B & C involves 4 loaded movements:
    i) Leaving A
    ii) Arriving at B
    iii) Leaving B
    iv) Arriving at C

5. Assume 2.5 loaded movements per cargo. (This was estimated by looking at past shipping patterns and depends on the number of ports being called on.)

6. From steps 1 and 5 we can calculate that during 1964–79 there were
$$19{,}000 \times 2.5 \text{ loaded movements}$$

7. Combining 2 and 6, the 'serious incident' rate is therefore
$$\frac{37}{(19000 \times 2.5)} = 0.0007789$$
$$= 7.8 \times 10^{-4} \quad \text{per loaded movement}$$

8. Allow for a slight degree of conservatism and rounding up we obtain.

$$10 \times 10^{-4} \quad \text{or} \quad 1 \times 10^{-3} \text{ per loaded movement.}$$

THE LANGUAGE OF UNCERTAINTY

9. None of the 'serious incidents' resulted in cargo loss. The probability of cargo loss must be less than the probability of a 'serious incident' by a factor of at least 25. This is because in more than 25 serious incidents there had been no cargo loss. Therefore the estimated probability of cargo loss must be less than

$$= \frac{1}{25} \times 10^{-3} = 0.04 \times 10^{-3}$$

$$= 4 \times 10^{-5} \quad \text{per loaded movement.}$$

10. It has been shown that 60% of shipping accidents involving tankers occur in restricted areas or in ports where damage to people and property can occur. Therefore the probability of cargo loss in the river or at a jetty

$$= 0.6 \times 4 \times 10^{-5} = 2.4 \times 10^{-5} \quad \text{per loaded movement}$$

It is easy to pick holes in this sort of estimate and in particular to question the repeated assumption that the past is a guide to the future. But before you criticise the approach it is as well to remember that something should be put in its place. Whilst recognising that some of the assumptions could have been replaced by equally valid ones which would have led to a different final result, at least a figure has been obtained by a process which can be audited. The Published risk may be less or more than that perceived by interested groups such as a pressure group in the vicinity of a port. But at least the calculation which produced the figure and the validity of the data on which it is based can be discussed rationally. This avoids the danger of a war of words opening up over what might otherwise be a purely subjective assessment.

How can this probability be interpreted? It suggests that if the past is reflected in the future, then in the long term a proportion 2.4×10^{-5} of loaded movements will result in cargo loss in or near a jetty. By inverting the rate, we can thereby convert it to an average number of loaded movements before a serious incident leads to cargo loss in or near a jetty.

$$\text{Average no of movements to cargo loss} = \frac{1}{(2.4 \times 10^{-5})}$$

$$= 41667 \text{ loaded movements}$$

Given 1000 loaded movements, say, per year through a specified port, the above can be converted to

QUANTITATIVE METHODS

$$\frac{41667}{1000} = 42 \text{ years to cargo loss in or near a jetty } on\ average$$

4.4 SUBJECTIVE PROBABILITIES: those based on intuition

4.4.1 We have just seen how probabilities can be estimated by an objective, auditable process. In some situations, there is no relevant past experience on which to base a calculation. In that case, probabilities can only be derived by basing them on the intuitive feel of an 'expert' or 'experts'. An example will illustrate the process.

A salesman approaching a prospect for the second time has an intuitive feel for the chance of his clinching a deal. Of course this is, to some extent, a reflection of his past experience but the market is forever changing, and therefore a computation based on the recorded proportion of past second calls being clinched would be useless. Yet as he parks his car in the prospect's car park and sets off for his second meeting the salesman will surely have some gut feel for the likelihood of his clinching a deal. If we could convert that gut feel into a value on the probability scale, it would be termed a subjective probability. The process by which such probabilities are arrived at cannot be clearly defined. That being the case, can such a probability have any meaning?

Suppose the salesman puts the probability of clinching a deal at 0.7. The odds equivalent of that is '7 to 3 on'. We can interpret that probability as implying that the salesman should be equally prepared to give or be given a bet at those odds. If he takes the odds, he would put down a £7 stake and collect £3 in the event of the sale being clinched together with the return of his stake. If, on the other hand, he gives the odds, he would be ready to pay the gambler £3 plus the return of his stake if the deal is clinched. The idea of creating a hypothetical gambling situation may seem a bit bizarre, but the technique is used in business to help test the validity of business executive's subjective probabilities generated for use in investment risk analysis procedures. In real life the process might go something like this.

Analyst: The decision we take at next week's board meeting seems to depend critically on whether International Computers (IC) bring out their new model before the end of the year. What probability would you put on the likelihood of that happening?

Executive: I don't think it's all that likely – let's say 0.1 then.

Analyst: Let me follow that up a little. Suppose you were a betting

THE LANGUAGE OF UNCERTAINTY

man, which of the following would you prefer to choose? You must choose one or the other.

A	B
Put down a stake of £1 and receive £9 + stake if I C bring out their new model.	Accept a stake of £1 and pay £9 + stake if I C bring out their new model.

Executive: Like a shot! Option A. Given my feelings about the chances involved, A is much more attractive than B.

Analyst: I see. Well let me change the odds a little and then see how you feel about it. Which of the following would you choose?

A	B
Put down £3 and receive £9 if I C bring out their model	Accept a stake of £3 and pay out £9 if I C bring out their model.

Executive: A seems a poor deal. To risk £3 for £9 when I feel that the chance of winning is poor doesn't attract me. I'll plump for B but not with enthusiasm.

This process continues until the executive is indifferent as to which bet to choose. This point could come perhaps at odds of 2 to 9 against. This would then imply that

probability that IC will bring out their model $= \frac{2}{11} = 0.18$

Given the approximate nature of the method this had better be rounded off to 0.2.

The process has led to an uplift of the original probability. The method is not without its difficulties. If the sums are too small, the executive won't be able to take the bets seriously and if they are too large, his reasoning may be influenced by the fear of loss or the desire for gain. An alternative way of getting people to think of probabilities is by employing the idea of a modified roulette wheel. To get someone to see what a probability of 0.1 'feels' like, you can ask them to imagine a roulette wheel which has only 10 numbers on it. The number **1** being marked in red and the others marked in black (I have indicated red in bold type).

QUANTITATIVE METHODS

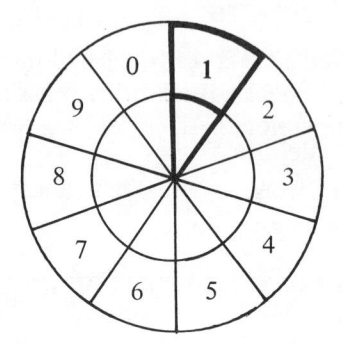

To face the prospect of an event which has a probability of 0.1 of occurring involves the same degree of uncertainty as facing the prospect of the wheel turning up the number 1. To portray a probability of 0.7 we need to imagine the digits 1 to 7 being coloured red to indicate that if any of them turn up this is equivalent to the occurrence of the event in question. You may well feel that these procedures amount to nothing more than a guessing game and the results are hardly verifiable. However I don't think that it is reasonable to attack the approach unless you have a more objective method to put in its place. To replace estimation of subjective probabilities with verbal expressions of likelihood is a process just as subjective as that described above and one which involves all the ambiguities demonstrated in the exercise laid out in the beginning of the chapter.

By training staff to be more precise about the degree of uncertainty that they face in their environment encourages a more disciplined approach to planning and forecasting. Training is essential to obtain useful results and the process of subjective estimation of probabilities by staff has to be built up over time and the results carefully monitored. In order to improve the estimating skill of staff, feedback on the accuracy of their previous forecasts should be provided. Of course poor estimation may not necessarily be an indication of a lack of skill on the part of the employee, it may be that the estimator has been operating with inadequate information about the problem at hand. Moore (1983) discusses in some detail the problem of subjective probability assessment. This readable book provides a comprehensive survey of the topic of risk with a minimum of technical complication.

THE LANGUAGE OF UNCERTAINTY

4.5 Random and Non-random Sequences
4.5.1 Simulation and Random Numbers

One of the prime functions of Management is exercising control over processes. This often involves making sense of sequences of events which are shrouded in uncertainty. For example the stock controller has to make sense of a sequence of demands for items of stock which rise and fall in an irregular way and decide whether there is evidence for a shift in the demand pattern which requires action on her part.

The administrator of a coronary care unit has to plan her facilities to meet a demand for the service which fluctuates from day to day. Naturally she has no control over the number of cases which arise each day and yet she still has to run the unit. A car manufacturer might accept that he must adjust overall 25% of the cars coming off the end of the production line. Of course this does not mean that every fourth car requires adjustment. Within the overall average level of 25% requiring adjustment a random pattern may arise. Management will, however, want to react sharply to any increase in this overall level. Their problem is how to distinguish a general rise in the percentage requiring adjustment from random fluctuations around an average level. In order to make sense of the sequences described above, the manager needs to get an intuitive feel for the look of random and non-random patterns. In particular he needs to be aware of the way in which totally random sequences can show superficially interesting features which are merely the products of chance. The stock controller faced with a series of freak high demands might react by raising stock levels unnecessarily in order to meet what seemed to her to be a new, higher level of demand.

Simulation provides a way of 'seeing' how random and non-random sequences behave and thereby gives managers the opportunity to get a feel for the sorts of patterns that can be expected. Consider, for example, the car manufacturer who expects overall 25% of the finished cars to require some sort of adjustment. What would we observe if we looked at a sequence of cars coming along the production line? To come to grips with the concept of randomness, it is necessary first to explain the nature of random numbers.

4.5.2 Sampling using Random Numbers

Imagine that you have a box containing 100 identical counters inscribed 01, 02, 03 . . . . up to 99, 00. Now suppose that you

QUANTITATIVE METHODS

were to draw a counter from the box after shaking it well and to write down the result. You then return the counter, shake it well and repeat the process. The result might be a sequence of numbers such as

36 93 41 73 29 36 44 . . . .

Such a sequence of numbers are known as random numbers. They are random in that each number as it comes out is equally likely to be any of the 100 numbers inscribed on the counters. The fact that 36 appears twice in this instance has no special significance. After the first '36' was drawn, the counter was returned and the box shaken, so its re-emergence was due to chance alone, 36 was no more or less likely to occur on that particular draw than on any other draw. In fact it can be shown that there is a one in five chance that in seven such two-digit random numbers at least one will be repeated. To the casual observer, the reappearance of the second '36' in the above sequence looks 'un-random'. Simulation will help you to appreciate the extent to which apparent order can arise in what are in fact purely random sequences. Random though these numbers are, they do possess certain predictable properties. For instance, in the very long run, we would expect each specified number to constitute 1% of the total numbers drawn.

Practically minded managers quite reasonably get a bit irritated at the thought of shaking boxes and drawing out counters and so on. Fortunately the above procedure can be replaced by reference to tables of random numbers. The numbers in Table 4.4 and in Appendix 7 , can be thought of as if they had been produced by the counter-drawing process described above, although in practice more sophisticated computer methods are used to generate them.

Table 4.4

A Sample of Random Digits

85	31	54	29	11
99	75	60	76	52
91	06	28	38	37
17	83	14	83	87
21	54	42	43	53

By allocating the random numbers in the right proportions, we can simulate the production process operating with an overall adjustment rate of 25%. To do this we allocate 25% of the random numbers to represent the arrival of a car requiring adjustment and the remaining 75% to represent those which pass the final inspection stage without adjustment.

THE LANGUAGE OF UNCERTAINTY

Random Number Allocation	Observed Effect
01 – 25	Car requires adjustment at end of line.
26 – 99, 00	Car OK at end of process

Now a sequence of random numbers can be used to simulate the arrival of a sequence of cars together with an indication of whether they require adjustment or not.

Random Number	Status of car leaving end of line
85	OK
99	OK
91	OK
17	ADJUST
21	ADJUST
31	OK
75	OK
06	ADJUST
83	OK
54	OK
.	.
.	.
etc.	etc

The results of a simulation of a sequence of 100 cars is shown in Table 4.5.

Table 4.5 : A Random Sequence

Car No.	Status	Car No.	Status	Car No.	Status	Car No.	Status	Car No.	Status
.	.	.	.	.	A	.	.	.	.
.	.	.	.	.	.	.	A	.	.
.	.	.	.	.	.	.	.	.	A
.	A	.	A	.	.	.	.	.	.
5	A	25	.	45	A	65	.	85	.
.	A	.	.	.	A	.	.	.	A
.	A	.	.	.	.	.	.	.	.
.	A	.	.	.	A	.	.	.	.
.	.	.	.	.	.	.	.	.	A
10	.	30	.	50	.	70	.	90	.
.	.	.	A	.	.	.	.	.	.
.	.	.	A	.	.	.	A	.	.
.	A	.	.	.	.	.	.	.	.
.	.	.	.	.	.	.	.	.	.
15	A	35	.	55	.	75	.	95	A
.	.	.	A	.	.	.	A	.	.
.	A	.	.	.	.	.	.	.	.
.	.	.	.	.	.	.	A	.	.
.	A	.	.	.	.	.	.	.	.
20	.	40	.	60	.	80	.	100	.

25% of cars overall require adjustment

133

QUANTITATIVE METHODS

Remember that as the sequence of numbers is random, it follows that the sequence of car status generated is also random. The way in which I have allocated the random numbers ensures that in the long run 25% of cars need adjustment but it also ensures that each car in the sequence has the same probability of being adjusted. The sequence of five defective cars, starting with car No. 4, arose by chance alone.

It is important to appreciate that random sequences will, if long enough, show at times what seem at first sight to be regular patterns. The production manager needs to realise this so that he can distinguish real changes in quality from random fluctuations. In examining Table 4.5, have a look for what seem to be regular features and try to get a feel for just how much regularity a random process can produce. These features have the same significance as the 'birds' and 'animals' that we can sometimes 'see' in pieces of dead wood lying around on a forest floor. Most of them look remarkably like dead wood but now and again some piece may attract our attention because of its resemblance to a familiar object. We may well take it home and show it to our friends commenting on its 'amazing likeness'. However we accept that it is the product of pure chance and recognise that the object was *selected* from many featureless specimens lacking in any interest.

But why should a practical, busy manager need to get an intuitive idea of the sort of patterns that can arise in random sequences. Well suppose that the car production manager calls for a spot check on two *successive* cars coming off the production line. They both require adjustment. He will need to know whether this is evidence of a systematic fault developing in the process or whether it is just bad luck. This is a problem in 'statistical inference' and reference to Table 4.5 demonstrates that it is quite possible for two successive cars to require adjustment even if the sequence of cars is a random one. As you can see, we obtained, by chance, one sequence of 5 and two of 2 cars in a row. The science of Quality Control provides rules which assist management to distinguish random sequences from those which arise from chance in a process which is stable. Tables which enable them to carry out appropriate *run tests* are available.

4.5.3 Non-random Sequences

In many business applications, non-random sequences can arise. Suppose that in the process of manufacture, cars need adjustment because of the malfunctioning of some vital piece of equipment or of some individual worker. In that case whole sequences of defective cars will be produced until the malfunction is detected and corrected.

THE LANGUAGE OF UNCERTAINTY

Table 4.6 shows a sequence of 100 cars which does not follow that which could reasonably be associated with a random process.

Table 4.6 : A Non-random Sequence

Car No.	Status	Car No.	Status	Car No.	Status	Car No.	Status	Car No.	Status
	.		.		A		.		A
	.		.		A		.		.
	.		.		A		.		A
	.		.		A		.		A
5	.	25	.	45	A	65	.		A
	A		.		.		.		.
	.		.		A		.		A
	A		.		A		.		A
	A		.		.		.		.
10	A	30	.	50	.	70	.	90	.
	A		.		.		.		.
	.		.		.		.		.
	A		.		.		.		.
	A		.		.		.		.
15	.	35	.	55	.	75	.		.
	.		A		.		.		.
	A		.		.		.		.
	.		A		.		.		.
	.		A		.		.		.
20	.	40	.	60	.	80	A	100	.

25% of cars overall require adjustment

Here most of the cars needing attention tend to come bunched together. There are three problem sequences:

    Car 6   to   Car 17
    Car 36   to   Car 48
    Car 80   to   Car 88

When a process is likely to produce this sort of pattern, one where defective cars tend to come in bunches, a different sort of control procedure may be required. Clearly in this case if any car found on the basis of a random check requires adjustment, then it seems likely that most of those in front and behind it will also need adjustment (unless you happen to start checking at the beginning or end of the sequence). Sampling output at regular intervals may then produce better results than the traditional sort of random sampling.

Exercise

Suppose a shop sells three brands of oil A,B & C, the market shares being 55%, 25% and 20% respectively. Use the random numbers in

QUANTITATIVE METHODS

Appendix 7 to simulate a long sequence of purchases. (Allocate 01–55 to brand A, 56–80 to brand B and 81–99, 00 to brand C). Then scan the resulting sequence and pick out what might seem to be non-random sequences or sequences which differ markedly from the average market shares shown above.

4.6 Conditional Probabilities

4.6.1 Suppose that an analyst has been charged with the task of assisting management in the assessment of market prospects for the following year. As part of this study a marketing executive is to be asked to assess the probability that she will be able to sell at least 1000 units of a product during the coming year. In arriving at a figure, she will have to weigh up a number of imponderables which might affect the outcome. These might include consideration as to

— whether her main competitor will have a comparable product on the market by next year.

— whether the product will prove attractive to the market.

— whether the quality of the product meets expectations.

   and many other factors.

Any probability she comes up with will depend on her subjective assessment of the above factors and others besides.

Suppose for the sake of argument that she decides on a probability of 0.4, a slightly worse than even money chance. The analyst might now pose a different question:

> 'What is the probability of selling at least 1000 units assuming that our main competitor does *not* manage to get his product onto the market in time.'

The executive is now being asked to estimate a *conditional probability,* that is a probability in which one of the factors which could affect the outcome is assumed to be known. Given that assumption, the executive may well feel able to raise the probability to, say 0.7, because one element of uncertainty has been eliminated from consideration. Note carefully that the state of the competition is still unknown. That doesn't prevent the executive from speculating on how she would feel *if* it were known and the facts in the company's favour.

Exercise

1. Calculate the conditional probability of drawing a heart from a

THE LANGUAGE OF UNCERTAINTY

shuffled pack from which one heart and one club have already been drawn without having been replaced.

2. In a game of poker what is the probability of being dealt a heart conditional on the following prior circumstances. Each of four players have been dealt 5 cards and so has the dealer. You are first in line to discard and draw some new cards. You were dealt four hearts and a club. You have discarded the club and in drawing one card, you hope to draw a heart from what remains of the pack to complete a 'flush'.

3. Suppose you are a burglar alarm salesman and find that 1 in 25 calls produces a sale. In what way might your estimate of the probability of making a sale be affected if it was conditional on

a) The prospect having invited you to call
b) You know that there has just been a burglary in the prospect's street
c) It is summer time.

4.7 Combining Probabilities : Complex Events

4.7.1 In many applications we need to find the probability of complex events occurring. These complex events are events which are made up of a combination of subsidiary ones. An example of such an event would be that of a power failure occurring in a hospital. Simplifying things a little, this event can be seen as one which is made up of two subsidiary events

1. The grid supply fails
2. The back-up generator fails

We need to find out how to combine the separate probabilities of the subsidiary events occurring into the single overall probability of the complex event occurring. To do this we will once again make use of such systems as simple gambling devices. Remember these suit our purpose because of the clear-cut structure of dice and playing card systems. They enable us to illustrate basic principles without getting tangled up in the complications of real world situations.

Consider first a combination of events involving a dice.

Probability in two throws   (6 on first) & (6 on 2nd)
of getting   throw   throw

                              (Event 1)   &   (Event 2)

QUANTITATIVE METHODS

Looking at all the possible combinations of the outcomes of throwing a dice twice we get

1 1	2 1	3 1	4 1	5 1	6 1
1 2	2 2	3 2	4 2	5 2	6 2
1 3	2 3	3 3	4 3	5 3	6 3
1 4	2 4	3 4	4 4	5 4	6 4
1 5	2 5	3 5	4 5	5 5	6 5
1 6	2 6	3 6	4 6	5 6	6 6

Intuitively we should accept that any one of these combinations are equally likely to occur. There are 36 possibilities and only one of them constitutes 2 sixes in a row. So we can say that

$$\text{Probability of 2 sixes in a row} = \frac{1}{36}$$

Could this probability have been deduced from the fact that we needed

$$\text{Probability of (Event 1 } and \text{ Event 2)}$$

where we knew that

$$\text{Probability of (Event 1)} = \frac{1}{6}$$

$$\text{Probability of (Event 2)} = \frac{1}{6}$$

It certainly looks as if all we need to do is to multiply the probabilities of the separate events together to yield the probability of the compound event.

$$\text{Probability of (Event 1)} \times \text{Probability of (Event 2)}$$

$$= \frac{1}{6} \times \frac{1}{6} = \frac{1}{36}$$

It turns out that this rule does indeed apply in general but only when the events are independent. Now if the issue of independence was solely a technical or academic matter it could perhaps be safely left to the statisticians. However it is a critically important issue and one in which management must involve themselves in practical applications because they are often better placed than the analyst to assess the extent to which events affect each other.

4.7.2 Dependent and Independent Events

First consider the issue within a clearly defined gambling situation.

THE LANGUAGE OF UNCERTAINTY

The outcome of the second throw of a dice is independent of the outcome of the first throw. This means that whatever the outcome of the first throw it has no effect or influence on the outcome of the second. If you accept that it is impossible to control the outcome of the thow of a dice then it follows that the outcome of the first throw cannot effect the result of the second.

Now consider the following two events:

Event 1   A club drawn at random from a shuffled pack of cards.

Event 2   A club drawn at random from the remainder of the same shuffled pack of cards.

In this case the outcome of event 2 depends on the outcome of the first event.

Either
The outcome of the first draw is a club in which case on the second draw there will only be 12 clubs among the 51 cards remaining in the pack in which case

$$\text{Probability of (club on 2nd draw)} = \frac{12}{51}$$

or
The outcome of the first draw is *not* a club in which case on the second draw there will still be 13 clubs remaining among the 51 cards in the pack in which case

$$\text{Probability of (club on 2nd draw)} = \frac{13}{51}$$

The two events are *not* independent events. Fortunately there is a rule for combining probabilities which ensures that the right practical questions are asked:

Rule for calculating the probability of two events occurring in association

     Probability of (Event 1 and Event 2)

=   Probability of (Event 1)

x   Probability of (Event 2 conditional on event 1 occurring in association)

QUANTITATIVE METHODS

Stating the rule in this form ensures that we ask whether the occurrence of the first event affects the chance of the second occurring. Where there is some degree of interdependence it requires us to find out and assess the degree of the effect. In real situations this means involving line management or their personnel because it is they, rather than the statistical expert, who have most knowledge of the way in which things interact in the field of application under consideration.

4.7.3 Example

Event 1 = a '6' on first throw of a dice

Event 2 = a '6' on second throw of a dice

Probability of (Event 1) = $\frac{1}{6}$

Probability of (Event 2 conditional on Event 1) = $\frac{1}{6}$

Because the occurrence of Event 1 has no effect on the chance of Event 2 occurring providing that the dice is thrown fairly. So

Probability of (Event 1 *and* Event 2) = $\frac{1}{6} \times \frac{1}{6} = \frac{1}{36}$

4.7.4 Example

Event 1 = a '9' on first draw from a shuffled pack.

Event 2 = a '9' on 2nd draw from a shuffled pack, the the first card not having been replaced

Probability of (Event 1) = $\frac{4}{52}$

Probability of (Event 2 conditional on event 1) = $\frac{3}{51}$

Because we have to take account of the changed structure of the pack resulting from the occurrence of Event 1.

4.7.5 Example *(Permission No. 6)*

Turning to a real-life example, in their major study of the risks arising from the industrial activity on Canvey Island (HMSO 1981), a calculation is presented for estimating the risk to individuals, located beside the Thames Estuary, from a major accidental release of LPG (Liquid Petroleum Gas). The probabilities involved are as follows:

Probability of a large LPG release after a collision in the estuary

THE LANGUAGE OF UNCERTAINTY

$$= 970 \times 10^{-6} \text{ per year}$$

or once every 1030 years on the average. This figure was calculated from historical accident records and an estimate of the expected river traffic.

Probability of the collision being within range of an individual on the Canvey Coast
$$= 0.2$$

This assumes that risk only arises for an individual within 2 km of the collision.

Probability of a drifting cloud arising
$$= 0.3$$

This figure derives from technical studies.

Probability of an individual being downwind
$$= 0.1$$

Providing that these events are all independent, the probability of an individual being at risk is found by multiplying all these probabilities together. That is

Probability (an individual is at risk) =

Probability (a large LPG release follows a collision which is within range of the individual, that the release is in the form of a drifting cloud and the individual is down-wind)
$$= 970 \times 10^{-6} \times 0.2 \times 0.3 \times 0.1$$
$$= 5.82 \times 10^{-6} \text{ per year}$$

Those vetting the calculation must not only ask themselves whether the individual probabilities are reasonable and valid in themselves but also whether the events are independent or not. For example, suppose the probability of an individual being downwind has been calculated on statistical evidence about prevailing winds in the area. Given that a collision were to take place, would any particular wind direction be more likely to be associated with the event than another? Is there a link between the risk of collision and the wind direction? In the age of sail this would almost certainly have been true. If the risk of the individual being down-wind has been calculated on all-year data on on wind directions, there could be a problem if collision risk were

QUANTITATIVE METHODS

greater in certain seasons. It is well known that the prevailing winds vary with the seasons. Note that the discussion is not a theoretical statistical discussion but is one which will draw in experts from a wide range of disciplines: meteorology, engineering, maritime experts and so on.

Exercise

In each of the following calculations decide what questions need to be asked about the assumption of independence between the events concerned. To do this you will have to use your imagination in considering the circumstances that might prevail in each case and whom you would want to question.

1. Suppose that past records suggest that the probability of as many as 5 people going to the stores in any 10 minute period is 0.2. Therefore the probability of as many as 5 people going to the stores in each of two successive 10 minute periods is 0.2 x 0.2 = 0.04. (The stores serves a workshop where about 20 mechanics work.)

2. An automatic safety device in an aircraft has a probability of failing of 0.0001 per flight. The device is triplicated in order to provide extra safety. If one device fails another is switched on. If two fail then the third is activated. Therefore the probability of total system failure on a flight is

0.0001 x 0.0001 x 0.0001 = 0.000000000001 = 10^{-12}.

4.8 More Complex Events : the Addition Rule

4.8.1 In many situations involving questions of risk and reliability, we need to calculate the probability of events which can come about in a number of different ways. For example, a car can suffer a blow-out *either* because one of its tyres runs over a sharp object *or* because it was inadequately pressurised *or* because its manufacture was faulty. In order to find a general rule for handling this type of situation first consider an example involving cards:

Probability of (drawing a black card from a shuffled pack)

= Probability of (*either* a club *or* a spade)

= Probability of (a club) + Probability of (a spade)

= $\frac{13}{52} + \frac{13}{52}$

= $\frac{26}{52}$

THE LANGUAGE OF UNCERTAINTY

In this case, the simple addition of the probabilities provides the correct answer for this *either/or* situation. This is only true because the two events involved are *mutually exclusive* events. They are 'mutually exclusive' because a card cannot be both a club *and* a spade at the same time. If a card is a club, then this *excludes* the possibility of its being a spade.

However if we needed to know the probability of a card being an ace or a club, then we have problems using the simple addition rule because drawing a club does not *exclude* the possibility of its being an ace. The simple addition of the probabilities in this case would give us the wrong answer:

Probability of (either a club or an ace)

is not $\quad \dfrac{13}{52} + \dfrac{4}{52} = \dfrac{17}{52}$

The reason is quite simply that the ace of clubs has been counted twice! To avoid this confusion and to make sure that the right questions are asked, we should use the following rule *which works in all cases*.

Probability of (*either* Event 1)
(*or* Event 2)

= Probability of Event 1
+ Probability of Event 2
− Probability of *both* Event 1 *and* Event 2

So in the example we have just been looking at:

Probability of (Either a club or an ace)
= Probability of (a club)
+ Probability of (an ace)
− Probability of (both a club and an ace)

$= \dfrac{13}{52} + \dfrac{4}{52} - \dfrac{1}{52}$

$= \dfrac{16}{52}$

the last term representing the selection of the ace of clubs. Note that this gives what we know to be the right answer because in a pack of cards there are indeed only 16 cards which are either clubs or aces, namely the 13 clubs and the three aces which are not clubs.

Note that the third term in the rule forces the user to ask himself

QUANTITATIVE METHODS

effectively whether the events are mutually exclusive or not.

4.8.2 The Addition Law for Small Probabilities

When dealing with very small probabilities, we can calculate the probability in 'either/or' situations by simply adding the probabilities. That this approximation works is demonstrated in the next example. Suppose that an engineer wishes to estimate the probability that either one or the other of two pumps will fail during the next 24 hours. Past performance suggests that there is likely to be two failures a year on average (assuming continuous running). He estimates the individual probability of failure for each pump as follows:

$$2 \text{ failures in } 365 \text{ days}$$

therefore

$$0.00548 \text{ failures in } 1 \text{ day.}$$

Using the 'either/or' formula

Probability of (Either pump 1 or pump 2 fails)

= Probability of (pump 1 fails)
+ Probability of (pump 2 fails)
− Probability of (both pumps fail)
= 0.00548 + 0.00548 − (0.00548 × 0.00548)
= 0.01096 − 0.00003

Note that the second term in the expression makes very little difference to the answer illustrating how the simple addition of *small* probabilities is adequate in most situations. Note also that the probability of both pumps failing assumes that their failures are independent events. In practice this is a question of engineering design. If the failure of one pump interferes with the operation of the other, by generating heat or fumes for example, then the *conditional* probability of the second pump failing could be much higher than the 0.00548 assumed here. Note that it needs an engineer to settle the issue of independence in this case, not a statistician.

4.8.3 Fault Trees

The development of the North Sea oil fields has led to an expansion of the 'risk business'. Companies specialise in assessing the risk of equipment failure leading to death or injury. Fault trees are often used to display the complicated logic of events which can lead to the catastrophic event under consideration. A *simplified* example of such a calculation follows.

On an oil rig, a gas conservation module has been designed to conserve

THE LANGUAGE OF UNCERTAINTY

light fractions which would otherwise be flared off. However the module is enclosed, and it contains pumps and compressor motors which could malfunction and as a result ignite any gas which has leaked and which has not been dispersed by the ventilation system. Fig 4.1 shows a simplified version of the system in the form of a *fault tree*.

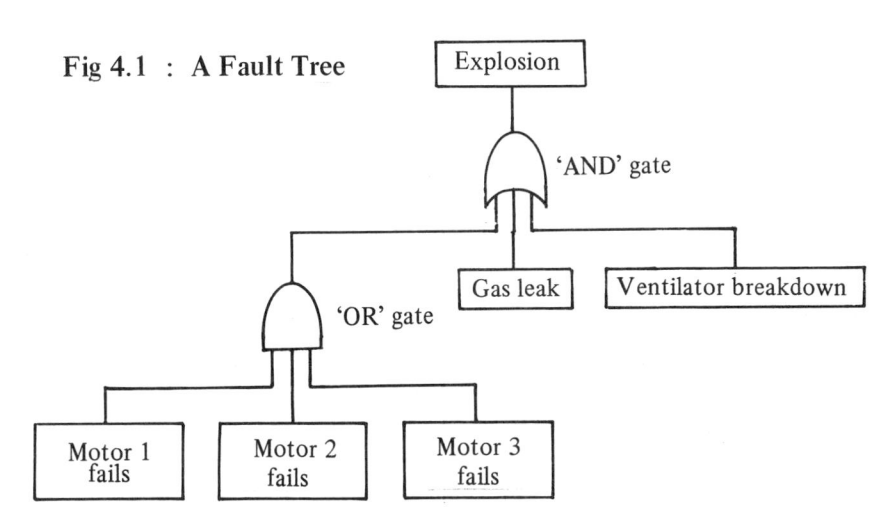

Fig 4.1 : A Fault Tree

```
                          ┌───────────┐
                          │ Explosion │
                          └─────┬─────┘
                                │
                              ╱─╲  'AND' gate
                             ╱   ╲
                ┌────────────┴─┬──┴────────────────┐
                │              │                    │
              ╱─╲       ┌──────┴──────┐   ┌─────────────────────┐
             ╱   ╲      │  Gas leak   │   │ Ventilator breakdown│
        'OR' gate       └─────────────┘   └─────────────────────┘
       ┌────┼────┐
       │    │    │
  ┌────┴┐ ┌─┴───┐ ┌─┴───┐
  │Motor│ │Motor│ │Motor│
  │  1  │ │  2  │ │  3  │
  │fails│ │fails│ │fails│
  └─────┘ └─────┘ └─────┘
```

The three motors which are potential sources of a spark feed into what is called an 'OR' gate because if motor 1 *or* motor 2 *or* motor 3 fail then a spark will be produced. That branch together with the other two branches feed into an 'AND' gate because one of the three motors must produce a spark *and* there must be a gas leak *and* the ventilation system must be malfunctioning otherwise the leaking gas would have been dispersed. The individual probabilities of failure during a 24 hour period are as follows

    Probability (a motor fails producing sparks) = 0.004
    Probability (a gas leak occurs) = 0.002
    Probability (ventilator fails) = 0.001

We start by simplifying the fault tree. First we calculate the probability of at least one of the motors failing and thus the probability of producing a spark. The probabilities are small and therefore we can simply add the probabilities together:

    Probability of (spark)
    = Probability of (one of three motors fail)
    = 3 x 0.004   =   0.012

QUANTITATIVE METHODS

So the simplified fault tree now looks like Fig 4.2.

Fig 4.2 : Simplified Fault Tree

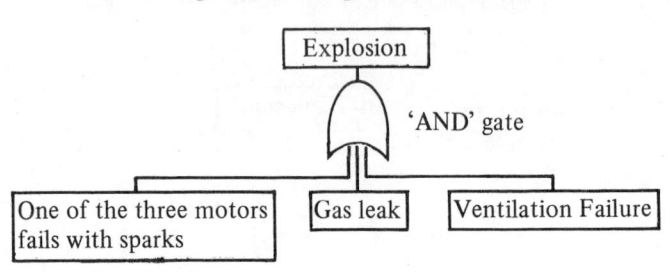

```
                    ┌─────────┐
                    │Explosion│
                    └────┬────┘
                         ∧  'AND' gate
          ┌──────────────┼──────────────┐
┌──────────────────┐ ┌────────┐ ┌──────────────────┐
│One of the three  │ │Gas leak│ │Ventilation Failure│
│motors fails with │ │        │ │                  │
│sparks            │ │        │ │                  │
└──────────────────┘ └────────┘ └──────────────────┘
```

Assuming that these three branches represent events which are independent, the probability of an explosion is the probability that there is a spark *and* that there is a leak *and* that there is inadequate ventilation

Probability of (explosion)
= 0.012 x 0.002 x 0.001
= 2.4×10^{-8} = 0.000000024

This is a very reassuring probability. But management would need to check out some of the following questions before assuming that the risk of explosion was so remote:

1. What is the source for the individual probabilities quoted? In particular were the figures obtained from tests carried out under conditions comparable to those which are likely to prevail on a North Sea oil-rig? For example salt in the air is likely to be a special feature of the North Sea environment.

2. Are the events independent? Could some factors causing a gas leak also cause failure of the ventilation system at the same time?

3. What other sources of sparking should be allowed for? In particular has human error been allowed for? For instance is it really possible to calculate the probability that someone will smoke illegally? Even if the oil companies had statistics on such infringements of the rules would they publish them, and in any case they would only know of those cases which were brought to their attention!

THE LANGUAGE OF UNCERTAINTY

Note that in this sort of calculation the mathematical part of the problem is the easy part. Answering the above questions will be time-consuming and will require imagination and experience and the ability to communicate with a wide range of specialists. In short it is a job for management. However it needs to be a management which understands the principles which underlie the risk calculations.

Exercise

1. Suppose a machine can fail because of bearing failure (probability = 0.0006 per working day) or because of the motor burning out (probability = 0.003 per working day). Calculate the probability of
   a) The machine failing during a working day
   b) The machine fails during a five day working week.

2. An aircraft auto-land system works on the 'majority vote' principle. Three identical channels A,B,C operate concurrently and the control system knows which channel, if any, is malfunctioning because it would then be behaving differently from the other two.

If two of the channels failed at the same time then the control would not know which, if any were operating correctly. Suppose the probability of failure during flight of an individual channel is 1×10^{-5}. The probability of failure of the system is therefore the probability that any two of the channels fail together (the probability of all three failing together being assumed to be negligible).

Probability of (AB, AC or BC failing together)

$= (1 \times 10^{-5} \times 1 \times 10^{-5}) + (1 \times 10^{-5} \times 1 \times 10^{-5}) + (1 \times 10^{-5} \times 1 \times 10^{-5})$

$= 3 \times 10^{-10}$

What factors could invalidate this calculation?

4.9 Expected Value and Utility

4.9.1 Expected Value: Using probabilities to value risky ventures

Managers often dislike any suggestion that their operations have anything in common with gambling. This applies even more to those who work in the public sector. However gambling situations do provide a useful starting point for discussing how to value risky business situations for the following reasons:

1. The probabilities in gambling situations can be calculated precisely as can the potential gains and losses.
2. Gambling situations have a relatively simple structure. They

QUANTITATIVE METHODS

allow discussion of the principles of decision making under uncertainty without the complications of the business situation obscuring the fundamental issues.

I knew a man once who was always prepared to toss a coin for a fiver. To most of us this is an unattractive pastime. We can represent the bet as follows:

Outcome	Probability of Occurrence	Gain
Head	½	+ £5
Tails	½	− £5

The gambler can see that in the long run he will win £5 half of the time on average and lose £5 on the other half. In repeated bets, the gambler should tend neither to accumulate winnings or debts. The *expected value* of the bet is calculated as the weighted mean of all the possible pay-offs, the weights being the probabilities of each pay-off arising.

Expected Value =

   the sum of   (monetry gain or loss,   x   probability of that gain)
                   the pay-off   or loss

So in the case of the coin tossing bet we get

Expected value   =   (£5 x ½)   +   (−£5 x ½)

                            £2.5   +   (−£2.5)

                        =   £0.0

The term 'expected value' is one of the many thoroughly misleading terms used in quantitative work. Far from being the value 'expected', it is only an average value, a weighted mean which measures the mean value of the bet in the long run. From the way it has been calculated it is only meaningful

1. Where the same bet is repeated so that a long run exists over which an average can apply.
2. Where the bet is one of many similar bets on offer. Then if only bets which have positive expected values are taken on, a net gain will be registered over the series taken as a whole.

To amplify point (2), consider a professional gambler faced with two bets. He makes a living from exploiting his superior knowledge of the precise probabilities of each proposal. In each case the stake is £10 and the odds on offer are shown together with the true probability

THE LANGUAGE OF UNCERTAINTY

derived from probability theory and the true expected value:

Bet 1 : In three cards drawn from a pack (with replacement), none are hearts.

Bet 2 : In four dice thrown, the total number on the faces adds up to 6 or less.

	Bet 1	Bet 2
Odds offered	evens	200 to 1
Equivalent probability	1/2	1/201
On winning	+ £10	+ £2000
On losing	– £10	– £10
True probability	$\frac{27}{64}$	$\frac{15}{1296}$
True expected value	– £1.56	+ £13.32

Faced with the odds on offer, the gambler would reject the first proposal because it has a negative expected value but would accept the second one with a positive expected value based on the true probabilities. Even if the bets were isolated, the gambler knows that by always accepting proposals which have a positive expected value, he will, on average, make a profit *in the long run*.

But does the theory of gambling have anything to do with the real world of business? Some speculative financial dealings are pure gambles. For instance, in the stock market, the 'stag' buys new issues of shares with money that he has not got and gambles on being able to sell them at a higher price at the end of the trading account using the proceeds to pay for the shares, and pocketing (hopefully) the profit. But even in more normal business dealings, management is faced with propositions where the value of the pay-off depends on forces and events beyond their control. If the probability of each of the possible pay-offs can be estimated then the expected value can be estimated. These probabilities are likely to be subjective probabilities based on the judgment of individuals or groups of experts. Providing that the 'mean value' interpretation of expected value is meaningful in the situation under study, then this measure provides a rational basis for choosing between courses of action.

Exercise:

1.(a) An antique dealer has bought a picture for £800. She is almost certain that it is seventeenth century in which case she can re-sell it for

QUANTITATIVE METHODS

£1800. On the other hand it may be a nineteenth century copy in which case it will only be worth £400. If the probability of its being genuine is O.8, calculate the expected net profit on the deal.

b) How low could the probability of the picture being genuine fall to while still leaving a positive expected net profit on the deal?

c) What precise meaning does the expected value have for the antique dealer?

2. A company has an option to buy a site. It believes that if it buys, the site might turn out to be very lucrative (+ £100,000, probability 0.2). It is more likely to show only a modest profit of (+ £10,000, probability 0.7) and there is a small risk of a bad loss (− £50,000, probability 0.1).

a) Calculate the expected value of the deal.

b) What precise meaning does the expected value have for the company?

c) Under what circumstances would the answer to (b) be invalid?

4.9.2 Utility : individual attitudes to risk

Different individuals and different companies do not have the same attitude to risky ventures. This is not necessarily an indication of irrational behaviour on their part. A large company with a lot of liquid assets might be relatively unconcerned about the possibility of a potential loss of £500,000, a loss which might be catastrophic for one of their weaker competitors. The way in which individuals differ in their attitudes can be easily demonstrated. Look at Table 4.7.

Table 4.7

	Bet 1	Bet 2	Bet 3
Heads	win £1	win £10	win £100
Tails	lose £1	lose £10	lose £100

In each case the expected value is zero and so in theory we should all be indifferent as to whether we take the bet or not. Unless you have a moral aversion to gambling, you will probably be indifferent as to whether you take up bet 1 or not.

But suppose that you had to take Bet 3 *or bargain to get out of it by offering to pay an agreed sum!* Faced with the prospect of throwing a coin to win or lose £100, each of us would react differently. The true gambler might enjoy the prospect, but to many ordinary rational

THE LANGUAGE OF UNCERTAINTY

people, the prospect of winning £100 is far outweighed by the prospect of losing £100. The measure of expected value assumes that these two prospects balance out. In a once-off situation, for a victim of limited resources, they do not.

Quite frankly many individuals would pay to get out of the bet. They would pay certain cash down rather than face the possibility of loss just as we all do with insurance policies. Each individual will, however, be prepared to pay a different sum.

Exercise

Interrogate some of your friends and colleagues on the basis of Table 4.7. Face them with a clear choice. They must take the bet or negotiate a payment to get out of it. It's then your job to interrogate them in order to find out just how much you can extort from them before they say 'hell, if you want that much I'll take the bet'. When you've finished compare the results obtained from different individuals. The answers to Bet 3 should display the greatest differences because it involves the highest potential gains and losses.

Note that it is the once-off nature of the bet that produces the difficulty. If Bet 3 were to be offered on a *regular basis* then I suspect that many more people's valuations would fall into the general line of indifference. The repetition of the bet allows losses to be balanced out by gains.

A company facing a series of different opportunities none of which involves exceptional gains or losses, can use expected value to help choose between options involving risk. Although they will lose some and win some, the company will see this as a 'swings and roundabouts' situation. They need to remember, however, that in some situations there may be a possibility of coming off the roundabouts so hard that they may never get a chance on the swings! For that reason, management will quite rightly allow the possibility of severe loss (or exceptional gain) to influence their valuation of a risky business opportunity.

Exercise : Drawing up a Utility Function

We have seen that different individuals place a different valuation on risky proposals when these involve large gains or losses on a once-off basis. You are now invited to try and draw up a *utility function* for an individual which will provide a profile of that person's attitude to risk within a specific range of monetry values. You will require the

QUANTITATIVE METHODS

cooperation of one or more colleagues who will ask to place a value on each of a number of 'bets'. You need to explain that these represent simplified financial ventures. Some of these are attractive and your colleagues may argue that *you* would need to pay *them* to get them to drop the opportunity of taking the bet. Some of the bets are very unattractive and most people should rationally be prepared to pay to avoid being left on risk. If they complain that the situations are too artificial, asking why they should have to pay cash or take the bet, you can remind them that when, for example, they insure the contents of their house, they are prepared to pay out hard cash to avoid taking a risk of loss and that in that situation they must choose one or the other!

The procedure is illustrated in Table 4.8 where I have filled in the monetry valuations as they might have been provided by two hypothetical respondents. You of course will replace these with the results derived from your own enquiries. Don't work through the 'bets' in the order shown in table 4.8. Start with one at one extreme and then move to one at the other extreme and so on. In the first attractive bet, a risk averter might accept as little as £55 to drop the bet whereas the risk taker could insist on as much as £95 before he will forego the bet. In the last bet, a very poor prospect, the risk averter will pay £90 to avoid the bet, whereas the risk taker will only pay £55.

Table 4.8 : Utility Functions for two hypothetical Respondents

1,000 utility units	+£100	0.9	0.8	0.6	0.4	0.2	0.1
(0 utility units)	-£100	0.1	0.2	0.4	0.6	0.8	0.9
Expected utility		900	800	600	400	200	100
Value assigned by a Risk Averter		+ £55	+ £20	− £20	− £55	− £80	− £90
Value assigned by a Risk Taker		+ £95	+ £88	+ £70	+ £38	− £15	− £55

As there is no absolute scale of utility, I have arbitrarily set + £100 to equal 1000 utility units and − £100 to equal 0 utility units. The idea is to produce a scale for relative measurements. Don't let the arbitary nature of the scale worry you. Think of good old British fahrenheit with its arbitary 0 well below freezing point and the boiling point of water at 240°. Although using different absolute values from those of the centigrade scale, both can be used to measure temperature relativities. Fig. 4.3 on page 153 provides a graphical representation of the two contrasting utility functions, the expected utility of each bet being plotted against the monetry value provided by the two hypothetical respondents.

THE LANGUAGE OF UNCERTAINTY

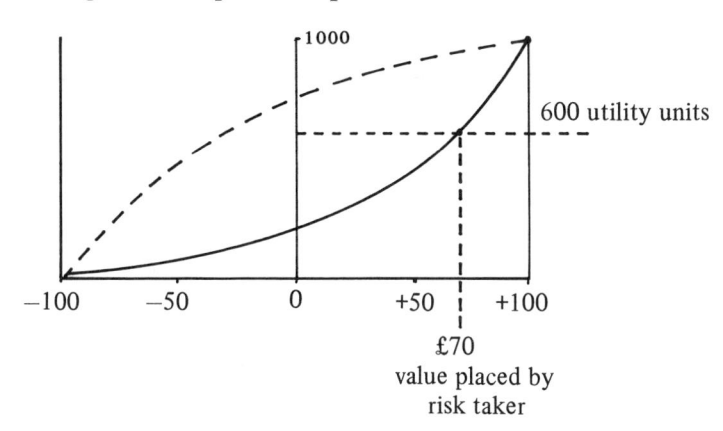

Fig 4.3 : Graphical Representation of Table 4.7

```
       1000
        |         ___----
        |     __--     /
        |   /-------------- 600 utility units
        | /          |    /
        |/           |   /
        |           |  /
        |          | /
   -100  -50    0  +50 | +100
                      £70
                 value placed by
                    risk taker
```

Note from the graph how little the risk taker distinguishes between different losses and how his utility rises rapidly for higher monetry values. Do remember that these are hypothetical curves. What you get from your colleagues are likely to show considerable inconsistencies. In no way should you expect them to conform to the graphs shown. Once you have obtained your own results, use the two curves as a bench-mark for classifying your own results. The main value of the exercise is what you learn during the process of drawing up the functions. Once a consistent utility function has been obtained. monetry values can be replaced by utilities and decisions made on the basis of maximising expected utility.

Obtaining the utility function for a company would be a difficult task. The range of monetry values would have to be much larger and groups of decision makers would not be able to agree on the valuations to be placed on the 'bets'. However the process of seeking agreement would be instructive because it would force the decision making group to seek agreement on the general issue of the company's attitude to risky ventures with the political complications of the decisions, which always arise, set aside for once!

CHAPTER 5 : SIMPLIFYING DATA

This chapter shows how very straightforward techniques can be used to simplify and clarify data.

5.1 Making the Desert Bloom : Rounding and Selecting

Table 5.1 contains some fascinating data derived from the Annual Abstract of Statistics. I say 'fascinating' but you might understandably disagree when faced with such a block of undigested data. To most people, Table 5.1 is as arid as an unwatered desert. Fortunately a few simple techniques can put a bit of life into it.

The first thing to do is to quite simply get rid of most of the figures! Not all the digits in a number carry the same amount of information. Suppose you win £563,141 on the pools. Most of what you need to know is given by the position and value of the first digit. 5. This gives you a good idea of your future life-style. The second digit is just a sweetener and the rest is irrelevant until you put the finishing touches to your investment portfolio. Table 5.1 tells us that in 1973 361,724 postal orders were sent. Very precise. But would the general reader lose anything if that figure were cut to 361,720 or 361,700 or for that matter 362,000. What if we go the whole way and round off to two significant figures. That will get rid of two thirds of the digits in that row for a start while leaving as much of the *information* that the general reader needs as was there before.

Postal Orders (units of 10 millions)

1971	1972	1973	......	1979	1980	1981
43	34	36		17	15	12

These simplified figures provide the general reader with the long term trend in a clear form. Don't be worried about pruning too severely. Cut the figures back to what your audience can cope with. When you over-do it, it's usually pretty obvious. Refer the readers to appendices if you think they may need more detail.

In Table 5.2, a bit of life begins to show through. The numbers have been stripped down to the minimum allowing long term trends to come strongly to the fore. Summarising such data in words requires care. Be selective, keep it simple and let the numbers speak for themselves. Here is my version.

Trends in Postal, Telegraph and Telephone Services 1971–1981

Considerable change has taken place in the ten years up to 1981. The

SIMPLIFYING DATA

Table 5.1 : Postal, Telegraph and Telephone Services

	Unit	1971	1972	1973	1974	1975	1976	1977	1978	1979	1980	1981
Letters Posted	Millions	10500	10550	10790	11010	10878	9903	9383	9485	9965	10207	9969
Postal orders	Thousands	434620	342251	361724	360631	303756	224752	192231	180308	169989	153947	121636
Telegrams	"	25831	26950	27021	27525	25532	21053	18676	17312	16601	15546	13670
Telex Connections	Number	32945	37774	43139	48995	54256	59142	64804	71586	79503	85752	89930
Telephone Calls (total inland)	Millions	10747	12029	12144	13238	14313	15156	15956	17303	19122	19857	20175
Telephone Calls (total international)	Thousands	18821	21963	25412	29178	36252	44326	54603	70537	86930	106427	116599
Television Licences	Thousands	15943	16658	17125	17325	17701	17729	17994	18042	18389	18300	18667
of which Colour	Thousands	610	1635	3332	5558	7580	8628	9928	10983	12131	12901	13780

(Permission No. 6)

TABLE 5.2 : Postal, Telegraph and Telephone Services
(Adapted from Table 5.1)

	Unit	1971	1972	1973	1974	1975	1976	1977	1978	1979	1980	1981
Letters posted	Billions	10.5	10.6	10.8	11.0	10.9	9.9	9.4	9.5	10.0	10.2	10.0
Postal Orders	Millions	43	34	36	36	30	22	19	18	17	15	12
Telegrams	Millions	26	27	27	28	26	21	19	17	17	16	14
Telex Connections	Thousands	33	38	43	49	54	59	65	72	80	86	90
Telephone Calls (total inland)	Billions	11	12	12	13	14	15	16	17	19	20	20
Telephone Calls (total international)	Millions	19	22	25	29	36	44	55	71	87	106	117
Television Licences (total)	Millions	15.9	16.7	17.1	17.3	17.7	17.7	18.0	18.0	18.4	18.3	18.7
Television Licences (colour)	Millions	0.6	1.6	3.3	5.6	7.6	8.6	9.9	11.0	12.1	12.9	13.8

(Permission No. 6)

SIMPLIFYING DATA

number of letters posted over the period has remained stable but other services show a mixture of growth and decline.

Whilst postal orders and telegrams have declined by a factor of 4 and 2 respectively, inland telephone calls have doubled and telex connections have trebled. Surprisingly, international telephone calls have increased six-fold.

Whilst the number of television licences has shown a modest increase overall, colour licences have grown to become a majority of all licences issued.

Note how I have further simplified the scale of the increases and decreases in my report. I can do this because the reader has immediate access to Table 5.2 and furthermore has the reference to the original source in Table 5.1. People are frightened of simplifying numbers. Some would feel that the process used to produce Table 5.2 was in some way 'cheating' and 'inaccurate'. But if my report were to be based on Table 5.1 rather than on Table 5.2, would I have to change a single word? Certainly not. I have thown away detail but not any relevant information as far as the reader is concerned. Perhaps the problem starts in the schools where we used to be given large chunks of arithmetic to do. In my case, unless every digit was correct the answer was declared to be 'wrong'. Precision was everything, you got no credit for getting roughly the right answer. It was a training guaranteed to develop a mixture of fear and respect for precision arithmetic. So start now and regain control. Knock your figures down to the level of accuracy you require and and develop the skills of approximate arithmetic.

Exercise *(Permission No. 6)*

1. Simplify the following table and write a summary containing no more than 100 words which will be of interest to the general public.

Building Societies in Great Britain
(Adapted from HMSO 1983)

	1971	1973	1975	1977	1979	1981
Societies on Register (number)	467	447	382	339	287	253
Share investors (thousands)	11568	14385	17916	22536	27878	33388
Depositors (thousands)	655	672	677	760	797	995
Borrowers (thousands)	3896	4204	4397	4836	5251	5490

QUANTITATIVE METHODS

2. Simplify the following table and write a summary in no more than 100 words describing its contents.

Turnover (£) for four subsidiaries of a holding company broken down by region

	A	B	C	D
North	37992	637241	7322241	639491
South	141558	523992	34297	584363
Scotland	136293	76395	278513	639412
Export	317492	196345	873994	757219

5.2 Percentages

Percentages provide a simple yet powerful means for making sense of complex quantitative information. However, as with all simple techniques, there are pitfalls to avoid, and their effectiveness and safety depends on knowing how and when to use them correctly. Percentages are mainly used to enable us to compare figures on a common basis.

5.2.1 Example

Suppose we have information on wastage from 5 different departments as follows:

Table 5.3

Department	Total number of employees at start of year	Number of leavers
A	120	10
B	46	2
C	2300	135
D	620	25
E	590	49

It is difficult at a glance to see whether the wastage is proportionately higher in one department than in another because, with the exception of D and E, the size of the departments is so different. Looking at the latter two, both containing about 600 employees, the wastage is obviously higher in E than in D.

But what about department C? There have certainly been a lot of leavers, but is that not simply because that department has so many employees? By calculating the proportion of leavers relative to the size of the department and expressing the result as a percentage, comparison becomes possible. Table 5.4 gives the results as well as demonstrating how the calculations are carried out.

SIMPLIFYING DATA

Table 5.4

Department	Leavers as a proportion of number of Employees	Leavers as a percentage of Employees (Column 2 x 100)
A	10/120 = 0.083	8.3
B	2/46 = 0.043	4.3
C	135/2300 = 0.059	5.9
D	25/620 = 0.040	4.0
E	49/590 = 0.083	8.3

Although the proportions and percentages are really giving the same information, most people in business find percentages easier to handle. Rounding off the percentages presents a neat clear picture:

Table 5.5

Department	Size of Department	Wastage %
A	120	8
B	46	4
C	2300	6
D	620	4
E	590	8

Note that I have quoted the size of each department. This is to remind the user that each percentage has been calculated on a different base. The user can then see that, although Department C has a lower wastage rate than Department A, it is applied to a much larger number of people.

5.2.2 Example

In a production process scrap losses are inevitable. Management will however want to keep a tight control on the scrap rate. A company producing components for nuclear power stations is faced with this problem. Batches of these components go through a number of stages, the scrap rate being about 10% overall. Here the batch sizes are usually of the order of 100 components but considerable variation around that figure occurs. Here are some typical figures:

Table 5.6

Batch Number	Batch Size	Number Rejected	% Reject	% Reject (Rounded)
1	120	10	8.3	8
2	110	14	12.7	13
3	140	7	5.0	5
4	85	12	14.1	14
5	130	6	4.6	5

QUANTITATIVE METHODS

Note how the comparison of the % rejects is more effective than a comparison of the number of rejects. Even though the batch sizes do not differ greatly, the ranking of the batches in order of numbers rejected is slightly different from that for percentage rejected.

5.2.3   Example

Percentages are increasingly used to make sense of complicated statistical information presented in company annual reports. Reproduced in Table 5.7 (Page 161) is information on the sources of revenue for British Airways scheduled services between 1972 and 1981.

The task of comparing the breakdown between the three categories of revenue over time is made almost impossible, not only because of the sheer volume of digits, but also because of the effects of inflation. Converting to percentages I obtain the results in Table 5.8 (Page 161).

Quite enlightening I think you will agree. Suddenly we can see how the make-up of the airline's revenue has shifted away from mail towards Passenger and Baggage over the years. Freight presents a more variable picture with recent decline.

But there are still far too many figures and you might well wonder why some columns add up to 100 and some to 99.99. Well, because the figures have been rounded off to two decimal places, the columns will not necessarily add up to precisely 100. The total should be shown as precisely 100 because a set of percentages should logically do so.

A further cleaning up operation will be needed to round off all percentages. There are two versions on page 162. In Table 5.9 I have rounded off to one decimal place and in Table 5.10, to the nearest whole percentage point.

You may feel that the rounding in Table 5.10 is a bit too drastic. Although this simplification does indeed bring out the long term trend quite impressively, it obscures some of the interesting detail which can still be seen in Table 5.9. Once again note how all columns are shown as adding up to 100. Note also in Table 5.9 how 88.0 is written instead of 88 to indicate that the percentage has been rounded to one place of decimals. If you are working a lot with statistical tables, you will find some very useful guidelines and many original ideas in Ehrenberg (1982).

SIMPLIFYING DATA

Table 5.7 : 1980/81 British Airways Annual Report & Accounts

Year ended 31st March	1972	1973	1974	1975	1976	1977	1978	1979	1980	1981
Results										
Scheduled Services										
Revenue–Passenger & Baggage (£m)	299.3	360.5	444.3	526.6	660.0	898.6	965.1	1,191.4	1,409.9	1,489.5
Revenue–Mail (£m)	21.5	20.2	21.1	22.3	23.6	32.7	33.0	36.2	39.8	41.0
Revenue–Freight (£m)	41.9	55.2	68.4	83.8	82.1	105.3	115.3	131.4	152.7	161.7
Revenue–Total (£m)	362.7	435.9	533.8	632.7	765.7	1,036.6	1,113.4	1,359.0	1,602.4	1,692.2

Table 5.8 *(Derived from Table 5.7)* Percentage Version: Rounded to 2 places of decimals

	1972	1973	1974	1975	1976	1977	1978	1979	1980	1981
Revenue–Passenger & Baggage (%)	82.52	82.70	83.23	83.23	86.20	86.69	86.68	87.67	87.99	88.02
Revenue–Mail (%)	5.93	4.63	3.95	3.52	3.08	3.15	2.96	2.66	2.48	2.42
Revenue–Freight (%)	11.55	12.66	12.81	13.24	10.72	10.16	10.36	9.67	9.53	9.56
Revenue–Total (%)	100.00	99.99	99.99	99.99	100.00	100.00	100.00	100.00	100.00	100.00

(Permission No. 3)

QUANTITATIVE METHODS

Table 5.9 *(Derived from Table 5.7)* Rounded to 1 place of decimals

	1972	1973	1974	1975	1976	1977	1978	1979	1980	1981
Revenue–Passenger & Baggage (%)	82.5	82.7	83.2	83.2	86.2	86.7	86.7	87.7	88.0	88.0
Revenue–Mail (%)	5.9	4.6	4.0	3.5	3.1	3.2	3.0	2.7	2.5	2.4
Revenue–Freight (%)	11.6	12.7	12.8	13.2	10.7	10.2	10.4	9.7	9.5	9.6
Revenue–Total (%)	100.0	100.0	100.0	100.0	100.0	100.0	100.0	100.0	100.0	100.0

Table 5.10 *(Derived from Table 5.7)* Rounded to whole numbers

	1972	1973	1974	1975	1976	1977	1978	1979	1980	1981
Revenue–Passenger & Baggage (%)	83	83	83	83	86	87	87	88	88	88
Revenue–Mail (%)	6	5	4	4	3	3	3	3	2	2
Revenue–Freight (%)	12	13	13	13	11	10	10	10	10	10
Revenue–Total (%)	100	100	100	100	100	100	100	100	100	100

SIMPLIFYING DATA

Exercise *(Permission No. 6)*

1. Use percentages to simplify and clarify the data in Exercise 2 on page 158. Summarise the main features of the data in less than 100 words.

2. The number of industrial stoppages in all industries and services has almost halved in the ten years between 1971 and 1981. Draw up a separate table to show the percentage breakdown of stoppages between different industries. Write a report containing *no more than 100 words* summarising the table.

Industrial Stoppages *(Adapted from HMSO, Annual Abstracts 1983)*

Number of Stoppages beginning in Each Year

	1971	1973	1975	1977	1979	1981
All Industries & Services	2228	2873	2282	2703	2080	1338
Mining & Quarrying	138	304	217	272	309	305
Metals, Engineering, Shipbuilding & Vehicles	1107	1342	1045	1124	848	434
Textiles	70	92	72	77	42	26
Clothing & Footwear	27	31	45	38	27	13
Construction	234	217	208	248	170	59
Transport & Communications	269	298	189	247	180	157
All other Industries & Services	383	591	517	705	521	353

5.3 Problems with percentages

As we have seen, percentages can be used to clarify complicated data. It would be a good idea however to see how things can go wrong. This isn't a 'knocking' exercise, Its just a question of knowing the dangers so as to avoid them. You don't detract from the usefulness of a car by pointing out the ways that they can cause death or injury when incorrectly handled.

5.3.1 Percentage of what? — The concealed base

A Personnel manager might be excused for being disturbed to hear that 50% of one department in his organisation had left in one month. To many people, 50% seems to imply a lot of people but in fact it does nothing of the sort. If, for example, you have a typing pool with

QUANTITATIVE METHODS

four typists and two of them, friends perhaps, both leave to go to another firm then you are left with a wastage rate of $\frac{2}{4}$ x 100 = 50%. As long as Management is in direct contact with the detailed operations of the organisation, there is little danger of confusion. But where management relies on summary statistics for its view or 'window' onto the organisation, it is especially necessary to avoid misleading statistical measures.

The problem arises when we forget that you get nothing in this world without paying for it. We saw how wastage figures can be difficult to assess when the department sizes vary. Percentages certainly do enable us to measure wastage on a comparable basis. But in doing so, the absolute size of the base, in this case the size of the department, disappears. The method employed to clarify one aspect of the situation creates a potential for confusion in another. For that reason, in Table 5.5, I showed the size of the department as well as the percentages. Then, given both columns, it is possible for the reader to reconstruct the approximate original number of leavers. Thus 8% wastage in department E implies

$$\frac{8}{100} \times 590 = 47.2$$

i.e. about 47 leavers; whereas 8% wastage in department A implies

$$\frac{8}{100} \times 120 = 9.6$$

i.e. 9–10 leavers.

Because the percentages in Table 5.5 were rounded, the number of leavers calculated above will not necessarily come out to round figures. If you think that this is going to cause your audience some concern then you should take care to avoid rounding off your percentages too drastically. The rule to remember when faced with a percentage is to ask yourself or, even better, the source of the percentage direct,

PERCENTAGE OF HOW MANY?

This will ensure that you focus your attention on the base on which the percentage has been calculated. This is the way to 'talk back' to a percentage in situations like the following where percentages are being used to 'bully' and exaggerate.

> 'Last week we had to reject 30% of a batch of finished product! Things can't go on like this you know.

'30% of how many?'

'Well, it was a small batch, I admit, only 27 units.'

SIMPLIFYING DATA

5.3.2 How percentages can exaggerate

Another commonly occurring situation where the magnitude of the base is a potential source of confusion lies in what accountants call 'variance analysis'. Look at the following example from a set of management accounts.

Table 5.11

Item	Variance as % of budget
Special alloy	87.5
Stainless Steel Sheet	3.8

If we focus on the magnitude of the variance as a percentage of the budgeted value, then our attention is drawn to the special alloy where the actual expenditure has been almost double that budgeted. On the other hand, the expenditure on stainless steel sheet has been a mere 4% over budget. If we look at the total picture

Table 5.12

	Budget	Actual	Variance	Variance as % of Budget
Special Alloy	400	750	350	87.5
Stainless Steel Sheet	29,000	30,000	1,100	3.8

and focus on the actual monetary variances then we can see that 3.8%, being 3.8% of £29,000, represents a larger sum of money and therefore, perhaps, a larger potential source of saving than the over-expenditure on the special alloy. In fact both ways of presenting variances can be useful for the manager attempting to exercise control over expenditure. The high percentage variance could be evidence of a lack of control in the spending department, a sign of slackening discipline or poor forecasting. A high absolute monetary variance indicates a suitable area, perhaps, for concentrating effort to achieve significant savings.

5.3.3 Spurious Averaging of Percentages

The fact that the base of the percentage is concealed can lead to problems when calculating an average percentage. Referring back to Table 5.6, consider what is the mean percentage reject rate? To simply calculate the mean of the percentages themselves would be naive and incorrect.

$$Spurious\ mean\ =\ \frac{8+13+5+14+5}{5}\ =\ 9\%$$

QUANTITATIVE METHODS

The only meaningful mean percentage scrap rate is

$$\text{Mean scrap rate} = \frac{\text{Total number scrapped}}{\text{Total of all batches}}$$

$$= \frac{10 + 14 + 7 + 12 + 6}{120 + 110 + 140 + 85 + 130} = 8.4\%$$

This could also have been calculated by producing a weighted mean of the percentage scrap rates per batch.

$$\text{Mean scrap rate} = \frac{(120 \times 8.3) + (110 \times 12.7) + \ldots \text{etc.}}{120 + 110 + \ldots \text{etc.}}$$

$$= 8.4\%$$

An extreme example should clarify any misunderstanding. Suppose the labour wastage for two departments was as follows:

Table 5.13

Department	Size	Leavers	% Wastage
A	10	2	20
B	1000	2	0.2

$$\textit{Spurious average \% wastage} = \frac{(20 + 0.2)}{2} = 10.1\%$$

$$\text{True mean \% wastage} = \frac{(2 + 2)}{(1000 + 10)} \times 100$$

$$= \frac{4}{1010} \times 100$$

$$= 0.4\%$$

In this extreme case the spurious average is a long way out because it wrongly gives the same weighting to the wastage in the very small department as to the small one. The spurious percentage would, if applied to the combined departments, imply

$$\frac{10.1}{100} \times 1010 = 102.01$$

$$= 102$$

suggesting 102 leavers instead of 4!

Exercise

A company uses three raw materials A,B,C. The percentage price increase just announced together with last years expenditure on these items is shown below.

SIMPLIFYING DATA

Last years expenditure on raw materials (£)	Percentage increase in price
232,000	19
17,500	37
1,230,000	2

Calculate the mean percentage increase in price for the company's raw materials.

5.4 Comparing Percentages – Significance

5.4.1 Percentages are often produced for the purpose of comparison with other percentages. The presentation in Table 5.5 invites a comparison of the wastage rates in five departments, that in Table 5.6 shows the varying percentage of rejects in 5 batches.

If we isolate the last two departments shown in Table 5.4 we are faced with the problem of deciding whether the difference between 4.0% 8.3% is one which is worthy of note or not. The instinctive reaction of most people would be to accept that these figures suggest that a real difference exists between the departments as regards wastage. As to whether investigation of the causes or action is required is another matter. Perhaps both figures are below the limits set as tolerances by the personnel department or perhaps we have a good idea why such a difference is to be expected. Perhaps there have been recent staff problems in Department E, for instance.

Now look at batches 3 and 5 in Table 5.6 on page 159. I think that most people would instinctively feel that the difference between these figures was not worthy of note. They would be seen as being 'about the same'.

This distinction between differences which are not worthy of note, the sort of differences which can be explained in terms of chance variations, and differences which have their source in real underlying causes, opens up the subject of *Statistical Significance*. At this stage you need merely note that some differences between percentages could just be the product of chance variation especially when the base is small. A more detailed coverage of this concept will be covered in Chapter 10.

5.5 Pareto Analysis: a powerful application of percentage analysis

Pareto Analysis is a technique which employs percentages in a way which helps to bring out the relative importance of the components of

QUANTITATIVE METHODS

large quantities of statistical information. It provides the manager and the analyst with a simple technique which helps him to decide where to concentrate his limited valuable time and effort.

5.5.1 Example

Suppose that you were setting out to improve the efficiency of a stock control system. Typically stock control systems are characterised by the large number of different items held in stock. Analysis of all these items is a daunting task. It seems sensible to classify the items and then apply a level of analysis to each class which ensures that the majority of management time is invested on those items which show the highest potential savings. The base data is shown in Table 5.14.

Table 5.14

A company has 10,000 parts held in store. The following figures represent a random sample of last years expenditure on 20 items in £ per annum.

85	27	835	18
8	106	7	6
4624	41	275	20
165	2064	16	6
8	470	614	65

The pareto analysis proceeds as, follows the results being shown in Table 5.15 on page 169.

Step 1: Rank the usage figures in descending order and sum the total usage (col 3).

Step 2: Calculate the usage for each item as a % of the total usage. Thus for the first item, with a usage of £4624 out of a total of £9460 we obtain a percentage of $\frac{4624}{9460} \times 100 = 48.9\%$.

Step 3: Calculate the cumulative percentage usage for the ranked items and the rank as a percentage of the maximum rank. Thus the first ranked item, $\frac{1}{20} \times 100 = 5\%$ of the total constitutes 48.9% of the total usage. The first and second items, $\frac{2}{20} \times 100 = 10\%$ of the total items, cover between them $(48.9 + 21.8) = 70.7\%$ of the total annual usage.

Step 4: On a piece of graph paper, draw a vertical scale marked 0% to 100% and a horizontal scale marked likewise. Label the horizontal scale 'Cumulative Percentage of items' and the vertical scale, 'Cumulative Percentage of usage'. Columns 2 and 5 of Table 5.15 can now be plotted on the graph as a Pareto Curve.

SIMPLIFYING DATA

Table 5.15 : Pareto Analysis based on Table 5.14

1 Rank Number	2 Rank as % of % of Total (Cumulative)	3 Usage (£)	4 Usage as % of	5 Cumulative usage as % of Total	1 Rank Number	2 Rank as % of Total (Cumulative)	3 Usage (£)	4 Usage as % of Total	5 Cumulative usage as % of Total
1	5	4624	48.9	48.9	11	55	41	0.4	98.7
2	10	2064	21.8	70.7	12	60	27	0.3	99.0
3	15	835	8.8	79.5	13	65	20	0.2	99.2
4	20	614	6.5	86.0	14	70	18	0.2	99.4
5	25	470	5.0	91.0	15	75	16	0.2	99.6
6	30	275	2.9	93.9	16	80	8	0.1	99.7
7	35	165	1.7	95.6	17	85	8	0.1	99.8
8	40	106	1.1	96.7	18	90	7	0.1	99.9
9	45	85	0.9	97.6	19	95	6	0.05	99.95
10	50	65	0.7	98.3	20	100	6	0.05	100.0

Total Usage : £9460

169

QUANTITATIVE METHODS

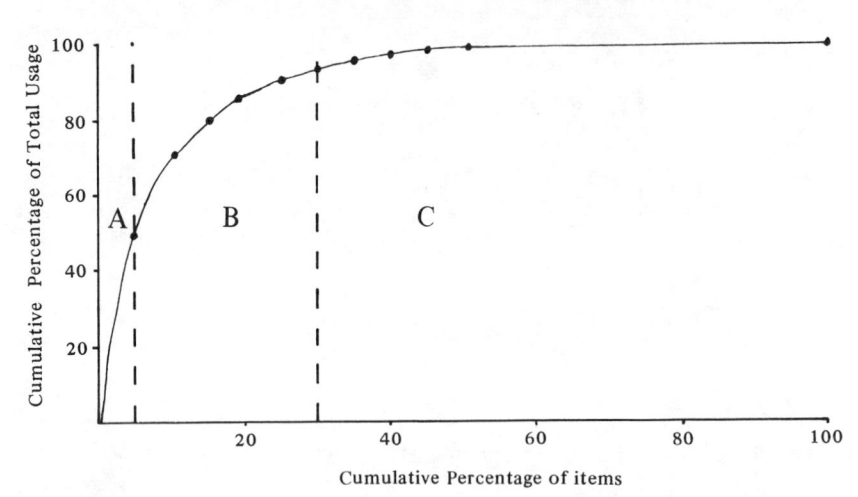

Fig 5.1 : Pareto Curve based on Table 5.15

The resulting curve is shown in Figure 5.1 the degree of flexing in the curve is a measure of the extent to which a high proportion of the total annual turnover is concentrated in a small proportion of the items. The way I have divided the items into 3 categories is somewhat arbitrary but the result provides a useful basis for starting detailed analysis. The procedure has acquired the term 'ABC' analysis.

Category A: 5% of items comprising 49% of the total value.

Category B: 25% of items comprising another 45% of the total value.

Category C: 70% of items comprising the remaining 6% of the total value.

By analysing a mere 5% of items the analyst can get to grips with almost half of the annual stock turnover. Thus elaborate analysis concentrated on relatively few items would be an efficient way of seeking large potential savings.

Conversely, relatively crude techniques can be applied to the great majority of items, 70% in all, generous safety margins being allowed to make up for the cursory nature of the analysis. Because such a loose approach will apply to less than 10% of the stock in value terms, the purchasing manager runs little risk of incurring large financial penalties.

SIMPLIFYING DATA

5.5.2 Example

The situation facing a manager required to cut waste in a factory making roofing felt provides another example of Pareto analysis. Roofing felt, such as might be used for covering a garage or garden shed, is made up of a number of ingredients some of them expensive and some of them cheap. The product basically consists of strong paper, sometimes lined with special material, coated with bitumen on which a variety of materials can be laid, some sort of sand (aggregate) being a common component, one which can be provided in a number of different colours.

Table 5.16 : Materials Usage in Roof Coverings

		Usage (£)	% of Total			Usage (£)	% of Total
1.	Aggregates	33,803	28.7	7.	Asbestos	7.478	6.3
2.	Rag	21,145	17.9	8.	Packaging	7,323	6.2
3.	Polyester	14,643	12.4	9.	Rope Brown	4,716	4.0
4.	Glass Fibre	9,378	8.0	10.	Aluminium	1,043	0.9
5.	Bituman	8,847	7.5	11.	Polythene	629	0.5
6.	Hessian	8,806	7.5				
					Total	117,811	

An obvious starting point would be to start looking at those materials with the highest unit value, such as Aluminium sheet, used in some special orders. The Pareto analysis suggests a different approach (Fig. 5.2). In this version the individual percentage frequencies are shown in ranked order together with the curve.

Fig 5.2 : Pareto Analysis based on Table 5.16

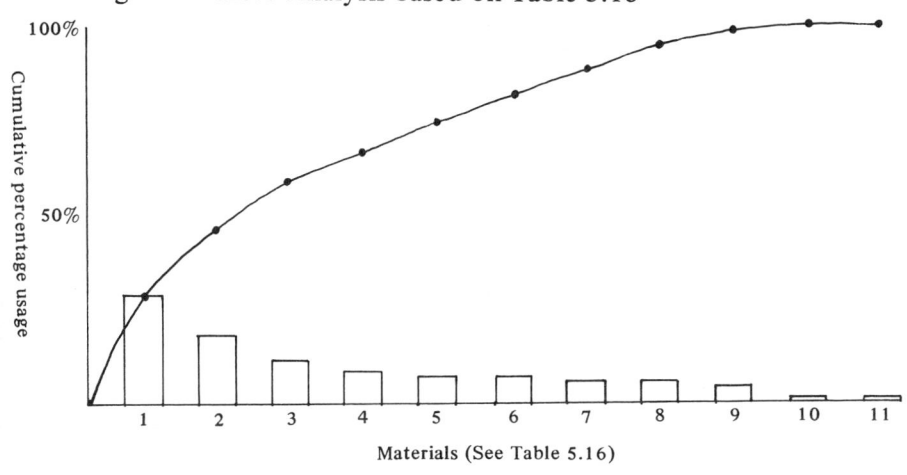

QUANTITATIVE METHODS

It turns out that an unromantic material, sand (aggregates), constitutes 28% of the potential materials savings, whereas a highly-priced item, polythene, constitutes only a negligible percentage of these. In fact the manager concerned was able to obtain dramatic savings by fitting up the machinery with buckets to trap clean sand trickling down to the ground under the machines. Before his action, it had been allowed to fall on the ground from where it could not be recovered. Misled by its low unit *price*, people had not taken account of the high usage involved and the consequently high potential for savings.

Pareto analysis is widely used in Quality Circle practice to help highlight areas for concentrating effort. This use is discussed in detail in Ishikawa (1983).

5.5.3 Example

Canon and Galvao (1980) describe an application which illustrates the special features that characterise stock problems in different organisations. In 1979, in Brazil, importers were required to deposit a high percentage of the total value of the import licence with the state owned bank. Not only was this sum devalued by the high inflation rates experienced in that country, but no interest was paid on the deposit either. Effectively this doubled the value of an imported item. The company needed a quick improvement in its financial position. Its total stock amounted to $1M, and the compulsory deposit was about $0.4M. The first stage of the analysis categorised the stock items by country of origin.

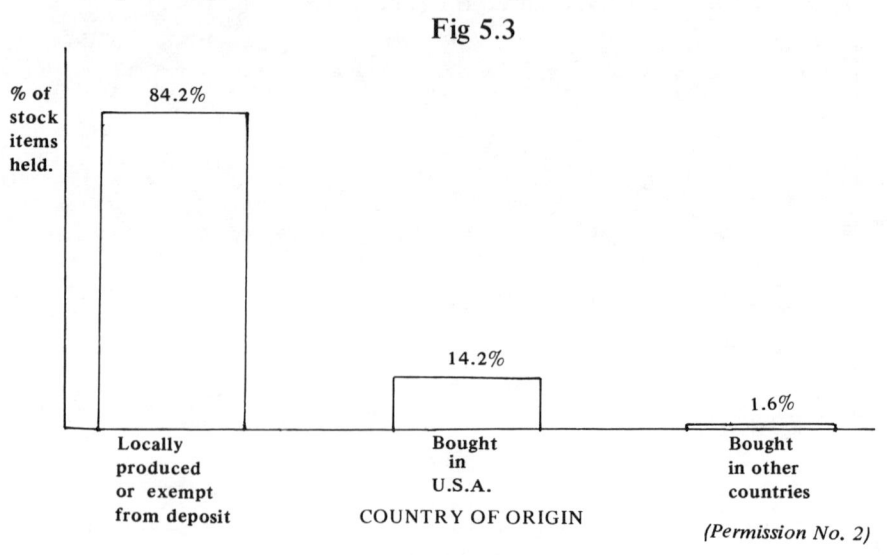

Fig 5.3

% of stock items held.

84.2% — Locally produced or exempt from deposit

14.2% — Bought in U.S.A.

1.6% — Bought in other countries

COUNTRY OF ORIGIN

(Permission No. 2)

SIMPLIFYING DATA

This tells us that only for a small proportion of the *items* was a deposit required. The next stage is to look at a pareto curve splitting the items up on an ABC basis.

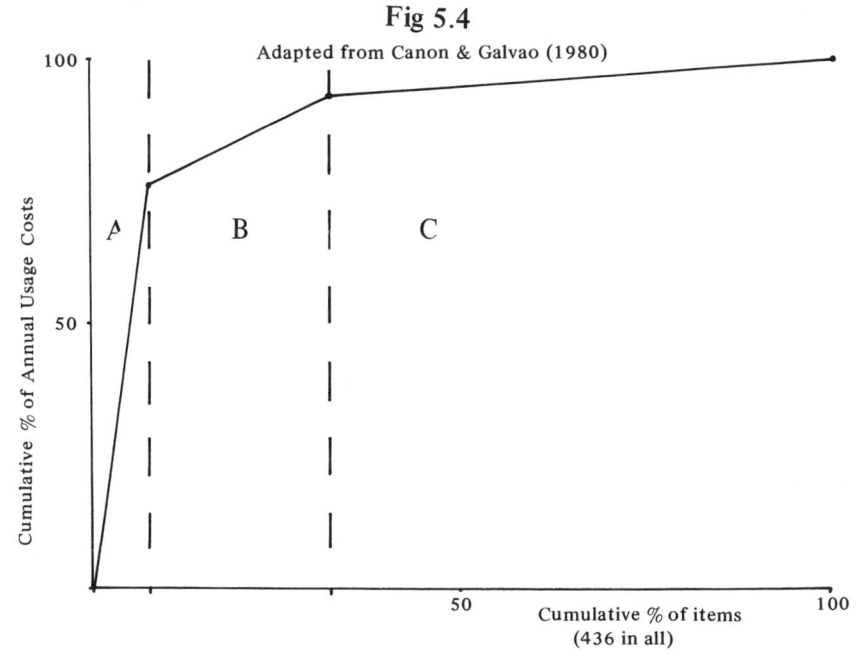

Fig 5.4

Adapted from Canon & Galvao (1980)

which can also be expressed as in Figure 5.5

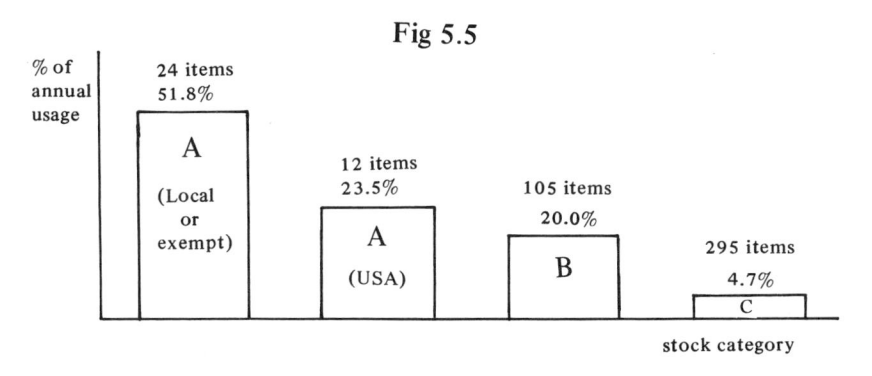

Fig 5.5

This indicates that 75% of stock usage (51.8% + 23.5%) involved only 36 items (24 + 12) and a breakdown of the 'A' items by source shows that nearly a quarter of the annual usage (23.5%) involved merely 12 imported items which were subject to punitive deposit regulations.

QUANTITATIVE METHODS

Rigorous control of these 12 items produced about 30% reduction in stock-related costs and highlighted the need to find alternative exempt sources of supply.

Exercise

1. Suppose the following data represents the value (£) of goods sold to 20 customers by a firm. Use Pareto analysis to write a brief report on the market.

2347	36987	456	589	9578
12478	5836	1147	89256	956
367	1258	632	2589	487
1105	2009	2598	258	632

2. How could pareto analysis be used in your own organisation? Try and get some relevant data and carry out your own analysis

5.6 Pictorial representation of data : Bar Charts

I've deliberately left this section to the end of the chapter. Simple tables of numerical information in a digestible form are an effective way of getting information across and key numbers can be emphasised by marking them with a highlighting pen. However graphs and charts can enhance the message by endowing the data with a shape that gives it impact. The bars in Fig 5.3 on page 172, for example, do not tell us anything that is not contained in the numbers 84.2%, 14.2% and 1.6%. But the different sizes of the bars do help to emphasise the relativities especially for people who have difficulty in assimilating numbers.

5.6.1 Problems with Bar Charts

Table 5.17 shows the drop in passenger car production in the United Kingdom up to 1981.

Table 5.17 : Passenger Car Production in the United Kingdom 1972-1981 (thousands): Annual Abstracts, 1983

	1972	1978	1979	1980	1981
Total	1920	1220	1070	920	950
Up to 1000 cc	250	150	130	160	230
1000 cc – 1600 cc	1030	700	620	520	530
1600 cc – 2800 cc	570	310	280	210	150
2800 cc	80	70	50	40	50

(Permission No. 6) (figures rounded)

In Fig 5.6 the numbers in each year are represented by bars whose whose length is porportional to the numbers involved.

SIMPLIFYING DATA

Fig 5.6

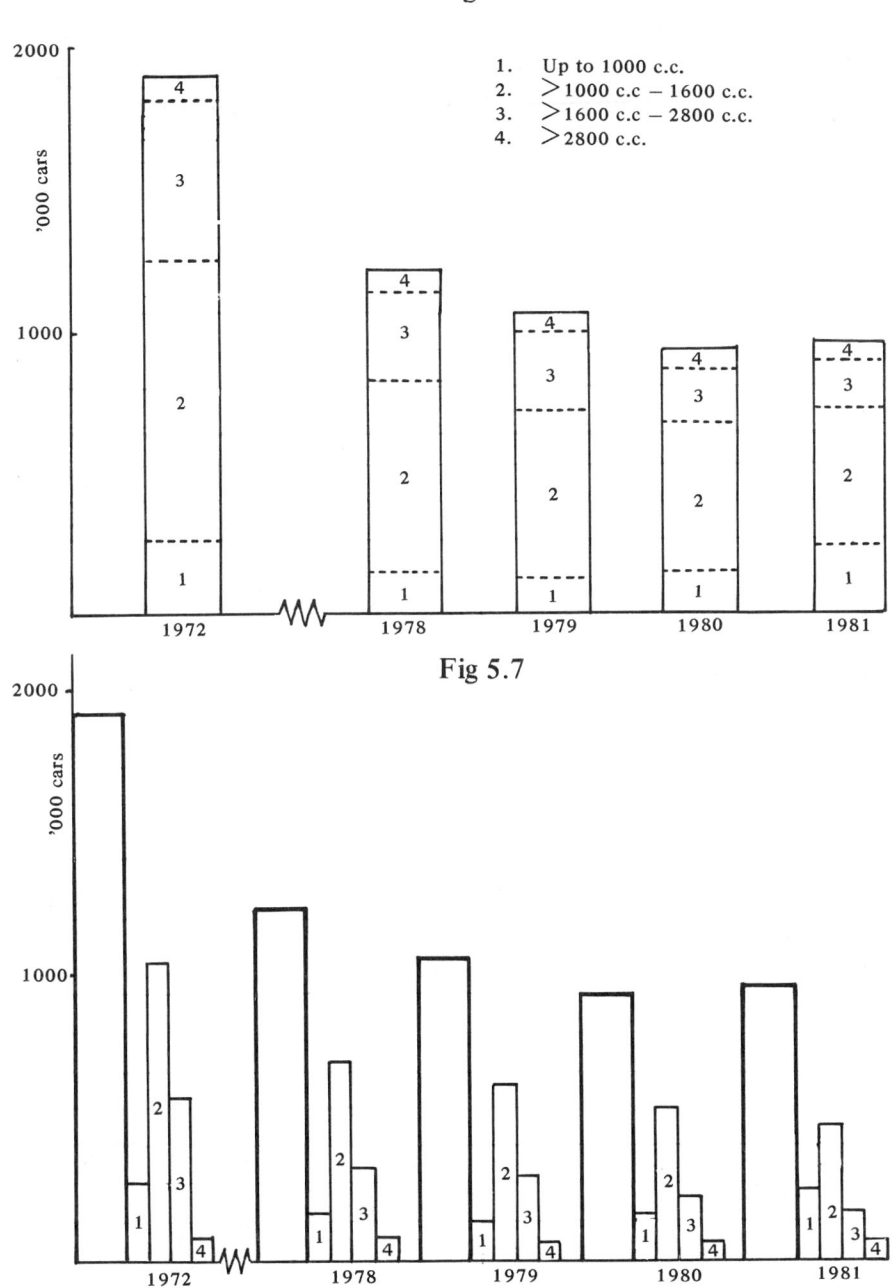

1. Up to 1000 c.c.
2. >1000 c.c – 1600 c.c.
3. >1600 c.c – 2800 c.c.
4. >2800 c.c.

Fig 5.7

QUANTITATIVE METHODS

To show the breakdown by engine capacity, a *component bar chart* can be used. Of the two versions, Fig 5.7 is preferable to Fig 5.6 because the values of the component parts can be read off the left-hand scale more easily in the second version. If the percentage breakdown is to be emphasised rather than the trends in total levels, a *percentage component bar chart* can be drawn.

Fig 5.8

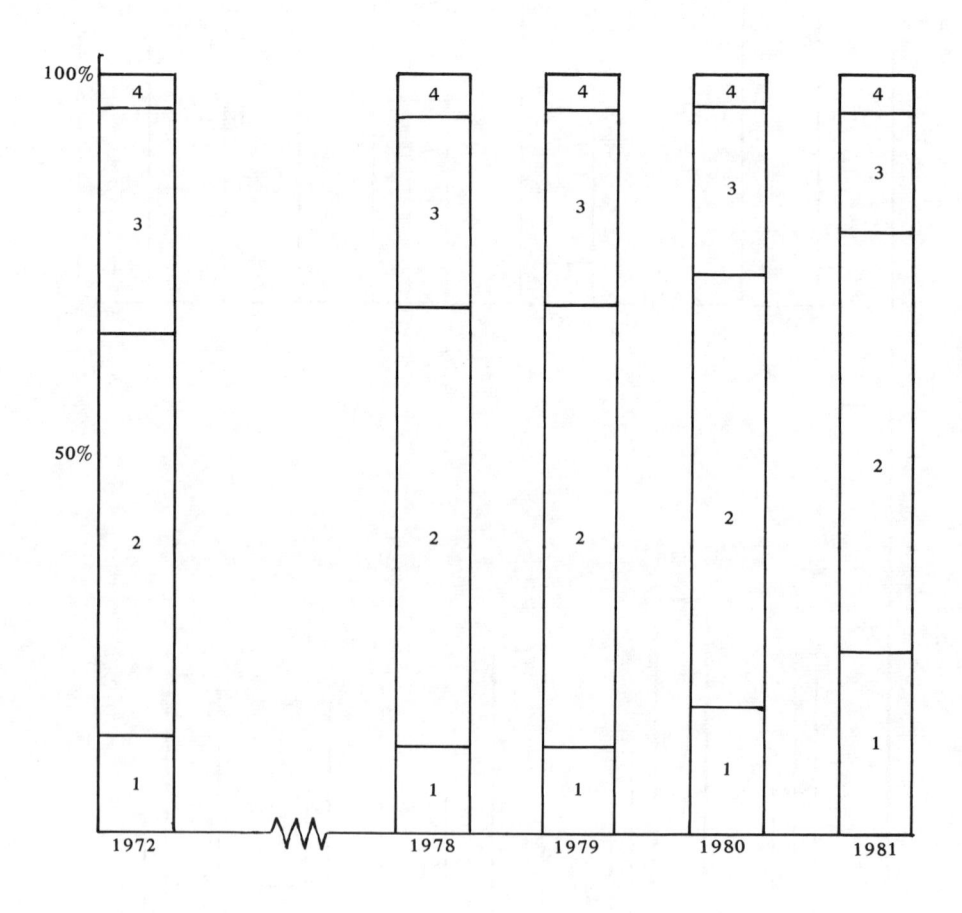

SIMPLIFYING DATA

It always used to be thought that supplementing bar charts with numerical information caused confusion. Now computer graphics are helping to re-write the rule books. I can't demonstrate the effects here, but colour, when cleverly used, enables you to pack a VDU screen with information of a mixed numerical and pictorial nature. The different colours help prevent the brain from becoming overloaded with information. You can find good examples of the use of colour in the annual reports of major companies and on financial television programmes such as the 'Money Programme'. Cheap computer graphics are now widely available on inexpensive microcomputers.

5.7 Using Pictures

The increasing accessibility of cheap computer graphics including animation facilities will increasingly lead people to use pictures to help tell the story behind the data. Care must be taken not to distort the information contained in the underlying figures.

5.7.1 Pie Charts

Pie charts are a popular and effective way of showing the relative size of the component parts of a figure, you will find many examples used in annual reports where colour is extensively used to highlight the segments of the chart. I will illustrate the way to draw them up by referring to Fig. 5.3 on page 172. Clearly 84.2% of the pie must be allocated to locally produced or exempt items. There are 360 degrees in a circle and so I allocate $360 \times \frac{84.2}{100} = 303$ degrees of the circle to this category which I can do using a protractor.

Figure 5.9 : Pie chart representation of Fig 5 showing required angles

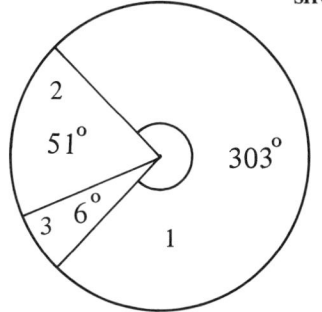

1. Locally produced or exempt

2. Bought in U.S.A.

3. Bought in other countries

Care needs to be taken when comparing two pie charts of different sizes. Suppose a company has sales for products as shown in Table 5.18.

QUANTITATIVE METHODS

Table 5.18 : Sales of two products (Units sold)

Product	A	B	Total
Year 1 sales	5	30	35
Year 2 sales	41	55	96

I want the 'pies' to show the change in product mix but suppose at the same time that I want the relative size of the pies to indicate the increase in sales units. If I draw the Year 1 pie with a diameter of 2 centimetres then the Year 2 pie needs to have an *area* $\frac{96}{35}$ = 2.7 times the area of the first pie. This is because the viewer will compare the relative size of the two pictures and these should reflect the increase in total sales. As the area of a circle is proportional to the *square* of the diameter of a circle, the Year 2 pie should have a diameter = 2 x$\sqrt{2.7}$ = 3.3 cms.

Fig 5.10 : Pie chart showing relative sales and market shares for two products A & B (See Table 5.18)

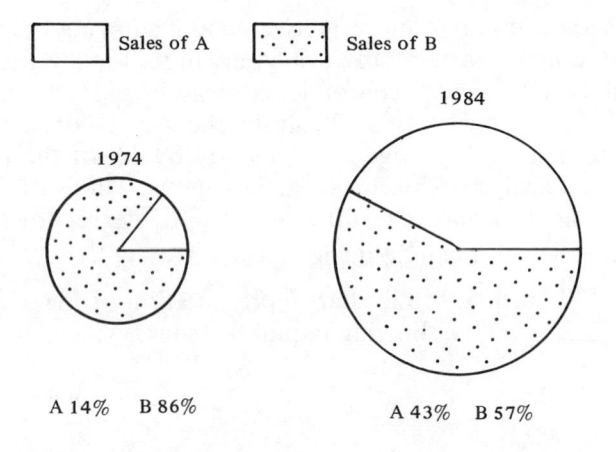

☐ Sales of A   ▦ Sales of B

1974

1984

A 14% B 86%   A 43% B 57%

5.7.2 Squares and Boxes

In representing the total sales figures in Table 5.18 above in pictorial form, the visual impact of the picture must be fair and its size proportional to the figures being compared. Fig 5.11 shows the total sales figures compared on a fair and an unfair basis.

SIMPLIFYING DATA

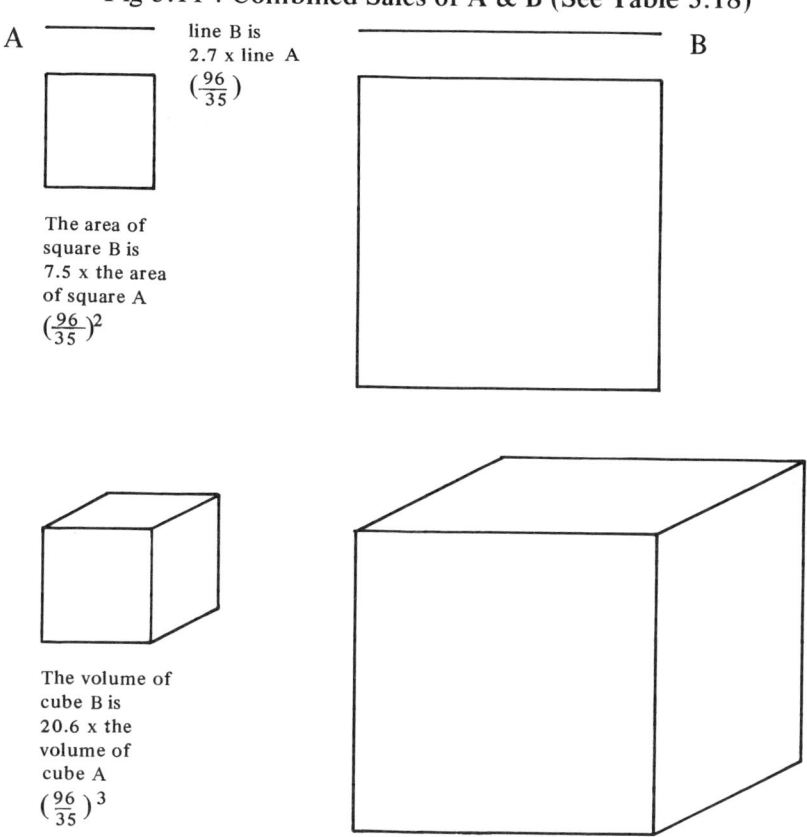

Fig 5.11 : Combined Sales of A & B (See Table 5.18)

A ——————   line B is   —————————————— B
                2.7 x line A
                $(\frac{96}{35})$

The area of
square B is
7.5 x the area
of square A
$(\frac{96}{35})^2$

The volume of
cube B is
20.6 x the
volume of
cube A
$(\frac{96}{35})^3$

Note the dramatic exaggeration produced by the cube. If you *must* compare cubes then it should have a side which is a factor $\sqrt[3]{\frac{96}{35}} = 1.4$ times the 1984 cube.

5.7.3 Picture Bars

In 1981 954,000 cars were produced compared with 1,920,000 in 1972. Some people like to liven up the bar chart destined to represent this change by making the 'bar' consist of little cars.

Fig 5.12 : Production of Passenger Cars (UK)

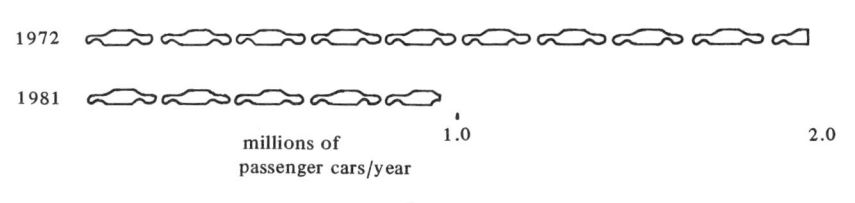

1972 🚗🚗🚗🚗🚗🚗🚗🚗🚗

1981 🚗🚗🚗🚗🚗
                      millions of   1.0   2.0
                      passenger cars/year

QUANTITATIVE METHODS

Although the effect can be a bit irritating, it is not misleading because all the cars are made of the same dimensions and so, in effect, a simple bar chart has been drawn. However, if two cars are drawn with the heights of the bonnets, say, of length proportional to the production figures, a misleading effect will be produced because the eye will compare the relative areas occupied by the two pictures.

Fig 5.13 : Misleading Version of Fig 5.12

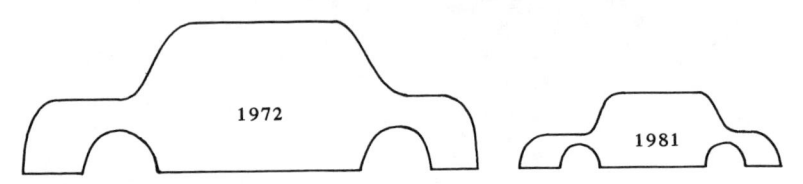

Computer graphics experts should be restrained. An excess of enthusiasm for what is pictorially exciting could lead to distortion of the facts.

5.8   Problems with Graphs

The 'Gee Whiz' effect

Since Darrell Huff christened it in his classic book (Huff 1973), the 'gee whiz' graph has been seen less frequently of late. By truncating the vertical axis and foreshortening or stretching the horizontal axis, the same graph can be made to undergo apparent changes as shown in Fig 5.14. Examine the graphs carefully and satisfy yourself that whatever their shape *they are all saying the same thing.* Even so it's hard not to see the rise in Fig 5.14b as 'steeper' in some way than 5.14a.

Fig 5.14a : Letters & Telephone Calls 1971–1981
(from Table 5.1)

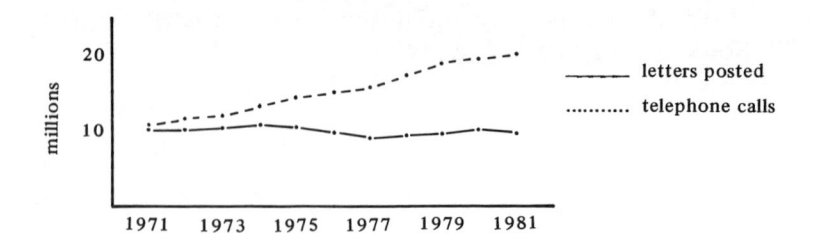

SIMPLIFYING DATA

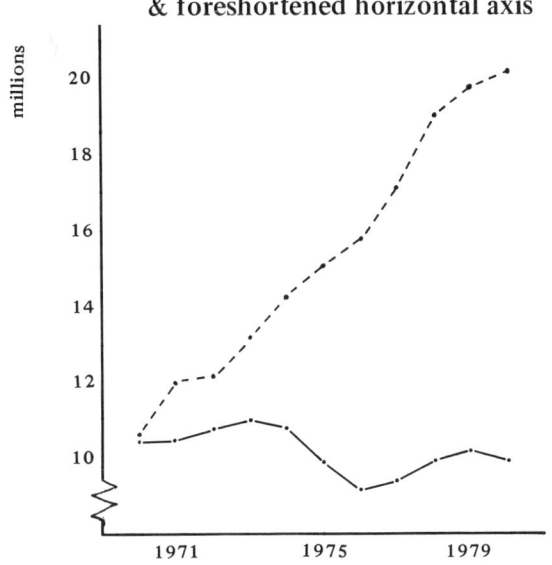

Fig 5.14b : Version of 5.14a with truncated vertical axis & foreshortened horizontal axis

Often it is quite reasonable to truncate the axes and this should be indicated by a clear break in the line as demonstrated in Fig 5.14. Just remember that most people will not examine the axes very carefully so the scope for misinterpretation is quite large.

Exercise

1. Use graphs to supplement your summary in Exercise 1 on page 157.

2. Use graphs to show the trends in Table 5.17 on page 174. Be careful with the horizontal axis.

A further discussion of graphs and the use of semi-log paper will be found in Chapter 8, page 285.

CHAPTER 6 : COMPOUND INTEREST & DISCOUNTING

The first section, 6.1, demonstrates the breadth of applicability of the concept of interest payments. Section 6.2 shows how compound interest is calculated, while Section 6.3 indicates how the effects of inflation can be forecast. Sections 6.4 to 6.7 show how future money can be valued using present value techniques and Sections 6.8 and 6.9, which end the chapter, cover Investment Appraisal and Decision Analysis.

6.1 When Compound Interest Applies

When you borrow money you usually have to pay interest to the lender. For example many people have mortgages and the greater part of the monthly payments represents interest paid to those who have deposited funds with the society. Most people expect to earn interest on any money that they have left over after keeping their bank account running and providing themselves with sufficient ready cash. In fact many people nowadays run their current account from a building society.

The interest rate is usually expressed as a percentage rate per annum. So 11% per annum means that interest will be paid out at a rate of £11 per year for every £100 invested. Although interest is sometimes calculated over a whole year, it is often calculated over a shorter period. So, for example, a building society advertising a *rate* of 11% per annum will in fact pay out interest of £5.5 per £100 every 6 months.

Apart from the familiar examples of building society and bank deposit accounts, there are many other situations where the laws of interest are applicable and yet which are not commonly recognised as such. It's important to realise that the concept of interest is vital to all financial transactions. So before dealing with the technicalities of the subject, take a look at the following cases.

6.1.1. Delayed Payments

I recently received a bill for £2500 for the fitting of a new roof. I had already set aside the sum in a building society account earning interest at a rate of 8% per annum after tax. When the invoice arrived my first reaction was to pay the sum immediately. I don't like bills hanging over me, and after all I had the exact sum carefully set aside. It then occurred to me to calculate the interest that I could earn on the

COMPOUND INTEREST & DISCOUNTING

£2500 if I were to delay the payment for a few days. I have always been aware of how surprised some traders are when I pay them promptly so this time I felt I could allow a modest time period to elapse. The calculation goes as follows:

$$\frac{8}{100} \times £2500 \times \frac{1}{365} = £0.55 \text{ per day}$$

So each day the bill is delayed, the sum I had set aside for its payment earned 55p. A weeks delay would be worth £3.85. A month (30 days) would earn me no less than £16.50.

While I was inwardly debating the morality of the situation, a sharp note came from the contractor reminding me that the payment terms were 'on receipt of invoice'. Clearly this particular firm understood the costs involved in delayed payments and if I had attempted to ignore their letter, they would probably have made some threat to my credit standing. However, despite their prompt action in this instance, it is my experience that many traders delay an extraordinary amount of time before even bothering to send out an invoice. If they read this chapter and as a result speed up their clerical procedures a little, then they can rapidly cover the cost of this book. During the period of high interest rates in the seventies, some large and powerful firms made a practice of delaying large bills sent in by small suppliers. They compounded this essentially unethical procedure by artificially querying the invoice to increase the delay.

6.1.2. Bills of Exchange

An ordinary pound note has written on it

> 'I promise to pay the bearer on demand the sum of One Pound'
> —Bank of England

Of course if you try to enforce this promise all you will get is another pound note to take its place. Now suppose the Bank of England offered to sell today the following promise in the form of a bill which does not pay interest.

> 'I promise to pay the bearer in 1 years time the sum of £100'
> —Bank of England

Assuming that the Bank of England will pay up (for if it did not then the whole foundations of business and the relevance of this book would largely disappear), just what sort of price should a prospective buyer pay for the bill? By buying the bill, the purchasers are effect-

QUANTITATIVE METHODS

ively depositing money with the Bank of England now and being repaid one year later. They will therefore require to be paid interest and as the bill itself carries no interest, they will surely pay less than its repayment value now. If they expect 7% on loans to the government they might pay £93.46 for the bill in question. Why? Well, they are parting with £93.46 for a year and will expect to be paid 7% interest. Their calculation is laid out below:

Principal = £93.46

One years interest at 7%
= $\frac{7}{100}$ x £93.46 = £6.54

Sum to be repaid plus interest = £100.00

In paying only £93.46 for the bill now, the buyer has *discounted* the bill, recognising that to buy it is effectively to lend for a year at interest.

6.1.3 Stockholding

A dealer stocks car parts for sale in a high street shop. Amongst the many items in stock are two parts: one is a lamp unit which costs £5 and another is a portable tyre pump costing £10. Table 6.1 shows how the stockholding of these parts changes over a six month period.

Table 6.1

End of month	Lamp Units at £5	Pump Units at £10	Value of stock held £ (units x price)	Value of stock held £ (sum of col. 4)
January	10	100	50 + 1000 =	1050
February	100	90	500 + 900 =	1400
March	80	70	400 + 700 =	1100
April	50	60	250 + 600 =	850
May	30	50	150 + 500 =	650
June	80	20	400 + 200 =	600
				£5650

The mean value of his holding during the 6 months has been £$\frac{5650}{6}$ = £942 per month. If the dealer had invested that sum at, say, 8% he would have earned

£942 x $\frac{8}{100}$ = £75.36 over a year

COMPOUND INTEREST & DISCOUNTING

or £37.68 over 6 months.

In this case, the interest rate is the *opportunity cost* of capital tied up in stock. It is the cost of losing the opportunity to invest the sum in an interest-bearing deposit (or some other profitable activity) rather than investing it in stock which does not earn interest. Of course the cost of stocking may be offset by a resulting increase in sales.

In all the examples mentioned, the interest rate provides a common link. We need now to understand how interest works.

6.2 How Interest Works

Interest rates vary from day to day in response to government decisions and policies and to market forces. On any one day, however, a wide range of interest rates are to be found depending on

1. The amount involved
2. The period during which money is tied up
3. The riskiness of the loan

Most Financial institutions have higher rates available for larger sums or in accounts where a minimum balance must be held. The way rates are influenced by the period of the loan can be seen in the following Local Authority deposit rates on 16th December 1983 (minimum amount not stated)

Overnight	$8\frac{3}{4}$
7 days notice	$8\frac{7}{8}$
One month	$9\frac{3}{16}\%$
Two months	$9\frac{5}{16}\%$
Three months	$9\frac{1}{2}\%$
One year	$10\frac{1}{8}\%$

Risky loans, such as those made by a pawnborker or a money lender are always at higher rates of interest.

6.2.1 Calculation Interest Over Short Periods

Interest rates are usually quoted on a per annum basis. Often,

QUANTITATIVE METHODS

however, we need to work out the interest payable over relatively short periods. You will have noted in the rates quoted that interest is even payable on an overnight basis. What would £500,000 earn on an overnight basis (1 day) at an annual rate of $8\frac{3}{4}\%$?

$$£500{,}000 \times \frac{8.75}{100} \times \frac{1}{365} = £119.86$$

Note that we first calculate the annual interest payable and then scale down the sum depending on the fraction of a year applicable. Calculations like this demonstrate that careful cash management can literally pay dividends.

This technique can be used to decide whether a cash discount should be accepted on an invoice. Suppose a trader has received an invoice for £632 and is offered a 1% discount on immediate payment. The trader would normally pay within 60 days. He can earn 6% net on money deposited.

$$\text{Value of discount} = £632 \times \frac{1}{100} = £6.32$$

Interest earned on £632 over 60 days

$$= £632 \times \frac{6}{100} \times \frac{60}{365} = £6.23$$

It seems to be worth taking the discount. However we must be sure that 6% is the correct opportunity cost of capital. Maybe it is true that the most the trader can earn on deposit is 6%. Suppose however that he has an overdraft on which he is paying 10%. In that case he can effectively 'earn' 10% by reducing his overdraft by £632 for 60 days instead of paying the bill promptly. The comparison then looks like this

$$\begin{aligned}
\text{Value of discount} &= £6.32 \\
\text{Saving on overdraft for 60 days} &= £632 \times \frac{10}{100} \times \frac{60}{365} \\
&= £10.39
\end{aligned}$$

and the decision now goes the other way. The trader must bear in mind that there are unquantifiable benefits to be gained by being a prompt payer and disbenefits from gaining a reputation for being a slow payer.

COMPOUND INTEREST & DISCOUNTING

Exercise

1. Calculate the interest payable on the following (all rates are per annum):

    i)   £463 at 11% for 1 year
    ii)   £213 at 14% for 6 months
    iii)   £339 at 10% for 29 days
    iv)   £39,560 at 12% overnight

2. A businessman is due to invoice a customer for £14,500. He is currently paying 14% on his overdraft and he knows that the customer usually takes 2 months to pay. How much is immediate payment by the customer worth to the businessman?

3. On the 1st January, in anticipation of a price rise, a factory buys 10 units of a product at a cost of £120 each. It uses 6 units at the end of April when the price has risen to £125 and uses the other 4 at the end of June by which time the price has risen to £130. The store pays 16% per annum on its overdraft. Assuming negligible warehousing and insurance costs, and that the store could have obtained goods on demand from its suppliers as and when when required, was it worth their while stocking up in advance?

4. A company is offered a 2% discount on £23,000 worth of goods which it needs in 5 months time providing that they pay cash now. They would normally pay on delivery and their overdraft costs them 12%. Should they accept the offer?

6.2.2 Compound Interest

When people place money in the deposit account of a bank or in the building society, they often leave the interest payments in their account thereby earning interest on the interest payments themselves. Their deposit is then said to be earning *compound interest*. If they get the interest payments paid to them on a regular basis as it arises, then the payments are referred to as *simple interest*. The following numerical example will illustrate the principles involved.

Example

What does £100 accumulate to over 3 years earning interest at 8% per annum?

The working is laid out in the following table

QUANTITATIVE METHODS

Table 6.2

	Amount on Deposit at start of Year	End of Year Interest	Amount Carried Forward
1.	100.00	8.00	108.00
2.	108.00	8.64	116.64
3.	116.64	9.33	125.97

The interest paid at the end of year two can be thought of as consisting of two parts:

1. Interest on original £100 = 8.00
2. Interest on £8.00 interest earned in Year 1 = 0.64

Total Year 2 interest = 8.64

But of course it is not necessary to break down the sums involved in this way. So the £9.33 interest paid at the end of year 3 is simply calculated as

$$£116.64 + \left(£116.64 \times \frac{8}{100}\right) = £125.97$$

In most cases we don't need to know the way in which the sum desposited grows from year to year. All we need to know is the sum to which our deposit will accumulate in the specified number of years. The following formula will provide the answer

The principal (the sum invested) placed on deposit for a number of time periods at a stated interest rate per period will accumulate to:

$$\text{Principal} \times \left(1 + \frac{\% \text{ Rate per period}}{100}\right)^{\text{No. of Periods}}$$

So applying this formula to the example shown in Table 6.2 we get:

$$£100.00 \times \left(1 + \frac{8}{100}\right)^3$$

$$= £100.00 \times (1.08)^3 = £100.00 \times 1.2597$$

$$= £125.97$$

The quantity

$$\left(1 + \frac{\% \text{ Rate per period}}{100}\right)^{\text{No. of Periods}}$$

COMPOUND INTEREST & DISCOUNTING

is known as the *compound amount factor* and tables of factors are available in Appendix 5a on page 457.

6.2.3 Fractional Years

When a fractional number of years is involved then proceed as in the following example. What is the compound interest earned on £485 at 11% for 6½ years?

£485 at 11% for 6 years + ½ years interest on the amount accumulated at the end of the 6th year.

$= £485 \times (1 + \frac{11}{100})^6$

$+ \frac{1}{2}$ years interest on the same.

$= £485 \times 1.87 + \frac{1}{2}$ years interest on the same

$= £907.15 + (907.15 \times \frac{11}{100} \times \frac{1}{2})$

$= £907.15 + £49.89$

$= £957.04$

The answer will be different, however, if interest is compounded more frequently than on an annual basis.

Exercise

1. Calculate
     i) £332 on deposit at 11% for 6 years
     ii) £192 on deposit at 7% for 4 years
     iii) £3,097 on deposit at 14% for 11 years
     iv) £1,000 on deposit at 10% for 50 years

2. Calculate
     i) £413 on deposit at 13% p.a. for 3.5 years
     ii) £391 on deposit at 11.5% p.a. for 6 years and 2 months

6.2.4 Compounding Other than Annually

Sometimes interest is compounded more than once a year. Most building societies add the interest twice a year and your credit card does so monthly. As the interest itself starts to earn interest before

QUANTITATIVE METHODS

waiting until the end of the year, such a method of compounding effectively increases the interest rate. In Table 6.3 you can see the effect or reworking the example of Table 6.2 on page 188 with twice-yearly compounding. The interest rate is now effectively 4% per 6-month period.

TABLE 6.3

Year	Amount on Deposit	End of Half-year Interest	Amount Carried forward
0.5	100.00	4.00	104.00
1.0	104.00	4.16	108.16
1.5	108.16	4.33	112.49
2.0	112.49	4.50	116.99
2.5	116.99	4.68	121.67
3.0	121.67	4.87	126.54

Note that at the end of the first half of Year 1, £4 ($\frac{£8}{2}$) interest has already been added to the principal. By the end of the first year this small half-yearly interest has contributed 16p to the interest earned in the second half of the first year. Comparing this result with that shown in Table 6.2, you can see that the final sum is (£126.54 − £125.97) = £0.57 higher than is the case when interest is compounded annually. In fact it gives the same result as would be obtained by compounding *once* a year at a rate of 8.16% instead of 8%.

Table 6.4 shows the effect of different compounding arrangements on the effective annual interest rate.

TABLE 6.4
Annual Rate of 8% Compounded at Different Frequencies

Once a year	8
Twice a year	8.16
Four times	8.24
Monthly	8.30
Daily	8.32

So it is well worth finding out the precise basis on which compounding is carried out when comparing deposit arrangements. The same applies to loans when you need to know the basis on which the interest that you will be required to pay is calculated. When a credit card company charges 2% per month, say, this is compounded monthly. So a £100 debt accumulates to

$$£100 \times (1 + \frac{2}{100})^{12} = £126.82$$

190

COMPOUND INTEREST & DISCOUNTING

in a year. Therefore the annual equivalent rate of interest is 26.82% and not 12 x 2 = 24%.

From Table 6.4 you can see that it is possible to have interest added on a continuous basis and indeed some banks do offer such a facility. However it is not quite as advantageous as it seems at first sight, being only marginally more advantageous than compounding twice yearly.

Example

Calculate the value of £2500 on deposit at 12% p.a. compounded quarterly over 5 years.

Effectively we have $\frac{12}{4}$ = 3% interest per quarter over 5 x 4 = 20 quarters. Therefore we will end up with

$$£2500 \times (1 + \frac{3}{100})^{20}$$

= £4515.28

Computational Note: these are unpleasant calculations to carry out. If you have an $\boxed{x^n}$ key (see page 66) then all you need do is:

$\boxed{1.03}$ $\boxed{x^n}$ $\boxed{20}$ $\boxed{=}$ $\boxed{x}$ $\boxed{2500}$

or on your personal computer type in

PRINT ((1+3/100)↑20)*2500

For details see section A6.2.2 on page 420.

Exercise

Calculate

i) £340 compounded twice yearly for 3 years at 10% per annum.

ii) £10,000 compounded monthly for 1 year at 15% per annum.

iii) £10,000 compounded daily for 1 year at 15% per annum.

iv) £13,426 compounded quarterly for 3 years at 8% per annum.

6.3 Allowing for Inflation

The cause of inflation does not concern us here. It is a fascinating and controversial subject in its own right and this book will limit itself to

QUANTITATIVE METHODS

explaining how to cope with the phenomenon. Inflation is the term given to the tendency for monetry prices to rise along a broad front. Not all prices rise by the same amount but various averages of price levels, or price indices as they are called, show a steady upward trend. The rate of increase varies but the direction in the UK has always been the same, upward, since before the war. The effect of such inexorable rises in price levels has a much more dramatic effect than is often appreciated. Table 6.5 shows the effect of various projected growth rates on two items over a period of 20 years: a house costing £30,000 and a salary of £10,000 per annum.

Table 6.5
Value (£'000) in 20 Years Time

Projected inflation rate	1%	5%	10%	15%	20%
House	36.6	79.6	201.8	491.0	1150.1
Salary	12.2	26.5	67.3	163.7	383.4

Note the enormous difference that a few percentage points can make. If you remember that the sum owed on your house is fixed or decreasing in value, you can understand why house purchase makes sense during a period of inflation.

6.3.1 Calculating Future Prices Under Inflation

Always remember that when considering particular items, specific inflation rates will be different. Various costs and prices for different products will almost certainly inflate but they will tend to do so at different rates. (See Section 8.4.4 on page 267). Let us calculate the estimated future price levels for a product which costs about £10 now, a shirt, say. Assuming an inflation rate of 10%. we need to increase the price by 10% per annum. This is exactly the same calculation as we used for compound interest. The general rule is :

Estimated price in a specified number of years time assuming a specified inflation rate is given by

Current price x $(1 + \frac{\text{\% Inflation rate}}{100})^{\text{No. of Years}}$

So in two years the shirt would cost

£10.00 x $(1 + \frac{10}{100})^2$ = £10.00 x $(1.10)^2$

COMPOUND INTEREST & DISCOUNTING

$$= £10.00 \times 1.21 = £12.1$$

and in Table 6.6 you can see how the price might be expected to change over the next 10 years. Check out the figures for yourself.

Table 6.6

Year	5%	10%	15%
1	10.5	11.0	11.5
2	11.0	12.1	13.2
3	11.6	13.3	15.2
4	12.2	14.6	17.5
5	12.8	16.1	20.1
6	13.4	17.7	23.1
7	14.1	19.5	26.6
8	14.8	21.4	30.6
9	15.5	23.6	35.2
10	16.3	25.9	40.5

So applying a level of inflation which seems quite possible in 1983, you can see that prices can be expected to double within about 10 years.

To emphasise just how critical the assumption about the rate of inflation is, Table 6.6 also shows the estimated future price assuming 5% and 15% inflation. The dramatic differences shown in Table 6.6 demonstrate the need for managers to monitor inflationary trends and build them into their investment appraisal procedures. This matter will be taken up on page 217.

6.3.2 Varying Inflation rates Year by Year

Sometimes it would be unreasonable to assume that prices will rise steadily or we have forecasts available for varying future inflation rates.

Example

Consider a car costing £5,000 on 1/1/84. Suppose the specific inflation rates for the next 4 years are forecast as

Year	Rate of Price Increase
1984	4
85	6
86	8
87	12

QUANTITATIVE METHODS

What is the forecast price of the car in 1987?

End of '84 price = £5,000 x $(1 + \frac{4}{100})$

End of '85 price = End of '84 x $(1 + \frac{6}{100})$ etc.

So the end of '87 price =

£5,000 x $(1 + \frac{4}{100})$ x $(1 + \frac{6}{100})$ x $(1 + \frac{8}{100})$ x $(1 + \frac{12}{100})$

= £5,000 x 1.33346 = £6667.32

which is NOT the same as averaging the rates to 7.5%. This gives the *wrong* answer of £6677.35.

Exercise

1. Calculate the price in 10 years time of a house costing £40,000 today assuming

    i) 5% per annum inflation
    ii) 10% per annum inflation
    iii) 15% per annum inflation
    iv) 20% per annum inflation

2. Repeat exercise 1 but applying it to a car costing £5000 today.

3. In 1976 a wine connoisseur bought wine at £2 per bottle. Assuming that his costs of warehousing are effectively zero and that there is no breakage, what is the cost per bottle to him at the end of 1983? Interest rates paid by him over the years have varied as follows:

Year	Interest Rate Paid
1976	13
77	10
78	9
79	15
1980	15
81	13
82	13
83	10

6.4 Valuing Future Money

The businessman deals in future money, and future money is governed

COMPOUND INTEREST & DISCOUNTING

by the laws of compound interest. Any investment made will generate revenues and costs that will not accrue until some time in the future. However the manager must make decisions now which means that he must have some way of placing a value on these future cash flows.

As we have already seen, interest rates govern the value of money tied up over time. If we can delay payments, then we can earn interest in the meanwhile on the payment money. If we can encourage our debtors to pay us sooner, then we can put the cash received on deposit to earn interest or put it to profitable use.

Because of the ability of money to earn interest or be put to work, future money is not as valuable as the same sum today. The process of valuing future money is known as *discounting*. The word comes from a procedure that has taken place for centuries in the city of London.

6.4.1 The Principle of Discounting

To value a future sum we need to ask 'How much would I need to have today to be equivalent to that future sum?' Take £100 received in two years time for instance. With interest rates at 10% say, I would value the future £100 as £82.64 because if I invested £82.64 at 10%, then in 2 years it would become £100.

$$\text{Present value} \times \left(1 + \frac{10}{100}\right)^2 = £100$$

From which it follows that

$$\text{Present value} = \frac{£100}{\left(1 + \frac{10}{100}\right)^2} = £100 \times \frac{1}{\left(1 + \frac{10}{100}\right)^2}$$

or in general

Present value of future sum $= \dfrac{\text{Future sum}}{\text{Compound amount factor}}$

$= $ **Future sum x Discount factor**

So the discount factor is just the reciprocal of the compound amount factor and vice versa. By using the 1/x key on your calculator, discount factors can be readily found. Tables of discount factors can be found in Appendix 5b on page 459, but you should try and calculate some of them directly for yourself.

QUANTITATIVE METHODS

6.4.2 The Treasury Bill Tender

It is well worth while spending a little time looking at this well established procedure. It will remind us that there is nothing 'new' or 'gimmicky' about the discounting process. The Bank of England regularly offers varying quantities of Treasury Bills for tender by the banks discount houses and a few other specialised institutions. These bills are in various denominations from £5,000 to £250,000 and they mature 91 days on from the date on which they are taken up by the purchasing institution. The crucial point is that they are paid for 91 days before the maturity date and they do not pay interest so that in effect the Bank of England is offering future money for tender.

Consider a bank which is considering tendering for a £5,000 bill which will pay out with something which approximates to certainty 91 days later. Suppose they argue that they require an annual interest rate of 11% on money lent to the government. They will then ask themselves:

> 'What sum should we invest today such that when the bill matures, we will get our money back together with an amount of interest equivalent to 11% per annum?'

Suppose they tendered £4,866.54 for the bill, then the transaction would look like this:

Principle repaid on maturity of bill	£4866.54
Effective interest paid by Bank of England	£ 133.46
Sum paid on maturity of bill	£5000.00

So at that price, £133.46 interest has been earned over 91 days on an investment of £4866.54. That represents an equivalent annual rate of interest of

$$\frac{£133.46}{£4866.54} \times 100 \times \frac{365}{91} = 11\%$$

The factor $\frac{365}{91}$ being used to scale up the interest rate from a 91 days basis to an annual basis.

Discount houses and banks of course use tables to work out the tender price which equates to a given annual rate of interest. The process is then known as discounting and it is clearly nothing more than applying inverted compound interest.

COMPOUND INTEREST & DISCOUNTING

6.4.3 Discounting as Inverted Compound Interest

A businessman is due to receive £10,000 in 3 years time. What is the present value of this sum discounted at 12%?

$$£10{,}000 \times \frac{1}{(1 + \frac{12}{100})^3}$$

$$= £10{,}000 \times \frac{1}{1.405}$$

$$= £10{,}000 \times 0.71178$$

$$= £7117.80$$

But what does this figure mean? Well if the businessman had £7117.8 now and were to invest it at 12%, it would amount to

$$£7117.8 \times (1 + \frac{12}{100})^3$$

$$= £7117.8 \times 1.4049$$

$$= £10{,}000$$

after 3 years of compound interest. Note that discounting is nothing more than inverted compound interest.

If 12% is the best rate of return the businessman can obtain over the next three years, then he should be indifferent when faced with the choice of £7117.8 now or £10,000 in three years time.

If he finds that £7117.8 is greatly preferable to £10,000 in three years time, then it must be that the businessman feels that he can earn more than 12% on money now, perhaps using the sum to avoid having to borrow at a rate of interest higher than 12%, and therefore a higher rate of discount should have been applied to the future sum. If, when interrogated, his indifference point turned out to be £6,900, this would imply a discount rate of 13.2%.

6.4.4 Breaking a Trust

Suppose that a certain charity is the residual legatee of a trust. The life interest is held by Mr X who is likely to live for another 5 years. At the moment he receives interest only, the charity receiving nothing. When Mr X dies, the charity will receive £1,000,000.

QUANTITATIVE METHODS

Mr X's solicitors suggest that the charity accept a lump sum now, both parties agreeing to break the trust and thereby obtaining liquid capital now. The charity will pay 9% on capital raised for building if it needs to carry out a building programme.

The present value of £1,000,000 received in 5 years time discounted at the charity's cost of capital is

$$= £1,000,000 \times \frac{1}{(1 + \frac{9}{100})^5}$$

$$= £1,000,000 \times 0.650 = £650,000$$

The charity now argues that any sum negotiated over this figure would be more valuable than £1,000,000 in 5 years time. Of course in practice they would not be sure how long the life tenant of the trust fund would survive and would be operating with an average figure based on actuarial statistics.

6.4.5 Discounting is not the same as allowing for Inflation

People often confuse discounting with making allowance for inflation. The charity knows full well that the £1 in 5 years time will buy less than it will today. This is reflected *to some extent* by the high rate of interest that it has to pay for borrowed money which it used in determining its discount rate. However even if inflation vanished as a phenomenon, interest rates would still exist although they would, of course, be lower than those levels that prevail today. So with no inflation, future money would still be discounted but at a lower rate.

6.4.6 Price Discounts

A company has received an invoice for £3,146. Normally they would tend to delay payment for about 4 months. What is the present value of this payment in the future? The company's overdraft costs them 14%.

The effective interest rate over a period of 4 months

$$= \frac{14}{3} = 4.67\%$$

Therefore the present value

$$= £3,146 \times \frac{1}{1.0467}$$

$$= £3,146 \times 0.9554 = £3,006$$

COMPOUND INTEREST & DISCOUNTING

As the company can 'earn' the equivalent of 14% per annum by not increasing their overdraft, they would prefer to delay payment unless the discount for immediate payment were to bring the sum payable down to something near £3,006. Therefore the price discount required from the creditor would have to be

$$\frac{£(3146 - 3006) \times 100}{£3146}$$

$$= 4.45\% \text{ on the invoice value.}$$

No wonder things get rough when interest rates rise.

6.4.7 Valuing Gilts by discounting

A £100 government bond with a nominal interest rate of 6% will be redeemed at par in 2 years time, interest of £3 per bond being payable twice yearly. A prospective purchaser expects to earn 13% on funds invested in the market. Ignoring tax complications, what is the present value of the gilt-edged security?

The buyer is in effect purchasing the following stream of cash receipts (note that the interest is calculated as 6% of the nominal value of the bond, £100, and not on its market price):

```
                                    +100
        +3      +3      +3          +3           Cash (£) in
├───────┼───────┼───────┼───────────┤
0       ½       1       1½          2            Year
```

The purchaser discounts at $\frac{13}{2}$ = 6.5% per ½ year.* The calculation can be laid out as:

End of Year	Discount Factor	Cash Receipt	Present Value of Cash Receipt
½	0.9390	3	2.817
1	0.8817	3	2.645
1½	0.8278	3	2.483
2	0.7773	103	80.062
			88.007

So by paying £88 for the stock, the purchaser will effectively earn 13 13% on his investment over the period.

* See note on page 427

QUANTITATIVE METHODS

Calculations such as these carried out by the market determines the price of gilts. Each bond has slightly different tax implications and cash flow timing advantages for different buyers which complicates the valuation process.

Exercise

1. Calculate the present value of the following:
   i) £140 received in 2 years time discounted at 12% per annum
   ii) £2,300 received in 5 years time discounted at 8% per annum
   iii) £1,400 received in 8 years time discounted at 11% per annum.

2. Calculate the present value of the following
   i) £2,300 received in 5 days time discounted at 13% per annum
   ii) £140,000 received in 3 weeks time discounted at 17% per annum
   iii) 3,000,000 received in 2 days time discounted at 15% per annum.

3. You are due to receive £32,000 today. Your debtor has problems and suggests paying you £32,100 in 10 days time. Calculate the present value of his proposed payment using a discount rate of 8% per annum. Comment on the result.

4. A Treasury bill (paying no interest) is due to be redeemed for £5,000 at par in 29 days time. If you expect to earn 13% on money, what price would you be prepared to pay for it? What other factors would you take into account?

6.5 Equal Payment Series

In the example in 6.4.7, a stream of equal interest payments had to be discounted. Similarly, in valuing leasing arrangements, a stream of equal payments is involved. A short-cut method may be used to cope with this cash flow pattern. We derive a *present value factor for an equal payment series* for a given % rate of discount.

COMPOUND INTEREST & DISCOUNTING

Present value factor for a stream of equal end-of-year payments of £1 is given by

$$\frac{1 - \frac{1}{\left(1 + \frac{\% \text{ rate}}{100}\right)^{\text{No of Periods}}}}{\frac{\% \text{ rate}}{100}}$$

(See Tables in Appendix 5c on page 460)

or expressed differently

$$\frac{1 - \text{present value factor for a single payment in n periods time}}{\frac{\% \text{ rate}}{100}}$$

N.B: All the formulae in this chapter are summarised in Chapter A.6 on page 428.

6.5.1 Example

What is the present value of 3 end-of-year payments of £200 discounted at 7%?

```
              +200      +200      +200   Cash Flow
       |────────|─────────|─────────|
       0        1         2         3    Year
```

The present value factor (which will then have to be multiplied by 200) is given by

$$= \frac{1 - \frac{1}{\left(1 + \frac{7}{100}\right)^3}}{\frac{7}{100}}$$

$$= \frac{1 - \left(\frac{1}{1.225}\right)}{0.07}$$

$$= \frac{1 - 0.8163}{0.07} = 2.6243$$

201

QUANTITATIVE METHODS

(For calculation on personal computer see Section A 6.5 on page 422)

So as we are dealing with £200 per period, the present value of the stream is given by

£200   x   2.6243   =   £524.86

Note that the value 0.8163 is the present value factor for a single payment and can be found in tables (see Appendix 5b on page 459) Note also that we get the same result as that obtained by discounting the individual payments year by year.

£200   x   0.9346   =   £186.916
£200   x   0.8734   =   £174.688
£200   x   0.8163   =   £163.260
                          £524.86

6.5.2 Example : Payments at the beginning of the year

What would happen in the previous example if the payments were made at the beginning of the year instead of at the end? We would then have this picture

```
+200      +200      +200           Cash Flow
 |         |         |     |
 0         1         2     3       Year
```

We can then treat the problem as consisting of one payment of £200 now i.e. already at present value, together with an equal payment series over *two* years. The present value is therefore equal to

$$£200 \;+\; \frac{1 - \frac{1}{(1+\frac{7}{100})^2}}{\frac{7}{100}} \times 200$$

=   £200   +   1.808 x £200   =   £561.60

As you might expect, the result is higher than the result in 6.5.1.

6.5.3 If we apply the rule for equal payment series to Example 6.4.7 on page 199, we get

202

COMPOUND INTEREST & DISCOUNTING

```
                              +100    Cash
         +3      +3     +3     +3     Flow
    ├─────┼──────┼──────┼──────┤
    0    ½      1     1½      2      Year
```

We had 6.5% per ½ year period applied to 4 equal payments of £3. Therefore the present value factor for the equal payment series is

$$= \frac{1 - \frac{1}{(1 + \frac{6.5}{100})^4}}{\frac{6.5}{100}} = \frac{1 - 0.777}{0.065}$$

$$= \frac{0.2227}{0.065} = 3.426$$

Therefore the present value of the cash flows is
= present value of interest + present value of redemption value.

$$\begin{aligned} &= \quad £3 \times 3.426 \quad + \quad £100 \times 0.7773 \\ &= \quad £10.278 \quad\quad\quad + \quad £77.73 \\ &= \quad £88.01 \end{aligned}$$

which confirms the result already arrived at earlier.

6.5.4 Example : Free credit arrangements

Suppose the Gas Board were to offer for sale a cooker costing £250. To encourage buyers, the Board offers interest-free credit. The purchase price can be paid off in 12 equal end of month payments of $\frac{£250}{12}$ = £20.83 per month. Suppose that a customer can earn 8% on his investment account. What is the present value of the stream of payments?

The effective interest rate per month is $\frac{8}{12}$% or 0.667% per month. Therefore the present value factor for equal payments is

$$\frac{1 - \frac{1}{\left(1 + \frac{0.667}{100}\right)^{12}}}{\frac{0.667}{100}} = 11.495$$

* Assuming monthly compounding: See note on page 427.

QUANTITATIVE METHODS

Therefore the present value of the payments made to the Gas Board is

= £20.83 x 11.495 *
= £239.44

The saving of £250−£239.44 = £10.56 amounts to a discount of $(\frac{£10.56}{£250}) \times 100 = 4.2\%$ on the purchase price.

A purchaser paying 25% per annum on his well-used credit card, should discount at $\frac{25}{12}\% = 2.083\%$ per month. The present value factor for the equal payments series then becomes

$$\frac{1 - \dfrac{1}{(1.02083)^{12}}}{0.02083} = 10.522$$

Therefore the present value of the payments is

= £20.83 x 10.522
= £219.17

which amounts to an effective discount rate of 12.3% on the purchase price.

As you would expect, the Gas Board's interest-free credit offer is more attractive to a purchaser in debt and paying high interest charges than one who has money on deposit at rates which are inevitably lower than lending rates.

6.5.5 Example: 'Annual Percentage Rate' (APR)

In some commercial dealings, a rate of interest is quoted but calculated on the sum borrowed rather than on the reducing balance owed. For example suppose a man buys a car for £10,000 at an interest rate of '9% per annum over 3 years. The repayment schedule is as follows:

interest 3 years at 9% on the sum borrowed	= 3 x £900	= £ 2,700
capital repayment	=	= £10,000
		£12,700

The customer is to pay three end of year payments to clear the debt of $\frac{£12,700}{3} = £4,233$'

To find the 'true annual rate of interest' which makes allowance for the repayment of capital year by year, we need to find by trial and error that discount rate which will make the present value = £10,000

* 11.507 Compounding Annually)
(see note on page 427)

204

COMPOUND INTEREST & DISCOUNTING

```
        £4233         £4233         £4233    Cash Paid
    |_____|_____|_____|
          1             2             3       Year End
```

Discount at 13%   =   £4233   x   2.361 = £9994

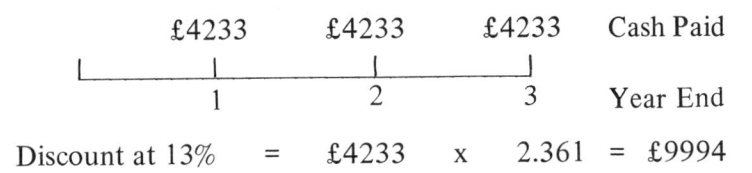

So the declared interest rate of 9% on the sum borrowed is equivalent to 13% on the more conventional reducing balance basis. As part of its attempt to secure 'truth in lending', the Consumer Credit Act (1974) laid down that advertisements of credit show the true annual rate of interest. This is known as the 'Annual Percentage Rate' or 'APR' (Dobson 1979). It is found by the trial and error method described above. (Also see Exercise 3 on page 216).

Exercise

1. Calculate the present value of
   i) £2000 p.a. received at the end of each of 5 years discounted at 10%
   ii) £350 p.a. received at the end of each of 10 years discounted at 13%
   iii) £1200 p.a. received at the end of each of 9 years discounted at 4%
   iv) As for (iii) but assuming the payments are received at the beginning of each year.

2. Calculate the present value of   (Compounded periodically)
   i) £10 per month for 2 years discounted at 11% p.a.
   ii) £100 per quarter for 5 years discounted at 13% p.a.
   iii) £1 per day for 1 year discounted at 9% p.a.

3. Suppose you are entitled to £500 a year for 5 years (end of year payment).
   i) What is the present value of these payments assuming a discount rate of 5%?
   ii) Repeat (i) but applying a discount rate of 10%

4. A businessman is owed £1400 which is due to be paid today. Accepting that the debtor has problems, he agrees to accept payment in 4 equal interest-free monthly payments, the first being made *now*. How much has he lost on the deal? The businessman is paying 13% on his overdraft (compounded monthly, see note on page 427).

QUANTITATIVE METHODS

5. Suppose you have just bought a bond issued by a company repayable in 30 years time. It is secured on the assets of the company and the nominal rate of interest is 3% on the nominal value of the bond which is £100. This bond will therefore pay out £3 per annum for 30 years. You only paid £25 for the bond because interest rates have gone up and £3 on your investment of £25 gives an effective interest rate of 12% which is the going rate. Suddenly the company goes bankrupt and you find that interest payments will cease but the Official Receiver will now repay the *nominal* value of the bond in 3 years time. Assuming a discount rate of 12%, calculate the value of the bond now. What do you think will happen to the price of the bonds on the Stock Market?

6.6 Capital Recovery

We have seen how to convert a stream of payments to present value. Often one needs to convert a sum at present value into an equal payment series. The building society needs to do this when calculating a repayment schedule for a mortgage.

A person borrows £20,000 to be repaid in 20 equal end-of-year payments, interest being paid at 9% per annum. We need to multiply the capital sum by an appropriate *capital recovery factor*:

$$\frac{\frac{\text{Discount rate}}{100}}{1 - \left(\dfrac{1}{1 + \frac{\text{Discount rate}}{100}}\right)^{\text{No. of periods}}}$$

$$= \frac{0.09}{1 - \left(\dfrac{1}{1.09}\right)^{20}}$$

$$= \frac{0.09}{1 - 0.1784} = 0.1095$$

Therefore the yearly repayments are

= £20,000 × 0.1095
= £ 2,190

or £182.5 per month.

If interest is calculated twice annually we have then effectively $\frac{9\%}{2}$ or

COMPOUND INTEREST & DISCOUNTING

4 ½% per half-year over 40 ½-year periods. The capital recovery factor is therefore

$$= \frac{0.045}{1 - (\frac{1}{1.045})^{40}} = 0.0543$$

Therefore the half-yearly repayments are

= £20,000 x 0.0543
= £ 1,086 per 6 months period

or £181 per month. The difference of £182.5 − £181 = £1.5 arises because in the second case an element of the capital is repaid twice yearly instead of once. (See Appendix 5c on Page 460 for factor tables.)

6.6.1 Example

A company pays £3,000 cash down for a 3-year maintenance contract on a new machine. For this sum all maintenance costs will be covered. What is the effective monthly maintenance charge? Calculating this as $\frac{£3000}{(12 \times 3)}$ = £83.33 per month *understates* the cost because it ignores the loss in interest over the three year period. Faced with the choice of paying £3,000 or £83.33 per month we would choose the latter. We could deposit the £3000 to earn interest and it would be sufficient to cover the monthly charges as they arose leaving accumulated interest over.

Assume an interest rate of 7% per annum. This implies a monthly interest rate of $\frac{7}{12}$ = 0.583% per month.[*] The capital recovery factor for 36 monthly periods is therefore

$$= \frac{0.00583}{1 - (\frac{1}{1.00583})^{36}}$$

= 0.03088

Therefore the equivalent monthly cost is given by

= 0.03088 x 3000
= £92.63

The meaning of this quantity is this. If £3,000 were placed on deposit earning interest at a rate of 7%,[*] then it would furnish a sequence of 36 end-of-month payments of £92.63. It is also true to say that the present value of the sequence of monthly payments is £3,000. The statements are equivalent. Therefore the sum above is equivalent to the capital sum, £3,000, payable for maintenance.

[*] compounding monthly
(see note on page 427).

QUANTITATIVE METHODS

Exercise

1. A woman borrows £20,000 to buy a house repaying the sum over a period of 20 years. Calculate her repayments assuming 8% interest and
    i) 20 single end of year payments
    ii) Repayments at the end of every 6 months

2. A company purchases a truck for £8,000. It will have a life of 6 years after which it will have no value and will be scrapped. Calculate the equivalent annual cost of the vehicle assuming an interest rate of 12% p.a.

3. A trader is owed £35,000 today. His debtor asks to pay over 8 months but is prepared to pay 11% interest on the sum outstanding. Calculate a schedule of 8 equal end of month payments.

6.7 Investing for the Future

Suppose a regular sum is placed on deposit earning compound interest. To what will it accumulate? The sum is given by multiplying the regular sum by the following compound interest factor for an equal payment series:

$$\frac{(1 + \frac{\% \text{ interest rate}}{100})^{\text{No. of Periods}} - 1}{\frac{\% \text{ interest rate}}{100}}$$

6.7.1 Example

A person deposits £500 at the end of each of the next 10 years in anticipation of his retirement. To what will it accumulate assuming an interest rate of (i) 5%, (ii) 15%?

i) $$\frac{(1 + \frac{5}{100})^{10} - 1}{\frac{5}{100}}$$

= 12.58

Therefore the deposits will have accumulated to

12.58 x £500 = £6,290

after 10 years

COMPOUND INTEREST & DISCOUNTING

ii) At 15% interest, the compound amount factor for the equal payment series is given by

$$\frac{(1.15)^{10} - 1}{.15} = 20.30$$

and therefore the payments will accumulate to

20.30 × £500 = £10,150.

Exercise

A person who owns a house valued at £40,000 today decides not to move house. He had intended borrowing an extra £20,000 to buy a house worth £60,000 and on which he would have paid 10% interest with no capital repayments. Instead he intends to place on deposit at 8.5%, the interest he would have paid out. To what will this sum accumulate in 10 years?

If he had bought the house, assuming that house prices rise by 5% p.a. would he have been better off to increase his mortgage?

6.7.2 The Sinking Fund Factor

By inverting the formula just employed, we can find out how much to set aside in order to accumulate a specified sum in the future. We need to multiply the target sum by a *sinking fund factor* which is as follows

$$\frac{\frac{\% \text{ rate}}{100}}{\left(1 + \frac{\% \text{ rate}}{100}\right)^{\text{No. of Periods}} - 1}$$

Example

A person wants to have £20,000 to buy an annuity in 20 years time. How much does he have to invest at the end of each of the next 20 years assuming an average interest rate of 8%?

The sinking fund factor is given by

$$\frac{\frac{8}{100}}{\left(1 + \frac{8}{100}\right)^{20} - 1}$$

= 0.02185

209

QUANTITATIVE METHODS

Therefore the required regular sum is given by

$$0.02185 \times £20,000$$
$$= £437$$

6.7.3 Inflation proofing

If the required sum must be maintained in real terms then the target sum should be inflated on the basis of some estimate of the average inflation rate over the period in question.

Example

In the preceding example, if inflation is expected to average 6% on average, then the required regular sum will now be

$$0.02185 \times £20,000 \times (1 + \tfrac{6}{100})^{20}$$

(the third term being the compound amount factor which inflates the target sum over 20 years at the inflation rate of 6%).

$$= 0.02185 \times £20,000 \times 3.207$$
$$= £1,401.5$$

This should be compared with the £437 which was the required sum before allowing for inflation.

The problem is that it is difficult to forecast the inflation rate. Table 6.7 below shows how the required regular amount varies with projected rate

Table 6.7

Projected Inflation Rate (% p.a.)	Required Annual Deposit (£ p.a.)
5	1160
6	1402
7	1691
8	2037
10	2940
15	7153

Note that an error of just 1 percentage point above 6% leads to an extra

$$\frac{(£1691 - £1402) \times 100}{£1402} = 20.6\%$$

COMPOUND INTEREST & DISCOUNTING

on top of the annual payment required. That's why running an index-linked pension fund isn't much fun!

Exercise

Check and extend Table 6.8 and draw a graph showing how the required annual payments depend on projected inflation rates varying between 0 and 20%

6.8 Investment Appraisal

6.8.1 Cash Flow Analysis

In order to evaluate an investment proposal you need first to lay out the expected cash outflows and inflows. Suppose that an investment £600,000 in machinery now will allow production of 300 units in the first two years and 200 units in the third and fourth years. The sales price is estimated as £1,000 per unit. Material costs and labour costs amount to £100 and £200 per unit respectively. At the end of four years, the machinery will have to be scrapped and it will then have a value of £50,000. The cash flows involved are laid out in Table 6.8 and are assumed to be at year end (allowance for inflation will be discussed on page 217).

Table 6.8 : Cash Flows for an Investment Proposal (£'000)

	Capital Outlay	Sales Revenue	Materials Cost	Labour Cost	Net Cash Flow
Now	− 600				− 600
End Year 1		300	− 30	− 60	+ 210
End Year 2		300	− 30	− 60	+ 210
End Year 3		200	− 20	− 40	+ 140
End Year 4	+ 50	200	− 20	− 40	+ 190

NPV at 8% = £25.2 (£'000)

Only costs which arise if the investment is undertaken should be included in such analysis. Depreciation should *not* be included nor should apportioned overheads unless they represent the true opportunity cost of carrying out the project. The test question in case of doubt is: 'If this project were not undertaken, would there be cost savings? If, for example, the machinery used factory space which could have been rented out or otherwise profitably used, then the opportunity cost of that space should be included. If the space would not otherwise be profitably used, then the overhead apportioned for administrative purposes should not be included as it is not a cash flow. Interest payments should not be included. These are taken account of in the discounting process to be discussed in the next section.

On the revenue side, capital allowances and tax benefits should be included even though they may be only indirectly earned by, for for example, reducing the organisations overall tax liability. The test question is: 'If this project is undertaken will there be a decreased tax liability? If the answer is 'yes' then the tax saving should be included. (Any further coverage of tax is beyond the scope of this book and details vary from organisation to organisation and it will therefore be excluded from all further examples. Remember, however, that *tax plays a crucial role in investment appraisal* and specialist advice is required).

If, by carrying out the investment, expenditure elsewhere can be avoided, then that expenditure should be included as if it were a positive cash inflow resulting from the investment. Thus in the case of a project which employs workers who would otherwise have been made redundant, it would be correct to show the redundancy payments, which no longer need to be paid, as a cash benefit in the investment appraisal!

The initial capital cost should exclude *sunk costs*. These are capital costs relevant to the proposed investment *but which have already been spent and cannot be recovered*. For example suppose a company has invested a million pounds in developing a new product. In assessing the worth of the product they should calculate the present and *future* outgoings required to bring it to the market place together with the future benefits. Writing off past expenditure may be embarrassing from a political point of view but it should not affect the valuation of the future prospects of the project.

6.8.2 Discounted Cash Flows

Look at Table 6.8 on page 211. The net cash flows arising from an investment of £600,000 amounted to a total of £210,000 + £210,000 + £140,000 + £190,000 = £750,000. However the calculation involves the adding together of money received at different points in time in the future. In section 6.4 on page 194, we saw that valuing future money involves the process of discounting. The discount rate employed should be the *opportunity cost of capital*. If unlimited funds are available, then this will be the interest rate charged for these funds. If capital rationing prevails, then the opportunity cost of

COMPOUND INTEREST & DISCOUNTING

capital will be the return that could be obtained on alternative investments.

The cost of capital may be the rate the investor is charged for funds used for other purposes. For example, a person evaluating an investment opportunity who pays 12% on her long term overdraft and who is able to obtain 8% by placing money on deposit would discount the cash flows at 12%. By taking up the opportunity she foregoes the opportunity to reduce her overdraft which would thereby have effectively 'earned' her 12% on her capital. A number of different ways of evaluating investment opportunities follow.

6.8.3 Net Present Value

The net present value (NPV) of an investment is found by discounting each element of the cash flow at the appropriate discount rate. For the investment shown in Table 6.8 and using a discount rate of 8% we obtain the result as follows.

Table 6.9: Calculation of NPV for Proposal shown in Table 6.8 £'000

Discounted net cash flows

End of Year	Net Cash Flow	8% Discount Factor	Discounted net cash flow
1	210	0.9259	194.4
2	210	0.8573	180.0
3	140	0.7938	111.1
4.	190	0.7350	139.7
			625.2

less initial investment of £600

Net present value (NPV) = £25.2

This value can be interpreted as follows: if the investment was financed by borrowing at 8% then the investment would produce a surplus of £25,200 at present value after allowing for interest and repayment of capital. A negative NPV would imply that a deficit would be incurred after allowing for financing the investment. Note that discounting to present value automatically allows for interest payments.

Exercise

1. Calculate the NPV as shown in Table 6.9 but using discount rates

QUANTITATIVE METHODS

of 10% and 12%. Comment on the results.

2. A company has the choice of buying a machine for £2,000 and paying £200 per annum maintenance charges. The life of the machine will be 5 years at the end of which it will have an estimated scrap value of £500. Alternatively the company can lease the machine for £600 per annum payable at year end. In this case there will be no scrap value and all maintenance charges will be included within the leasing charge. Compare the net present value of the two proposals discounting at 12%.

6.8.4 Internal Rate of Return (IRR)

The IRR of an investment is that discount rate which makes the net present value equal to zero. Fig 6.1 shows the graph of NPV for the data of Table 6.8 plotted for various discount rates. It shows that the internal rate of return is fractionally under 10%. The graph should make it clear just what the IRR means. For a conventional investment (investment now, returns later) it marks the cut off point for the opportunity cost of capital. If the cost of capital exceeds the IRR then the investment is not a profitable one.

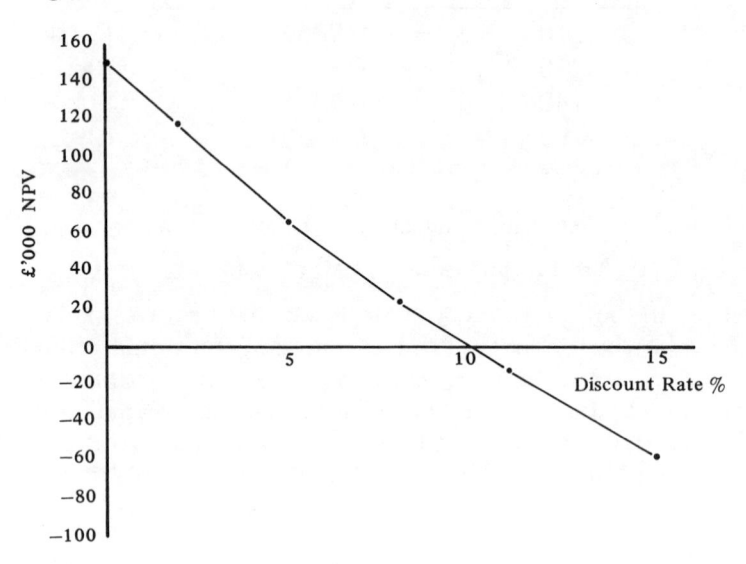

Fig 6.1 : Calculation of IRR for the Example in Table 6.8

COMPOUND INTEREST & DISCOUNTING

Although the IRR can therefore be used to sort out those investments which are profitable from those which are not, it can *not* be used to choose between profitable alternatives. Fig. 6.2 shows a graph of NPV against discount rate for two *competing* or *Mutually exclusive* investments A and B. You can see that the IRR of A(22.5%) exceeds that of B(16.5%). This merely says that A is profitable for discount rates up to 25% whereas B is only profitable up to 16.5%. However if the opportunity cost of capital is 10% then the NPV at 10% for B (£22,000) is higher than that for A(£17,500)! At the opportunity cost of capital, B is more valuable than A and it remains so for discount rates up to 12.5%.

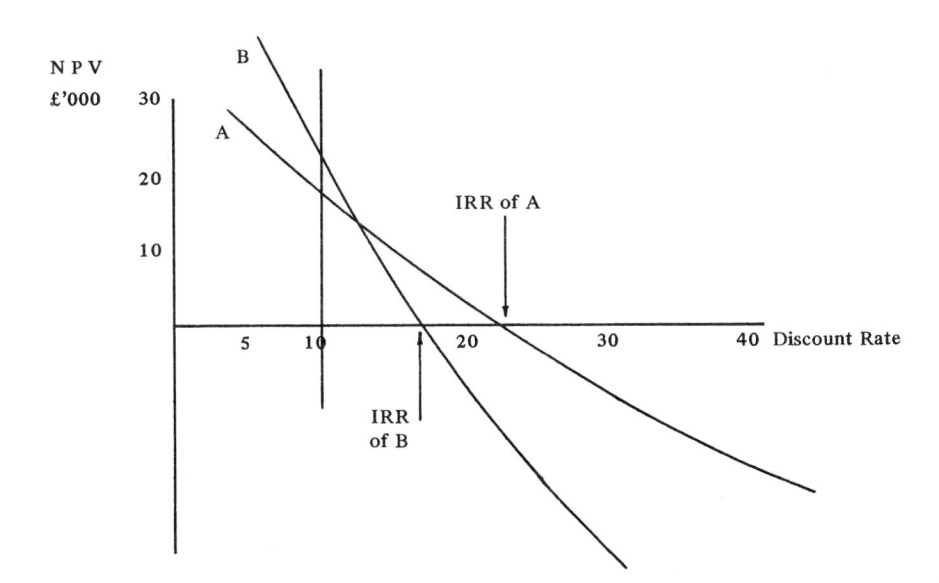

Figure 6.2 : IRR of Two Competing Proposals

Exercise

1. A company has a choice of investing (a) £10,000 and receiving £7,000 at the end of each of the next two years or (b) for the same sum invested, receiving a single sum of £40,000 in 7 years time. Calculate the NPV of both investments at 10% discount rate and by plotting NPV against discount rate, find the IRR for both investments. Which is the more valuable investment?

2. (This one is for IRR fans). A mining company is investigating a proposal to dig a mine at a cost now of £400,000. They expect net

QUANTITATIVE METHODS

returns of £600,000 and £560,000 at the end of years 1 and 2 respectively but they expect a net *loss* at the end of year 3 of £800,000 because of being required to dismantle machinery and to landscape the site which is of outstanding beauty. They can raise the money by borrowing at 15%. Calculate the NPV at 15% and find the IRR by plotting the NPV against discount rates between 0 and 70%. Explain what the IRR for this unconventional investment means! (Be prepared for some surprises.)

3. Some strange interest rates can be quoted but all loans now have to show the true annual percentage rate (APR). A car company advertises 'interest calculated at 5.95% per annum *on the amount financed*' with a repayment period of 36 months. That means a £1,000 loan will incur interest at £59.5 per annum for all three years even though the capital will be paid off in equal instalments! Thus the monthly repayments of capital and interest will amount to 36 payments of £32.74 ($\frac{1000}{36} + \frac{59.5}{12}$). Calculate the IRR of the company's investment of £1,000 assuming that it receives 36 payments of £32.74 at the end of the next 36 months. (For this you can calculate the equal payment series discount factor, see page 200). The APR will be the IRR multiplied by 12 to convert it to an annual rate. (The answer lies between 0.4 and 1.25% per month). So the APR can be found by working out the IRR of a repayment schedule.*

6.8.5 Discounted Payback

Traditionally payback has been and remains a popular basis for evaluating investment proposals. This measures the number of years that it takes for the investors to 'get their money back'. Often this method has been employed without discounting in which case it does not achieve what it claims. Suppose an investor borrows money at 10% and invests £10,000 to generate net cash inflows of £2,000 per annum for 8 years. It would be quite misleading to say that he 'gets his money back' after 5 years because this would take no account of the loss of interest on the sum borrowed.

A modified version of payback measures the number of years for the *discounted* net cash flows to equal the initial sum invested. Discounting at 8% in the above example, Table 6.10 shows how the discounted payback can be found.

*This method assumes monthly compounding.

COMPOUND INTEREST & DISCOUNTING

Table 6.10 : Discounted Payback

End of Year	Net Cash Return	8% Discount Factor	Discounted Return	Cumulative Discounted Return
1	2000	0.926	1852	1,852
2	2000	0.857	1714	3,566
3	2000	0.794	1588	5,154
4	2000	0.735	1470	6,624
5	2000	0.681	1362	7,986
6	2000	0.630	1260	9,246
7	2000	0.583	1166	10,412

The discounted payback is seen to be just less than 7 years whereas the conventional payback is 5 years. However the discounted payback really does tell you how long it takes to get your money back *plus interest at the stated discount rate.* Of course any form of payback is dangerous if it is used as the only criterion of investment worth. After all, investment is carried out for profit. If all you want is your money back as quickly as possible, then place it on deposit and you can have it back whenever you want it! As a supplementary criterion to the valuation of the investment by means of the NPV, it is useful.

6.8.6 Allowing for Inflation

Inflation affects the estimates of future cash revenues and costs incurred in any investment proposal. Also the market's perception of inflation prospects has a strong influence on interest rates in general and an organisation's opportunity cost of capital is in turn affected by the general level of interest rates. It is essential that the cash flows discounted at the opportunity cost of capital should allow for estimated inflationary growth in price and cost levels. An example will illustrate the dangers of confusing this issue. Look again at Table 6.8.[*] Suppose that we have new information indicating that sales revenues, materials costs and labour costs are all going to increase at 10% per annum. Some people may think that as all these components are increasing at the same rate then the effects of inflation will cancel out. Not so! Table 6.11 shows the situation assuming compound growth at 10% for all components.

[*] On page 211.

QUANTITATIVE METHODS

Table 6.11 : Cash Flows from Table 6.8 Assuming 10% inflation. (£ ' 000)

	Capital Outlay	Sales Revenue	Materials Cost	Labour Cost	Net Cash Flow
Now	– 600				
End Year 1		330	– 33	– 66	+ 231
End Year 2		363	– 36.3	– 72.6	+ 254.1
End Year 3		266.2	– 26.6	– 53.2	+ 186.4
End Year 4	+ 73.2	292.8	– 29.3	– 58.6	+ 278.1

NPV at 8% = £184.1
(£ '000)

Note the enormous difference in the NPV compared with the value when no adjustment is made (£25.2). The example illustrates the importance of adjusting for inflation and not calculating future cash flows in terms of today's price levels.

In estimating the future cash flows, allowance can be made for differential price increases. Suppose it is believed that revenue will increase at 6% p.a. but materials costs will rise at 10% and labour costs at 12% p.a. The scrap value of the machinery will increase in value by only 4% p.a.

Table 6.12 : Cash Flows from Table 6.8 showing differential Inflation (£ '000)

	Capital Outlay	Sales Revenue	Materials Cost	Labour Cost	Net Cash Flow
Now	– 600				
End Year 1		318	33	67.2	217.8
End Year 2		337.1	36.3	75.3	225.5
End Year 3		238.2	26.6	56.2	155.4
End Year 4	+ 58.5	252.5	29.3	62.9	218.8

NPV at 8% = £79.2

Note that although costs are increasing at a higher rate than the sales revenue, the NPV is still greater than when no allowance for inflation is made. Clearly if organisations fail to bring inflation into their investment appraisal then they will grossly underestimate the benefits of investing. Carsberg and Hope (1976) suggest that incorrect handling of inflation by management may have contributed to a UK failure to invest.

COMPOUND INTEREST & DISCOUNTING

Of course by introducing estimates of the effects of inflation, a highly subjective element is introduced into the evaluation. 'What if' programmes of the 'spread sheet' variety allow the user to see how sensitive their evaluation is to estimates in inflation rates (see Chapter 11, page 383).

6.9 Decision Tables and Decision Trees

The decision maker has a problem when deciding between competing investment proposals. Although in theory he should choose that proposal which has the highest NPV, the value of the NPV is usually not known with certainty. Inflation is just one of the many unknown factors which could affect the valuation of a proposal. A payoff table helps the decision makers to face up to the problem by showing all the competing decisions together with their respective NPV's under different assumptions about future conditions.

Table 6.13 : Illustrative Payoff Table for an Investment Decision. (NPV £ '000)

		'States of Nature'	
		Competitor's Product on the market	Competitor's Product NOT on the market
Possible Actions	Plan A	−£10	+ £200
	Plan B	+ £20	+ £25
	Plan C	+ £5	+ £40

Table 6.13 shows the sort of result which would arise where the decision maker's valuation of three alternative marketing plans depends on the actions of their main competitor.

Plan A   Launch a product which encroaches on the main competitor's traditional market. If they are working on a similar product and launch it then a loss will be incurred.

Plan B   Launch a non-controversial product. It's market success is almost assured whatever the main competitor does.

Plan C   Launch a safer product which can cope with a certain

QUANTITATIVE METHODS

amount of competition but which will be reasonably successful in the absence of competition.

The main advantage of having a payoff table is that it disciplines the decision maker into quantifying all possible combinations of Action and States of Nature. Each value for the NPV shown in the table would require detailed calculations of cash flows before the NPV value could be obtained. The decision maker is therefore forced to look at all possible combinations before 'political' considerations rear their ugly head in the decision making process.

6.9.2 Opportunity Loss or Regret Tables

The opportunity loss concept can be useful to decision makers.

Table 6.14 : Opportunity Loss (Regret) Table
Derived from Table 6.13 (NPV £ '000)

	Competition	No Competition
A	30	0
B	0	175
C	15	160

The first column was calculated as follows. If the main competitor's product is on the market then, with hindsight, the best decision would have been to choose Plan B (gaining £20) (see Table 6.13). If Plan A had been chosen an opportunity loss of £30 (the difference between + £20 and − £10) would have been incurred. The difference between the payoff arising and the best one possible for that set of market conditions is a measure of the decision maker's regret. A decision maker wishing to minimise the potential regret or opportunity loss would choose A because in that case the regret would be limited to £30. Other plans could involve him in higher regrets.

6.9.3 Expected Monetry Value (EMV)

If subjective probabilities can be assigned to the states of nature then each plan can be assigned an expected monetry value. If the probability of the competitor NOT being involved is 0.8, then the EMV of the three proposals (see Table 6.13) would be

$$\text{EMV of A} = -£10 \times 0.2 + £200 \times 0.8 = £158$$
$$\text{EMV of B} = +£20 \times 0.2 + £25 \times 0.8 = £24$$

COMPOUND INTEREST & DISCOUNTING

EMV of C   =   + £5 x 0.2 + £40 x 0.8   =   £33

A careful re-reading of Section 4.9 on page 147 will remind you that EMV only provides a clear-cut decision when the situation is a repeated decision or one of many similar decisions. Remember that major capital investment decisions do NOT often fall into that category.

6.9.4 Decision Trees

Some investment decisions are multi-stage processes. The final outcome depends partly on decisions which are made later on in time. This makes some decisions very complex and these can be effectively portrayed in the form of a *Decision Tree*. The main advantage of such trees is the clear way they display the choices of action, present and future, which are open to decision makers. Drawing up such a tree does not pre-suppose anything about the way in which the tree is analysed. Fig 6.3 shows a very simplified decision tree for a product launch.

**Fig 6.3 :   Simplified Decision Tree for Launching a Product
(Costs in £'000 at present value)**

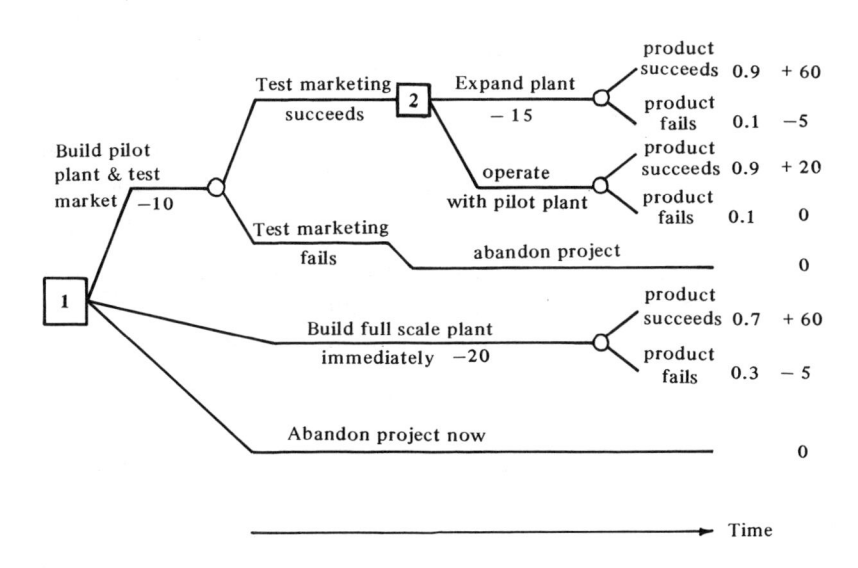

```
                                                              product
                                                              succeeds  0.9   +60
              Test marketing      Expand plant
              succeeds         [2]   -15                      product
                                                              fails     0.1   -5
Build pilot
plant & test                          operate                 product
market  -10                           with pilot plant        succeeds  0.9   +20
                                                              product
              Test marketing                                  fails     0.1    0
              fails              abandon project
                                                                               0
[1]
                                                              product
              Build full scale plant                          succeeds  0.7   +60
              immediately  -20
                                                              product
                                                              fails     0.3   -5

              Abandon project now
                                                                               0

                                                        → Time
```

QUANTITATIVE METHODS

Each square represents a numbered decision point. Note how the tree displays the options available together with their consequences in monetary terms. The probabilities of product success in the top branch are conditional on a successful test market whereas those on the middle branch reflect the experts view now. The costs shown are cumulative so that if a pilot plant is built, then expanded and the product then fails, the net cost will be $-10 -15 -5 = 30$.

The traditional analysis using Expected Monetary Value (EMV) rolls back the decision from right to left. Given successful test marketing, at decision point 2 the plant would be expanded (EMV = +53.5 − £15 = £38.5) as opposed to continuing with the pilot plant (EMV= +£18). (A more cautious decision, however, would be to continue with the pilot plant incurring less risk of loss). Remember that for large scale decisions EMV is not an appropriate criterion for choice and the tree may be better simplified by eliminating branches on the basis of a range of criteria, some quantitative and some qualitative, following discussion with all those concerned.

Whatever method is used to analyse the decision tree, it provides an effective means of communicating the options open to management and displaying them against a time scale. Wells (1982) offers an example of the use of this technique as a communication aid in the Imperial Group. Phillips (1982) discusses the use of decision trees as part of a process in which the tree is used to provide a framework to *help* all those involved in the decision, aiming to give them a deeper understanding of the issues. In both these examples subjective probabilities were used in the modelling process but calculation of an 'optimum decision' was not sought.

For too long Decision Trees have been associated with the search for optimum decisions using expected monetary value as a sole criterion. They need a new lease of life being used flexibly and undogmatically.

CHAPTER 7 : CORRELATION AND REGRESSION — A STATISTICAL MINEFIELD

Sections 7.1 to 7.3 discuss the principles of correlation analysis with special emphasis on the problems of correctly identifying cause and effect relationships. 7.4 to 7.8 describe the way in which the degree of correlation can be measured and its significance determined. Sections 7.9 to 7.10 deal with linear regression.

7.1 I've described the subject of correlation and regression as a minefield. Those who work in this area should indeed tread carefully. There are many hidden dangers lying in what may seem at first sight to be quite simple situations. So if this is the case, why bother?

Businessmen are interested in the association between variables. For example marketing managers expect high levels of advertising to be associated with high levels of sales otherwise they wouldn't do it. But what is the precise relationship between the two? How many extra sales will they get for each extra £1 of advertising expenditure? A department store manager will expect cold weather conditions to be associated with high sales of gloves and scarves. Given forecasts of temperatures in the coming months, can the association allow him to forecast sales levels? A management accountant expects production costs to vary with the level of production. Can she use the association between these two variables as the basis for a budgeting system, laying down standard costs as a basis for the control of expenditure? A local authority spending more on home visits to the elderly expects such action to be associated with some improvement in the welfare of the community, but to what extent? In running an organisation, private or public, we are inevitably driven to consider the association between variables and are, as a result, tempted onto dangerous ground. The experience will be rewarding provided you remember the following guidelines

1. Never lose touch with your common sense
2. Gain an *understanding* of the techniques involved
3. Match your ambitions to the quality of your data.

Once you have understood the techniques, allow your common sense to monitor and check the conclusions arrived at. Remember that cheap calculators and personal computers now make light work of the computational aspect of the techniques. In particular remember the

QUANTITATIVE METHODS

third rule. Your common sense tells you that no mathematical technique can allow you to extract complex information from data which you know to be faulty, crude or deficient. Yet some people become mesmerised by the sheer power of technology. Momentarily they get hypnotised by the output from the computer. You the manager, the non-specialist, have the experience of the work area which is essential to ensure that analysis operates at a level appropriate to the quality of information available. Much of the technical detail is therefore relegated to Chapter A7 so that you can concentrate on basic principles and understanding.

7.2   Plotting Scatter Diagrams

When one variable influences another variable, such as the influence of the air temperature on the quantity of gas consumed in a home fitted with gas central heating, then the values of the two variables can be expected to show a degree of correlation and this correlation will show up on a scatter diagram. A set of data is shown in Table 7.1 and and the corresponding scatter diagram is shown in Figure 7.1 on Page 225.

Table 7.1 : Gas Consumption & Mean Temperature in a home

Month	Mean Temp. (C)	Cubic Feet '000
January	3.1	123
February	6.3	115
March	5.4	108
April	9.0	102
May	11.3	45
June	14.3	50
July	15.0	34
August	16.3	2
September	15.2	18
October	9.6	52
November	7.0	46
December	6.0	119

Note carefully how the scatter diagram in Figure 7.1 has been constructed. Because the direction of the causal link is quite clear, it is conventional to plot the gas consumption on the vertical axis. It is termed the *dependent* variable, depending as it clearly does on the temperature of the environment of the central heating system. Temperature, the *independent variable* in this example, is plotted

CORRELATION AND REGRESSION – A STATISTICAL MINEFIELD

Fig 7.1

Consumption per month (cubic ft '000)

[Scatter plot showing monthly gas consumption vs mean daily air temperature, with points labelled Jan (~120, ~3), Dec (~120, ~5), Feb (~115, ~5), March (~100, ~5), April (~100, ~9), Oct (~52, 9.6), Nov (~45, ~7), May (~50, ~11), June (~52, ~15), July (~45, ~15), Sep (~25, ~14), Aug (~5, ~16). Horizontal dashed line at 52,000 cubic ft and vertical dashed line at 9.6 divide the plot into four quadrants.]

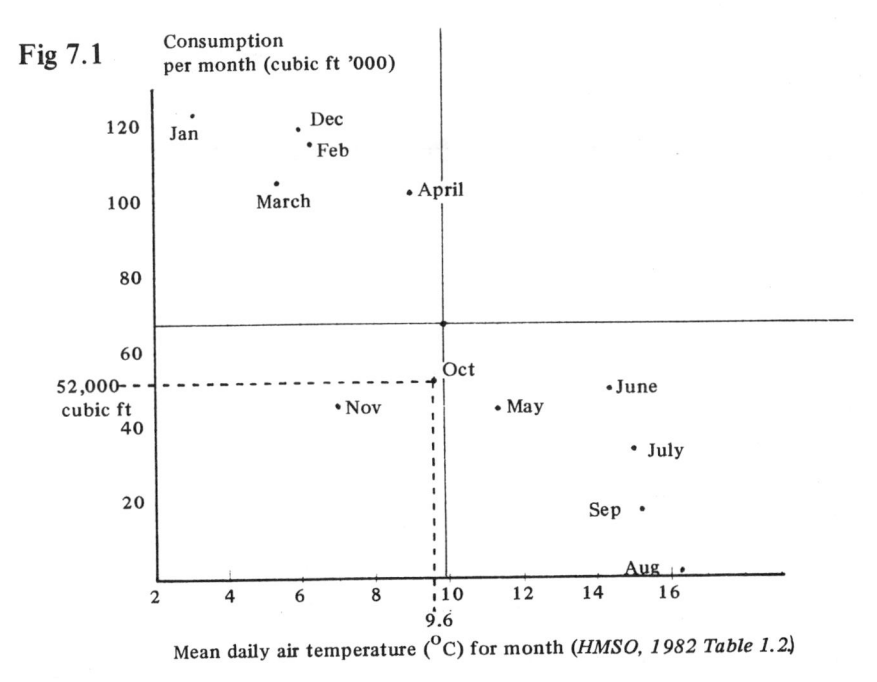

Mean daily air temperature (°C) for month (*HMSO, 1982 Table 1.2*)

along the horizontal axis. Each pair of readings defines one point on the graph. So, for example, the October figures of 52,000 cubic feet and 9.6 C are plotted by imagining a vertical line drawn up from 9.6 C and a horizontal line drawn across from 52,000 cubic ft. The point represents the intersection of these two lines. In this instance it is worth labelling each point with the month of the year. This makes it easier to identify interesting features. Looking at Fig 7.1 there is a clear tendency for the hotter months to be associated with relatively low consumption of gas and vice versa.

Figure 7.1 also shows the graph divided into four quadrants by the drawing of horizontal and vertical lines through a point representing the mean of both columns, the 'centre of gravity' of the data. The tendency for the points to occupy the upper left and lower right quadrants indicates that these two variables are negatively correlated, meaning high values of one variable are associated with low values of the other and vice versa. Because the points are labelled, it is easy to identify exceptions to the general tendency. The November figure represents a lower consumption of gas than one would expect given the temperature for that month. Further investigation might throw some light on the reasons for this. Perhaps the central heating broke

QUANTITATIVE METHODS

down in that month or perhaps there was a gas strike. The owner could have been on holiday (unlikely, but this could explain the particularly low August figure) or could have been on an economy drive. The important point to register is that there exists no statistical technique that will resolve such questions. Investigation and discussion with those qualified to give an opinion is essential. But the technique is powerful enough all the same. It provides an excellent starting point for discussions between the analyst and the manager.

Looking at the graph as a whole, note that although a correlation exists between the variables, it is not a precise one. Even with a central heating system automatically responding to the air temperature, there will be a host of other factors which will affect the gas consumption such as the following

1. Gas is not only used for heating. Would gas used for cooking show the same relationship with temperature?

2. A number of transient personal factors will affect the setting on the thermostat. The visit of a friend who likes to be warm. There will be extended periods when the house is empty during the day, for instance during the school term in a house where the mother works, and as a consequence the heating will be programmed to switch off in order to conserve energy.

3. In the autumn or early spring some people will tend to put on the heating regardless of the temperature. For example some public authorities put on the heating in buildings on a specified date in the year even if there is a heat wave in progress!

Factors like those given above tend to cloud the relationship between gas consumption and air temperature even though a direct causal relationship between the two variables cannot be denied.

7.3 Causality: a critical Issue

7.3.1 When there is a direct causal link between two variables such as temperature and gas consumption then we can expect to observe a correlation between the values of those two variables, but not a perfect one because of the interference of outside factors. It does NOT follow, however that because a correlation exists between two variables, there exists a direct causal relationship. The logical fallacy to avoid here is a well known one: it is true that all dogs are animals but not true to say that all animals are dogs!

It is worth looking at a few ludicrous examples to make the point

CORRELATION AND REGRESSION – A STATISTICAL MINEFIELD

quite clear. There exists, I am assured, a correlation between the number of storks nests in Alsatian towns and the number of births there. Amusing though it might be to argue the point, there is no basis for assuming that this is evidence for an alternative mechanism for childbirth. Even more importantly, any attempt by the authorities to effect birth control by shooting the storks would not be successful. The source of the correlation is quite easy to find. Storks make their nests on houses, and families live in houses. The more families, the more houses. The more houses the more storks.

A stupid example you might think. But if one of your staff suggested that because sales were positively correlated with salesmen's expenses, that therefore all salesmen's expense accounts should be increased, would the logic seem ridiculous in that instance? There may or may not be a causal link.

The mean monthly temperature in my unheated bathroom is negatively correlated with the sales of thermal underwear in Harrods. I am sure you will believe me. But you would be right to be sceptical if I proposed to corner the market in thermal underwear and then refrigerate my bathroom during the summer in an attempt to make a killing. Both the temperature in my house and in most houses in the northern hemisphere are negatively correlated with the sales of winter clothing: the lower the temperature the higher the sales. The correlation between my house's temperature and Harrod's sales of thermal underwear arises because both variables are correlated with a third factor, and nothing I do to my bathroom will affect the sales figure.

When looking at the degree of correlation between variables, remember these examples and beware. Now consider a couple of examples which are less extreme but which, all the same, present some difficulties. In these less ludicrous cases it is very easy to make the mental jump from the existence of a correlation to the belief that a direct causal link exists. This is particularly true in Multiple Regression which is discussed on page 387.

7.3.2 Example

Table 7.2 shows figures for the number of cinema admissions in Great Britain between 1970 and 1980 together with an average admission price which I have converted to 1980 price levels in the third column using the RPI (Real prices and indices are discussed later in Chapter 8).

QUANTITATIVE METHODS

Table 7.2

Year	Number of Admissions (millions)	Average Price of Admissions (New Pence)	Average price at 1980 price levels (New Pence)
1970	193	30.6	110.4
1971	176	34.2	112.7
1972	157	37.9	116.6
1973	134	43.2	121.8
1974	138	50.1	121.8
1975	116	61.2	119.7
1976	104	73.0	122.5
1977	103	82.6	119.7
1978	126	93.7	125.4
1979	112	113.4	133.8
1980	96	141.3	141.3

(Permission No. 6)

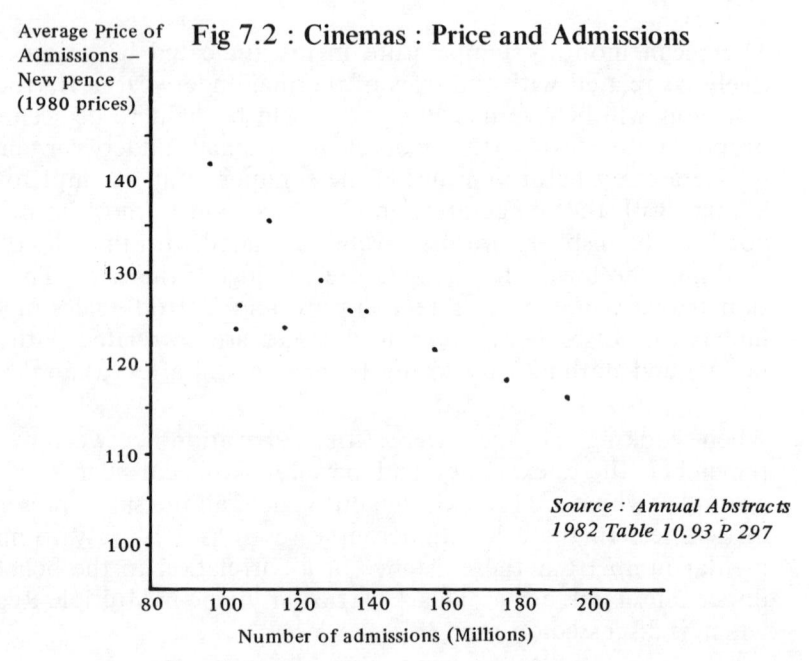

Fig 7.2 : Cinemas : Price and Admissions

Source : Annual Abstracts 1982 Table 10.93 P 297

Drawing up the scatter diagram in Fig 7.2 there is no doubt that there is a clear negative correlation between the two variables. As prices have risen in real terms, so admissions have fallen. But is there a direct causal relationship operating here and if there is, *in which direction is it operating?* Is it that the relatively high prices have kept the customers away or is it that the fall-off of customers has led cinema owners to raise prices so as to maintain the level of their takings?

CORRELATION AND REGRESSION – A STATISTICAL MINEFIELD

Perhaps it is a combination of both, a vicious circle, in which the direction of the causal relationship can change from one year to the next. Remembering the caution I urged earlier on, we should remember that here we are dealing with a time series and that admissions will be negatively correlated with any variable which has been increasing over the 11 years in question, the development of colour television for example. To come to any definitive conclusion we would need to carry out an extensive investigation into changing attitudes and practices in the entertainment field during the period in question.

7.3.3 Example

Fig 7.3 shows the relationship between the number of flying hours flown by a fleet of aircraft using a particular type of engine and the number of engines failing over a 21 month period.

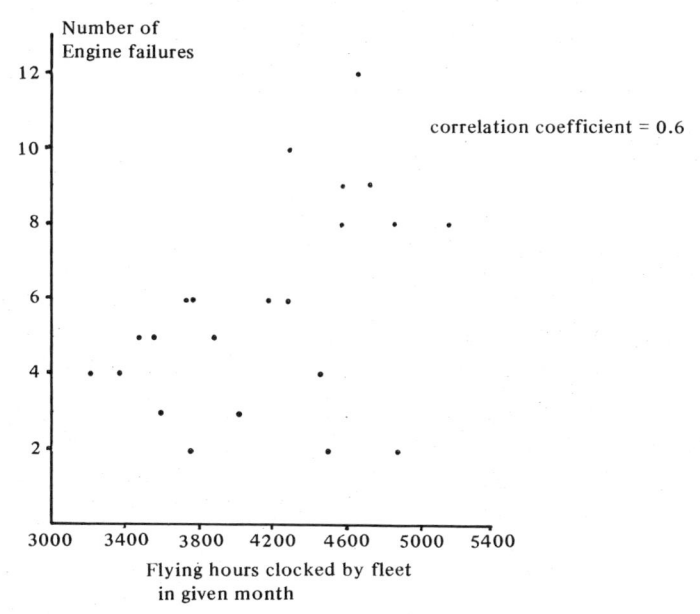

Fig 7.3 : Engine Failures and Flying Hours

correlation coefficient = 0.6

Flying hours clocked by fleet in given month

It seems reasonable to expect a positive correlation here, and indeed there is one, although the situation is blurred by a number of outliers. It is tempting to deduce from this diagram that it should be possible to forecast engine failures from projected flying hours for the planning period accepting of course that the degree of scatter means that the forecast would be subject to a certain amount of error. Is there not a trap here for the unwary? Flying hours in a given month follow

QUANTITATIVE METHODS

seasonal patterns. An airline is most busy during the summer and therefore any correlation between engine failures and flying hours means that there will also be a correlation between engine failures and any variable which is correlated with airline traffic. The weather is one possibility. Flying hours are at a peak when it is hot, and when it is hot there is dust in the air and there are also a lot of birds flying around. During the summer when the airline is at its busiest, aircraft utilisation is very intense and relatively more flights are made to holiday resorts. Perhaps it is one of these factors which is responsible for the correlation.

Note also that the plot consists of 21 months data only. Common sense suggests that from so little data no firm conclusions could be drawn. The diagram is useful, however, in opening up the problem. It provides a starting point from which the next step would be to carry out a more detailed examination of the specific instances of failure. What was the nature of each failure? What comments did the crew make on their flight report? What was the verdict of the engine overhaul team which dealt with the failed engine when it came into the workshops? More detailed information would be needed to arrive at even tentative conclusions.

7.4 Measuring Correlation

The examples discussed so far have demonstrated the need for the relationships between variables to be approached with a degree of caution. It is now time to look at some of the technicalities of how correlation is measured and how the relationship between variables can be put to use. I will start by discussing a classic example, the relationship between cost and the level of production. It is a situation which has widespread relevance in public and private organisations and one where a direct causal link can be reasonably assumed to exist.

7.4.1 Table 7.3 shows 9 weeks data on the number of units produced of a particular product together with the direct materials cost for that product.

Table 7.3 : Weekly Costs & Production levels

Week Number	Direct Materials (£)	Units of Production
1	210	30
2	405	60
3	382	105
4	480	141
5	690	172
6	510	206
7	805	251
8	904	283
9	793	323

CORRELATION AND REGRESSION – A STATISTICAL MINEFIELD

A scatter diagram for this data is shown in Fig 7.4. On it I have marked the 'centre of gravity' which is the point determined by the mean of the costs (£575) and the mean production level (175 units).

Fig 7.4 : Direct Materials Cost and the level of Production

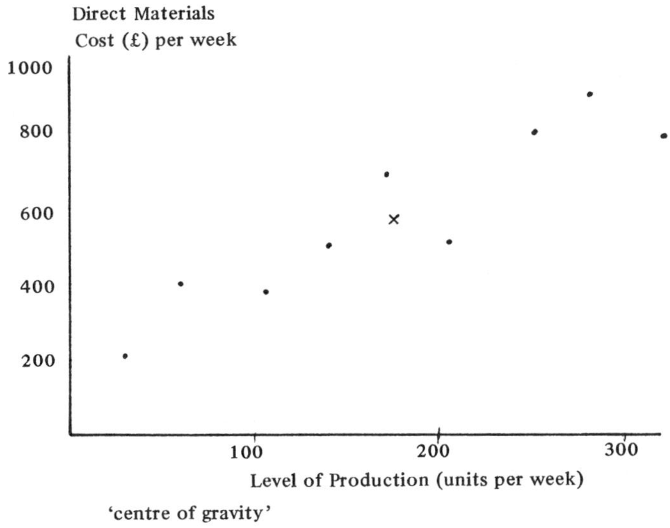

```
Direct Materials
Cost (£) per week
1000|
    |                              •
 800|                        •         •
    |                   •
 600|              ×
    |           •     •
 400|      •  •
    |
 200|   •
    |_____
         100      200      300
      Level of Production (units per week)
```
'centre of gravity'

The degree of correlation seems to be very high. How can this be measured in some objective way?

Fig 7.5a represents the extent to which each cost figure deviates from its mean value of £575. When the deviation is negative, that is when the cost is less than the mean figure, the deviation has been represented by a dotted line. Fig 7.5b does the same for the production level figures, showing how they vary around the mean level of 175 units.

As you can see, when the production level exceeds its mean level, the same tends to be the case with the cost figures. In fact only on two occasions do the costs move in opposite directions, in week 1 and week 4. In both these cases the deviations are small. Fig 7.5c shows the direction of the deviations, positive if they are above the mean and negative if below.

231

QUANTITATIVE METHODS

Fig 7.5 : Covariation of Direct Materials & Units of Production (see Table 7.3)

	above or below mean Materials	above or below mean Units	sign of product
a	b	c	
MEAN = £575	MEAN = 175 Units		
		+	−	−
		+	+	+
		−	−	+
		−	+	−
		−	−	+
		−	−	+
		+	+	+
		+	+	+
		−	−	+

200 400 600 800 1000   0 100 200 300 400
DIRECT MATERIALS COST   NO OF UNITS PRODUCED

Remembering that − x − = +, you can see that multiplying the deviations in most cases results in a positive quantity. This product

(Production level − mean level) x (cost − mean cost)

is a measure of the co-variation of the two variables whose mean value is known as the *covariance* of the two variables. When it has been standardised by the individual variances of the two variables (see A7. on page 430), it provides a measure known as the coefficient of correlation, a measure that lies between two limits +1 and −1.

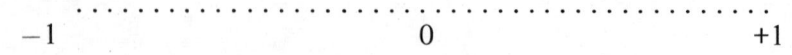

```
. . . . . . . . . . . . . . . . . . . . . . . . . . . . . . . . . . . . . . . . . . . .
−1                          0                         +1
```

Coefficients on the positive side indicate that
— High values of one variable tend to be associated with high values of the other

Coefficients on the negative side indicate that
— High values of one variable tend to be associated with low values of the other.

CORRELATION AND REGRESSION – A STATISTICAL MINEFIELD

From Fig 7.5c it is clear that the covariance is going to be positive because the only two pairs of deviations yielding a negative product are the small ones. Of course if the two variables had tended to move in opposite senses around their respective mean values, the resulting covariance would have been negative. If there is very little correlation between the variables, then the elements of the covariance will tend to cancel out and the correlation coefficient will tend to be 0. In the case of Fig 7.5, the correlation coefficient turns out to be very close to 1, +0.92 to be precise.

By contrast, Table 7.4 shows 9 weeks maintenance costs for the same weeks as were shown on Table 7.3.

Table 7.4

Week Number	Direct Maintenance (£)	Units of Production
1	57	30
2	21	60
3	82	105
4	33	141
5	54	172
6	23	206
7	106	251
8	24	283
9	52	323

Exercise

1. Plot a scatter diagram for this data. You will find that there is little suggestion of a correlation between the variables.

2. Represent the co-variation of these two variables using the method shown in Fig 7.5. Note how the deviations around the respective means of the two variables show no significant co-variation. Of the products of the deviations, 4 are positive and 5 are negative. The correlation coefficient in this case works out as +0.07, a value very close to 0.

7.5 Getting a feel for the Correlation Coefficient

Before going any further it would be a good idea to get some feel for the relationship between the correlation coefficient and the degree of scatter that can be observed in a scatter diagram. In Fig 7.6 a sequence of data sets is laid out. In each case the number of pairs of data is indicated together with the correlation coefficient, r. Look carefully at these in turn and try to summarise in your mind, or on paper, what the correlation coefficient tells you.

QUANTITATIVE METHODS

Fig 7.6 : Examples of Scatter Diagrams
a – i

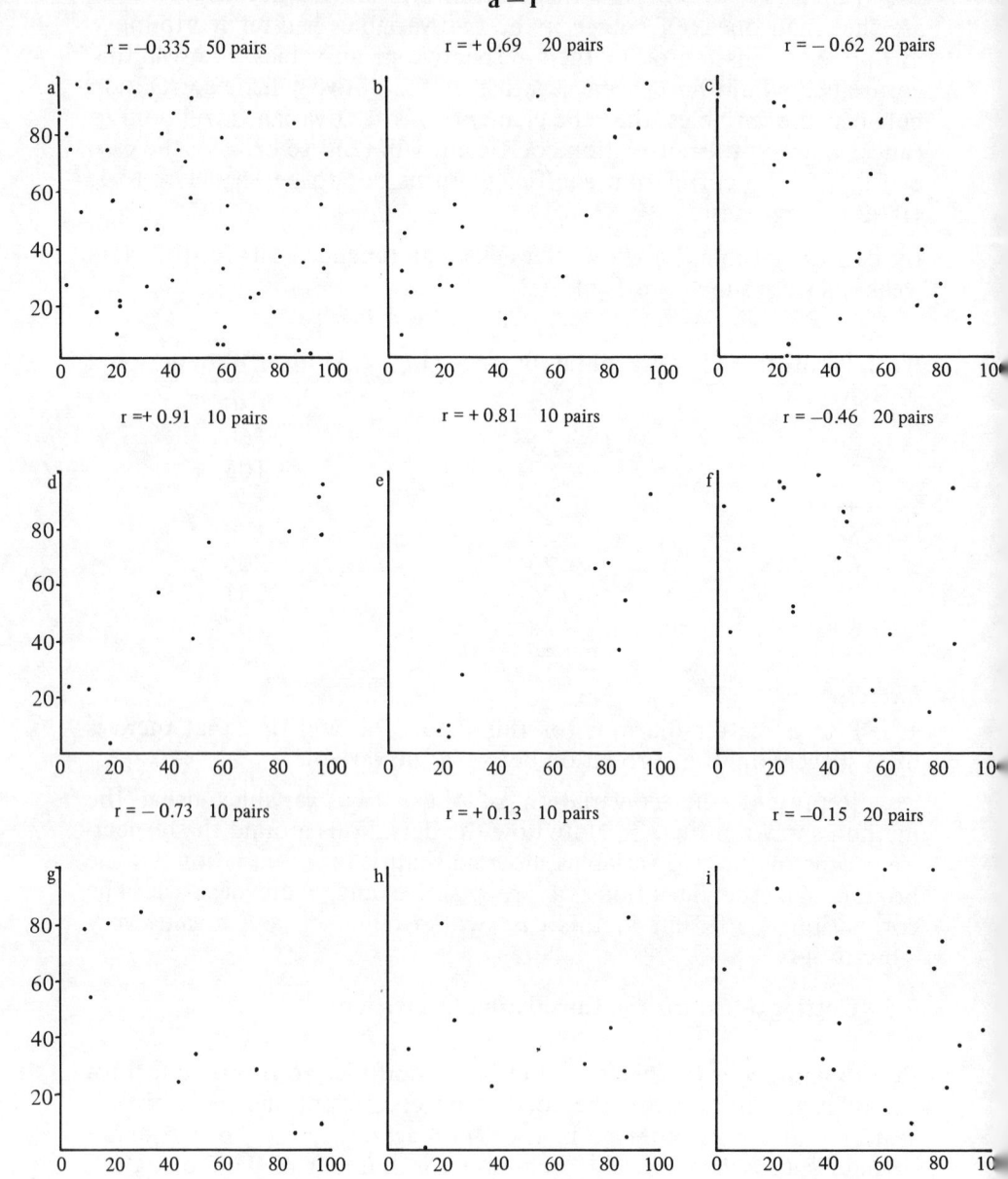

a) r = –0.335   50 pairs

b) r = +0.69   20 pairs

c) r = –0.62   20 pairs

d) r = +0.91   10 pairs

e) r = +0.81   10 pairs

f) r = –0.46   20 pairs

g) r = –0.73   10 pairs

h) r = +0.13   10 pairs

i) r = –0.15   20 pairs

Look at sets c, f and i. As your eye runs down the page notice how the clearly negative pattern in (c) moves towards the so-called 'plum pudding' effect in (i) in which no marked pattern can be discerned. This decrease in correlation is mirrored in the way the correlation coefficient moves towards 0 from -0.62 to -0.15. Note that although in set (i) the coefficient is technically negative, it is hard to see much sign of it in the scatter of points. Next compare (b) and (c) side by side. The absolute value of the correlation coefficient is about the same in both cases but the difference in sign is reflected in the trend of the scatter of points. Set (b) slopes up to the right while (c) slopes up to the left.

Set (a) at first sight shows no correlation. Close inspection, however, shows that there is tendency for the points to congregate in the upper left and the lower right quadrants and this indicates a definite negative correlation. But note that the value is far from 1.0. This is to be expected given the wide scatter of the points. Set (h) shows that low absolute correlation, +0.13 in this case, is not necessarily associated with a 'plum pudding' effect. The scatter shows an apparent sort of regularity, two rough columns of points side by side, but with no upper-left/lower right or lower-left/upper-right tendency which would push the coefficient towards 1.0.

7.6   The Problem of Significance

7.6.1 In your study of the examples in Fig 7.6, you will have noticed that there are examples where the correlation coefficient has a value near 0 and yet there seems to be no real degree of correlation visible. For example, in no case is the correlation coefficient actually equal to zero. What we need is some way of distinguishing those instances where the correlation is worthy of note, from those which have nothing to say. I must now make a confession. All the data sets shown in Fig 7.6 consist of *pairs of uniform random numbers.* However, I have *selected* these sets from a large number of samples using a computer programme. Now you might think at first, that it is odd that random numbers can show correlation, but they can. Think of the operation of the roulette wheels on two gaming tables placed side by side in a casino. By chance alone you might get pairings like this (the wheels bear numbers from 0 to 36).

Wheel 1	Wheel 2
34	28
12	3
27	31

producing a positive correlation. Of course you might just happen to get negative correlation such as

QUANTITATIVE METHODS

Wheel 1	Wheel 2
17	33
35	2
11	29
1	31

or, what is much more likely, you will get no notable degree of correlation at all.

But you must still be wondering why I thought it worthwhile to correlate random numbers! Well we need to decide whether a correlation coefficient is worthy of note or whether it is to be put down to chance associations. In order to do this I set the computer to work correlating pairs of random numbers (computers do that sort of thankless task very efficiently!). From the results we will be able to see just how likely random correlations are likely to arise. The examples in Fig 7.6 were all carefully *selected*. Fig 7.7 however, shows the distribution of all the correlation coefficients produced by the computer. In order to produce these distributions, the programme sampled uniform random numbers, allocated them arbitrarily into pairs and then calculated the correlation coefficients. Having done this it slotted them into class intervals.

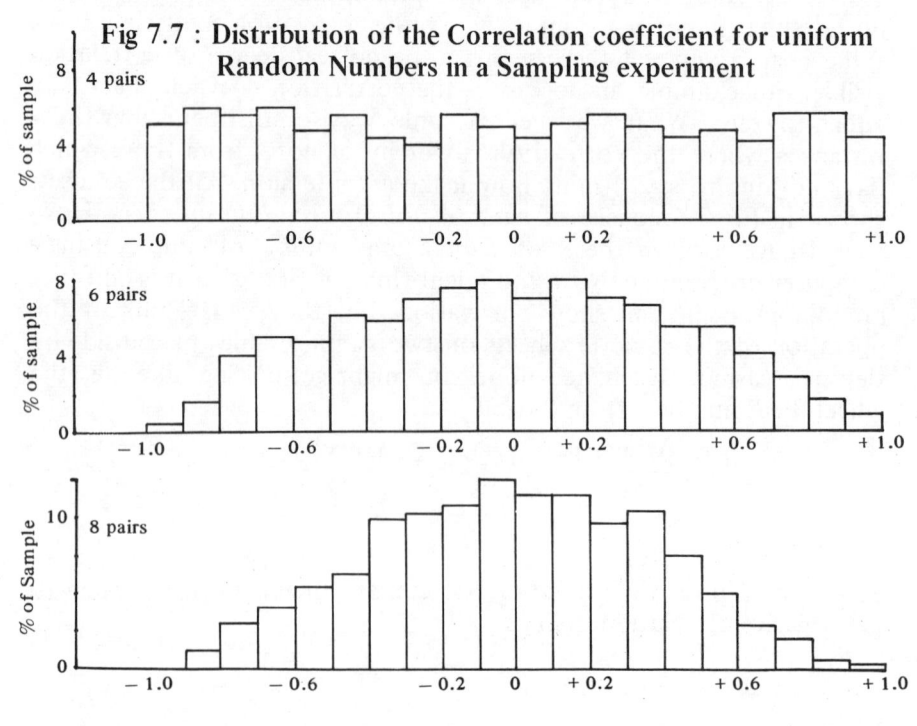

Fig 7.7 : Distribution of the Correlation coefficient for uniform Random Numbers in a Sampling experiment

236

CORRELATION AND REGRESSION— A STATISTICAL MINEFIELD

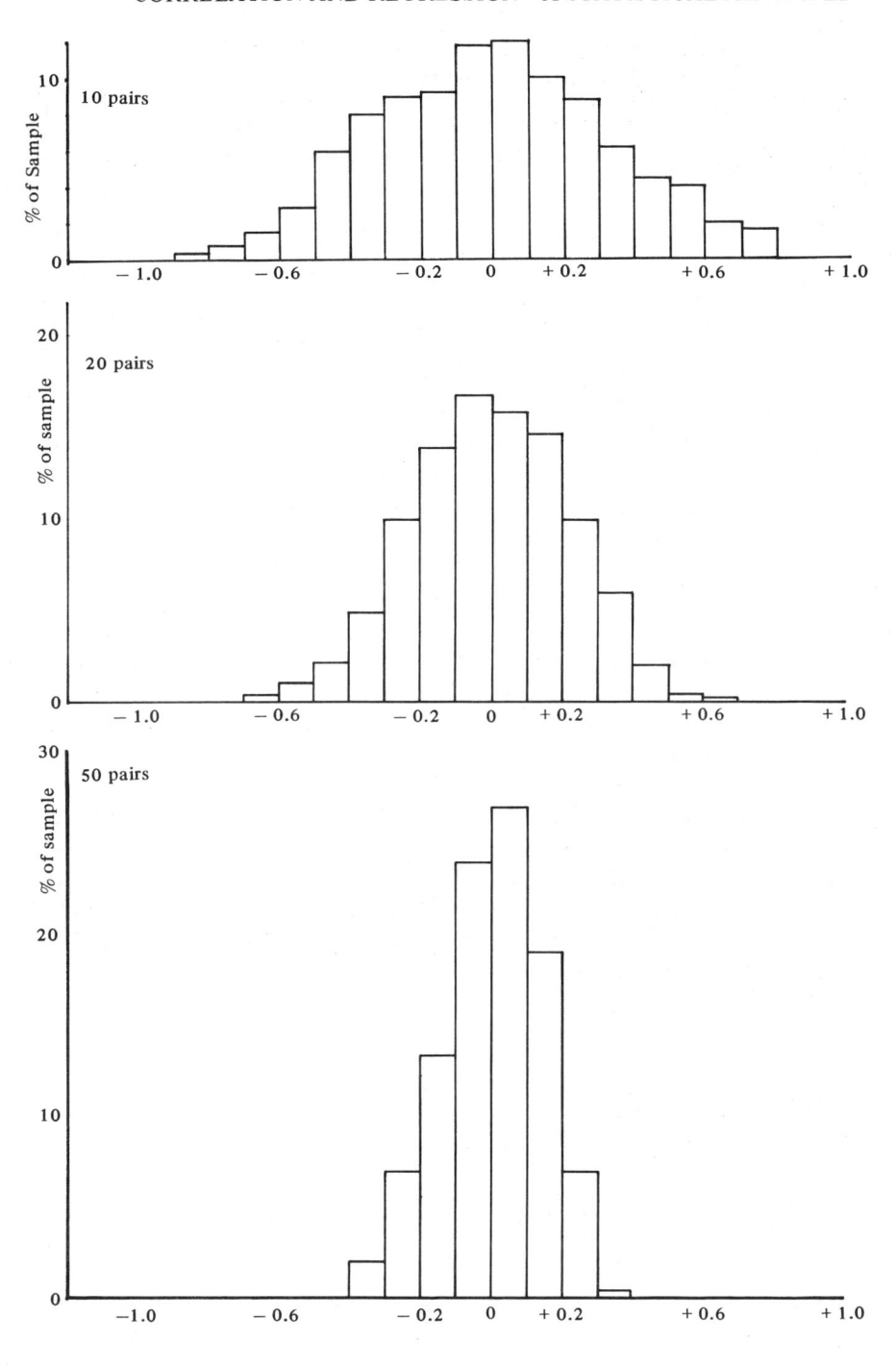

QUANTITATIVE METHODS

The most striking thing to notice is that the picture changes dramatically depending on the number of pairs of data correlated. With only 4 pairs of random numbers, correlation coefficients cover the whole spectrum from −1 to +1. In fact the extreme values were − .998 and +.994 respectively. However with 10 pairs, correlation coefficients above +/− 0.7 were rare and with 20 pairs most correlation coefficients fell between the limits +/− 0.5 while with 50 pairs, no coefficients more than +/− 0.4 were found. So clearly although random numbers can indeed show a degree of correlation, the experiment described above sets distinct limits to what is likely to occur. We can use this discovery to help decide when a correlation coefficient is likely to have occurred by chance or not.

Obviously from what has been said above, if we found 50 pairs of data with a correlation coefficient of 0.6 then we could argue that this could not have occurred by chance alone because such a high coefficient was never observed in the sampling experiment. We would describe such a coefficient as being *highly significant*. A value for the correlation coefficient of 0.22, however, would not give a clear-cut answer. The distribution based on 50 pairs suggests that such a value is unlikely to have occurred by chance but could conceivably have done so. Such a value we would describe as being *possibly significant*. A value of 0.15 is the sort of value which could well have occurred by chance. We would describe it as being *not significant*.

7.6.2 It must be stressed that the detection of a non-significant correlation coefficient does not mean that there is no association between the two variables concerned. All the sampling experiment has shown is that a coefficient of 0.15 based on 50 pairs is consistent with the hypothesis that there is no relationship between the two variables and has arisen merely by chance. However *it is also consistent with the hypothesis that there is a relationship between the variables.*

Think of the analogy with a court of law. Suppose that evidence is produced by the police connecting a driver with a hit and run accident. The jury may well think that the evidence is consistent with the defendant's guilt. What they also have to consider is whether it is also consistent with his innocence. The man was knocked down by a red car driven by a man with a broken nose. The defendant has a red car, a broken nose and a dent in the front bumper. This evidence is consistent with the assumption of his guilt. However there are other people with red cars and broken noses. The defendant's physiognomy and the state of his car is also consistent with the hypothesis that

CORRELATION AND REGRESSION – A STATISTICAL MINEFIELD

someone else did it. All the jury can do is to consider how many people there are with such a car in such a state and driven by such a man! They will probably decide that 'it would be too much of a coincidence' to assume that some other person was involved, and would consequently convict.

When faced with a marginal correlation coefficient we must weigh up the odds. However we are not in a court of law. Unlike the court of law we are not obliged to give a clear-cut verdict. We may be content to proceed on the basis that 'there may be a meaningful correlation' or 'it seems unlikely that the observed correlation is of any significance', and proceed with caution. We can look for other evidence to help out or defer the decision to a later date. For that reason what we need is a rough guide to the significance of the correlation coefficient. This is provided in Fig 7.8. I have deliberately made the boundary between the area of significance and non-significance a diffuse one (see shaded area). No sharp demarcation exists.

Fig 7.8 : a guide to the Significance of the Correlation Coefficient

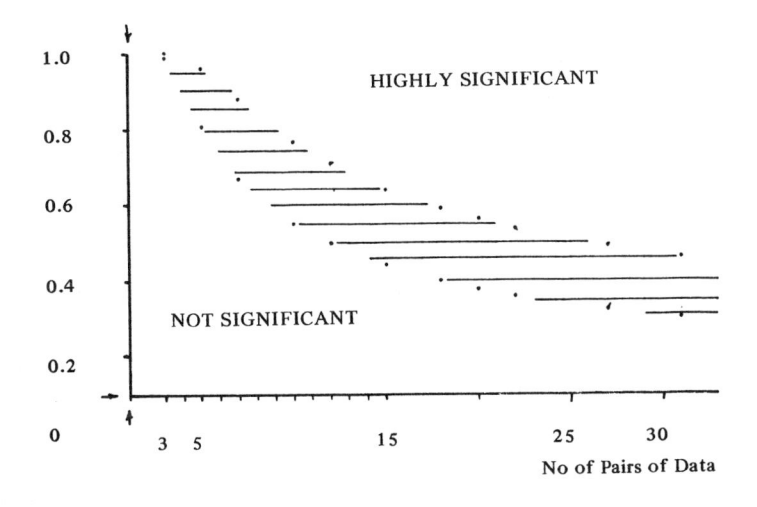

HIGHLY SIGNIFICANT

NOT SIGNIFICANT

No of Pairs of Data

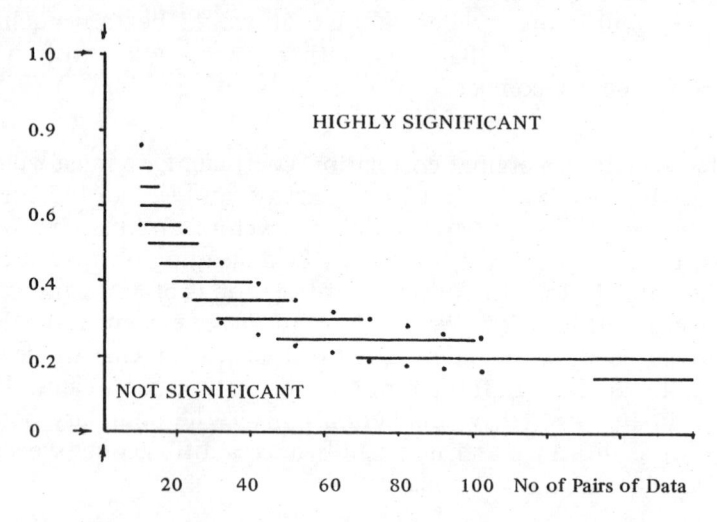

QUANTITATIVE METHODS

(N.B: The shaded area is bounded by the 1% & 10% 2-tail significance levels.)

Remember the following vital provisos to interpreting the correlation coefficients.

1.   A significant value for r does *not* mean that a causal relationship can be assumed.

2.   A non-significant value does *not* mean that no causal relationship exists. This is particularly true for small numbers of pairs of observations.

Now it is time to leave the theory and look at some examples from the real world.

7.6.3   Example: You get what you pay for ??

How much fat should there be in minced beef? The outcome of a court case brought by Hampshire County Council against a butcher was that the justices of the Queen's Bench Division concluded that the price was crucial in determining the quality demanded. The implication seemed to be that where quality is an issue, price is a relevant consideration in determining the 'quality demanded'. A survey was carried out into the relationship between the fat content of mince and its price. This was done between July and December 1981.* Ten

* This work was conducted by the London Chief Environmental Health officer's group and coordinated by officers from Hammersmith & Fulham Borough Council (as requested by letter).

CORRELATION AND REGRESSION – A STATISTICAL MINEFIELD

London boroughs cooperated in producing a total of 118 samples, these were analysed and one of the factors measured was the fat content.

Most people would expect that there would be a high degree of negative correlation between the price of mince and its fat content. Negative because the higher the fat content, the lower the price should be. A glance at Fig 7.9 shows that this is not the case.

Fig 7.9 : The Price of Mince & Fat Content

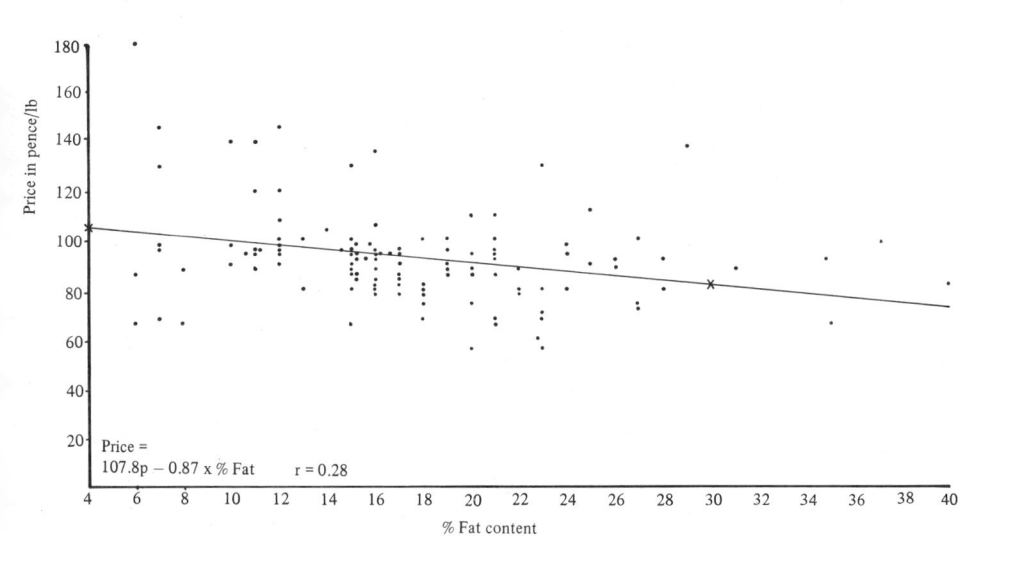

Price = 107.8p − 0.87 x % Fat   r = 0.28

(Permission No. 5)

There is a surprisingly wide scatter or points so that, for instance, in the fat content ranging from 6% to 8% prices ranged from between 146p per lb to 65p per lb. For those items where the fat content exceeded 20%, the price ranged between 138p per lb and 56p per lb. And yet there is a distinct degree of negative correlation. The coefficient works out to 0.28, and reference to Fig 7.8 indicates that this value is highly significant. What does that phrase 'highly significant' mean?

QUANTITATIVE METHODS

It means that it is very unlikely that such a correlation coefficient could occur by chance alone. (Remember the way in which random numbers could produce correlations by chance association). In this case that doesn't tell us too much. We expected a correlation anyway. Note, however what the degree of significance does *not* tell us! The fact that the coefficient is 'highly significant' does *not* mean that the degree of correlation is high. In fact, as you can see, the degree of correlation is very low. It's just that with as many as 118 observations, even a low degree of correlation is unlikely to arise by chance.

7.6.4 Example

Refer to Fig 7.3 on page 229. The correlation coefficient there is 0.6. From Fig 7.8, it is clear that this is a highly significant correlation. But remember that only tells us that there is something in the relationship worthy of note. It does not tell us that flying hours are a cause of engine failure. The coefficient is merely a measure of the association between the variables and not an indication of causal mechanisms.

7.6.5 Example

Fig 7.10 shows 6 pairs of observations of the age and length of service of the employees of a company in West London.

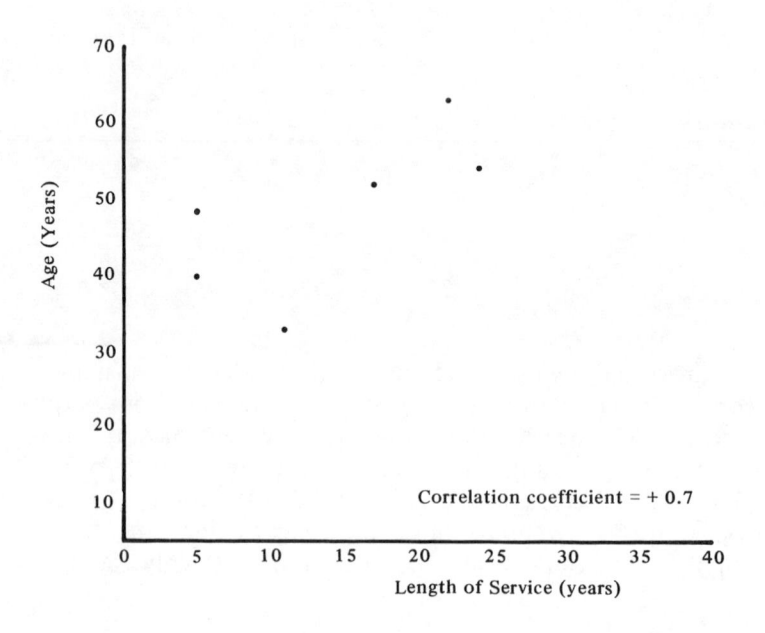

Fig. 7.10 : Age & Length of Service (Small Sample)

Correlation coefficient = + 0.7

CORRELATION AND REGRESSION – A STATISTICAL MINEFIELD

The coefficient of correlation is quite high, 0.7, but unfortunately for 6 pairs of readings Fig 7.8 tells us that a value as low as that is not 'significant'. What does this mean? Does this mean that here is statistical evidence that there is no relationship between age and length of service in this organisation? An unlikely story your common sense will tell you! Let's get this quite clear. The fact that the correlation coefficient is 'not significant' merely tells us that such a value *could* have occurred by chance, not that it *did* occur by chance. Look at Fig 7.7 again. The simulation experiment showed that for only 6 pairs of values, the correlation coefficient of quite random numbers can vary across the whole spectrum. I got one value as high as 0.98 by chance alone! So its hardly surprising that statistical theory is reluctant to allow us to call the value of 0.7 significant.

When you get a non-significant statistic *with low sample sizes* then it is as well to recognise that the evidence is inconclusive. For 6 pairs of values the correlation has to be very strong indeed for the effect to be distinguished from that which can be expected from chance alone. More data is required to reach a conclusive decision. In fact if we add a further 43 pairs to the 6 pairs of values in Fig 7.10, we obtain the scatter shown in Fig 7.11. The correlation coefficient is only marginally higher than for the smaller sample, but now Fig 7.8 tells us that it is highly significant.

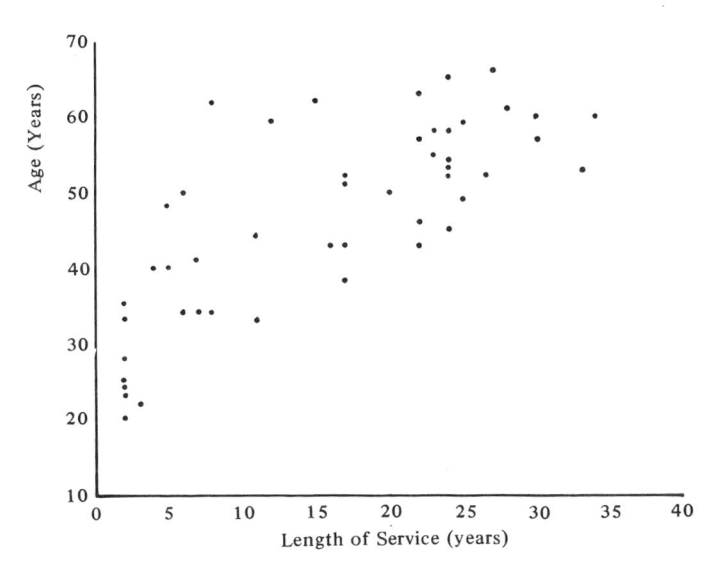

Fig 7.11 : Age and Length of Service (large sample)

QUANTITATIVE METHODS

This conclusion tallies with our common sense. A small number of values associated could have been a fluke. A large number convinces us that this cannot be so.

Exercise

In each of the following examples plot the data in the form of a scatter diagram. Guess the value of the correlation coefficient. Then check your answer and use Fig 7.8 on page 239 to assess the degree of significance of the coefficient. Then try and think of two or more different causal mechanisms which could account for the degree of correlation.

1. The figures which follow represent the sales per month together with the corresponding advertising expenditure for a perfume in a highly competitive market

| Sales per month (cases) | 10 | 15 | 18 | 35 | 32 | 38 |
| Monthly Expenditure on Advertising (£'000) | 7 | 6 | 12 | 14 | 18 | 20 |

2. The following figures represent the age together with the output in terms of the number of repairs carried out on a particular day by 24 operators in an electronics service centre. The repairs involved are not all the same, and some are on new models and others are on models which have been around for years.

Output 60 55 55 58 62 52 55 60 50 63 58 58 52 55
Age   20 30 40 45 35 45 50 45 50 60 35 50 55 60

Output 45 48 60 65 45 47 50 45 50 60
Age   60 62 40 30 50 55 60 65 40 30

7.7 The Correlation Matrix

When a large number of variables are involved, it is sometimes useful to have a look at a correlation matrix. This sets out the correlation coefficients of every variable against every other variable. The National Bus Company annual report for 1980 gives figures for its subsidiaries for 8 variables. These are as follows

CORRELATION AND REGRESSION – A STATISTICAL MINEFIELD

1. Net Revenue after interest and taxation – Historical Accounting
2. Net Revenue after interest and Taxation – Current cost Accounting
3. Support Payments
4. Traffic Revenue
5. Passenger journeys
6. Vehicle Mileage
7. Traffic Vehicles
8. Net Assets Employed

Below is shown the correlation matrix for this set of variables.

	1	2	3	4	5	6	7	8
1	1.00							
2	.94	1.00						
3	−.16	−.24	1.00					
4	−.05	−.3	.64	1.00				
5	−.02	−.18	.52	.88	1.00			
6	−.11	−.36	.62	.98	.85	1.00		
7	−.18	−.42	.72	.95	.83	.94	1.00	
8	.39	.22	.49	.73	.70	.70	.62	1.00

You can see that the relationship between Traffic Revenue (4) and Vehicle mileage (6) has in fact a correlation coefficient of 0.98, a very high figure indeed. This high correlation is partly explained by the fact that the traffic revenue includes subsidy payments from Local Authorities. These will tend to balance out those routes where there is a low revenue per mile travelled.

Exercise

Discuss possible reasons for the negative correlation between variables 3 and both 1 and 2. Also discuss the correlation between variables 4, 5, 6 and 7.

7.8 Hidden Dangers in Correlation

I have already highlighted the main danger, namely that a correlation between two variables will be interpreted as a causal relationship between two variables. Remember, before you decide that one variable is directly influencing another, you must find evidence of

QUANTITATIVE METHODS

how this takes place. Remember the storks. The correlation I accept, now show me a stork carrying a baby in its beak!

It is particularly important not to misinterpret the concept of significance. A low degree of correlation can be highly significant (see Fig 7.9) and a high figure for so little data can be non-significant (see Fig 7.10). Sort out that apparent paradox before you proceed. Two more potential problems are worth highlighting.

7.8.1 Insufficient range of Data

When data on two variables covers an insufficient range, no correlation may be apparent. If from Fig 7.3 on page 229, we took merely all the months where flying hours had been 4,200 or less, there would seem to be no relationship between the variables, the correlation coefficient being then only +0.191. You can see what the scatter diagram would be like by covering all of Fig 7.3 to the right of 4,200 flying hours. Care should therefore be taken before dismissing the hypothesis that an association exists between two variables when the data only covers a limited range.

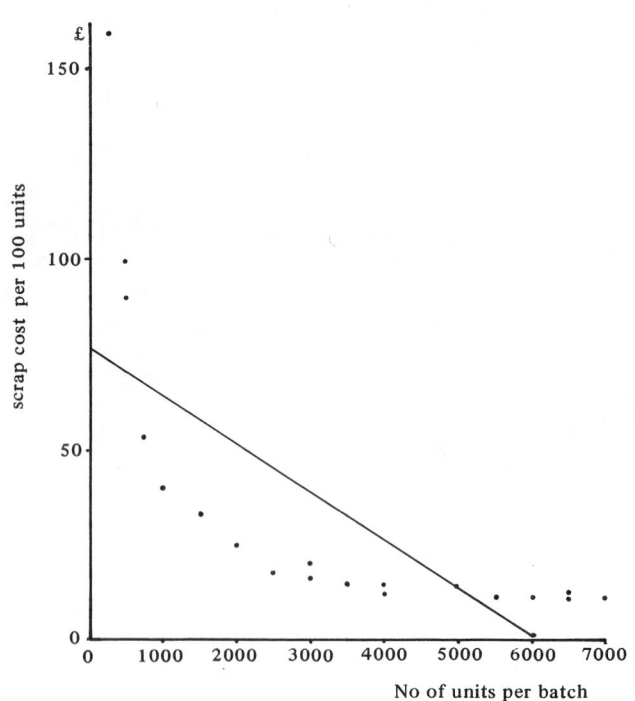

Fig 7.12 : Scrap cost & batch size

CORRELATION AND REGRESSION – A STATISTICAL MINEFIELD

7.8.2 Non-linear relationships

Look at Fig 7.12 on previous page. It is a hypothetical set of data representing the relationship between the batch scrap loss in £ per 100 units plotted against the number of units per batch. There is a very close relationship between the two variables and yet the correlation between the two variables is only −0.71. This is because the relationship does not follow a straight line trend. The correlation coefficient as it is normally calculated assumes that the relationship between the two variables concerned follows a straight line basis. (If the scrap loss in £ rather than in £/100 units were plotted, a straight line relationship would be obtained.)

For this reason it is time to open up the subject of straight line regression.

7.9 Straight Line Regression

Fig 7.4 represented the relationship between the direct materials cost and the level of production. Given the shape of the association, it seems quite appropriate to draw a straight line through this data, but which line should we draw?

If you are in a hurry and have no computational facilities to hand, then there is a quick and effective way of drawing a good line.

7.9.1 Semi-Averages

First calculate the mean of both variables. In this case we obtain

    Mean cost   =   £575

    Mean level of production   =   £175 units

These two points define a 'centre of gravity' for the data pairs just like the one shown in Fig 7.1. Through this point, a number of different lines can be drawn, although having a 'pivot point' helps to pin down the range of lines that can be reasonably drawn (see Fig 7.13 on page 248). The two lines I have drawn seem to me to represent the outer extremes of possible lines that 'fit' the data.

If you have a little more time for the job, there is one refinement you can add to this method. It involves the following steps:

1. Draw a line vertically through the centre of gravity

2. Separate the pairs of values lying to the left and right of that vertical line

QUANTITATIVE METHODS

Fig 7.13 : Regression Lines drawn 'by eye' through the centre of gravity

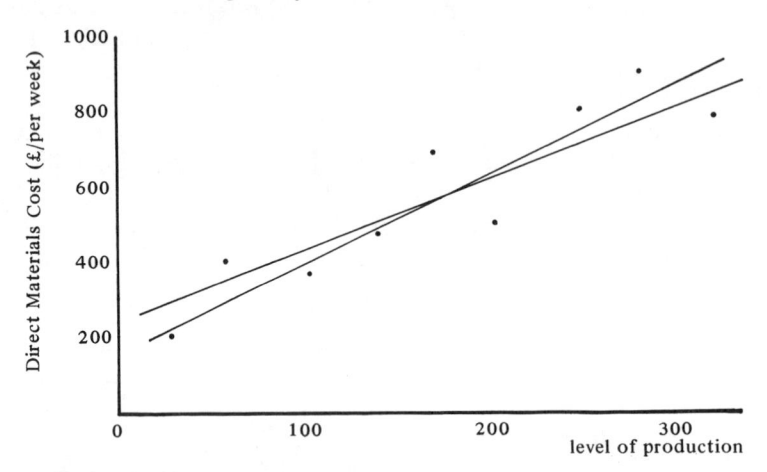

3. Calculate the separate centres of gravity of these two sets of data and mark them on your graph.

4. Draw a line through the centre of gravity that goes as near as possible to the subsidiary centres of gravity.

Applying this approach to the data in Table 7.3 on page 230 and Fig 7.4, the data separates into the following two sets;

Materials Cost	Production Level	Materials Cost	Production Level
690	172	793	323
210	30	510	206
405	60	904	283
382	105	805	251
480	141		

Mean cost = £433

Mean production level = 102 units

Mean cost = £753

Mean production level = 266 units

In this particular instance (Fig 7.14 on page 249) the three points are almost exactly in a straight line. This will not always be the case. When they are not so aligned, make sure that your line goes through the overall centre of gravity.

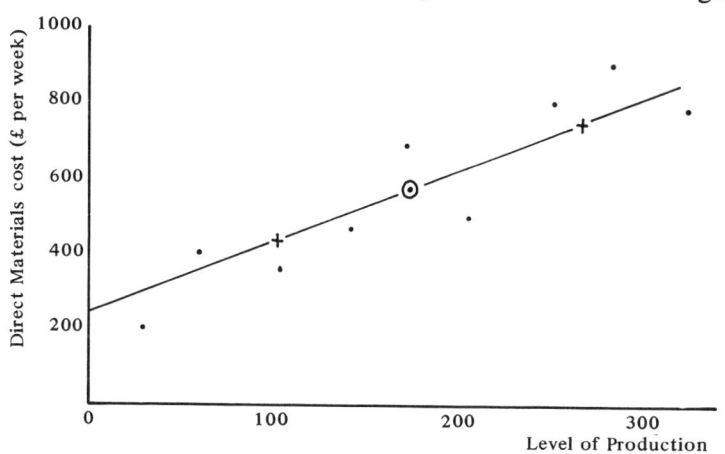

CORRELATION AND REGRESSION – A STATISTICAL MINEFIELD

Fig 7.14 : Line fitted using method of semi averages

You may feel that the method described doesn't produce results which are very much better than you could obtain by fitting the line by eye alone. However, it does reduce the possibility of bias. When people have a vested interest in the result, then they may tend to manipulate the line to produce a result which suits them. The method of semi-averages provides an objective method which is simple to implement and does not require heavy computation.

Exercise

Fit a straight line to the data contained in the exercises shown on page 244.

7.10 The Least Squares Regression Line

This is the most commonly used method for fitting a straight line to a set of data. We will concentrate here on understanding the principles underlying the method and the problems of making use of the results while the computational details are to be found in Section A7 (p 430).

When a line is fitted to a set of data, it is done with the purpose of predicting one variable from the other. The line fitted in Fig 7.14 would let us predict material costs given the level of production planned. For instance given a planned level of production of 200 units, the line suggests that the direct material costs would be £620. However the scatter of the points around the line suggests that such a forecast must be subject to some error. For instance if we take a production level of 283 units, the line suggests that the cost would be £785 whereas the data on which the line is based tells us that the

QUANTITATIVE METHODS

actual cost was £904, an error of +£119. If we take a production level of 30 units, the line suggests a materials cost of £295 whereas in fact the cost was only £210, an error −£85. We shouldn't be surprised, the line was drawn through mean values and therefore it attempts a compromise between the different pairs of data.

The least squares line employs statistical theory to find that line which minimises a measure of the errors that the line produces in predicting values of the dependent variable. Instead of minimising the sum of the errors, however, it minimises the square of those errors as represented diagrammatically in Fig 7.15. Such a criterion will tend to require a line that avoids large errors, as these, when squared, will produce large values.

Fig 7.15 : Errors and squared errors

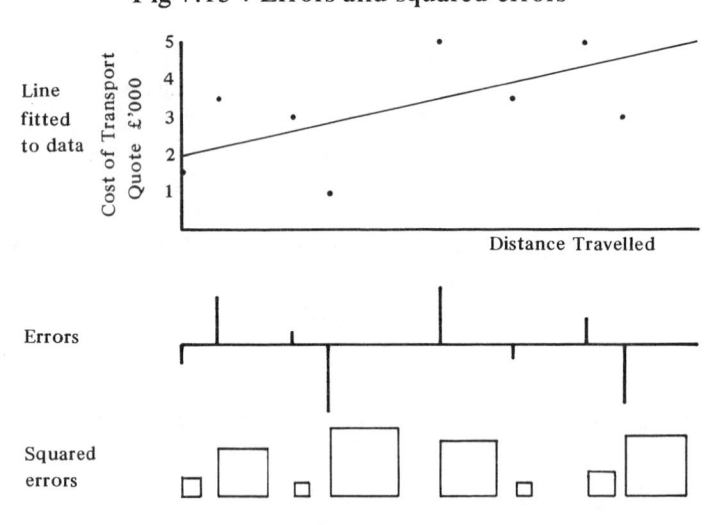

7.10.1 Fitting the Regression Line

The line is best found by using a computer programme. Manual calculation is messy and details are given in A7.10 on page 431. The output from the program will be an equation of the form

Dependent variable = Constant + Slope x Independent Variable

For example the least squares line which fits the data of Fig 7.13 is

Materials cost = £202.7 + 2.14 x Production level

It is important to be able to fit such a line. The method is quite easy. Take any two values for the production level within the range displayed in the scatter diagram and calculate the corresponding value for the materials cost.

CORRELATION AND REGRESSION – A STATISTICAL MINEFIELD

Production Level	2.14 x Production Level	Estimated Materials Cost (Col 2 + £202.7)
100	214	416.7
200	428	630.7
300	642	844.7

Now plot the results and connect them with a straight line. I have calculated three points. This means that if I have made a mistake in calculating one of the values it will show up as the three points should all lie on the same straight line.

Fig 7.16 shows the line appropriate to the materials cost data. Note that it is not the same as that shown in Fig 7.14.

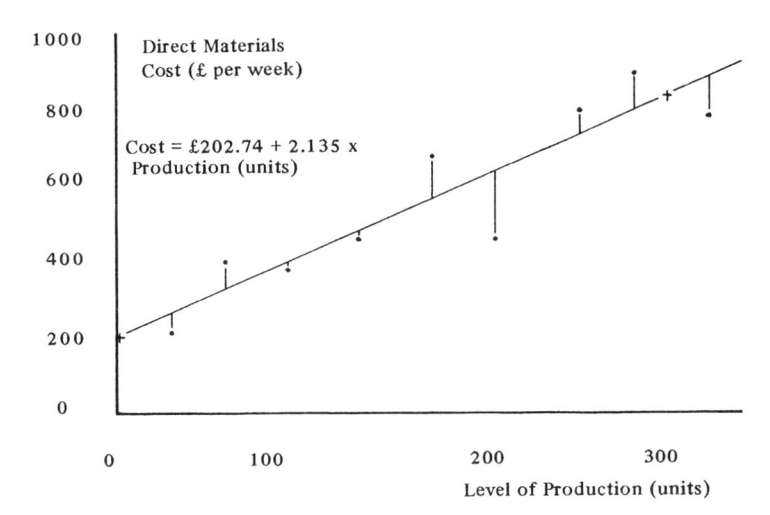

Fig 7.16 : Regression Line showing Residuals

Direct Materials Cost (£ per week)

Cost = £202.74 + 2.135 x Production (units)

Level of Production (units)

Exercise

Draw up the following lines on graph paper:

1. Monthly electricity consumption (£) = 1000 + 0.15 x (tons of product produced per month)
   (Maximum monthly production is 1000 tons)

2. Sales (£'000) = −5 + 1.5 x (number of salesmen employed)
   (usually 5–10 salesmen employed)

3. Monthly sales in Branch (£'000) = 16.5 − 1.3 x (number of main competitors within 1 mile).

QUANTITATIVE METHODS

7.10.2 Residuals

Fig 7.16 shows not only the regression line but also the errors between the actual values for the materials cost and those predicted by the line. These are known as the *residuals*, because they represent the errors 'left over' after fitting the line. The line fitted ensures that the sum of the squared residuals is minimised.

Examination of the residuals will often help to avoid major misunderstandings. Look again at Fig 7.12 on page 246. A computer programme gives a regression line as follows:

Scrap cost = £76.8 − 0.0125 x No of units per batch

If you fit this line to the date (for 1000 units, cost = £64.3 and for 5000 units, cost = £14.3), the line runs across the curve of the points because the computer is fitting a *straight line only*. Such a line is clearly inappropriate in this case.

If you have a scatter diagram in front of you this would be immediately obvious. If you didn't, however, you might be deceived by the relatively high correlation coefficient. However plotting the residuals against the number of units per batch, you obtain a striking effect, Fig 7.17.

Fig 7.17 : Residual Scrap cost and Batch size for inappropriate straight line

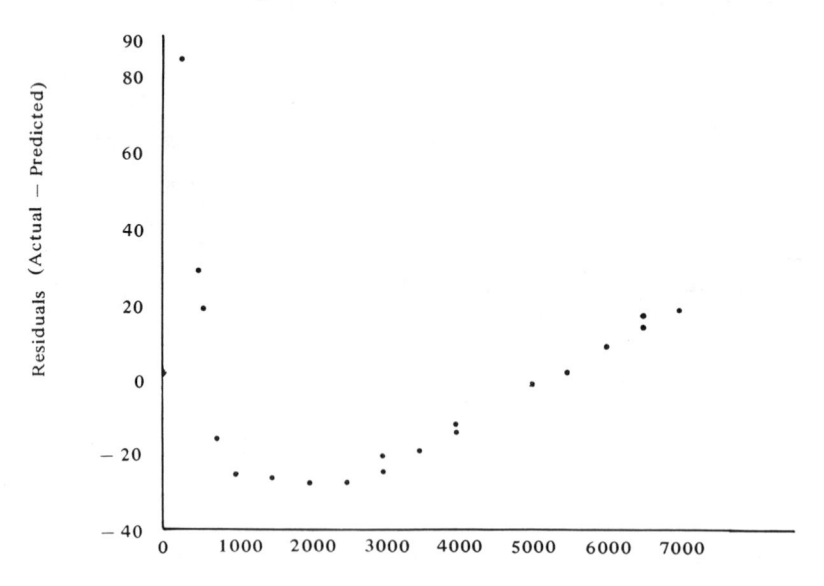

CORRELATION AND REGRESSION – A STATISTICAL MINEFIELD

Such regular patterns in the residuals are usually a sign that the line fitted is, in some way inappropriate and some investigation is called for. In the case of Fig 7.12 a curve would obviously fit the data much better.

7.10.3 Explained and Unexplained Variance

These technical terms are so widely used in applied regression analysis that they had better be discussed right away. In particular the word 'explained' can be misleading and requires careful understanding. If you don't like too many technicalities, go straight on to the next chapter.

Fig 7.16 showed the least squares line fitted to the materials cost/ production level data. Having fitted the line, we saw that there were *residuals* left over, measuring the extent to which the line did not fit the data. We say however that the line has 'explained' to some degree the variation of the cost figures.

Fig 7.18 shows the variation of the cost figures around their mean of £575. This is the variation that has to be 'explained'. Remember that statisticians find it better to measure this variation in terms of the squares of these deviations and they give to the mean of these squared deviations the name 'variance' see page 112 . In the absence of the regression line all of this variance would remain 'unexplained'. Now look at Fig 7.16. As a result of the line, the errors are much reduced. The residuals, squared and summed are referred to as the 'unexplained variance' or to use a technical term, the 'residual sum of squares'.

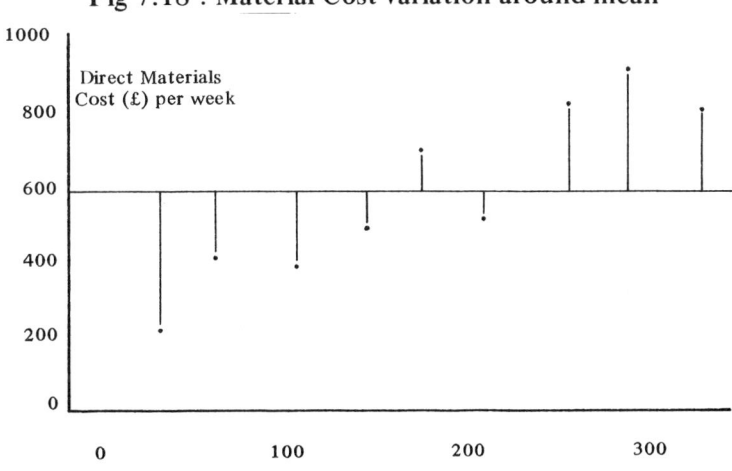

Fig 7.18 : Material Cost variation around mean

QUANTITATIVE METHODS

The details for the materials cost example are shown below. The squaring of deviations makes a mess of things but it is worth seeing what is happening in numerical terms as displayed in Table 7.5.

Table 7.5

1	2	3	4	5	6
210	− 365.4	133550	267	− 57	3226
405	− 170.4	29051	331	+ 74	5498
382	− 193.4	37421	427	− 45	2019
480	− 95.4	9110	504	− 24	567
690	+ 114.6	13123	570	+ 120	14401
510	− 65.4	4283	643	− 133	17580
805	+ 229.6	52696	739	+ 66	4399
904	+ 328.6	107949	807	+ 97	9409
793	+ 217.6	47330	892	− 99	9882
		434512			66981

The columns have the following meaning:

Col. 1 The actual material costs on which the line is based. (See Fig 7.16).

Col. 2 The deviation of each cost figure from the mean cost figure as displayed in Fig 7.18 (rounded).

Col. 3 The square of column 2. The mean of these is the 'variance' of the materials cost, that which needs to be 'explained'.

Col. 4 The cost figure predicted from the regression line. Each production level figure will generate a cost figure by reading off from the regression line (see Fig 7.16 rounded).

Col. 5 The residual cost. Col. 1 − Col. 4. These are the values that you can see on Fig 7.16. They represent the difference between the actual cost figures and those that would be predicted from production level figures by using the regression line.

Col. 6 The squared residuals. The least squares regression line guarantees that the sum of these is minimised.

The total variance to be explained amounts to $\frac{434512}{9}$. The 'unexplained' variance amounts to $\frac{66981}{9}$. It follows that

$$\frac{66981}{434512}$$ of the variance of the costs remains

'unexplained' or a proportion of 0.154 or 15.4% That means that the regression line has 'explained' a proportion 0.846 or 84.6% of the variance in the materials costs. Remembering that the correlation coefficient is 0.92, you will note that the correlation coefficient squared gives the proportion of the variance explained *by a least squares regression line*

$$(0.92)^2 = 0.846$$

Although this may all seem very technical it is important to grasp because many reports that managers have to read will employ some of the technical terms used above.

7.10.4 'Linear' Regression

We have seen that the correlation coefficient relates to the degree of fit of the straight line regression model. This serves to emphasise that the correlation coefficient, as it is normally calculated, assumes a straight line relationship even when one is inappropriate. So the straight line which fits Fig 7.12 on page 246, with a correlation coefficient of -0.711 implies that a proportion $(-.711)^2 = .51$ of the variation in scrap cost is 'explained' by the number of units per batch. A glance at the graph shows that the fit of the points to a *curve* would be much better than that and that a curved relationship would 'explain' a much higher proportion of the variance in scrap costs than a straight line would.

The term 'explain' has been cautiously put in quotes. To the uninitiated it might seem to imply that the regression has unravelled a causal relationship between the variables. Careful study of the example above will remind you that all the *explanation* consists of is a measurement of the extent to which the movement of one variable is associated with the movement of another. Remember the temperature of my unheated bathroom 'explains' a fair proportion of the variance of the sales of thermal underwear in Harrods. The association is not however a direct one but an indirect one. The only thing about my bathroom which throws any light on the sales in Harrods is its temperature and the same degree of 'explanation' would be provided by any other unheated bathroom or, more reliably, by the temperature on the Air Ministry roof.

Just to ram the point home refer back to Fig 7.6b where the correlation coefficient of 0.69 between two sets of random numbers (carefully selected by me of course) implies that 48% of the variance of one

QUANTITATIVE METHODS

set of random numbers is 'explained' by the other!

7.10.5 Use of Regression in Planning

A good example of when regression analysis is useful is in providing a basis for fixing budgets. In the example we have been using (Table 7.3 and Fig 7.4), the mean level of material costs was £575 while the mean level of production was 175 units. Crudely speaking that gives a mean level of $\frac{£575}{175}$ = £3.3 per unit produced. This figure, if used as the basis for forecasting the material cost per unit for budgeting purposes, would imply the relationship shown by the dotted line in Figure 7.19. Compared with our regression line, you can see that the dotted line will tend to underestimate the materials cost at low levels of production and exaggerate the cost at high levels of production. The reason is that the regression line implies that the materials cost at very low levels of production would be far from negligible. It seems to suggest that there is a *fixed cost* component of about £200 regardless of the level of production together with a *variable cost* of £2.1 per unit (the slope of the line).

Fig 7.19 : Effect of ignoring fixed/variable cost breakdown

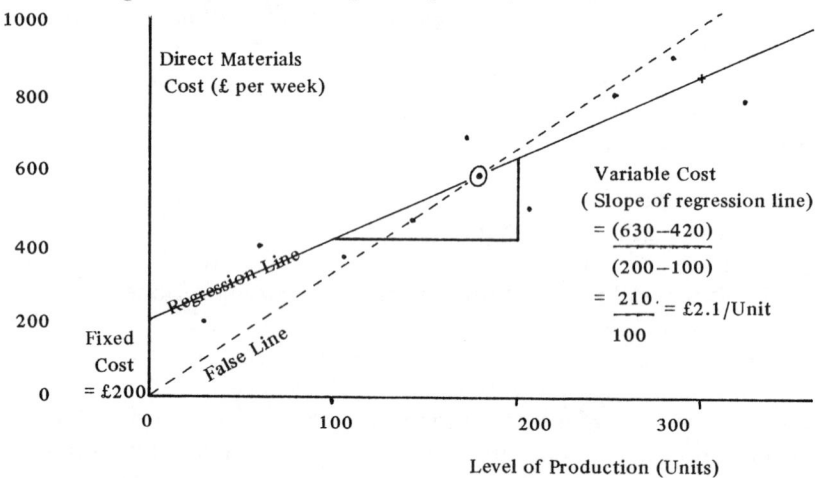

[Graph: Direct Materials Cost (£ per week) vs Level of Production (Units). Shows Regression Line and False Line (dotted). Fixed Cost = £200. Variable Cost (Slope of regression line) = (630−420)/(200−100) = 210/100 = £2.1/Unit]

A failure to recognise the fixed/variable structure of the costs can have serious economic consequences. Suppose a sudden order comes in for tender which will raise the level of production from 200 units to 300 units. The regression line suggests that materials should be costed at £2.1 for every extra unit whilst the other method suggests £3.3, a figure 57% too high. By exaggerating the cost, too high a price might be tendered and the order lost. Our analysis suggests that the *marginal materials cost* of each extra unit is £2.1 per unit.

CORRELATION AND REGRESSION – A STATISTICAL MINEFIELD

The errors involved in the example are relatively modest. If we turn to the maintenance costs (Table 7.4) where there is no evidence of any significant relationship then the errors can be very striking. The mean maintenance cost was £50 while the mean production level was 175 units. That suggests £0.29 per unit produced. This is equivalent to the relationship shown by the dotted line in Fig 7.20 The regression line, however, is almost horizontal and since the correlation coefficient was not significant and could well have occurred by chance, it would seem best to treat it as horizontal. This would imply a maintenance cost of £50 per week regardless of the level of production. In other words the regression analysis suggests that the maintenance cost is wholly fixed, the mean cost method (the dotted line) suggesting that it is wholly variable.

Fig 7.20 : Effect of ignoring fixed/variable cost breakdown (little correlation)

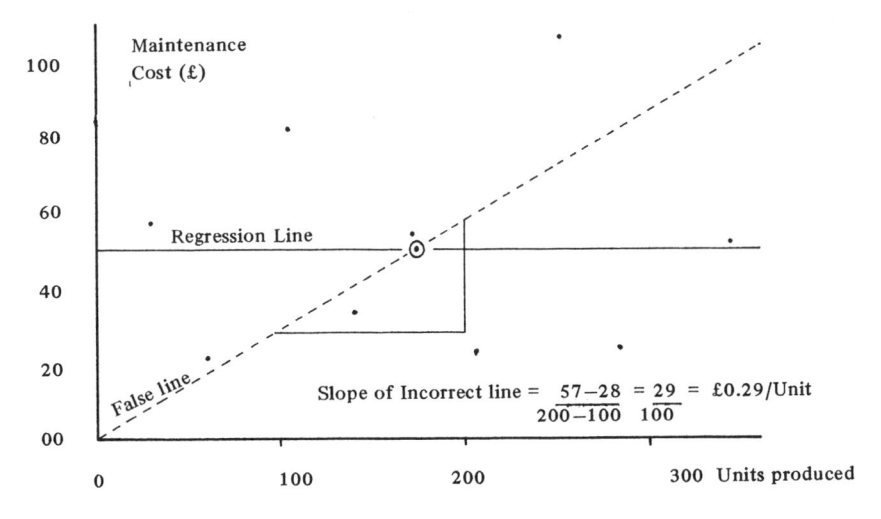

Slope of Incorrect line = $\dfrac{57-28}{200-100} = \dfrac{29}{100} = £0.29/\text{Unit}$

In this case, if cost is not treated as fixed and the false dotted line is used, then important errors will be incurred. In particular, raising the production level will be assumed to cost an extra £.29 per unit instead of costing nothing. This in conjunction with other misinterpretations of cost behaviour would exaggerate the cost of increasing production and lead to the company possibly turning orders away.

7.10.6 Multiple Regression

Multiple Regression is employed when the dependent variable depends on more than one independent variable. The calculations require use

QUANTITATIVE METHODS

of the computer and discussion will form part of Chapter 11 where it will provide an example of how computer packages can be used and misused by managers.

7.10.7 Linear Limitations

Because straight (linear) regression is the easiest to handle, we should not make the mistake of assuming that all relationships fall into that category. Fig 7.12 on page 246 is one example that we have already looked at. Others to watch out for are situations where step functions or changes in slope apply. Fig 7.21 suggests a few situations where some common sense will avoid inappropriate straight line fits.

Fig 7.21 : Some Typical Non-linear Relationships

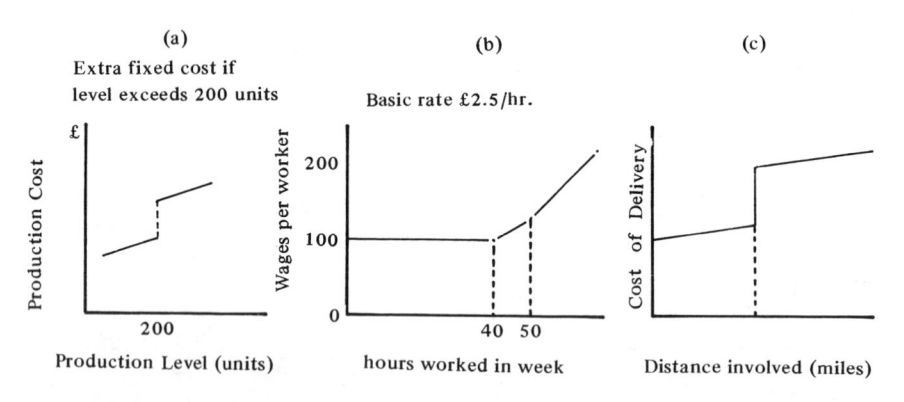

In Fig 7.21a extra fixed costs are incurred if the level of production exceeds a level of 200 units. Beyond a certain point, additional facilities are required to increase the level of production and this results in a sudden 'step' in costs. In 7.21b wages are fixed up to the guaranteed 40 hour week. The line thereafter has two slopes because of the two overtime rates applicable. Time and ¼ up to 49 hours and double time thereafter. In Fig 7.21c, a fixed cost is incurred for deliveries beyond a certain distance because of obligatory overnight stops.

These examples illustrate the dangers of projecting a relationship beyond the range of the data provided. Whenever you are looking at an approximately straight line relationship, use your common sense to ask yourself about when things are likely to change.

CHAPTER 8 : TRACKING THINGS IN TIME

Sections 1 — 4 discuss the problems that inflation creates for those studying time series involving monetary values and shows how index numbers can be used to solve them. The remaining sections, 5 — 8, discuss methods of analysing time series.

8.1 : The Inflation Fog

Have you ever had to find your way in the fog? You can see things in the immediate vicinity all right, but you can't see where you're going and what's worse, you can't see *where you've come from.* Landmarks that you've just passed vanish from sight. Things which were familiar and immediately recognisable are no longer present. The result is that you lose your bearings. I think inflation has the same effect on our sense of direction in money matters.

Inflation describes the tendency of prices to rise on a broad front over an extended period of time. There are a few exceptions but in general, over the past ten years and more, the prices of cars, washing machines, cigarettes, apples, oil, the membership fee to the AA, bus fares, the cost of a telephone call and most other items have risen. Most salaries have risen over the same period so that many people have been able to go on buying the items and services just as they used to before. But those on fixed incomes suffer the humiliation of finding that their pensions buy less and less as the years go by.

The truth is that most people can afford to ignore inflation. They grumble about it of course, a bit like the way they grumble at the weather, but they have come to rely on the 'expanding' pay packet and soon forget the way prices used to be even in the recent past. Every now and then a price sticks in the mind. People remember what they paid for their house, their car and a few other special things, but in general the broad advance of prices confounds our appreciation of relative price changes. Whisky, beer and cigarettes have all 'gone up', but have they all gone up to the same extent? The 'inflation fog' obscures the relative movement of prices so that it is difficult to see what has become relatively cheaper and what is relatively more expensive.

When you think of it, it is extraordinary. As you read this page you

QUANTITATIVE METHODS

could probably tell me without hesitation the rough price of a pint of beer in the local, the price of a coffee in the canteen and the price of your daily paper. But could you give me the same prices as they were five years ago? Unless you have an extraordinary memory your mind will go blank. Refer to objective evidence, past bills or papers and you'll get a shock. To follow relative price movements you need to be able to remember prices as they were and at the same time calculate the percentage increase in your head. Even with the prices to hand, the arithmetic can be unpleasant without a calculator. Just by looking, which of the following price increases is higher in relative terms?

1982 Price	1984 Price
236.49	276.21
71	89

Matters aren't helped by the official indicator, the Retail Price Index (RPI). Based on this published measure the television and radio journalists tell us by how much 'prices have risen'. These pronouncements add to the confusion by suggesting that all prices are rising at the same rate which is certainly not true.

8.2 By how much have prices gone up: Price Relatives

Suppose a house is sold for £18,000 in 1975 and sold for £65,000 in 1984. How can the increase in price be expressed? The price has more than trebled since 1975, the precise amount can be calculated as $\frac{£65,000}{£18,000} = 3.61$. It is more usual to multiply by 100 and then say that the 1984 price relative is 361 (1975=100). In this way the prices of a product during the advance of time can be converted to a sequence of price relatives

Table 8.1

	1980	1981	1982	1983	1984
Price of raw Material £ per ton	32.19	28.47	41.57	68.29	93.15
Price relative (1980=100)	100	88.4	129.1	212.1	289.4

(Permission No. 6)

You can see immediately that the relative price has changed over time. The figures tell us that between 1980 and 1984, the raw material price has risen by a factor of 2.89 or by 189%. When looking at a number of different items, this technique is very useful in picking out those items

TRACKING THINGS IN TIME

which are of special interest.

Exercise

1. Look at the following table and, without using a calculator, rank the items according to what you perceive to be the size of the increase between Year 1 and Year 2. Once you have done that, calculate the price relatives (Yr.1 = 100) and see if your rankings were correct.

Item	Price (£) Year 1	Price (£) Year 2
A	346	392
B	285	305
C	4.2	4.9
D	87	92
E	113	138

2. A company orders raw materials from three different sources. The pattern of price changes over the past 5 years is shown below. Without doing any calculations but just relying on your impression of the figures as they stand, jot down a few comments on the way supplier's prices have changed in relative terms during the period. Once you have done this, then convert each row into a set of price relatives (Year 1 = 100).

	YEAR 1	2	3	4	5
Supplier A	27.6	30.4	33.9	37.0	40.3
Supplier B	26.9	22.9	28.2	33.6	41.7
Supplier C	28.1	35.7	39.1	39.9	40.2

I think that you will agree that the price relatives make spotting trends much easier.

8.3 Price Indices

Price relatives tell us how individual prices and costs have varied in time. In order to cope with the 'inflation fog' we need to know how prices and costs have changed within broad categories of items such as 'raw materials', 'foodstuffs', 'share prices' and so on. A problem arises because each of these categories is made up of a number of different items and the price of each of these is likely to have been increasing or decreasing at different rates.

QUANTITATIVE METHODS

8.3.1 Shopping Baskets

A trip to the local supermarket will provide you with clear evidence that the ordinary family includes a very wide range of items in their shopping basket. So let's have a look at a pretty spartan household who live off nothing but tea, bread and milk! Table 8.2 shows how the price per unit of these items has varied over a hypothetical three year period.

Table 8.2 : Price changes over a three year period for a household

	Year 1	Year 2	Year 3 (Current year)
Bread p/loaf	50	60	70
Milk p/bottle	20	22	22
Tea p/packet	40	60	100

(Permission No. 6)

Exercise

Calculate the price relatives for each of the three items consumed by this household (Year 1 = 100).

From the price relatives that you have just calculated you will have seen that the price of these items has not gone up steadily. The price of milk has stabilised because of pressure within the EEC and the price of tea has risen because of competition for supplies in the developing world. Suppose we wanted to know by how much this household's food prices had gone up in the three year period. It would be quite *incorrect* to average the Year 3 price relatives thereby yielding an overall figure of 167 because this would take no account of the relative quantities of the three items consumed by the household. If we knew how much of each item the family bought, then we would calculate the increase in prices *weighted by the quantity consumed*. The result would be a *Price Index*.

Table 8.3 shows the quantities of the three commodities consumed by the family. This will provide the *weights* used for constructing a price index.

Table 8.3 : Average Weekly Consumption for the Household in Table 8.2

	Year 1	Year 2	Year 3 (Current year)
Bread (loaves per week)	14	14	14
Milk (bottles per week)	14	12	8
Tea (packets per week)	1	1.5	2.0

TRACKING THINGS IN TIME

Each column can be looked on as a weekly shopping basket typical for that particular year. Table 8.3 shows that the contents of that typical basket have not remained the same as time has passed. This poses a dilemma. Which shopping basket (the weights) should be used to measure the increase in prices? There are two simple ways of doing this.

1. Compare the cost of Year 1's basket with what that basket would have cost if it had been bought at current price levels. This is known as the 'Laspeyre Index' or *base year weighted* index.

2. Compare the cost of the current year's basket with what it would have cost if it had been bought at Year 1 price levels. This is called a 'Paasche Index' or *current year weighted* index.

Both these methods can be used to calculate a price index and the calculation and results are shown in Table 8.4.

Table 8.4 : Two price Indices for the Household

Laspeyre Method (Base Year Weighted)

	Yr 1 Consumption	Yr 1 Price/Unit	Yr 3 Price/Unit	Yr 1 Expenditure £/Week	Yr 1 Expenditure at Year 3 prices £/Week
Bread	14 loaves/week	50p	70p	7.00	9.80
Milk	14 bottles/week	20p	22p	2.80	3.08
Tea	1 packet/week	40p	100p	0.40	1.00
				10.20	13.88

Price Index for Year 3 = $\frac{13.88}{10.20} \times 100 = 136.1$

Paasche Method (Current Year Weighted)

	Yr 3 Consumption	Yr 1 Price/Unit	Yr 3 Price/Unit	Yr 3 Expenditure at Year 1 prices (£/Week)	Yr 3 Expenditure (£/Week)
Bread	14 loaves/week	50p	70p	7.00	9.80
Milk	8 bottles/week	20p	22p	1.60	1.76
Tea	2 packets/week	40p	100p	0.80	2.00
				9.40	13.56

Price Index for Year 3 = $\frac{13.56}{9.40} \times 100 = 144.3$

QUANTITATIVE METHODS

You may find it very frustrating that there are two answers to this problem and both of them are correct! But you must recognise that measuring price changes when the pattern of consumption is changing is essentially an impossible task. Try taking things to extremes and you will see what I mean. Imagine what the typical shopping basket would have been 100 years ago. It would have included things that no longer exist today. Servants' wages, candles and hay for horses would have appeared in the 'shopping basket' of the well-off. Major items that we take for granted today would not have been around at all 100 years ago. Repairs to car, electricity bills and so on. Clearly in the long run the task is impossible and all we can hope for is some reasonable and consistent measure.

Perhaps you're wondering why we can't simply compare the cost of the current basket with the cost of Year 1's basket. The result $\frac{13.56}{10.2}$ = 132.9 measures the relative *expenditure* between the two years but does not tell us whether that is due to a change in prices or a change in the quantity consumed. In other words a household's expenditure can go up because prices go up OR because the quantities consumed go up. You can't tell which is the case just by looking at the relative change in total expenditure.

Both indices calculated in Table 8.4 show changes in price levels by holding consumption levels fixed. They differ only in the year chosen to fix the consumption level. You might think that the current year weighted version (Paasche) is the obvious one to use. But because this measure compares todays basket of goods to what they would have cost in the base year it follows that each year not only do you have to find out what all the new prices are but also you have to find out what the new pattern of consumption is. This can be expensive.

8.4 Price Indices

8.4.1 The Index of Retail Prices (RPI)

This series of index numbers gives an indication of the relative change in retail prices, that is the prices that you and I pay in our everyday lives. The base of the current series is 15/1/74 = 100. The index is the weighted mean of a set of indices for 11 different categories of *expenditure*. These are shown in Table 8.5 together with the 1983 weights which total 1000.

Table 8.5 : Components of the retail Price Index with weights

1.	Food	203
2.	Transport and Vehicles	159
3.	Housing	137
4.	Clothing and Footware	74
5.	Alcoholic Drink	78
6.	Miscellaneous Goods	75
7.	Services	63
8.	Durable Household Goods	64
9.	Fuel and Light	69
10.	Meals bought and consumed Outside the Home	39
11.	Tobacco	39
		1,000

(Permission No. 6)

So the index for 1983 assumed that 20.3% of expenditure was on food and 6.9% was on fuel and light. You can see straight away that when movements in this index are used to describe changes in the 'cost of living' or 'inflation' then certain categories of people will be poorly represented. Pensioners, for example, might spend a much higher proportion of their meagre income on food and heating. Sharp increases in these items would affect the pensioner much more harshly than the change in the overall index might indicate. The weights shown are, of course, average weightings. If you keep detailed personal accounts you can check and see how they compare with your own personal weightings for these categories.

Table 8.6 : General Index of Retail Prices (15 Jan 1974 = 100)

Annual Averages

Year	Price Index	Food Index	Weight	Housing Index	Weight	Tobacco Index	Weight
1963	54.0						
1964	55.8						
1965	58.4						
1966	60.7	53.3	298	57.1	113	73.3	77
1967	62.2						
1968	65.2						
1969	68.7						
1970	73.1						
1971	80.0						
1972	85.7						
1973	93.5						
1974	108.5	106.1	253	105.8	124	115.9	43
1975	134.8	133.3	232	125.5	108	147.7	46
1976	157.1	159.9	228	143.2	112	171.3	46
1977	182.0	190.3	247	161.8	112	209.7	46
1978	197.1	203.8	233	173.4	113	226.2	48
1979	223.5	228.3	232	208.9	120	247.6	44
1980	263.7	255.9	214	269.5	124	290.1	40
1981	295.0	277.5	207	318.2	135	358.2	36
1982	320.4	299.3	206	358.3	144	413.3	41
1983	335.1	308.8	203	367.1	137	440.9	39

(Derived from Employment Gazette March 1984 & Annual Abstracts 1983)

(Permission No. 6)

QUANTITATIVE METHODS

Table 8.6 shows the index values for 1966 and for recent years. This is a sort of DIY table. I've left some space so you can bring it up to date by referring to the published statistics. I have also shown the individual indices for food, tobacco and housing so that you can see how the component price relatives and the weightings can change over the years.

The 1983 value for the RPI, 335.1, indicates that retail prices in general have more than trebled since 15/1/1974. The indices for Food, Housing and Tobacco remind us that the RPI is only an average and that it conceals major differences between the categories. The tobacco index, for example, shows a relatively high increase because of the recent policy of successive governments to penalise smokers. The changes in the weights are also of interest. Food has constituted a decreasing percentage of expenditure since 1966. As tobacco prices have risen above the general level of prices, the drop in the weighting reflects the decreasing number of smokers. In the case of housing, however, as the index has increased with higher interest rates, the weights have also increased. People with mortgages have to pay up when the 'price' of money goes up. They don't have much choice.

8.4.2 Changing the Base

Suppose that you were mainly interested in changes during the period 1979 onwards. It might make things clearer in that case to convert the index to one in which 1979 = 100. This is done as follows.

$$\text{New index} = \frac{\text{Old index}}{\text{New base year index}} \times 100$$

Thus 1980's figure for the RPI becomes $\left(\frac{263.7}{223.5}\right) \times 100 = 118.0$, and that for 1983 becomes 150.0. This procedure makes identifying relative changes with respect to the new base year much easier. The RPI itself has had its base changed twice within the range of figures shown in Table 8.6. Prior to 1974 the index was based on 16/1/62 = 100 so that for 1970 the index was 140.2 and on 15/1/74 the *old* index was 191.8 ∴ Converting to the new 1974 base, the 1970 figure becomes

$$\frac{140.2}{191.8} \times 100 = 73.1$$

As shown in Table 8.6

Exercise

Produce a new index series up to 1981 (1979 = 100) for Food, Tobacco and Housing. Thus for Food in 1980, the new value is $\frac{255.9}{228.3}$ x 100 = 112.1. What effects does this new version of the index help to highlight.

8.4.3. The Limitations of the RPI

The RPI gives *an* indication of how the prices facing *an* average consumer are changing in time. When the index goes from about 100 in 1974 to about 200 in 1978, this indicates that the price of *a* typical 'basket' of goods and services has doubled during that period. *A* typical consumer would need to have doubled his earnings during that period in order to have maintained his 'standard of living'. I have used the indefinite article to remind you that an index such as the RPI is only an average and therefore other equally valid indices could have been constructed. It's an expensive business updating indices so it's just as well to use the ones available 'off the hook' and be aware of their limitations.

Always bear in mind that the RPI is constructed as a measure of the cost of living to the man in the street. It was not designed for the businessman importing electronic equipment from the USA or for one operating an air freighting service. Different organisations may require more relevant indices to give them an indication of how *their* prices are changing. The costs for the importers will be affected by fluctuations in the sterling/dollar exchange rate. Their basket of goods and services can go up overnight with a sudden change in the money markets. The costs for the company providing an air freighting service will be very sensitive to fuel costs and therefore, as we have seen in recent years, can suffer sharp changes because of political changes in different parts of the world.

8.4.4 Indices of Wholesale Prices

Other price indices exist of course. The Department of Industry publishes indices of wholesale prices for materials purchased by manufacturing industry. Fig 8.1 (page 268) shows how some *selected* items have varied since 1975.

These index numbers measure changes in the prices of goods purchased by organisations within different industrial categories and therefore provide for such companies a better measure of the 'cost of living' than the RPI. Fig 8.2 (page 268) illustrates indices of output which are produced by the Department of Trade and Industry.

Note how different commodities can vary greatly in the degree to which prices have changed. Our obsession about inflation and how 'it' goes up at a quoted rate should not let us forget that although nearly all prices go up some go up more than others.

QUANTITATIVE METHODS

Fig 8.1 : Indices of wholesale prices purchased by three Industries

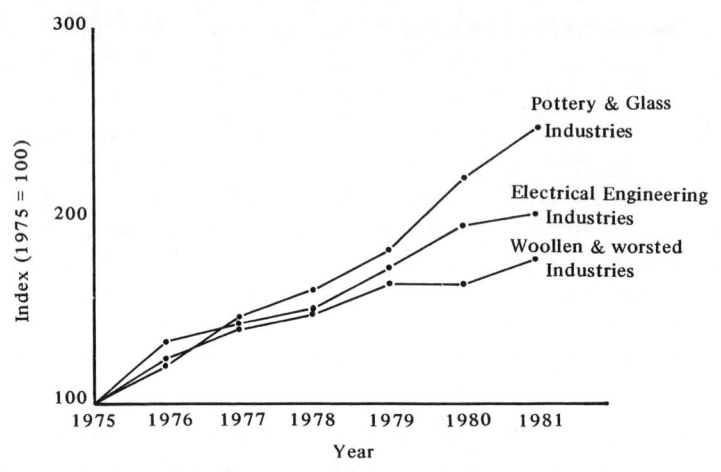

Fig 8.2 : Indices of wholesale prices of Selected Commodities produced in the U K

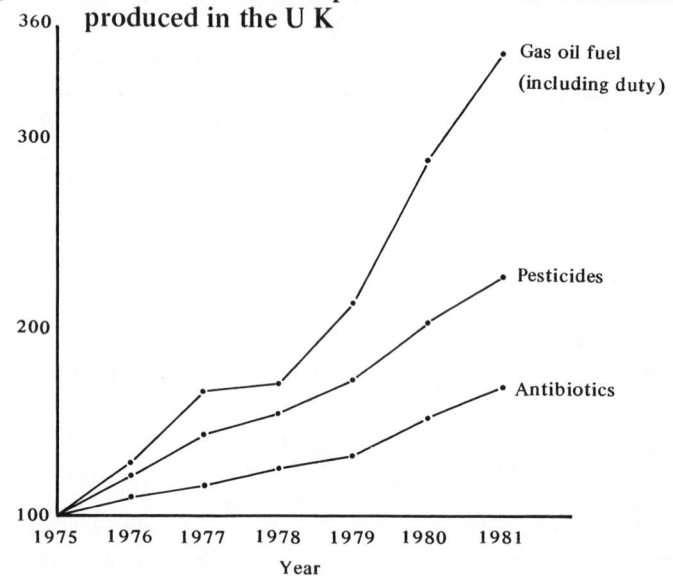

8.4.5 Real Price Changes, Deflating a Series

Price Indices can be used to clear away the inflation fog. Inflation suggests to us that 'everything is going up' and yet, as we have seen, there are marked differences between different items. Time series of prices can be converted to a common base of today's average price level. Table 8.6 says that the index for 1966 was 60.7 and that for 1983 was 335.1. That means that in a very general sense that prices have gone up by a factor of $\frac{335.1}{60.7} = 5.52$ and that therefore you would need £5.52 in 1983 to buy goods and services worth £1.00 in 1966. It is possible therefore to convert 1966 prices to a value which is comparable to 1981 prices. The rule is

$$\text{Price at current level} = \frac{\text{Old Price} \times \text{Current Index Value}}{\text{Old Index Value}}$$

The process is known as deflating the series. So using the RPI let's sweep away the inflation fog and see how the price of a number of familiar goods has varied in terms of 1983 purchasing power.

'Just think of how expensive spirits are these days! Beer too is a terrible price. Why, I remember the days when you could get . . . .' A familiar line overheard in the bar. But because of 'inflation fog' it is difficult to have any clear idea of whether things are more expensive in real terms than in the 'good old days'. Table 8.7 shows how the price of a bottle of spirits costing £7.15 in 1983 and a pint of beer costing 60p in the same year have varied over a 20 year period.

Table 8.7 : Typical Prices of Spirits & Beer with deflated (1983) equivalent prices (See note on page 434)

Year	Spirits £/bottle	RPI (15.1.74=100)	Spirits Real price £/bottle	Beer P/pint	Beer Real price P/pint
1963	2.10	54.0	13.03	7.8	48.4
1965	2.42	58.4	13.89	8.9	51.1
1967	2.58	62.2	13.90	9.5	51.2
1969	2.51	68.7	12.24	10.5	51.2
1971	2.42	80.0	10.14	12.0	50.3
1973	2.32	93.5	8.31	14	50.2
1975	3.29	134.8	8.18	20.5	51.0
1977	4.38	182.0	8.06	29.5	54.3
1979	4.77	223.5	7.15	38.5	57.7
1981	6.29	295.0	7.15	50.5	57.4
1983	7.15	335.1	7.15	60	60.0

(Derived from Economic Progress Report No 161, Oct 1983, Treasury) *(Permission No. 6)*

Values for the RPI are also shown and these have been used to calculate the price of the two items in terms of 1983 prices. So, for example, the price of a bottle of spirits in 1965 expressed in equivalent 1983 terms is calculated as

$$£2.42 \times \frac{335.1}{58.4} = £13.89$$

This price can be interpreted as follows. What people paid for a bottle

QUANTITATIVE METHODS

of spirits in 1965 would buy goods and services worth £13.89 in 1983. In fact in 1983 a bottle of spirits only cost £7.15 so that the *real cost* of spirits has fallen since 1965. So Table 8.7 allows us to follow the real cost of spirits and beer with inflation eliminated by bringing all prices onto a 1983 basis. The fog of inflation has been blown away and the result is quite dramatic. The series shows that spirits which seem to cost so much these days have tumbled in real terms while beer has risen. Close scrutiny of Table 8.7 shows what happened. The price of spirits (including duty) remained virtually unchanged between 1965 and 1973 during which time the general level of prices rose by a factor of $\frac{93.5}{58.4}$ = 1.6. If the monetary price of an item remains static while prices in general are rising then the real cost of that item must be falling. The government has always been careful to manipulate the duty on tobacco and drink to provide a source of revenue without letting prices rise so high as to drive away the consumer.

Refer back to page 228 and note that I deflated the price of cinema tickets so as to eliminate the effects of inflation and correlate real costs against admission numbers.

Exercise

1. Calculate the real cost at 1983 price levels for the following items (Use the RPI figures in Table 8.7. The figures show the approximate monetary costs in the years in question.

Year	63	65	67	69	71	73	75	77	79	81	83
Wine p/bottle	44	56	55	75	74	72	107	128	137	171	200
Cigarettes p/packet	19	23	23	26	26	27	42	55	66	90	108
Petrol p/gallon	24	26	27	33	35	37	74	91	113	154	180

2. A man inherited some family shares in 1963 since when he feels they have 'done very well'. Calculate how the value of the shares has changed over time using the RPI values given in Table 8.7.

Year	63	65	67	69	71	73	75	77	79	81	83
Share Price (pence)	35	37	34	38	42	46	67	87	107	136	150

3a. Convert the following figures for the average weekly earnings of full-time men into real earnings in 1981 equivalent values. Use the RPI figures in Table 8.6 on page 265. What has been the trend in real earnings?

Year	75	76	77	78	79	80	81
Average weekly Earnings	59.2	70.0	76.8	86.9	98.8	121.5	136.5

(Annual Abstracts 1983)

3b. Convert the original series to an earnings index with 1975 = 100. Carry out a similar change of base for the RPI and compare the results.

4. A man retired on a fixed pension of £5,000 a year in 1970. Calculate his pension over the years expressed in deflated 1983 terms and plot a graph of the results.

5. A woman retired on an index-linked pension in 1970. The terms were £2,500 per annum but to be increased along with the increase in the RPI. Calculate her annual pension and compare it with that received by the pensioner in (4) above. (For example in 1971, referring to the RPI figures in Table 8.6, her pension would be $\frac{80.0}{73.1}$ × £2,500 = £2,736.) What has her pension been in real terms?

8.4.6 'Deflating' Time Series using other indices

You must be careful not to use the RPI for deflating all series. The RPI is a measure of the level of general prices of goods and services. For industrial users, an index more relevant to prices that affect them should be used. In the following example special indices have been used.

Table 8.8 shows the value of stock purchased in the first three months of 1982. It was all sold in July 1982 for £10,000. Crudely speaking, the gross profit is the revenue less the cost of the goods sold, that is £10,000 − £8,000 = £2,000. However the profit is exaggerated because to replace that stock would cost more than £8,000 because the price of stock has gone up. Using an 'All Stocks Price Index' provided by the Board of Trade, the profit can be calculated using the replacement cost of the stocks.

QUANTITATIVE METHODS

Table 8.8

	Purchase Value	Stocks Index	Deflated Value (July)
January	2,000	217.0	2,038
February	3,000	218.6	3,034
March	3,000	218.9	3,030
April		219.7	
May		220.6	
June		220.5	
July		221.1	

The total replacement cost of the stock in July would be £8,102. Therefore costing the stock at replacement value reduces the profit to £1,898. The government now allows stock relief for tax purposes but the precise calculations are beyond the scope of this book.

8.5 The Manager and Time Series

Managers have a well established cartoon image. They sit at their desks while on the wall behind them a graph zig-zags up or down to match the expression on the manager's face. In fact Time Series really are a vital part of manager's working material. Managers have to preserve a keen sense of the passage of time and time series provide them with a picture of how vital measures of performance such as costs, sales, scrap rates, wastage rates and complaints have varied in the past. These series usually contain information which is relevant to decisions which have to be taken about present and future operations.

Between controlling current operations from hour to hour at one extreme and long term forecasting at the other, there is no clear dividing line. However these two activities are so different at the extremes that it is useful to talk about short term and long term forecasting. Just remember that there is a hazy area in the middle which I shall avoid calling medium term forecasting for fear of entering into a sterile semantic debate. For short and long term forecasting the statistician has techniques to help the manager. There is however a magic ingredient that the manager must add himself before stirring: common sense and knowledge of the area under study.

8.6 Short term Forecasting

8.6.1 Smoothing Using Moving Averages

One of the most awkward things about time series is that they have a

TRACKING THINGS IN TIME

tendency to jump about in a sort of haphazard manner. *Smoothing* is the term given to the process of ironing the series out so that the viewer can see the underlying trend. Moving averages (means) provide provide a simple way of doing this. Suppose a new salesman has been taken on. The weekly business he has been able to obtain is shown in Table 8.9

Table 8.9 : Smoothing a series using Moving Averages

Week No	1	2	3	4	5	6	7	8	9	10
Sales £ '000	6	2	8	2	12	10	4	4	14	12
4 week moving total				18	24	32	28	30	32	34
4 week moving average				4.5	6	8	7	7.5	8	8.5

The moving total is simply the sum of four weeks sales (18 = 6 + 2 + 8 + 2) and the moving average (mean) is that total divided by 4. As the moving totals overlap, a short-cut method is available as follows:

moving total for week 5 = moving total for week 4
+ (week 5 sales − week 1 sales)

Thus the moving total for week 5 is calculated as follows:

24 = 18 + (12 − 6)

As the total moves on by one week, the new week is added and the sales 5 weeks previously 'fall off'. Fig 8.3 (page 274) shows how the moving average smoothes the time series.

Exercise

Extend Table 8.9 by adding the following sales data for weeks 11 to 20.

| 11 | 8 | 14 | 13 | 12 | 10 | 9 | 15 | 8 | 16 |

The choice of 4 weeks over which to average was quite arbitrary. In practice you need to experiment in order to find the best results. The main disadvantage of this method is the abrupt way in which information 'falls off' the average. Look at the moving total for week 4. All the sales values for weeks 1 to 4 are included in the total of 18. Just one week later and the sales value for week 1 is no longer considered relevant. This abrupt switch from data being relevant to being non-relevant defies common sense. Still, the moving average method, crude though it may be, has the advantage of being easy to carry out and easy to explain.

QUANTITATIVE METHODS

Fig 8.3 : A Time Series smoothed using a Moving Average

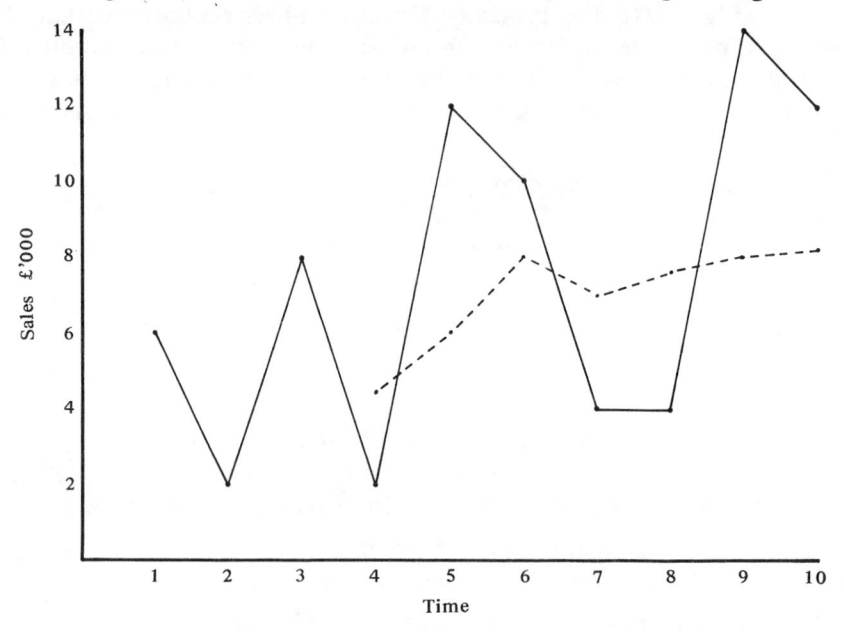

Fig 8.4 : A Time Series smoothed by Exponential Smoothing

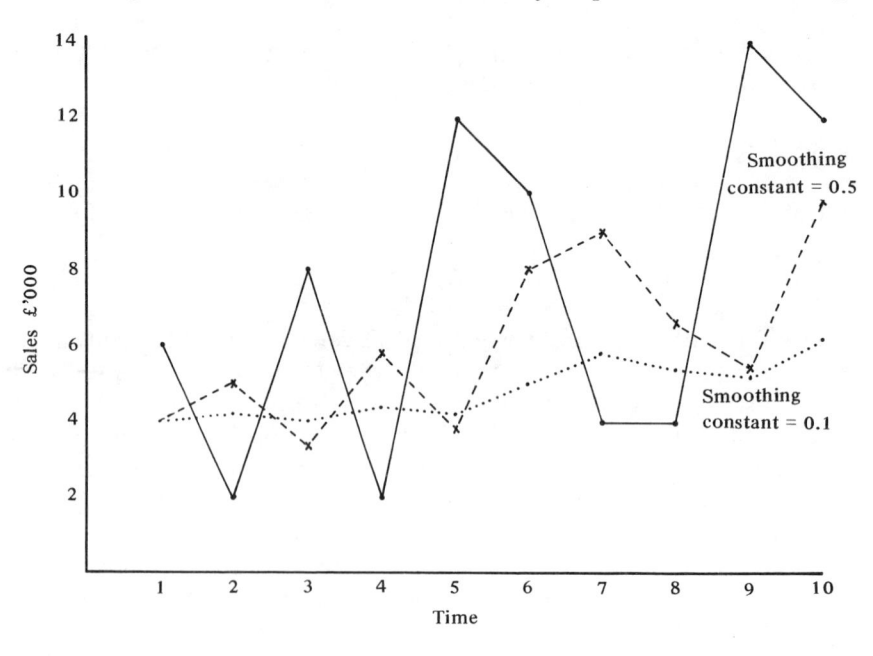

TRACKING THINGS IN TIME

8.6.2 Exponential Smoothing

This more sophisticated technique has the advantage of being more rational and flexible. What we do is to monitor the extent to which the time series deviates from the smoothed series and then adjust the current smoothed value by a *fraction* only of that deviation.

New smoothed value = Old smoothed value + a fraction of (Time series value − old smoothed value)

This fraction is known as the *smoothing constant*. If it is small then the smoothed series will only adjust slowly to fluctuations in the time series. Table 8.10 shows two versions (an initial smoothed value of 4 is assumed in both cases.

Table 8.10 : Exponential Smoothing of a Time Series = 0.1

Smoothing Constant = 0.1
(SC)

Month	Sales	Smoothed Value	Deviation	SC x Deviation	New Smoothed Value
1	6	4	+ 2	+ 0.2	4.2
2	2	4.2	− 2.2	− 0.2	4.0
3	8	4.0	+ 4	+ 0.4	4.4
4	2	4.4	− 2.4	− 0.2	4.2
5	12	4.2	+ 7.8	+ 0.8	5.0
6	10	5.0	+ 5.0	+ 0.5	5.5
7	4	5.5	− 1.5	− 0.2	5.3
8	4	5.3	− 1.3	− 0.1	5.2
9	14	5.2	+ 8.8	+ 0.9	6.1
10	12	6.1	+ 5.9	+ 0.6	6.7

Smoothing Constant = 0.5
(SC)

Month	Sales	Smoothed Value	Deviation	SC x Deviation	New Smoothed Value
1	6	4	+ 2.0	1.0	5.0
2	2	5.0	− 3.0	− 1.5	3.5
3	8	3.5	+ 4.5	+ 2.2	5.7
4	2	5.7	− 3.7	− 1.8	3.9
5	12	3.9	+ 8.1	+ 4.0	7.9
6	10	7.9	+ 2.1	+ 1.0	8.9
7	4	8.9	− 4.9	− 2.4	6.5
8	4	6.5	− 2.5	− 1.2	5.3
9	14	5.3	+ 8.7	+ 4.4	9.7
10	12	9.7	+ 2.3	+ 1.2	10.9

Note the way in which the new smoothed value is carried forward to the next period so that column 6 provides the value for column 3 in next period and so on. Note also in week 5 how little the smoothed series reacts with a smoothing constant of 0.1, the deviation of 7.8 only leading to an adjustment of 0.1 x 7.8 = 0.78 = 0.8. With a smoothing constant of 0.5, the smoothed series is much more sensitive.

QUANTITATIVE METHODS

From Fig 8.4 on page 274 you can see that the smoothing constant acts somewhat like an adjustable shock absorber. A small smoothing constant produces a very smooth series but one which reacts only slowly to persistent change. A larger smoothing constant reacts faster but is less stable overall and tends to move out of phase with the original time series as it tries in vain to react to the random fluctuations of the series.

For smoothing a series it is usually best to use a smoothing constant of somewhere between 0.1 and 0.2. The calculations are not complicated and can be easily programmed for a personal computer and the result is, in many ways, more satisfactory than that provided by moving averages. The simple moving average gives equal weight to all the values contained within the chosen period (4 weeks in Table 8.9) and *no weight* to those values which fall beyond if (see page 273). The Exponential Smoothing system is in effect a moving average in which the weights decrease back in time (see page 436 for technical details). The weights are shown in Table 8.11 together with those for a normal moving average.

Table 8.11 : Exponential Smoothing seen as a Weighted Moving Average

(Weights sum to 100)

Week No	Initial Value	1	2	3	4	5	6	7	8	9	10
4 week moving average		0	0	0	0	0	0	25	25	25	25
Exponential Smoothing											
SC = 0.5	0.1	0.1	0.2	0.4	0.8	1.6	3.1	6.2	12.5	25	50
SC = 0.1	34.9	3.9	4.3	4.8	5.3	5.9	6.6	7.3	8.1	9	10

The reason for showing these weights (they are not necessary for using the system) is so that you can appreciate the inner logic of the system. As you 'turn up' the smoothing constant as if it were a dial, you are effectively increasing the rate at which you discount past data. With a smoothing constant of 0.5, the weighting for the initial value is effectively zero unlike the case with a value of 0.1 where it still has some influence 10 time periods later! Whatever the value chosen you avoid the sharp break which arises with the moving average.

8.6.3 Short Term Forecasting

For many purposes, notably stock control, there is a need for routine short-term forecasts. They should be insensitive to minor fluctuations

TRACKING THINGS IN TIME

in demand but should respond to significant changes without the need for human intervention. A stock control system will typically consist of many thousands of items and manual control is therefore not a serious option. Exponential smoothing provides the basic idea for many such systems although in practice, sophisticated elaborations are developed to suit particular situations. Fig 8.5a shows a pattern of demand over 12 weeks together with two smoothed series, one using a smoothing constant of 0.1 and the other 0.5. With a value of 0.1 a stable forecast is provided for the first 9 weeks whilst using a value of 0.5, the forecast makes a futile attempt to follow the ups and downs of the series. Once a sudden jump in demand takes place in week 10, the 0.1 version is hopelessly slow in raising the forecast to the new required level. The 0.5 version does much better.

Fig 8.5a : Exponential Smoothing Responding to a Step in the Series

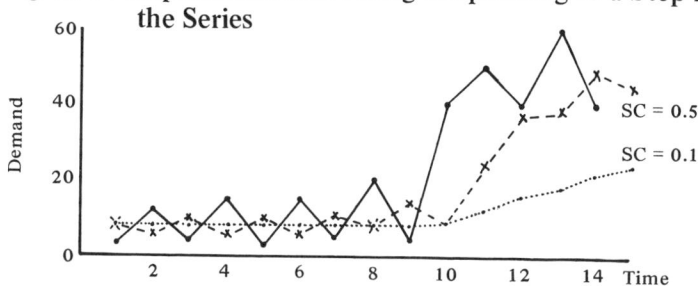

Fig 8.5b : Forecast error with Smoothing Constant = 0.1

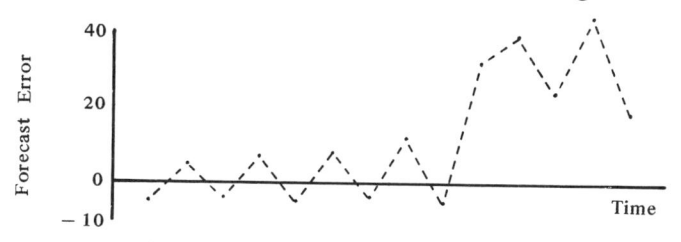

It is possible to operate a system which gets the best of both worlds. A low smoothing constant of 0.1, say, provides stable forecasts when little of significance is occurring. Common sense tells us that when the forecast lags behind the series itself then a series of errors of the same sign will occur. A computer stock control system can be programmed to automatically jump the forecast when a run of errors of the same sign arise. Look at Fig 8.5b. By week 12, the persistent shortfall of more than 20 could lead the control system to make an abrupt shift upwards in the forecast after which a low value of the smoothing constant would provide stable forecasts at the new level.

QUANTITATIVE METHODS

More sophisticated versions of *adaptive forecasting* exist such as the Box-Jenkins technique. These involve more complicated error analysis.

Exercise

Using an initial forecast of 40, simulate a simple exponential forecasting system with smoothing constants of 0.1 and 0.3 using the following data

20,60,10,70,50,20,60,60,15,70,60,75,50,90,40,95,75

8.6.4 Cusum Charts

Cusum Charts provide an effective means of detecting changes in trends in time series. They are simple to construct but are tricky to interpret. For the manager trying to control expenditure or performance who is keen to spot slight shifts away from the norm, they offer a very powerful aid.

Instead of plotting a series of values over time, we plot the cumulative deviation of these values from some fixed norm or target. Suppose a manager expects sales of 20 units per week from salesman. It would be unreasonable to expect exactly that level of sales each and every week. As long as the mean sales per week are 20 then all will be well. Table 8.12 shows how the Cusum value for the sales can be found and the results are shown in Fig 8.6 on page 279.

Table 8.12

Sales	18	23	19	21	19	20	18	23	21	24	23	25	21
Sales−20	−2	+3	−1	+1	−1	0	−2	+3	+1	+4	+3	+5	+1
Cusum	−2	+1	0	+1	0	0	−2	+1	+2	+6	+9	+14	+15

Sales	25	23	19	18	21	19	20	19
Sales−20	+5	+3	−1	−2	+1	−1	0	−1
Cusum	+20	+23	+22	+20	+21	+20	+20	+19

The time series can be split up into 3 phases. During weeks 1 to 7, the sales hover around 20. The cusum therefore remains around 0, the deviations above and below 20 roughly cancelling each other out. From weeks 7 to 15, however, the cusum rises sharply because there is a sequence of sales values above 20 which results in the cusum accumulating a sequence of positive deviations and growing accordingly. From weeks 15 to 21 sales average out below 20 so that the cusum falls slightly.

TRACKING THINGS IN TIME

Fig 8.6a : A Time Series

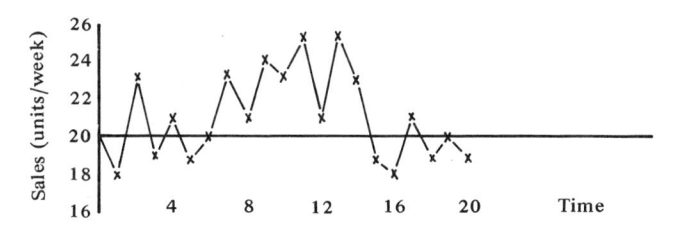

Fig 8.6b : Cusum for Fig 8.6a

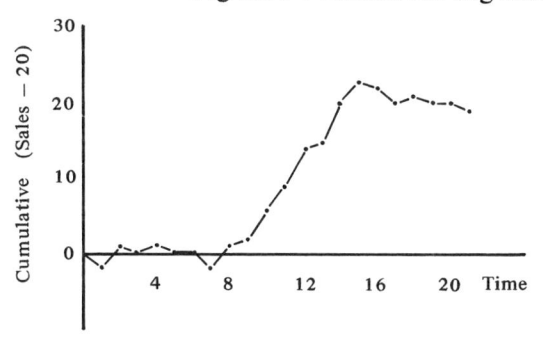

Note that the cusum shows up trends much more dramatically than in the original time series. It is, however, easily misinterpreted. The casual observer looking at Fig 8.6b will *incorrectly* say that sales rose to stabilise at a new higher level. This is *not true*. The vital thing to remember is that the relevant fact about a cusum is whether it is rising, falling or running level. The position of the plot above or below the O line is a reflection of the past, not of what is happening currently. A cusum will rise if the current values are, on average, above the target and it will do so whatever has happened in the recent past.

The idea is illustrated in Fig 8.7

Fig 8.7a : Cusum monthly Expenses for a Salesman

279

QUANTITATIVE METHODS

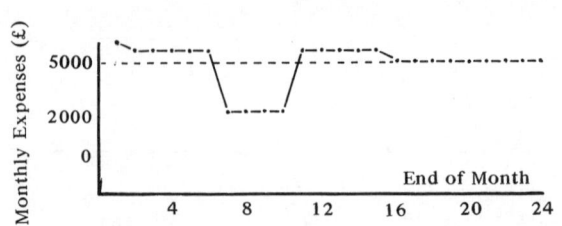

Fig 8.7b

Expenses between months 1 and 6 run at the *same level* as between months 10 and 15. Although the cusum is located below the line in one case and above it in the other, the cusum is rising at the same rate in both cases. During both these periods £3,000 surplus expenses are accumulated in the cusum over 5 months which is equivalent to £600 per month over the target of £5,000. This means that expenses must have been running at a level of £5,600 on average during both the periods in question. Note also that between months 15 and 24 the cusum stays level and therefore over this period expenses averaged £5,000 a month even though the cusum has levelled out below the 0 line! A guide to interpretation is provided in Fig 8.8.

Fig 8.8 : A guide to the Interpretation of the Cusums of (Series − Target)

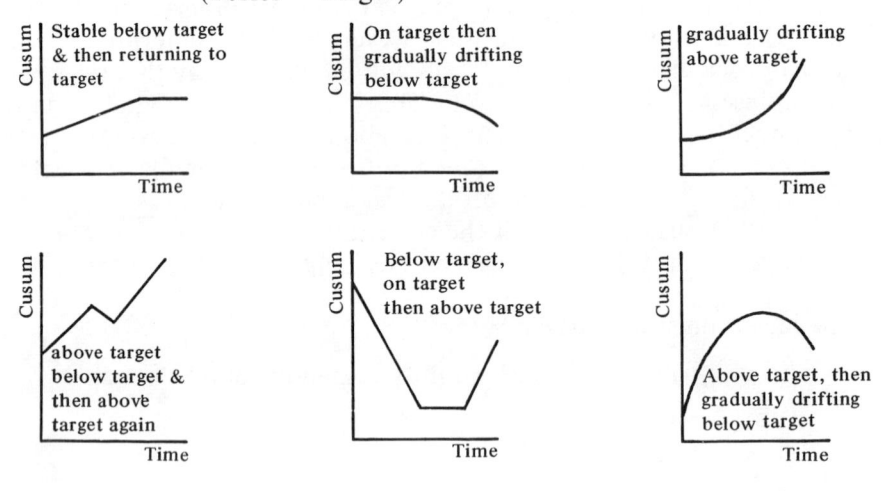

Exercise

Data has been collected on the successive times taken to do a particular job by an operator. It is expected to take 25 minutes on the average. Plot the data in the form of a normal time series and then underneath it plot a cusum using a target value of 25 minutes and

TRACKING THINGS IN TIME

comment on the result.

Time	40	40	35	25	25	20	30	20	30	25
(minutes)	30	20	30	35	25	35	45	40	50	40
	55	50								

Example

The use of the cusum charts for budgetary control is illustrated in the next example where instead of a fixed target, the cusum plotted is the cumulative deviation between actual and budgeted scrap cost. In this situation budgeted scrap is related to planned production levels and the type of material being worked on and it therefore varies from week to week. In accountants' terms this is the cumulative variance, not to be confused with the statistician's 'variance' defined on page 110. The data is shown in Table 8.13.

Table 8.13 : A Cusum used for Budgetary Control (£'000)

Week No	1	2	3	4	5	6	7	8	9	10
Actual Scrap	4.1	11.3	9.3	10.2	8.9	9.3	10.8	10.0	11.7	10.6
Budgeted Scrap	5.2	9.8	11.8	10.7	9.2	13.3	8.6	12.5	11.0	10.9
Deviation	−1.1	+1.5	−2.5	−0.5	−0.3	−4.0	+2.2	−2.5	+0.7	−0.3
Cusum	−1.1	0.4	−2.1	−2.6	−2.9	−6.9	−4.7	−7.2	−6.5	−6.8

Week No	11	12	13	14	15	16	17	18	19
Actual Scrap	12.7	11.0	10.2	8.2	5.9	10.9	11.8	9.4	5.4
Budgeted Scrap	12.0	10.9	11.2	8.2	8.4	10.3	13.2	12.6	9.7
Deviation	+0.7	+0.1	−1.0	0	−2.5	+0.6	−1.4	−3.2	−4.3
Cusum	−6.1	−6.0	−7.0	−7.0	−9.5	−8.9	−10.3	−13.5	−17.8

The cusum is plotted in Fig 8.9 and it shows that the performance compared with budget is very good.

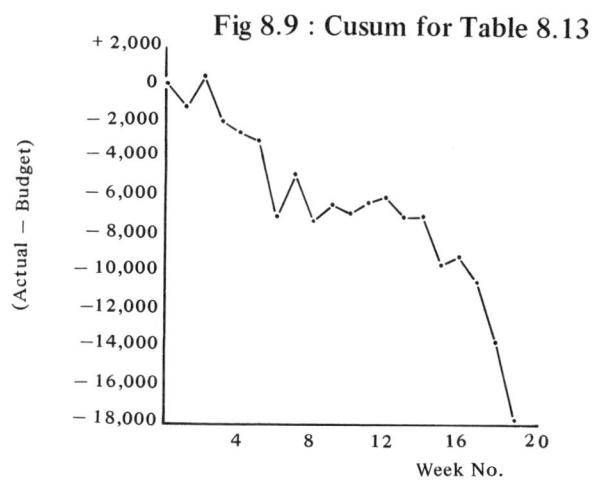

Fig 8.9 : Cusum for Table 8.13

QUANTITATIVE METHODS

From weeks 1 to 6 the company is on average about 1,100 under budget per week. From weeks 7 to 14 is at or about budget level but from week 15 on, the performance is very much better than budget. Note how dramatically the cusum shows up shifts in series. This is why it is particularly good at exposing very small changes in trends.

8.7 Long Term Forecasting
8.7.1 Sense and Nonsense about Forecasting

Some people say that forecasting the future is more of an art than a science. Now I don't believe that they really think that forecasting has got anything to do with Picasso and Beethoven, what they are really trying to say is that it is difficult. They are quite correct. Treat with the deepest suspicion anyone who claims that he can forecast the future. Take it from me, anyone who finds a way of accurately forecasting the future won't waste his time talking to you and me. A fortune awaits them elsewhere.

There is only one way to attempt to forecast the future and that is to understand what is going on in the world and particularly those processes that affect the area you are particularly interested in. The past can only be a useful guide in a fairly stable world. For example to forecast the future sales for a new product you need to understand the market, the place of your product within it and the state of the competition. To guess how things are likely to go in the future you need to understand how markets change. All the statistician can do is to offer techniques which can help the manager to *understand* the way things change in his relevant world.

Forecasting is not an art, it is a science. Psychiatry, too, is a science. It is a difficult one and often leads to inconclusive results because of the complexity and inaccessability of the human mind. Psychiatrists have, despite their difficulties, developed analytical techniques and drug treatments which help without providing the whole answer. The science of forecasting too is difficult because the world around us is complex and subject to a web of interacting forces which cannot be clearly measured and understood. So the job needs to be tackled using a broad range of techniques: statistical analysis, survey methods, advice from informed experts and so on.

8.7.2 Understanding Trends

A trend is a trend is a trend
The trouble is, will it bend
Will it carry on up
Or suddenly drop
And come to a premature End?   *Anon*

TRACKING THINGS IN TIME

Despite the lessons of the seventies there are still some cases of 'linear lunacy' when people believe that forecasting is synonymous with fitting linear regression lines to trends. Remember that trends bend and end. Far from assuming that trends will continue into the future, the forecaster should be consciously seeking to detect the inevitable point in time when the trend changes.

Think of the typical way in which things evolve. They grow, reach one or more levels of stability and then decay. Fig 8.10 shows how the sales of a new product might change in time.

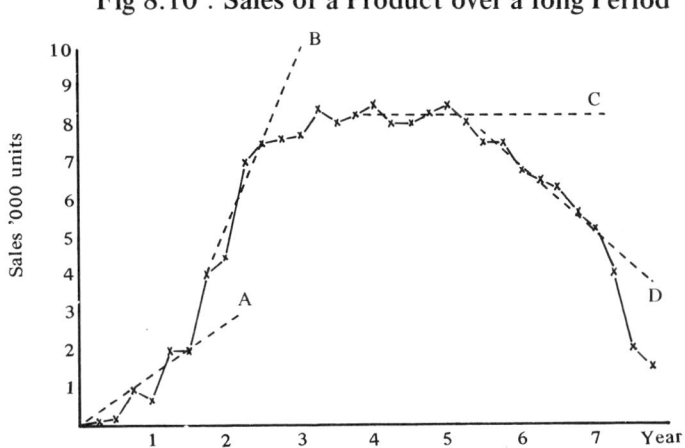

Fig 8.10 : Sales of a Product over a long Period

Analysis carried out in year 1.5 might suggest a straight line trend projecting to A. By year 2.5 the trend begins to look as if it is heading for B. By year 5, the trend seems to be stable and level and a linear projection to C would seem reasonable. By year 7, a straight line projecting to D would seem to fit. Now Fig 8.10 is not meant to be a demonstration of the futility of linear trend fitting. It is meant to show the ephemeral nature of such fits. Over short term periods of 1 to 2 years, a straight line may fit the data well. Furthermore the projection provides a standard against which to look for shifts in the trend. The projection to A is made at time 1.5. By year 2, comparison of the actual sales with the projection will give a clear indication of the upward thrust of sales. By year 3.5, the actual figures will make it clear that the projection to B has been overoptimistic.

QUANTITATIVE METHODS

Exercise

On 29.4.84, the *Sunday Times colour supplement* published an article entitled 'The Mile : a sprint to the year 2000' in which they asked 'What is the future of the mile record?' The graph below shows how the mile record has fallen since Roger Bannister ran the first four-minute mile. Fit a trend line to the data (by eye will do) and use it to project the mile record in the years 1990, 2000 and finally 3000. What are the problems of projecting trends in this case? In the article John Walker is reported as being convinced that a 3 min. 30 sec. mile will be run by the year 2000, other runners are convinced that 3:40 is the limit. What does the graph suggest?

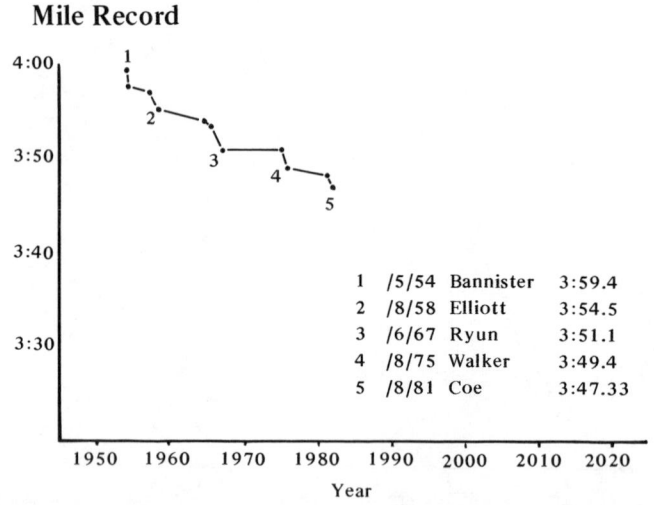

Mile Record

1	/5/54	Bannister	3:59.4
2	/8/58	Elliott	3:54.5
3	/6/67	Ryun	3:51.1
4	/8/75	Walker	3:49.4
5	/8/81	Coe	3:47.33

So we can see that straight line projections are perfectly reasonable providing that they are seen as provisional and are used to help define the evolution of the more complex trend. Cusums can be useful here. In Fig 8.10 the projection to B is the line defined by the following equation.

$$\text{Sales ('000 units)} = -4.5 + 4.83 \times \text{(Years)}$$

Table 8.14 on page 285 shows the sales from years 1.5 to 3.5 together with the projected value from the trend line (calculated from the above equation and a cusum of the difference between them.

Once a projection has been made, the cusum of the difference between actual and projected sales gives an early warning of any persistent deviation from the projection.

TRACKING THINGS IN TIME

Table 8.14 : The Use of a Cusum to detect movement away from a trend

Year	Sales	Projected Sales	Difference	Cusum
1.5	2.0	2.7	− 0.7	− 0.7
1.75	4.0	4.0	0	− 0.7
2.0	4.5	5.2	− 0.7	− 1.4
2.25	7.0	6.4	+ 0.6	− 0.8
2.5	7.5	7.6	− 0.1	− 0.9
2.75	7.7	8.8	− 1.1	− 2.0
3.0	7.8	10.0	− 2.2	− 4.2
3.25	8.3	11.2	− 2.9	− 7.1
3.5	8.0	12.4	− 4.4	−11.5

Exercise

Based on past trends, a straight line projection of sales has been made yielding the equation

Sales = 10 + 2.25 x (months)
(units per month)

Suppose that the following figures represent next years data as it arises arises. Plot them on a graph and superimpose the projection on your graph. Then separately calculate and plot the cusum of the difference between actual and projected values.

Month No	1	2	3	4	5	6	7	8	9	10	11	12
Actual sales (units per month)	14	13	20	20	20	22	30	35	33	40	50	50

8.7.3 Curve Fitting and Log Paper

A glance at Fig 8.10 will suggest that trends can often be better expressed in the form of a curve. Special computer programs exist providing a least squares curve fitting procedure but don't be ashamed of fitting curves by eye. In any case remember that any curve fitted can only be provisional. In Fig 8.10, even if the analyst suspects at year 1.5 that a growth curve is appropriate, there is nothing in the data itself to suggest just how steeply the curve will rise. There may, however, be other sources of information to suggest the growth potential, and close monitoring of the actual figures as they arise will help to avoid any major errors.

8.7.4 Log Paper

Fitting curves is a tricky process. Special graph paper can help. When

QUANTITATIVE METHODS

compound growth is a possibility, log graph paper can be used. Fig 8.11a shows two products whose sales are increasing in time. A is growing on a compound basis, i.e. at a roughly constant *rate* per year, whilst B is growing on a linear basis, is by a constant *amount* each year. Fig 8.11b shows the same data plotted on log paper.

Figure 8.11a & b

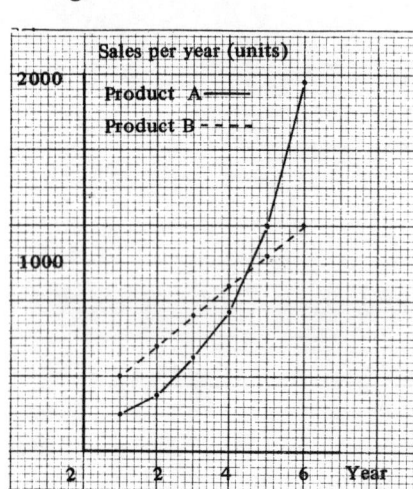

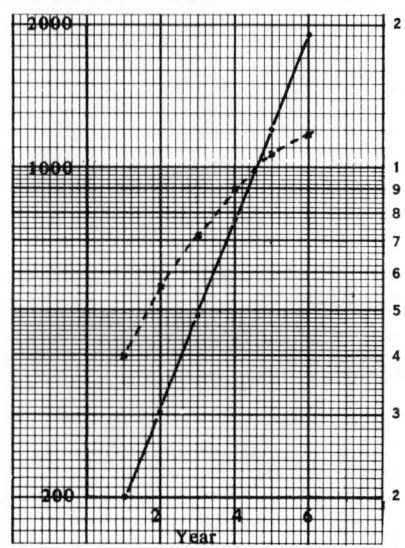

Look carefully at the right hand axis. There is no zero and between the value of 1,2,4 and 8 there is equal spacing (on a normal graph there would be equal spacing between 1,2,3 and 4). Anything growing at a constant *rate* will now plot as a straight line. Thus 1 unit in year 1 doubling each year would grow to 2,4 and 8 in successive years producing a straight line plot.

Fig 8.11b shows product A as growing at a constant rate while B, on this form of paper, shows up as a curved line. Log paper can therefore be used as a diagnostic for early signs of compound growth. Try it out on some series relevant to your own work. Sometimes log paper is used simply to compress the vertical scale for convenience. Where this is going to mislead the unobservant viewer, it should be avoided.

8.8 Decomposition of Time Series

8.8.1 Seasonal Effects

Time series are complicated by the existence of seasonal effects. In fact the identification and quantification of such effects is the most useful service that time series analysis can provide. Seasonality is not simply a summer–winter affair. Consider the following:

TRACKING THINGS IN TIME

1. An airline does peak flying in summer when people go on holidays, but it also has mini–peaks at Easter and Christmas. Its engineering maintenance section, however, has its peak in the winter when flying is at its lowest.

2. Demand for salads is obviously highly seasonal. However the pattern of seasonality has changed in recent years with imported goods being flown in from abroad.

3. Traditionally turkey sales have been the seasonal food par excellence, sales being largely restricted to Christmas. Recently, however, advertising has been used to encourage sales more evenly throughout the year.

Seasonal effects like these can be so pronounced as to make the study of trends almost impossible. For this reason it makes sense to correct for the seasonal effect and thereby de-seasonalise the series so that a trend can be identified. Equally once a trend has been identified on some basis or other, the seasonal effect needs to be applied to the projection in order to produce forecasts for different times of the year.

8.8.2 Modelling Time Series

A time series is a reflection of one aspect of a complex process. The values for sales, for example, will depend on the decisions of innumerable customers and competitors with the added complication of once-off effects such as strikes, heat-waves and so on. Large companies can afford to carry out in-depth studies of markets which allow them to delve into the complexities at the root of sales. A cheaper, simpler and quicker analysis has to operate with a simple *model* of the process.

A model is a representation of the real-life system. It does not attempt to represent the whole system in all its complexity or richness of detail. It concentrates instead on representing one or more aspects of the system in a simple form which will enable the user to make useful decisions regarding the real-world system. For example, a model of an aircraft for wind tunnel experiments need represent only the external shape of the aeroplane, scaled down of course. The inside of the model could be solid or empty. A model of the plane for planning seating arrangements, however, should have no roof and would need no wings. The internal lay-out of the model would, however, have to be carefully modelled to scale.

A simple model of a Time series assumes that the series is made up of

QUANTITATIVE METHODS

three components: a trend, a seasonal element and lastly a residual element which fluctuates in an essentially unpredictable way. It has to account for all effects not explicitly recognised within the model.

Sometimes other components will have to be added to make the model usable. For example the effect of strikes could be allowed for to explain sudden rises or falls in the series.

To model the seasonal effects in a time series a fundamental question has to be answered. Does the seasonal effect operate additively or multiplicatively? Does the seasonal peak *add* sales to the underlying trend or *amplify* them by some factor. Different models can be proposed depending on the answer to that question. Two such models are:

Additive Model
 Series = Trend + Seasonal Deviation + Residual

Multiplicative Model
 Series = Trend x Seasonal Factor x Residual

Other models could be proposed but these two will do to illustrate the process of model fitting. The model that is eventually chosen will be the one which fits the facts best, i.e. which explains the observed time series to date.

8.8.3 The Additive Model

Table 8.15 shows the sales data which will be used to demonstrate the method. The first thing to do is to fit a trend. Once a trend has been fitted we can obtain the seasonal deviation by subtraction.

Table 8.15 : Quarterly Sales '000 units over a 4 Year Period

Year	1	2	3	4
1	6	12	10	3
2	7	15	11	5
3	10	25	20	9
4	9	24	21	7

Quarters

Series − Trend = Seasonal Deviation + Residual

From this an average seasonal deviation can be calculated and used to de-seasonalise the data.

As this is quarterly data, I have used a centrally weighted moving

TRACKING THINGS IN TIME

average. Annual moving averages provide a good estimate of trend because each value gives equal weight to all the quarters thereby evening out the seasonal effects. The method is shown in Table 8.16.

Table 8.16 : A Centrally weighted moving average

Year & Quarter	Series Value				
1–1	6			6	Quarterly
1–2	12		12	24	Average
1–3	10	+	10	= 20	$= \frac{63}{8}$
1–4	3		3	6	
2–1			7	7	= 7.9
	31		32	63	

An ordinary moving average centres awkwardly between quarters. By overlapping two years as shown, the resulting mean is centred on Year 1 quarter 3 and it still gives equal weighting to all quarters. The complete analysis is shown in Table 8.17 and the series with the trend superimposed is shown in Fig 8.12.

(Note: for monthly data a similar scheme will work. Overlapping January – December with February – January produces 24 months data centred on July, all months being given equal weighting).

Fig 8.12 : Time Series & Centrally weighted moving Average

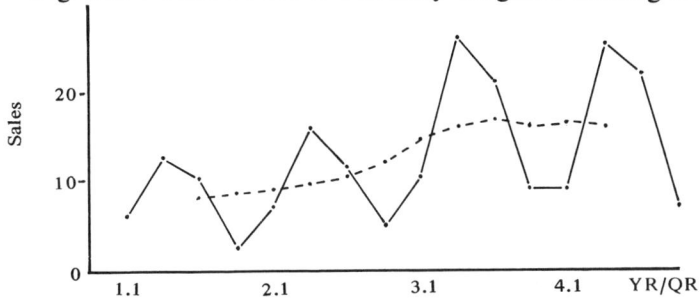

Notes on Table 8.17 on page 290

1. The 8-quarter moving total for Yr 1 Qr 4 is made up as follows:

    12 + 10 + 3 + 7   =   32   = 67
  +   10 + 3 + 7 + 15   + 35

2. Col 4 = $\frac{\text{Col 3}}{8}$ because Col 3 is the sum of 8 quarters data.

QUANTITATIVE METHODS

Table 8.17 : Decomposition of a Time Series (Additive Model)

	1 Series	2 Moving Total (4 Qtrs.)	3 Moving Total (8 Qtrs.)	4 Trend	5 Series-Trend	6 Seasonal Deviation	7 Series −Seasonal Deviation
YR/QR	A	M.T	M.T	T	A−T	S	A−S
1 − 1	6					− 4.1	10.1
1 − 2	12	31				+ 7.9	4.1
1 − 3	10	32	63	7.9	+ 2.1	+ 2.4	7.6
1 − 4	3	35	67	8.4	− 5.4	− 6.2	9.2
2 − 1	7	36	71	8.9	− .9	− 4.1	11.1
2 − 2	15	38	74	9.2	+ 5.8	+ 7.9	7.1
2 − 3	11	41	79	9.9	+ 1.1	+ 2.4	8.6
2 − 4	5	51	92	11.5	− 6.5	− 6.2	11.2
3 − 1	10	60	111	13.9	− 3.9	− 4.1	14.1
3 − 2	25	64	124	15.5	+ 9.5	+ 7.9	17.1
3 − 3	20	63	127	15.9	+ 4.1	+ 2.4	17.6
3 − 4	9	62	125	15.6	− 6.6	− 6.2	15.2
4 − 1	9	63	125	15.6	− 6.6	− 4.1	13.1
4 − 2	24	64	124	15.5	+ 8.5	+ 7.9	16.1
4 − 3	21					+ 2.4	18.6
4 − 4	7					− 6.2	13.2

3. Col 5 = Col 1 − Col 4. This removes the trend from the series leaving the seasonal and residual components.

4. Col 6 contains the mean seasonal deviation for each quarter. So from Col 5 we get for quarter 1

$$\frac{(-1.9) + (-3.9) + (-6.6)}{3} = -4.1$$

Check the others for yourself.

5. These mean seasonal deviations are subtracted from the original series (Col 1) to produce a de-seasonalised series in Col 7 (see Fig 8.13).

It is important that you don't see this as *the* way to decompose the series. After all the series was not put together this way in the first place! It may or may not be a useful way of handling it. The proof of the pudding is in the eating. A glance at Fig 8.13 leads us to suspect that we haven't been very successful as the de-seasonlised series still seems to reflect the seasonal pattern. Look at the dips at 1−2 and

TRACKING THINGS IN TIME

2—2 and the rising values at 3—2 and 4—2. It looks as if the seasonal deviation of + 7.9 for quarter 2 overcompensates for the series at lower values and undercompensates at higher values of the series.

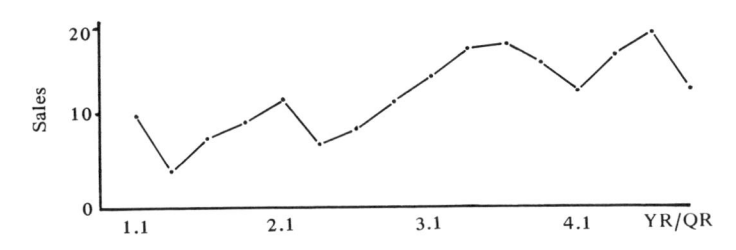

Fig 8.13 : De-seasonalised Series (Additive)

We are of course using a fixed seasonal deviation. A simple multiplicative model would use a fixed *factor* and this would lead to a higher adjustment in absolute terms later on in the series and a lower adjustment early on. This suggests that a more successful model could be developed.

8.8.4 A Multiplicative Model

$$\text{Series} = \text{Trend} \times \text{Seasonal Factor} \times \text{Residual}$$

from which it follows that

$$\frac{\text{Series}}{\text{Trend}} = \text{Seasonal Factor} \times \text{Residual}.$$

The calculations are shown in Table 8.18

Table 8.18 : Decomposition of a Time Series (Multiplicative Model)

YR/QR	1 Series	2 Trend	3 Series/Trend	4 Seasonal Factor	5 Series/Seasonal Factor
1 — 1	6			0.70	8.6
1 — 2	12			1.60	7.5
1 — 3	10	7.9	1.27	1.21	8.3
1 — 4	3	8.4	0.36	0.46	6.5
2 — 1	7	8.9	0.79	0.70	10.0
2 — 2	15	9.2	1.63	1.60	9.4
2 — 3	11	9.9	1.11	1.21	9.1
2 — 4	5	11.5	0.43	0.46	10.9
3 — 1	10	13.9	0.72	0.70	14.3
3 — 2	25	15.5	1.61	1.60	15.6
3 — 3	20	15.9	1.26	1.21	16.5
3 — 4	9	15.6	0.58	0.46	19.6
4 — 1	9	15.6	0.58	0.70	12.9
4 — 2	24	15.5	1.55	1.60	15.0
4 — 3	21			1.21	17.4
4 — 4	7			0.46	15.2

QUANTITATIVE METHODS

Notes on Table 8.18

1. Col. 3 is obtained by dividing the series (col 1) by the trend factor (col. 2)

2. Col. 4 is obtained by averaging the col. 3 values for each quarter

e.g. for quarter 1 $\quad \dfrac{0.79 + 0.72 + 0.58}{3} = 0.7$

3. The series is de-seasonalised by *dividing* by the appropriate factor. So for 1–1 6 becomes $\frac{6}{0.7}$ = 8.6. Compare this with the way the de-seasonalisation was carried out in the additive version by subtracting a seasonal deviation.

The resulting de-seasonalised series (col. 5) can be seen in Fig 8.14. The result is definitely more successful than that shown in Fig 8.13. *In this instance* a multiplicative model has produced better results.

Fig 8.14 : De-seasonalised Series (Multiplicative)

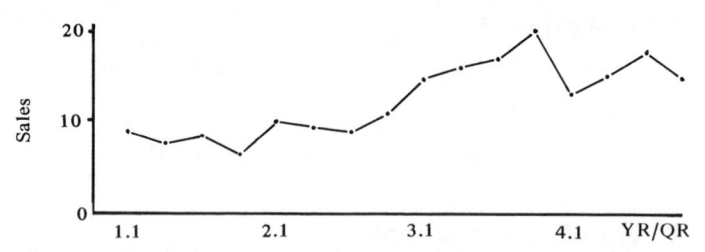

Exercise

1. The following data gives the expenses incurred in running an operation together with seasonal *factors* applicable to each month. De-seasonalise the data.

Month	1	2	3	4	5	6	7	8	9	10	11	12
Expenses (£'000)	14	18	20	42	76	180	215	210	156	83	28	20
Seasonal Factor	.3	.4	.4	.8	1.3	2.8	3.1	2.7	2.0	1.0	0.3	0.2

2. Analyse the following quarterly figures for the demand for an item of stock using both additive and multiplicitive models

Year & Quarter	1–1	1–2	1–3	1–4	2–1	2–2	2–3	2–4	3–1	3–2	3–3	3–4
Demand (units)	64	124	132	132	106	72	140	143	107	86	80	94

TRACKING THINGS IN TIME

3. Get hold of some time series relevant to your work and apply some of the techniques discussed in this chapter. If they are monetary time series extending over more than a year, deflate them to current price levels first.

8.8.5. The Catch 22 of Time Series Analysis

In order to estimate seasonal effects and trends a large amount of data is required. By the time you have collected a lot of data, everything has changed anyway. That is the Catch 22 of time series analysis. Many textbooks use as examples long economic time series where it is indeed possible to estimate sophisticated components. The world of business is much more fleeting.

Look at the Quarter 1 seasonal deviations listed on page 290 and in Table 8.17. With so little data the mean deviation of -4.1 is not going to be very accurate. With so little data it would be foolish to speculate on whether there was a significant decreasing seasonal deviation with the passage of time, from -1.9 in year 2 to -6.6 in year 4. And yet three years is a long time in the life of a product and decisions must be made. The moral is that in the world of business you often have to be content with fairly simple models of time series because of the poor quantity of relevant data available.

But suppose that you really want to know whether the seasonal component is shifting in time as has been the case with many seasonal food products? With only a few years data, unless the effects are very pronounced, you cannot detect such changes from the data alone. What you have to do is to resort to alternative sources of information, from buyers and salesmen for example.

To show you how misleading short time series can be, in Fig 8.15 on page 294, I have simulated a time series of the following form

$$\text{Series} = 10 + 5 \times (\text{time period}) + \text{residual}$$

The residual component (see page 439 for details) produces a random scatter around a straight line, the underlying straight line being superimposed on the series.

These simulated time series show how deceptive a time series can be. An attempt to carry out too sophisticated an analysis would lead you to trying to 'explain' the dip at period 4 and the 'peak' in period 7 in

QUANTITATIVE METHODS

Fig 8.15 : Simulated Time Series
Series = 10 + 5 x (Time) + Residual

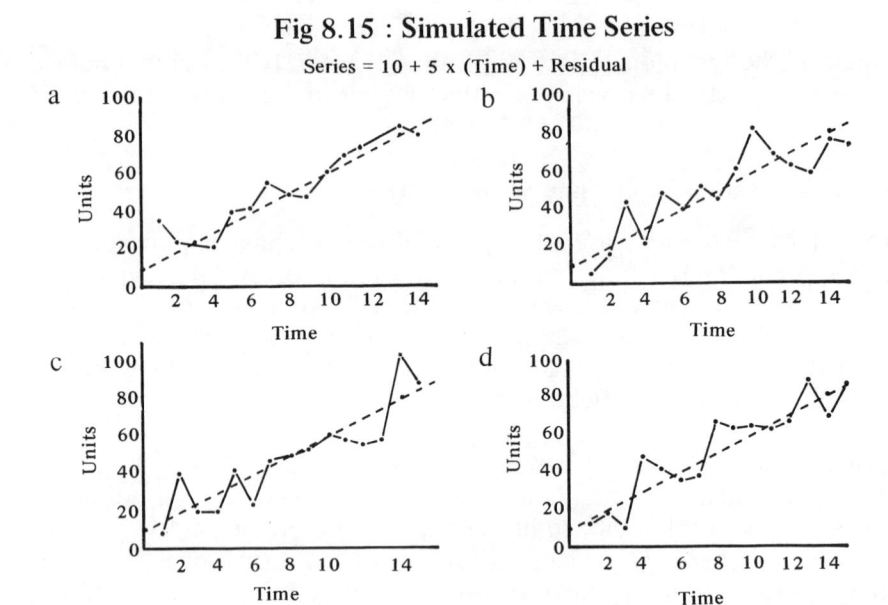

Fig 8.15 a. This is yet another example of the fundamental problem of statistical significance. The variations around the straight line are all, by definition, not statistically significant. This is because they were all produced using random numbers in a computer routine and used to perturb the straight line in a random fashion. The only way you can distinguish real effects from chance effects is to get lots of data. Catch 22, remember?

Time series analysis is a vital technique for management. It needs to be carried out in a realistic frame of mind. All conclusions should be seen as provisional. Expect things to turn out differently and monitor actual results against your projections, modifying these accordingly. Use more than one technique and above all, seek understanding.

CHAPTER 9 : FINDING OUT BY SAMPLING

Sections 9.1 and 9.2 introduce the idea of populations and samples and distinguish between bias and error. Sections 9.3 to 9.5 deal with bias in detail and Sections 9.6 to 9.7 sampling error. The special circumstances of finite populations are covered in Section 9.8, the important technique of stratification in Section 9.9 and the chapter ends with a brief discussion of surveys in Section 9.10.

9.1.1 Populations and Samples

'The electors of Finchley', 'our customers', 'the company's 20 workshop machines', 'households in Ealing' are all examples of populations which may be of interest to a manager. As an election approaches, the voting intentions of the electors of Finchley as a whole are of interest to the campaign managers. Whether a company's customers are satisfied with the service provided is obviously of vital interest to the marketing department. The wear on the company's 20 workshop machines will be a factor in deciding when to replace all or part of them. In each of the above cases there is a population which can be defined.

The population means all those entities which are of interest for a particular purpose. Clear definition is required. For an area sales manager, the relevant population may be only those customers in his area alone. A group marketing manager will perhaps be concerned with a larger population consisting of customers in all areas. For another purpose the population might be defined as all customers with a turnover of more than £1 million. In each case it is the whole population which interests the investigators, but lack of time and/or money or just good sense may lead them to carry out investigations by examining a limited number of the members of the population only. This process is known as sampling.

9.1.2 Attributes and Variables

It is useful to think of each member of the population as being associated with a number of attributes. An attribute is a characteristic which is either possessed or not possessed by the member of the population. A customer of the company either did or did not place an order last month. A vehicle in the fleet is roadworthy or not, as laid down in the regulations. An elector of Finchley has said that he/she will vote for one of four parties in a forthcoming election or that

QUANTITATIVE METHODS

he/she 'doesn't know'. Each elector can be said to fall into one of these five categories. A household in Ealing either does or does not have access to running hot water or has partial or shared access.

The information that the manager or researcher requires will be the proportion of the population which possesses a particular attribute and this can then be expressed in percentage terms: the percentage of the electors who say they will vote for each party, the percentage of the fleet cars that are roadworthy and so on.

We can also measure variables associated with each member of the population. The *amount* spent by customers last month or the *length of time* they have been with the company. We could be interested in the *mileage* clocked up by a vehicle, or its *age*. The *number of members* in a household in Ealing or the *length of time* during which they have lived in the borough could interest a social worker. The *attitude* of an elector towards the government as measured on an attitude scale or the *distance* that their house is from the polling booth could be of relevance to a political campaign manager. In each of these cases the value of the variable can be measured on some sort of continuous scale.

9.1.3 Population Percentages and Means

When taking a sample we are often interested in the percentage of the population possessing a given attribute or the mean value for a chosen variable. We would like to be able to say something like:

'40% of the electors of Finchley intend to vote Conservative'

" 20% of our vehicle fleet is not roadworthy'

'The median number of miles clocked up by our fleet last month was 1460'.

'The mean number of members in a household in Ealing is 2.8'.

In order to be able to make such definitive statements about the population, it will, in theory, be necessary to measure or interrogate the whole population. If the population is small, then this is quite possible. The mean mileage for a company's whole vehicle fleet could be readily found without any need for sampling. Measuring the opinions of the entire electorate of Finchley would be out of the question. It follows therefore that statements about large populations in practice can only be *inferred* from the sample obtained. Such inferences are likely to be inaccurate for the simple reason that the sample leaves out a large part of the population.

FINDING OUT BY SAMPLING

9.2 The Twin Pillars: Bias and Sampling Error

Common sense tells us that the estimates of a population percentage or average based on a sample must differ from the true values for the population because the sample only represents a small part of the population. It is important to understand that this inaccuracy comes in two forms, *bias* and *sampling error*. In essence bias is error which arises from the inadequate way in which the sample is selected. In repeated sampling the population percentage or average will tend to be under-or over-estimated usually because certain sections of the population have been over-or under-represented in the sample. Sampling error arises from a combination of the limited size of the sample and the inherent variability of that which is being measured. You can have a large sample which is biased and yet which is precise or you can have a very small sample which is unbiased yet imprecise and of course you will often have a mixture of the two.

To clarify this point, think of the population percentage or mean as the bull's eye of a target on a shooting range and the bullets fired at the target as samples trying to estimate the population parameter which is of interest.

Fig 9.1 : Precision & Bias in Hitting a Target

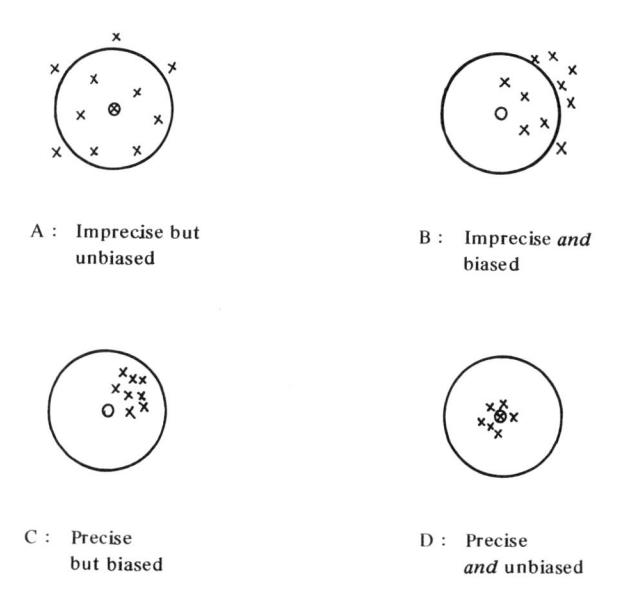

A : Imprecise but unbiased

B : Imprecise *and* biased

C : Precise but biased

D : Precise *and* unbiased

QUANTITATIVE METHODS

The result in Fig 9.1A is not encouraging for the marksman. The shots scatter widely around the bullseye and yet even so, there is no sign of bias, that is a tendency to shoot high or low and/or right and left. The shooting in result B lacks precision and also shows a tendency to shoot to the right. Result C is encouraging. Although the shots show bias, with a tendency to shoot up and to the right, it shows precision in the sense that it is consistent shooting. This is encouraging, because if the bias can be conciously allowed for, then the marksman can be trained to compensate for the bias and hit the bull with the same high degree of precision as before.

The task of estimating time or costs for planning purposes can pose the same problem. Suppose that Table 9.1 shows the estimates produced by two estimators Smith and Jones. They were required to estimate the time it would take to write a computer programme.

Table 9.1 : Time Estimates for two Estimators (Days)

Smith			Jones			
Actual	Estimate	% Error	Actual	Estimate	% Error	Estimate ÷ 1.2
20	22	+ 10	20	25	25	21
40	38	− 5	40	47	18	39
18	21	+ 17	18	21	17	18
30	28	− 7	30	36	20	30
25	30	+ 20	25	31	24	26

Jones' estimates at first seem to be less reliable as they always involved errors of about 20%. But looking at the pattern of errors for both estimators you can see that Smith's errors scatter around the target whilst Jones are consistently about 20% over the actual. Compensating for Jones' tendency to overestimate by dividing by 1.2, the adjusted estimates are very reliable. These are shown in the last column of Table 9.1. All this means that paradoxically Jones' estimates are more consistent and usable than Smith's even though they are biased. Corrected for bias they provide a very accurate set of forecasts.

(Note that to compensate for a 20% increase, you divide by 1.2. You do not reduce the figure by 20%! So, for example to restore a cost increase of 30% on goods originally costing £100 you divide the new price, £130, by 1.3 giving £$\frac{130}{1.3}$ = £100, the original price. Reducing it by 30% would give the *wrong* answer, £130 − $\frac{30}{100}$ of £130 = £91.)

9.3 Bias arising from an Inadequate Sampling Frame

To understand how bias can arise we need to study the way in which a sample is taken.

9.3.1 The Random Sample and the Sampling Frame

The simplest form of sample is a random sample. Each member of the population is notionally given a number and random numbers can then be used to select those members of the population to be included in the sample (see page 132). To take a random sample of the electors of Finchley, a number needs to be assigned to each member on the list and random numbers will then ensure that each of the electors on the list has an equal chance of being chosen for the sample and that any personal bias by the sampler is kept at bay. Later other forms of sampling will be discussed (see page 327).

The list of the members of the population which forms the basis of the sample is known as the *sampling frame.* In the case of the election at Finchley, the sampling frame is the electoral register which contains a list of all those eligible to vote either now or in the near future together with some people who are no longer eligible or who have died. For electoral opinion polling it constitutes a good sampling frame because it actually defines legally who has the right to vote.

As a sampling frame for asking householders in Ealing about their access to running hot water, the electoral register is inadequate because it would produce a biased sample. The list of electors would exclude all foreigners (not eligible) and, more importantly, all householders who didn't get round to registering or those whose landlords did not bother to inform the authorities or deliberately avoided registering the tenants. Now these excluded groups are likely to include many families who might be living in poor conditions without access to hot water. If the purpose of the survey was to estimate the proportion of households with adequate facilities, then a sample based on the electoral register would be likely to underestimate the proportion.

9.3.2 The Literary Digest Fiasco

A famous example of an inadequate sampling frame leading to biased results arose in the 1936 presidential election. 2,376,523 questionnaires were sent out by mail and yet the magazine failed to predict a Roosevelt victory (Gallup 1972). 'With a sample that big we can't go wrong', they thought. The sampling frame used consisted of lists of car and telephone owners. However the political opinions of car and telephone owners were biased towards the right wing republican Landon rather than the more liberal Roosevelt. This classic example illustrates the need to think hard and long about the relevance of any proposed sampling frame and to consider whether any significant number of the target population are excluded from that list.

In some cases a large section of the population can be excluded by the sampling frame without leading to bias. It depends on the purpose of the sample. For example a sample of telephone owners would give a biased estimate of income in the population as a whole but might give an unbiased estimate of height. After all why should telephone owners be any shorter or taller than those without a phone? Knowledge of the field of study is essential. Managers with their long experience of the business environment must take an active role in avoiding bias. They need to exercise their imagination when appraising the sampling frame, trying to think who might be excluded and whether exclusion will affect the estimate obtained. They must avoid the temptation to 'leave it to the experts'. They are the experts.

9.3.3 Pseudo Random Sampling

Ideally a sampling frame is a complete and up to date list of the target population. When this is not available, some substitute must be used and this may not be a numbered list. Suppose you want to take a sample of motorists and see what they think of buying a new motoring magazine which you intend to launch on the market. The list of registered car owners held by the government would provide a pretty good sampling frame if it was accessible. However, unlike the electoral register, it is not commercially available. Suppose as an alternative you decide to stand at the entrance to an urban car park in a shopping centre in London on Saturday morning and interrogate car users on arrival. The sample is now going to be all those motorists in or visiting London using that particular car park on that Saturday morning.

Now you might feel that such a sample could provide a reasonable sample of the motoring public at large. It cannot produce a truly random sample because not all members of the target population have an equal chance of being chosen, and the method does allow the possibility of bias arising from the way you make the choice of car consciously or un-consciously. Even if you try and interview all car users as they arrive, there will be times when you will have a choice to make and in the field it is hard to do that randomly.

It does, however, offer a *cheap* and *speedy* source of information. You need now to use your *imagination* in trying to assess the significance of having excluded large sections of the population. These will include motorists who live in the country, motorists who don't live or visit London, motorists who live locally, less affluent motorists, perhaps motorists who are DIY fans and who prefer to use their Saturdays for tinkering with their cars and putting into practice what they have read about in motoring magazines! There will also be motorists who are present but who refuse to take part in your survey. With imagination you may be able to think of other excluded groups some of whom could lead to bias with respect to the matter under study, the readership of motoring magazines.

Don't forget, however, that even a biased sample can be valuable as long as you are aware of the possibility of bias. A cheap and quick sample such as the one described could provide valuable preliminary feedback on the initial attitude of some motorists to a new magazine. Only if we want to use the results of such inadequate samples for making definitive statements about motorists in general do we risk making serious errors.

Exercise

In each of the following cases you are given the target population and the characteristic to be measured together with a proposed sampling frame. In each case think of how the population available via the sampling frame differs from the target population. Consider which members will be excluded by the sampling frame and the extent to which sample results will be likely to be biased as a result. In each case stretch your *imagination* and try hard to think of who will slip through the net and whether it is likely to matter.

1. You would like to know what proportion of managers in the UK have studied Statistics. You propose to send a questionnaire to a sample of people subscribing to the Financial Times.

2. You would like to find out how many people in a local Authority are satisfied with the welfare services provided for the sick and elderly. You need to get a rough idea fast, so you propose to sample people who live in the borough by phoning names drawn from the local telephone directory.

3. You want to start up a health food shop in a provincial town. You propose to sample shoppers passing down the main street of that town on one weekday morning and on one Saturday morning in August.

QUANTITATIVE METHODS

4. You wish to try out a new anti-rust product on a sample of the motorists in the UK. You propose to send a trial offer to a random sample of the subscribers to the AA and the RAC.

5. You want to sample the views of people who are concerned with the effects of pollution on the environment with a view to assessing their political affiliations. You propose to send a questionnaire to a sample of members of the National Trust.

9.4 Bias arising from Non-response

Even if you have an adequate sampling frame, bias can arise if some of those sampled do not respond to an enquiry or are inaccessible for some reason. The person who slams the door in your face is a refusal. The person who is away when you call is inaccessible and it is useful to distinguish the two cases. The bias resulting from both these situations can be massive as is illustrated in the following examples.

9.4.1 The Postal Vote

The electoral register would seem to provide a good sampling frame for sampling voting intentions. After all it contains a numbered list of the names and addresses of all those entitled to vote. What more could you ask for? Unfortunately sampling from it can produce biased results. Some people will refuse to respond to specific written or verbal questions, the 'don't knows' of the opinion pollsters, and some people will be inaccessible. Those who 'don't know' may be spread over the three parties in roughly the same proportion as for those who do respond but there is a possibility of bias. Labour voters might be unwilling to admit to a change of traditional loyalty to a middle-class pollster.

There is a strong likelihood that the inaccessible group will be biased towards the Conservative party. They will include those on the electoral roll who are away or who have moved and who are entitled to a postal vote. Now although there may only be a small bias against Labour in that group as a whole, richer people tend to move homes more often and are more likely to be Conservative voters. The important point is that this group's voting intentions will only be turned into votes if a postal vote is arranged and the Conservative party is well known to be very much more efficient at organising that vote.

The electoral register has a major defect. Although it is an excellent list of those eligible to vote it is not a reliable list of those who *will* vote.

9.4.2 The Impatient Customers

One of the ways of avoiding bias is to actually do some of the fieldwork yourself. This holds true even if you are a senior manager empowered to pay other people to do the donkey work. By doing so you may see potential sources of bias that you could not have imagined.

Some years ago a survey of the customers using a garage on one of the approach roads to the city in North London was carried out. The petrol company that owned the garage wished to know whether the existing customers would continue to use the garage if it was converted to self-service. At the time of the survey it was a sleepy garage run by a single operator who seemed to be on friendly terms with many of his clientele. Now he had decided to retire to the country and 'progress' was moving in on the station. The sampling procedure seemed reasonable. It was proposed to interview all customers using the station during a whole week and ask them to fill in a questionnaire which would establish the type of customer that they were, their existing usage and which would ask the key question:

> 'This garage will shortly be converted to a self-service station; will you continue to use it?'.

There was no reason to believe that the customers passing through the station in that particular week would not be representative of the customers as a whole. Taking part in the survey I was surprised to find that quite a high proportion of the motorists using the garage refused to answer any questions. Most of them were visibly in a hurry on their way into London and annoyed at being detained. Some went part way along with the questionnaire but abandoned it long before the key question came up and then raced off. We stemmed the flow somewhat by always sending a male interviewer to a female driver. People don't like to be rude, it seems, to people of the opposite sex.

One or two of the customers, however, seemed to have all the time in the world. They really enjoyed answering the questionnaire having a good think over each question and making quite sure that the answer they had given really was appropriate. Once it was completed, I noticed that many of them went off to have a chat with their old friend the operator. By actually doing the fieldwork I was able to see at first hand that the population being sampled was clearly split between those who were in a hurry and those for whom the garage was merely one stop on their daily social round. Now clearly if these two groups differ with respect to the key question being asked then

QUANTITATIVE METHODS

bias will be introduced. I needed to ask myself 'Would people who did *not* reply to the question be more or less likely to use the garage if it became self-service than those who *did* reply?'

The answer is that there would almost certainly be a difference. It was obvious from the impatience shown by some drivers that they were in a great hurry to get to work, surely just the people who would appreciate a self-service system with no waiting. The people who had plenty of time to answer the questionnaire were just the sort of people who appreciated personal service and who would probably seek a more socially rewarding friendly garage elsewhere. It was clear that the sample would inevitably produce a strong bias against approving the self-service proposed. But remember, biased though such a survey is, it is well worth doing as long as the extent of the bias is recognised. This example highlights the need to see a survey, particularly a preliminary survey, as a learning experience and not just an estimating procedure.

9.4.3 Redundant Workers

A company carried out a survey of workers who they had made redundant within the previous 15 months and who were still seeking employment. The purpose of the survey was to find out how many of these workers had managed to find jobs in the meantime. The population was therefore a finite one and consisted of about 300 workers whose situation was not known at the time of the termination interview. The sampling frame was essentially sound and consisted of the names and addresses of the entire population under consideration as of about 2 years previous.

Questionnaires were sent out by post to the whole of this limited population and a sample of those not replying were contacted by phone. This telephone back-up provided a check on some of the non-respondents but two groups of non-respondents were inaccessible.

1. Those who did not have telephones or who were ex-directory
2. Those who had moved away.

The first of these two groups did not cause much concern. Telephones are so widely used these days that it seemed unlikely that accessibility by telephone would be related in any way to the key question in the questionnaire:

'Do you now have a job?'

The second of these two groups are potentially more important. People who have 'gone away' after being made redundant are quite likely to have moved to take up a job or to enter into some sort of self-employment or possibly to retire. There was therefore a possibility of underestimating the proportion of the population who had found a job by sampling only those who were still to be found at their old addresses. Fortunately in this case the 'gone away' group was relatively small so that the potential bias was relatively insignificant.

Exercise

In each of the following situations, try and identify that part of the population which is either inaccessible or which is more likely not to respond. Consider the extent of the bias which could result.

1. A random sample of manual workers in a large manufacturing company will be chosen from an up-to-date staff list. They will be interviewed in July and asked their views on the introduction of new shift-working proposals.

2. A high street wine merchant decides to sample customers from her mailing list with a view to finding out if they are interested in Australian wines. The list consists of all those who have attended formal wine tastings and all those customers who have bought a dozen bottles or more at a time have been invited to join the list.

3. A trust concerned with birth control methods wishes to carry out a survey to estimate the proportion of men who would be prepared to have a vasectomy as a means of family planning once they have been fully informed of the facts. The proposal is to send information to a sample of men drawn from the electoral register and ask them if they are willing to have an in-depth confidential interview in their own homes.

9.5 Bias arising when sampling from unstable populations

The electoral register represents a relatively stable population because even though the population of the constituency is in a state of flux, it remains the definitive list of those allowed to vote. Some populations are in a state of rapid evolution and there may be no valid sampling frame open to the researcher. The following examples will help to illustrate the problem.

9.5.1 The Mould Circuit

One of the high cost items involved in casting metal into ingots is that of the moulds used. Before metal can be poured into the moulds these need to be lined and any minor repairs carried out. They

QUANTITATIVE METHODS

are then trundled into the casting area and metal poured into them. Once this has cooled sufficiently, the mould is recycled. There comes a time, however, when the mould must be scrapped. When this is done, the statistical records office is informed and the number of castings that the mould had received before being scrapped is recorded against the mould number for future reference and analysis.

Suppose that you are working on a cost model. This is a statement of the way in which the costs of a product are broken down into different components. Management need to know, as part of this study, what the cost of moulds contributes to the cost of the material cast. To answer this they need to know how much the company spends on moulds in order to produce a ton of cast metal. This would normally be found by calculating:

$$\frac{\text{Cost of Mould}}{\text{Mean tons of metal cast by that mould}} = \frac{\text{Cost of Mould}}{\text{Mean number of casts achieved} \times \text{capacity of mould (tons)}}$$

At the moment only one type of mould, A, is used but a new mould type, K, has been recently introduced with a view to it possibly replacing type A. The company have provided you with information on the life (in casts achieved) of moulds recently scrapped together with relevant capacity and cost information. This is shown in Fig 9.2

Fig 9.2 : Capacity & Mean life of 2 Mould types

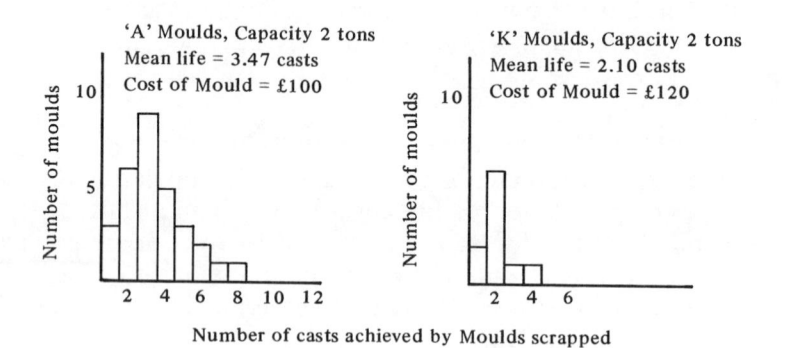

'A' Moulds, Capacity 2 tons
Mean life = 3.47 casts
Cost of Mould = £100

'K' Moulds, Capacity 2 tons
Mean life = 2.10 casts
Cost of Mould = £120

Number of casts achieved by Moulds scrapped

Exercise

Can you see any problems about using the data as presented? Think hard about the sampling frame being used and what potential for bias it contains.

FINDING OUT BY SAMPLING

The sampling frame certainly is the main source of the problem. At first sight the K mould looks as if it is a very poor bet. Given the mean lives as they are shown in Fig 9.2. We would say that

$$\text{Mould Cost per ton using A} = \frac{£100}{3.47 \times 2} = £14.4 \text{ per ton cast}$$

$$\text{Mould Cost per ton using K} = \frac{£120}{2.10 \times 2} = £28.6 \text{ per ton cast}$$

However the sample of lives for mould K is extremely *biased*. It is biased because the K mould has only recently been introduced and the sampling frame only consists of those moulds which have been scrapped. Moulds that are still in the mould circuit being used again and again, are still out there doing a good job. The first ones to be scrapped will, of course, be the *bad ones.* We are trying to sample from a population in the early stages of evolution. In fact in this situation there is no valid sampling frame because early on there will be some K moulds, the good ones, that have not yet been scrapped so that there is no way by which their final lives can be determined because these will be determined in the future. Of course we could get some indication from the number of casts achieved to date by K moulds in the circuit if that data were to be accessible. The A moulds are a long established population and the mould type has been in use for long enough for scrapped moulds to be representative of both good and bad moulds.

In some cases the population never reaches a stable state. Cars may rust before the long-run life of the engine can be determined. Long before a component's life has been determined, new modifications may be brought in. As a result the population mean has no stable value that can be measured.

Exercise

1. An airline has just installed a new modification of an altimeter. The data for 5 altimeters scrapped to date shows a mean life of only 400 flying hours. The mean life of the old type was 2,000 flying hours. Why might the result be biased? How would you estimate the true mean life?

2. A new drug has been given to 100 seriously ill patients at various times over the past 5 years. The mean number of years survived by members of this population is 1.5 years. Does this information provide a reasonable basis for estimating the survival of patients using the drug?

QUANTITATIVE METHODS

3. A company has just carried out a sample of workers it has made redundant over the past 2 years. Some of these workers have since found jobs but those who left 2 years ago took longer on average to find a job than those who left only a year ago. Comment on the results.

9.6 Sampling Error: Attributes

Sampling error is the error that arises from the limited size of the sample. With a big enough sample, and in the absence of bias, it should be possible to obtain a near perfect estimate of the population parameter required. The estimate based on smaller and more realistic samples can be expected to deviate from the true population figures. Statisticians have uncovered laws which govern the extent of this error. By using the result of these studies, it is possible to predict very accurately the degree of precision that an ideal sample can offer.

However it needs to be stressed once again that the statistician's calculation of sampling error assumes an unbiased sample. As we have seen earlier in this chapter, the elimination of bias is not easy and its effects are difficult to quantify. It follows therefore, that in most situations, statements of sampling error should be interpreted as statements of minimum error applicable before bias is taken into account.

9.6.1 The Sampling Distribution of a Percentage

Suppose that we want to estimate the percentage or proportion of a population which possesses a given attribute by taking a sample. We will need to know the degree of sampling error to be attached to the estimate, that is how far away from the population percentage is the percentage given by the sample likely to be. To get an idea of the way in which statistical theory can help, we will look at a very simple example with a ridiculously small sample. However by taking a very small sample, you will be able to see how, in principle, theory can be used to calculate the sampling error. In that way we will only need to employ very basic probabilities.

Suppose a company manufacturing breakfast cereal wished to know what percentage of households have a box of their product in their kitchens. What would happen if they were foolish enough to base their enquiries on a sample of only 2 households. Let us assume for the moment that unknown to them, 30% of the population have the product when they are carrying out their survey, and will say 'yes' if asked. With a sample of 2, either 0, 1 or 2 will say 'yes' and we can calculate the probabilities of each of these results as shown in Table

FINDING OUT BY SAMPLING

9.2 using the concepts of probability developed in Chapter 4.

Table 9.2

Number saying 'yes'	% in sample	Sample responses		Probability calculation		Probability of given no. saying 'yes'
0	0	N	N	0.7 x 0.7	=	0.49
1	50	Y	N	0.3 x 0.7	=	0.42
		N	Y	0.7 x 0.3		
2	100	Y	Y	0.3 x 0.3	=	0.09
						1.00

Note the two ways in which a sample result of 50% could arise in the sample: either the first member of the sample says 'yes' and the other 'no' Y N, or the other way round, N Y.

The resulting probability distribution is the theoretical sampling distribution of percentages. It is called a sampling distribution because it indicates how samples drawn from the population behave in theory. In this case it shows how likely different sample percentages would be if the population percentage were to be 30%. Similar calculations can be used to handle larger samples (see page 441). As you can see, the sample is unlikely to show 100% saying 'yes' but is likely to show either 0% or 50%.

Exercise

Confirm that if the population percentage saying 'yes' were 60%, then the sampling distribution for a sample of size 2 would be as shown in Table 9.3.

Table 9.3

% in Sample saying 'yes'	Probability of occurrence
0%	0.16
50%	0.48
100%	0.36

A comparison of Tables 9.2 and 9.3 shows that, not surprisingly, a sample of 2 would be useless for predicting the population percentage.

What about using a larger sample size? Fig 9.3 shows the theoretical sampling distribution of the percentage saying 'yes' for different

QUANTITATIVE METHODS

sample sizes. These have been calculated using essentially the same methods as were used for the sample of size 2.

Fig 9.3 : Sampling distribution of the Percentage in a Sample (Population Percentage possessing a given attribute = 30%)

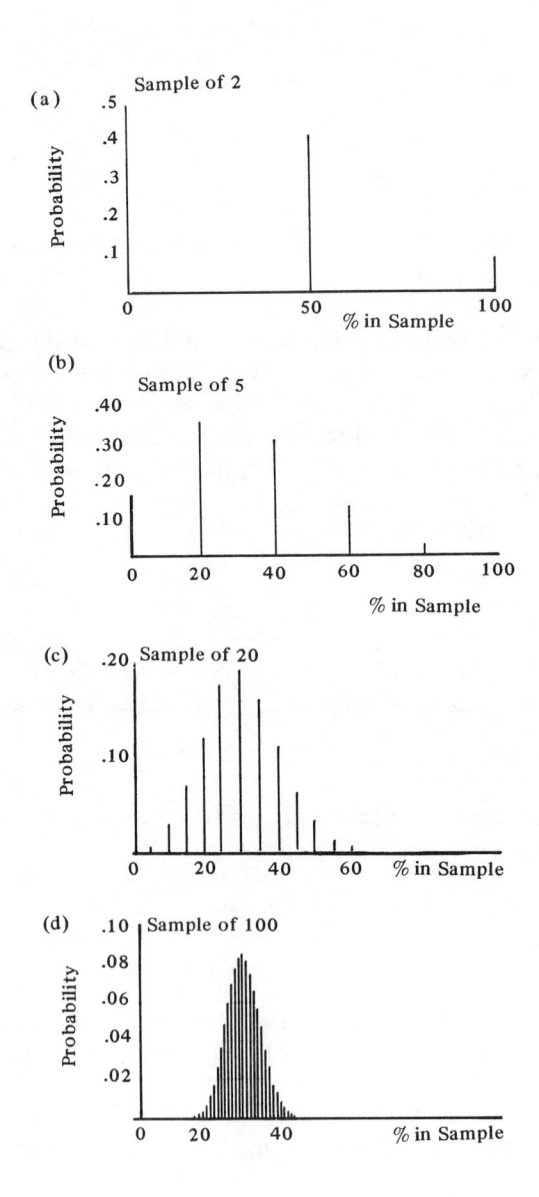

(a) Sample of 2

(b) Sample of 5

(c) Sample of 20

(d) Sample of 100

FINDING OUT BY SAMPLING

Note how the percentages likely to be produced by the sample are scattered over a progressively more limited range as the sample size is increased. With the tiny sample of 2, a sample could easily indicate anything from 0% to 100% 'yes' whereas with a sample of 100, the range runs from about 18% to 42%. This scattering of sample results around the population figure of 30% applies *even if the sample is completely unbiased.* Fig 9.3 provides a visual impression of sampling error. You will probably be surprised by the extent of the spread of the error for a sample of 100 when compared with that of size 20. Although 100 is 5 times 20, the error has not been reduced by a factor of 5. Clearly there are some surprises in the way samples behave.

9.6.3 The Normal Distribution

Sampling distributions for large samples follow a distribution which is symmetrical and bell-shaped and which is known as the 'normal' distribution. There is a precise and well documented relationship between the scatter of values around the mean and the standard deviation (see page 462). Appendix 1 contains a summary of that relationship. The distribution occurs widely in the natural world but in the world of business, its main importance lies in its importance in interpreting information derived from samples.

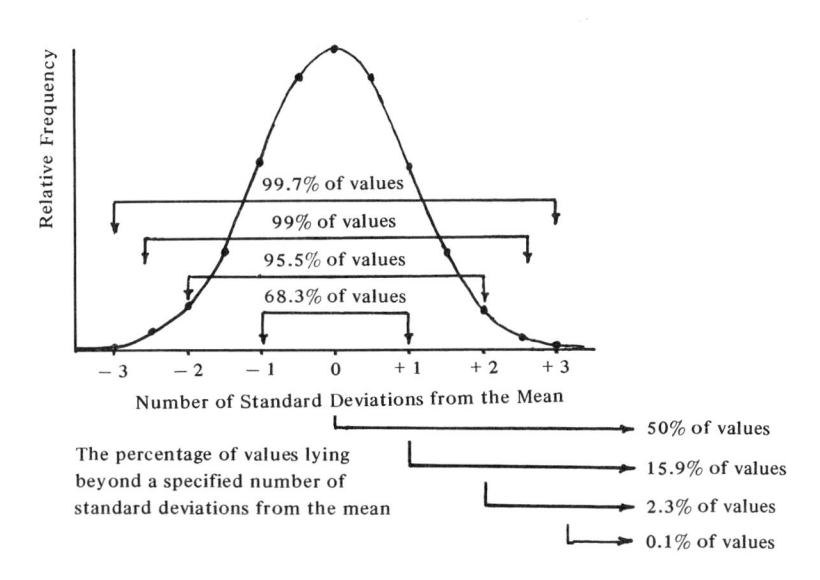

Fig 9.4 : The Normal Distribution

QUANTITATIVE METHODS

As you can see from Fig 9.4, most of the distribution lies within 3 standard deviations of the mean, about 95% lies within 2 standard deviations and 99% within 2.6 standard deviations.

Looking at Fig 9.3d, you can see that the sampling distribution of the percentage for large samples roughly follows a similar bell-shaped distribution. It is only approximately normal and you can see that there is in fact a small degree of skewness to the right. For most purposes we can say that for samples of 50 or more and for population percentages lying between 10% and 90%, the sampling distribution of the percentage approximately follows a normal distribution. Referring back to Fig 7.7 on page 236, you can see that the sampling distribution of the correlation coefficient also tends to follow a normal distribution for large sample sizes. This is a further illustration of the tendency of sampling distributions to follow the normal distribution providing reasonably large samples are taken.

9.6.4 The Standard Error

In Chapter 3 various measures of dispersion were discussed. To measure sampling error, the standard deviation of the sampling distribution is used and it is referred to as the *Standard Error*. It is calculated as

$$\text{Standard Error of the percentage} = \sqrt{\frac{\text{Population \% x (100} - \text{population \%)}}{\text{sample size}}}$$

So for a sample of 100 and a population percentage of 30% as in Fig 9.3d, the standard error is given by

$$\sqrt{\frac{30 \times (100 - 30)}{100}} = \sqrt{21} = 4.6\%$$

For *large samples* the standard error can be interpreted as follows:

Roughly 95% of sample percentages will lie within 2 standard errors of the population percentage

This follows because the sampling distribution approximately follows the normal distribution. Applying this in the case of 9.3d, where the standard error is 4.6%, this would suggest that 95% of the sample percentages would lie within 2 x 4.6% = 9.25% of the population percentage of 30%. They would therefore cover a range of 21% to 39%. Fig 9.3d confirms this prediction.

If a sample of 1,000 were taken, the standard error would be

FINDING OUT BY SAMPLING

$$\sqrt{\frac{30 \times (100 - 30)}{1000}} = 1.45\%$$

and so, in that case, 95% of sample percentages should lie within about 3% (= 2 x 1.45) of the true figure.

9.6.5 Diminishing Returns

As you might expect, with increasing sample size the sampling error, as measured by the standard error, decreases. However the square root sign in the standard error formula means that

The standard error is proportional to $\frac{1}{\sqrt{\text{sample size}}}$.

Now this means that to halve the sampling error, the sample size must be quadrupled. This means that increasing the sample size has a disappointing effect on the sampling error. Look at Fig 9.3c and d. In going from a sample size of 20 to one of 100, an increase in the sample size by a factor of 5. the scatter has only been reduced by a factor of 2¼ (= $\sqrt{5}$). This unpleasant fact means that there is a law of diminishing returns for samples. As the sample size increases, so the corresponding error reduction becomes smaller. This is illustrated in Fig 9.5.

Fig 9.5 : How the Standard Error of the Sample Percentage Reduces with sample size

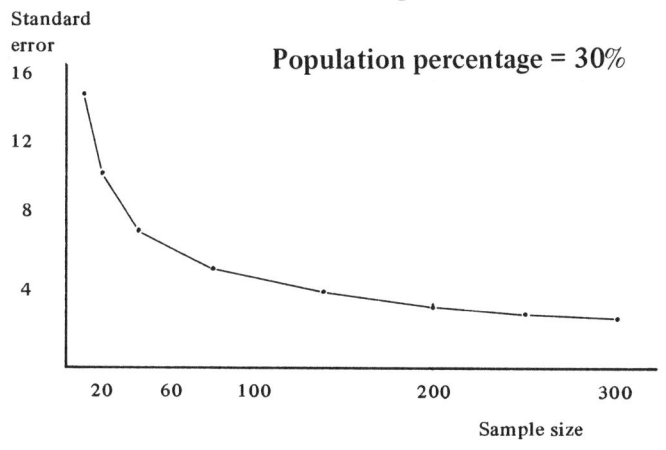

Note how relatively disappointing the reduction in standard error becomes for large samples.

9.6.6 Confidence Limits

The theoretical distributions shown in Fig 9.3 show how the

313

percentage in a large number of samples of the given sizes would behave. Of course the researchers only have *one* sample and therefore *one* percentage. They do not know the population percentage, after all that is why they are taking a sample in the first place! However they can use the sample percentage to estimate the standard error of the population. They can then say that:

> 'We do not know where our one sample percentage is located within the sampling distribution. Maybe it is above or below the true population value. We can, however, be roughly 95% confident that our sample percentage is no further than 2 standard errors from the population percentage'.

I say 'roughly 95% confident' because the standard error is not known with certainty and has to be estimated from the sample percentage, and also the sampling distribution only approximately follows a normal distribution. Approximate 95% confidence limits can be attached to the sample estimate as follows

$$\text{Estimate of Population Percentage} = \text{Sample \%} \pm 2 \times \sqrt{\frac{\text{Sample \% }(100 - \text{Sample \%})}{\text{Sample size}}}$$

and for approximately 99% confidence limits we can use the properties of the normal distribution to replace the factor 2 with the factor 2.6 (see page 311).

Example

In a sample of 120 invoices taken from a large batch, 20% were incorrectly laid out. Confidence limits for the population percentage based on that sample are:

$$95\% \quad 20\% \pm 2 \times \sqrt{\frac{20 \times 80}{120}} \quad \text{or} \quad 20\% \pm 7.3\%$$

$$99\% \quad 20\% \pm 2.6 \times \sqrt{\frac{20 \times 80}{120}} \quad \text{or} \quad 20\% \pm 9.5\%$$

So whatever the sample says we can only be really confident that the true percentage correct is above 10% and less than 30%. Pretty vague, you might say, but then samples can only give an idea of the underlying population. Although the estimates are vague, at least we now know how vague they are.

Do remember that the above limits assume an unbiased sample. Where a degree of bias may be present, your estimate may be much worse than the confidence limits suggest. As a result you should view confi-

FINDING OUT BY

dence limits as setting a lower limit to the degree of er[r] estimate. This means that however perfect the sampling [the] sampling error expressed in the confidence limits represents the very least error that can be incurred.

Exercise

1. In a sample of 2,500 motorists, 45% were found to be interested in a new product. Estimate the population percentage interested with 95% and 99% confidence.

2. 51% of a sample of 60 customers were satisfied with the after-sales service of a company. Estimate the percentage in the population as a whole with 95% and 99% confidence.

9.6.7 Required Sample Size

Given that the error to be attached to an estimate decreases with sample size, it should be possible to work out how big a sample is needed in order to reduce the sampling error to some specified level. The following rule provides the required sample size for 95% confidence given a rough estimate of the percentage to be estimated and the required error within which the estimate is to be made.

$$\text{sample size required} = \frac{4 \times \text{Percentage estimate} \times (100 - \text{Percentage estimate})}{(\text{Required error})^2}$$

and for 99% confidence, the 4 should be replaced by 6.8.

Example

Suppose market researchers want to estimate the percentage of TV viewers who saw the company's commercial on a given night. They hope that the figure will be at least 60% of those viewing that night. How big a sample should they take to estimate the figure with an error of only ± 1%?

$$\text{Required Sample size} = 4 \times \left(\frac{60 \times (100 - 60)}{1^2} \right) = 9{,}600$$

This figure should come as a bit of a shock. But of course ± 1% would be a very precise estimate and probably be more precise than any potential bias. If the required accuracy were only ± 2%, then the sample size needed would come down to 2,400. Note that by halving the required precision, the required sample size comes down by a factor of 4. This is just one of the surprises that sampling theory has in store.

QUANTITATIVE METHODS

Exercise

1. Confirm that if the error required to predict a population percentage of about 60% is ± 5% then the required sample size is 384.

2. Calculate the required sample size to estimate the population percentage to the nearest 5% given that the population percentage is believed to be about (a) 20% (b) 30%. Compare the result to that of the first question (assume 95% confidence in both cases).

9.6.8 Small Samples

As a glance at Figs 9.3a and b demonstrates, small samples will only give very imprecise estimates of the underlying population percentage. Not only is the sampling error large but also the sampling distribution cannot be assumed to follow a normal distribution. The binomial distribution should be used (see page 441) but remember that small samples have a much greater chance of being quite unrepresentative of the population and should be avoided where possible.

9.7 Sampling Error : Variables

A distinction between attributes and variables was made in Section 9.1.2 on page 295 and 296. We need to see now how sampling error is calculated when variables are sampled. Typical samples might be a work study sample of the *time* to complete a specified task, an auditor sampling invoices to estimate the mean *value* of a batch of invoices or a quality control engineer wishing to estimate the mean *weight* of cans of dogfood coming off a production line.

9.7.1 The Sampling Distribution of the Mean

It is not often that we can examine a large population in its entirety. All that we know about the population mean we need to infer from the sample mean. However in order to understand how sample means behave, I propose to imagine a population about which we have perfect knowledge and then use simulation techniques to study the sampling distribution.

Imagine a company proposing to open a service centre for a large retailing chain. Machines which require repair will be sent to the centre and it is necessary for the company to estimate the mean repair time. Given that prediction, it will be possible for the company to predict the number of repair manhours they will need for given forecasts of throughput of machines requiring repair. Suppose that unknown to the company repair times have the distribution shown in Fig 9.6a

FINDING OUT BY SAMPLING

Figure 9.6 : Simulated Sampling Distribution of the Mean for various sample sizes and a bimodel Population

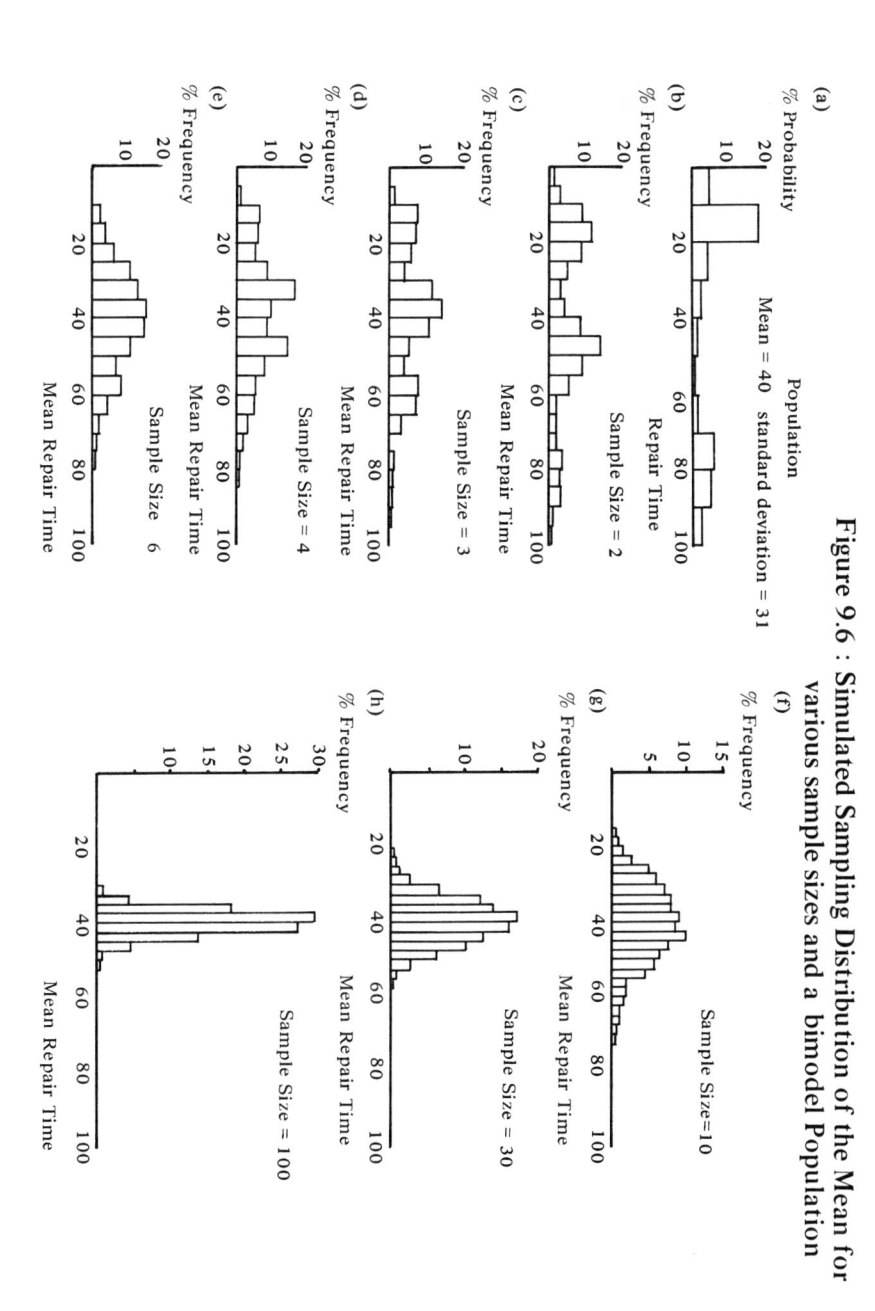

QUANTITATIVE METHODS

As you can see, the population of repair times have an irregular distribution which is bimodal and very different from a symmetrical distribution like the normal distribution. It has a high degree of dispersion around the mean of 40 minutes and is bimodal, and so the standard deviation is relatively large. Remember that the company carrying out the sample does not have this information. They are in the dark and will sample from the distribution in an attempt to estimate the population mean. Fig 9.6 shows the results of a simulation carried out in order to show what might happen if a large number of different sized samples were taken.

Fig 9.6b shows the distribution resulting from collecting 5,000 sample means of size 2. The computer sampled 2 repair times from the population shown in Fig 9.6a. It calculated the mean of the sample and repeated the process 5,000 times. As the population has 2 peaks, the distribution of the means of samples of size 2 could be expected to have 3 peaks. The sample might pick up 2 short jobs giving a sample mean of about 15 minutes. If 2 long jobs were sampled, a mean of about 80 minutes would be the result. But if it took one from each peak of the distribution, the sample would come out in the middle at, say, 50 minutes. Note that although very few repairs take 50 minutes, the mean of a sample of 2 repair times would be likely to yield such a value, e.g.
$$\frac{15 + 85}{2} = 50$$

Fig 9.6b shows the three peaks very clearly. But note how widely the sample means are dispersed ranging from almost 0 to 100. This confirms what our common sense tells us, namely that an estimate based on a sample of size 2 would be subject to a considerable amount of sampling error.

Now look at the rest of Fig 9.6 and note two important features:

1. As the sample size increases, the dispersion of the sample means, the sampling error, decreases.

2. As the sample size increases, the shape of the sampling distribution of the mean becomes more and more symmetrical and tends to resemble the normal distribution. Even for this irregular distribution the tendency is evident for a sample of size 6 and is well established by a sample size of about 30.

9.7.2 The Standard Error of the Mean

You will recall that the standard error of the mean is the standard

FINDING OUT BY SAMPLING

deviation of the sampling distribution (page 312). Statistical theory says that its magnitude should be given by

$$\frac{\text{standard deviation of the population}}{\sqrt{\text{sample size}}}$$

So for a sample of 100 repair times, given that the standard deviation of the population is 31, the standard error should be $\frac{31}{\sqrt{100}} = \frac{31}{10} = 3.1$. The actual standard deviation of the sample means of size 100 in the sampling experiment was 3.12, a result close to what theory predicts.

9.7.3 Confidence Limits for Estimates of the Mean

For samples of size 100 then, the theoretical standard error is 3.1 minutes and the distribution of the sample means follows a normal distribution. According to the laws of the normal distribution (page 311) 99% of sample means should lie within 2.6 standard errors of the mean of the population, i.e. 40 mins ± 2.6 x 3.1 or 40 mins ± 8.1 mins thereby covering a range of roughly 32 to 48 minutes. A more detailed breakdown of Fig 9.6h (see Fig 9.7) bears out this statement.

Fig 9.7 : Simulated Sampling Distribution for the means of Samples of size 100 (See Fig 9.6 h)

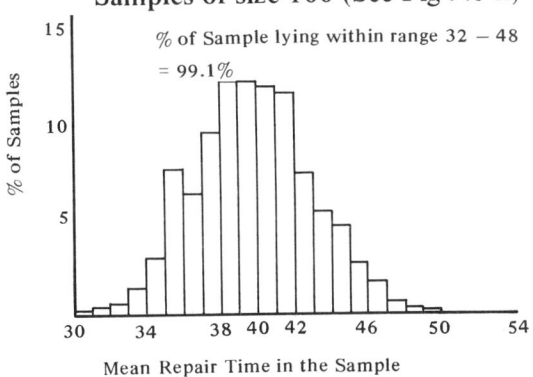

% of Sample lying within range 32 – 48 = 99.1%

(Histogram: x-axis "Mean Repair Time in the Sample" ranging 30 to 54; y-axis "% of Samples" ranging 0 to 15)

So far this has all been theory illustrated by a sampling experiment. In practice the analysts or researchers only have one sample mean of a specified size. They do not know what the population mean is. The standard deviation of the sample can, however, be used to estimate the value of the standard error. Now they know that whether the sample mean is above or below the population mean, they can be roughly 95% confident that the sample mean lies no more than 2 standard errors from the true mean of the population. Confidence limits can therefore be set as follows:

QUANTITATIVE METHODS

Best estimate of population mean = Sample Mean ± 2 x standard error for given sample size

= Sample Mean ± 2 x $\dfrac{\text{standard deviation of the sample}}{\sqrt{\text{sample size}}}$

and for 99% confidence limits, a figure of 2.6 should be used instead of 2.

9.7.4 Diminishing Returns

We have already seen (on page 313) that sampling can be disappointing. Suppose an auditor has sampled 36 invoices from a large batch and found that they have a mean value of £156 and a standard deviation of £140. Estimates of the mean value of the batch are as follows:

95% confidence limits: £156 ± 2 x $\dfrac{£140}{\sqrt{36}}$ = £156 ± £47

99% confidence limits: £156 ± 2.6 x $\dfrac{£140}{\sqrt{36}}$ = £156 ± £61

Now suppose that a more accurate estimate is required and the auditor decides to double the sample size to 72 invoices. What would the confidence limits become then? Assuming that the estimate of the standard deviation remains unchanged, they would become:

95% limits: ± £33   99% limits: ± £43

What has happened? Surely with twice as much information, the error should be halved? Unfortunately not. Remember that the formula for the standard error contains the *square root* of the sample size. This means that to halve the sampling error, the sample size would have to be *quadrupled*!. Refer back to Fig 9.5 on page 313. The same law of diminishing returns applies to the estimation of the mean as applied in that case.

Remember too that the 95% and 99% confidence limits should be treated as the minimum level of error to be associated with an estimate. Bias could mean that even with a large sample and a consequently low sampling error, the estimate could still turn out to be very inaccurate.

Exercise

1. A work study engineer has sampled 40 job times and found a

FINDING OUT BY SAMPLING

mean time of 6 minutes and a standard deviation of 4 minutes. Estimate the overall mean job time with confidence limits.

2. Using the results of (1) above, derive confidence limits for the number of jobs that can be carried out in an 8-hour day assuming 2 minutes delay between successive jobs.

3. Recalculate (1) assuming that 400 job times have been sampled.

4. A sample of 25 invoices from a large batch has a mean value of £225 with a standard deviation of £15. Estimate the mean value of the invoices in the batch, with confidence limits.

5. Using the result of (4) above, derive confidence limits for the total value of the batch assuming that there are 6,500 invoices in all.

9.7.5 Small Samples

Two problems arise with small samples.

i) The estimate of the standard error based on a small sample may be very inaccurate and in that case special factors have to be used.

ii) As Figure 9.6 shows very well, the sampling distribution of the mean for small samples may not follow a normal distribution. If the population is near-normal or at least roughly symmetrical then this problem does not arise.

At this point things start to get very technical and a detailed discussion can be found on page 444. People rarely set out to take small samples, but in surveys, small samples often arise because of a partitioning of the population. Suppose a sales manager wants to estimate the planned purchases of his customers next year. A large sample of customers could be asked to state their intentions. The manager might then be interested in the views of a subset of the population, perhaps those customers who have been buying from the company for more than 5 years. Once the customers in the sample who meet that criterion have been isolated, a sample of 4 or 5 might be all that was available and small sampling conditions, with all the complications that that implies, would be encountered. For that reason *Stratified Sampling* is often used to provide a way out of such problems (see page 324).

9.7.6 Required Sample Size

Following the logic of Section 9.6.7 on page 315, it follows that :

QUANTITATIVE METHODS

$$\text{sample size required for 95\% confidence} = \frac{4 \times \left(\text{Estimated standard deviation of population}\right)^2}{(\text{Required error})^2}$$

and for 99% the 4 should be replaced by 6.8. The estimated standard deviation of the population is often obtained from a preliminary sample.

Exercise

A company has carried out a preliminary test on a new instrument and found that the sample had a mean life of 520 hours with a standard deviation of 350 hours. How big a sample would be needed to predict the mean life to within (a) 10 hours and (b) 1 hour?

9.8 Finite Populations 'the Great Sampling Fallacy'

As you have seen, it is the size of sample obtained that determines the precision of an estimate. Many people believe, however, that it is the percentage of the population sampled that counts. They will incorrectly worry about whether a 10% or a 20% sample is sufficient. This is a fallacy. A sample of 100 cheques from a batch of 1,000 tells us roughly the same about the batch as a whole as a sample a of 100 cheques taken from a batch of 2,000 cheques! This is so even though in one case a 10% sample has been taken, and in the other a 5% sample has been taken. People find this hard to believe especially as common sense tells us that if a very high percentage of a population is sampled, then we must have almost complete knowledge about the population in question and consequently an estimate based on such a high percentage sample should be very precise.

To resolve this problem, we need to have another closer look at the formula for calculating the standard error. The formula for the standard error used so far should in fact be multiplied by the following factor:

$$\text{Finite Population Correction factor} = \sqrt{\frac{\text{Population size} - \text{sample size}}{\text{Population size}}}$$

(see page 444 for coverage for small samples)

So for a sample of 100 cheques taken from a batch of 1,000, the standard error should be multiplied by a factor of

$$\sqrt{\frac{(1000-100)}{(1000)}} = \sqrt{\frac{900}{1000}} = 0.95$$

FINDING OUT BY SAMPLING

In other words, the standard error should be reduced by 5% to take account of the fact that 10% of the population has been sampled, a very marginal adjustment I think you will agree. If a 100 cheques were sampled from a population of 2,000, then the factor would be 0.97 implying a reduction in the normal standard error of only 3%. Fig 9.8 shows how the finite population factor varies as the percentage of the population sampled varies.

Figure 9.8 :
Finite Population Correction Factor for the Standard Error (attributes and variables)

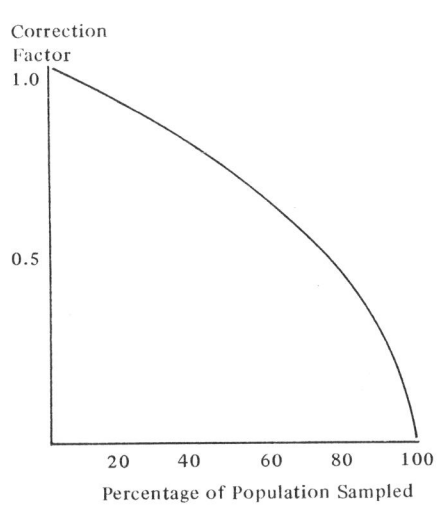

It really does come as a surprise that you have to sample 75% of the population before the normal standard error is reduced by $\frac{1}{2}$ and having sampled 99% of a population, the standard error has still 10% of its normal value! Clearly unless you are sampling a large proportion of a population, you can simply ignore the factor.

Example 1

An engineer wishes to check 150 machines. He suspects that about 25% of them are unsafe. He decides to check out 50 of them at considerable expense. How precisely will he be able to estimate the percentage which are faulty? Confidence limits are given as:

$$\pm 2 \times \sqrt{\frac{25 \times (100-25)}{50}} \times \sqrt{\frac{150-50}{150}}$$

$$= \pm 12.2\% \times 0.82 = \pm 10\%$$

Note that allowing for having sampled one third of the population lation results in only a modest reduction in the ordinary standard error expression.

QUANTITATIVE METHODS

Example 2

A sample of 130 bank accounts out of a total of 150 were selected at random. The mean balance is £230 with a standard deviation of £290 Given that they had sampled over 80% of the population, management felt that they should have a pretty accurate estimate of the mean balance of the population of 150 accounts. The result is quite surprising. The estimate with 95% confidence limits is

$$£230 \pm 2 \times \frac{£290}{\sqrt{130}} \times \sqrt{\frac{150-130}{150}}$$

$$\pm £50.9 \times 0.365$$
$$\pm £18.6$$

The correction factor does effectively reduce the standard error considerably, but the residual error is still unpleasantly high. As you can see, sampling is hard work.

9.9 Stratification

Where a population is very diverse, it may be much more efficient to divide the population up into a number of sections or *strata* and sample from each of these separately. There are two good reasons why this may be a good idea.

9.9.1 Adequate Coverage of Small Groups

An important section of the population may be small in number and may consequently be poorly represented in a purely random sample. By sampling from that small section separately a representative sample overall can be ensured. Suppose, for example, that a company wants to take a sample of 30 of its 5,000 customers in order to estimate the quantity of business being done. What would happen if 10% of the customers (that makes 500 in all) are particularly big and account for no less than 95% of sales. Within samples of 30 we would expect to find only 3 such major customers on average. Such a small sample of the major group would lead to an inaccurate estimate of the contribution coming from the most significant section of the population. In such an instance, it would be much more sensible to stratify the population into 500 large customers and 4,500 small customers and determine adequate samples for estimating the means of each taken separately.

9.9.2 Reduction of Sampling Error

Where there is considerable variation *between* sections of the

FINDING OUT BY SAMPLING

population *within* which there is little variation, it is more efficient to stratify the population. An exaggerated example will serve to illustrate the point. Suppose a company offering a vehicle tuning service on site wanted to estimate the sales potential of its customers nationwide. This will involve salesmen making enquiries with specific customers about their vehicle fleet in the coming year. The figures for an earlier year are shown in Table 9.4.

Table 9.4

Vehicle Fleet Size	No of Companies (North)	No of Companies (South)	No of Companies Overall
0 – 10	100		100
10 – 20	700		700
20 – 30	100	100	200
30 – 40	100	800	900
40 – 50		100	100
Mean	17	35	26
Standard Deviation	7.5	4.5	10.9

The customers are equally split between North and South and note that *within* the regions there is little variation but that there is a large difference *between* regions. If the company sampled from the overall population and required an estimate to ± 2 vehicles, it would need a sample of

$$\frac{4 \times 10.9^2}{2^2} = 119$$

If on the other hand it tackled each region separately within which the variation as measured by the standard deviation is much smaller, it would need separate samples of

$$\frac{4 \times 7.5^2}{2^2} = 56 \text{ and } \frac{4 \times 4.5^2}{2^2} = 20$$

The total sampling bill will now be smaller for the population as a whole. Clearly imaginative stratification can save you money.

9.10 Surveys

Anyone intending to carry out a survey should consult a detailed source such as the comprehensive, yet readable, Moser and Kalton (1971). Some of the major issues to be thought out are as follows.

9.10.1 Purposes

A survey should have a clearly defined purpose and this should be

QUANTITATIVE METHODS

subject to revision before the survey is implemented. Ask yourself:

1. Who needs the information and why? Are there not other cheaper sources of information?

2. For what purpose will the information be used? The answer to this question will affect the degree of detail and the precision required.

3. Which is more important? Quantitative precision or an in-depth study of a possibly biased sample? Is the latter not a good preliminary step in any case?

All these questions are worth answering before blundering into the expense of a full-blooded survey. A quick, cheap and biased survey can save you a lot of money if it leads you to reassess the purpose or need for a survey. Bias is only vicious when its presence is ignored or undetected. Of course no reliable *estimates* can be based on such a crude trial survey.

9.10.2 Planning a Survey

A survey requires detailed planning. A few vital features which are often neglected follow.

1. Provide for non-response in advance. Section 9.4 has shown how non-response can introduce bias. Of course your plan should ensure that you know who has replied to a questionnaire. If forms are returned un-named to ensure anonymity, then unless they are coded, you will be unable to say who the non-respondents are, and as a result you will be unable to check the non-responding population for special features so as to estimate any bias.

2. The twin pillars of bias and sampling error (9.2) need to be given separate consideration. Remember that whereas the control of sampling error is a technical matter, the avoidance of bias requires the active involvement of management for it is they who have knowledge of the population under consideration. Careful attention to sampling methods are required, and above all the exercise of *imagination* in foreseeing problems before they arise.

3. Plan the processing and analysis of the results in advance and in detail. Give your friendly statisticians or computer experts some dummy responses well in advance of your survey and explain your objectives. Such experts are usually only too pleased to give advice when there is still time for them to have some influence. For instance questionnaires can be designed so that it is easy to transfer the data

to the computer for analysis. This can save money.

4. Carry out a pilot survey, however crude, and try to do some of it *yourself*. This will enable you to get some idea of the suitability of the sampling frame. You will be able to estimate the variability of the population so that the required sampling size can be estimated. A dummy run will enable you to assess the scale of the non-response problem and if a questionnaire is involved, you will almost certainly be able to clarify ambiguities in the form once trial fieldwork has taken place.

9.10.3 Sampling Methods

Simple random sampling is rarely used. Researchers proposing to interview a random sample of householders in this country would be led a merry dance. From the suburbs of London, the random numbers might lead them to a remote farm on the moors of Devon and from there to the coast of Wales and to the Industrial centres of the North of England. Such a Cook's tour would be prohibitively expensive. The inevitable pressure to save time and money has led to special forms of sampling.

1. *Cluster Sampling* when a number of discrete sections of the population are chosen at random and the whole of that section is then sampled. For example an aeroplane flight is chosen at random and then *all* of the passengers on the flight are then interviewed.

2. *Multistage Sampling* is similar to cluster sampling except that in this case only a sample of the chosen cluster is sampled. This can be done in a number of stages. A town, for example, might be sampled and then a further stage could be introduced by sampling a ward at random within that town. At that point, a random sample can be chosen which can be assessed at a reasonable cost.

3. *Quota Sampling* is a form of stratified sampling procedure, but one carried out by the fieldworker. Have you ever walked past an interviewer in the street and felt offended that they didn't ask you to help? Sometimes they don't seem to give you a glance and then pounce on someone immediately behind you. It is probably that the interviewer has been instructed to ensure that the sample contains predetermined quotas of 'typical' people and your quota has been filled. The idea is to ensure that the sample is representative of the population as a whole.

Of course such a system is difficult to control even with experienced

QUANTITATIVE METHODS

fieldworkers. The potential for bias is very great. The method assumes that the fieldworker can assess the status of the passer-by, a task which is difficult to do objectively. But it does have one great advantage. It is cheap, it is quick, and experienced market researchers seem to get reliable results from it.

Note: A Summary of the principle formulae relating to sampling statistics can be found on page 446.

CHAPTER 10 : DRAWING CONCLUSIONS

The chapter opens with a section on experimentation (10.1 and 10.2) and then reintroduces the concept of significance, this time on a formal basis (10.3 and 10.4). The chapter concludes with a discussion of some well-known significance tests (10.5).

10.1 Experiments in Business

There are three principal areas of business where formal experiments are an important feature. In Research and Development new products and processes are investigated in a formal scientific environment. In Quality Control, experimentation with new methods of production is carried out to raise or at least maintain quality standards. In Market Research, finding out about the impact of new products or packaging on the consumer plays a vital role in maintaining momentum in the market place. Elaborate experiments are sometimes carried out in shops when the response of the public is measured.

Outside these well established fields, informal experimentation of a cruder kind takes place even though it is not thought of as formal experimentation. A factory lay-out is changed and its general effectiveness observed. A subordinate is moved to a new position in order to see 'how he gets on'. A new organisation structure is instituted and its efficacy commented on at a later date. Such pseudo-experiments are taking place all the time on an uncontrolled basis. But even though the general business environment does not often permit formal experiments to be carried out, at least an understanding of what is ideally required, will help the manager to appreciate the dangers inherent in such pseudo-experimentation.

10.1.1 The Essentials of an Experiment

In an experiment, a *treatment* is applied to an experimental group or entity and the resulting effect observed. The scientist in his laboratory can rigorously control the environment so that any observed effect can be deemed to have been caused by the treatment. Also by his control of the environment, the experiment can usually be repeated under identical conditions.

In most business situations, however, including market research conditions, control of the environment is very difficult. Suppose a new TV commercial is tried out nationally and the subsequent change in sales measured. Clearly it would be unjustifiable for the researchers

QUANTITATIVE METHODS

to assume that any increase or decrease in sales had definitely been caused by the commercial. So many other factors in the environment could have changed at the same time as its transmission: action by competitors, the weather, trends in public taste and so on.

Suppose a local authority were to change the lay-out in all their libraries at the same time and then measure the public reaction to the services provided in the following year. It could not be assumed that any observed change in their reaction was due solely to the change in lay-out because of all the other changes which may have taken place: trends towards video, changes in the price and availability of books in the shops and so on.

10.1.2 The Need for Controls

In order to make allowances for possible changes in an uncontrollable environment, a *control group,* which does not receive the treatment, needs to be set up. This control group is then exposed to the same environmental conditions as is the *experimental group.* It is important that the units should be assigned to these two groups on a random basis so as to avoid bias. So a new commercial could then be run in a limited number of TV areas (the experimental group) while the existing commercial could run in other areas (the control group), care being taken to make the two groups as similar as possible from a geographical and demographical point of view.

The local authority could divide the libraries under its control into two groups on a random basis, changing the lay-out in one group and not in the other. In this case there could be problems arising from having two systems running simultaneously in the same area especially as users may well make use of more than one branch. Controls aren't always easy to set up in the world of business.

10.1.3 Simple Designs

In an *after-only* design, the effect due to the treatment is assessed by observing the state of the two groups, the experimental and the control, after the treatment. For instance, two groups of patients suffering from arthritis could be given treatment in the form of pills. The experimental group is given pills containing the drug being tested, the control group being given a pill containing a harmless ingredient (the placebo). This is called a *blind trial.* If the nurse or doctor administering the treatment does not know which patients are being given the drug and which are not, then the experiment is called a *double-blind trial.* The experimental design ensures that the participants cannot know whether they have been given the drug or the placebo. If they did, of course, this knowledge could affect their perception of their symptoms. The double-blind design prevents the doctors' knowledge of which patients have been treated, from affecting their assessment of the patient's health after receiving the treatment. This sort of design is useful in Market Research trials where the views of customers on the taste of new products are sought.

Sometimes it is advisable to establish the state of the groups before any treatment has taken place. In a *before-after* design, both the experimental and control groups are measured before and after the treatment. This design has the advantage that it will help to pick up any change which arises from carrying out the experiment itself. If the people or groups of people involved are affected by taking part in the experiment, then this effect will show up in *both* groups. The need for this precaution was highlighted in the famous Hawthorne experiments when it was found that simply by observing groups of workers, production improved even though no treatment had been applied.

10.1.4 More Complicated Designs

'Design of Experiments' in most textbooks refers to the planning of complex experiments which have been widely used in Science, Technology and Agriculture and also to some extent in Market Research. The different treatments are applied to units collected together in *blocks*. These might be groups of comparable stores each of which is to be treated with a different type of display, the selection of the store to be given a particular treatment within the block being chosen on a random basis. A planned allowance can be made for differences between blocks, i.e. between groupings of comparable stores in the above example. Within blocks, the stores will be similar in size and product range, between blocks there may be large differences.

Factorial experiments allow for treatments to be made at more than one level. In a store experiment, the different levels might be different amounts of discount applied. *Interaction* effects can also be teased out in tightly controlled experiments. Cox (1958) provides an intensive, yet relatively non-mathematical coverage of the subject.

10.2 Pseudo-Experiments

Ordinary managers don't usually see themselves in the business of carrying out experiments. They usually associate the formal testing of

QUANTITATIVE METHODS

hypotheses by the systematic collection of data, with the world of the scientist. However businessmen do find themselves making changes and coming to conclusions about the effect of those changes on the basis of observations of the world about them.

A brand manager for a company selling personal computers might offer a free gift to the customer with each machine sold 'as an experiment'. In the month following the introduction of the scheme he observes a 20% increase in sales. Similarly a Production manager might add 5 minutes to the morning tea break and then in the following week observe a 10% increase in output.

If after introducing the free gift there is an observed increase in sales then, because there is no control group, there are several hypotheses which could account for the results. These could include

1. Purchasers were attracted by the offer of a free gift and therefore encouraged to buy a computer.

2. The competition had unexpected problems that month so that customers were more inclined to buy from this company.

3. There was a seasonal uplift in sales in the month following the introduction of the free gift which had nothing to do with the treatment.

Unfortunately in the world of business, public and private, it would be difficult to set up the controls necessary to eliminate some of these competing hypotheses. In the case of the free gift offer, controls could have been established by operating the scheme in some sales areas only (the experimental group) and not in others (the control group). In theory such a procedure should help to distinguish hypotheses 2 and 3 from the first. If the first hypothesis applied then the increase in sales would be limited to the experimental areas alone, but if either 2 or 3 were operating then the increase should be detectable in all areas.

Even though controlled experiments cannot always be carried out in business in the fullest sense, the manager does at least need to be conscious of the limited conclusions that he can draw from the uncontrolled pseudo-experiments that he must inevitably carry out as part of his day to day duties. Always bear in mind in such situations that more than one hypothesis may be consistent with the observed facts.

10.2.1 Pseudo-experiments with time series

There are many situations where no properly controlled experiment

DRAWING CONCLUSIONS

can be carried out even in theory. This situation occurs when the treatment is applied to the whole population. This happens when a government brings in a new law, when a company changes its name or when a local council changes a local bye-law. All you can do is to observe the time series before and after with no control group to help determine whether observed changes in the time series after the treatment are due to the treatment or to other factors. The classic example arises after elections. You must have heard the old cry. 'Since the X party came to power, prices have gone up, exports have gone down etc, etc.' To which the appropriate reply is that since the X party came to power, a lot of other things have happened as well, and these could have affected the economic indicators.

Regression artifacts are one particularly tricky effect to handle in understanding time series. They arise when an extreme result, which must occur from time to time in any series, produces a response from the manager. The lower value which inevitably follows is erroneously ascribed to the treatment. Campbell (1972) describes the case of a severe crackdown on speeding offences in Connecticut. This was instituted because of a peak in accidents in 1955 when there were 324 deaths. In 1956 deaths fell to 284. Looking at Fig 10.1, the time series taken as a whole shows a fairly random variation prior to the crackdown.

Figure 10.1 : Connecticut Traffic Fatalities 1951–59 (Campbell 1972)

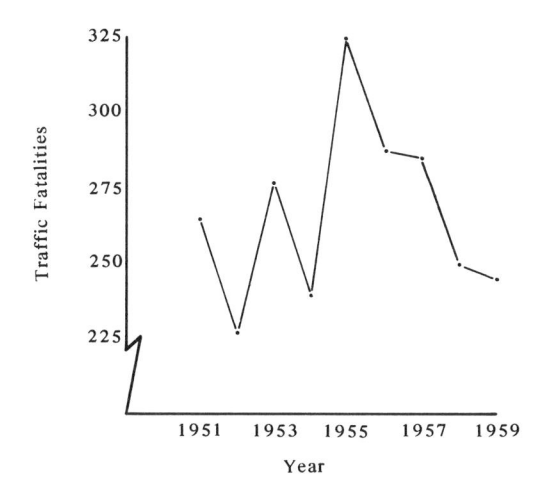

QUANTITATIVE METHODS

It *may* be that the crackdown was effective but of course any such change in the law is likely to be brought in at a crest in the time series and so a fall would be expected even if it were quite ineffective. Clearly in any quasi-experiment of this kind, sufficient time should be allowed to elapse before any conclusion is arrived at. The politicians can't usually wait that long!

10.3 Significance Once Again

When the treatment has been applied in any experiment, a difference between the experimental and control groups may be observed. Even if the experiment has been effectively controlled, it is always possible that the difference may have arisen because of random fluctuations within the two groups. If the observed difference lies within the bounds of everyday variation, then although the treatment may well have had some effect, we will have no means of being sure. However if the difference or the magnitude of the effect is greater than that which could reasonably have occurred by chance, then it is termed a *significant effect*.

The concept of significance has arisen at several points in this book already. On page 309 the way in which percentages can show insignificant differences was discussed and illustrated using simulation techniques. On page 236 a sampling experiment was used to indicate how significant correlation coefficients can be identified. In each case the statistician's contribution consists of showing the extent to which variations can arise *by chance alone*. A formal *test of significance* within an overall experimental design aims to distinguish effects arising from treatments which are larger than those which could reasonably have been expected to occur by chance. Managers need to take action when real effects are present but do not want to waste money trying to respond to mere random fluctuations.

For these reasons the formal process of significance testing needs to be understood. But there are many different tests and each presents its own difficulties. Here we will concentrate on the basic principles only and, to remove the statistical complications from the issue, a very simple example will be used to illustrate the main features of the procedure.

10.3.1 A Classical Significance Test

The classical significance test is a bit of a logical tongue-twister. Before

DRAWING CONCLUSIONS

discussing an example in detail, the steps are summarised below.

1. The status-quo is assumed to prevail until evidence to the contrary is produced. This assumption is given in the form of a quantitative statement called the *Null Hypothesis.*

2. The users specify the degree of change in the population which they would consider worthy of note.

3. An alternative hypothesis is set up which will be adopted if the status-quo Null Hypothesis is rejected.

4. A *test statistic* is chosen which will be derived from the sample and which will form the basis of the test e.g. the number of defects in a sample.

5. A sample is taken which is large enough to provide sufficient *power* to detect the degree of change specified in (2) above.

6. Assuming that the Null Hypothesis is true, the sampling distribution of the test statistic is found. This describes the extent to which the test statistic can vary in the absence of any effect. A set of extreme values, the *critical values,* are specified. These are chosen so that their occurrence is improbable enough to warrant the rejection of the Null Hypothesis if they arise in the sample. This degree of improbability is known as the *significance level* of the test.

7. The sample is taken, and the decision to reject or accept the Null Hypothesis follows depending on whether the test statistic falls within the critical range of values specified.

All this technical jargon will be illustrated by an example.

10.4.1 An Example from Quality Control

Suppose a company manufactures radar tubes. The product is a complex one and the company reluctantly accepts a failure rate of 10% within the first month of operation with the customer. Any increase above this rate would require immediate investigation but any false alarm would be embarrassing and costly. In order to check on the reliability of the process the company proposes to take a small sample of the final product and test the units to destruction. The test will indicate whether the tubes are defective and liable to fail or not in the first month, and they want to use the results to check on whether the 10% status quo still prevails. The number of defective tubes arising in the sample will constitute the test *statistic.*

We will consider what happens if a sample of 2 were to be taken. Now of course such a small sample is ridiculously small, but it has been

QUANTITATIVE METHODS

chosen so that the statistical theory involved is simple to understand and does not obscure the fundamental principles brought to light.

10.4.2 The Null Hypothesis

In a classical significance test, the first step is to assume that no change in the status quo has taken place. In the example described, this means that the following *Null Hypothesis* is set up:

> The defect rate is 10%, i.e. the chance of selecting a defective tube as part of the sample is 0.1.

This procedure is analogous to the situation in the courts where the assumption is made that the prisoner is innocent until proved guilty. This assumption is not made because people believe that the prisoner really *is* innocent, but is a procedural device to throw the onus of proof on to the prosecution's evidence leaving innocence as the default verdict in the event of that evidence being insufficient. In addition, an alternative hypothesis is set up. In this case this will state that the defect rate is greater than 10%.

10.4.3 The Sampling Distribution of the Test Statistic under the Null Hypothesis

The jury in a court case is asked to consider whether the evidence presented is consistent with the prior assumption of innocence. The company making radar tubes needs to consider in advance what sample results are consistent with the prior assumption of a 10% defective rate. Because we have chosen a small sample, some very simple probability provides the answer.

Assuming that the Null Hypothesis is true and only 10% of tubes are defective, we can calculate the probability that a sample of 2 tubes will contain 0, 1 or 2 defectives. The probability distribution is shown in Table 10.1.

Table 10.1 : Theoretical Sampling Distribution for the Number of Tubes Failing. 10% Defects overall : Sample of 2

Number of tubes failing	Probability Calculation	Probability of given number failing
0	0.9 x 0.9	0.81
1	0.1 x 0.9 0.9 x 0.1	0.18
2	0.1 x 0.1	0.01 1.00

DRAWING CONCLUSIONS

So on the assumption that the Null Hypothesis is true and the status quo prevails, it is possible to have 2 defectives in a sample of 2, but such an event would be unlikely. The sampling distribution in Table 10.1 allows us to be quite specific.

Assuming that the Null Hypothesis is true, there is only a 0.01 chance (1%) of getting 2 defectives in a sample of 2.

10.4.4 Choosing Critical Values for the Test: Significance Levels and Errors of Type I

A jury is asked to acquit if there is 'reasonable doubt' about a case although the term is never, and indeed can never be quantified. When faced with the evidence, the jury has to ask itself whether an innocent man would have said that, would an innocent man have done that, behaved like that? It is the jury's sense of the sort of behaviour which is consistent with innocence that leads the jury to a verdict. There must come a time in their deliberations when they decide that although it is conceivable that the defendant could be innocent in the face of the evidence, it is stretching the bounds of likelihood too far, and a conviction ensues.

The company making tubes is also faced with a dilemma. How many defectives can turn up in the sample and the result still be deemed to be consistent with the Null Hypothesis that only 10% of tubes overall are defective? In a significance test, reasonable doubt is defined as a probability and is termed the *level of significance* of the test. A critical level of extreme sample outcomes is set such that the probability of their occurrence is less than a specified probability. That probability is called the *level of significance* of the test.

The levels used are usually 5% and 1%. The arbitary nature of these accepted conventional levels are discussed somewhat irreverently in Skipper et al (1967).

In the case of the radar tubes, if the company operates at the '1% significance level', then it declares 2 defectives to be the critical value because there is only a 1% chance of such an extreme result in the event of the Null Hypothesis being true. If they eventually take a sample of 2, find 2 defectives and as a result reject the Null Hypothesis, then they accept that they incur the risk of making an error. Rejecting the Null Hypothesis when it should be accepted is called an *error of Type I*. It is analogous to convicting the innocent man in court. The relationship between the different errors is shown in Table 10.2.

QUANTITATIVE METHODS

Table 10.2 : Errors of Type I and II

	Null Hypothesis True	Null Hypothesis False
Reject Null Hypothesis	Error of Type I	OK
Accept Null Hypothesis	OK	Error of Type II

. . . .

	10% defectives overall	Greater than 10% defectives overall
2 defects are found and the company *rejects* the 10% figure	Error of Type I	correct Decision
0 or 1 defects are found and the company *accepts* the 10% figure	Correct Decision	Error of Type II

By accepting a 1% risk of making an error of Type I, the company recognises that if a large number of samples of size 2 are drawn from tubes which are 10% defective, the accepted quality level, then on average 1 in 100 samples will show 2 defectives and lead to the rejection of the Null Hypothesis when it should have been accepted. Why should they accept such a risk at all? The problem is that if they did not accept some risk they would never come to a decision. Quality could deteriorate and the company continue to explain poor sample results as being freak results consistent with normal quality overall.

If you have ever done jury service, then you will have faced the risk of making an error of Type I face to face. The evidence almost convinces you that the defendent is guilty, and yet. . . . could it not be that he is innocent and that a series of extraordinary coincidences have created an erroneous impression? In the end every jury has to accept some degree of making an error of Type I.

10.4.5 Errors of Type II : the Power of a Test

With a critical value of 2 defectives, the company has a 1% chance of making an error of Type I, that is of saying that things have changed even though the average defective rate is unchanged. That doesn't seem too bad. But Table 10.2 suggests that another form of error is possible. Suppose that the underlying defective rate really did increase but only 0 or 1 defectives turned up in the test sample. According to

DRAWING CONCLUSIONS

the rules laid down, the Null Hypothesis would be accepted. For instance, suppose 20% of tubes were defective overall. Table 10.3 shows the sampling distribution for the number of defectives in a sample of 2 in that case.

Table 10.3 : **Sampling Distribution for the Number of Tubes Failing. 20% defects overall : sample of 2**

Number of Tubes failing	Probability Calculation	
0	0.8 x 0.8	0.64
1	0.2 x 0.8 0.8 x 0.2	0.32
2	0.2 x 0.2	0.04

Sadly, although the underlying defective rate has doubled to 20%, the chances of getting the critical value of 2 defectives in the sample, and as a result rejecting the Null Hypothesis, is very slim.

Not surprisingly, the test based on a sample of 2 turns out to be lacking in *power*. Fig 10.2 shows a *power curve* for this test. It shows how the probability of rejecting the Null Hypothesis varies with the underlying defective rate. The test is so weak that even if the true defect rate were 50%, the chance of the test picking it up would be only 0.25.

Fig 10.2 : **Power Curve for a Test**

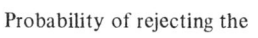

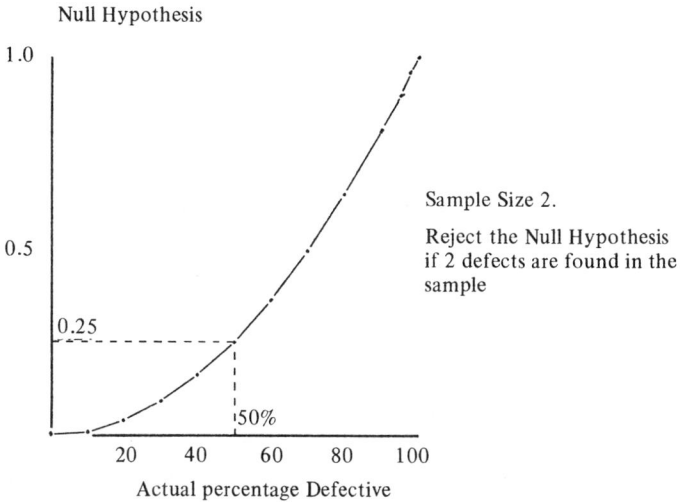

QUANTITATIVE METHODS

Clearly in designing a test, it is necessary for the test to be powerful enough to detect the sort of change in the population which is of economic importance. The feeble power of the test shown in Fig 10.2 accords with common sense. Given that we are obtaining so little information, how could the test be anything but a weak one? How could it possibly discriminate between good and bad quality?

Exercise

Look at Fig 10.2. If the overall defective rate were (a) 40%, (b) 80%, what would be the chance of rejecting the Null Hypothesis?

With more information gathered in the sample, the situation improves. If a sample of 20 were taken, then the sampling distribution for the number of defects assuming the Null Hypothesis is true is shown in Table 10.4.

Table 10.4

Number of Defects	Probability of number of defects	Probability of stated number of defects *or more*
0	.1216	
1	.2701	
2	.2852	
3	.1901	
4	.0898	
5	.0319	.0432
6	.0089	.0113
7	.0020	.0024
8	.0003	
9	.0001	

For a significance test at the 1% level for this larger sample size, the critical number of defects will be 6 or more. This is because if the Null Hypothesis applies and the underlying defect rate is 10%, then the chance of getting 6 or more defectives and thereby rejecting the Null Hypothesis will be roughly 1%. In other words, the chance of making an error of type I will be about 1%.

The company could alternatively adopt the rule: 'Reject the Null Hypothesis if a sample of 20 shows 5 or more defectives'. Table 10.4 says that the chance of making an error of Type I is less than 5% likely. As a result such a rule would provide a test operating at the 5% level.

DRAWING CONCLUSIONS

10.4.6 Balancing Type I and II Errors

By definition, a significance test set at the 5% level will involve the user in a higher risk of making an error of Type I than one set at the 1% level. However this is balanced by a decreased chance of making an error of Type II. In a legal system, if it is made easier for juries to convict, then more innocent people will be convicted but on the other hand fewer guilty people will go free. Fig 10.3 shows the power curves for tests carried out at the 5% and the 1% level using a sample of size 20. Note that if the underlying quality of tubes changed to 20% defective, then the 1% test would only have a 0.19 chance of picking up the change whereas the 5% test would have a 0.37 chance of doing so.

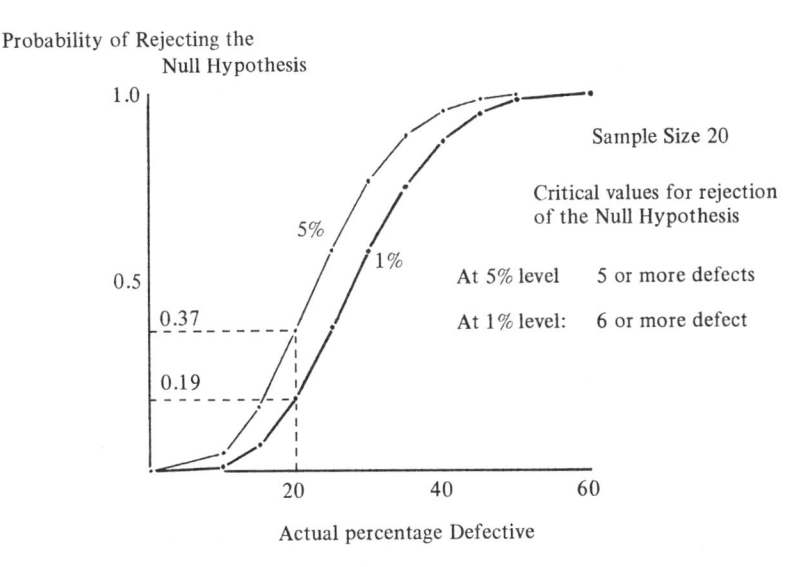

Fig 10.3 : Power Curves for a Test

So in any significance test, there must be a balance between the two errors. For a given sample size, one error can only be reduced by increasing the other and vice versa.

10.4.7 Problems with the Court Analogy : Interpreting a null result

There is one major snag about using the court analogy in order to understand the way a significance test works. In a court of law, if a man is acquitted, then he leaves the court 'without a blemish on his character'. Now in Scotland, there is a third verdict, that of 'not proven', and in a significance test, 'not proven' is very often a more appropriate 'verdict'.

341

QUANTITATIVE METHODS

In the example on page 336 suppose the company samples 2 tubes and finds one defective. According to the rules of the test, the Null Hypothesis cannot be rejected. This does not mean that the Null Hypothesis has been shown to be true. Remember, you are not obliged, as in a court of law, to send the acquitted defendent out a 'free man'. If you are running a business, then treating the results of a quality control sample or a market research sample as being inconclusive is perfectly reasonable.

Table 10.1 on page 336 does indeed say that 1 defective in a sample of 2 is possible even if the underlying rate is 10%. 1 defective in 2 is certainly consistent with the assumption that quality remains unchanged. *But it is also consistent with the assumption that quality has deteriorated'.* The test is so lacking in *power* that the finding of 1 defective is consistent with a whole range of possible quality states. Think of the legal analogy. A man was seen driving away from the scene of the crime in a red Ford car. The police arrest you, and the only evidence is that you drive a red Ford. That evidence is consistent with the assumption of your being innocent (lots of people have Ford cars) and also with the assumption that you are guilty (the thief was seen driving a red Ford). There is not enough evidence to eliminate one of the two hypotheses.

Now look at Fig 10.3. For a 1% significance test using a sample of 20, the power of the test is very high for quality deteriorating to 40% or more. In that situation a test would have been likely to lead to the rejection of the Null Hypothesis.

Exercise
1. If, unknown to the company, quality had fallen to 40% defective, use Fig 10.3 to calculate the chance that a test at the 1% level would lead to the rejection of the Null Hypothesis?
2. Repeat (1) with a 50% defective level
3. Repeat (1) and (2) using the 5% significance test.

We conclude then that a null result can only be interpreted in the light of the power of the test. This agrees with intuitive common sense. If you ask someone whether they can see someone walking along a hillside a mile away, and they declare that they can see no one, then your interpretation of that statement depends critically on whether they have good eyesight or not! So the statement

'No significant change in quality was observed'

does not mean that quality *is* OK. It means that the sample evidence is consistent with unchanged quality and only if the test was powerful enough to detect the sort of change that would cause concern to the company can they feel reassured.

10.4.8 What Significance Tests don't tell you

We have seen that significance tests may not show up major changes in the status quo if the tests employed are not powerful enough. Equally they will show up unimportant differences if they are very powerful. Recently a major police search of lock-up garages failed to locate a suspected arms cache but inevitably all sorts of petty criminals were apprehended. This was hardly surprising as the search was on such a scale that it was certain that some small fry would be netted.

A statistically significant difference is merely one that is unlikely to have occurred by chance. As to whether it is an *important* difference or not, is for the user to say. The word 'significant' has a special meaning in statistical work and must not be taken to be a synonym for 'important'. This issue is discussed in Gold (1969). Bakan (1967) pointed out that the editors of psychological journals tended only to publish articles based on research which showed highly significant results in the statistical sense. Now academics have to publish to be seen to be performing well. It follows therefore that there was a high incentive for them to do research which leads to significant (statistical) results as opposed to research which is significant (noteworthy advance in human knowledge). To obtain statistically significant results, large sample sizes are required which produce powerful tests capable of showing up small differences.

Anyone carrying out significant tests in practice should study Henkel and Morisson (1970). This collection of readable papers, some of which have just been referred to, sheds light on many of the controversial aspects of classical significance testing with very few technical complications. Liebermann (1971) provides a more technical collection but one which contains much of interest.

10.4.9 The 'Onceness' of Significance Tests

One common abuse of significance tests arises when a whole series of tests is carried out and the significant ones are picked out as one might pick ripe cherries from a basket. To avoid this sort of nonsense, remember what significance means. In 100 tests, *by definition* 1 in 100 will be significant at the 1% level and 1 in 20 at the 5% level even if the Null Hypothesis is true!

QUANTITATIVE METHODS

It is tempting for researchers in search of significance and publishable results to sift through data in search of the significant result. For that reason, in order to interpret a significance test, it is necessary to know the whole experimental background to the test. That means knowing how many null results were obtained before or after the published result was recorded.

10.4.10 The Bayesian Alternative

The classical significance test has a distinctly conservative air about it. The fact that the status quo is assumed to apply until evidence is found which is sufficient to invalidate it, should irritate all with a touch of revolutionary blood in their veins! This in-built conservatism makes sense in a court of law where it puts the onus of proof on to the prosecution to prove its case. It is also a good idea when testing new drugs. The new drug is assumed to show no improvement over 'the devil we know' until evidence to the contrary is established.

There are other situations where sampling is carried out with a view to improving our knowledge of the population and where it is not appropriate to cast the experiment in a Yes/No or Either/Or framework. Think of a company drilling for oil. As the cores come up from the sea bed, they are examined and the prospector's view of the likelihood of oil being present changes with each sample. *Bayesian statistics* provides the theoretical infrastructure for this sort of situation. A clear summary is provided by L'Esperance (1971).

The classical position sets up a hypothesis and then calculates the likelihood of specific sample results which result from that hypothesis. The Bayesian approach is to modify the prior probability of a hypothesis given a sample result. This probability is known as a posterior probability because it works *back* from the sample to the hypothesis.

For example a surgeon could assign a prior probability to the chance that a patient has a specified disease, 0.2 say, based on a preliminary examination. Following further tests, he could use Bayes' theorem (see page 447 for details) to produce a modified probability that the patient has that disease. This would be the posterior probability. This could have dropped to 0.1 as a result of the tests. The process could be repeated as the patient has more and more tests until a diagnosis is arrived at, and when treatment can be prescribed. At each stage the probability of various diseases changes so that the probability of a number of different hypotheses is being amended.

DRAWING CONCLUSIONS

Managers are likely to come across these concepts with the development of *expert systems*. An expert system is an information system which contains a *knowledge base* and a sophisticated updating programme. In a medical version, given a particular patient's symptoms, it could calculate the probability of specific diseases (hypotheses) and recommend further tests. Once the results are fed in, using Bayesian principles, it can progressively adjust the probabilities.

Such a system has also been developed for diagnosis in fault-finding in systems maintenance. The 'symptom' or malfunction may not give the engineer an immediate, clear-cut diagnosis. (Think of your own car and all the hypotheses that can explain the symptoms 'Car won't start'). The expert system will suggest further tests to the engineer or ask for further information until the probability of some hypothesis becomes much larger than any other. The same idea has been applied in geological research. Where will it be applied next? (see page 393).

10.5 Some Well Known Significance Tests

10.5.1 Sample Mean compared against Population Mean : Attributes

Suppose that a company selling computers believes that 40% of a target list of companies already possess a machine. To check this figure, 100 companies will be sampled via a telephone call by sales representatives. A classical significance test might set up the following hypotheses:

Null Hypothesis: 40% of the companies possess a computer
Alternative Hypothesis: some other percentage applies.

Note that the alternative hypothesis chosen does not make any prior assumption about whether the researcher expects a higher or a lower figure than 40%. This is then a *two-tailed test*. (A *one-tailed test* would have required an alternative hypothesis which would have specified whether the percentage was higher or lower than 40%).

Suppose that the company decides to operate at the 5% significance level. In that case, from page 311 we know that sample percentages have a normal distribution around the mean percentage of 40% and with a standard error of $\sqrt{\frac{40 \times 60}{100}} = \sqrt{24} = 4.9\%$. That implies that 95% of sample means will fall within 2 x 4.9 = 9.8% either side of 40% in theory. The critical values for the sample percentage will now be 49.8% or greater and 30.2% or less. These two critical sets of values, or regions, constitute the 'two tails' and 5% of sample percentages should fall within them. Now when the sales representatives complete their survey, *an automatic decision can be made* to reject the

QUANTITATIVE METHODS

Null Hypothesis if the sample percentage lies within these critical ranges.

Of course the company could simply ignore its prior estimate of 40% and simply choose to make an estimate on the basis of the sample with confidence limits. Small samples (less than 50 values, say, pose special problems here).

Exercise

1. If the sample shows that 54% of the companies already possess a computer, what can we conclude?

2. If the proportion in the sample turned out to be 34%, could we say that this 'proved' that the Null Hypothesis was true?

10.5.2 Sample Mean against Population Mean : Variables

Suppose that a company has long accepted that the mean time to travel between two sites is 1.6 hours. As part of a cost-cutting exercise. it wishes to test the validity of this assumption by taking a reasonably large sample. Now the means of large samples follow a normal distribution around the population mean with a scatter measured by the standard error (page 318). From past recorded travel times, the standard deviation time is believed to be about 1.2 hours. It has been decided that a sample of 30 trips will be taken. The test proceeds by setting up a Null Hypothesis and an alternative hypothesis. Because of the industrial relations implications, the researchers decide to carry out a test at the 1% level which gives them a low risk of a Type 1 error.

Null Hypothesis: Mean time between sites = 1.6 hours.

Alternative hypothesis: Mean time is *not* 1.6 hours (2-tail test).

The standard error is estimated to be $\frac{1.2}{\sqrt{30}}$ = 0.22 hours. So 99% of sample means will fall within 1.6 hours ± 2.6 x 0.22 hrs = 1.6 hrs ± 0.57 hrs. A carefully controlled sample of 30 runs using different drivers at different times of the week can now be taken. If the mean time falls outside the limits shown above, i.e. in the 'two tails' beyond those limits, the Null Hypothesis can be rejected at the 1% level. Note that the critical values should ideally be predetermined. If they are calculated after the results of the experiment are known, then as the critical values depend on the degree of significance chosen, the terms of the experiment could be drawn up to suit the experimenter who nearly always has some vested interest in the outcome.

DRAWING CONCLUSIONS

Small samples (less than 30, say) pose special problems (see page 444)

10.5.3 Control Charts and Interpreting Repeated Significance Tests

In Quality Control situations, a form of repeated significance test is required. Fig 1.1a on page 2 illustrates the fact that the output of many mechanical processes produces items whose dimensions approximately follow a normal distribution. It therefore follows that even the means of small samples will follow that orderly distribution. Control lines can therefore be set for the means of samples on the same basis as the critical regions defined for a 2-tail test.

Example

Suppose that a machine, when it is functioning correctly, should produce parts with a mean dimension of 20 cms and a standard deviation of 0.2 cms. Samples of 4 parts are taken on a regular basis and the means plotted. 'Warning' limits, are typically set at ± 2 standard errors and 'Action' limits set at ± 2.6 standard errors. Fig 10.4 shows the chart with a sequence of sample means plotted.

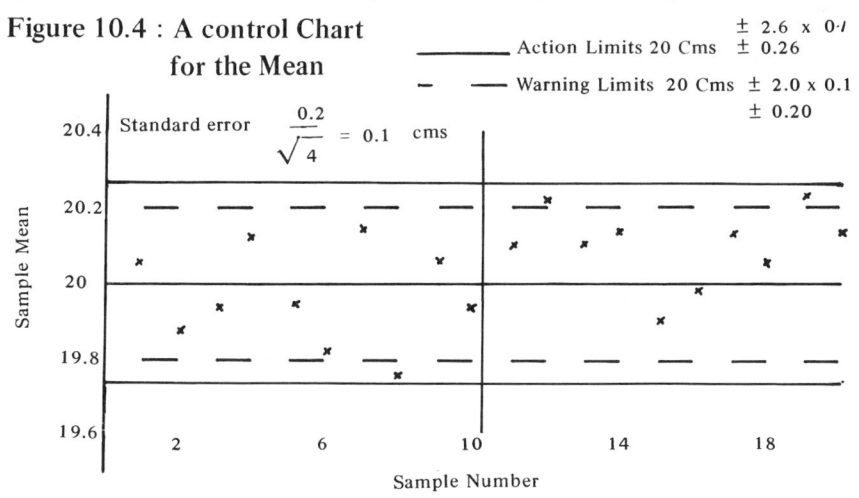

Figure 10.4 : A control Chart for the Mean

Action Limits 20 Cms ± 2.6 x 0.1 ± 0.26

Warning Limits 20 Cms ± 2.0 x 0.1 ± 0.20

Standard error $\frac{0.2}{\sqrt{4}} = 0.1$ cms

From the way the control lines have been set up, we know that 95% of sample means should lie within the warning limits and 99% within the 'Action' limits. Superficially each sample taken resembles a 2-tail test of significance, a sample mean falling outside the 'Warning' limit being significant at the 5% level.

However, referring back to Section 10.4.9 on page 343 you will recall

QUANTITATIVE METHODS

that a significance test is interpreted on a once-off basis. With the repeated samples on a control chart, the whole sequence must be read and interpreted. In the first 10 samples, one mean falls outside the warning limit but then 1 in 20 should do so even if the process is on target. Therefore the first 10 sample means *taken as a whole* are not of great significance.

In samples 11 to 20, taken as a whole, the process mean is clearly out of control even though no sample mean actually exceeds the 'action' limit. (For a good survey of Quality Control see Caplan (1982)).

10.5.4 Two Independent Samples: the t Test and the Mann-Whitney U Test

Testing for the significance of the difference between two sample means arises very frequently in business. We have already seen that the concept of experimentation is relevant over a wide area of business activity. In a properly controlled experiment, the outcome of the experiment will consist of measuring the difference that has arisen between the experimental group and the control group.

For example, a sample of bank clerks who have undergone a new course of training could be compared with respect to speed in operating terminals against a control group who have been subjected to the traditional training methods. The Null Hypothesis set up will assert that there is no difference between the terminal speed for clerks trained by the two different methods. Any difference, it will be initially assumed, has arisen through the inherent variation between clerks. After all, it would be amazing if the two groups clocked up exactly the same operating speeds, so some difference can certainly be expected.

The alternative hypothesis will say that there is some difference. If the direction of the difference is specified, then a one-tail test is carried out. If the direction of the difference is not specified, then a two-tail test is required.

The standard error of differences needs to be estimated and critical values for the difference can be evaluated. (See page 450 for details.) Special care should be taken when comparing small samples. The 't' test is the most powerful test available to do this job. It is termed a *parametric* test because it requires calculation of the means of the sample and estimates of standard errors. It also requires that the measurements be on either an *interval scale* where the distances

DRAWING CONCLUSIONS

between any two values on that scale are of known magnitude such as on the centigrade temperature scale, or a *ratio scale* where the scale has, in addition, a true zero point such as on the scale of weights, where zero really does mean the absence of weight.

All these restrictions, together with special problems with small samples, and the technical complications required for estimating the standard error, makes the 't' test powerful but fragile. There are situations where it is safer to use a *robust* test which, while less powerful, makes fewer assumptions and where there is an added advantage that an *ordinal* scale will suffice. Measurements on an ordinal scale cannot be used to produce valid means and standard deviations, but they can be ranked. If two respondents give values of 1 and 5 on a 10 point attitude scale measuring peoples feelings towards smoking in trains, the first can be said to have a stronger attitude than the second but the mean of the two, 3, has no precise meaning. In market research, an example could be the scores given by customers to the taste of a product on a scale from 1 to 10. In Personnel management, the scores could be those assigned to workers reflecting their performance as perceived by an assessor.

Example

Suppose a controlled marketing experiment has been carried out to measure how the customer's symptoms respond to a modified version of a cough mixture. A control group has been given the normal brand, the experiment being carried out using unlabelled bottles on a *double-blind* basis. The degree of discomfort is measured by an objective test using a 10 point scale with 10 representing the maximum discomfort. The results are shown in Table 10.5

Table 10.5 : Two Independent Samples

Experimental Group E (new mixture)	Control Group C (old mixture)
1	9
3	7
6	4
1	10
8	4
2	

The Mann-Whitney 'U' test first involves setting up the Null Hypothesis that the two populations from which the two samples have been drawn have the same distribution so that the chance that the score given to a member of the experimental group exceeds that given to a member of the control group is 1/2 or the equivalent of tossing a coin. The alternative hypothesis will be that one population tends to produce higher scores than the other. If the population which tends to produce larger values is specified, then a one-tail test is carried out. Note that because this is a non-parametric test, no assumptions about the means and standard deviations are required.

The scores for all 11 people taking part in the experiment have been ranked and are shown in Table 10.6.

Table 10.6 : Ranking of Combined Scores for the 2 Samples in Table 10.5

Score	1	1	2	3	4	4	6	7	8	9	10
Origin	E	E	E	E	C	C	E	C	E	C	C
Overall Rank	1.5	1.5	3	4	5.5	5.5	7	8	9	10	11

Table 10.7 shows how the resulting ranks are distributed between the experimental and control groups.

Table 10.7 : Reallocation of Ranks to Samples

							Rank Sum	Mean Rank
Experimental Group	1.5	1.5	3	4	7	9	26	4.3
Control Group	5.5	5.5	8	10	11		40	8.0

Under the Null Hypothesis, the average ranks allocated to the two samples should be the same, but as you can see, the control group seems to have collected most of the larger rankings. This seems to imply that the medicine given to the experimental group must be more effective than that given to the control group. The 'U' test helps us to tell whether this effect could have merely occurred by chance. Unfortunately calculating the critical values from the rank sums is somewhat complicated. The details are to be found on page 450, but in this case the conclusions are that such an extreme result in favour of the new medicine (one-tail) had a 0.04 chance of occurring by chance alone and we would therefore reject the Null Hypothesis at the 5% level. If we had been operating the test on a stricter 1% significance level, we would be unable to reject the Null Hypothesis. Remember,

DRAWING CONCLUSIONS

however, that the power of a test using such small samples is quite low and may not be sufficient to uncover any effect present.

10.5.5 Contingency Tables

When a sample is broken down so as to show the numbers which fall into different categories, differences can appear which may at first sight seem to be of interest, but which could have arisen merely from sampling error. The significance of these differences can be assessed using the χ^2 test (Chi-square).

Example

Suppose that a company operating on two sites carries out a survey to find out worker's attitudes to a new bonus scheme. The results can be expressed in the form of a *contingency table* (Table 10.8).

Table 10.8 : Contingency Table, observed frequencies

	Factory 1	Factory 2	Row Total
Number in favour	20	100	120
Number against	30	30	60
Number of 'Don't know's'	50	70	120
	100	200	300

Now the Null Hypothesis states that there is no difference between the attitudes in the two factories. So what would the table look like if the two factories were each to give responses in the same proportions as the proportion overall? Well, overall $\frac{120}{300}$ were in favour, so on that basis we would have expected $\frac{120}{300} \times 200 = 80$ in Factory 2. The full 'Expected' table is shown in Table 10.9.

Table 10.9 : Expected Frequencies Assuming Null Hypothesis to be true

	Factory 1	Factory 2	Row Total
In favour	40	80	120
Against	20	40	60
Don't know	40	80	120
	100	200	300

N.B: The *expected* frequencies should *never* fall below 5 and should ideally be as high as 10. If this is not so categories should be

QUANTITIVE METHODS

combined. If in this instance there had been a few 'Unavailables', 'Sick' or 'Refusals', these could have been combined into the 'Don't know' category so as to meet the requirements of this constraint. (See Liebermann (1971) for a fascinating debate on this issue).

The extent to which Tables 10.8 and 10.9 differ is a measure of the discrepency between what actually happened and that which could have been expected if there was no real difference between the two factories. The test statistic used goes by the uncompromising title of χ^2 (Chi-square). It is *a* measure of the difference between the two tables and its calculation is illustrated in Table 10.10.

Table 10.10 : Calculation of Chi-square from Tables 10.8 & 10.9

Factory 1

$$\frac{(20-40)^2}{40} = 10.0$$

$$\frac{(30-20)^2}{20} = 5.0$$

$$\frac{(50-40)^2}{40} = 2.5$$

Factory 2

$$\frac{(100-80)^2}{80} = 5.0$$

$$\frac{(30-40)^2}{40} = 2.5$$

$$\frac{(70-80)^2}{80} = 1.25$$

Chi-square = Sum of $\frac{(\text{Observed} - \text{Expected Frequencies})^2}{\text{Expected Frequencies}}$ = 26.25

'Degrees of Freedom' = (Rows–1) x (Columns–1) = (3–1) x (2–1) = 2

Comparing the value of Chi-square with the 1% critical values for this measure shown in Appendix 3 and using the appropriate number of degrees of freedom we can see that the results are highly significant.

The degrees of freedom in a contingency table represents the minimum number of entries that define the whole table given the row and column totals. So for example in Table 10.8 on page 351, given any 2 values the rest of the table can be reconstructed. For example if I know that there are 20 in favour and 30 against in Factory 1, I can deduce that there must have been 50 'Don't Know's' because the column total is 100. Once I know the Factory 1 figures, I can deduce the Factory 2 figures from the row totals. There are therefore 2 degrees of freedom in all.

As in every statistical test of significance, attention must be paid to the experimental procedures. The technical aspects of the test all assume that the two samples are independent and the data has been

DRAWING CONCLUSIONS

collected without any bias. In this case there is plenty of scope for bias. Was the survey carried out in the same circumstances? Were the questions posed in the same way and were they unambiguous?

Exercise

Three independent samples of consumers are taken in 3 regions and their current brand of product used was identified and the results are shown in the following table.

Brand of Product

	A	B	C	D
North	30	64	4	2
South	50	80	7	3
Scotland	37	50	12	1

Is there evidence that there is a significant difference between the market shares in the three regions?

10.5.6 Paired Samples : the 't' test and the Sign Test

Paired samples arise in an experimental design in which there is measurement before and after the treatment. This could be customer attitudes before and after seeing an advertisement, or a patient's symptoms before and after receiving a dose of drug. When the measurements are on an interval scale, and where a number of hard assumptions hold true, then the powerful but 'fragile' 't' test can be used. In this case the Null Hypothesis would state that the underlying mean of the differences should be 0 (see page 451 for details).

A robust non-parametric alternative is the sign test. Here, the sign of the change with each pair of observations 'before' and 'after' is all that is recorded. Under the Null Hypothesis, there should be as many positive signs as negative signs and the probability of any pair producing a change of one sign or the other is 0.5, just like throwing a coin. In other words, in carrying out a sign test we are in effect calculating the probability of getting as few heads as the critical value in a specified number of throws (one-tail test), or as few of either face when doing a two-tail test.

Example

Suppose 20 patients suffering from arthritis were given a placebo (a harmless ineffective treatment) as part of a controlled experiment involving a new drug. (Another group was given the real treatment).

QUANTITATIVE METHODS

Of these 20, 16 claimed that their symptoms had improved after the 'dummy' treatment. Is there evidence that merely taking part in the experiment has improved the patients perceptions of his own symptoms?

The sign test uses as a test statistic, the number of + or − signs *whichever is the smaller*. Where no change has taken place, the pair is removed from the sample and the sample size reduced accordingly. In this case we use (20−16) = 4 as the test statistic. Appendix 4 shows critical values of this test statistic for use at the 5%, 1% and the ½% level on a one-tail test. For a two-tail test the column heading should be doubled. Reference to this table shows that we can reject the Null Hypothesis at the 1% level. This means that there is less than a 1% chance of getting as few as 4 heads in 20 throws of a coin.

If we had been doing a two-tail test at the 1% level we would have to use the ½% column in Appendix 4. In that case we would not have been able to reject the Null Hypothesis because the chance of getting as few as 4 of the same sign, + or −, is more than 1%.

Siegel (1956) provides a friendly guide to non-parametric tests. He includes discussion of a special version of the sign test, the Wilcoxon Test, which takes account of the *magnitude* of the difference arising in paired observations providing that these differences can be ranked. This offers a powerful and robust alternative to the 't' test.

Exercise

1. The performance of 40 machine operators was assessed one month before and one month after undertaking a special training course. 30 showed an improvement, 5 no change, and the performance of 5 had deteriorated. Is there any evidence that the course had some effect?

2. In a blind trial, 12 members of the public, were given a normal food product and one containing a new experimental food additive. The ordering of each pair was randomised so that 6 had the modified product first, and 6 the normal first. In 10 cases overall the new product was preferred. Is there evidence that the additive has improved the product? Why might a double-blind trial be advisable in this case.

CHAPTER 11 : MANAGING WITH THE COMPUTER

This chapter starts by discussing some of the essential terminology of modern computing (11.1) to clarify some key terms and then proceeds in sections 11.2 to 11.4 to discuss various aspects of programming from a non-specialist manager's point of view. The chapter ends with a discussion of spreadsheet systems (11.5) and packages (11.6).

11.1 Getting Computers Into Perspective

Putting a chapter on computers in any book is asking for trouble these days. Things are moving so fast that such an inclusion would seem to guarantee built-in obsolescence. However certain fundamental concepts and principles should hold good for the coming decade and as the handling of quantitative techniques is being revolutionised by the spread of personal computers and local terminals which give direct and immediate access to powerful and sophisticated databases, quantitative techniques and computers are now inextricably interrelated.

11.1.1 The Information Technology (IT) Revolution

The word 'revolution' has been much abused. Tinkering with a car design or a washing powder formula can in no way justify the advertiser's use of such a word. A revolution is a process which brings about fundamental and irreversible change in a system, and a glance back at the state of Industry and Commerce 20 years ago should convince all of us of the revolutionary effect of computer and telecommunications technology on business and society in general. Just to give one example, think of how petrol stations have changed in a few years and the way that change has affected the speed and quality of service, and the effect it has had on employment levels and then realise that similar changes have been changing, and will continue to change other industries.

Being in the middle of a revolution, is a bit like being on a mystery tour. You can see out of the coach, of course, and note the way the scene outside is changing in the short term, and while you can piece together the route so far, the final destination remains unknown. There's not much that you can do about it either. Looking out of the 'coach window' it is clear that the information revolution is still in progress. Faster and cheaper computers are still coming on the market.

QUANTITATIVE METHODS

More developments are promised in the near future. Manufacturing processes are still being reorganised on an automated basis. There is plenty of steam left in it yet.

Some of the current trends are clear to see. There will be a steady move towards all management staff in most organisations making use of terminal equipment linked to remote or local computers on a regular basis. Managers will be expected to take their use as a matter of course, to be able to discuss their future needs and contribute to the further development of such systems. Data will increasingly be available in electronic form only, and its manipulation made easier for those who can get to grips with the system. This trend will bring with it serious new problems for the accuracy and relevance of data which are discussed at length in Chapter 12 on page 395.

11.1.2 Some Essential Definitions

Faced with the volume of words being produced on the subject of computers and the variety of systems themselves, it would be a futile task to set out to describe the modern computer in any detail. All I propose to do is to define some essential terms which will arise in the later discussion about managers and their relationship with the machine. Books in this field aren't much use if they're more than 2 years old, and the output of computer journals is so vast that ordinary managers are best advised to keep their eye on the technology pages of the *Financial Times*. Each year there is at lease one major supplement which will do a lot to keep them up to date.

Fig 11.1 shows the essential *hardware* devices which go to making up the modern computer system.

The term 'Hardware' refers to the physical devices in the system, mechanical and electronic. Put it this way, if hardware malfunctions you need someone with a screwdriver or a soldering iron. Although you may well suffer from hardware malfunctions, sorting out the mess is strictly for the technicians. Now that the hardware is so cheap, hardware problems are becoming less and less important. Whole units can be pulled out and replaced at little cost.

All the units outside the central processing unit are collectively referred to as peripherals. However micros, small compact computers, which can have a semi-independent existence outside the *mainframe* (central computer), while still being connected to it, are not peripherals in the ordinary sense. The whole micro/mainframe

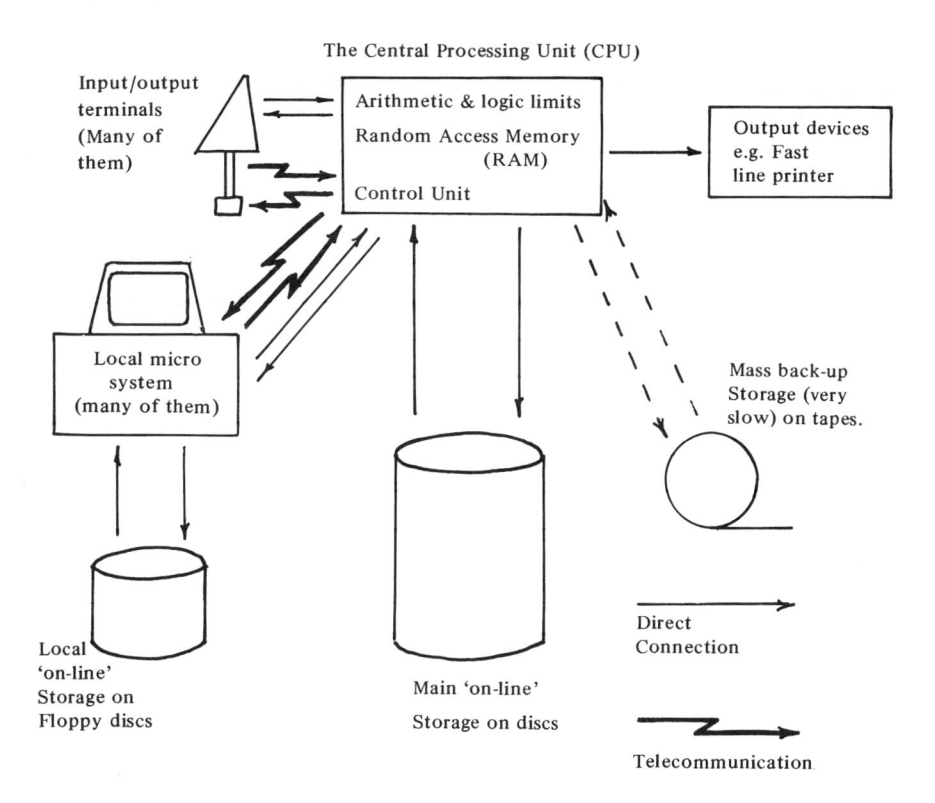

Figure 11.1 : An outline of a Modern Computing System

[Diagram showing: The Central Processing Unit (CPU) containing Arithmetic & logic limits, Random Access Memory (RAM), and Control Unit; connected to Input/output terminals (Many of them), Output devices e.g. Fast line printer, Local micro system (many of them), Local 'on-line' Storage on Floppy discs, Main 'on-line' Storage on discs, and Mass back-up Storage (very slow) on tapes. Legend shows Direct Connection and Telecommunication symbols.]

distinction is becoming blurred as *distributed processing* with a devolution of computing power to small local computers is being developed within larger systems.

On the input side, the trend is increasingly towards direct input by means of a VDU which can also act as an output device. This means that there is less paper involved and interactive communication between the user and the system is becoming the norm. The old days of batch processing with cards going in one end and mountains of line-printer paper coming off the other end to be taken away on fork-lift trucks, are happily drawing to a close.

It is wisest to treat the Central Processing Unit (CPU) of the computer as a complicated 'black box'. Arithmetic and logic is carried out at speeds which we can barely grasp and which, in any case, move

QUANTITATIVE METHODS

upwards year by year, and the quantity of Random Access Memory (RAM) is a critical factor in determining the power of the system. When this RAM is inadequate, and there is a version of Parkinson's law which ensures that it always is, *back-up storage* is required.

Magnetic tapes are mainly used as cheap mass storage. They are the only things which can be seen moving in a computer room these days so they are still very popular with television and film producers who have them whirring away amongst colourful flashing lights in the Sci-Fi spaceships of the 21st century consuming vast quantities of power!

It is Discs, rather than tape, which are *at the moment* the most important back-up medium. On a mainframe computer with vast capacity for storage, whole libraries of statistical and other quantitative packages can be made available *on-line* within seconds of being required. Other packages can be held *off-line* which means that they are held in the library and have to be manually or mechanically loaded before being made available on-line. On the micro, the floppy version of discs has given the personal computer a power which would have staggered us 10 years ago and although many micro users still struggle on with cassette tapes, I predict that every micro user will be using some form of disc system by 1990. Of course discs themselves may have been replaced by then!

All this hardware is controlled by *software*. Software consists of programs which tell the computer and its peripherals what it should do. The *operating system* is the program which stage-manages the whole operation. Its role is a bit like the old-fashioned shop-keeper who ensures that his assistants get the goods into the shop, makes sure that the customers are dealt with, checks on what is in the till and the state of stocks, calling up the suppliers when necessary. All user managers need to do is to be sure that someone somewhere knows a lot about operating systems when a system is being designed.

The operating system is an example of system software, *Application Software* refers to the programs that make the computer do useful work for the managers using the system. *Programming Languages* are used to enable the instructions for the machine to be set out. The machine actually operates in a special language, machine language, which is specific to a particular machine. Users prefer to express their demands in languages which are not specific to a particular machine and the operating system arranges for special programs, *compilers* and *interpreters*, to convert these to machine language. Thus

PRINT 5*3

MANAGING WITH THE COMPUTER

will be understood by *all* BASIC interpreters. The machine instructions generated within the computer will differ between machines. A similar situation arises in a car. All accelerators, when depressed, make the car go faster. All brakes, when depressed, slow it down. The precise way in which these operations are implemented under the bonnet differs widely from car to car and most of us are happy to keep the 'bonnet' of the computer firmly closed!

The nearer a language is to ordinary English, the higher the *level* of the language. Very high level languages written in near-English which managers can use directly will be extensively developed in the next decade (see page 377). The ultimate in high-level languages will be spoken English.

All the hardware and software described above permits the computer to handle large quantities of data with an increasing degree of user-interaction. With many different users all wanting different sets of information but with considerable overlap with each other, some kind of organised *Data base system* becomes necessary. The current misuse of this important concept is aptly described by Wooley (1983):

> '... The term 'database' became first a buzzword, and later a Humpty Dumpty word. (When I use a word, it means exactly what I want it to mean)...What I want 'database' to mean today is this: a collection of data in a single repository according to a logical structure which captures the interrelationships, establishes control over redundancy, and allows data independence in applications programs'

For example sales figures need to feed into files used for sales forecasting, stock control and profitability assessment. If each of these users maintains their own separate files, considerable redundancy will arise because so much data will be common to all three users. A database system will contain programs which maintain centralised files but allow each user to have what will seem to them to be an independent filing system. If an application program changes its requirement, then all the other users will be protected from interference because the database system acts as a go-between. Remember, however, that database systems are extremely complex and expensive, but it is clear that they will rapidly become standard in large organisations. Martin (1982) provides a friendly introduction to this topic.

11.1.3 The Input/Output (I/O) Barrier

For years managers have been repelled from systems which are

QUANTITATIVE METHODS

difficult to talk to or listen to. They have felt the presence of an invisible barrier between them and the alien world inside the system.

I watched recently a delightful film about the life of penguins in their natural habitat. On the shore they were hopelessly clumsy, shuffling about awkwardly with their useless flippers hanging by their sides, an essentially comic picture. Then they staggered down to the shore and the instant that they entered the water, a total transformation took place. They cut through the water at breathtaking speed, turning and flashing as they hunted their prey.

The same contrast exists with data inside and outside the computer. Inside, the data in the form of numbers and letters held in coded form, can be stored, retrieved, sorted, operated on and compared at speeds which pack hundreds of thousands of operations into a second. With satellite communications, this data can also be shunted around the globe in times measured in seconds. Once outside the computer, like the penguins on shore, data is clumsy to handle and time-consuming to manipulate. Inside the computer, data is in its natural medium and yet managers in the past have often preferred to deal with it on paper, a medium that they are used to and which they can handle without special training. The barrier between their world and that of the computer has been too awkward to overcome. Recent developments have opened up an era in which that barrier will progressively disappear.

Until recently, time-consuming data conversion processes were required to input data or programs into the computer. They would first have to be punched onto cards or tape and then input into the machine in batches. Now data can be input into terminals with a Visual Display Unit (VDU) attached which allows whole pages to be built up and checked or edited before filing. Programs can be accessed with little delay, the necessary 'housekeeping' being handled internally by the operating system about which the manager need know little except at the purchase or planning phase of a system's development. Increasingly data can be captured at source. For example identity labels can be automatically read on the shop floor and the price labels on goods in a supermarket can be automatically read at the check-out point by means of the printed bar codes on the packet. Easy-to-use package programs (see page 386) and spreadsheet systems (see page 378) have now enabled nonspecialists to use computers with a minimum of training.

Getting data out of the computer has been a tedious process too.

A person can draw up a table of figures given a few relatively vague guidelines. The computer can be told how to do a lot of arithmetic or sort items with a few concise instructions, but telling it to tabulate information in neat columns with appropriate headings, used to require step by step instructions which took up a large part of the program. Woe betide the manager who suggested that the output format should be changed to suit them! With the report-writing languages coming in to greater use now, managers will be able to specify reports to meet their own requirements so that the last barriers between the manager and the computer are progressively being demolished (see page 377). Fear of the computer based on an out-of-date image of what is available will hinder the survival chances of the manager in the years to come. Computers are going to be easier and more exciting to use and they are going to be more orientated towards you, the user. So stick around and don't jump off the mystery tour just yet!

11.1.4 'User-Friendship'

The current trend in both input and output is towards more direct contact between management and the computer system at all levels. It is essential therefore that managers should insist on systems which are *user-friendly*. This term describes systems which are designed to make life easy for the end users and require a minimum of technical knowledge on their part. Such systems are orientated towards meeting the needs of the users rather than the users having to orientate themselves towards the system's needs. This fundamentally new approach has only recently become feasible, because to meet the special needs of a wide range of different users at the same time, the system needs to be fast and contain large quantities of memory, and this was difficult until really cheap and powerful computers became readily available.

A typical unfriendly system leaves the user stranded, or bombarded by rude and incomprehensible commands written in the language with which the system programmers, but no one else, are familiar. For example, on some time sharing systems, each user is required to log into the system using a 'user code'. This is an unfriendly start. Why not require the user's name and let the computer convert it to a code internally using a look-up list? A dialogue that I witnessed proceeded as follows (the computer responses are printed in italics):

LOGIN ACB1324

PLEASE LOGOUT

QUANTITATIVE METHODS

>Puzzled, the user tried again.
>LOGIN ACB1324
>*PLEASE LOGOUT*
>LOGIN ACB1324
>*PLEASE LOGOUT*
>LOGIN ACB1324
>*PLEASE LOGOUT*   etc, etc,

After a screenful of this banal conversation, the user turned to me and furious with frustration, shouted: 'I want to log into the system, so why the hell does it keep on telling me to log out?'. Now this system is being quite logical according to the rules laid down within its programs. A time sharing system allows many different users to use the same terminal one after the other. The previous user had left the terminal without logging out so that the system quite reasonably would not allow the next user on without the situation being rectified.

The system is unfriendly because it left the user stranded. You don't have to have a very sophisticated operating system to be able to send a helpful message such as:

>ANOTHER USER IS ALREADY USING THIS TERMINAL. IF YOU ARE A NEW USER, YOU MUST FIRST TYPE 'LOGOUT' BEFORE ATTEMPTING TO LOG IN.

Of course the problem lies not with the complexity of programs required but rather in the attitudes required of the system designers. Some of them still believe that users should adapt their behaviour to suit the system rather than the other way round. Their monopoly of computer power until recently gave them the final say. However cheap micros being sold direct to non-specialist users by hungry salesmen has brought a wind of change into the computer world. The next generation of computer systems will be much more polite and very, very friendly.

Another unfriendly characteristic of many systems is the coded error message. Certain conditions make it impossible for the computer to proceed with the program. An unfriendly system will 'crash', depositing an obscure message on the screen which means nothing to the non-specialist without reference to a manual. This is not acceptable to the general user. Most languages have *error trapping* procedures by which the error condition can be caught in mid-air as it were, and examined internally, before the user even knows that anything has gone wrong.

The snag can then either be automatically allowed for, or an English language statement be produced advising the users of the problem *and offering them some options for how to proceed*. So don't accept unfriendly error messages from your system. Once you mention 'error-trapping' to the computer boffins, they'll know that you know that they have been passing the buck!

11.1.5 The 'What-if' revolution

The trend has been, and will continue to be towards faster computers with larger and cheaper storage facilities. These two factors taken together have permitted a fundamentally new approach to using computers. In the early days, once the program was loaded there was usually a long delay before the results came back. This might be as long as 24 hours. The fast speeds that even personal computers can now achieve means that calculations can be carried out in real time and the results displayed shortly after the posing of the problem. This continuity between question and answer means that the new questions that most answers tend to provoke can be immediately tried out. Instead of using the computer to find out *the* answer to *a* question, it can be used to explore a whole range of answers to a whole series of questions. Each run enables the user to pose the question: '*What* would happen *if* such and such were the case'.

It is reasonable to use the word 'revolutionary' in this context because the whole way in which the users relate to computers changes radically when they feel that they are conversing with it as opposed to serving it.

11.2 Should Managers be Able to Program

11.2.1 Managers and Managers : Programs and Programs

It is difficult to talk about managers in general terms and in this book, the word has been used in its widest sense. There are of course a whole body of managers in the world of Information Technology who may have started out as programmers and who still need to know in detail about programming and they will probably be skipping this chapter anyway. There is another group of managers who have a strong quantitative background, such as engineers and research scientists, for whom programming has always been a valued skill even in the days when computers were expensive, unfriendly, slow, clumsy and relatively inaccessible.

For the majority of managers, there have been essentially two schools of thought.

QUANTITATIVE METHODS

1. Until you have written a program, you can't really get to grips with the way computers work.

2. Programming is a specialist skill and should be left exclusively to the programmers.

As is so often the case in such debates, 'all have won and all shall have prizes'. I support the first view so long as we remember that the word 'program' covers everything from a 2 or 3 line *routine* to a 1,000 line program of great complexity. Given the ready availability of personal computers, managers will find that if they take the trouble to acquire enough expertise to write 5–20 line routines for small useful jobs, they will not only obtain a better understanding of the nature of computers, their strengths and their weaknesses, but they will also find that the computer on their desk can do useful work for them even when just acting as an extension to the calculator.

Before doing this, it is essential to buy a cheap computer if you don't have one already. Just reading about programming is a bit like reading about how to drive a car. Do you remember when you first tried to coordinate clutch and accelerator? Would a description in a book have really helped much? For the sort of simple routines I will be describing in this chapter, a simple and cheap machine will do. There are lots of second-hand machines around now going for a song, but make sure you get the manual as well!

11.3 Basic Basic

11.3.1 What are Programs

There is nothing mysterious about programs. Chapter 2 is full of programs, programs for operating the calculator. There you will have found sequences of operations laid out which enable you to manipulate numbers within the calculator, making use in some cases of the memory store. They differ from the programs that you can write for the personal computer in that

1. Typically there is only sufficient memory to store one number and no facility for storing instructions as such. (There are, however, some programmable calculators on the market, which function as small and rather inadequate computers).

2. The sequence of operations is manually operated

This lack of memory in the ordinary calculator means that if you are doing complicated calculations, it will be necessary to write down

MANAGING WITH THE COMPUTER

separate stages of the calculation on paper as you proceed. On a personal micro-computer, such intermediate results can be temporarily stored and later recalled from one of the many memory locations available. The need for manual operations on a calculator, means that the process of calculation is relatively slow and unreliable. Looking at calculator routines such as that for currency conversion in Section 2.6.1 on page 57, it would seem a logical step to be able to store not just the numbers, but the sequence of operations themselves and call them down ready for use, the user merely putting in the data when required. After all, each calculation involves laboriously bashing out the same set of keys. All of the additional facilities required are available on the computer.

So you can see that the computer can be usefully viewed as a logical development of the familiar calculator. The computer stores the sequence of operations, or *instructions*, in the form of a program (how it does this is of no interest to most of us) and when the program is 'run', the computer follows through the sequence of instructions in order. For example the sequence in Fig 11.2 written in BASIC will, on most micros, convert francs into pounds. The instruction **LIST**, given direct to the machine, instructs the machine to list the instructions in line number sequence. In doing so, it will automatically re-order any lines that have been added, a facility which makes editing programs very easy. The instructions are numbered so that the natural order of operation can be changed if necessary. An explanation of each instruction is provided.

Figure 11.2 : A Program to convert Pounds into Francs

```
LIST
   20 PRINT "HOW MANY FRANCS TO THE POUND ";
   30 INPUT R
   40 PRINT "HOW MANY POUNDS ";
   50 INPUT S
   60 PRINT "SUM IN FRANCS = "; S*R
   70 PRINT
   80 GOTO 40
```

Line 20: Print the characters within quotes. The characters have no meaning for the computer, but they remind the user of what he is to do next.
N.B: The ' ; ' in BBC BASIC holds the printer at the end of the string of characters instead of moving on 1 line. Different dialects of BASIC use different characters for this purpose. Refer to the manual or, if you are allergic to manuals, use trial and error, ' : ' or ' , ' being strong contenders.

QUANTITATIVE METHODS

Line 30: Wait for a number to be fed in on the keyboard and store it in a location which the user will refer to as R. It will over-write any value currently held in that location. Note that the number means nothing to the computer because it is merely a machine. It is the users who know what it means and they must instruct the computer to do things with it to achieve *their* objective.
N.B: Some versions of **BASIC** allow *named variables* so that in this instance **INPUT RATE** would be permissable. When you can use this facility programs become much easier to follow.

Line 40: Print the characters within quotes.

Line 50: As for Line 30, the stored number to be referred to as S.

Line 60: Print the characters within quotes and then follow them with the result obtained by multiplying the numbers held in locations R and S.

Line 70: Print a blank line to separate successive calculation.

Line 80: The next instruction to be obeyed is Line 40. This effectively jumps the program unconditionally. The result is that the user will find that after getting the first result, the computer will be automatically ready to do a new calculation.

I have deliberately spelled out the meaning of these instructions in the mundane terms that the machine understands. Hopefully this will help to emphasise the mechanical character of a computer program. Fig 11.3 shows the result of running the program. The instruction **RUN** given directly to the machine, instructs the machine to work through the sequence of instructions in order.

Figure 11.3 : The Program in Fig 11.2 is 'Run'

```
>RUN
HOW MANY FRANCS TO THE POUND ?13.4
HOW MANY POUNDS ?20
SUM IN FRANCS = 268

HOW MANY POUNDS ?125
SUM IN FRANCS = 1675

HOW MANY POUNDS ?1300
SUM IN FRANCS = 17420

HOW MANY POUNDS ?2
SUM IN FRANCS = 26.8

HOW MANY POUNDS ?
```

MANAGING WITH THE COMPUTER

The program as it stands is never-ending and therefore untidy. One way out of this would be to find some way of indicating to the computer that no more values are needed. A negative number of pounds means nothing and will therefore never arise. So, by slotting in the following instructions, we can get the computer to stop by inputting a negative number.

     55 IF S < 0 THEN 1000
     1000 STOP

The computer will now examine each value of S inserted and if it is negative, instead of going on to instruction 60, it will jump to instruction 1000 and then stop. Once added the lines will be automatically put in correct sequence and so the program will now look as in Fig 11.4.

Figure 11.4 : Program incorporating a conditional jump together with a flow diagram.

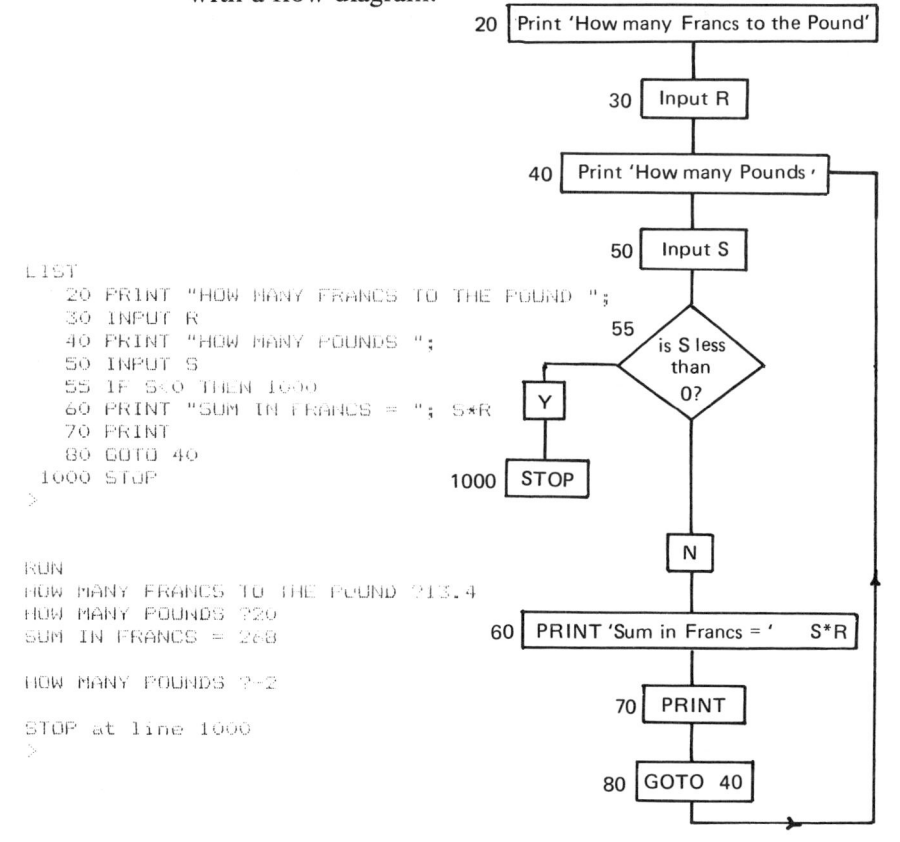

```
LIST
    20 PRINT "HOW MANY FRANCS TO THE POUND ";
    30 INPUT R
    40 PRINT "HOW MANY POUNDS ";
    50 INPUT S
    55 IF S<0 THEN 1000
    60 PRINT "SUM IN FRANCS = "; S*R
    70 PRINT
    80 GOTO 40
  1000 STOP
>

RUN
HOW MANY FRANCS TO THE POUND ?13.4
HOW MANY POUNDS ?20
SUM IN FRANCS = 268

HOW MANY POUNDS ?-2

STOP at line 1000
>
```

367

QUANTITATIVE METHODS

Note that no very complicated I/O instructions are needed to produce a useful little routine which will save a lot of time when a large number of similar calculations are required.

11.3.2 Example

Small routines are particularly useful for costing purposes. This is because costing procedures often remain the same even though the figures change from case to case and with the passage of time. The costing procedure can then be preserved in the form of a program and brought out for use when required. Also costs are often not known with certainty and a program allows re-calculation with a minimum delay.

For example, suppose that the cost of a contract is calculated as follows:

1. The material cost is obtained by calculating the cost of the components used, the component cost in dollars being first converted into pounds sterling.

2. The labour cost is calculated from the hours needed multiplied by the wage rate per hour.

3. To the total cost, a percentage allowance for scrap and wastage must be made.

A program to carry out this job is shown in Fig 11.5 together with the results of a run.

Figure 11.5 : a simple Program for Costing

```
10 REM    N=NUMBER OF COMPONENTS
20 REM    C=COST PER COMPONENT IN DOLLARS
30 REM    R=EXCHANGE RATE, $ PER £1
40 REM    H=LABOUR HOURS FOR CONTRACT
50 REM    L=LABOUR RATE, £ PER HOUR
60 REM    P=PERCENTAGE SCRAP ALLOWANCE
100 REM   ASSIGN VALUES TO VARIABLES
110 N=4
120 C=492
130 R=1.4
140 H=46
150 L=3
160 P=4
200 REM CALCULATE CONTRACT COST
210 PRINT "MATERIALS COST £";N*(C/R)
220 PRINT "LABOUR COST £";H*L
230 PRINT "TOTAL COST, ALLOWING FOR SCRAP = £";(N*(C/R)+(H*L))*(1+P/
240 PRINT
250 PRINT
```

MANAGING WITH THE COMPUTER

```
RUN
MATERIALS COST £1405.71429
LABOUR COST £138
TOTAL COST, ALLOWING FOR SCRAP = £1605.46286

>
```

Note that

1. I have made no attempt to 'clean up' the output. Input/Output procedures differ enormously from machine to machine and they tend to obscure the essential logic of the program. If you run it on your own machine you can clean it up for yourself.

2. **REM** for 'remark' is a line ignored by the computer. It is used to provide commentary on what the program is supposed to be doing, a sort of built-in documentation. Such 'remarks' are invaluable later on. You may know how your program works now, but you just come back to it in a few months time!

3. Note the use of brackets in Line 230 (see page 72 for guidance).

11.3.3 Loops and 'What If?'

Suppose that in the previous example, the number of labour hours required was not known with certainty. I could then use a powerful facility to ask the computer to automatically calculate the costs for a sequence of values for the number of hours rather than just one figure. This builds *sensitivity analysis* into the program, showing how sensitive the cost is to a change in labour hours required. Such a task would be time consuming for us mortals, but computers are excellent at doing repetitive arithmetic and have no feelings, so they never get bored. The program is shown in Fig 11.6.

Figure 11.6 : A costing Program using a loop for Sensitivity Analysis

```
LIST
    10 REM    N=NUMBER OF COMPONENTS
    20 REM    C=COST PER COMPONENT IN DOLLARS
    30 REM    R=EXCHANGE RATE, $ PER £1
    40 REM    H=LABOUR HOURS FOR CONTRACT
    50 REM    L=LABOUR RATE, £ PER HOUR
    60 REM    P=PERCENTAGE SCRAP ALLOWANCE
```

QUANTITATIVE METHODS

```
100 REM  ASSIGN VALUES TO VARIABLES
110 N=4
120 C=492
130 R=1.4
150 L=3
160 P=4
165 REM   LOOP STARTS HERE
170 FOR H=40 TO 50 STEP 2
200 REM CALCULATE CONTRACT COST
205 PRINT "ASSUMING LABOUR HOURS = ";H
210 PRINT "MATERIALS COST £";N*(C/R)
220 PRINT "LABOUR COST £";H*L
230 PRINT "TOTAL COST, ALLOWING FOR SCRAP = £";
240 PRINT                         (N*(C/R)+(H*L))*(1+P/100)
250 PRINT
260 NEXT H
1000 STOP
>
```

```
RUN
ASSUMING LABOUR HOURS = 40
MATERIALS COST £1405.71429
LABOUR COST £120
TOTAL COST, ALLOWING FOR SCRAP = £1586.74286


ASSUMING LABOUR HOURS = 42
MATERIALS COST £1405.71429
LABOUR COST £126
TOTAL COST, ALLOWING FOR SCRAP = £1592.98286


ASSUMING LABOUR HOURS = 44
MATERIALS COST £1405.71429
LABOUR COST £132
TOTAL COST, ALLOWING FOR SCRAP = £1599.22286


ASSUMING LABOUR HOURS = 46
MATERIALS COST £1405.71429
LABOUR COST £138
TOTAL COST, ALLOWING FOR SCRAP = £1605.46286


ASSUMING LABOUR HOURS = 48
MATERIALS COST £1405.71429
LABOUR COST £144
TOTAL COST, ALLOWING FOR SCRAP = £1611.70286


ASSUMING LABOUR HOURS = 50
MATERIALS COST £1405.71429
LABOUR COST £150
TOTAL COST, ALLOWING FOR SCRAP = £1617.94286
```

MANAGING WITH THE COMPUTER

For the program in Fig 11.6, I've modified Fig 11.5 as follows:

1. Line 140 has been deleted.

2. I've added **FOR** and **NEXT** statements on lines 170 and 260. At line 170 first time round, the computer will set H equal to 40 and then carry out the calculations down as far as line 260. Here the instruction **NEXT H** makes the computer return to line 170, increase H by 2, the magnitude of the **STEP**, on round this loop until it has carried out the sequence with H equal to 50.

Thus a *loop* has been set up between lines 170 and 260. The results, as you can see, show the user how the total costs vary within the range of hours assumed.

3. I've slipped in a line 205 which indicates, on the output, the hours which have been assumed in each calculation.

The **FOR. . .NEXT** statement is very flexible. On most computers. I could have said

$$170 \text{ FOR } H = 40,41,45,53$$

and the computer would then have carried out the calculations with these specified values rather than the values set at regular intervals shown in Fig 11.6. You can use the **FOR** statement to do sensitivity analysis on your business calculations.

11.3.4 Building-in Conditions

We have seen that computers can do arithmetic and store and carry out instructions. They also have the ability to compare numbers or *strings* (groups of letters and other characters, often mixed) and depending on the result of that comparison, alter the sequence of operations carried out. This trick is carried out using an **IF** statement. The facility can rapidly lead to complicated programs in which the computer moves around the instructions in a complex way. However some modest uses of this facility can be useful in producing useful routines for non-specialists.

Example

Suppose a personnel officer has data on the number of people in each department at the beginning and end of the year. She needs to print out the percentage increase or decrease during the year. Fig 11.7 shows a program which will achieve this end.

QUANTITATIVE METHODS

Figure 11.7 : Program with Branching

```
LIST
  100 REM N1 = NUMBER IN DEPARTMENT AT BEGINNING OF THE YEAR
  110 REM N2 = NUMBER IN DEPARTMENT AT END         OF YEAR
  120 PRINT "INPUT N1 AND N2 SEPARATED BY A COMMA."
  130 PRINT "(TO TERMINATE, INPUT NEGATIVE VALUE FOR N1)";
  140 INPUT N1,N2
  150 IF N1<0 THEN 1000
  160 IF N1 > N2 THEN 310
  170 REM IF THE COMPUTER REACHES THIS INSTRUCTION THEN N2 MUST,
  171 REM EXCEED OR EQUAL N1,OTHERWISE IT WOULD HAVE JUMPED TO LINE 310
  180 REM
  190 REM SO IT FOLLOWS THAT THE SIZE OF THE DEPARTMENT MUST HAVE INCREASE
  200 PRINT "% INCREASE IN DEPARTMENT = ";((N2-N1)/N1)*100;"%"
  210 PRINT
  220 REM NOW RETURN FOR NEW VALUES
  230 GOTO 120
  300 REM
  310 REM THE COMPUTER COMES HERE IF N1>N2 AND SO IT FOLLOWS THAT
  311 REM THE DEPARTMENT MUST HAVE DECREASED IN SIZE
  320 PRINT "% DECREASE IN DEPARTMENT = ";((N1-N2)/N1)*100;"%"
  330 PRINT
  340 GOTO 120
  350 REM
  360 REM
 1000 STOP
>




RUN
INPUT N1 AND N2 SEPARATED BY A COMMA.
(TO TERMINATE, INPUT NEGATIVE VALUE FOR N1)?100,120
% INCREASE IN DEPARTMENT = 20%

INPUT N1 AND N2 SEPARATED BY A COMMA.
(TO TERMINATE, INPUT NEGATIVE VALUE FOR N1)?342,278
% DECREASE IN DEPARTMENT = 18.7134503%

INPUT N1 AND N2 SEPARATED BY A COMMA.
(TO TERMINATE, INPUT NEGATIVE VALUE FOR N1)?-6,-7

STOP at line 1000
>
```

MANAGING WITH THE COMPUTER

The flow diagram for this program is shown in Fig 11.8. It leaves out statements not essential to the logic and shows how **IF** statements can produce logically complicated programs.

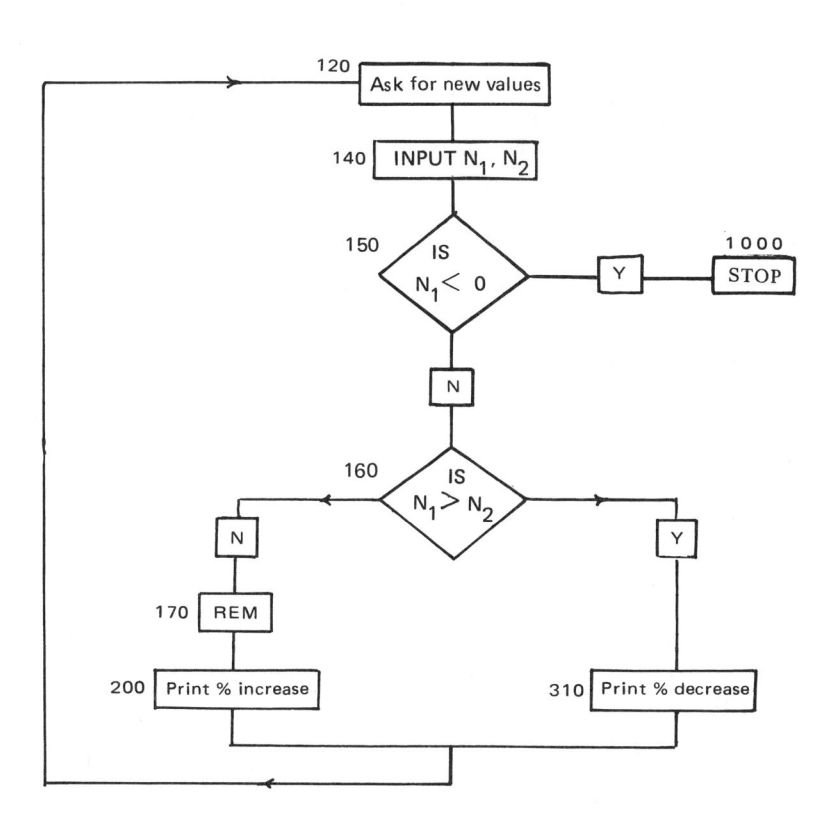

Figure 11.8 : Flow diagram for Fig 11.7

QUANTITATIVE METHODS

Exercise

1. Write a program which will input a percentage rate of discount and will then calculate the selling price given the normal price of a series of items of goods.

2. Adapt the program shown in Fig 11.6 on page 369 & 370 to make the scrap allowance 20%.

3. Adapt the program shown in Fig 11.4 on page 367 to print the results for a range of exchange rates between 10 to 15 francs to the pound.

4. Write a program to calculate the selling price of goods from the cost price. If the cost price is under £10, a mark-up of 40% applies. If £10 or over, a mark-up of 30% applies. VAT should be added at a rate of 15% on all items.

5. Modify the program in (4) so that a variable discount rate, set up at the beginning of the program, is applied to all goods whose selling price exceeds £20.

6. Modify the program from (5) above so that the £20 break-point becomes a variable set at the beginning of the program.

7. A small transport company calculates its delivery charges on the basis of a fixed cost of £10 plus 30p per mile plus payment for the driver at £3 per hour. For each quote, the distance and the number of hours involved is estimated. Write a program to calculate the charge for a series of quotes, quoting the charge with and without VAT at 15%.

8. Modify your answer to (7) so that if the number of hours exceeds 8, an additional fixed charge of £30 is added to allow for an overnight stop.

9. Modify your answer to (8) so that the cost for a range of hourly rates between £2.5 and £4 is calculated for each quote. (NB: In the **FOR** statement, a fractional **STEP** value is permitted in most dialects of BASIC).

11.3.5 Incorporating Procedures or Subroutines

It is difficult to describe to someone who has never programmed just how easy it is to build in self-contained blocks of program which do certain specific jobs such as sorting, data vetting and fundamental statistical operations. Once these procedures have been written in a general form, they can be used over and over again, without modification, in a variety of different programs.

MANAGING WITH THE COMPUTER

In the program we have looked at, a procedure should be used to vet the data. It would carry out the following functions:

1. Ensure that a number has indeed been fed in and not some other characters accidentally input which would 'crash' the program (like stones fed into the food processor instead of raisins!).

2. Ensure that the number fed in lies between a minimum and a maximum pre-set for each application.

Writing the procedure is somewhat technical, but you can get some friendly computer boffin to give you a copy of his own procedure which you can then incorporate in any program you write which involves data input. All you would have to do is to append it to your program and 'call' it when required. The programme in Fig 11.2 would then have the structure of Fig 11.9. If a correct number is input, the user will be unaware that a vetting process is in progress.

Figure 11.9 : a Simple Program calling a Procedure

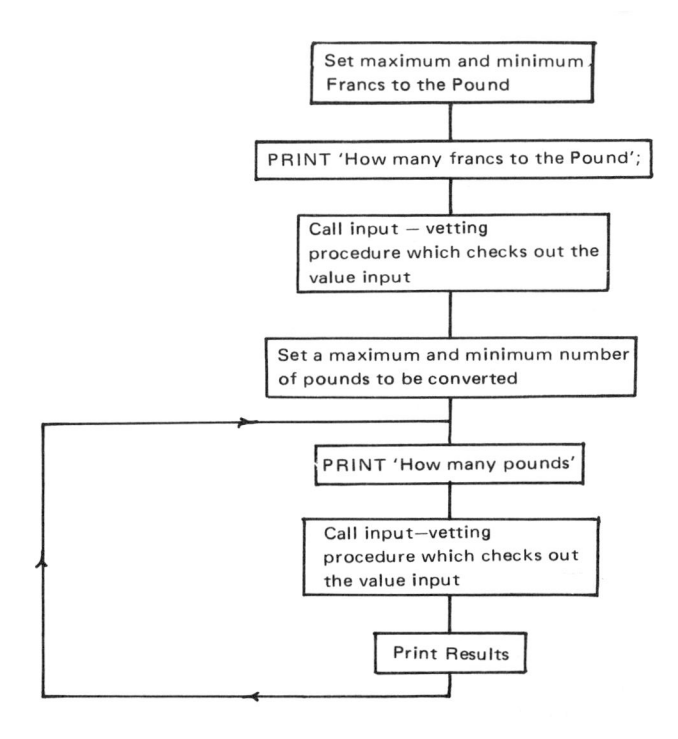

```
┌─────────────────────────────┐
│ Set maximum and minimum     │
│ Francs to the Pound         │
└─────────────────────────────┘
              │
┌─────────────────────────────┐
│ PRINT 'How many francs to the Pound'; │
└─────────────────────────────┘
              │
┌─────────────────────────────┐
│ Call input — vetting        │
│ procedure which checks out the │
│ value input                 │
└─────────────────────────────┘
              │
┌─────────────────────────────┐
│ Set a maximum and minimum number │
│ of pounds to be converted   │
└─────────────────────────────┘
              │
┌─────────────────────────────┐
│ PRINT 'How many pounds'     │
└─────────────────────────────┘
              │
┌─────────────────────────────┐
│ Call input—vetting          │
│ procedure which checks out  │
│ the value input             │
└─────────────────────────────┘
              │
┌─────────────────────────────┐
│ Print Results               │
└─────────────────────────────┘
```

QUANTITATIVE METHODS

In fact if you decide to do serious programming, you will find that it is best to build up your program as a series of procedures or subroutines. Such a methodology is known as *structured programming*. Programs then consist of a sequence of self contained procedures as shown in Fig 11.10.

Figure 11.10 : Structured Programming, an example

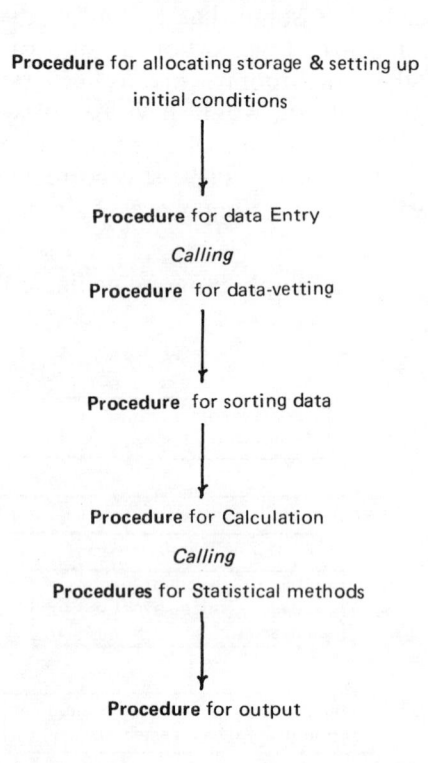

Procedure for allocating storage & setting up initial conditions

↓

Procedure for data Entry

Calling

Procedure for data-vetting

↓

Procedure for sorting data

↓

Procedure for Calculation

Calling

Procedures for Statistical methods

↓

Procedure for output

The advantages are that since each section is now independent, they can be separately tested. Also procedures can be interchanged between programs and the logical structure of the program is clear. Some forms of BASIC make structured programming easier than others, so get advice before buying a machine.

11.4 Power to the User!
11.4.1 Crystal Balls

Predictions of the future are always interesting when viewed in retrospect. Some of the main trends can always be foreseen, but many of the essential elements of change are always unforeseeable. Macaulay (1830) had a go when he looked 100 years into the future:

> 'If we were to prophesy that in the year 1930 a population of 50 millions, better fed, clad and lodged than the English of our time, will cover these islands. . . . that cultivation, rich as that of a flower-garden, will be carried up to the very top of Ben Nevis and Helvellyn, that machines constructed on principles yet undiscovered, will be in every house, that there will be no highways but railroads, no travelling but by steam, that our debt, vast as it seems to us, will appear to our great-grandchildren a trifling incumbrance, which might easily be paid off in a year or two, many people would think us insane.'

Well, he got the population and the bit about the national debt right, but his imagination could not foresee the limitations of steam or the possibilities of powered flight; and as for cultivating the top of Ben Nevis. . . . . ! It seems that predictions of this kind always end up as a mixture of sense and nonsense.

Unfortunately we, who have no choice but to live and work in the era of the computer revolution, need to make predictions about the level of change taking place in the computer field in order to be able to manage our careers within an organisation, and we will find it no easier than our forefathers did. All that we can do is to keep revising our assessment of what is possible on an *annual* basis!

It does seem safe to predict that there will be a rapid development of direct end-user development of computer systems. This will result in much power being returned to the individuals and departments from whom it was snatched when autocratic, centralised data processing started to automate manual systems in the early days. The legacy of that period is a population of managers many of whom fear or despise computers and their peripheral equipment. New developments providing user-friendly software for use in the manager's own office will offer great opportunities for those who have the imagination to see the possibilities opened up by a very small investment in developing the new skills required.

11.4.2 Managers will Create their own Applications Software

We have seen that managers can be expected to use **BASIC** only to the

QUANTITATIVE METHODS

extent of using it to treat the computer as a powerful calculator. Until recently the idea of managers themselves writing large applications programs to use the computer to help with areas such as Forecasting, Stock Control, or Financial and Production Planning, was laughable. Martin (1982), in 'Application Development Without Programmers', provides essential and relatively friendly reading for managers who want to know how the computer is likely to affect them over the next 10 years especially if they work for large organisations. Martin lays out two contrasting images of how computers are used in organisations in order to develop applications.

1. An over-worked DP department tries to clear a back-log of requests for development on the computer, these requests being centrally controlled. All applications are implemented by special-purpose programs written by professional programmers under the guidance of systems analysts who attempt to liaise with the end-user. The programs themselves will usually be incomprehensible to the end-user.

2. The end-users, create the applications themselves, locally, using sophisticated application generators linked to data-base systems. These application generators will be complex interactive friendly programs which will guide the end-users as they specify their requirements. Such systems will inevitably be expensive in order to provide a service which is sufficiently general to allow the end-users to create totally new applications. The DP departments will be kept busy maintaining the complex systems required.

Before deciding that the imminence of this prospect has been exaggerated, let us have a look at some special software which already allows users to write their own programs to implement quantitative techniques without using a programming language in the conventional sense of the word.

11.5 Spreadsheets

The potential for end-user application creation is well exemplified by the popularity of *spreadsheet systems*. The moment they arrived on the scene, they started to sell micros. Working managers suddenly found that they could program a computer to do what they wanted without calling on specialist help or learning a language like **BASIC**. They also found that the software required cost £100 or so and ran on a machine costing about £1,500. The fact that busy line managers were prepared to buy the machines behind the Data Processing

MANAGING WITH THE COMPUTER

Department's back just so as to be able to use this software, was evidence of how managers can, and indeed will, grasp back the initiative in the computerised environment when given the opportunity.

11.5.1 How Spreadsheets Work

A spreadsheet system is a clever interactive programme which manipulates data and text, displaying it in a grid format on a screen, columns or rows being numbered or designated by letters. It has access to statistical and mathematical routines which it fetches and implements when required.

The users are presented on the screen with a matrix of columns and rows whose width they can alter to suit their requirement. Into the cells of this matrix they can enter numbers or text (see Fig 11.11).

Figure 11.11 : Spreadsheet Display : A simple Financial Application

	E	F	G	H	I	J	K	L	M	N
6	Product									
7	Report	198*								
8		Month No	1	2	3	4				
9	Product X	Units Sold	1100	1200	1400	1500				
10										
11		Revenue								
12		Costs								
13		*********	**	**	**	**				
14		Profit								
15										

QUANTITATIVE METHODS

Any cell in the matrix can clearly be defined by giving its coordinates (like a map reference). The number 1100 is in cell G9 for example. The system goes out of its way to be extra friendly by allowing the user to designate a cell simply by moving the cursor (a light spot on the screen), to the required cell. In effect the user merely has to 'point' at it. In fact systems are on the market already in which you literally touch the screen to designate a cell. The 'mouse' is another device which is now available. When this device is moved around the table top, the cursor on the screen moves.

Having indicated the required cell, the user can enter numbers or text and they will appear in neat columns and/or rows on the screen. So clever user-orientated software has smashed one of the main Input/Output barriers which makes programming in **BASIC** and other languages so tedious for the non-specialist.

11.5.2 What puts the 'Spread' into Spreadsheets

One problem arises fast when filling up a spreadsheet. The amount of data will rapidly extend beyond the limits of the screen. Yet another ingenious feature of the system works as follows. The system allows the user to work on what seems to him to be a vast sheet containing hundreds of rows and columns. The screen then acts as a 'window' into that sheet. In Fig 11.11, for example, the window has E6 in the top left-hand corner. On direct command or by 'knocking' the cursor against the side or bottom of the screen, the software automatically readjusts the section of the spreadsheet displayed to the user. Of course all of this reshuffling is done automatically and requires no skill on the part of the user. It is thus possible to build up long time series or entire balance sheets with this facility for virtually unlimited extension of the spreadsheet.

Hidden from sight above the display shown in Fig 11.11, vital parameters 'float' above the main report sheet. By moving the 'viewing window' up and one column to the left, you can see in Fig 11.12 (page 381), that the sales price for the product and the costs expressed as a % of sales are stored and can be used by giving the references G1 and G2 respectively.

Once the numbers are in columns or rows on the screen, values derived from them can be generated by means of simple commands which avoid the 'mathematical' appearance of BASIC programming. So for instance, we can calculate the value for the revenue by moving the cursor to G11 in Fig 11.11 and entering G9'*G1, and 3300 (1100

MANAGING WITH THE COMPUTER

units at £3 each) will now appear in G11. Note that even though G1 does not appear on the display, it is still present as far as the computer is concerned.

Figure 11.12 : Spreadsheet with Window moved upwards

	D	E	F	G	H	I	J	---
1	Product X		Sales Price	3	£			
2		Costs as	% of Revenue	60	%			
3								
4		Estimated	growth rate	10	%			
5								
6		Product						
7		Report	198*					
8			Month No	1	2	3	4	
9		Product X	Units Sold	1100	1200	1400	1500	

11.5.3 What puts the Power into Spreadsheets

A *Replication* or copying facility is useful and time saving for copying the contents of one cell into another. Chunks of text such as 'Product' or 'Profit' can be copied into designated cells to save time. But what really gives spreadsheets their power is the ability to copy *the way in which* the contents of a cell have been calculated.

Spreadsheets are not merely electronic writing pads, they are really a programming language operating at a high level, storing both numbers *and instructions* and carrying out those instructions when requested (c.f. **RUN**, in **BASIC**). The logical inter-relationship between stored numbers and instructions is something that programmers tend to visualise largely in their heads! It's almost as if chess had always been played blind-fold (traditional programming) and someone suddenly invented playing the game on the chessboard (spreadsheets)!

So at G11, not only is the number 3300 stored, but also the way in which it was calculated. This means that having obtained G11 with

QUANTITATIVE METHODS

one operation, we can ask the system to *replicate* the process by which it was produced from H11 through to J11. By labelling G9 in some way (different spreadsheet systems use different methods so I have used '), we can indicate that as the calculation moves from G11 to H11 and on to I11, the contents of G9, H9 and I9 are used in the computation rather than G9 each time. As G1 was not 'marked' as requiring relative treatment, it remains as a constant throughout the replication process. Thus just one instruction leads the machine to carry out all the following.

Multiply H9 x G1 and put the result in H11
Multiply I9 x G1 and put the result in I11
Multiply J9 x G1 and put the result in J11

The result is shown in Fig 11.13 where only a limited part of the whole spreadsheet is displayed.

Figure 11.13 : Spreadsheet : Calculation of Revenue

	F	G	H	I	J	K
9	Units Sold	1100	1200	1400	1500	
10						
11	Revenue	3300	3600	4200	4500	
12	Costs					

Assuming that costs are 60% of revenue as indicated by the number held in G2, we can proceed to calculate the costs in G12 as (G2/100)*G11 ', replicating the result from H12 through to J12. Following that operation it is possible to define profit in G14 (refer back to Fig 11.11) as G11 '− G12 ' and replicate that calculation from H14 through to J14 giving the result shown in Fig 11.14 on page 383.

The full power of this replication facility can now be realised. The spreadsheet system has memorised the way in which the entire matrix has been calculated. So now the contents of G1 could be changed to £4 and that of G2 to 80%, changes which require two new entries taking seconds to carry out. Using the *recalculate* facility which requires the depression of a single key or takes place automatically, the entire spreadsheet can be recalculated as in Fig 11.15 (page 383). Remember that in a practical application, it would be very much larger than the example shown here.

382

MANAGING WITH THE COMPUTER

Figure 11.14 : Spreadsheet : Calculation of Profit

	F	G	H	I	J	K
9	Units Sold	1100	1200	1400	1500	
10						
11	Revenue	3300	3600	4200	4500	
12	Costs	1980	2160	2520	2700	
13	*****	**	**	**	**	
14	Profit	1320	1440	1680	1800	

Figure 11.15 : Spreadsheet : Recalculation with Changed Parameters

	F	G	H	I	J	K
9	Units Sold	1100	1200	1400	1500	
10						
11	Revenue	4400	4800	5600	6000	
12	Costs	3520	3840	4480	4800	
13	****	**	**	**	**	
14	Profit	880	960	1120	1200	

QUANTITATIVE METHODS

It is often useful to use the replication facility for projecting series. Using the estimated growth rate of 10% held in G4 (see Fig 11.12), we could project the sales figures by defining K9 to be J9'*(1+G4/100), replicating the result from K9 into the future. Each successive sales figure will be 10% greater than the previous one. By changing the contents of G4, the projection will change in a flash when recalculated.

11.5.4 Built-in Functions

In section 11.3.5 on page 374, we saw that in **BASIC** a powerful aid exists in the facility to build in subroutines that do specific jobs. Because a spreadsheet system is, in effect, a programming language in new guise, the same facility exists to some extent in current spreadsheet systems and no doubt will become more highly developed in later versions.

To calculate the quarterly profit, for example, we could move the cursor to G16 and then use a special function which would look something like

SUM (G14 to I14)

which automatically sums the cells along the 14th row between the limits indicated. With appropriate text entered into E16 and F16, the results are shown in Fig 11.16. Other functions are usually available to automatically calculate the mean, the net present value, and other commonly requested statistics.

Figure 11.16 : Spreadsheet using SUM function

	E	F	G	H	I	J
11		Revenue	3300	3600	4200	4500
12		Cost	1980	2160	2520	2700
13		**********	**	**	**	**
14		Profit	1320	1440	1680	1800
15						
16	Quarterly	Profit =	4440			

MANAGING WITH THE COMPUTER

Most systems will allow the user to calculate the correlation coefficient and line of regression for specified pairs of columns or rows between specified limits. In fact most of the techniques found in this book can be implemented on spreadsheet systems.

Exercises

The following exercises assume that you have familiarised yourself with some sort of spreadsheet system. A good tip is to work through the building up on the screen of someone else's spreadsheet. My manual has 2 or 3 of them at the end which spell out *exactly* what you enter (it's like playing a chess game from a book). I suspect that you will learn a lot quicker using that method than trying to fathom the manuals.

The following suggested exercises will demonstrate that most of the techniques in this book can be implemented on a spreadsheet. When building up a table, make sure that you never enter a number if it can be calculated from the entries already on the screen.

1. Enter Table 5.3 on page 158, and calculate the wastage rates as shown in Table 5.5.

2. Try the simple exercise on page 262.

3. Repeat the exercises in Chapter 3 with and without using special functions such as those that automatically calculate the mean.

4. Enter the first three columns of Table 6.1 on page 184 and calculate the last column and its total.

5. Reconstruct Table 6.3 on page 190, then change the interest rate and re-calculate.

6. Reconstruct Table 6.6 on page 193. See how quickly you can change the percentage rates and re-calculate.

7. Reconstruct Table 6.7 on page 210, but tabulate it vertically for a complete series of interest rates along which you can scan when necessary.

8. Construct Table 6.8 on page 211, and try changing the discount rate and recalculating.

9. Try and derive Table 6.14 on page 220 from Table 6.13. Change Table 6.13 and recalculate.

10. Use the appropriate special function to calculate the correlation coefficient and regression line for Tables 7.1 on page 224, 7.2 on page 228, and 7.3 on page 230.

QUANTITATIVE METHODS

11.   Try calculating Table 8.4 on page 263. Change the Year 1 prices and recalculate.

12.   Reconstruct Tables 8.9 on page 273, Table 8.10 on page 275 and Table 8.12 on page 278.

13.   Repeat the exercise on page 285.

11.6   Packaged Goods

Spreadsheet systems and other financial planning systems are designed to provide non-specialist users with a general purpose planning aid. When employing them, users need to have identified the problem and decided how it should be solved. Then the spreadsheet helps them to build up the solution method on the screen.

Packages provide a more restricted service. What has been 'packaged' is a specialised, and often very complicated, set of quantitative procedures. Examples would include Network or Critical Path Analysis for project planning, Linear Programming (LP) for resource allocation, or mixed packages of statistical methods, especially forecasting techniques.

In line with the trends already identified, these packages are becoming more and more user friendly. This trend brings with it new dangers. A spreadsheet system displays to the users in friendly form the calculations they are carrying out and controlling. A package is often seen as providing *the* solution to the problem rather than being an aid to its solution. Computational techniques of great complexity and sophistication can indeed be encapsulated in a package, but the package cannot provide the technical expertise and judgment combined with a knowledge of the area where the application is to be implemented which is essential when using these techniques. (Expert systems, discussed on page 393 may get over this problem to some extent). As Barnett (1982) puts it

> 'The widespread availability of sophisticated computer packages has put mathematical bazookas in the hands of some people who would be dangerous with an abacus.'

Whereas in spreadsheet applications, the users build up the logic of the situation themselves, the package tempts the user to feed data into the 'black box' and wait for the results to come out the other end. Computer salesmen often encourage this attitude because what they sell is the package and the machine. They do not sell the expertise to put them to good use, therefore there is a danger that they will suggest that the package can stand on its own.

11.6.1 Multiple Regression

A good example of a 'mathematical bazooka' is provided by *Multiple Regression*. When discussing Linear Regression on page 247, it was clear that more than one variable is needed to 'explain' the variation in an observed variable. Sales of goods depend not just on advertising levels but also on the activity of competitors, economic conditions, the number of salesmen employed and so on. Manpower wastage in departments may well depend on the location of the department in the country, the level of seniority, average age of the personnel and so on. To explain the variation in any one variable, it would seem reasonable to study the correlation of the dependent variable with large numbers of potential independent or predictor variables which are, inevitably, inter-correlated amongst themselves. A technique that could tease out a simple prediction model from all that data is potentially attractive to management.

Suppose a study on factories were carried out with data being collected on many of the variables that could conceivable affect accidents. A Multiple Regression package could automatically select those variables which taken together best 'explain' the variation in the incidence of accidents between different factories and produce a predictor equation such as the following.

Expected number of accidents per year in a factory =

```
    3.4
+   0.0001  x  (Number of Employees)
-   0.01    x  (Annual sum spent on safety)
+   2.1     x  (Dummy variable indicating whether the factory is
               classed as 'heavy industry' or not)
```

NB: The *Dummy variable* is a variable that takes on the value 0 or 1 depending on whether or not some condition applies. In this case it is an indicator of the nature of the work carried out in the factory. Using this model, a factory with 800 employees spending £3,500 on safety and classified as 'heavy industry' would yield the following predicted number of accidents:

Expected number of accidents =

```
    3.4
+   0.0001  x  800
-   0.0001  x  3500
+   2.1     x  1            =   5
```

These predictions could then be compared with actuals and the residuals examined just as on page 252. Such an end product is

QUANTITATIVE METHODS

attractive. The package seems to have sorted out from all the possible predictor variables just three significant variables. However the dangers of misuse are great.

The package will not ask how the amount 'spent on safety' is defined. It will not ask whether the amount spent on safety is not correlated with some other variable, such as the quality of management in the factory which might be the true contributor to accident reduction. After all, good management might well provide good supervision which is effective in reducing accidents. At the same time such management might spend money on safety in the mistaken belief that it was effective. It's the old cause and effect problem to the resolution of which the computer package can contribute *nothing*. Sorting that problem out requires field work and communication with those involved in safety affairs.

The package will not 'know' it it is being misused. In some published work, arbitrary numerical codes have been fed into packages as 'variables'. For example, suppose that you want to indicate a predictor variable which will indicate whether the factory is in the North, South, East or West of the country. It is totally invalid to allocate codes as follows:

Regional Predictor 'variable'	=	1 if in North
	=	2 if in West
	=	3 if in South
	=	4 if in East

Given such a phoney 'variable', the package will blindly correlate such arbitrary codes, caclulating means and standard deviations which have no meaning. In fact, three dummy variables are needed for this job, and the values assigned to them will depend on the location of the factory as follows:

	Dummy Variable Number		
	1	2	3
North	0	0	0
West	1	0	0
South	0	1	0
East	0	0	1

Now for example, the coefficient of dummy variable 1 will measure the effect of a location in the West over that of the North taken as an arbitrary baseline, variable 2 the effect of being in the South and so on.

The complication described above is only one example of some of the technical complications which can arise in doing regression analysis. The truth is that a multiple regression package will provide the skilful user with the computational procedures to arrive at useful results as long as the package is being used as part of an overall study under the guidance of an experienced statistician. A study by Doyle et al (1979) provides a readable account of a multiple regression study in which great care was taken to step carefully through the 'minefield'.

This study was aimed at finding models which would help the management of the Yorkshire Bank to control its 180 branches. By analysing its existing branches, the bank wanted to predict a number of variables such as the number of personal accounts that a branch would obtain, the average balance of a personal account and several others besides. The predictor variables used in the analysis of the existing branches included

- % of self employed in the trading area
- population over 65 " " " "
- region of the country (4 dummy variables)
- number of major retailers within a specified distance of the branch
- whether the branch had a night safe (dummy variable)

As well as carrying out extensive preliminary research, three principle problems had to be tackled.

1. *Multicollinearity* leading to unreliable results arises when the multiple regression package is asked to examine variables which are highly correlated. A whole group of variables are, for instance, correlated with the population of the trading area. Skill was needed in handling the choice of predictor variables for each run.

2. The direction of causality cannot be assumed. Turnover is highly correlated with branch floor area. That doesn't necessarily mean that large floor areas *cause* a high turnover. It could be that the expectation of turnover caused a large floor area to be installed in the first place!

3. The team took care to validate their results. They divided the 180 branches into 2 data sets of size 90. They then derived a model based on one half and then looked to see if the other half highlighted the same predictor variables.

Management used their results to screen potential branch sites and to estimate the business potential of existing ones. Six pages of good sense which are well worth reading if you intend to handle this particular bazooka for yourself!

QUANTITATIVE METHODS

Another problem with packages is that the user often assumes wrongly that they are accurate. A rather technical paper by Lachenbruch (1983) compares the accuracy of a number of Multiple Regression packages and suggests some hints for how to test them for yourself.

11.7 Simulation Models

Computer simulation techniques have always played a significant role in assisting in management decision making. The idea of constructing models on which controlled experiments can be carried out is an attractive one. Random numbers have already been used on page 133 for sampling, and a simple simulation experiment was used on page 236 to explain the behaviour of a sampling distribution.

Building up and validating simulation models requires the same sort of careful planning and fieldwork by experts as is required for the implementation of Multiple Regression, and a full coverage is beyond the scope of this book. However the following very simplified example will illustrate how the simulation process can throw light on business problems, especially problems that involve queues.

Example

Suppose that as part of a process in a manufacturing company machines are put in the one available test rig and subjected to three testing processes. These are carried out independently, but at the same time, by three engineers. The time to test can vary greatly and each testing process can take anything up to 30 minutes. The percentage frequency distributions for process times, as obtained by work study, are shown in Table 11.1.

Table 11.1 : % of Frequency Distributions for Each of 3 testing processes

Time (in Minutes)	Process A % frequency	Process B % frequency	Process C % frequency
0 – 10	10	80	40
10 – 20	70	15	30
20 – 30	20	5	30
	mean time = 16 minutes	mean time = 7.5 minutes	mean time = 14 minutes

As the processes are carried out at the same time, the overall test time will depend on which of the three processes takes the longest on any particular occasion.

MANAGING WITH THE COMPUTER

Try and answer these questions straight away. How long will the overall testing time take on average? If a machine arrives every 20 minutes during a continuous 8-hour day, how big a queue is likely to build up? How much overtime, if any, will have to be worked at the end of a typical day to clear any back-log?

The simulation approach is to sample typical process times and then work out in numerical terms how the system will behave. Random numbers can be used to generate samples of the three process times from the ogives (see page 88) of the distributions shown in Table 11.1. This procedure is shown in Fig 11.17.

Figure 11.17 : Ogives for Table 11.1 showing Random Sampling Method

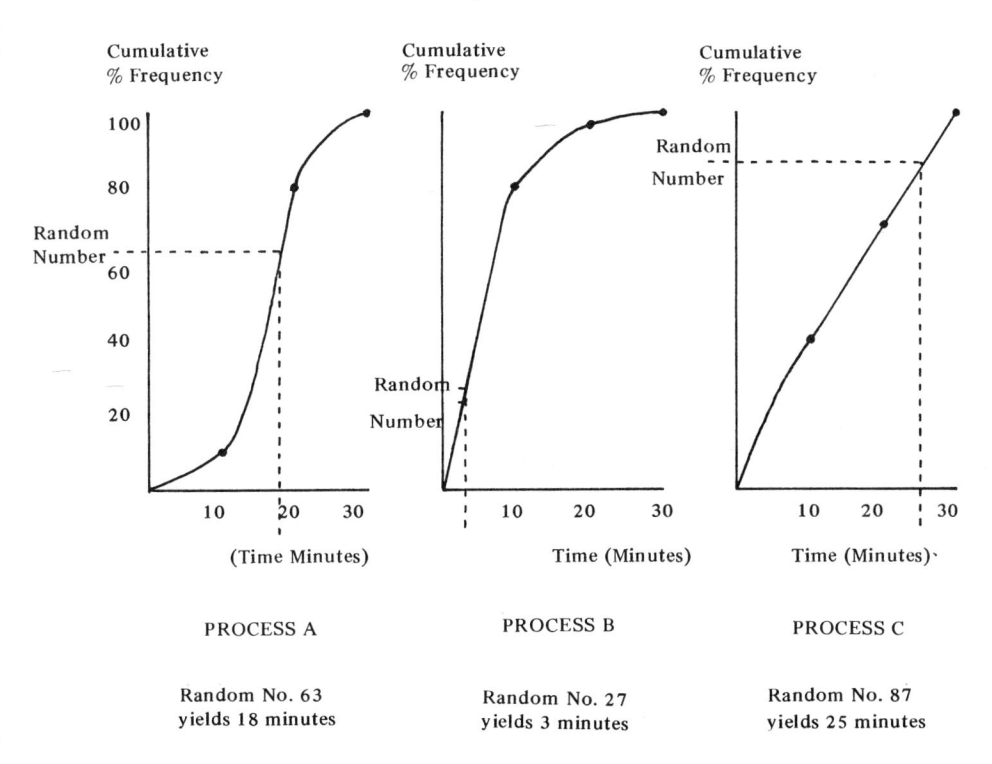

PROCESS A

Random No. 63
yields 18 minutes

PROCESS B

Random No. 27
yields 3 minutes

PROCESS C

Random No. 87
yields 25 minutes

In Table 11.2, the simulation procedure is tabulated. Note that it can be carried out in purely numerical terms and is therefore ideally suited to the computer. For each machine, the longest of the three process

391

QUANTITATIVE METHODS

times determines the overall processing time. When a machine arrives, if an earlier machine is still being processed, then it will have to wait, forming a queue. The computer can deduce that a machine will have to wait by testing to see whether the arrival time is earlier or later than the 'Job finish' time of the previous machine.

Table 11.2 : Simulation of a Day of Testing (part only)

M/C No.	Arrival Time	Process A Random Number	Time	Process B Random Number	Time	Process C Random Number	Time	Overall Time	Job Starts	Job Finished	M/C Delay
1	0:00	63	18	27	3	87	25	25	0:00	0:25	
2	0:20	02	2	69	8	17	4	8	0:25	0:33	5
3	0:40	52	18	98	24	85	24	24	0:40	1:04	
4	1:00	81	20	17	2	63	17	20	1:04	1:24	4
5	1:20	37	16	99	26	60	16	26	1:24	1:50	4
6	1:40	95	26	20	2	30	7	26	1:50	2:16	10
7	2:00	38	16	96	21	21	5	21	2:16	2:37	16
8	2:20	36	16	48	5	32	8	16	2:37	2:53	17
9	2:40	75	20	07	1	89	26	26	2:53	3:19	13
10	3:00	30	15	68	7	22	5	15	3:19	3:34	19

The times are given in clock-times starting at 0:00 for the sake of clarity. Thus, for example, machine number 3 arrives at 0:40, 40 minutes into the simulation and is finished 24 minutes later at 1:04.

Exercise

1. From Table 11.2, work out the 'queue profile'. That means drawing up a chart which shows how the queue size varies as the simulation proceeds. For example, when machine 2 arrives, it has to wait for 5 minutes before starting testing. A queue of 1 forms therefore at 0:20 and disappears at 0:25. Continue the process after completing the next exercise.

2. Note how the delays seem to be building up, and also the high overall testing time. Carry on the simulation to the end of the 8-hour day using the random numbers in Appendix 7. Then compute the mean delay and overtime needed at the end of the day.

On a series of 10 runs the following results were obtained:

MANAGING WITH THE COMPUTER

- Mean overall testing time = 19.6 mins per machine.
- On most days, the queue did not exceed 2 but on 1 day it was as high as 4.
- 72% of machines suffered some delay (mean = 17 mins)
- Mean overtime worked = 17.8 mins.

High speed computers can repeat simulations like the above very rapidly so that the long-run effects can be judged and experiments carried out. In the situation described above, such experiments might include the following:

1. What would be the effect of having 2 testing rigs?

2. What would be the effect of reducing the time for process 3 by 25% by buying better equipment?

Simulation has been widely used in the past, but it too is being affected by the computer revolution. The latest development is to produce *visual simulation models,* many of them in colour, in which instead of the results being displayed in numerical terms as in Table 11.2, they are displayed on a screen in colour, in diagrammatic form. In a model of a car assembly plant, for instance, an animated display representing the essential features of the plant allows the simulation to be validated by non-specialist staff who can literally see if the model is a reasonable representation of reality before experimentation takes place. It provides yet another example of the trend to end-user involvement.

11.8 Expert Systems

An *Expert System* is a complex set of programs designed to assist a user by drawing inferences based on the contents of a *knowledge base.* This knowledge is not just a computerised encyclopaedia, it also consists of the interrelationship between the items of knowledge. Communication with the user will be conversational. When interrogated, the machine will systematically build up a picture of the user's requirement and initiate its own questions addressed to the user. A significant feature of such systems is that they can explain the logical path which led to the conclusion arrived at. This offers the exciting prospect that using such systems will be an enlightening and

QUANTITATIVE METHODS

stimulating experience for the user. Unlike the case when dealing with a human 'expert', the expert system will go into any level of detail required by the user. There will be no status problem on either side. In the privacy of their own rooms, users will be able to ask for detailed explanations that they would find embarrassing when dealing with a human 'expert'.

Another feature of expert systems is that they will include programs that can refine the knowledge base in the light of experience. Systems are being developed which will analyse past experience and work out rules for guiding users and modify these rules when necessary. Clearly such systems already have a great potential in medicine where the accumulation of experience is so vast and scattered around the globe, and where the need for diagnosis is so pressing. Similarly, in aircraft maintenance, diagnosing faults in complex systems is difficult. Engineers all over the globe are facing similar problems on the same make of aircraft. Expert systems are already being applied in this field.

Ordinary line managers can expect to be using such systems in their own domain within the next decade. Books like this could then be replaced and become subsets of general business problem solving expert systems which would advice managers about quantitiative techniques appropriate to their problems. It is not clear what the intelligent fifth generation of computers will be like. If they are well designed, they should be very interesting to use.

CHAPTER 12 : PROBLEMS WITH DATA

The first three sections of this chapter discuss the ways in which faulty or misleading data can be recorded. Sections 12.4 and 12.5 deal with cost data and government statistics and the last section, 12.6, makes some positive suggestions for improving matters.

12.1 Garbage in, but what comes out?

Those responsible for information systems have always been concerned to try and improve the quality of information being input. Recently they have taken to using the old saying:

'Garbage in, garbage out'

The idea is that if an information system, particularly a computerised one, is fed with poor or faulty data, then the output of the system and all the analysis based on it will be worthless. I think the saying is misleading. One of the things that can be said about garbage is that it has an unmistakable air about it which makes it difficult to be mistaken for anything else! Now the trouble is that if you feed nonsense data into an information system then the system will produce something which will be worthless but which will not look like nonsense. It will be 'garbage' dressed up as information. The information system will have given it the appearance and trappings of meaningful data. This deception is particularly true when the information system is being run on a a computer.

12.1.1 Laundering Data

When you look at source documents produced at the supervisory level where much data stems from, you can often get an idea of the degree of care that has gone into its preparation. You may find that forms have been neatly and carefully filled out and clarificatory comments attached to missing items. On the other hand you may find that the figures have been scribbled on the form together with scarcely legible cryptic comments, meaningful to the author's close associates perhaps, but to no one else. There may also be unexplained gaps on the form. Faced with source documents, an employee can not only get an idea of the quality of the information in front of him, he should also be able to identify the originators and having done so, check out any curious details with them face to face.

. Even a torn old shirt looks quite impressive when it comes back from

QUANTITATIVE METHODS

the laundry. Neatly folded and packaged, it only betrays its true state when you try and wear it. Computer systems 'launder' data in a similar way. By the time data appears as computer output, it has acquired a deceptively pure and convincing appearance. Numbers appear in neat columns and written comments, if any, appear in a standard typeface obliterating any evidence of the degree of care taken in their preparation. The pages have authoritative headings declaring what the figures represent. The entire output has a homogenous de-personalised appearance which helps to endow it with an air of authority which may not be deserved. Only careful scrutiny and cross-checking can show up any deficiencies. But because it comes from the computer, the output is given an aura of authority which tends to discourage scepticism.

12.1.2 Facing up to Reality

There are two approaches to the data problem. One is to ignore it and to develop and use techniques on the assumption that the data is pure or ought to be. The other approach is to face up to the problem and do something about it. If you want to take the first approach then you had better skip the rest of this chapter. If you grapple with the second approach, you won't get a Ph.D out of your efforts, it is a field of study which has little academic status, but you will find that it has its own rewards. Studying data, how it is generated, and how it can be corrupted can be interesting. It has its amusing moments and can pay dividends.

It is difficult to structure a discussion on data quality. What follows is inevitably anecdotal. Hopefully the examples described will encourage you to seek out your own examples within your own organisation. Remember, the control of data quality is not a problem specific to computer–based information systems, it is common to all such systems. It is just that computers have cut off many of the natural checks that people used to be able to apply in manual systems.

12.2 Problems in Recording Data

Organisations have tended to get bigger in recent years. This results in greater efficiency but on the other hand the planners, the accountants and other users of data have become much more remote from that critical moment when an individual scribbles figures on a summary sheet at 2 AM on the night shift. To get to grips with the data recording problem we need to find out what can go wrong with the recording process and pay some attention to the extent to which people are motivated to get things right.

PROBLEMS WITH DATA

12.2.1 Who cares?

A keen student of quantitative methods once set out to put into practice some of the techniques of stock control that she had been taught. She set to work to identify the demand for different items of stock. As she worked through the figures, much to the embarrassment of the stock control staff, serious discrepancies began to appear and soon a discrepancy of half a million pounds between the stock on the shelf and that indicated in the books had turned up. The reason was quite banal. Staff had carelessly added together different units. Single items, dozens and batches and all been totalled together.

A simple blunder, you might say. A badly run company, perhaps. But couldn't it happen in your organisation? It could, especially if those responsible for recording data have no incentive to get the figures right. Motivation is a key factor here. When the originators of data have little interest in the destination of the figures they are producing and when no one seems to care whether they are right or wrong, then quality will deteriorate, however sophisticated a computer is used.

Exercise

Choose some set of data which *you use* within your organisation but which you do not originate yourself. Find out the precise way in which the data are recorded and consider the extent to which the recording process could be imperfect. Pay particular attention to the motivation of staff involved.

12.2.2 A False Alarm : By-passing the System

Sometimes data gets misrecorded because staff, motivated by a wish to get things moving, by-pass the paperwork system or 'bend' it to get results which they genuinely believe will meet the goals of the organisation. The figures generated then mislead those who are trying to understand the organisation by analysing the statistics produced by the information system. The next example took place in the accounts office of a highly successful company making components for power stations. The company is part of a group which keeps a tight control on its subsidiaries by means of financial indicators supplied monthly by the company's chief accountant. The accountant is therefore very concerned about the scrap rate amongst the components because this affects the measures of efficiency by which the company's performance is assessed.

The process consists of a number of stages. At the end of the process

QUANTITATIVE METHODS

batches of components of various sizes are packed up and sent to the power station. The wastage rate during the long process is usually about 10%. It is measured by comparing the starting size of the batch and comparing it with the number of good units still in the batch at the end of the process. One day the accountant noticed a batch showing a recorded wastage rate of 30%. Very concerned, he was determined to find out the cause of this alarming instance.

After an investigation lasting several hours and involving considerable ill-feeling between him and the Production manager, the solution was found. Three batches with the identical specification, and destined for the same customer, were nearing the end of the process and were undergoing their final quality checks. Two batches were ready for delivery but the third was still incomplete. The customer was in a hurry and wanted immediate delivery, being ready to accept part of the order only if necessary. Motivated by a commendable desire to keep the customer happy, Sales and Production agreed to transfer some good units from the third batch which was still being finished off, so as to increase the size of the part delivery.

The number left in the third batch was obviously now reduced in number, and so on the record sheet it looked as if it had suffered considerable losses during its passage through the process. The losses from three batches were effectively concentrated onto this one single batch. This misled the accountant into wasting time on what turned out to be a 'wild-goose chase'.

12.2.3 Ignorance of the System

Often data is misrecorded through ignorance of the system and how it is supposed to work. This is more easily picked up in a manual system or in a small organisation when analysts will know or suspect that a novice is at large. If a computer based system is involved, then the system will assume that everyone using the system is acquainted with the correct procedures. Only very sophisticated computer systems are actually programmed to be suspicious!

For example, a quality control engineer working for a company making sophisticated electronic equipment, was examining records showing the number of new units made each month, the number despatched without faults and the number despatched after rework had been needed. He was interested in estimating the efficiency of the process and seeing how it had varied in time.

PROBLEMS WITH DATA

He found that the number of units which had required re-working had suddenly fallen at a certain point in time and remained at zero up to the present. Now from his direct knowledge of the process and the company, he knew that the process was not trouble free and that re-working was in fact still taking place. After a long search which involved him in talking to the supervisory staff involved, the solution to the mystery was revealed. It turned out to be quite simple. A new clerk had taken over and he had not realised that it was necessary when recording despatches, to differentiate normal components from those which had been re-worked.

12.2.4 Improving Data Recording

What can one do to improve the quality of data recorded? Here are some positive suggestions.

1. If the data is fed into the computer, then make sure that there are adequate checks on its validity *at the point of entry*. Real-time access to files allows very sophisticated checks to be carried out. When this is done, any mistake can be displayed immediately to the originator of the data who will learn from the instant feedback.

2. When data is eventually found to be incorrect, make sure that those responsible are made aware of the fact. Even if the mistake is fairly trivial, it will show that someone is taking an interest. If people know that they can input 'garbage' into a system and no one seems to care, then they won't care either. Remember that people relish any opportunity for making a fool of the computer.

3. Ensure that those who are responsible for data entry, know what the data is required for. Check out on what really is motivating them as *they* perceive it. If nobody is motivating them to produce accurate data, be it by means of stick or carrot or a sense of pride, then quality will not be achieved. Quality control for data should learn a few lessons from production quality control techniques. In particular, the new Japanese-led approach which encourages people to take a pride in being responsible for quality through Quality Circles, could be applied to improving data.

12.3 Deceptive Data : Things aren't always what they seem to be

Even if data has been accurately recorded, it may not represent what the user believes it to be. This can often result in spectacular misunderstandings. The problem is particularly prevalent in computer systems. This is because computers tend to rely on a relatively small

QUANTITATIVE METHODS

number of channels of information whereas humans can always supplement the official channels with information derived from informal contacts within the organisation and a general awareness of what is 'reasonable'. Human beings can easily give data the 'common sense test'. When doing so, they are bringing all their accumulated experience of business to bear when checking just one single item. It is much more difficult for computers to do so because everything has to be made explicit in the program. That's why computer system designers often fall back on exhorting the originators of data to be sure to do a good job. They then just hope for the best.

12.3.1 Example : Recruitment Lead Times

In controlling manpower levels in an organisation it is necessary to allow for some delay between the recruitment process being initiated and a recruit being found. This I will call the recruitment lead time. An analyst seeking to improve the control of establishment levels needed to know how long these lead times were. The information provided is summarised in Fig 12.1.

Figure 12.1 : Recruitment lead times

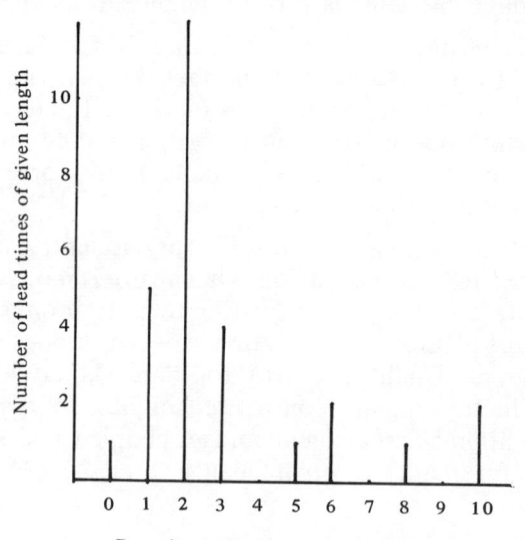

At first glance, there seems to be a very wide range of figures although the process usually takes 2 weeks. On consulting the personnel manager concerned, it was found that although the figures do in fact accurately record the time elapsing between the request for the post to be filled and the recruit accepting, in some cases, the post had been

PROBLEMS WITH DATA

deliberately held in suspense. There were a number of reasons for this being done; a need to fit in with end of year budgetary constraints, or delays while details of the post were being discussed. So although *officially* a recruitment was recorded as being pursued, *unofficially*, but known to all concerned, no efforts were being made to progress the matter. Once these instances had been allowed for, only one genuine lead-time above 3 weeks remained.

This example illustrates the need to check out data at source, wherever possible with those who actually originated it, or at least with those who are familiar with the relevant environment. In this case the personnel officer was acting perfectly sensibly. However the information system was not sophisticated enough to allow the originator to register the interruption to the normal procedure.

12.3.2 Data Processing : Human and Computer

The preceding example illustrates the need for data to be checked out at source. This requirement is difficult to meet when dealing with large centralised computer systems. A computer receiving the recruitment lead-time figures would typically treat them as follows:

ACCORDING TO THE PROGRAM HELD IN MEMORY, I AM TO COMPUTE THE DIFFERENCE BETWEEN THE FIGURE LABELLED 'RECRUITMENT STARTED' AND THE FIGURE LABELLED 'OFFER ACCEPTED' AND LIST THE RESULT UNDER THE HEADING 'RECRUITMENT LEAD-TIME'.

Remember that the computer is not thinking. It is merely executing the instructions held in its memory and unless actually instructed to do so, it will not subject the data to any validity checks.

As Gall (1978) puts it in his viciously amusing critique of systems:
'The real world is what is reported to the system. If it isn't official, it hasn't happened'.

The computer system will only get its information from those sources which it is told to use. Even if it has other relevant sources to hand which it could theoretically use to cross-check the data it is working on, and it could do so with an access time measured in millionths of a second, it will not make use of them *unless specifically instructed to do so.*

By contrast, the human data processor will have a much richer view of the environment around him with a large number of points of

QUANTITATIVE METHODS

contact, many of them unofficial, with other members of the organisation. Apart from the official memos he receives, he will overhear things said in the canteen, discuss business matters in general in the company sports centre over a pint, and thereby have access to a wide range of sources of information. He will often have held positions in other areas which will have provided him with a broad view of the organisation's workings and even though he may no longer have any official connection with these other areas, he will use this experience whenever the opportunity arises.

On receiving the recruitment dates shown in Fig 12.1, a human data processor, because of his awareness of what is reasonable, might well want to check out the figures in an attempt to understand the reasons for the extreme figures. He will probably be able to pick up the phone and ring a colleague with whom he may have no formal links and clear up the matter.

Human processors, inaccurate, inconsistent and slow though they may be, have potentially sophisticated abilities for filtering information. In designing an information system, the great danger lies in failing to appreciate the fundamentally different mode of operation of the computer and the human. The extent to which new developments will enable us to get the best of both methods will be discussed on page 411.

12.3.3 Example : 'Concealed Data'

Sometimes the data that the user really wants to use lies concealed from view because of the workings of the system which produces it. Fig 12.2 on page 403 is a time series which shows the number of units of stock *issued* at the stores in an engineering workshop.

You will note that the issues seem to be highly variable with large peaks and prolonged troughs. Now in order to calculate re-order levels, it is necessary for a stock control system to forecast the mean level of demand and the variability of demand. While awaiting stock replenishment from the supplier, an allowance can then be made for mean demand during lead-time and in addition provide safety stock to allow for any freak demand during that period.

It is quite likely that 'issues' could be read as being synonymous with 'demand'. Issues are easy to monitor because when stock is issued at a stores counter, paperwork obviously has to be raised to account for the items leaving the stores. If that is the case, then the data shown in

PROBLEMS WITH DATA

Fig 12.2 might suggest a highly erratic demand pattern and a large and expensive safety stock would have to be held to protect the company against the possibility of sudden 'demands' for as many as 20 units in 1 week.

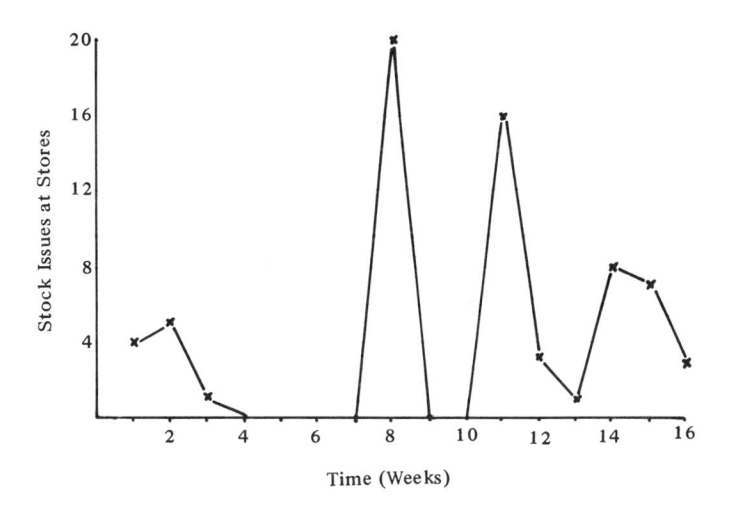

Figure 12.2 : Issues of an Item of Stock from Stores

Fig 12.3 shows the actual pattern of 'demand'. The extraordinary thing you will note is that the pattern of demand is quite unlike the pattern of issues. Only in the first two and the last two weeks do the series coincide.

Figure 12.3 : Demand for an Item of Stock (C.F. Fig 12.2)

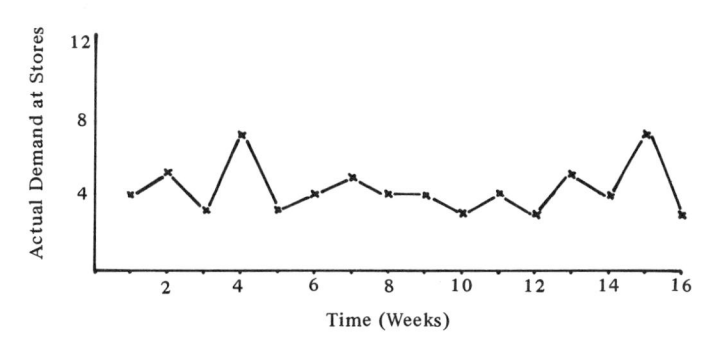

QUANTITATIVE METHODS

Far from being erratic, as the issues would seem to indicate, the demand for this item is very steady and it would be most unfortunate if a computer system attempted to modify its forecast of *demand* by responding to large perturbations in the time series of *issues*.

What is the solution to this apparent riddle? Table 12.1 shows the origin of the pattern of demand and issues already shown in Figs 12.2 and 12.3.

Table 12.1 : The Relationship between Demand and Issues

Week No.	True Demand	Receipts from Supplier	Issues at Stores	Stock Remaining in Store	Accumulated Shortages
				10	
1	4		4	6	
2	5		5	1	
3	3		1		2
4	7				9
5	3				12
6	4				16
7	5				21
8	4	20	20		5
9	4				9
10	3				12
11	4	20	16	4	
12	3		3	1	
13	5		1		4
14	4	20	8	12	
15	7		7	5	
16	3		3	2	

At the beginning of Week 1 there are 10 items in Stock. For two weeks demand was met from stock and therefore issues and demand were identical. In week 3, however, although the demand was for 3 items, only 1 item was issued because *there was only 1 item left in stock*. The un-met demand of two items is therefore accumulated in the form of 'shortages' or 'back-orders' and the people who requested these items must await new supplies. By the time these arrive, in week 8, accumulated shortages of 21 units have built up, during which time, of course, no issues have been made. In week 8, a demand for 4 items plus the accumulated shortages of 21 consumes the new batch which has just arrived from the supplier, still leaving shortages of 5 units to be met later.

Careful examination of Table 12.1 will show how deceptive the issues figures would be if they were assumed to equate to demand. As you can see, the true damand pattern lies concealed beneath the observable issues. To prevent a computer system mis-reading the situation, it

PROBLEMS WITH DATA

would be necessary to provide the machine with a record of accumulated shortages. Of course measuring unmet demand can be difficult. Recording official shortages will help, but people may not go to the stores because they know from the 'grapevine' that the item is out of stock and so no shortage will be recorded.

One story that has probably been around for some time tells of the stock control computer system that noticed that 'demand' for one of its items had fallen to zero and remained there for some time. In fact what had happened was that there had been a delay at the suppliers and the order was still being eagerly awaited. By the time it arrived, the item had been deleted from the catalogue by the computer. The system had decided that as no one seemed to want the item, after all there were none being issued, it had better be eliminated!

Another story that has gone the rounds tells of the company that stocked 2" and 3" bolts. One day the company ran out of 2" bolts. The fitter accepted 3" bolts, reluctantly agreeing to cut them down to 2" rather than await the stock on order. As a result the computer registered an increased demand for 3" bolts and cut the forecast for 2" bolts. As a result, there was soon another stock-out and once again 3" bolts were drawn from stores and cut down to size. Now only 3" bolts are held in stock!

Exercise

1. Re-read the above section and then consider how sales data for an item or service might be an unreliable indicator of the true demand.

2. Think of real-life situations and consider how difficult it would be to actually measure the true demand for a product or service and get it officially recorded in the information system.

12.3.4 Misleading Outliers

Always treat extreme values with a bit of suspicion. Another stock control example will illustrate the general point. Even if demand at the stores has been accurately monitored, the true demand could still be concealed and thereby mislead the stock control system. We will consider the effect, for instance, of trayholding on issues at a store. Trayholding is the common practice whereby someone goes to the stores and draws more units than are needed straight away. These are then held in the workshop as 'the tray' and act effectively as a secondary store. We do the same at home when we stock up with a months supply of flour or detergent rather than buy small quantities as and when we need them.

QUANTITATIVE METHODS

When the quantity on 'the tray' drops to a low level, the fitter will go to the stores and obtain a new supply. The trouble is that someone who does not understand the practice, a carelessly programmed computer for instance, will be in danger of misinterpreting the spikey pattern of demand that results at the stores. Fig 12.4 shows a pattern of issues which suggests trayholding.

Fig 12.4 : Issues from Stores Arising from 'Trayholding'

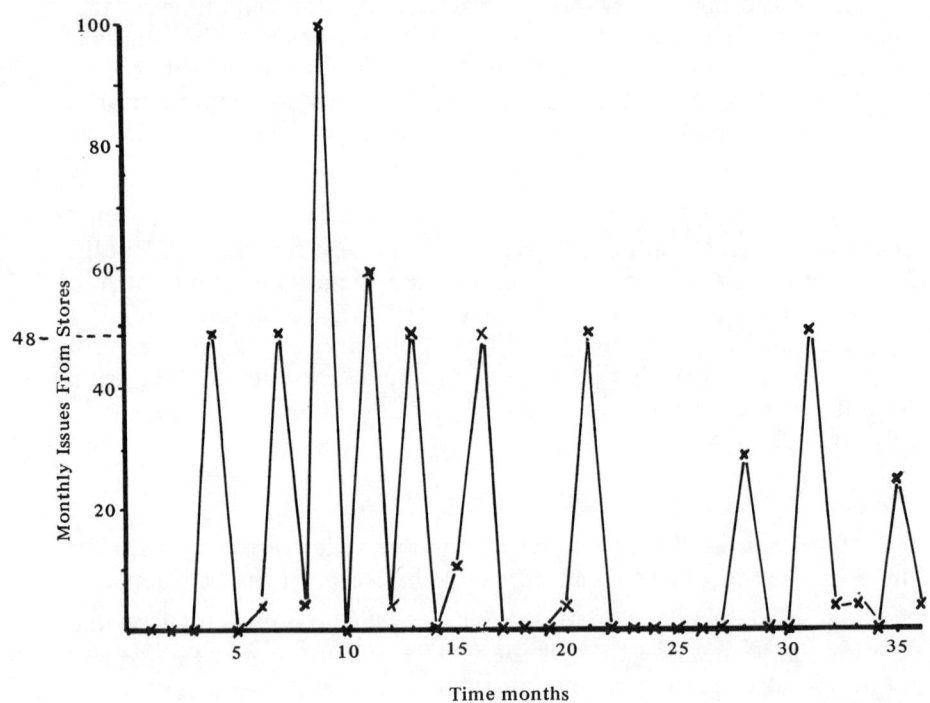

To any human observer, the recurrance of issues of round figures of 4 dozen (48) or, in one case 100, suggests bulk supply for trayholding rather than supply to meet immediate demand. Faced with such a pattern, a human controller would not worry if stock levels in the stores were allowed to fall to a level where it might not be possible to supply a full 48 on demand. The fitter could be simply told to accept 'enough to be going on with' and await the arrival of further supplies. Of course a computer would not 'recognise' 48 as a round number of dozens *unless it had been programmed to do so* and it would be in danger of treating this item as a highly erratic one requiring a large safety stockholding to 'protect' the organisation against 'unpredictable' peaks in 'demand'

PROBLEMS WITH DATA

There are other possible explanations for large spikes such as the 100 items issued. Suppose a subsidiary were to call the stores and ask them if they could help them out with a temporary shortage. The friendly store, having plenty in stock, agrees to help with a large delivery. Unfortunately there is no official procedure to account for this worthy transaction so it goes into the computer as a normal issue. The computer system is now in danger of reading the situation as one where sudden demands of 100 *from the customer* may arise and therefore it raises stocks in consequence. An exceptional helping hand offered to another part of the organisation because surplus stocks were available now results in excess stock holdings for the company for some time to come. Now look again at Figs 1.5b & c on page 16.

12.4 Cost Data

Some of the most frequently used data in business is, of course, cost data. As profit can be defined as the difference between selling price and cost, cost data is directly linked to profitability data as well. It would be nice if cost figures could be looked on as something solid hard and indisputable. Unfortunately this is not so. Cost figures are not absolute quantities, but depend on what the users want to do with them. As there are many different users in a business, inevitably all of the cost data in the system cannot be designed to suit or be appropriate for all these users.

To illustrate how cost data needs to be tailored depending on the use to which it is to be put, consider how you would calculate the cost of your car being used by another person. Assume that Road Tax is £80 and insurance is £150. You usually drive 10,000 miles a year. Every 5,000 miles a service costing £40 minimum is required. This figure excludes occasional repairs. The car does about 30 miles to the gallon and a gallon of petrol costs £2.00. There are therefore fixed costs of at least £230 per annum and a variable cost of at least 7.5p per mile for routine service and petrol. The fixed costs are those which remain the same regardless of the level of activity. Variable costs are those which vary with that level.

How suppose that a good friend wishes to borrow your car to drive 100 miles. He says that he will re-imburse you for the *cost* of using your car. Clearly you could charge him for the petrol and an appropriate proportion of the service charge without being considered mean. You might also charge him for some notional depreciation or 'wear and Tear' but you would recognise that such a procedure would be highly subjective. There is no easy way by which the reduction in

QUANTITATIVE METHODS

value of the car over a journey of 100 miles could be objectively assessed.

And what about the fixed costs? Would you charge for tax and insurance? If you did, would you apportion the fixed cost on the basis of a day's usage, charging $\frac{1}{365}$ of (£80 + £150) which is 63p or would you charge on the basis of mileage, $\frac{100}{10,000}$ of (£80 + £150) which is £2.3? Perhaps you would not make any charge for the fixed costs on the grounds that you would have to pay these costs whether the car is used or not.

Clearly the cost you end up with depends on some objective values (petrol and service), some subjective items (estimated wear and tear) and some items which depend on your policy and attitudes towards your friends (contribution to tax and insurance). Of course if the loan of the car was on a commercial basis, it would be logical to include the fixed costs in your 'cost' calculation. You might then want to make a generous allowance for 'wear and tear' and you might also include an estimate of the cost of your being deprived of the car for a day, an opportunity cost or inconvenience charge as it were. Such a charge would naturally be very subjective.

Exercise

Imagine that in your cellar at home you have 5 bottles of cheap wine for which you paid £1.80 a bottle 6 months ago and which are still freely available in your local off-licence at a price of £2. You also have 10 bottles of cheap wine bought in a French supermarket. The price labels are still on them saying that you paid 5F, 50p say, for each of them. What cost would you quote if you agreed to provide 'at cost' 10 bottles of wine early one Sunday morning to

      a)   Your best friend
      b)   A friend of a friend who is in a jam

N.B: The 5F stickers can be easily peeled off and you are paying 18% per annum on your overdraft! (This example is for illustrative purposes only and the transaction would, of course, be illegal in practice.)

12.4.1 'Costs' rather than 'the cost'

It is important to understand that costs in business are usually established by accountants for a particular purpose. As the same sort of cost information may in fact be needed for a number of different purposes, a number of different purpose-built cost figures should theoretically be provided. What often happens is that one figure gets used for a whole series of situations even when it is quite inappropriate.

Take the situation when a car manufacturer is faced with a one-day stoppage. The 'cost' of the strike can be calculated in a number of different ways.

1. The showroom value of the cars that were not produced that day. This will provide the media with a suitably high figure under the heading 'production valued at such-and-such was lost today'.

2. The profit on the cars due to be produced that day. A number of different profits can be calculated depending on the extent to which fixed costs and overheads are included in the figure.

3. The *opportunity cost* of the strike. This is the nearest thing to the 'true cost'. It is calculated by considering what the company has lost by having suffered the strike or, alternatively, what would the company have gained if the strike had not taken place. Of course such a cost would be difficult to calculate. For instance if supplies of cars are badly needed by the showrooms, then the strike may lead to lost sales. But if the showrooms are full then the opportunity cost may be zero. In fact, it may be that the company is better off than if it had been working. The strike could have enabled them to reduce costly stocks and save on wages at the same time!

12.4.2 Accounting Procedures

Any organisation can be broken down into a number of separate components for costing purposes. These components of the organisation are known as *cost centres*. These are the smallest segments or collection areas of activity for which costs are brought together and might be based on products, sales areas or departments. Some direct costs can be unambiguously allocated to specific cost centres. Direct material costs could, for instance, be allocated to the cost centre for a particular model in a car plant. Accountants, however, have to allow for some general costs which are not directly associated with a particular cost centre. What they then do is to *apportion* them to cost centres. In doing so they have to make some assumption. So the heating bill for the assembly plant might be apportioned to the car models on the basis of the relative number of each model being produced. If the models A and B are made in the ratio of 2 to 1, then the heating costs might be apportioned in the same ratio.

QUANTITATIVE METHODS

They might, however, apportion them on the basis of value throughput or, perhaps, on the basis of the labour content on the grounds that the heating is there for the benefit of the workforce. The point to bear in mind is that many costs that appear as data will depend to some extent on the way in which the accounting system is operated and that method may not have been designed for the purpose that you have in mind. In particular you must find out whether the costs include an apportionment of overheads. If they do, it is essential to understand the basis on which this has been done. Inevitably changes in procedures can affect costs. As Graham (1982) puts it

> 'Data on any organisation are valid only as far back as the last change in accounting procedures'

A bit exaggerated, of course, but in handling data it is better to be cautious than gullible.

It is worth being careful when asking accountants for data that you don't get fobbed off with readily available data prepared for another purpose. There is a simple test. When you make your request, see if the accountant asks you what you want the data for. If he doesn't enquire, be suspicious. You may be getting what Gene Woolsey (1975) in one of his many amusing iconoclastic articles calls the 'Give the kid a number' treatment, the number in question being anything to get rid of you and your query! Remember that accountants are busy people and they are in charge of a complex system and you may not rank high on their list of priorities.

12.5 Government Statistics

For the manager in private industry, understanding the accounting system in his organisation is a first priority. For the manager in the public sector, Government statistics, and how the data contained within them is generated, is vital. As with the accounting procedures within an organisation, it is important to appreciate that public statistics do not just happen, they are compiled and constructed by civil servants and the precise way in which this is done effects their validity for the user. Morrison (1976) quotes an example of how local authorities record a 'permanent solution' when homeless households make no further contact with the authority for 6 months after leaving the temporary accommodation provided. Here 'permanent solution' really means 'the case is now closed'. If the family returns at a later date they are registered as a new case. The statistics are clearly misleading unless the procedure for assembling them is understood. A procedure designed for statistical convenience can thus affect the quality of the resulting data.

PROBLEMS WITH DATA

Irvine et al. (1979) includes many articles which stress the 'social construction of data' produced in official statistics. A classic example is provided by crime statistics where the figures given for crime tend to reflect police activity in response to public and Home Office pressure rather than measuring the true level of crime. For example, if public concern over 'mugging' rises, then it would be surprising if the police did not respond to this pressure by devoting more resources to clearing up cases in that category. This will then be reflected in the published figures which will show an 'increase' in that category of crime.

A Government concerned with keeping inflation down will be tempted to try and influence the Retail Price Index (RPI) because its value at a particular time of year will be used to index items such as state pensions. Because the RPI includes mortgages (see page 264), and these are affected by interest rates and the Government can affect interest rates, the Government can influence, to some extent the values that the official statistic will show. 'Unemployment' and 'Inflation' have become the subject of political debate and successive values for Government statistics are now given headline status. It is not surprising that Governments now use their power to influence the figures if they can.

Turning to the actual process of generating the values, GSS(1979) remind us of how bored many people are who do much of the form filling necessary for the production of routine statistics and give an interesting insight into how Government statistics are produced.

12.6 Being Positive

I have said much about the problems that arise with data. But because there are problems does not mean of course that data is worthless, it just means that we need to be careful when using it and recognise that some data is very much better than others. Data is interesting. Once you have recognised that it does not represent some absolute truth, it can be a rewarding experience checking its validity or relevance to the particular application at hand.

Perhaps when dealing with data we should proceed as a jury does when dealing with witnesses in a court of law. Some witnesses are supposed to be reliable because of their status, others seem convincing when examined but in any case the jury will check out the statement of one against the other. In the search for the truth, it is the cumulative impression which decides matters. Data, like evidence in

QUANTITATIVE METHODS

court, needs to be pondered carefully, and wherever possible it should be cross-checked against alternative sources. For example sales figures can be checked against movements of stock and production figures for consistency.

12.6.1 Checking Data at Source

One result of the continuing developments in computer systems will be an improvement in the general quality of data. In the early days of computing, data was punched onto cards or tape and then entered into the computer on a batch basis. So, for example, all stock transactions would have been batched together and the master file updated once a week. Only then, with access to the stock master file, could the data be properly checked and inconsistencies and errors be detected.

Clearly any mistakes found during the run, were being found many days after the creation of the error. Now it is becoming economic to collect data at source via remote terminals. Modern developments in cheap microcomputers make it easy and feasible to provide these terminals with enough memory and a small processor. This makes them sufficiently intelligent to subject the data to a range of validity checks *on the spot*. These checks will ensure that the data is within reasonable limits. If not, then the errors are immediately notified to the terminal operator and it is even possible then for the terminal to lock itself until the matter is cleared up. The immediate feedback provides an incentive for the terminal operator to get things right and learn from the errors.

Even more intelligent terminals can be linked up with the main database files or at least to extracts from those files held on floppy discs within a computer linked locally to the terminal. In this case, in addition to simple validity checks, more complex consistency checks can be made in real-time and once again, any problems *instantly* referred to the terminal operators before they have proceeded to the next item. Once the operators find that the information system 'cares' about the quality of data, they are more likely to aim at improving their performance.

12.6.2 Involving People

One of the depressing aspects of the early data processing system was the way people seemed to be down-graded by the system. For example, in the early seventies, a new production control system was being introduced in an engineering complex. Until that point in time,

PROBLEMS WITH DATA

the system had operated on a paperwork basis which was kept going by a team of clerks and a group of ingenious trouble-shooters. The new system employed pre-punched cards to identify items passing through the workshops. Use of the new system was explained to the users in such a way as to imply that absolutely *no skill* was required to input the data. All the operators had to do was to put in this card, key in a few figures, pull a lever and the computer would do the rest. Not surprisingly, people felt that they were being down-graded to the status of a mere appendage of the machine. Each mistake made by the system was then relished by the workforce.

New developments under way will tend to de-centralise computing systems, with intelligent terminals in offices, on the shop floor and in advice centres. Advances in telecommunications and their link-up with computer systems, will provide mobile terminals for workers such as salesmen and health visitors, enabling them to feed in data as it is generated in the field, have it checked and also receive feedback and back-up information on the spot. Hopefully this will improve the quality of data and from a psychological point of view give people the impression that the system is reaching out to them, 'listening' to them and supporting them rather than treating them as mere data feeders for a distant system.

With people interrogating the system on a day to day basis, there will be a new incentive for data quality to be improved. If it is clearly out of date, defective or misleading, the credibility of the system will suffer. By giving ordinary employees access to the system, errors should come to light fairly quickly.

We have seen how misleading the generalisations based on data can be. With a terminal in every office, it will be possible for the originators of data to vet these summaries. Once the information system is seen as being more friendly and more useful to small people in the organisation, there will be a greater willingness on their part to point out deficiencies together with suggestions for improvements.

APPENDIX CHAPTERS

The following chapters provide:

a) A technical back-up to certain numbered sections in the main chapters. Mathematical notation is freely used.

b) A summary, where appropriate, of material.

c) Short computer routines in **BBC.B BASIC**. These routines will run on most machines with a few minor changes, and in some cases the output will need to be formatted for your own specific machine.

Note: In this version of **BASIC**

i) ; holds the print position in a **PRINT** statement

ii) Text printed out is placed in double quotes

To make these routines compatible with other machines these two features may require attention.

CHAPTER A.3 : SUMMARISING DISTRIBUTIONS

A3.2   The Sigma Notation

Traditionally the Σ sign is used to indicate the operation of adding up data. It is equivalent to the SUM function found in most spreadsheet systems (see page 378). Being a Greek letter it has the effect of making quite simple operations look obscure and alien and it has been responsible for putting thousands of managers off studying even elementary quantitative methods. It is not used, therefore, in the main part of this book but it is worth mastering if you want to be able to cope with standard text-books, journal articles and the appendices of many management reports.

Mathematical notation is used to explain how quantitative operations can be done in general terms. Letters are used to represent variables of interest. A set of n data items can be represented symbolically as

$$x_1, x_2, \ldots, x_i, \ldots, x_n$$

x_i being a way of describing the ith item or any item.

Now the sum of the data set can be designated by $\sum_{i=1}^{n} x_i$ which says that the data set should be summed from the first to the nth, i.e. the last, item. The mean, $\bar{x}$, is given as follows

$$\bar{x} = \frac{x_1 + x_2 + \ldots x_n}{n} = \frac{\Sigma x_i}{n}$$

When there is no ambiguity, the sum of a data set is often simply given as $\sum_{1}^{n} x$ or $\sum_{i} x$ or Σx.

When you see a Σ sign, it is a good idea to think the sum of a column of figures. Refer back to Table 3.2 on page 84. If the number of class intervals is denoted by k, the assumed mid-point is denoted by x, and the frequencies denoted by f, then the sum of the frequencies is denoted by Σf_i and the last column which was obtained by multiplying the class interval mid-points by the frequencies, by $\Sigma f_i x_i$. Now the mean of the frequency distribution can be denoted by

$$\bar{x} = \frac{\Sigma f_i x_i}{k}$$

A3.9.6 Measures of Dispersion (refer to page 104)

Absolute values are denoted by enclosing the value within two upright lines so that

$$|4 - 2| = +2 \qquad |1 - 6| = +5$$
$$|2 - 4| = +2 \qquad |5 - 2| = +3$$

So the mean absolute deviation (M.A.D.) from the mean for the n values is given by

$$\text{M.A.D.} = \frac{\Sigma |x_i - \bar{x}|}{n}$$

By a particularly perverse quirk of history, statisticians have decided to represent the standard deviation by a small, as opposed to a capital, sigma σ. Nobody is going to change things now but it does mean that the formula for the standard deviation contains two different sigma signs both denoting different things! The formula for the standard deviation (see page 113) is built up as follows.

$(x_i - \bar{x})^2$ The squared deviation of a data item from its mean

$\Sigma(x_i - \bar{x})^2$ The sum of the squared deviations from the mean

$\dfrac{\Sigma(x_i - \bar{x})^2}{n}$ The Variance σ^2

$\sqrt{\dfrac{\Sigma(x_i - \bar{x})^2}{n}}$ The Standard Deviation σ

CHAPTER A4 : THE LANGUAGE OF UNCERTAINTY

A4.5.2 Producing Random Numbers on the Computer

A sample of random numbers is shown in Table 4.4 on page 132 and in Appendix 7 on page 463. Such numbers can be produced in most versions of BASIC by using a special function **RND**. The precise way in which the function works varies from machine to machine so you will need to get precise details for your machine from its manual. Usually the random numbers produced are uniformly distributed between 0 and 1 (see Fig A4.1).

Fig A4.1

```
LIST
   100 REM  PRINT 5 RANDOM NUMBERS BETWEEN 0 AND 1
   200 FOR I = 1 TO 5
   300 PRINT RND(1)
   400 NEXT I
   500 END
>RUN
0.831321611
0.844469216
0.353857762
0.378537402
0.445161781
>
```

The source of these is best thought of as a long circular chain of numbers into which **RND** (1) jumps at random. On most machines you can *initiatialise* the stream of numbers. This ensures that you can break into the sequence at the same point each time which makes the sequence repeatable, a quality that is essential in simulation experiments where the same random pattern must be repeated in different experiments. The numbers produced are really *pseudo-random numbers,* numbers which satisfy the tests for randomness, but which are in fact quite predictable to the computer program producing them.

The idea is illustrated in Fig A4.2 as it operates in **BBC.B BASIC**.

(* 1.8E−3 is computer shorthand for 1.8×10^{-3} or 0.0018).

Fig A4.2

```
LIST
   100 REM TO PRINT THE SAME SEQUENCE OF 5 RANDOM NUMBERS TWICE
   200 FOR K = 1 TO 2
   300 Z = RND(-3)
   400 FOR I = 1 TO 5
   500 PRINT RND(1)
   600 NEXT I
   700 PRINT
   800 NEXT K
   900 END
```

```
>RUN
0.992782623
0.847648606
1.8121372E-3  *
0.50093087
0.740674505

0.992782623
0.847648606
1.8121372E-3  *
0.50093087
0.740674505
```

Fig A4.2 (Cont.)

To obtain random integers, the random numbers between 0 and 1 can be multiplied by an appropriate power of 10 and only the integral part taken (see Fig A4.3).

Fig A4.3

```
LIST
 100 REM   PRINT 5 RANDOM 2-DIGIT PAIRS
 200 FOR I = 1 TO 5
 300 PRINT INT(100*RND(1))
 400 NEXT I
 500 END
>RUN
          32
          63
           6
           5
          76
```

A4.7   Probability Laws : Multiplication or 'AND'

The laws of probability are usually expressed in a concise algebraic notation.

Let E_1 and E_2 represent two events. Then the probability of the two events occurring together or in association is given by

$$Pr(E_1 \text{ AND } E_2) = Pr(E_1) \times Pr(E_2 / E_1)$$

the last part of the expression indicating the probability of E_2 arising *conditional* on E_1 occurring in association with it. For independent events

$$Pr(E_2 / E_1) = Pr(E_2 / \bar{E}_1)$$

$\bar{E}_1$ representing the non-occurance of the event E_1 and the multiplication law becomes simply

$$Pr(E_1 \text{ AND } E_2) = Pr(E_1) \times Pr(E_2)$$

A4.8   Probability Laws : Addition or 'OR'

Using the same notation, the addition law becomes

$$Pr(E_1 \text{ OR } E_2) = Pr(E_1) + Pr(E_2) - Pr(E_1 \text{ AND } E_2)$$

If the two events are *mutually exclusive*, then $Pr(E_1 \text{ AND } E_2) = 0$ and the addition law becomes simply

$$Pr(E_1 \text{ OR } E_2) = Pr(E_1) + Pr(E_2)$$

CHAPTER A6 : COMPOUND INTEREST AND DISCOUNTING

A6.1 (see page 182)

The material in Chapter 6 can be very concisely expressed by using algebraic notation. First the following terms need to be defined.

- I = the interest rate expressed as £ per £1 per annum. As this is usually a fraction, it is often quoted as a percentage, as 100I%. Thus I = 0.12 is the same as 12%.
- N = the number of time periods involved
- P = the Principal or the capital sum involved

So the simple interest for 1 day at an interest rate of £I per £1 per annum is given by

$$I \times P \times \frac{1}{365}$$

which in BASIC becomes:
```
PRINT I*P*(1/365)
```
So for the example of 6.1.1 on page 183, we get
```
PRINT 0.08*2500*(1/365)
0.547945205
```

A6.2.2 Compound Interest (see page 187)

£P invested at a rate of interest of 100I% for N periods will accumulate to
$$P(1+I)^N$$

The expression $(1+I)^N$

is known as the *compound amount factor* (see Appendix 5a on page 457. The example on page 188 becomes in BASIC
```
PRINT P*(1+I)^N

>PRINT 100*(1+0.08)^3
 125.9712
```

6.2.4 Compounding other than annually (see page 189)

If interest is charged at 100I% per annum, but compounded K times per year, then the sum will accumulate to

$$P\left(1 + \frac{I}{K}\right)^{NK}$$

So the example on page 190 becomes in BASIC

```
PRINT P*(1+(I/K))^(N*K)

>PRINT 100*(1+(0.08/2))^(3*2)
126.531902
>
```

A6.3 Allowing for Inflation

If 100I% is the inflation rate per annum and P is the current price, then the estimated price in N years time will be given by

$$P(1 + I)^N$$

So Table on 6.6 on page 193 could be calculated as follows

```
.1ST
    50 REM   A PROGRAM TO PROJECT FUTURE PRICES UNDER INFLATION
    51 REM   AT CONSTANT RATES PER ANNUM
    52 REM
   100 REM   SET UP THE PRICE OF THE ITEM
   200 P=10
   300 REM   SET UP THE RANGE OF YEARS
   400 FOR N= 1 TO 10
   500 PRINT N;
   600 REM   SET UP INFLATION RATES
   700 FOR I= 5 TO 15 STEP 5
   800 PRINT P*(1+I/100)^N;
   850 NEXT I
   900 PRINT
   940 NEXT N
   960 END
   990 REM NB: REQUIRES OUTPUT FORMAT SPECIFIC TO YOUR MACHINE
```

N.B: Different prices can be employed by changing line 200. By replacing it with an INPUT statement, different values can be read in at the terminal. Different inflation rates can be investigated by changing the limits in line 700.

6.4.1 Discounting (see page 194)

Let P be the future sum received in N periods time. Then the present value (PV) of that sum discounted at 100I% per period can be calculated as

$$\frac{P}{(1 + I)^N}$$

In BASIC, applied to the example of 6.4.3 on page 197, we get

```
PRINT P/(1+I)^N

>PRINT 10000/(1+0.12)^3
7117.80247
```

The same result can be found by multiplying the Principal by the *discount factor*

$$\frac{1}{(1+I)^N}$$

In BASIC the factor for the above calculation is given by

```
PRINT 1/(1+I)^N
```

```
>PRINT 1/(1+0.12)^3
0.711780248
```

A6.5   Equal Payment Series (see page 200)

Given a series of N equal future payments (or receipts) at *year end*, the present value factor discounting at 100I% is given by

$$\frac{1 - \frac{1}{(1+I)^N}}{I}$$

In BASIC, applied to the example of 6.5.1 we get

```
PRINT (1-1/(1+I)^N)/I
```

```
>PRINT (1-1/(1+0.07)^3)/0.07
2.62431604
```

A6.6   Capital Recovery Factor (see page 206)

To recover £P lent today in N equal end-of-period payments with interest charged at 100I% per period, the sum should be multiplied by the factor

$$\frac{I}{1 - \frac{1}{(1+I)^N}}$$

In BASIC applied to the example of 6.6 on page 206, we get

```
PRINT (I/(1-(1/(1+I)^N)))
```

```
>PRINT (0.09/(1-(1/(1+0.09)^20)))
0.109546475
```

A6.7 Cumulative Compound Interest Factor (see page 208)

To find out what £P deposited at the end of each of N periods will amount to at the end of the Nth period with interest charged at 100I% per period, the sum £P should be multiplied by the factor

$$\frac{(1+I)^N - 1}{I}$$

In BASIC applied to the example of 6.7 on page 208, we get

```
PRINT ((1+I)^N-1)/I

>PRINT ((1+0.05)^10-1)/0.05
12.5778925
>PRINT ((1+0.15)^10-1)/0.15
20.3037182
```

If the payments are made at the *beginning* of each of the N periods, the factor will be

$$\frac{[(1+I)^N - 1](1+I)}{I}$$

which in BASIC applied to the previous example is

```
PRINT (((1+I)^N-1)/I)*(1+I)

>PRINT (((1+0.05)^10-1)/0.05)*(1+0.05)
13.2067871
>
```

A6.7.2 The Sinking Fund Factor (see page 209)

The regular equal sum required per period to accumulate to a target sum of £P after N periods is obtained by multiplying £P by the factor

$$\frac{I}{(1+I)^N - 1}$$

in BASIC applied to the example of 6.7.2 on page 209 we get

```
PRINT I/((1+I)^N-1)

>PRINT 0.08/((1+0.08)^20-1)
2.18522088E-2
```

(remember that $2.18E-2 = 2.18 \times 10^{-2} = 0.0218$)

If the payments are made at the beginning of the periods, a smaller factor is required because interest gets to work sooner and the revised factor is given by

$$\frac{I}{[(1+I)^N - 1](1+I)}$$

and in BASIC

```
PRINT I/(((1+I)^N-1)*(1+I))

>PRINT 0.08/(((1+0.08)^20-1)*(1+0.08))
2.02335267E-2
>
```

A6.7.3 Inflation Proofing

If the target sum is expressed in current monetary values but an allowance for $100J\%$ inflation per period is required, then the factor assuming end-of-year payments becomes

$$\frac{I(1+J)^N}{(1+I)^N - 1}$$

or in BASIC

```
? PRINT (I*(1+J)^N)/((1+I)^N-1)

>PRINT (0.08*(1+0.06)^20)/((1+0.08)^20-1)
7.008299941E-2
>
```

So Table 6.7 on page 210 can be produced as follows

```
LIST
  50 REM   PROGRAM TO CALCULATE REGULAR SAVED SUM TO ATTAIN A FUTUR
 100 REM   SET UP TARGET SUM REQUIRED                          TARGE
 200 P=20000
 300 REM   SET UP INTEREST RATE (%)
 400 I= 8
 500 REM   SET UP NUMBER OF PERIODS
 600 N=20
 700 FOR J = 5 TO 15
 800 PRINT J;" ";(P*(I/100)*(1+(J/100))^N)/((1+(I/100))^N-1)
 900 NEXT J
 970 END
 990 REM   NB: REQUIRES OUTPUT FORMAT SPECIFIC TO YOUR MACHINE
>
```

If you run the program, in order to get neat columns and headings, you will of course have to format the output to suit your machine.

A6.8.2 Discounted Cash Flows (see page 211)

Calculations such as those used to produce Table 6.8 on page 211 are easily carried out on a *spreadsheet system* (see page 378). The columns (or rows) of costs can be built up on the screen and a net cash flow column constructed. This can then be converted to a discounted net cash flow column and added up to obtain the net present value. On many spreadsheet systems, NPV and IRR functions are available which can be applied directly to the net cash flow columns.

Using **BASIC**. the elements of cash flow can be conveniently held in *arrays*. When examining the annotated program shown in Fig A6.1 refer to Table 6.8 and the calculations which follow it. **Fig A6.1**

```
LIST
100 REM    READ IN ELEMENTS OF CAPITAL, SALES REVENUE, MATERIALS COST,
101 REM LABOUR COST   INTO C( ),S( ),M( ), & L( ) RESPECTIVELY
150 REM    FIRST RESERVE SPACE INCLUDING F( ) FOR NET CASH FLOW
200 DIM C(20),S(20),M(20),L(20),F(20)
250 REM    NOW READ IN NUMBER OF PERIODS FROM DATA FILE
300 READ N
350 FOR K= 0 TO N
400 READ C(K),S(K),M(K),L(K)
450 REM    CALCULATE NET CASH FLOW AS YOU GO
500 F(K)=-C(K)+S(K)-M(K)-L(K)
550 NEXT K
600 PRINT "INPUT THE DISCOUNT RATE AS %   ";
650 INPUT I
660 REM    CONVERT % RATE TO A RATE PER £1
670 I=I/100
680 REM    ACCUMULATE NET PRESENT VALUE IN LOCATION   A    STARTING WITH
681 REM    YEAR 0   I.E. INITIAL NET CASH FLOW
700 A= F(0)
750 FOR K= 1 TO N
800 A= A + F(K)/(1+I)^K
850 NEXT K
900 PRINT "NET PRESENT VALUE = ";A
930 PRINT
940 PRINT " DO YOU WANT A NEW DISCOUNT RATE ....Y/N ";
960 INPUT Z$
980 IF Z$="Y" THEN 600
990 END
994 DATA 4
995 DATA 600,0,0,0
996 DATA 0,300,30,60
997 DATA 0,300,30,60
998 DATA 0,200,20,40
999 DATA -50,200,20,40
>RUN
INPUT THE DISCOUNT RATE AS %   ?8
NET PRESENT VALUE = 25.2777824

 DO YOU WANT A NEW DISCOUNT RATE ....Y/N ?Y
INPUT THE DISCOUNT RATE AS %   ?5
NET PRESENT VALUE = 67.7269248
```

Fig A6.1 (Cont)

```
DO YOU WANT A NEW DISCOUNT RATE ....Y/N ?Y
INPUT THE DISCOUNT RATE AS %  ?10
NET PRESENT VALUE = -0.580561519

DO YOU WANT A NEW DISCOUNT RATE ....Y/N ?Y
INPUT THE DISCOUNT RATE AS %  ?12
NET PRESENT VALUE = -24.6916163

DO YOU WANT A NEW DISCOUNT RATE ....Y/N ?N
```

As can be seen from the re-runs at the end of Fig A6.1, the IRR can be found by trial and error or by drawing a graph from the values for the NPV calculated at different discount rates.

To allow for inflation, values for specific inflation rates for the components of cash flow can be input to R1, R2, R3 and R4, say, and lines such as the following added.

```
LIST
   420 C(K) = C(K)*(1+(R1/100))^K
   421 S(K) = S(K)*(1+(R2/100))^K
```

which will inflate the cash flows by an appropriate amount before they are discounted.

Technical Note: Complications over Compounding

1) In Table 6.4 on page 190 we have seen that interest at a rate of 8% per annum gives an effective annual return of 8.16% when compounded twice yearly and 8.3% when compounded monthly. To find the rate per half-year or per month which will produce an effective rate of 8% we need to calculate

$$\sqrt{1 + \frac{8}{100}} = 1.0392 \quad \text{whence } 3.92\% \text{ compounded per ½ year NOT 4\%}$$

OR

$$\sqrt[12]{1 + \frac{8}{100}} = 1.00644 \quad \text{whence } 0.644\% \text{ compounded per month NOT } \frac{8}{12}\%$$

(The 12th root is found by trial and error or from the computer).

2) When using the factor for an equal payment series as in Examples 6.5.3 and 6.5.4 on page 203, interest is assumed to be compounded periodically. Thus example 6.5.3 assumes an annual *rate* of 13% compounded twice yearly equivalent to an effective annual return of 13.42% to the investor, and in example 6.5.4, an annual rate of 8% compounded monthly is equivalent to an effective annual return of 8.3%

3) If in Example 6.5.4, the customer earns 8% compounded *annually*, then the present value of the payments is calculated as

$$£20.83 \times \frac{1}{\left(1 + \frac{1 \times 8}{12 \times 100}\right)}$$

$$+ \quad £20.83 \times \frac{1}{\left(1 + \frac{2 \times 8}{12 \times 100}\right)} \quad \text{allowing for 2 months interest } not \text{ compounded}$$

+ \quad etc...

SUMMARY OF FINANCIAL FORMULAE

Compound Amount Factor (see page 188) or
What £1 will become when invested at Compound interest?

```
£1                                    ?
|___|___|_____|
Now                  A Number of Periods in the Future
```

$$? = \left(1 + \frac{\% \text{ rate of interest per period}}{100}\right)^{\text{No of Periods}}$$

N.B   This can also be used to calculate the future price of an item costing £1 now when applying an appropriate inflation rate.

Discount Factor (see page 195) or
What is the present value of £1 received in the future discounted at an appropriate discount rate?

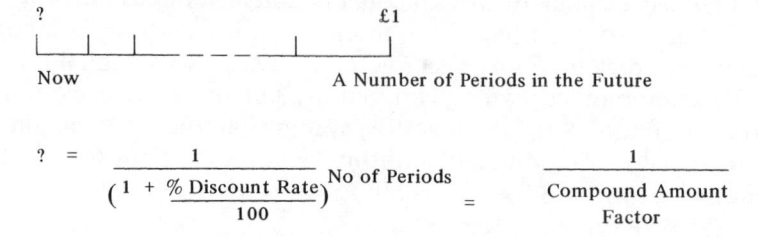

```
?                                    £1
|___|___|_____|
Now                  A Number of Periods in the Future
```

$$? = \frac{1}{\left(1 + \frac{\% \text{ Discount Rate}}{100}\right)^{\text{No of Periods}}} = \frac{1}{\text{Compound Amount Factor}}$$

Present Value Factor for an Equal Payment Series (see page 201) or
What is the present value of £1 per period received at the end of a series of time periods discounting at an appropriate discount rate

```
?    £1  £1      £1   £1
|___|___|_____|___|
                     A Number of Periods in the Future
```

$$? = \frac{1 - \left(\frac{1}{1 + \frac{\% \text{ Rate}}{100}}\right)^{\text{No of Periods}}}{\frac{\% \text{ Rate}}{100}} = \frac{1 - \text{Single Period Present value factor}}{\frac{\% \text{ Rate}}{100}}$$

Capital Recovery Factor (see page 206) or
What equal end-of-period payment streams will pay off £1 borrowed today within a specified number of periods, allowing for a specified rate of interest?

```
£1   ?   ?              ?   ?
|____|___|_____ ____ __|___|
 Now              A Number of Periods in the Future
```

$$? = \frac{\frac{\% \text{ Interest Rate}}{100}}{1 - \left(\frac{1}{1 + \frac{\% \text{ Interest Rate}}{100}}\right)^{\text{No of Periods}}} = \frac{\frac{\% \text{ Interest Rate}}{100}}{1 - \text{Present Value Factor (single period)}}$$

Cumulative Compound Interest Factor (see page 208)   or
What will £1 per period accumulate to after a specified number of periods at a specified rate of compound interest.

```
     £1  £1           £1  £?
|____|___|_____ ____ _|___|
 Now              A Number of Periods in the Future
```

$$? = \frac{\left(1 + \frac{\% \text{ Interest Rate}}{100}\right)^{\text{No of Periods}} - 1}{\frac{\% \text{ Interest Rate}}{100}} = \frac{\text{Single Period Compound Amount Factor} - 1}{\frac{\% \text{ Interest Rate}}{100}}$$

Sinking Fund Factor (see page 209)   or
What will have to be invested at the end of each of a specified number of periods at a given rate of interest so as to accumulate to £1 in the future?

```
     ?   ?            ?   ? £1
|____|___|_____ ____ _|___|
 Now              A Number of Periods in the Future
```

$$? = \frac{\frac{\% \text{ Interest Rate}}{100}}{\left(1 + \frac{\% \text{ Interest Rate}}{100}\right)^{\text{No of Periods}} - 1}$$

$$= \frac{\frac{\% \text{ Interest Rate}}{100}}{\text{Single Period Compound Amount Factor} - 1}$$

If the payments are to be made at the *beginning* of each period instead of the end, then the factor calculated above should be divided by $\left(1 + \frac{\% \text{ interest rate}}{100}\right)$

CHAPTER A7 : CORRELATION AND REGRESSION

A7.4 Measuring Correlation

The data from Table 7.3 on page 230 is reproduced below in Table A7.1 in a modified form with 'Direct Materials', the dependent variable, labelled 'y' and 'Units of Production', the independent or predictor variable, labelled 'x'. This is a universal convention and the dependent variable should always be plotted on the vertical 'y' axis.

Table A7.1

Week Number	Direct Materials y	Units of Production x	y^2	x^2	xy
1	210	30	44100	900	6300
2	405	60	164025	3600	24300
3	382	105	. .	. .	. .
4	480	141	. .	. .	. .
5	690	172			
6	510	206			
7	805	251			
8	904	283			
9	793	323	. .	. .	. .
Sums	5179	1571	3414739	354845	1076156
	Σy	Σx	Σy^2	Σx^2	Σxy

Means $\bar{y} = 575.4$ $\bar{x} = 174.6$

The correlation coefficient is defined as

$$r = \frac{\text{Covariance of } x \text{ and } y}{\sqrt{\text{variance of } x \ \times \ \text{variance of } y}}$$

$$= \frac{\frac{\Sigma(x-\bar{x})(y-\bar{y})}{N}}{\sqrt{\frac{\Sigma(x-\bar{x})^2}{N} \times \frac{\Sigma(y-\bar{y})^2}{N}}}$$

but for computational purposes the following version is preferable

$$r = \frac{N\Sigma xy - \Sigma x \Sigma y}{\sqrt{(N\Sigma x^2 - (\Sigma x)^2) \times (N\Sigma y^2 - (\Sigma y)^2)}}$$

Avoid confusing $(\Sigma x)^2$ with Σx^2.

$(\Sigma x)^2$ means adding up the x's and squaring the result.

Σx^2 means squaring each of the x's and summing the resultant squares

Note that the ingredients of the horrible expression above for 'r' are all sums of columns shown in Table A7.1 on page 430, and given those sums, the value of 'r' can be calculated in one swashbuckling line of **BASIC**.

```
PRINT (9*1076156-1571*5179)/((9*354845-1571^2)*(9*3414739-5179^2))^0.5
0.919699541
```

Of course it makes sense to get the computer to calculate all the sums as well. This will be done on page 432 once the regression line has been defined.

A7.10 The Least Squares Regression Line

A regression line is required to estimate the values of y from the values of x. These estimates we will denote by y^{est}, and the line should be fitted to the data so that the sum of squared errors between actual values of y and those predicted by the line, are minimised. This means that the squared residuals

$$(y - y^{est})^2$$

should be minimised.

Any straight line can be defined by an equation of the form

$$y = a + bx$$

where a is the intercept on the vertical (y) axis and b is the gradient or slope of the line. The values which minimise the sum of the squared residual errors are given as follows

$$\text{The gradient of the line} \quad b = \frac{\Sigma xy - N\bar{x}\bar{y}}{\Sigma x^2 - N\bar{x}^2}$$

$$\text{The intercept } a = \bar{y} - b\bar{x}$$
$$\text{of the line on the } y \text{ axis}$$

A program to calculate the correlation coefficient and regression line in **BASIC** (BBC.B) follows in Fig A7.1. As before, the output will need cleaning up to suit your own computer.

Fig A7.1

```
LIST
   100 REM   READ NUMBER OF PAIRS OF VALUES
   120 READ N
   140 REM   READ N SUCCESSIVE PAIRS OF DATA
   160 FOR K = 1 TO N
   180 READ Y,X
   200 REM   ACCUMULATE RELEVANT SUMS AS FOLLOWS
   220 REM   S1    =    SUM OF X
   230 S1=S1+X
   240 REM   S2    =    SUM OF X SQUARED
   250 S2=S2+X^2
   260 REM   S3    =    SUM OF Y
   270 S3=S3+Y
   280 REM   S4    =    SUM OF Y SQUARED
   290 S4=S4+Y^2
   300 REM   S5    =    SUM OF X*Y
   310 S5=S5+X*Y
   320 NEXT K
   400 REM   NOW ALL THE NECESSARY SUMS HAVE BEEN ACCUMULATED
   420 REM   AND THE CORRELATION COEFFICIENT CAN BE CALCULATED
   440 PRINT "CORRELATION COEFFICIENT = ";
   460 PRINT (N*S5-S1*S3)/((N*S2-S1^2)^0.5*(N*S4-S3^2)^0.5)
   480 PRINT
   490 PRINT
   500 PRINT "REGRESSION LINE "
   510 PRINT
   520 PRINT "SLOPE OR GRADIENT ";
   540 B=(S5-N*(S1/N)*(S3/N))/(S2-N*(S1/N)^2)
   560 PRINT B
   580 PRINT "INTERCEPT ON VERTICAL AXIS = ";
   600 A=(S3/N)-B*(S1/N)
   620 PRINT A
   800 DATA 9
   801 DATA 210,30,405,60,382,105,480,141,690,172
   802 DATA 510,206,805,251,904,283,793,323
   900 STOP
>RUN
CORRELATION COEFFICIENT = 0.919699542


REGRESSION LINE

SLOPE OR GRADIENT 2.13515968
INTERCEPT ON VERTICAL AXIS =   202.74046

STOP at line 900
>
```

The residuals could be calculated by 'restoring' the data file (see your manual, but **RESTORE** may work) and then re-reading the data and calculating

$$Y - (A + B*X)$$

or alternatively the pairs of values could have been stored in pre-dimensioned arrays when read in on line 180 thus

READ Y(K), X(K)

and the residuals could then be calculated without having to re-read the data.

A7.10.2 Explained and Unexplained Variance

Refer to Table 7.5 on page 254. The 6 columns of that table can be defined as follows:

Col 1 y the actual material costs

Col 2 $(y - \bar{y})$ the deviations of the y values from their mean

Col 3 $(y - \bar{y})^2$. The mean of this column, $\frac{(y - \bar{y})^2}{N}$ is the variance which needs to be 'explained'.

Col 4 y^{est}, the values estimated from the regression line

Col 5 $(y - y^{est})$, the residuals or $(y - (a + bx))$

Col 6 $(y - y^{est})^2$. The mean of this column is the variance 'unexplained' by the line.

Note on Table 7.5 on page 254.

Columns 3 and 6 are accurate figures based on the precise equation Materials Cost = 202.74046 + 2.13516 (units of Production). The column 5 figures are rounded off, and so when squared, will not give precisely the same value as shown in column 6.

CHAPTER A8 : TRACKING THINGS IN TIME

A8.3 Price Indices (see page 261)

If P_0 = the price of goods in the base year

P_N = the price of goods in the current year

Q_0 = the quantity of goods consumed in the base year

Q_N = the quantity of goods consumed in the current year

then the two forms of index discussed 8.3 can be defined as

<table>
<tr><td align="center">Laspeyre
(base-year weighted)</td><td align="center">Paasche
(current-year weighted)</td></tr>
<tr><td align="center">$\dfrac{\Sigma\, P_N\, Q_0}{\Sigma\, P_0\, Q_0}$</td><td align="center">$\dfrac{\Sigma\, P_N\, Q_N}{\Sigma\, P_0\, Q_N}$</td></tr>
</table>

A8.4.5 A Note on Table 8.7 (see page 269)

The prices for spirits and beer have been obtained indirectly from the relative price changes shown in the Treasury source indicated and have assumed a 1983 price of £7.15 for a bottle of spirits and 60p for a pint of bitter (public bar). The resulting figures for spirits require some comment. The price of spirits (and beer) is strongly influenced by the amount of duty charged. On April 1973 spirits became liable to VAT at the same time as the duty was reduced. The average price of spirits was greatly affected by the rise of supermarket and cut-price outlets. Of course typical prices are difficult to specify where there is such a diversity of products and outlets in existence.

Deflation Calculations

On a spreadsheet system, the RPI covering the relevant period can be held in a row or column and drawn on when necessary to deflate a series.

In **BASIC**, the RPI, or any other suitable index, can be read into an array as shown in Fig A8.1 below

Fig A8.1

```
LIST
   50 REM   DEMONSTRATION OF DEFLATION USING THE RPI
  100 REM   READ RPI VALUES INTO AN ARRAY
  110 DIM R(30)
  120 FOR I = 1 TO 21
  130 READ R(I)
  140 NEXT I
```

Fig A8.1 (cont)

```
150 REM   THE INDEX FOR YEAR Y IS NOW HELD IN R(Y-1962)
160 REM
170 REM   READ IN 3 YEARS DATA FROM TABLE 8.7
171 REM   AND PRINT DEFLATED VALUE IN TERMS OF 1983 MONEY
180 FOR I = 1 TO 3
190 REM   READ YEAR AND VALUE
200 READ Y,X
210 PRINT "YEAR = ";Y
220 PRINT "VALUE = ";X
230 PRINT "INDEX = ";R(Y-1962)
240 PRINT "REAL VALUE ";X*(R(1983-1962)/R(Y-1962))
250 PRINT
260 NEXT I
300 STOP
500 DATA 54.0,55.8,58.4,60.7,62.2,65.2,68.7,73.1,80.0,85.7,93.5
501 DATA 108.5,134.8,157.1,182.0,197.1,223.5,263.7,295.0,320.4,335.1
510 REM
520 DATA 1977,4.38,1979,4.77,1981,6.29
```

```
YEAR = 1977
VALUE = 4.38
INDEX = 182
REAL VALUE 8.06449451

YEAR = 1979
VALUE = 4.77
INDEX = 223.5
REAL VALUE 7.15179866

YEAR = 1981
VALUE = 6.29
INDEX = 295
REAL VALUE 7.14501356
```

A8.6.1 Moving Averages (see page 272)

Spreadsheet systems can easily be organised to produce moving averages. By saving the display, they can be periodically updated.

Very simple **BASIC** programs can do the job, as shown in Fig A8.2 on the following page.

Fig A8.2

```
LIST
  50 DIM X(20)
 100 REM   MOVING AVERAGES FOR WEEKLY DATA
 120 REM   FIND OUT HOW MANY WEEKS IN MOVING AVERAGE
 140 PRINT "HOW MANY WEEKS IN MOVING AVERAGE ";
 160 INPUT K
 180 REM   READ NUMBER OF WEEKS DATA AVAILABLE
 200 READ N
 220 REM   CHECK THAT THERE ARE AT LEAST K WEEKS DATA
 221 REM   ( >= MEANS 'GREATER OR EQUAL TO' )
 240 IF N>=K THEN 320
 260 REM IF YOU GET HERE, THERE IS NOT ENOUGH DATA TO COMPUTE A MOVING
 280 PRINT "INSUFFICIENT DATA AVAILABLE"                              AVER
 300 STOP
 320 REM   IF YOU GET HERE, THERE IS SUFFICIENT DATA TO PROCEED
 340 REM   SO READ DATA INTO AN ARRAY X( )
 360 FOR I = 1 TO N
 380 READ X(I)
 400 NEXT I
 420 REM   CALCULATE SUCCESSIVE MOVING AVERAGES (MEANS)
 440 M=0
 460 FOR I = K TO N
 480 M=0
 500 FOR J = (I-K+1) TO I
 520 M=M+X(J)
 540 NEXT J
 560 PRINT "PERIOD NO ";I;" MOVING TOTAL = ";M;" MOVING AVERAGE = ";M
 580 NEXT I
 600 STOP
 800 REM   DATA FOR TABLE 8.9
 820 DATA 10
 821 DATA 6,2,8,2,12,10,4,4,14,12
 900 REM
 920 REM   FORMAT OUTPUT TO SUIT YOUR MACHINE
```

A8.6.2 Exponential Smoothing (see page 275)

A Technical Note

Let V_T = the smoothed value for period T

X_T = the actual value for period T

α = the smoothing constant

then $V_T = V_{T-1} + \alpha(X_T - V_{T-1})$

which can also be written

$$V_T = \alpha X_T + (1-\alpha) V_{T-1} \quad \ldots\ldots\ldots\ldots 1$$

That this can be viewed as a weighted moving average can be demonstrated by recognising that going back one period,

$$V_{T-1} = \alpha X_{T-1} + (1 - \alpha) V_{T-2} \quad \ldots\ldots\ldots \quad 2$$

Substituting for V_{T-1} in equation 1 above we get

$$V_T = \alpha X_T + (1 - \alpha) \times \text{R.H. Side of} \ldots\ldots\ldots \quad 2$$

$$= \alpha X_T + \alpha(1 - \alpha) X_{T-1} + (1 - \alpha)^2 V_{T-2}$$

Now if $\alpha = 0.5$ and $T = 10$ then the weighting for X_{10} and X_9 are 0.5 and 0.5 x 0.5 = 0.25 as shown in Table 8.11 (in percentage form). For the other weightings, substitute for V_{T-2} and proceed as before.

Computation

As with moving averages, spreadsheet systems can be easily programmed to carry out exponential smoothing procedures.

The **BASIC** program in Fig A8.3 below is applied to the data of Table 8.10 on page 275.

```
LIST
  50 DIM X(50)
 100 REM   SIMPLE EXPONENTIAL SMOOTHING
 120 REM   READ IN NO OF DATA ITEMS AND INITIAL SMOOTHED VALUE
 140 READ N,V
 160 REM   NOW READ IN DATA ITEMS
 180 FOR I = 1 TO N
 200 READ X(I)
 220 NEXT I
 240 REM   NOW CALL ON USER FOR THE VALUE OF THE SMOOTHING CONSTANT
 260 PRINT "INPUT SMOOTHING CONSTANT ";
 280 INPUT A
 300 IF A <0 THEN 700
 320 IF A>1 THEN 700
 340 REM   NOW CALCULATE SUCCESSIVE SMOOTHED VALUES
 360 FOR I = 1 TO N
 380 V=A*X(I)+(1-A)*V
 400 PRINT "PERIOD NO ";I;"  SMOOTHED VALUE = ";V
 420 NEXT I
 440 STOP
 700 PRINT "SMOOTHING CONSTANT OUTSIDE RANGE 0 TO 1, TRY AGAIN "
 710 PRINT
 720 GOTO 260
 730 REM
 800 REM   NO OF DATA ITEMS AND INITIAL SMOOTHED VALUE
 820 DATA 10,4
 840 REM   THE  DATA ITEMS
 860 DATA  6,2,8,2,12,10,4,4,14,12
 870 REM
 900 PRINT "SMOOTHING CONSTANT OUTSIDE RANGE 0 TO 1, TRY AGAIN "
 910 PRINT
 920 GOTO 260
 950 REM
 960 REM   FORMAT OUTPUT TO SUIT YOUR MACHINE
```

A8.6.4 Cusums (see page 278)

The Cusum accumulates the deviation of values x from a fixed target K thus

$$\sum_T (X_T - K)$$

the results in Table 8.12 on page 278, can be easily computed on a spreadsheet system or in **BASIC** as shown in Fig A8.4 below

```
LIST
   40 REM   SIMPLE CUSUM ROUTINE
   50 DIM X(50)
  100 REM   READ IN NO OF ITEMS AND SALES DATA
  120 READ N
  140 FOR I = 1 TO N
  160 READ X(I)
  180 NEXT I
  200 PRINT "WHAT IS THE TARGET VALUE";
  220 INPUT K
  240 PRINT "CUSUM VALUES AS FOLLOWS "
  260 C=0
  280 FOR I = 1 TO N
  300 REM   ACCUMULATE CUSUM IN C
  320 C=C+X(I)-K
  340 PRINT I;
  360 PRINT "    ";C
  380 NEXT I
  400 STOP
  600 DATA 21
  610 DATA 18,23,19,21,19,20,18,23,21,24,23,25,21,25,23,19,18,21,19,20
  700 REM
  720 REM FORMAT OUTPUT TO SUIT YOUR MACHINE
```

A8.7.2 Monitoring Trends with Cusums (see page 282)

This procedure is demonstrated in **BASIC** as shown in Fig A8.5 below

```
LIST
   50 REM   A PROGRAM WHICH PRINTS CUSUM DEVIATIONS OF
   51 REM   ACTUAL FIGURES FROM THE PROJECTED STRAIGHT LINE TREND
   52 REM   AS IN TABLE 8.14
  100 DIM X(50)
  200 REM   READ IN THE COEFFICIENTS A & B OF
  201 REM   THE EQUATION OF THE PROJECTED STRAIGHT LINE
  220 READ A,B
  240 REM   READ IN THE NUMBER OF DATA ITEMS, AND THE DATA INTO THE
  260 READ N                                              ARRAY X( )
  280 FOR I = 1 TO N
  300 READ X(I)
  320 NEXT I
  340 REM   PRINT CUSUM OF ACTUAL-PROJECTED VALUES
  360 C=0
```

Fig A8.5 (cont)

```
380 FOR I = 1 TO N
390 REM  SET UP YEAR AND QUARTER.
391 REM   I.E. FOR I=1, T=1.25+0.25 =1.5, THAT IS HALF WAY THROUGH
392 REM   EACH TIME PERIOD ADVANCES BY 0.25 OF A YEAR      YEAR 1
395 T=1.25+I*0.25
400 C=C+X(I)-(A+B*T)
420 PRINT "PERIOD NO ";T
440 PRINT "ACTUAL = ";X(I)
460 PRINT "PROJECTED = ";A+B*T
480 PRINT "ACTUAL-PROJECTED = ";X(I)-(A+B*T)
500 PRINT "CUSUM = ";C
510 PRINT
520 NEXT I
600 STOP
700 REM
720 REM
800 REM  STRAIGHT LINE PROJECTION, INTERCEPT AND GRADIENT
820 DATA -4.5,4.83
840 REM NO OF DATA ITEMS AND DATA
860 DATA 9
880 DATA 2.0,4.0,4.5,7.0,7.5,7.7,7.8,8.3,8.0
```

A8.8.5 Note on Fig 8.15 on page 293

The Time Series was simulated by calculating

$$a + bT + RS$$

where a = the intercept of the projection = 10
  b = the slope of the projection = 5
  T = time
  R = a normally distributed random number with mean = 0 and standard deviation = 1.
  S = standard deviation of the residual disturbance to be superimposed on the straight line (= 10 in this case).

R can be calculated as shown in Fig A8.6 below

```
LIST
  100 REM  PRINT OUT 10 NORMALLY DISTRIBUTED RANDOM NUMBERS
  150 FOR I= 1 TO 10
  200 S=0
  250 FOR W = 1 TO 12
  300 S=RND(1)+S
  350 NEXT W
  400 S=S-6
  450 PRINT S
  500 NEXT I
  550 STOP
>
```

```
RUN
 1.06818117
-0.668179832
-0.869235851
-0.14090123
-0.591054892
 0.5693508
-2.38106775
-1.11733134
 0.123681653
-0.761344811

STOP at line 550
>
```

CHAPTER A9 : FINDING OUT BY SAMPLING

A9.6 Sampling Theory (see page 308)

It is useful to distinguish Population and Sampling parameters as follows

	Population	Sample
Size	N_p	N
Mean of a variable	μ	$\bar{x}$
Standard deviation	σ	s
Proportion possessing an attribute	P	p

A9.6.1 The Binomial Distribution (see page 308)

If the proportion in a large population possessing a particular attribute is P, then the probability that x members in a random sample of N will possess that attribute is given by

$$^NC_x \, P^x \, (1-P)^{N-x}$$

where $^NC_x = \dfrac{N!}{x! \, (N-x)!}$ $N! = N \times (N-1) \times (N-2) \times \ldots \times 3 \times 2 \times 1$

$0! = 1$

Where $N!$ is difficult to calculate or compute, use Stirling's approximation

$$N! = \sqrt{2\pi} \cdot e^{-N} \cdot N^{N + \frac{1}{2}}$$

So for Fig 9.3b on page 310, where $N = 5$ and $P = 0.3$,

$Pr(x = 1$ in a sample of 5, i.e. 20%)

$= \dfrac{5!}{1! \, 4!} \, (0.3)^1 \, (1 - 0.3)^{5-1}$

$= \dfrac{5 \times 4 \times 3 \times 2 \times 1}{1 \times 4 \times 3 \times 2 \times 1} \, (0.3)^1 \, (0.7)^4$

$= 0.36$

and for Fig 9.3c, where $N = 20$ and $P = 0.3$.

$Pr(x = 6$ in a sample of 20, i.e. 30%)

$$= \frac{20!}{6!\ 14!} (0.3)^6 (0.7)^{14}$$

$$= 38760 \times 0.000729 \times 0.006782$$

$$= 0.192$$

Tables of the Binomial distribution for a limited range of sample sizes can be found in Murdoch and Barnes (1975) referred to from now on as M & B. These tables are cumulative, giving the probability of x or more members of the sample possessing the given attribute (N.B: M & B use r instead of x in these tables, so beware).

The Poisson Distribution as an Approximation to the Binomial

The Binomial Distribution is a tedious thing to calculate and M & B quote values for N = 2,5,10,20,50 and 100 only. Where P is less than about 0.2 and N is reasonably large, more than 50, say, then the cumulative Poisson distribution (M & B Table 2) can be used, tabulated for values of NP, the expected number of arisings in the sample.

Lets see how good the approximation is for P = 0.15, N = 40 and x = 4.

Poisson

$$Pr(x=4) = \frac{e^{-NP}\cdot(NP)^x}{x!} = \frac{e^{-40 \times 0.15}\cdot(40 \times 0.15)^4}{4!}$$

$$= \frac{0.00248 \times 1296}{4 \times 3 \times 2 \times 1} = 0.1339$$

The same result can be found in M & B, Table 2, under column 6.0, the expected number of arisings in the sample. The probability of x = 4 being

$$Pr(x \geqslant 4) - Pr(x \geqslant 5) = 0.8488 - 0.7149.$$

Binomial

The above approximation can now be compared with the true result of

$$^{40}C_4 (0.15)^4 (0.85)^{36} = 0.1331$$

The Poisson result showing an error of less than 1%.

The Normal Distribution as an Approximation to the Binomial

If *NP* is reasonably large and $P > 0.1$, then the value of x approximately follows a normal distribution with

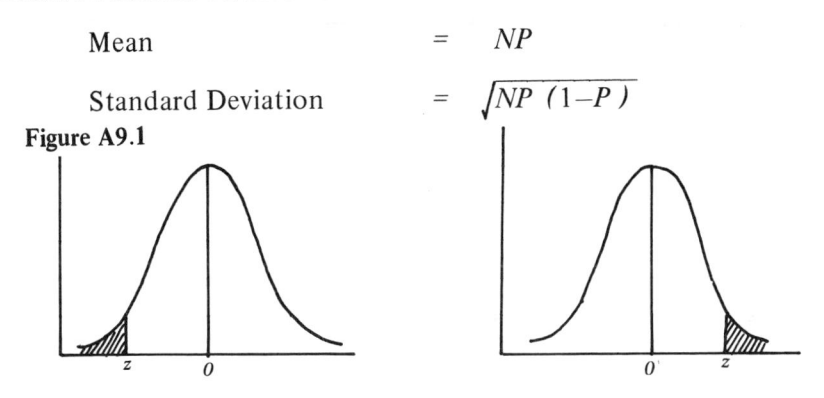

Mean $= NP$

Standard Deviation $= \sqrt{NP(1-P)}$

Figure A9.1

Appendix 6 on page 462 shows the precise probability that a standardised normally distributed variable

$$z = \frac{(x - \mu)}{\sigma}$$

will yield a random observation which lies beyond a specified value i.e. the shaded area above. ('z' is effectively the number of standard deviations that x is from the mean in absolute terms). In this application with $\mu = NP$ and $\sigma = \sqrt{NP(1-P)}$, the standard error for x, we get

$$z = \frac{x - NP + 0.5}{\sqrt{NP(1-P)}}$$

with $N = 40$, $P = 0.15$, $NP = 6$ and $\sqrt{NP(1-P)} = 2.26$. To obtain the probability that $x \geqslant 4$, we need to take account of the fact that we are fitting a *continuous* normal distribution to a *discrete* binomial distribution.

Figure A9.2 : A detail of the normal curve fit

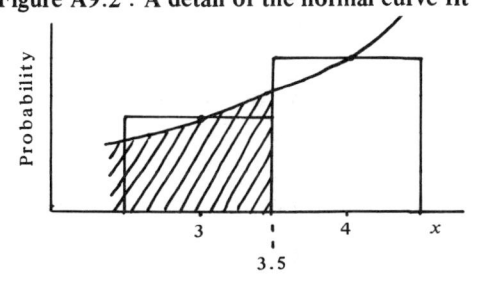

We need first to calculate the shaded left-hand tail, the addition of 0.5 to the top of the expression should now be clear.

$$Pr\left(z > \frac{|3.5 - 6|}{2.26}\right) = Pr(z > 1.11)$$
$$= 0.1335$$

So $Pr(x \geqslant 4) = 1 - 0.1335 = 0.8665$ which compares with the true Binomial value of 0.8698 an error less than 1%.

A9.7.5 Problems with Small Samples (see page 321)

Little can be deduced from *small* samples taken from populations whose distribution deviates from a known distribution except that the percentage of items falling beyond C standard deviations from the mean is *not more* than $\frac{100}{C^2}$ *(Chebyschev's Inequality).*

Even if the population is normally distributed or at least not far from being so, the following special factors still need to be taken into account.

1. If the sample itself is used to estimate σ, the population standard deviation, then the '*t*' distribution must be used (M&B Table 7) to replace the factors 2.0 and 2.6 used for 95% and 99% confidence limits respectively. The appropriate factors are given in the columns headed 0.025 and 0.005 respectively tabulated against degrees of freedom $(N-1)$. Thus for a sample of size 4, say, 3.182 would replace 2.0 and 5.841 would replace 2.6. This coupled with a large standard error leads to very broad confidence limits (see page 313). These factors can also be obtained from Appendix 2.

2. In estimating the standard deviation of the population from a sample, the following modified formula with $N - 1$ in the denominator should be used to obtain an unbiased result

$$\text{Estimate of } \sigma = \sqrt{\frac{\Sigma(x - \bar{x})^2}{N - 1}}$$

A9.8 Finite Population Correction Factor—Small Population sizes
(see page 322)

The precise formula is

$$\sqrt{\frac{N_p - N}{N_p - 1}} \quad (N_p = \text{Population size})$$

As this formula produces such surprising results, it is worth demonstrating. Take a mini-population of size 4 thus:

$$2 \quad 4 \quad 11 \quad 15$$

for which $\mu = 8$, $\sigma = \sqrt{\dfrac{\Sigma x^2}{N} - (\bar{\mu})^2} = 5.244$

The theoretical standard error of the mean for samples of size 2 is therefore

$$\dfrac{5.244}{\sqrt{2}} \cdot \sqrt{\dfrac{4-2}{4-1}} = 3.028$$

and by definition this should be the same as the standard deviation of the means of all possible samples of size 2.

Sample	2,4	2,11	2,15	4,11	4,15	11,15
$\bar{x}$	3.0	6.5	8.5	7.5	9.5	13.0

The mean of all these sample means is 8 and the standard deviation is indeed 3.028.......... QED.

SUMMARY OF RESULTS: ATTRIBUTES

Standard Error of the Percentage $= \sqrt{\dfrac{\text{Population \%} \times (100 - \text{Population \%})}{\text{Sample size}}} = 100\sqrt{\dfrac{P(1-P)}{N}}$

Standard Error of the Proportion $= \sqrt{\dfrac{\text{Population Proportion} \times (1 - \text{Population Proportion})}{\text{Sample size}}} = \sqrt{\dfrac{P(1-P)}{N}}$

Standard Error of the Number in a Sample possessing a given attribute $= \sqrt{\text{Sample size} \times \text{Population Proportion} \times (1 - \text{Population Proportion})} = \sqrt{NP(1-P)}$

95% Confidence Limits ± 2.0 x standard error
99% Confidence Limits ± 2.6 x standard error

Required Sample size to Predict Population to ± Required Error with 95% (or 99%) Confidence

$\dfrac{4 \text{ x (or 6.8)} \quad \text{\% estimate} \times (100 - \text{\% estimate})}{(\text{Required error})^2}$

SUMMARY OF RESULTS : VARIABLES

Standard Error of the Mean $= \dfrac{\text{Standard Deviation of the Population}}{\text{Sample size}} = \dfrac{\sigma}{\sqrt{N}}$

Confidence Limits (As for attributes)

Required Sample size for 95% (or 99%) Confidence Limits

$\dfrac{4 \text{ x (or 6.8)} \quad (\text{Estimated standard deviation of the population})}{(\text{Required error})^2} = \dfrac{4\sigma^2}{E^2}$

Finite Population Correction Factor $\sqrt{\dfrac{\text{Population size} - \text{Sample size}}{\text{Population size} - 1}} = \sqrt{\dfrac{N_p - N}{N - 1}}$

N.B: (the −1 can be left out except when dealing with small populations)

CHAPTER A10 : DRAWING CONCLUSIONS

A10.4.5 Note on Table 10.4 (see page 340)

This table shows the Binomial distribution and part of its cumulative version with $N = 20, P = 0.10$. For example

Pr (5 defects in a sample of 20)

$$= {}^{20}C_5 \ (0.1)^5 \ (0.9)^{15}$$
$$= 15504 \times 0.00001 \times 0.2059$$
$$= 0.0319$$

Table 1 in M & B gives the cumulative figure 0.0432.

A10.4.10 Bayes Theorem

The theorem will be set out within a hypothetical example. Suppose a distributor of chickens to butchers obtains the birds from two farms, Buckdale (B) and Rosemount (R) packed in boxes of 10. The birds are made up of two varieties, Plymouth Rock (PR) and Rhode Island Red (RIR), but in the plucked form these are identical as far as the customers are concerned. Each farm provides a different proportion of the market and the percentage of each variety at the farms is different.

Farm	Variety PR	RIR	Fraction of Total Market Supplied
Buckdale	80%	20%	$\frac{3}{4}$
Rosemount	40%	60%	$\frac{1}{4}$

The boxes of birds delivered to the butchers are effectively a mixture of boxes from the two farms and the butchers do not know the source of their supply. The purchase of a chicken by a customer can be seen as a two-stage process as follows.

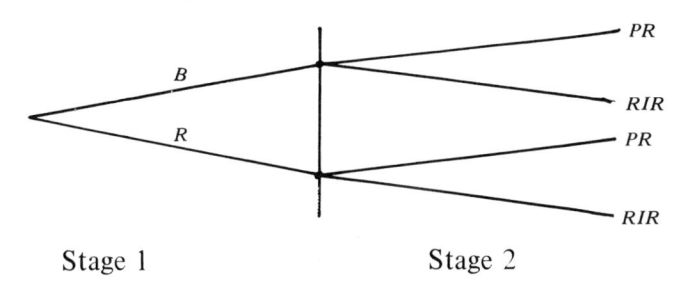

Stage 1   Stage 2

In stage 1, a box supplied to a butcher comes from either Buckdale or Rosemount. The *prior probability* of these origins can be stated as

$$Pr(B) = \frac{3}{4}$$

$$Pr(R) = \frac{1}{4}$$

We can now calculate the probability of a customer being served a particular variety of bird given that it was taken from a box coming from a specified farm.

$$Pr(PR/B) = \frac{80}{100} \qquad Pr(RIR/B) = \frac{20}{100}$$

$$Pr(PR/R) = \frac{40}{100} \qquad Pr(RIR/R) = \frac{60}{100}$$

N.B / means 'conditional on'

These probabilities of second-stage events conditional on knowledge of the first stage are known as *likelihoods*.

Suppose that a customer finds that the bird purchased is contaminated. There is no way of knowing the exact source of the bird, but the prior probability that it came from Buckdale is $\frac{3}{4}$ ($Pr(B) = \frac{3}{4}$). But suppose that the health inspector provides the additional information that the bird was a 'Plymouth Rock'. Can this information be used to modify the prior probability that the bird came from Buckdale? This would then be a *posterior probability* of a first-stage event conditional on a second stage event.

$$Pr(B/PR)$$

and as such it is a revised prior probability.

We will work out the answer using common sense first. For every 400 birds, 300 come from Buckdale and 100 from Rosemount.

	Number of Birds	Number of 'Plymouth Rock'
Buckdale	300	80% of 300 = 240
Rosemount	100	40% of 100 = 40
	400	280

Therefore if a customer has a 'Plymouth Rock', the chances that it came from Buckdale are $\frac{240}{280} = \frac{6}{7}$.

448

The same result is obtained from Bayes' Theorem which says that for a two-stage process with first stage events, E_1 and E_2 and second stage events F_1 and F_2

$$Pr(E_1/F_1) = \frac{Pr(E_1) \cdot Pr(F_1/E_1)}{Pr(E_1) \cdot Pr(F_1/E_1) + Pr(E_2) \cdot Pr(F_1/E_2)}$$

or in our example

$$Pr(B/PR) = \frac{Pr(B) \cdot Pr(PR/B)}{Pr(B) \cdot Pr(PR/B) + Pr(R) \cdot Pr(PR/R)}$$

$$= \frac{\frac{3}{4} \times \frac{80}{100}}{\frac{3}{4} \times \frac{80}{100} + \frac{1}{4} \times \frac{40}{100}}$$

$$= \frac{6}{7} = 0.86$$

The arguments about the validity of Bayes' Theorem start when *subjective* prior probabilities are employed. Short readable critiques of the Bayesian approach (and much else besides) can be found in Sprent (1979) and Ehrenburg (1982).

A10.5.1 Test for Attributes

The test statistic for comparing a sample proportion p against a population proportion P is given by

$$\frac{|p - P|}{\sqrt{\frac{P(1 - P)}{N}}}$$

and should be compared with the critical values for one and two-tail tests shown in Appendix 1 on page 453.

A10.5.2 Test for Variables

The test statistic for comparing a sample mean $\bar{x}$ with a population mean μ is

$$\frac{|\bar{x} - \mu|}{\frac{\sigma}{\sqrt{N}}} \quad \text{(for large samples, > 30 say)}$$

and should be compared with the critical values of the normal distribution shown in Appendix 1 on page 453.

With small samples, if s, the sample standard deviation, is used to estimate σ, then a denominator of $N-1$ should be used (see p. 444) and the result should be compared with the critical values of the 't' distribution in Appendix 2 on page 454, with $(N-1)$ degrees of freedom.

A10.5.4 Test for the Difference between Sample Means

Given two large samples of size N_1 and N_2 with means of $\bar{x}_1$ and $\bar{x}_2$, and sample standard deviation s_1 and s_2. The test statistic

$$\frac{(\bar{x}_1 - \bar{x}_2) - (\mu_1 - \mu_2)}{\sqrt{\frac{s_1^2}{N_1} + \frac{s_2^2}{N_2}}} \quad \text{(for large samples)}$$

Should be compared with the critical values for the normal distribution for one and two-tailed tests as shown in Appendix 1 on page 453.

For small samples, the two populations must be normal or near normal and have the same standard deviation. The test statistic is the same as above but it should be compared with critical values for the 't' distribution with $(N_1 + N_2 - 2)$ degrees of freedom, shown in Appendix 2 on page 454.

N.B.: (Strictly speaking s_1 and s_2 should be replaced by a pooled estimate of the common standard deviation given by

$$\sqrt{\frac{(N_1 - 1)s_1^2 + (N_2 - 1)s_2^2}{N_1 + N_2 - 2}}$$

The Mann-Whitney 'U' Test (see page 348)

Given two samples N_1 and N_2, the sum of the ranks from the combined samples which attach to the first sample are denoted by R_1, and that of the other by R_2. Then

$$U_1 = N_1 N_2 + \frac{N_1(N_1 + 1)}{2} - R_1$$

$$U_2 = N_1 N_2 + \frac{N_2(N_2 + 1)}{2} - R_2$$

So in the example on page

$$U_1 = 6 \times 5 + \frac{6 \times 7}{2} - 26 = 25$$

$$U_2 = 6 \times 5 + \frac{5 \times 6}{2} - 40 = 5$$

The smaller of these two, $U = 5$, forms the test statistic. Tables are bulky and can be found in Siegel (1956). The 5% and 1% critical values (one-tail) for these sample sizes are 5 and 2 respectively

For large sample sizes, the test statistic

$$\frac{U - \frac{N_1 N_2}{2}}{\sqrt{\frac{1}{12} N_1 N_2 (N_1 + N_2 + 1)}}$$

can be compared with the critical values of the normal distribution in Appendix 1 on page 453.

A10.5.5 The Chi-Square Test

The general formula for computing Chi-square from the observed and expected frequencies of a contingency table is

$$\chi^2 = \Sigma \left[\frac{(O - E)^2}{E} \right]$$

A10.5.6 Paired Samples: 't' test

A 't' test can be applied if the distribution of the N paired differences D is normally distributed. Under the Null Hypothesis, the mean difference between paired readings in the long run should be 0, so the test statistic is

$$\frac{\bar{D} - 0}{\frac{S_D}{\sqrt{N}}} \quad \text{where } S_D = \sqrt{\frac{\Sigma(D_i - \bar{D})}{N - 1}}$$

and the result compared with the appropriate critical value of the 't' distribution.

APPENDIX 1 : CRITICAL VALUES OF THE NORMAL DISTRIBUTION

Under 'One-tail' is shown the percentage of values in a Normal distribution which lie at *one* extreme of the Normal distribution located c standard deviations from the mean.

Under 'Two-tail' is shown the percentage of values which lie at *both* extremes of the Normal distribution located c deviations either side of the mean.

One–Tail	Critical Value (c)	Two-Tail	Critcial Value (c)
10%	1.28	10%	1.64
5%	1.64	5%	1.96
1%	2.33	1%	2.58
0.1%	3.09	0.1%	3.29

For confidence limits, the two-tail values for the appropriate significance level should be used as a factor for the standard error. For 95% use the 5% value, for 99%, use the 1% value.

In relevant significance tests, the absolute value of the test statistic should exceed the critical value shown for a statistically significant effect to be established.

A detailed table of the Normal distribution can be found in Appendix 6 on page 462.

APPENDIX 2 : HOW THE CRITICAL VALUES FOR THE 't' DISTRIBUTION VARY WITH THE DEGREES OF FREEDOM

The graph shows how the critical values in Appendix 1 increase with decreasing degrees of freedom.

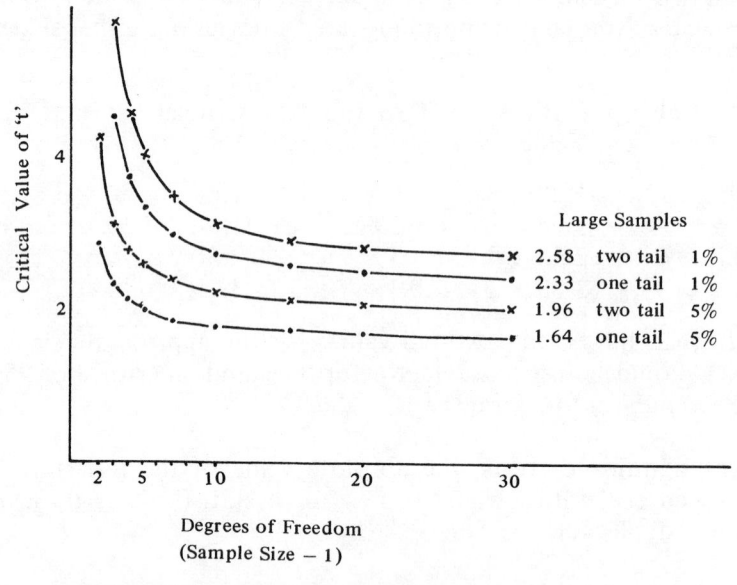

Large Samples
- 2.58 two tail 1%
- 2.33 one tail 1%
- 1.96 two tail 5%
- 1.64 one tail 5%

For 95% confidence limits use two tail 5% values
For 99%   "   "   " two tail 1% values

For 95% confidence limits, use two-tail 5% values
For 99% confidence limits, use two-tail 1% values
with $(N-1)$ degrees of freedom in each instance.

For most purposes, given the accuracy of data available, the approximate values above will suffice. For precise values see M&B Table 7 or many advanced statistics text books.

APPENDIX 3 : HOW THE CRITICAL VALUES FOR THE CHI–SQUARE DISTRIBUTION (χ^2) VARY WITH DEGREES OF FREEDOM

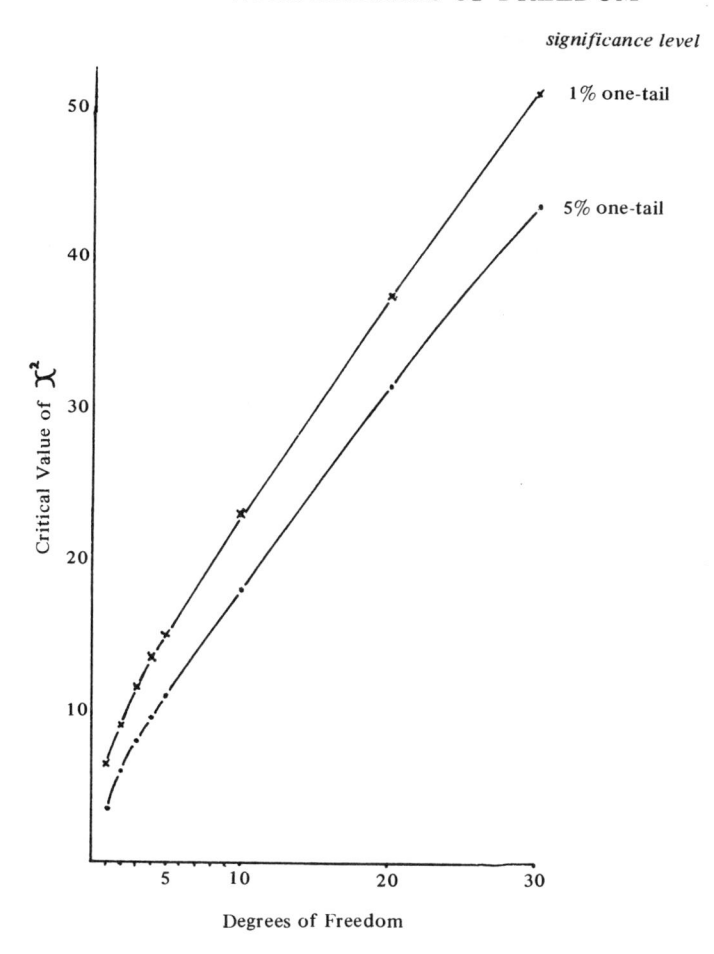

When testing for significant differences within a contingency table, the value of χ^2 should exceed the critical value for specified level of significance.

For precise probabilities see **M & B**, Table 8.

APPENDIX 4 : CRITICAL VALUES OF THE SIGN TEST

The probability that the number of + or − signs, whichever is the smaller, is less than or equal to the critical value shown for the given sample size, is less than or equal to the value shown in the column heading (one-tail).

CRITICAL VALUES

Number of pairs	10% 5%	2% 1%	1% ½%	two-tail one-tail
5	0			
6	0			
7	0	0		
8	1	0	0	
9	1	0	0	
10	1	0	0	
11	2	1	0	
12	2	1	1	
13	3	1	1	
14	3	2	1	
15	3	2	2	
16	4	2	2	
17	4	3	2	
18	5	3	3	
19	5	4	3	
20	5	4	3	
25	7	6	5	
30	10	8	7	
40	14	12	11	
50	18	16	15	

APPENDIX 5a : COMPOUND AMOUNT FACTORS OR INFLATION FACTORS

The table shows the value of £1 in Y periods time earning compound interest at the given % rate per period.

OR

The Table can be read as giving the price in Y periods time of an item costing £1 now assuming inflation in the future at the given % rate per period.

Y	1%	2%	3%	4%	5%	6%	7%	8%	9%	10%	11%	12%
1	1.01	1.02	1.03	1.04	1.05	1.06	1.07	1.08	1.09	1.10	1.11	1.12
2	1.02	1.04	1.06	1.08	1.10	1.12	1.14	1.17	1.19	1.21	1.23	1.25
3	1.03	1.06	1.09	1.12	1.16	1.19	1.23	1.26	1.30	1.33	1.37	1.40
4	1.04	1.08	1.13	1.17	1.22	1.26	1.31	1.36	1.41	1.46	1.52	1.57
5	1.05	1.10	1.16	1.22	1.28	1.34	1.40	1.47	1.54	1.61	1.69	1.76
6	1.06	1.13	1.19	1.27	1.34	1.42	1.50	1.59	1.68	1.77	1.87	1.97
7	1.07	1.15	1.23	1.32	1.41	1.50	1.61	1.71	1.83	1.95	2.08	2.21
8	1.08	1.17	1.27	1.37	1.48	1.59	1.72	1.85	1.99	2.14	2.30	2.48
9	1.09	1.20	1.30	1.42	1.55	1.69	1.84	2.00	2.17	2.36	2.56	2.77
10	1.10	1.22	1.34	1.48	1.63	1.79	1.97	2.16	2.37	2.59	2.84	3.11
11	1.12	1.24	1.38	1.54	1.71	1.90	2.10	2.33	2.58	2.85	3.15	3.48
12	1.13	1.27	1.43	1.60	1.80	2.01	2.25	2.52	2.81	3.14	3.50	3.90
13	1.14	1.29	1.47	1.67	1.89	2.13	2.41	2.72	3.07	3.45	3.88	4.36
14	1.15	1.32	1.51	1.73	1.98	2.26	2.58	2.94	3.34	3.80	4.31	4.89
15	1.16	1.35	1.56	1.80	2.08	2.40	2.76	3.17	3.64	4.18	4.78	5.47
16	1.17	1.37	1.60	1.87	2.18	2.54	2.95	3.43	3.97	4.59	5.31	6.13
17	1.18	1.40	1.65	1.95	2.29	2.69	3.16	3.70	4.33	5.05	5.90	6.87
18	1.20	1.43	1.70	2.03	2.41	2.85	3.38	4.00	4.72	5.56	6.54	7.69
19	1.21	1.46	1.75	2.11	2.53	3.03	3.62	4.32	5.14	6.12	7.26	8.61
20	1.22	1.49	1.81	2.19	2.65	3.21	3.87	4.66	5.60	6.73	8.06	9.65

Y	13%	14%	15%	16%	17%	18%	19%	20%	21%	22%	23%	24%
1	1.13	1.14	1.15	1.16	1.17	1.18	1.19	1.20	1.21	1.22	1.23	1.24
2	1.28	1.30	1.32	1.35	1.37	1.39	1.42	1.44	1.46	1.49	1.51	1.54
3	1.44	1.48	1.52	1.56	1.60	1.64	1.69	1.73	1.77	1.82	1.86	1.91
4	1.63	1.69	1.75	1.81	1.87	1.94	2.01	2.07	2.14	2.22	2.29	2.36
5	1.84	1.93	2.01	2.10	2.19	2.29	2.39	2.49	2.59	2.70	2.82	2.93
6	2.08	2.19	2.31	2.44	2.57	2.70	2.84	2.99	3.14	3.30	3.46	3.64
7	2.35	2.50	2.66	2.83	3.00	3.19	3.38	3.58	3.80	4.02	4.26	4.51
8	2.66	2.85	3.06	3.28	3.51	3.76	4.02	4.30	4.59	4.91	5.24	5.59
9	3.00	3.25	3.52	3.80	4.11	4.44	4.79	5.16	5.56	5.99	6.44	6.93
10	3.39	3.71	4.05	4.41	4.81	5.23	5.69	6.19	6.73	7.30	7.93	8.59
11	3.84	4.23	4.65	5.12	5.62	6.18	6.78	7.43	8.14	8.91	9.75	10.7
12	4.33	4.82	5.35	5.94	6.58	7.29	8.06	8.92	9.85	10.9	12.0	13.2
13	4.90	5.49	6.15	6.89	7.70	8.60	9.60	10.7	11.9	13.3	14.7	16.4
14	5.53	6.26	7.08	7.99	9.01	10.1	11.4	12.8	14.4	16.2	18.1	20.3
15	6.25	7.14	8.14	9.27	10.5	12.0	13.6	15.4	17.4	19.7	22.3	25.2
16	7.07	8.14	9.36	10.7	12.3	14.1	16.2	18.5	21.1	24.1	27.4	31.2
17	7.99	9.28	10.8	12.5	14.4	16.7	19.2	22.2	25.5	29.4	33.8	38.7
18	9.02	10.6	12.4	14.5	16.9	19.7	22.9	26.6	30.9	35.8	41.5	48.0
19	10.2	12.1	14.2	16.8	19.7	23.2	27.3	31.9	37.4	43.7	51.1	59.6
20	11.5	13.7	16.4	19.5	23.1	27.4	32.4	38.3	45.3	53.4	62.8	73.9

So £150 earning interest at 17% per annum for 14 years will become

$$£150 \times 9.01 = £1,351.50$$

OR

A car costing £5,000 today and subjected to inflation at 8% per annum for 3 years will cost

$$£5,000 \times 1.26 = £6,300$$

APPENDIX 5b : DISCOUNT FACTORS

The table shows the present value of £1 received at the end of Y periods time, discounting at the given % rate of discount.

Y	1%	2%	3%	4%	5%	6%	7%	8%	9%	10%	11%	12%
1	.990	.980	.971	.962	.952	.943	.935	.926	.917	.909	.901	.893
2	.980	.961	.943	.925	.907	.890	.873	.857	.842	.826	.812	.797
3	.971	.942	.915	.889	.864	.840	.816	.794	.772	.751	.731	.712
4	.961	.924	.888	.855	.823	.792	.763	.735	.708	.683	.659	.636
5	.951	.906	.863	.822	.784	.747	.713	.681	.650	.621	.593	.567
6	.942	.888	.837	.790	.746	.705	.666	.630	.596	.564	.535	.507
7	.933	.871	.813	.760	.711	.665	.623	.583	.547	.513	.482	.452
8	.923	.853	.789	.731	.677	.627	.582	.540	.502	.467	.434	.404
9	.914	.837	.766	.703	.645	.592	.544	.500	.460	.424	.391	.361
10	.905	.820	.744	.676	.614	.558	.508	.463	.422	.386	.352	.322
11	.896	.804	.722	.650	.585	.527	.475	.429	.388	.350	.317	.287
12	.887	.788	.701	.625	.557	.497	.444	.397	.356	.319	.286	.257
13	.879	.773	.681	.601	.530	.469	.415	.368	.326	.290	.258	.229
14	.870	.758	.661	.577	.505	.442	.388	.340	.299	.263	.232	.205
15	.861	.743	.642	.555	.481	.417	.362	.315	.275	.239	.209	.183
16	.853	.728	.623	.534	.458	.394	.339	.292	.252	.218	.188	.163
17	.844	.714	.605	.513	.436	.371	.317	.270	.231	.198	.170	.146
18	.836	.700	.587	.494	.416	.350	.296	.250	.212	.180	.153	.130
19	.828	.686	.570	.475	.396	.331	.277	.232	.194	.164	.138	.116
20	.820	.673	.554	.456	.377	.312	.258	.215	.178	.149	.124	.104

Y	13%	14%	15%	16%	17%	18%	19%	20%	21%	22%	23%	24%
1	.885	.877	.870	.862	.855	.847	.840	.833	.826	.820	.813	.806
2	.783	.769	.756	.743	.731	.718	.706	.694	.683	.672	.661	.650
3	.693	.675	.658	.641	.624	.609	.593	.579	.564	.551	.537	.524
4	.613	.592	.572	.552	.534	.516	.499	.482	.467	.451	.437	.423
5	.543	.519	.497	.476	.456	.437	.419	.402	.386	.370	.355	.341
6	.480	.456	.432	.410	.390	.370	.352	.335	.319	.303	.289	.275
7	.425	.400	.376	.354	.333	.314	.296	.279	.263	.249	.235	.222
8	.376	.351	.327	.305	.285	.266	.249	.233	.218	.204	.191	.179
9	.333	.308	.284	.263	.243	.225	.209	.194	.180	.167	.155	.144
10	.295	.270	.247	.227	.208	.191	.176	.162	.149	.137	.126	.116
11	.261	.237	.215	.195	.178	.162	.148	.135	.123	.112	.103	.094
12	.231	.208	.187	.168	.152	.137	.124	.112	.102	.092	.083	.076
13	.204	.182	.163	.145	.130	.116	.104	.093	.084	.075	.068	.061
14	.181	.160	.141	.125	.111	.099	.088	.078	.069	.062	.055	.049
15	.160	.140	.123	.108	.095	.084	.074	.065	.057	.051	.045	.040
16	.141	.123	.107	.093	.081	.071	.062	.054	.047	.042	.036	.032
17	.125	.108	.093	.080	.069	.060	.052	.045	.039	.034	.030	.026
18	.111	.095	.081	.069	.059	.051	.044	.038	.032	.028	.024	.021
19	.098	.083	.070	.060	.051	.043	.037	.031	.027	.023	.020	.017
20	.087	.073	.061	.051	.043	.037	.031	.026	.022	.019	.016	.014

So the present value of £137 received at the end of 4 years time and discounted at 11% is given by

$$£137 \times 0.659 = £90.28$$

APPENDIX 5c : CAPITAL RECOVERY FACTORS

The Table shows the amount to be repaid at the end of each of the next Y periods to repay £1 borrowed today at the given % rate of interest.

The reciprocal of these factors (1 divided by the factor) gives the present value of an equal payment series of £1 received at the end of each of the next Y periods discounted at the given % rate of interest.

Y	1%	2%	3%	4%	5%	6%	7%	8%	9%	10%	11%	12%
2	.508	.515	.523	.530	.538	.545	.553	.561	.568	.576	.584	.592
3	.340	.347	.354	.360	.367	.374	.381	.388	.395	.402	.409	.416
4	.256	.263	.269	.275	.282	.289	.295	.302	.309	.315	.322	.329
5	.206	.212	.218	.225	.231	.237	.244	.250	.257	.264	.271	.277
6	.173	.179	.185	.191	.197	.203	.210	.216	.223	.230	.236	.243
7	.149	.155	.161	.167	.173	.179	.186	.192	.199	.205	.212	.219
8	.131	.137	.142	.149	.155	.161	.167	.174	.181	.187	.194	.201
9	.117	.123	.128	.134	.141	.147	.153	.160	.167	.174	.181	.188
10	.106	.111	.117	.123	.130	.136	.142	.149	.156	.163	.170	.177
11	.096	.102	.108	.114	.120	.127	.133	.140	.147	.154	.161	.168
12	.089	.095	.100	.107	.113	.119	.126	.133	.140	.147	.154	.161
13	.082	.088	.094	.100	.106	.113	.120	.127	.134	.141	.148	.156
14	.077	.083	.089	.095	.101	.108	.114	.121	.128	.136	.143	.151
15	.072	.078	.084	.090	.096	.103	.110	.117	.124	.131	.139	.147
16	.068	.074	.080	.086	.092	.099	.106	.113	.120	.128	.136	.143
17	.064	.070	.076	.082	.089	.095	.102	.110	.117	.125	.132	.140
18	.061	.067	.073	.079	.086	.092	.099	.107	.114	.122	.130	.138
19	.058	.064	.070	.076	.083	.090	.097	.104	.112	.120	.128	.136
20	.055	.061	.067	.074	.080	.087	.094	.102	.110	.117	.126	.134

Y	13%	14%	15%	16%	17%	18%	19%	20%	21%	22%	23%	24%
2	.599	.607	.615	.623	.631	.639	.647	.655	.662	.670	.678	.686
3	.424	.431	.438	.445	.453	.460	.467	.475	.482	.490	.497	.505
4	.336	.343	.350	.357	.365	.372	.379	.386	.394	.401	.408	.416
5	.284	.291	.298	.305	.313	.320	.327	.334	.342	.349	.357	.364
6	.250	.257	.264	.271	.279	.286	.293	.301	.308	.316	.323	.331
7	.226	.233	.240	.248	.255	.262	.270	.277	.285	.293	.301	.308
8	.208	.216	.223	.230	.238	.245	.253	.261	.268	.276	.284	.292
9	.195	.202	.210	.217	.225	.232	.240	.248	.256	.264	.272	.280
10	.184	.192	.199	.207	.215	.223	.230	.239	.247	.255	.263	.272
11	.176	.183	.191	.199	.207	.215	.223	.231	.239	.248	.256	.265
12	.169	.177	.184	.192	.200	.209	.217	.225	.234	.242	.251	.260
13	.163	.171	.179	.187	.195	.204	.212	.221	.229	.238	.247	.256
14	.159	.167	.175	.183	.191	.200	.208	.217	.226	.234	.243	.252
15	.155	.163	.171	.179	.188	.196	.205	.214	.223	.232	.241	.250
16	.151	.160	.168	.176	.185	.194	.203	.211	.220	.230	.239	.248
17	.149	.157	.165	.174	.183	.191	.200	.209	.219	.228	.237	.246
18	.146	.155	.163	.172	.181	.190	.199	.208	.217	.226	.236	.245
19	.144	.153	.161	.170	.179	.188	.197	.206	.216	.225	.235	.244
20	.142	.151	.160	.169	.178	.187	.196	.205	.215	.224	.234	.243

So to repay £10,000 over 4 years at an 18% rate of interest requires 4 annual end-of-year payments of

$$£10,000 \times 0.372 = £3,720$$

The present value of £200 per period for 15 periods discounting at 23% per period is

$$£200 \quad \times \quad \frac{1}{0.241} \quad = \quad £829.88$$

APPENDIX 6 : NORMAL DISTRIBUTION TABLES

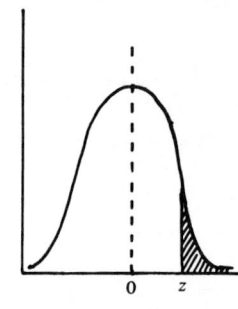

This table shows the probability that a standardised Normal variable will be greater than

$$z = \frac{x-\mu}{\sigma}$$ Thus with $z = 1.96$

there is a proportion 0.025 in the tail of the distribution. Thus 2.5% of values lie above a point 1.96 standard deviations above the mean. 0.47% of values lie above a point 2.6 standard deviations above the mean.

z	0.00	0.01	0.02	0.03	0.04	0.05	0.06	0.07	0.08	0.09
0.0	0.5000	0.4960	0.4920	0.4880	0.4840	0.4801	0.4761	0.4721	0.4681	0.4641
0.1	0.4602	0.4562	0.4522	0.4483	0.4443	0.4404	0.4364	0.4325	0.4286	0.4247
0.2	0.4207	0.4168	0.4129	0.4090	0.4052	0.4013	0.3974	0.3936	0.3897	0.3859
0.3	0.3821	0.3783	0.3745	0.3707	0.3669	0.3632	0.3594	0.3557	0.3520	0.3483
0.4	0.3446	0.3409	0.3372	0.3336	0.3300	0.3264	0.3228	0.3192	0.3156	0.3121
0.5	0.3085	0.3050	0.3015	0.2981	0.2946	0.2912	0.2877	0.2843	0.2810	0.2776
0.6	0.2743	0.2709	0.2676	0.2643	0.2611	0.2578	0.2546	0.2514	0.2483	0.2451
0.7	0.2420	0.2389	0.2358	0.2327	0.2296	0.2266	0.2236	0.2206	0.2177	0.2148
0.8	0.2119	0.2090	0.2061	0.2033	0.2005	0.1977	0.1949	0.1922	0.1894	0.1867
0.9	0.1841	0.1814	0.1788	0.1762	0.1736	0.1711	0.1685	0.1660	0.1635	0.1611
1.0	0.1587	0.1562	0.1539	0.1515	0.1492	0.1469	0.1446	0.1423	0.1401	0.1379
1.1	0.1357	0.1335	0.1314	0.1292	0.1271	0.1251	0.1230	0.1210	0.1190	0.1170
1.2	0.1151	0.1131	0.1112	0.1093	0.1075	0.1056	0.1038	0.1020	0.1003	0.0985
1.3	0.0968	0.0951	0.0934	0.0918	0.0901	0.0885	0.0869	0.0853	0.0838	0.0823
1.4	0.0808	0.0793	0.0778	0.0764	0.0749	0.0735	0.0721	0.0708	0.0694	0.0681
1.5	0.0668	0.0655	0.0643	0.0630	0.0618	0.0606	0.0594	0.0582	0.0571	0.0559
1.6	0.0548	0.0537	0.0526	0.0516	0.0505	0.0495	0.0485	0.0475	0.0465	0.0455
1.7	0.0446	0.0436	0.0427	0.0418	0.0409	0.0401	0.0392	0.0384	0.0375	0.0367
1.8	0.0359	0.0351	0.0344	0.0336	0.0329	0.0322	0.0314	0.0307	0.0301	0.0294
1.9	0.0287	0.0281	0.0274	0.0268	0.0262	0.0256	0.0250	0.0244	0.0239	0.0233
2.0	0.0228	0.0222	0.0217	0.0212	0.0207	0.0202	0.0197	0.0192	0.0188	0.0183
2.1	0.0179	0.0174	0.0170	0.0166	0.0162	0.0158	0.0154	0.0150	0.0146	0.0143
2.2	0.0139	0.0136	0.0132	0.0129	0.0125	0.0122	0.0119	0.0116	0.0113	0.0110
2.3	0.0107	0.0104	0.0102	0.0099	0.0096	0.0094	0.0091	0.0089	0.0087	0.0084
2.4	0.0082	0.0080	0.0078	0.0075	0.0073	0.0071	0.0069	0.0068	0.0066	0.0064
2.5	0.0062	0.0060	0.0059	0.0057	0.0055	0.0054	0.0052	0.0051	0.0049	0.0048
2.6	0.0047	0.0045	0.0044	0.0043	0.0041	0.0040	0.0039	0.0038	0.0037	0.0036
2.7	0.0035	0.0034	0.0033	0.0032	0.0031	0.0030	0.0029	0.0028	0.0027	0.0026
2.8	0.0026	0.0025	0.0024	0.0023	0.0023	0.0022	0.0021	0.0021	0.0020	0.0019
2.9	0.0019	0.0018	0.0018	0.0017	0.0016	0.0016	0.0015	0.0015	0.0014	0.0014
3.0	0.00135									
3.1	0.00097									
3.2	0.00069									
3.3	0.00048									
3.4	0.00034									
3.5	0.00023									
3.6	0.00016									
3.7	0.00011									
3.8	0.00007									
3.9	0.00005									
4.0	0.00003									

APPENDIX 7 : TABLE OF RANDOM DIGITS

6501500337	3595974586	6580973186	2380996315	9877412797
7332389986	9747641047	9470353408	2612433497	6167657494
4261856865	9197828386	6883593214	8783154079	6845368589
3542088370	7913339509	2237519315	1339883934	5874412968
9950571447	0376968228	1959944732	4315685915	3574023689
3571552035	5374185397	3357706828	1158897465	7015605948
4683097088	0632422620	5450240570	6739737797	5990658914
4081420061	8832328128	5000711014	9053128732	2510241000
3796148655	7388464596	4024433919	7147439586	4028449846
9767393772	4757818310	9400552863	9617750115	1565389367
9788639045	8963659922	6470765921	7063717691	6755286193
9643558476	7356062002	3200949233	1038447766	5746716804
3479331468	0625222002	9682240328	9432838252	0740289242
7154859291	2437299330	9459032709	0759655453	5550134980
8454251347	9043691852	7718408029	6036344435	6396759920
4522713557	9355292547	1091873894	3367500450	0445912503
6962739129	1681395921	9571822824	5053065466	4345354797
6855122502	2743172183	1926111268	8902977308	7235898087
0711159485	0642593437	3862215122	4368496150	6313405207
4736092475	3069558939	1149005537	3963462240	3918413811

ANSWERS TO EXERCISES

p27   1(i)   Numbers per week   0   1   2   3   4   5   6   7   8   9
                    Item A frequencies   3   7   13   9   6   5   2   2   2   1
                    Item B frequencies   2   9   22   12   4   1

       (ii)   Higher safety stocks are required for item A. In a week, demand for B is unlikely to exceed 5 whereas with A, it could be as high as 8 or 9.

       2.   Time   0–   10–   20–   30–   40–   50–   60–   70–   80–
              Frequency   3   16   13   5   7   2   1   1

             The extremes beyond 50 need to be investigated. A more detailed breakdown of the figures by repairman or time of the week would be interesting.

       3.   Range of data is 66.8 – 41.3 = 25.5 suggesting intervals of 2.5

Weight   40–   42.5–   45.0–   47.5–   50–   52.5–   55–   57.5–   60–   62.5   65–
             2   2   9   8   3   7   2   3   2   5   3

             Questions: Why are controls so bad? Is it possible to break down the data by operator and day? How accurate is the weighing machine, are the operators trying to over-shoot to ensure a minimum of 40 kilos?

p32   1.   In plotting the distribution as a histogram, halve the frequencies in the last three intervals.

       2.   In plotting the histogram, note the following adjustments
                            10,000   –   <   12,000   halve the frequency
                            12,000   –   <   14,000   halve the frequency
                            14,000   –   <   20,000   divide by 6

p49   1.   Column totals : 199; 219; 208; grand total 626
             Row totals   : 168; 17: 76; 69; 65; 231 : grand total 626
             Note the way the grand total provides a built-in check.

       2(ii)   Working in thousands : 21 + 29 + 15 + . . . + 31 = 299
       2(iii)   297, 455, so the answer to (ii) is less than 1% above the true value.
       3(i)   0.0011 + 0.0009 + . . . + 0.0008 = 0.0054
       (ii)   0.005453, so that the error in (i) is only 1%.
       (iii)   1.134 + 0.926 + . . . + 0.776 = 5.453 thou

p53   1.   358.393
       2.   £5,707 in bills leaving £2,709 in the bank.
       3(i)   About 2,000 are accounted for leaving about 18,000 in store.
       (ii)   17,942
       (iii)   The figures calculated may well be inaccurate as some may have been miscounted.

p55   1.   (a) 0.918   (b) 61.596   (c) 0.014   (d)   0.5395
       2(ii)   Individual revenue items and the total
              310.5;   2,450;   20.8;   233.6;   62.1;   18;   51.2   Total £3,146.2

3(i) Roughly (in thousands) for order of magnitude
7 x 100 + 9 x 200 + 11 x 90 + 15 x 15
= 700 + 1800 + 990 + 225 = 3715
(ii) Accurate results (in thousands)
914.6 + 2075.472 + 985.732 + 219.48
= £4,195.284 exactly, (i) showing an 11% error over (ii)

P58 1. (a) 135.705 (b) 5.229 (c) 0.0018011
     2. (a) 12082.65 (b) 465.57 (c) 0.160363
     3. Dollars : 5066.49; 0.33; 1.23; 3.47; 9.95
     4. F.Francs : 47,369.91; 3.08; 11.5; 32.49; 93.06

p60 1. (a) 1820 (b) 0.1198 (c) 16.98 (d) 17.1429
        (e) 37,836.4 (f) 0.02727
     2. 5083; 2429; 1151
     3. 2473 kilos exclusively devoted to any one of the 5 products could produce these maximum numbers of units
        3,533; 82,433; 4,416; 6 (6.77 theoretical); 5 (5.67 theoretical)
     4. Factor the kilos up by 1.2 giving:
        2,944; 68,694; 3,680; 5; 4

p63 1. (a) Total frequency = 272. % frequencies : 31.6; 9.2; 14.3; 24.6; 8.5; 11.8
        (b) Total frequency = 146. % frequencies: 57.5; 29.5; 11.6; 1.4
     2. £: 794.5; 10.74; 313.88; 230.11
     3. (a) 60 minutes in an hour, so $\frac{60}{7.4+1} = 7$
        (b) 285
        (c) assuming that a 40 hour week consists of 5 days with 2 x 4 hour work periods around a meal break, then 30 minutes will be lost in each work period.
        5 x 2 x 3½ = 35 productive hours per week.
        Therefore the number of weldings = $\frac{35 \times 60}{7.4+1} = 250$.

p64 1. 80.5   2. 0.185 or 18.5%   3. (a) 0.763   (b) 0.538   (c) 0.076
p70 1. 1.1025   2. 1.0824   3. 1.219   4. 5.427   5. 5.895   6. 92.02
p71 1. 0.04   2. −6.34   3. 0.270
p73 1. 8.968   2. 16.023   3. −69.13
p79 1. mean = 5.43; median = 4; mode = 3
     2. mean = 7.75; median = 6.5; mode = 1
p92 1. median = 29.2; mean = 32.73
     2. median = 0; mean = 1.31
     3. A: mean = 3.2 mode = 2 median = 3
        B: mean = 3.2 mode = 3 median = 3
     4. From the frequency distribution
        mean = 28.3; median = 24.2; mode = 18
        Raw data: mean = 27.81; median = 23

466

p100 1(i) the mean (ii) possibly the mode (iii) the median, 50% of colleagues are above and below that figure.
   3. 1.5; three orders every two years
   4. Mode: not very helpful in this case as in 70% of weeks there are breakdowns.
   Median: ambiguous for discrete distributions e.g. 30% below and 45% above.
   Mean: good for estimating arisings during a specified period, but not a typical figure.
   (ii) 'we expect 18 breakdowns during a 10 week period'

p107 1. median = 1.32 hours; lower quartile = 0.9 hrs; uper quartile = 1.82; semi-interquartile range = 0.46. 25% of messages took longer than 1.82 hrs and the same percentage took no longer than 0.9 hrs. The central 50% is located within 0.46 hours of the median on average.
   2. semi-interquartile range = 7.5; upper decile = 48.5; lower decile = 21.5; 'The upper 10% of recruits are aged over 48.5, the lowest 10% of recruits are no more than 21.5 years old.'

	Median	Upper Q.	Lower Q.	S.I.R.
3. men<18 :	6.6	24.8	4.4	10.2
men 35–44 :	50.3	115	15.9	49.6
women<18 :	5.8	23.6	4.3	9.6
women 35–44:	27.1	59.4	9.1	25.2

   (i) Younger people haven't had time to be unemployed for very long. They may also find jobs more easily.

p121 1. (a) $\frac{13}{52}$ (b) $\frac{8}{52}$ (c) $\frac{20}{52}$
   2. (a) $\frac{18}{37}$ (b) $\frac{18}{37}$ (c) $\frac{9}{37}$ (d) $\frac{1}{37}$

p123 1. $\frac{158}{968} = \frac{1}{6.13}$; theoretically it should be $\frac{1}{6}$. Unless the die is biased, $\frac{1}{6}$ should be a better guide.
   2. $\frac{27}{163}$; is the next call to be made under similar circumstances?
   3. $\frac{25}{323}$; the presence of the engineer may well have affected the situation in some way. The figure may therefore be untypical
   4. $\frac{0}{3742}$; 0 might imply that it can never fail which is not true.
   5. $\frac{3}{632}$; 'accident' needs careful definition. A breakdown of figures by time of year and weather conditions would be invaluable.

p125 1. (a) 0.0001 (b) 0.0017 (c) 0.0000034
   2. (a) 3.7×10^{-3} or 37×10^{-4} (b) 7.3×10^{-5} or 73×10^{-6} (c) 10^{-6}
   3. Winter $\frac{2+1+3}{2 \times 52 \times (2+3)} = 0.008$; Summer $= \frac{2}{728} = 0.003$

   Problems of definition: is a puncture an 'accident'? Why not look at accident statistics for *all* lorries?

p136 1. $\frac{12}{50}$

2. Your card could be any of the 52 less 5 cards whose whereabouts are unknown. Of these, 13 less 4 are hearts so $\frac{9}{47}$

3. (a) & (b) a higher probability than on average
(c) lower than on average because of holidays

p142 1. If a large number go in one ten minute period, then there might be less chance of the same happening in the subsequent period.

2. If one device fails it may damage the others.
What is the probability of the switch-over device failing?

p147 1. (a) 0.0006 + 0.003 = 0.0036 assuming that the two failure modes are independent.
(b) 5 x 0.0036 = 0.018

2. A critical assumption is that all channel failures are independent events. If the same fault had been built in because of faulty maintenance, this would not be so.

p149 1. (a) 0.8 x (1800−800) + 0.2 x (400−800) = £720
(b) 0.286   (c) the long-term pay-off in a large number of such deals.

p157 1. Simple rounding is helpful. e.g. 1971 borrowers 3.9 millions.. Main contrast, increasing activity, decreasing number of societies.

2. Rounding e.g. Export, A320 thousand.

p163 1. % breakdown for each subsidiary e.g. for A: N 6%; S 22% (22.35 exactly); Scotland 22%; Export 50%. Note the built-in check: All percentages sum to 100.

2. Bring out contrasting trends. Is this a measure of stoppages or rather of industrial activity in each sector?

p167 5.1%: the % increases per item weighted by expenditure per item.

p174 1. Total 171,565; 5% of customers (1 in 20) were sold 52% of goods. Subsequent pareto points: 10%−73.6%; 15%−80.9% etc.

p.187 1(i) £50.93 (ii) £14.91   (iii) £2.69   (iv) £13.01

2. Reducing overdraft by £14,500 is worth £338.33

3. Allowing for 4 months interest April−end price = £126.4 and June−end price £128. Better to have bought all at end April for £125.

4. £22,540 now becomes £23,667 in 5 months time allowing for 12% interest, so not worthwhile.

p189 1. (i) £332 x 1.8704 = £620.97   (ii)   £192 x 1.3108 = £251.67
(iii) £3,097 x 4.2262 = £13,088.64 (iv) £117,391

2. (i) £634.65   (ii) £765.72

p191 (i) £455.63   (ii) £11,607.54   (iii) £11,617.74
(iv) £13,426 x 1.2682 = £17,027

p194 1(i) £65,156 (ii) £103,750 (iii) £161,823 (iv) £247,669
2(i) £8,144 (ii) £12,969 (iii) £20,228 (iv) £30,959
3. £2 x 2.517 = £5.03

p200 1. (i) £140 x 0.7972 = £111.61 (ii) £1,565.38 (iii) £607.46

468

2(i) discount rate for 5 days = 13 x $\frac{5}{365}$% : £2,295.91
(ii) discount rate for 3 weeks = 17 x $\frac{3}{52}$%:
£138,640.26 (iii) £2,997,536
3. £32,100 x 0.9978 = £32,029. So you are better off accepting his proposal.
4. £5,000 x 0.9898 = £4,949. Other factors, loss of flexibility over 29 days etc.

p205 1(i) £2,000 x 3.791 = £7,582 (ii) £350 x 5.426 = £1,899.1
(iii) £1,200 x 7.435 = £8,922 (iv) £1200 + £1200 x 6.733 = £9,279.6
2(i) at $\frac{11}{12}$% per month; £10 x 21.456 = £214.56
(ii) £100 x 14,539 = £1,453.9 (iii) £1 x 349.05 = £349.05.
3(i) £2,164.5 (ii) £1,895.4
4. Value of payments = $\frac{£1400}{4}$ + 3 similar end-of-year payments at $\frac{13}{12}$% per month = £350 + £350 x 2.9362 = £1,377.67 thereby losing £22.33 on the deal.
5. Discount £100 received in 3 years time at 12% = £89.29. Prior to bankruptcy the value of the bond was 3 x 8.055 + 100 x 0.0334 = £34.185, so that at £25 the bond was cheap. Clearly after the bankruptcy announcement prices will fall as the amateurs sell, they will then rise as the professionals buy.

208 1(i) £20,000 x 0.1019 = £2,038 (ii) 40 periods at 4%; £20,000 x 0.0505 = £1,010 per ½ year or £168.33 per month.
2. £8,000 x 0.2432 = £1,945.6 per annum.
3. Monthly interest rate $\frac{11}{12}$ %; £35,000 x 0.1302 = £4,557.37 per month.

p209 10% interest on extra £20,000 = £2,000 p.a. on deposit at 8.5% for 10 years = £29,670. With a new house, extra £20,000 equity increases at 5% per annum to £32,578, a much better deal. (N.B. the interest on a house loan may be subject to tax relief).

p213 1. At 10%, NPV = −£0.59. At 12%, −£24.68. As the discount rate increases, so the investment becomes unprofitable.
2. NPV (purchase) = − 2,000 − 200 x 3.605 + 500 x 0.5674 = -£2,437; NPV (lease) = −600 x 3.605 = −£2,163.

p215 1. IRR of (a)=£25.7% and of (b) = 21.9% but NPV of (a) is less than that of (b) at a 10% discount rate.
2. There are *two* IRR values! One at 8% and one at 59%. Check this result. The investment is profitable for discount rates between these rates.
3. About 0.9% per month or 10.8% per annum.

p233 2 Mean values: maintenance = 50.2; Production = 174.6
p244 Correlation coefficient = for (1) 0.91, for (2) −0.61
p245 Support payments are likely to apply to subsidiaries with relatively low revenues. High traffic revenue will tend to be associated with a high level of activity as measured by variables 5,6 & 7.
p249 1. intercept = 0.52, gradient = 1.88

469

	2.	Intercept = 68.4, gradient = -0.3
p251	1.	tons = 100, consumption = 1015
	2.	tons = 200, consumption = 1030, etc.
p261	1.	113.3; 107.0; 116.7; 105.7; 122.1
	2.	Supplier A: 100; 110.1; 122.8; 134.1; 146.0
p262		Bread: 100; 120; 140; Milk: 100; 110; 110
		Tea: 100; 150; 250
p266		Food: 100; 112.1; 121.6. Tobacco: 100; 117.2; 144.7
p270	1.	Wine: 273; 321; 296; 366; 310; 258; 266; 236; 205; 194; 200
		Cigarettes: 118; 132; 124; 127; 109; 97; 104; 101; 99; 102; 108
		Petrol: 149; 149; 145; 161; 147; 133; 184; 168; 169; 175; 180;
	2.	217.2; 212.3; 183.2; 185.4; 175.9; 164.9; 166.6; 160.2; 160.4; 154.5; 150.
	3.	(a) 129.6; 131.4; 124.5; 130.1; 130.4; 135.9; 136.5
		(b) 100; 118.2; 129.7; 146.8; 166.9; 205.2; 230.6
		100; 116.5; 135.0; 146.2; 165.8; 195.6; 218.8
	4.	In 1983 terms: 1970–£22,920; 1975–£12,430; 1980–£6,354
	5.	1970: £2,500; 1975: £4,610; 1980: £9,018. Actual monetary values, constant in real terms.
p273		Moving totals: 41; 45; 45; 46; 47; 49; 44; 46; 42; 48
p278		With 0.1, Forecasts: 38; 40.2; 37.2; 40.5; 41.5; 39.3; etc.
		With 0.3, '' 34; 41.8; 32.3; 43.6; 45.5; 37.9; etc.
p280		Cusum: 15; 30; 40; 40; 40; 35; 40; 35; 40; 40; etc.
p285		Cusum: 1.75; 0.25; 3.5; 4.5; 3.25; 1.75; 6.0; 13; etc.
p292	1.	46.7; 45; 50; 52.5; 58.5; 64.3; 69.4; 77.8; etc.
	2.	Deseasonalised additive: 87; 125; 118; 121; 129; 119; 126; 132; 130; 146; 146; 144
		Deseasonalised multiplicative: 78; 125; 119; 122; 129; 119; 126; 132; 130; 146; 144; 144
p301	1.	Not all managers read the F.T. – those that do may be more biased towards statistics. 2. People in need tend not to have telephones. 3. Health food fans may avoid shopping centres.
	4.	DIY enthusiasts may not bother with AA/RAC. 5. Middle class bias in the National Trust?
p305	1.	Effect of holidays 2. Australians more likely to have moved on. Sampling frame excludes casual Australian buyers.
	3.	Only those already interested are likely to cooperate.
p307	1.	The good ones are still flying. Evaluate part-life to date. 2. Long-term survivors still have some way to go. 3. Recent leavers can not, by definition, have taken a long time to get a job!
p315	1.	95%: 45% ± 2%; 99%: ± 2.6%
	2.	95%: 51% ± 12.9% 99%: ± 16.8%
p316	2.	256; 336
p320	1.	95%: 6 ± 0.4 2. From $(\frac{480}{7.3+2} = 52)$ to $(\frac{480}{4.7+2} = 72)$

	3.	95%: 6 ± 0.2 4. £225 ± £6 5. £1,462,500 ± £39,000
p322		4900; 490,000 (in theory!).
p340		0.16; 0.64
p342		1. 0.87 2. 0.98 3. 0.95; 0.995
p346	1.	Reject the Null hypothesis.
	2.	No. the result is consistent with the Null hypothesis and other hypotheses.
p353		Combine C&D: Now expected frequencies row by row are 34.4; 57.1; 8.5; 48.2; 79.9; 11.9; 34.4; 57.1; 8.5.
		Chi-square = 5.96; 4 degrees of freedom. Not significant.
p392	1.	Sample size 35, critical value 1%, one-tail = 10, therefore highly significant.
	2.	Critical value 1%, one tail = 1, therefore not significant.
p405	1.	Sales will not equate to demand if stocks are inadequate or if insufficient sales staff available. They can also be distorted by administrative procedures.
p408		Replacement cost of £2 makes most sense but for a friend you might (hypothetically) wish to share your cheap bottles.

REFERENCES

BAKAN, D   The test of significance in psychological research IN Henkel (1970).

BARNETT, A   Misapplication reviews: an introduction. *Interfaces* (12:5) Oct, 1982, pp.47–9

BRITISH AIRWAYS   *Annual report and accounts, 1980–1.*

CAMPBELL, D T   Measuring the effects of social innovations by means of Time Series IN J M Tanur (ed.) *Statistics: a guide to the unknown.* Holden-Day, 1972.

CAMPBELL, D T & H L Ross   The Connecticut crackdown on speeding: Time Series data in quasi-experimental analysis. *Law & Society Review* (3:1), 1968, pp.33–53.

CANEN, A G & R D GALVAO   An application of ABC analysis to control imported material. *Interfaces* (10:4), 1980, pp 22–4.

CAPLAN, R   *A practical approach to quality control.* Business Books, 1982.

CARSBERG, B & A HOPE   *Business investment decisions under inflation.* Institute of Chartered Accountants, 1976.

COX, D R   *Planning of experiments,* Wiley, 1958.

DOBSON, P   *Consumer credit.* Sweet & Maxwell, 1979.

DOYLE, P   *et al.* Management Planning and control in multi-branch banking. *Journal of the Operational Research Society* (30:2), 1979, pp.105–12.

EHRENBERG, A S C   *A primer in data reduction.* Wiley, 1982.

GALL, J   *Systemantics.* Wildwood House, 1978.

GALLAGHER, C & A METCALFE   How managers use numerate techniques, *Management Today* Dec. 1982, pp.33–8.

GALLUP, G   Opinion polling in a democracy IN J M Tanur (ed.) *Statistics: a guide to the unknown.* Holden-Day, 1972.

GOLD, D   Statistical tests and substantive significance IN Henkel (1970).

GOVERNMENT STATISTICIANS COLLECTIVE   *How official statistics are produced: views from the inside.* G S S, 1979, quoted in Irvine (1979)

GRAHAM, R J   Give the kid a number: an essay on the folly and consequences of trusting your data. *Interfaces* (12:3), 1982, pp.40–4.

H M S O

Annual abstracts of Statistics, 1983
- Average Weekly Earnings, Table 6.20
- Building Societies in Great Britain, Table 17.21
- Death Rates for men and women 1980, Table 2.30
- Indices of Wholesale Prices Purchased by Three Industries; Tables 18.2, 18.3
- Industrial Stoppages, Table 6.15
- Passenger car production in the U K, 1972–1981, Table 8.74
- Postal, telegraph & telephone services, Table 10.91

Annual Abstracts of Statistics, 1982 Cinema Price and Admissions, Table 10.93

Canvey : a second report... Office of the Health and Safety Executive, 1981

Economic Progress Report No 161, Treasury, Oct 1983 Typical prices of Spirits and Beer with deflated (1983) equivalent prices

Employment Gazette, December, 1983 Unemployment : Age & Duration, Table 2.6

Employment Gazette, March, 1984 General Index of Retail Prices, Components of the Retail Price Index with weights, Table 6.4

HENKEL (1970) *see*

MORISSON, D E & R E HENKEL (eds). *The significance test controversy: a reader.* Aldine, 1970.

HUFF, D *How to lie with statistics.* Penguin, 1973.

IRVINE, J, I MILES & J EVANS (eds) *Demystifying social statistics.* Pluto Press, 1979.

ISHIKAWA, K, *Guide to quality control.* Asian Productivity Organisation: printed by Nordica International Ltd, 1983.

LACHENBRUCH, P A Statistical programs for microcomputers. *Byte,* 1983. pp.460–70.

L'ESPERANCE, W L *Modern statistics.* MacMillan, 1971.

LIEBERMANN, B *Contemporary problems in statistics: a book of readings for the behavioural sciences.* O U P, 1971.

MACAULAY, T B Review of Southey's Colloquies on the Progress and Prospects of Society (1830) IN *Collected Essays.*

MARTIN, J *Application development without programmers.* Prentice-Hall, 1982.

MOORE P G *The business of risk.* C U P, 1983.

MOORE, P G & H THOMAS Measuring uncertainty, *Omega* (3) 1975, pp.657–72.

MORRISON, H New systems of statistics on homelessness. *Statistical News* (C S O), No. 35, Nov., 1976, quoted in IRVINE (1979).

MOSER, C A & G KALTON *Survey methods in social investigation.* Heinemann Educational, 1971.

MURDOCH, J Y & J A BARNES *Statistical tables.* MacMillan, 1975.

NATIONAL BUS COMPANY *Annual report, 1980*

PHILLIPS, L D Requisite decision modelling: a case study. *Journal of the Operational Research Society* (33), 1982, pp.303–11.

The price of mince and fat content: a survey conducted by the London Chief Environmental Health Officers' Group, coordinated by officers from Hammersmith & Fulham Borough Council. Unpublished report, 1981/2.

SIEGEL, S *Non parametric statistics for the behavioural sciences.* McGraw-Hill, 1956.

SISSOURAS, A A & B MOORES The 'optimum' number of beds in a coronary care unit. *Omega* (4:1), 1976, pp.59–65.

SKIPPER, J K Jnr. *et al.* The sacredness of .05: a note concerning the uses of statistic levels of significance in social science IN Henkel (1970).

SPRENT, P *Statistics in action.* Penguin, 1979.

TANUR, J M (ed.) *Statistics: a guide to the unknown.* Holden-Day 1972.

'VERITAS REPORT' (79–0670) IN T K JENSSEN & P LARSEN *Hazardous cargoes and public risk.* Veritas Paper Series No 80 P O 14, Sept. 1980.

WELLS, G E The use of decision analysis in Imperial Group. *Journal of the Operational Research Society* (33), 1982, pp.313–18.

WOOLEY, R N Database and the micro. *Journal of the Operational Research Society* (34), 1983, p.349.

WOOLSEY, R E D The measure of MS/OR application or let's hear it for the bean counters. *Interfaces* (5:2), 1975.

INDEX

Accounting procedures. 409-410
Addition (calculators) 42-50
    law (probability). 142-144
Additive models (time series) . . .288-291
Aiming point 5,8
Analysis, pareto. 167-174
Annual percentage rate (APR). . 204–205
Application software (computers) . . 358
APR(Annual percentage rate) . . .204-205
Asymmetrical distribution. 15
Averages 74-113
    calculation of 82-92
    definition 75-76
    misuse of. 79-82,102-104
    purpose of 75

Balance point (mean) 85-86
Bar charts 174-177
    percentage compound 176
Base year weighted index 263
BASIC (computer language) 365
Bayes Theorem 344-345
Bias (sampling) 297-308
Bills of exchange 183-184
Blind trial 330-331
Bonds. 199-200
Building society interest rates 182

Calculators, use of 40-73
    addition 42-50
    division. 58-63
    multiplication 53-58
    percentage 62-63
    subtraction. 50-53
Capital
    costs 212-213
    recovery factor 206-207
Cash flow 211-213
    discounted. 212-213
Causality. 226-230
Cause/effect relationships 223-230
Central processing unit (computers)
   356-358
Centre of gravity (means) 77-79
Charts
    bar 174-177
    Cusum 278-282,285
    pi 177-178

Chi-square 352-353
Class intervals (frequency distribution)
   23,25-31,33-36
    open ended 38-39
Cluster sampling. 327
Coefficient, correlation. 233-247
    matrix 244-245
Communication barriers 9-10
Compound
    amount factor 189,195
    interest 182,187-191
    inverted 197
Computer
    graphics (data representation). . . 177
    information systems 395-407
    languages. 358
    packages 386-390
    simulation techniques 390-393
Computers. 355-394
Concealed data 402
Conditional probability 136-137
Confidence limits (sampling) . . .319-320
Consumer Credit Act, 1974 205
Contingency tables 351-352
Continuous distribution 20
Control group 330
Correlation analysis. 223-247
    coefficient 233
    measurement 230-233
Cost
    data. 407-410
    centres 409
Covarience of variables 232
Credit, interest-free 203-204
Critical values (significance) 335
Current year weighted index
    263
Cusum charts 278-282,285

Data 395-413
    checking 412-413
    concealed 402-405
    cost 407-410
    handling 1-39
    'laundering' 395-396
    misrecording. 395-407
    processing 401-402
    recording. 395-407
    representation 154-181

bar charts 174-177
    percentages 158-174
    picture bars 179
    pi charts 177-178
Simplifying techniques. 154-181
Database 359
Decision
    tables 219
    trees 221-222
Decomposition (time-series) 290-292
Delayed payments . . . 182-183,198-199
Dependent variable 224
Depreciation 211
Deviation
    mean 109-110
    standard 112-113
Diminishing returns (sampling) . .313,320
Discount rates 213
Discs (computers) 358
Discounted
    cash flows 212-213
    payback 216-217
Discounting 183-184,195-200
    and inflation 198
Discounts 186,198-199
Discrete
    frequency distribution 20-21,90
    values 20
Dispersion 104-107
Distribution 1-39
    asymmetrical 15
    continuous 20
    discrete frequency 20-21
    frequency 1-39,83-86
Distribution
    irregular 17-20
    non-symmetrical 10
    quasi-symmetrical 10
    sampling 308-312,316-319
    symmetrical 10
Division (calculators) 58-63
Double-blind trial 331
Dummy variable 387-388

EMV (expected monetary value) .220-222
Error
    detection (calculators) 43-46
    trapping (computers) 362-363
    types (significance testing) . . .337-339
Expected
    monetary value (EMV) 220-222

value (probability) 147-151
Experimental group 330
Experimentation,329-334
    factorial 331
    pseudo- 331-334
Expert system (computers) . 393-394,345
Exponential smoothing 275-277

Factorial experiments 331
Fault trees 144-147
Finite population 322
Fixed costs 5,256-257
Floppy discs (computers) 358
Forecasting, ...272-294
    error 277
    long term 282-292
    short term 276-278
Frequency distribution 1-39
    compilation 21-25
    discrete 20-21,90
    mean of 83-86
    problems of 25-39
Future money, valuing 194-200

'Gee whiz' effect (graphs) 180-181
Gilt-edged securities 199-200
Government
    bonds 199-200
    statistics 410-411
Graphics, computer (data representation)
. . . . 177
Graphs, problems of 180-181

Hardware (computers) 356-359
Histogram 25

Independent variable 224
Inference, statistical 134
Inflation 191-194,159-272
    and discounting 198
    and investment 217-219
    proofing 210-211
Information systems 395-396
Input/output barrier 359-361
Interaction 331
Interest 182-222
    Compound 182,187-191
    inverted 197
    rates 182,185-187
    simple 187
Interest-free credit 203-204

Internal rate of return (IRR) . . .214-215
Interval scale. 348-349
Intuition (probability) 128-130
Inverted compound interest 197
Investment appraisal 211-219
IRR (internal rate of return). . . .214-215
Irregular distribution 17-20

Knowledge base (computers) 345,393-394

Laspeyre Index 263
Linear regression 255-258
    Limitations 258
Long term forecasting 282-294

Magnetic tape (computers). 358
Mainframe computers 356
Mann-Whitney U Test 349-350
Mean (averages) 75-79,83-86
    balance point 85-86
    deviation. 109-113
    frequency distribution 83-86
    standard error 318-319
    uses 92-97
    weighted 82-83
Median (averages) 76,86-90,97-99
Micro-computers 356,412
Minimum/maximum values
   104-105
Mode (averages) 76, 90-91, 99-100
Models (time series). 287-293
    additive. 288-291
    multiplicative 291-293
Mortgages 182
Moving averages 273-276,289
Multicollinearity 389
Multiple regression . . . 257-258,387-390
Multiplication (calculators) 53-58
Multiplicative models (time series)291-293
Multistage sampling. 327

Negative skew 12,14-15
Net present values (NPV)213-215,218-219
Non-linear relationships 247,258
Non-random sequences. . . . 131,134-135
Non-response,
    sampling 302-305
    surveys 326
Non-symmetrical distribution 10
Normal distribution. . . 311-312,318,347
NPV (net present value) 213-215,218-219

Null
    hypothesis 335-342
    result 341-342
Numeracy 40

Ogive graph 88
Open-ended class intervals 38-39
Operating systems. 358
Opportunity
    costs 185,212-214,409
    loss tables 220
Overall probability(complex event)137-142

Paasche Index 263
Packages (computers). 386-390
Paired samples. 353-354
Parametric test 348
Pareto analysis. 167-174
Payback, discounted 216-217
Payments, delayed . . . 182-183, 198-199
Payoff tables. 219-220
Percentages 158-174
    comparison of 167
    frequencies. 87-89
    pareto analysis. 167-174
Percentages
    problems of 163-167
    spurious averaging. 165-167
Peripherals. 356
Picture bars 179
Pi charts 177-178
Pilot surveys. 327
Population (sampling) 295-300
    finite 322
    mean 345-346
    percentage 296-298
Positive skew 14-15
Power curves. 339
Predictability 118-153
Price
    changes. 268-271
    discounts. 198-199
    indices 261-270
    relatives 260-261
Probability. 181-153
    addition law 142-144
    complex events 137-142
    conditional. 136-137
    scale of 119-122
    subjective 128-130
Production costs 5

479

Programming (computers) 364-378
    languages. 358-359,364-378
Pseudo experiments. 331-334
Pseudo-random sampling. 300-301

Quality control 335-347
Quartiles 105-106
Quasi-symmetical distribution. 10
Quota sampling 327

RAM (random access memory) 358
Random
    access memory (computers) 358
    numbers 131-134
    sampling 131,235,299-300
    sequences 131-134
Range (dispersion) 105-107
Ratio scale. 349
Real price (inflation) 268-271
regression
    artifacts 333-334
    linear. 255-258
    limitations 258
    lines. 248-251
    multiple 257-258
Regret tables. 220
Relative frequency 122-123
Regression 247-258
Residuals. 252-253
Retail Price Index (RPI)
    260,264-267,269-271,411
Risk analysis. . 124-128,144-147,150-153
Rounding (figures) 48
Run tests. 134

Sample
    mean 316-320,345-348
    size 315-316,321-324
Sampling. 131,295-325,348-351
    bias 297-308
    cluster 327
    distribution 308-312
    error 297,308-322
    and variables. 316,324-325
    frame. 299
    methods (surveys). 327-328
    multistage 327
    non-response. 302-305
    paired. 353-354
    pseudo-random 300-301
    quota. 327

    random. 299-300
    stratified 321
Scale of probability. 119-122
Scales (measurement). 348-349
Scatter diagrams. 224
Seasonality. 286-287
Semi-averages 247-249
Sequences 131-135
    non-random 131,134-135
    random. 131-134
Semi-interquartile range (dispersion)
    105-107,113
Short loan interest rates 185-186
Short term forecasting 276-278
Significance 235-240
    level. 335-337
    testing 334-354
Simulation. 131, 390-393
Sign test 353-354
Sinking fund factor. 209-210
Skew 12-15
    negative 12,14-15
    positive. 14-15
Small samples 321
Smoothing. 273-278
    constant 275-277
Software (computers) 358-359
Spreadsheets (computers) 378-384
Spurious average (percentages) . .165-167
Standard
    deviation. 112-113
    error 312-315,322,346
Statistical
    analysis. 3
    inference. 134
    theory 9
Statistics (Government). 410-411
Stock control 15-17
Stockholding 184-185
Storage (computers) 358
Straight line regression 247-258
Stratified sampling 321,324-325
Structured programming. 376
Subjective probability 128-130
Subtraction (calculators). 50-53
Sunk costs 212
Surveys. 324-328
    planning of. 326-327
Symmetrical distribution. 10

't' tests 348-349,353-354
Tally count (frequency distribution) . . 23
Tax liability 212
Test statistic 335
Testing 334-354
Time series 272-293,332-334
Trayholding 405-407
Treasury bills 196
Trends 282-287
Trials (experimentation) 330-331

Uncertainty 118-153
User-friendly (computers) 361
Utility (probability) 150-153
    function 151-153

Value, expected (probability) . . .147-151
Value factors 200-202
Variable costs 256-257
Variables 224-241,316
Variance 110,253-255
    analysis 165
Visual display unit (VDU) 357,360

Weighted
    mean (averages) 82-83
    moving average 276-277,289
Wholesale price indices 267-268